History of the Jews in Modern Times

History of the Jews in Modern Times

Lloyd P. Gartner
Tel-Aviv University

OXFORD
UNIVERSITY PRESS

OXFORD

UNIVERSITY PRESS

Great Clarendon Street, Oxford OX2 6DP

Oxford University Press is a department of the University of Oxford.
It furthers the University's objective of excellence in research, scholarship,
and education by publishing worldwide in

Oxford New York

Auckland Cape Town Dar es Salaam Hong Kong Karachi
Kuala Lumpur Madrid Melbourne Mexico City Nairobi
New Delhi Shanghai Taipei Toronto
With offices in
Argentina Austria Brazil Chile Czech Republic France Greece
Guatemala Hungary Italy Japan South Korea Poland Portugal
Singapore Switzerland Thailand Turkey Ukraine Vietnam

Oxford is a registered trade mark of Oxford University Press
in the UK and in certain other countries

Published in the United States
by Oxford University Press Inc., New York

ISBN 978-0-19-289259-1

Printed in the United Kingdom by
Lightning Source UK Ltd., Milton Keynes

Preface

It is a bold deed for an academic historian to undertake a general history of the Jews in modern times. Very few do so, for reasons which are familiar: too vast a field, lack of knowledge of large areas, too few relevant languages mastered, and so forth. Such reasons are intrinsically good, but their result is not. Besides, one must often face the skepticism of colleagues. The academic historians' inhibitions have brought about that general histories have been attempted by several popular authors who attempted a task clearly beyond them.

The accumulation of studies in modern Jewish history is overwhelming, especially during the past quarter century, in Hebrew and English. Just to master all the worthwhile writings would leave time and strength for nothing else. Yet I have thought to try, and will spare the reader further apologies.

There is the matter of ideology, a term very familiar to those brought up in Israel and in Zionist principles. The 'Jerusalem school', which has included some historians of the highest distinction, has seen the yearning for deliverance from Exile (*galut*) and Return as the central meaning of Jewish history. I live in Jerusalem but am unable to share this outlook. The yearning for deliverance and Return is unquestioned but it did not dominate Jewish life even when it ruled the minds of many religious, and later nationalist, intellectuals. Often deliverance and Return were forgotten or at least marginalized, and influential sectors of the Jewish people renounced them during the nineteenth and twentieth centuries. Return, in the secular form of Zionism towards the end of the nineteenth century, was highly controversial. At all events, this is not a book which fits the Jerusalem school.

Readers will notice considerable attention to the general historical framework into which Jewish history fits, and much space given to demography, economic, and social history, as well as the development of the Jewish community structure. In these respects I find myself following in the footsteps of my mentor, Salo Wittmayer Baron

(1895–1989). The reader will judge the validity of my viewpoint and the extent of my success.

I am indebted to friends and colleagues for their comments and suggestions, but this history is entirely my independent work. My late wife, Ruth S. Gartner, aided and supported me throughout our life together. To her beloved memory I dedicate this book.

Lloyd P. Gartner
August 2000

Contents

	Glossary	ix
1	The Heritage of Medieval Judaism	1
2	Glimmerings of a New Age	26
3	A Rift Opening, 1720–1780	61
4	Era of Revolution	95
5	Emancipation in Western Europe, 1815–1870	128
6	Travail in Eastern Europe, 1815–1881	162
7	Outposts	191
8	Age of Migration and Ideologies	213
9	From War to War, 1914–1939	267
10	Havens and National Home	319
11	Catastrophe, Recovery, and Triumph	347
12	A New Jewish World, 1950–1980	396
	Index	438

Glossary

aliyah beit, 'illegal' Jewish immigration to Palestine without certificate issued by the British Mandatory authorities.

Ashkenazic, pertaining to German Jews and their descendants in other countries.

Bar Mitzvah, occasion of a boy's attaining religious and legal maturity. The equivalent for girls is the *Bat Mitzvah*.

beit midrash, study hall for sacred literature in a community or a yeshiva.

beth din, a court adjudicating according to Jewish law.

bittahon, complete trust in God's benevolent interest.

devekut, communion with God, so intimate that consciousness of self is lost.

Eretz Israel, official Hebrew name for the area governed by British mandate from after World War I until 1948.

galut, exile from the homeland; a condition of existential alienation.

Ha'avara, agreement allowing Jews settling in Palestine to exchange German marks for proceeds from the sale of goods.

Haganah, illegal military defence organization in the *yishuv*.

hakham, lit. wise man; rabbinic head of a Sefardic community.

halakhah, Jewish law considered to be of Divine origin, and binding.

halutz, pioneer in Israel, especially in agriculture.

Hasidic, pertaining to certain mystical sects of Judaism.

Haskalah, Jewish Enlightenment movement of eighteenth century in central and eastern Europe.

hazaka, permanent right to some communal position, honour, etc.

hazan, cantor; official who chants prayers in a synagogue.

heder (pl. *hadarim*), lit. room; one-room elementary schoolhouse, usually the schoolmaster's dwelling.

herem, the ban, imposed by the community for offences which exclude one from social, economic, and religious participation.

hevra (pl. *hevrot, havarot*), a society.

hevra kadisha, communal society responsible for burial arrangements and cemetery upkeep.

hezkat ha-yishuv, permanent right to residence in a community.

Judenrat, body responsible for administration of Jewish community under Nazi rule.

kabbalah, Jewish mysticism.

kahal, executive body of a community.

kashrut, regulations determining the Jewish dietary laws.

kosher, ritually correct; faultless.

kehillah, the organized Jewish community.

kibbutz, kvutza, Israeli collective agricultural settlement.

kibbutz galuyot, ingathering of the exiles; mass immigration to the state of Israel.

kiddush, sanctification, usually over wine, before Sabbath and festival evening and daytime dinners.

Kiddush ha-Shem, voluntary martyrdom by a group or individuals.

ma'abarah, transit camp in use during mass immigration to Israel, especially 1951–5.

maggid, preacher.

Marranos, Spanish and Portuguese Jews converted to Christianity and their descendants.

maskil, adherent of the *Haskalah*, or Jewish Enlightenment.

mazzot, unfermented biscuits eaten on Passover instead of forbidden bread.

mehitza, physical partition between the sexes, as in the Orthodox synagogue.

midrash, free exegetical commentary on biblical books and individual verses.

minhagim, religious customs, not formally binding but generally practised in some locality.

Mishnah, codification of the oral law, ca. 200, by Rabbi Judah the Patriarch. The foundation text of the Talmud (q.v.).

Mishneh Torah, the code of *halakhah* (q.v.) composed by Moses Maimonides (1135-1204).

mitzvah, a religious obligation; a blessed service.

moshav, moshava, Israeli agricultural settlement with private family life and collective economy.

mussar, movement promoting ethical reflection and study of ethical literature.

parnassim, heads of a *kehillah*.

Pentateuch, first five books of the Torah.

rebbe, Hasidic religious leader.

rishonim, lit. the first ones; the commentators on the Talmud before the sixteenth century.

Rosh ha-Shanah, the Jewish New Year.

Sabbatianism, heretical movement accepting Sabbetai Zvi of Izmir as the Messiah.

Seder, the Passover eve home ritual.

Sefardic, pertaining to Sefarad (Spain) and Portugal and to Jews of that descent.

servi camerae, servants of the chamber, the subordination of the Jews in feudal society exclusively to the monarch.

shehita, slaughter of animals by the kosher rules.

shohet, a slaughterer of animals by the kosher rules.

Shulhan ʿArukh, lit. the set table; the code of *halakhah* (q.v.) composed by R. Joseph Karo (1488–1575).

Sukkot, Feast of Tabernacles, a festival lasting seven days.

tallit, shawl worn by men during prayer.

Talmud, compilation of the Palestinian and Babylonian schools' rulings and discussions, ca. 500. The central subject of Jewish study.

Talmud Torah, the study of the Torah; a school where such study is carried on.

Torah, the totality of biblical and Talmudic literature, held to be divinely inspired; sometimes only the Pentateuch.

Vaʿad Arbaʿ ʾArazot, Council of Four Lands, the council of Polish Jewry, ca. 1580–1764.

Vaʿad ha-medinah, the council of the Lithuanian lands, 1623–1764.

Vaʿad Leumi, National Council of Palestine Jews from 1920–1948.

yeshiva, academy for the advanced study of Torah; before ca. 1800 the circle of students of a rabbi.

yishuv, the collective term for the Jewish settlement in Palestine before the state of Israel.

zaddik, Hasidic saint and teacher.

zizit, fringes worn on the four corners of the outer garment or separately (Numbers 15: 37–41).

1

The Heritage of Medieval Judaism

The Jewish Map of 1650

Beneath the surface of events the multiplication of Jewish population is a cardinal fact in modern Jewish history. No more than one and a quarter million Jews lived in the world when Europe's ascent to global supremacy began about 1650. The number of Jews was far fewer than at the beginning of the Christian era, when there were approximately 8 million in the world-embracing Roman and Persian empires. 1650 was the low point after which the world's Jewish population climbed to approximately 16.7 million in 1939 on the eve of the Second World War and the Holocaust. The greatest increase, proportionately far higher than that of the general population, occurred in Europe and its New World offshoot between 1800 and 1914. On the other hand the Jews of North Africa and the Middle East increased little during these centuries and their importance in the world Jewish scene declined until the post-Second World War era.

The significance of population growth is not merely a matter of quantity. Population growth made the Jews a youthful people heavily burdened with dependants. It also meant that a very high proportion of available money and energy had to be spent on children's education and welfare. It constantly required new sources of livelihood. The search for livelihoods for this new young population probably intensified Jews' efforts to abolish or circumvent economic and other restrictions upon them. The needs which arose from population growth also greatly stimulated emigration to new lands, especially the United States of America. In 1650, where we start, all this lay in an unfathomable future.

The Heritage of Medieval Judaism

Almost all Jews lived solely within the rich but constricted world of Judaism. What constituted Judaism was laid down in the Bible and Talmud and a vast corpus of writings based on them. These were not merely a meticulously preserved heirloom but the substance of life and faith for almost all Jews. Like Islam and Christianity, Judaism claimed to be the truth. It is only a later conception that every religion is subjectively true for its believers and that emotional satisfaction and psychic benefits from religion count the most. Outwardly, Judaism may be characterized as a religion of divinely ordained law (*halakhah*) encompassing all conduct. The path of life for a Jew was set forth in the sacred writings and summed up by rabbinic sages in law codes, whose prime source was the Talmud and its early interpreters (*rishonim*). The most famous code was the *Mishneh Torah* ('Supplemental Torah') of R. Moses Maimonides (1138-1204) but that most commonly used was the *Shulhan Arukh* ('Set Table') of R. Joseph Karo (1488-1575). No code was final, as shown by the work of commentators and glossators which surrounded the printed text; Karo himself was the foremost commentator on Maimonides' code. Partial codes have been written since, and local or regional customs (*minhagim*) were as a rule respected by codifiers. Questions of *halakhah* in daily life were for communities' rabbis to decide, with major questions referred to renowned rabbis. The informal structure of halakhic authority permitted a good deal of individualism on the part of rabbis who were untrammelled by hierarchical restraint. From the diligent study of this oral Torah, itself a *mitzvah* (religious duty), were derived rulings in Jewish law when necessary for contemporary needs.

The emphasis on law emphasizes two additional characteristics of Judaism. First, it is an activist religion. The Jew must do or not do certain things, and religious merit is acquired by acts performed or avoided, especially in the face of danger or temptation. Faith and inward sincerity were expected but they did not substitute for actually performing a required *mitzvah*. The second point is that religious life is carried on within a time frame. Daily prayers had to be recited within specified hours, and the Sabbath and holidays and a gamut of religious obligations were likewise fixed by the clock. The clock governed the required interval between consuming meat and then dairy products afterwards, and even the formal conclusion of the Passover eve Seder.

Judaism was a highly rationalized religion which proceeded from the belief in a revelation at Sinai for eternity, which included the written Torah explicitly and the oral Torah of the later rabbis implicitly. Honour was paid to those distinguished in the study of the Torah. This was the main duty of rabbis, but there were many who were not rabbis and learned in the Torah. In the secular world one sought the new in knowledge and ideas, but the goal of rabbinic learning was instead deeper understanding of the ancient and given. These characteristics of Judaism—activism, the time framework, and rational intellectuality—when translated into secular terms became vitally important a few generations later to Jews who were finding their way in the modern world of capitalism, natural science, and rationalism.

Judaism was always in religious competition with Christianity, but Jews avoided debates with Christians over religion. Those who indulged even in amicable religious discussions might be punished by the community on account of the danger of allegations of 'profaning' or 'insulting' the majority religion. Christian authorities, for their part wary of the perils to innocent believers of Jewish 'subtlety', also opposed encounters between Jews and ordinary Christians. However, Jewish mastery of the Scriptures and the Hebrew language compelled Christians to resort, willingly or not, to Jewish teachers in order to learn the sacred tongue.

In the traditional Jewish community one was a Jew by birth in a Jewish family. Maturity brought membership in the community (*kehillah*), which was not merely a matter of choice or sentiment but compulsory. It entailed religious, social, and financial obligations, and the Jewish community had the authority to enforce them. In any case one could hardly live as a Jew without a Jewish community to be part of. Under the Old Regime society was composed of classes, and the members of each class possessed a defined legal status. 'Jew' was one such status.

Materially, the Jew lived better than did the mass of impoverished Christian and Muslim peasants, yet he was looked down on and disliked. It was possible to be kind and sympathetic to an individual Jew, but he was still descended from those who supposedly rejected and killed Jesus. The Jews as a people were under the curse of exile, their land lost and their Temple destroyed. Christianity challenged the Jews with its claim that exile and wandering showed that God rejected them, and this exile would endure until the Jewish people accepted Jesus at the end of days. Judaism had to provide a response to the Christians and also satisfying to themselves. Jewish teaching maintained that God had justly punished his people for their grievous moral and religious sins, and the fate of Jesus had nothing to do with it. Just as their sufferings in exile had been truly foretold by Scripture, so would the scriptural prophecies of their restoration also come to pass. God would reward his people and restore them to their Holy Land in glory. Punishment would be meted out to those who had afflicted them, and peace and plenty would endure forever under the kingship of the Messiah of the House of David.

It was a heroic conception, and at all times there were Jews who lost faith in it and converted to Christianity or Islam. As human nature would have it, some converts became missionaries to their former co-religionists and a few turned into informers and persecutors.

The Jews constituted what sociologists call a traditional society, meaning one based upon a common body of knowledge and values transmitted from the past. They were still united on this basis in the mid-seventeenth century, constituting a separate community which had relations with non-Jews as buyers and sellers or lessors and lessees, but rarely as partners and socially almost never. Given the gulf between the Jew and Christian ways of life and the restrictions of the Jewish dietary laws in particular, social contact between Jews and Christians was almost impossible. Christian no less than Jewish leaders disapproved and combated any tendency to socialize. In a few advanced circles in Holland and Italy common cultural interests brought a few men together. A handful of the Jewish élite looking after Jewish interests were involved in political affairs outside the Jewish community. There was no more contact than that.

Family and Community

The monogamous family was the social basis of Jewish life. Polygamy had long been suppressed notwithstanding its biblical sanction. Concubinage was likewise out of bounds. As a group, the Jews stood for chastity and rejected celibacy. Sexual life was decidedly approved of, but exclusively within the marital bond. The marriage of the young was arranged between their respective families. Brides' prosperous families often undertook to support the new couple for a given number of years. Procreation was in religious terms a 'positive Divine commandment', in fact given during the six days of creation (Genesis 1: 28). Birth control was prohibited and infanticide, widely practised and unofficially tolerated in the majority society, among the Jews was deemed plain murder. The seriousness with which the prohibition of birth control was taken is illustrated by the many halakhic queries put to rabbis concerning extreme medical situations. It might be allowed on the part of the woman, but even then not by the man. It was practically unheard of for a woman not to marry, while an unmarried man was regarded with disdain and moral suspicion. To 'be fertile and increase', as God enjoined Adam and Eve, produced a Jewish progeny probably larger than that of Christians. To be sure sexual life was not always virtuous; infidelity occurred and prostitution existed. The limited evidence which exists points not to the absence but to the rarity of illegitimate Jewish births.

Family meant parents and children. However, aged parents and relatives without their own families might live together in one household, as well as Jewish servants. The husband and father was the head of the family, although deference was due to elderly parents living in the household. A highly prominent role was reserved for the wife and mother, who was often her husband's business aide and collaborator. The man was often a merchant or a lowly pedlar who had to be absent from home for extended periods, and the woman took his place at home and in business. The same was true for widows. It has been argued that in addition to women's specific religious duties such as kindling Sabbath and holiday candles they had a sort of religious sub-culture expressed in Yiddish prayers, books, and special supplications. The coming of emancipation was to reduce, not augment, women's role by returning them to home life and charity work.

Family connections were socially and economically important, and distinguished ancestry was widely esteemed. Divorce, while regrettable, was acceptable in cases of impotence, infidelity (if by the wife, it was mandatory), and serious incompatibility. The halakhic skill of Sefardic rabbis was taxed by the marital, remarital, divorce, and inheritance problems of New Christians returning to Judaism with or without their spouse.

The rearing of children meant their induction into the values and practices of Jewish traditional society. In addition to what they experienced at home, children were taught the sacred texts by a tutor in prosperous families or in a communal school (Talmud Torah) among the poor. Most elementary teaching took place in a 'room' (*heder*) in the teacher's dwelling. The physical conditions were poor, the teacher was untrained, and studies consisted of prayer book recitation and Pentateuch. Few children went beyond this modicum. Girls were taught about the same by women schoolmarms, and mothers were assumed to train their daughters in wifely duties. Boys and girls from poor or unstable families frequently became house servants of middle-class Jewish families until a marriage was arranged. Not many boys reached what are today secondary levels, and very few reached a yeshiva, which until the nineteenth century was the circle of students in the house of a distinguished rabbi. It was maintained by the rabbi himself or by his community as a matter of prestige and religious merit, and students moved readily from yeshiva to yeshiva. In due course a student might be granted a letter authorizing him 'to teach and teach' matters permitted and forbidden by *halakhah* and, for the best students, 'to judge and judge' in a court of Jewish law (*beth din*). Such a man was now a rabbi.

Education in seventeenth-century Jewry and long thereafter in most parts of the Jewish world dealt exclusively with textual study and exposition.[1] The culture and language of the surrounding society found no

---

[1] An interesting parallel to Talmud study is found in Paul Oskar Kristeller, 'The Scholar and his Public in the Late Middle Ages and the Renaissance', in *Medieval Aspects of Renaissance Learning*, ed. and trans. E. P. Mahoney (Durham, NC, 1974), 6–10.

place, nor did any vocational or scientific or physical training. The goal among established families was to produce religiously devout and learned men whose worldly requirements could be attended to by inheriting a parental business or by an advantageous marriage. This dysfunctional and inadequate educational system was a vulnerable target for Haskalah (Jewish Enlightenment) reformers and for rabbis and others who realized its inadequacies. However, no basic change occurred until the advent of modern conditions swept away the old system.

In societies composed of chartered bodies, each possessing defined rights and obligations, it is understandable that the Jews likewise possessed charters and governed themselves autonomously. The corporate Jewish community (*kehillah*), an institution reaching back more than a thousand years, served the interests of the Jews as well as their rulers.[2] A half-century's existence of the Jewish state of Israel helps to place the *kehillah* in perspective. Unlike Israel or any other state, it was not founded on a territory. It had no functions of armed defence, and its foreign relations consisted of dealings with the ruling powers from a position of dependence. For all its spiritual strength, the *kehillah* recognized its subordination, indeed its helplessness, before the powers that be. On the other hand the modern state of Israel contains a large variety of political and religious viewpoints, while the *kehillah* was based on unanimity of viewpoint. Unlike modern democracies it was incapable of hospitality to intellectual variety.

The functions of the *kehillah* towards the outside society were financial and representative. Rulers found it convenient to hold the *kehillah* responsible for the taxes which the Jews had to pay. Thus, local communities as well as regional and country-wide federations of communities in Poland borrowed and lent money and undertook long-term indebtedness, while at least one *kehillah*, the major one of Amsterdam, paid a return on funds which local Jews placed with it for investment. The *kehillah* also could fix the rights of competing Jewish businessmen. Within Jewish life, it oversaw many charitable societies as well as the numerous synagogues which existed alongside the community's official

---

[2] Salo W. Baron, *The Jewish Community: Its History and Structure to the American Revolution* (3 vols., Philadelphia, 1942), is a comprehensive study, arranged mainly by topic.

house of worship. In some places, such as Bohemia and Poland, the *kehillah* included independent guilds of Jewish craftsmen. Communal institutions could include a hospice, in some places a hospital, and in Italy a hall for weddings and entertainments. An array of charitable societies undertook among other works to educate the poor, support widows and orphans, endow needy brides, care for the sick, attend lying-in mothers, arrange circumcision for newborn boys, and ransom captives wherever they might be held. Some societies, often composed of ladies, undertook such pious tasks as mending prayer shawls (*tallitot*) and show-fringes (*zizit*). There were regular groups to recite psalms or study the weekly synagogal Torah reading, Mishnah, Talmud, ethical works, or other sacred texts.

Of all these pious groups, the most important and honorific was the Holy Society (*hevra kadisha*) which buried the dead. It held the primacy not only because burial was a sacred obligation which had to be promptly discharged, and because washing and shrouding the dead before burial was accorded such high religious merit that men and women vied for the honour of co-optation to the Holy Society to perform the task. In addition, the Holy Society wielded considerable power. It controlled the community's cemetery and could bury a criminal or disreputable individual in a shameful location, to his and his family's permanent dishonour. It might even delay burial until the family paid his debt to the community or offered a donation within their presumed means. Such powers, needless to say, could be abused and sometimes provoked fierce quarrels.

All these works of kindness and piety could keep busy the minds and hands of the 1,000 to 2,000 persons who constituted an average urban *kehillah*. Communal affairs, pious deeds, religious observances, and sacred study could fill the social and spiritual world of the Jews within their framework of social separateness and communal autonomy, and they made for dense networks of social life. In addition, the authority and responsiblity of the Jewish community was great. The sundry rulers—kings, municipalities, bishops, dukes—whose toleration permitted the Jews to dwell in their territories levied taxes and exacted loans and 'gifts', and left it to the *kehillah* to divide the amounts among its members. Moreover, the *kehillah*'s oft exercised privilege to admit or exclude a person from the right of permanent residence (*hazakah* or *hezkat ha-yishuv*) was closely related to his capacity to pay taxes. Malefactors and troublesome dissenters could also be deprived of the right and be expelled. The *kehillah* was empowered to impose the ban (*herem*), by which someone was ostracized and boycotted until he mended his ways or submitted to the authority of the *kehillah*.

The executive body of the *kehillah* was the *kahal*. Although every member of the community had rights, this executive was far from a democratic institution. The process of election involved electoral bodies which elected yet other electoral bodies by drawing lots. Quite a few rules prohibited in-laws and relatives even to the third degree from serving together on the *kahal*. Yet, with all the rules, the management of the *kehillah* was usually in the hands of a hereditary and intermarried oligarchy. Men acquired their place in the oligarchy by virtue of wealth, family connections, and occasionally as rabbis; money and rabbinic learning were married. There were *kahal* members who used their position to further their private interests.

Every *kehillah* had its officials, from those who cleaned its buildings to clerks, teachers, beadles, and rabbi, who was the ranking if not necessarily the most powerful figure in the *kehillah*. He was employed, usually for a term of three to five years, as expositor of the Torah, judge, and occasional preacher. Rabbis often changed positions several times during their lives, whether for a higher income, a more scholarly atmosphere, or on account of disputes with local oligarchs. Many a community, however, basked in its rabbi's reputation for wisdom and learning, and a few rabbis were the authors of classic works which are studied and used to the present day.

Large urban *kehillot* often held sway over little rural ones. The small places were resentful and resisted particularly when, as they maintained, the large community assessed them disproportionately for taxes. Above the local level, regional councils of Jewish communities developed in Poland and Germany. The most ramified community structure was that existing in Poland and Lithuania. In 1580 Polish Jewry's regional community councils established the Council of Four Lands (*Va'ad arba arazot*), namely Little (south-west) Poland, Great (western) Poland, Red Russia (Galicia), and Lithuania. Mazovia in central Poland became the fourth land after Lithuania withdrew in 1623 to set up its own Council of the [Three] Lands (*Vaad ha-medinah*). The regions represented in both councils changed and increased until they were finally abolished in 1764. Two representatives from each land of the Polish council met annually during the fair at Lublin or Jaroslaw. Their main business was allocating taxes among the lands. Other matters inevitably came up, including refugee relief, the encouragement of Hebrew printing, regulation of moneylending practices, and so on. An unofficial activity during council sessions and fairs was match-making, presumably of country-wide mercantile dynasties.

The effective powers of the autonomous Jewish community were nowhere more extensive than in Poland. Communal bodies decided the terms of Jewish moneylending and tax farming, as well as the leasing from territorial lords of concessions like salt mines. Once a man held a concession for a specified number of years he had tenure rights (*hazakah*) and it was an offence to underbid him for the concession. Such rules, it must be added, were not always honoured nor could they be readily enforced against wealthy Jews well connected with Gentile rulers. Even so, this range of communal enactments bore witness to the diversity and inner strength of Polish Jewry in the mid-seventeenth century.

Jewish Dispersion

Probably half the world's Jews in 1650 lived in the Ottoman empire,[3] which extended from Persia through the Middle East and across North Africa to Gibraltar, and in Europe from Greece to the Balkans and

---

[3] Since population figures will be given repeatedly, it is desirable to explain their sources. Local Jewish communities sometimes enumerated their members, usually by household for taxation purposes. The question of family and household size becomes central, and scholars have laboured and disputed over it. In eastern Europe and Ottoman lands a general census was rare, and Poland, 1764, and Russia, 1897, are single cases. Modern states have taken detailed censuses, but in many countries they did not enumerate by religion. In the United States a proposal to do so brought a sharp debate. In such modern countries demographers have drawn up detailed estimates from incidental information in censuses, burial records, and even Jewish names in telephone directories. Israel has full Jewish population data.

Hungary. The Sublime Porte in Constantinople was the overlord, but its subject peoples' real masters were the almost independent provincial rulers. Turkey and the Ottoman empire's European lands, not to mention the Middle East, had been the home of Jewish communities since ancient times. Under Ottoman rule Jews and other minority religions enjoyed extensive communal autonomy. Not only Jews from Germany, Hungary, and Bohemia but thousands expelled from Spain in 1492 and Portugal in 1497 found a haven in Ottoman lands. Especially in such cities as Salonika and Constantinople, renamed Istanbul in the twentieth century, they kept their native tongues and transmitted them to their children, while also enriching the simple Turkish language. In Constantinople the Iberian refugees joined and soon dominated the diverse Jewish elements who had been forced to resettle there from many parts of the sultans' realm as part of the imperial method of repopulating the ruined metropolis after the conquest of 1453. On the other hand, Jews from Salonika were compelled to move to the island of Rhodes after the Ottoman conquest in 1525. Others voluntarily moved northwards into the Balkans, although Balkan Jewry only developed when it came under Christian rule long after. The eastern Mediterranean also had significant Jewish communities on islands such as Corfu and Crete, which were ruled by the Italian commercial cities of Venice and Genoa. Ottoman Jewry, like the empire itself, had passed its peak by 1650. Jews in the empire could still hold Christian slaves,[4] but they had to struggle against the monopoly privileges of Turkish guilds while setting up guilds of their own.[5]

Of the approximately 550,000 Jews who inhabited the rest of Europe, about 450,000 could be found in the broad stretches of the Polish-Lithuanian kingdom. Its 282,000 square miles included today's Ukraine, Baltic states, much of White Russia, and north-west Russia. Poland was the flourishing centre of world Jewry, its most important community from the Spanish expulsion until the Second World War. Expulsions had put an end to Jewish life in most of western Europe: England in

[4] Pierre Belon, *Les observations de plusieurs singularitez . . . en Grece, Asie, Iudee . . . et autres pays estranges* (Paris, 1588), 399–401.

[5] Gabriel Baer, 'Monopolies and Restrictive Practices of Turkish Guilds', *Journal of the Economic and Social History of the Orient*, 13 (1970), 145–65.

1290, France in stages from 1306 to 1394, Spain and Sicily in 1492, Portugal in 1497, and most of the German towns and principalities between 1350 and 1500. Jews continued to live in some of the German principalities, and small Jewish groups, mainly former Marranos returning to Judaism, were tolerated in England and the south of France from the late sixteenth century. The poet Ronsard wrote of their unpopularity: 'I do not like the Jews; they put to the cross / The Christ, the Messiah, who erases our sins . . .'[6]

All these were open and recognized Jewish communities, to be duly discussed below. Here we take note of a strange and tragic community of fate, although it hardly qualifies as a community and was not Jewish. Yet they were not quite Christians either. These were the New Christians (*nuevos cristianos*), the Marranos—literally, pigs—of Spain and Portugal. Large-scale conversion in Spain began in 1391, and Judaism's lawful existence on the Iberian peninsula ended in 1497. The New Christians' Christianity was thus not new in 1650. However, the fanatical Catholicism which made Spain and Portugal bastions of religious fervour kept the descendants of Jewish converts under permanent suspicion of religious indifference or heresy. A cloud of distrust and social exclusion hung even over those who were rich or highly placed. The Holy Office of the Inquisition had the assistance of Old Christian snoopers and informers, eager to uncover 'Judaizing' for the sake of heavenly and earthly rewards. There was indeed reason to doubt the Christian fidelity of many a New Christian, even in the face of the Inquisition's sanctions, which included confiscations, long imprisonment, and the notorious public 'act of faith' (*auto da fe*) which meant fiery death at the stake. On the other hand, a large proportion of the New Christians—one will never know how many—were passively conforming Catholics, and some were truly devout. Among the latter were no less than St Teresa de Jesus of Avila, co-patron saint of Spain and the great religious intellectual Juan Luis Vives. His aunt and cousins went to the stake and his mother's remains were exhumed and burned. The devout Vives avoided the Inquisition's attention by living abroad. The findings of research

---

[6] Quoted in Robert Mandrou, *Introduction to Modern France, 1500–1640: An Essay in Historical Psychology* (London, 1975), 79.

constantly lengthen the list of Spanish and Portuguese prelates, scholars, poets, and statesmen who were wholly or partially of Jewish descent. Much of Spain's imperial greatness was built upon the economic, cultural, and political talents of the descendants of Jews.

Investigating possible Jewish ancestry of Catholic Spaniards and Portuguese may appear a biographical detail or a racist undertaking. Long before the Nazi racial mania, however, 'purity of blood' (*limpieza de sangre*) was of central interest in Spain. Since the 'taint' of Jewish blood could cast discredit upon the loftiest nobles, the government took steps to suppress genealogical handbooks which exposed Jewish ancestry. Many New Christians sought certificates from the Inquisition attesting to their 'purity of blood', meaning the absence of recent Jewish forebears. The Society of Jesus, founded and led by Spaniards, went further. Ignatius Loyola, the founder, was an Old Christian, but his successor Diego Lainez and most of the early Jesuit leaders were New Christians. Yet the Jesuits embraced Spanish racism. Rules passed in 1594 and 1608 excluded candidates who were blemished by 'notoriously dishonourable' ancestors as far back as five generations. Only the great-great-grandson of a convert could become a Jesuit. This racist rule, unparalleled in the history of Christianity, was abandoned only in 1936 when the racial laws of Nazi Germany became an uncomfortable parallel.

The Hispanist Americo Castro and his disciples hold that self-doubt and fatalistic resignation (*vivir desviviendose*) is deeply characteristic of the Spanish mind and permeates Spanish culture. They argue that this mood originated in the New Christians' awareness of the contempt and exclusion they endured and the insecurity of their existence. Many who lived in opulence still felt this distrust. Such a status fostered fatalism and despair, the opposite of the buoyancy and confidence to be expected of the rulers of a vast new empire. The disdain of proper Spaniards for the large, talented body of New Christians who constituted Spain's mercantile middle class contributed substantially to Spain's decline, as Spaniards themselves noticed after 1600.

Marranos constituted an international commercial and financial bourgeoisie linked by family and religion, including those who returned to Judaism in safe countries. Family members who remained Christians were not excluded, however.[7] Marranism had inner qualities of its own. With Judaism prohibited, Marranism meant minimally the denial of Christianity. Prohibited Judaism and rejected Christianity meant in several famous cases, as we shall see, the negation by Marrano descendants of all religious orthodoxy. Within Spain, Marranism became more active during Spain's dynastic union with Portugal between 1580 and 1640, when Portuguese arrivals revived Spanish Judaizing after a century of Inquisitorial thoroughness had practically stamped it out. There were good reasons for the stubbornness of Portuguese Marranism in particular. While the Spanish Jews' conversions during the fifteenth century had been more or less voluntary, the Jews of Portugal, including thousands who had gone there from Spain in 1492 rather than convert, were not expelled but forcibly Christianized in 1497. Portugal's unwilling Christians had been permitted to practise Judaism openly until the Inquisition began its persecutions in 1534. Thus there were active and knowledgeable Portuguese crypto-Jews who came to Spain during the sixty years of dynastic union. One result, put by I. S. Revah, was that 'Portuguese Marranism came to reawaken popular hostility against all "New Christians", and to confine within a veritable "moral ghetto" Spanish Catholic families which had not known, or could not bring to be forgotten, their Jewish origins.'[8] Another French historian, however, sees not just Judaizing at the root of the Inquisition's persecutions. He correlates waves of persecution with the social tensions which accompanied economic fluctuations:

This tension normally manifests itself in exasperation at the encounter with minorities. Now the Inquisitorial tribunal, even more than the police of the contemporary state, acts on denunciations . . . in a Spanish world purged of dissidence the Judaizer in Mexico and Madrid plays the indispensable role of scapegoat, catalyst of the discontents which long-term economic readjustments involve.[9]

---

[7] I. S. Revah, 'L'Hérésie Marrane dans l'Europe du 15e au 18e siècle,' in *Hérésie et sociétés dans l'Europe pré-industrielle, 11e–18e siècles,* ed. Jacques Le Goff (Paris, The Hague, 1968), 327–37.

[8] I. S. Revah, 'Les Marranes', *Revue des études juives,* 118 (1959), 40.

[9] Pierre Chaunu, 'Pour un tableau triste du Méxique au milieu du XVIIe siècle: Le "Diario" de Gregorio Martin de Guijo', *Annales,* (January 1955), 83; also his 'Inquisition et vie quotidienne dans l'Amérique espagnole au xviie siècle', *Annales,* 11/2 (April–June 1956), 235.

The last great outburst of persecution occurred during the 1680s and 1720s. Later in the eighteenth century, attitudes to Marranos softened somewhat and the way opened for their gradual assimilation into Iberian society.[10] But the Jewish question haunted the Iberian countries for centuries after their Jews were expelled.

There were always New Christians like Juan Vives who sought to escape the oppressive atmosphere in which they lived but had no desire to return to Judaism. Seventeenth century France received some who only desired to be Catholics in peace. Of great significance, however, was the settlement in western Europe of New Christians who returned to Judaism. The history of the Jewish Diaspora can tell of Jews forced out of native lands who remained distinct groups within the Jewish communities of their new countries, long retaining international family ties and frequently business connections. German Jewish refugees after 1933 provide a recent example, and Spanish including Marrano Jewry after 1492 is an earlier one.

The New Christians who quit Spain tended to settle in coastal cities which were centres of international trade. Jews of Spanish and Portuguese origin were found in the Mediterranean coastal cities of the Ottoman empire as well as Venice and Leghorn (Livorno) in Italy, at a time when English and Dutch merchants in Turkey were overcoming Venice's commercial dominance. Dutch and English aggressiveness led the Atlantic economy, with its Baltic and North Sea arms, in replacing the ancient centrality of the Mediterranean. As expressed by Ralph Davis, 'the old focus of European wealth and mercantile influence was sinking back into the role of another Baltic, subservient to the requirements of the powers bordering the Atlantic Ocean . . .'[11] Jews were prominent in this development. The new Atlantic bases of the 'Portuguese merchants', as Marranos were euphemistically called, could be found along its coast in Bayonne, Bordeaux and Rouen in France, in London and Hamburg, and above all Amsterdam.

New Christians who returned to Judaism had to be careful. In Italy they

[10] Revah, 'Les Marranes', 40.
[11] Ralph Davis, 'England and the Mediterranean', in *Essays in the Economic and Social History of Tudor and Stuart England in Honour of R. H. Tawney* (Cambridge, 1961), 137; Robert Mantran, 'La Navigation vénitienne et ses concurrentes en Méditerranée orientale', *Mediterraneo e Oceano Indiano* (Florence, 1970), 374–87.

could return freely for a while even in the pope's own city of Rome. Yet in Ancona, also under the pope, a group of returned Jews went to the stake during the 1550s as Catholic apostates. Catholic France unofficially permitted New Christians to settle and become Jews. Similarly, Spain's enemy Protestant England allowed a colony of 'Portuguese merchants' to carry on quietly as Jews in Queen Elizabeth I's London. However, their leader, the queen's physician Dr Rodrigo Lopez, was put to death in 1594 after entangling himself in dangerous Anglo-Spanish diplomacy. The free city of Hamburg had a prosperous colony of returned Jews, while Antwerp in the Spanish Netherlands (today's Belgium), an important centre of New Christian Judaization in the sixteenth century, was extinguished when it was engulfed by war and Spanish persecutors. The most extensive return to Judaism came in Amsterdam.[12] Although there have long been conflicting sources about the origin of Amsterdam Jewry, it seems clear that New Christian refugees from Antwerp and other refugees who came directly from Portugal founded by 1600 what became the greatest Jewish community in the west before 1800. They were attracted by Holland's unique combination of toleration for the Jews which was unofficial from 1595 and official after 1614, its commercial prosperity, relative breadth of livelihood, and a communal life. Approximately 3,000 Jews, the great majority of them Sefardim, lived in Amsterdam. Free of Spanish rule after 1609 and independent from 1648, the Dutch republic received a major migration of New Christians who were leaving persecution and the economic crash of 1647–53 in Spain. However, their treaty right to visit Spain for trade as Jews without molestation was little respected.[13] Many who settled in Amsterdam exceeded the city's capacity to absorb them economically, and they were encouraged to settle in Dutch colonies. The Dutch republic reached its greatest days in the mid-seventeenth century with broad Jewish participation.

---

[12] Miriam Bodian, *Hebrews of the Portuguese Nation: Conversos and Community in Early Modern Amsterdam* (Bloomington, Ind., 1997).

[13] Jonathan Israel, 'Spain and the Dutch Sephardim, 1609–1660', *Studia Rosenthaliana*, 12 (1978), 42 ff.; idem, *The Dutch Republic and the Hispanic World 1606–1661* (Oxford, 1982), 47, 126, 135, 141, 146–7, 423–5; idem, 'Menasseh ben Israel and the Dutch Sephardic Colonization Movement', in Yosef Kaplan *et al.* (eds.), *Menasseh ben Israel and his World* (Leiden, 1989), 139–63.

We see that out of the extinct Jewish communities of Spain and Portugal new Jewish communities in France, England, and Holland came into existence. On the other hand, the number of New Christians in Germany outside Hamburg was negligible. In Poland they played some role only in the town of Zamosc, and as a handful of courtier-diplomats in the sixteenth century. On the other hand, ancient Jewish communities within the Ottoman empire, including Palestine, were augmented and invigorated.

The Jews of Italy's history reached back to Roman times, and embraced distinct cultural traditions and religious customs. Italian Jewry was never numerous, especially after the disastrous plague of 1630. Rabbi Simone Luzzatto of Venice, whose Italian *Discourse on the Jews of Venice* of 1638 is a forerunner of the sociology of the Jews, estimated 5,000 in his city, 4,500 in Rome, and 25,000 in all of Italy. By the mid-seventeenth century, however, Italian Renaissance magnificence was past and so also the Jews' significant if not outstanding role in it. The population and economy of the Italian peninsula were contracting, and regimes loyal to the Catholic Counter-Reformation took control. The papacy led the way. It had protected the Jews for a millennium, but turned against them from the 1550s with a series of drastic restrictions intended to show the proper way for Catholic rulers to treat them. By 1650 Roman Jewry was crowded into a plaguey ghetto, its livelihoods limited to handicrafts, second-hand clothing, and moneylending. One widely copied innovation was the ghetto, a term probably coming from Venice during the 1550s. A century of pressure by the papacy brought about the establishment of ghettos throughout Italy, into which not only the local Jews but also those from countryside villages were herded. Jewish communities in city-states of northern Italy such as Venice, Florence, Mantua, and Padua existed on the basis of contracts drawn for a fixed period. When they came up for renewal the contracts included the ghetto requirement. The intellectual and social freedom of Renaissance times was gone as the Jews were confined within walled quarters where they remained until the French revolutionary era. Hebrew books were subjected to censorship and Roman Jews had to appear regularly in church in order to hear missionary harangues against Judaism. Yet poetry, biblical study, and historiography, as well as mysticism and rabbinic learning, persisted among Italian Jews notwithstanding their lowered intellectual *élan*. Some young men still pursued medical studies at the University of Padua, joined there by a few Polish Jews.

North of Italy, the Protestant Reformation and the Thirty Years War passed through Germany when few Jews lived there. In the middle of the seventeenth century Jews lived mainly in the Rhine valley and Bavaria. Those in the Holy Roman Empire were, in a much misunderstood term, servants of the emperor's chamber (*servi camerae*). Far from meaning servitude or slavery, it meant that they were subject to the emperor as their ruler and judge. Their taxes also went to him, in return for imperial protection. Inevitably the emperor's overlordship stirred jurisdictional conflict with local rulers. By the seventeenth century the authority of the emperor as well as his protection of the Jews were only a myth. The Habsburg emperors concentrated on extending their personal rule over Austria and Bohemia and lands which they were wresting from Ottoman rule. They and many territorial magnates in their realm saw the advantage of allowing a limited number of Jews to settle in their lands to expand commerce and credit. New Jewish communities such as Ofen (later Budapest), Eisenstadt, and Pressburg (Bratislava) owe their beginnings to the ambition to enlarge and fortify their domains. Prague and Vienna exemplified the Jews' opportunities and insecurities. During the Middle Ages both had seen massacres and expulsion and then return. Viennese Jewry, not yet numerous but beginning to be influential at the Imperial court, had a relatively spacious quarter of its own, while Prague Jewry, which already existed during the First Crusade in 1096, succeeded in maintaining neutrality during the wars of religion and emerged unscathed. Yet it too was regularly threatened with expulsion.

Outside the Imperial domains, each ruler decided whether or not to admit Jews, and if so how many and on what terms. No Jews were yet permitted in the duchy of Brandenburg, soon to become Prussia. Most lived in the old Rhenish towns of Worms, Mainz, and Trier and especially Frankfurt am Main. Ruled by emperors, dukes and bishops, and municipal oligarchies, perhaps 100,000 Jews dwelt in German lands around 1650.

Poland was the centre of Ashkenazic Jewry. Polish Jewry's early medieval origins are shrouded in legend, but it is probable that some Jews migrated to Poland from Byzantine and Muslim lands. It is even possible that Jewish survivors of the Khazar kingdom near the Caspian Sea made their way to Poland after that kingdom's destruction during the thirteenth century Mongol invasions. But it was Jews from Germany and Bohemia continuously moving into Poland from the time of the Black Death until the seventeenth century who gave Polish Jewry its enduring character. Thanks to this immigration from the west and rapid natural increase, mid-seventeenth century Polish Jewry on the eve of its time of troubles was about four times as numerous as all of Jewry in the rest of Christian Europe.

Like the other classes of the Polish realm the Jews lived under a regime of charters and privileges, but one far more generous than those of Germany and Italy. The charters which the Polish monarchs or local rulers granted to individual Jewish communities did not vary much from each other. Jews could live where they wished, enjoy legal and communal autonomy, and make a living as they pleased. The great majority of Polish Jews lived in towns and villages owned and ruled by magnates, in a country without large towns whose inhabitants were mainly peasants. Jews constituted half or more of the urban population. Like other social and cultural groups, they tended to live in their own quarters, but there was no compulsory ghetto in Poland. City people strongly opposed Jewish charters, and some could purchase charters of their own permitting them 'not to tolerate Jews' (*de non tolerandis judaeis*) in their midst. The charters could be local, regional, or country-wide. Some individuals also possessed charters. The privileges granted by kings in the charters they gave became useless as royal power declined. Few of the charters which nobles granted were presented any more to the monarch for ratification. All charters had to be saved carefully since there was no other proof that they existed.[14] The numerous clauses in the Polish Jewish charters and popular literature of the time dealing with the sensitive subject of pawning and moneylending have fostered the false notion of a community of moneylenders. Jewish

---

[14] Jacob Goldberg, *The Jewish Society in the Polish Commonwealth* (in Hebrew; English title), 90–125; an abridged translation is in *The Jews in Poland*, ed. A. Polonsky (Oxford, 1986), 31–54.

moneylenders functioned, but credit extended by Jewish merchants was a more frequent method of lending. Commerce was the livelihood of most Polish Jews. Its scope ranged from international trade, especially the export of grain and raw materials from the large noble estates which were leased to Jews, down to retail shopkeeping. As Poland turned into a source of grain and timber and a market for western Europe's products, Polish cities stagnated and declined. Jews were drawn in growing numbers to countryside occupations as managers of nobles' estates, concessionaires of their liquor monopoly, and lessees of tolls and taxes. Urban Jewish craftsmen worked mainly in foodstuffs and garments and in furs and silver. Scholars have found Jews practising more than twenty trades in several towns, and in the important city of Lwow (Lemberg) no fewer than thirty-two trades had Jewish practitioners. In many communities there were Jewish guilds. One also finds a Jewish physician, engineer, or other professional, while paramedical barbers were quite common.

Polish Jewish population increased with Poland's size. Its tolerant rule of the Baltic lands was contested at various times by intolerant Muscovy, and Sweden. With the Baltic Protestant churches also opposed to Jewish settlement, Jews in Baltic lands were very few. In the vast Ukraine, however, Jews settled and spread far. S. Ettinger has found that in this fertile, little inhabited territory the number of known Jewish communities rose between 1569 and 1648 from 24 to 114, and there may have been others unrecorded. The size of individual communities also increased.

Poland had been the home of many Protestant sects, including even Socinians (Unitarians in the west). However, once the Renaissance and Reformation spent their force in Poland by the beginning of the seventeenth century, strong Catholic pressure was exerted against the sects. Jews played almost no role in the Polish Renaissance and it did not have any effect in broadening Jewish intellectual horizons. Despite its pronouncedly Christian character the Polish Renaissance showed little interest in Hebrew studies, and consequently Jews did not become teachers of Hebrew to scholarly Christians. Nor did any of the beleaguered Christian sects seek even an unofficial alliance with the Jews against overweening Catholic power. The gulf between Judaism and liberal Christianity was too wide even for such a brief, opportunistic connection. Catholic anti-Jewish agitation from the 1580s found support particularly among the Jews' urban competitors. Still, these seemed no more than annoyances. Compared with the rest of European Jewry only Polish Jewry possessed both large numbers and substantial freedom.

Humanism and Orthodoxy

Medieval Jewry bequeathed poetry, philosophy, science, ethical and sermonic literature, law codes, commentaries on Bible and Talmud, and linguistic studies, as well as popular vernacular literature. However, little of this was remembered in the mid-seventeenth century. Iberian Jewry was no more and oriental Jewry, which inherited some of the Iberian legacy, was unable to add much besides mysticism and liturgical poetry. Italian Jewry retained some of the Spanish spirit of poetry and linguistics. Thus we know of Mantua Jewry's theatrical troupe, which performed the first known Hebrew play. Some of the Spanish heritage remained vital among the Sefardic Jews of Amsterdam, where there was a cultivated group of philosophers, poets, writers, and physicians. Amsterdam was one of the few places where scientific interests were cultivated, mainly among Marrano intellectuals. Physicians, mainly graduates of Padua University, and a rare traditional Jew also displayed interest in science.[15]

Notwithstanding such humanistic interests Amsterdam Jewry and other centres of former New Christians demanded of their members religious conformity. Many Amsterdam Jews had once practised Judaism furtively at mortal peril and, like former New Christians elsewhere, they now wanted to adhere fully to Judaism as expounded and codified by rabbinic authorities. Besides, they believed that their continued enjoyment of religious tolerance in Holland demanded circumspection and the avoidance of anti-religious heresy. Discussing religion with outsiders was therefore forbidden, conversion of native Christians obviously so,

[15] David B. Ruderman, *Jewish Thought and Scientific Discovery in Early Modern Europe* (New Haven, 1995), esp. 11–13.

and no book could be published without the sanction of communal authorities. Questioning and dissent from normative Jewish faith and practice was put down by the community.[16] Was there a trace of the Inquisitorial past in the sternness with which these and other rules were enforced? Yet not every Jew submitted to this discipline. To be sure, most New Christians who became Jews did become adherents of rabbinic Judaism, Orthodox Jews in later terminology. Isaac Cardoso abandoned a fine career as a medical professor close to the Spanish royal court to become a Jew in Verona and the author of Jewish apologetics in Spanish. His brother Abraham also re-entered Judaism, but became the leading theologian of heretical Sabbatian messianism. There were also New Christians who came to Holland and France in order to be simply Christians relieved of the harassment and suspicion they underwent in Spain. They detested Judaism and some were willing to inform on conversos they had known.[17]

Among returned Jews there were also sceptics and rationalists who, after rejecting Catholicism, found Judaism not what they had imagined it to be from furtive Bible reading in Spain. Some of them sought the believable elements held in common by all religions. Early studies by C. Gebhardt and recent penetrating investigations by I. S. Revah have revealed a circle of Jewish deists and pantheists in mid-seventeenth century Amsterdam, negators of all positive religions. As we shall see, it was out of this background that Spinoza emerged.

There was bound to exist in Jewish life a gulf between adjustment to earthly realities and faith in redemption by Divine intervention. Faith in the advent of a redeemer was very vigorous in the seventeenth century, and not only among Jews. Persecution did not always rouse messianic expectations, nor did wealth and security necessarily dull them. After the great trauma of the expulsion from Spain, Sefardic Jewry had an activist messianism which demanded human effort to 'compel' the advent, unlike the relative passivity of the Ashkenazim. Sefardic messianism included a quest for personal redemption, especially by

[16] I. S. Revah, *Spinoza et le Dr. Juan de Prado* (Paris, The Hague, 1959); *idem*, 'Aux origines de la rupture Spinozienne: nouveaux documents', *Revue des études juives*, 123 (1964), 359–431 add important material on the heretical atmosphere among Amsterdam Marranos. [17] J. Israel, 'Spain and the Dutch Sephardim', 7 ff.

many who thirsted for it while they had to pretend they were Christians. The messiah would thus bring both personal and national redemption. During the sixteenth century, mysticism (*kabbalah*) began to play a major role as a doctrine which concentrated on the transcendental meaning of the coming of the messiah. By the middle of the seventeenth century this messianic kabbalism, which had started in the Galilean town of Safed one hundred years earlier, combined messianic passion with the contemplation of redemption's transcendental meaning. The combination was to explode a few years afterwards.

Modern Age Beginning

When the modern era in Jewish history began has been keenly debated for more than a century.[18] Neither in Jewish nor in general history do modern times, however they are defined, begin everywhere simultaneously. In Jewish life they arrived in regions such as western Europe centuries before their arrival in regions such as Yemen. Modern times are thus not defined by a date but by the appearance of certain new characteristics of individual and communal Jewish life. It is up to the historian to select those he or she considers the most important and begin modern Jewish history from their appearance. On the other hand some phenomena which appeared after the accepted onset of modern times reflect medieval ways and beliefs. For example, Sabbatianism began in 1665 and endured in various guises over 150 years, while Hasidism began during the 1750s and remains active to the present day. Neither bore the stamp of modernity even though they sounded some modern echoes.

What, then, are modern characteristics? This has been the real focus of the debate, and the answers given by historians reflect their scholarly and sometimes their personal outlooks.[19] Emancipation and liberalism,

[18] A brief, cogent statement is Michael A. Meyer, 'Where Does the Modern Period in Jewish History Begin?', *Judaism*, 24/3 (summer 1975), 329–38.

[19] This is conspicuous in the historian and theorist of Jewish autonomism Simon Dubnow, whose chronology of modern Jewish history is put mainly in terms of the loss of Jewish communal autonomy. See especially the introduction to his multi-volume world Jewish history, 'The Sociological View of Jewish History', in *Nationalism and History*, ed. Koppel S. Pinson (Philadelphia, 1958), 336–53.

Zionism and mass migration, science, capitalism, and population increase have all been brought into play to identify what is modern in the era of modern Jewish history.

Of the dates which have been proposed as the turning-point to modern times the earliest is 1492, the year of the expulsion from Spain and the discovery of America. However, the expulsion was but the last and greatest in a long series of medieval expulsions and America hardly figured in Jewish history before the seventeenth century when we exclude New Christians who sought to practise Judaism more safely in the remote Spanish territories. A British Jewish scholar has argued that the critical period is 1570-1620, when the prolonged Catholic–Protestant struggle stimulated a new, sceptical attitude towards religious and traditional controls. These were also the years of 'the beginning of Jewish re-entry into the mainstream of western civilization'.[20] This suggestive view of modern times rests on too few phenomena in too few places and is based on interpretations which are quite speculative. The philosopher of Jewish history Nachman Krochmal of Galicia, who died in 1840, found the end of a long cycle of decline in 1648, implying that a new and better era began then.[21] The year 1700 was proposed by a fervently Zionist historian as the year when *aliyah*, in his view the key to modern Jewish history, began. But the episode he cited was almost derisory, and his interpretation was idiosyncratic.[22] The modernization of Judaism by means of the Haskalah (Jewish Enlightenment) movement from about 1750, together with the French Revolution from 1789, have often been proposed, beginning with Heinrich Graetz, the greatest Jewish historian of the nineteenth century.[23] However, the process of modernizing change

---

[20] Jonathan I. Israel, *European Jewry in the Age of Mercantilism, 1550–1750* (Oxford, 1985), 1–2, 35–52.

[21] To be sure, he dismisses this in two sentences in his otherwise profound analysis. *The Writings of Nachman Krochmal*, ed. S. Rawidowicz (2nd edn., London, 1961), 112.

[22] B. Dinur, 'The Modern Period in Jewish History', *Be-Mifneh ha-Dorot* (Jerusalem, 1955), 26–9; translated in *Israel and the Diaspora* (Philadelphia, 1969). Dinur cites the *aliya* of a group led by Judah the Hasid. But they had Sabbatian purposes, Judah the Hasid died within a week of arrival, and the group dispersed.

[23] Heinrich Graetz, *Geschichte der Juden: Von Beginn der Mendelssohnchen Zeit (1750) bis in die neueste Zeit (1848)* (Leipzig, n.d. [c.1900]), to whom this is the fourth era of Jewish history, 'The Time of Awakening Self-Consciousness'.

began before the French Revolution, and the legal emancipation which the revolution brought was preceded by economic and intellectual emancipation. Moreover, how exaggerated were the hopes placed in emancipation has long been realized. The contemporary historian Jacob Katz claims that modern Jewish history begins with a change in Jews' self-consciousness about the meaning of their communal and social existence. He places this specifically in Berlin between 1750 and 1775, before the French Revolution, in Moses Mendelssohn's time and place. To be sure, Berlin Jewry itself remained for decades longer a traditional Jewish community.[24] Can the subjective experiences of very few people provide the turning-point of an age? Is modern Jewish history the product of inner experiences or of changes in objective circumstances?

Since there still must be some starting-point the most cogent one for modern Jewish history appears to be not in the eighteenth century but about 1650.[25] Then, a new secular view of the Jews began to be expressed. In the advanced societies of Holland and England Jews could live in relative freedom while capitalism provided the basis for their almost unfettered economic activity. Around 1650 western Europe and remote America were opening up to Jewish settlement, while east European Jewry's troubles were beginning—all characteristic of modern times. The Jewish community as a traditional society was visibly declining especially in western countries, to which Jews were beginning to emigrate from eastern Europe. All these were to become central themes during coming generations, and we therefore set the beginnings of modern Jewish history about 1650.

---

[24] Jacob Katz, *Massoret u-Mashber* (Tradition and Crisis) (Jerusalem, 1958), 247–70, 284-305; *Out of the Ghetto: The Social Background of Jewish Emancipation* (Cambridge, Mass., 1973), 46–59.

[25] This is presented tersely in Salo W. Baron, *A Social and Religious History of the Jews*, xi (New York, 1965), preface. It appears implicit in the periodization employed in the collective work of Hebrew University historians, H. H. Ben-Sasson (ed.), *A History of the Jewish People* (Cambridge, Mass., 1976), esp. in the opening sections on 'The Modern Period' by S. Ettinger (pp. 727–50).

2

Glimmerings of a New Age

Jewish communities felt deep kinship despite cultural differences, linguistic barriers, and the slowness and dangers of travel. In the absence of today's instant communication and secular organizations, the bond existed thanks to the belief which overrode every external difference, that the Jews were God's unique people with a common religion and destiny. Unless someone had migrated from there, he or she would have known little about Jewish communities even in nearby lands. Collective action was a matter for emergencies such as danger to physical security or wars. Yet the differences among communities were extensive. Before the nineteenth century the greatest line of difference could be found north and south of a line drawn approximately along the lower Loire river, the Alps, and the Danube. To its south, the heritage of medieval Spanish, Italian, and oriental Jewry was still reflected in interest in the general culture and in a diversified Jewish culture. A Venetian Jew had to dwell in the ghetto, a term which itself originated in Venice, but his language was Italian and he might be interested in music and art. The culture of Jews of Spanish descent in the Ottoman empire remained Spanish, and their language was Judaeo-Spanish, known as Ladino. The character of their culture went together with relatively easy-going religious practice, especially when compared with the stringent ways of northern and east European Jews. Africa and the Middle East including Palestine constituted another sphere south of the north–south divide. Ordinary Jews everywhere shared religious faith but the cultural divide, which included many differences in religious practice, made communication difficult when they met.

Ashkenazic Jewry's cultural interests, in contrast, centred almost exclusively on Talmud and related juridical and ethical studies. A mild earlier interest in secular and humanistic studies had been abandoned.

A specimen of this disappearing type was R. Manoah Hanokh ben Shmaryah (d. 1611) of Lemberg, who combined halakhic learning with commentaries on the Bible and medieval Hebrew scientific works. By the 1620s, however, the wandering Hebraic humanist Yosef Shlomo Delmedigo of Candia was denouncing Polish Jewry's new, exclusive concentration on rabbinic studies.[1] *Kabbalah* and mystical religion came to permeate their religious and intellectual life. No longer only a theosophy for the spiritual élite, mystical religion now concentrated on no less 'practical' an object than the final redemption of the Jews. The world-wide scope of the Sabbetai Zvi messianic explosion of 1666–7, to be discussed below, shows how deeply mystical theories of redemption had penetrated seventeenth-century Judaism.

The Distress of Polish Jewry

The combined kingdom of Poland and Lithuania made an imposing presence on the map of 1648. Extending south from the Baltic to the Black Sea and from the Oder to the Dnieper rivers, the realm was flat, fertile, and without defensible natural borders. Since the Middle Ages a land of refuge for Jews from western Europe, during the 1630s Poland received refugees from the Thirty Years War. Its manifold inner weaknesses brought twenty years of war, plague, and devastation to the Polish-Lithuanian kingdom starting in 1648 from which it never fully recovered. Jews, intimately tied to Polish-Lithuanian political and economic life, were affected by these developments, which set Jewish life in eastern Europe on a prolonged downward course.

The Ukraine was the unstable frontier region of the Polish-Ukrainian realm. From 1569, the burdens of Polish servility were fastened upon the hitherto free Ukrainian peasants, and a system of taxes and fees was imposed on them. Weddings, baptisms, and even the use of their churches were subjected to taxation. Jews made money as estate administrators and lessees of mills, distilleries, fishponds, orchards, toll stations, and even entire towns. They served Polish landlords and even Polish Catholic

---

[1] S. Buber, *Anshey Shem* [on Lemberg Jewry] (repr. Israel, 1968), 71–2; Yashar, *Mazref le-Hokhmah* (Odessa, 1865), 59–60, *Ma'ayan Ganim* (Odessa, 1865) 128–32.

priests, but Jews were included in the hatred felt by Ukrainians towards these masters. The state of affairs which existed on the eve of 1648 has been summarized by Salo W. Baron:

The geographic, numerical, and economic expansion of Polish and Lithuanian Jewry before 1648 often blinded the Jewish leaders, as well as the masses, to the instability inherent in the Jewish position in a society which favored the small minority of nobles and clergy, excluding the vast majority of burghers and peasants, along with the numerous other ethnic minorities. Jews and other ethnic groups owed their relative well-being to the protection extended them by kings, whose power was constantly declining. Protection by the aristocracy, on the other hand, depended entirely on the exigencies of the moment and the profitability to the magnates of maintaining the Jews. To increase that profitability Jews, like the lower gentry in the great landlords' service, often had to tighten the screws on the subject population, in order to obtain the greatest revenue possible for both the masters and themselves.[2]

The death of King Ladislas IV in 1648 and the interregnum until the Polish nobility elected his successor were the point when the Ukrainian uprising against the oppressive regime broke out under Cossack leadership. Ethnically linked to the Ukrainians, the freebooting Cossacks supposedly protected the Ukrainian borders against the Tatars. In 1648, however, Cossacks, Ukrainians, and Tatars joined forces under Bohdan Chmielnicki. They ravaged the Ukraine and south-eastern Poland, while the Tatar allies' main interest was plunder and captives for the slave market.

As the Shavuot (Pentecost) holiday approached in June 1648 terrified Jewish refugees from the countryside, bearing tales of carnage and murder of Jews and Polish Catholic landlords and priests, sought the shelter of fortified cities. Killing in that pre-technological era was not yet mechanized but savage—disembowelling, impaling, roasting on spits. Many Jews fled to the Tatar camp, preferring the perils of captivity with the chance of ransom by fellow Jews to the probability of a barbarous death. A chronicle written shortly after the event tells what transpired in the

---

[2] Salo W. Baron, *A Social and Religious History of the Jews*, 2nd edn., xvi (New York, 1976[?]), 216–17.

fortress city of Nemerov, crowded with Jews and Poles who came there for safety.

This region did not know yet of the king's death, and so they still hoped God would send the king and his hosts to their aid. Later, when they heard [of his death] they mourned deeply and wept in supplication . . . But when the Cossacks heard of the king's death they rejoiced heartily. Then fear and trembling fell upon the Poles, traffic ceased and roads were abandoned . . . About fifty Cossacks came to Nemerov deceitfully and sounded horns and bugles. The people all noticed the sounds; it seemed as though the Poles were coming jubilantly with cavalry. [This was done] so that the gates of the fort should be unlocked. The satanic deed succeeded . . . They killed about six thousand people in the city . . . several hundred were drowned or put to death in agony.

Tolchin, besieged by Chmielnicki's men, saved itself by delivering its Jews for slaughter. As the Cossacks divided into a westbound column heading for Lwow and other Galician cities and another moving north towards Lithuania, Jews fled deeper into Poland.

Lwow and many other fortified cities kept faith with the Jews and did not yield them up. But in some places, such as Pinsk, the Jews were turned over to be killed or robbed in order to buy safety for the others. They shared in the armed defence of some cities and paid heavily to buy off the attackers when that was possible. Group martyrdom, a conception nearly unknown among Polish Jews, first appeared at this time. Conscious martyrdom (*Kiddush ha-Shem*, sanctification of the Divine Name) has a complex history, and in Europe it probably first appeared in Rhenish communities somewhat before the First Crusade in 1096. The concept coursed through medieval France, Germany, and Austria as individuals and entire communities immolated themselves rather than accept apostasy. *Kiddush ha-Shem* reached a climax during the massacres which followed the Black Death of 1348–9, which were commemorated in the liturgy and by chroniclers. On the Ukrainian frontier before 1648–9, however, Jews were accustomed not to martyrdom but to self-defence. But now, the chronicle of Nemerov reports the tone of martyrdom:

In the synagogue, where the children of Israel's prayers were as the sacrifice of animals in the Holy Temple, the singers and cantor and beadles were slaughtered with knives, sacrificing themselves like rams and lambs and goats. May the fragrance of their sacrifice ascend to the Dweller on High . . . Then [Cossacks] destroyed the Lesser Temple [the synagogue].[3]

The chroniclers relate that as the Jews who had been ejected from the fortresses of Tolchin and Gomel awaited their fate, religious leaders exhorted them to embrace martyrdom as their ancestors had. Glossed over by the chroniclers, there were Jews who turned Christian to save their lives and usually returned to Judaism when they safely could. However, it is by no means clear that the Jewish victims of 1648 were even given the choice of conversion. Many twentieth-century Jews regard martyrdom with feelings ranging from scepticism to scorn. Influenced by the extremes of the Holocaust during the Second World War and the defence of Israel, they feel that only forcible resistance and aggressive defence merit respect. During the Deluge of 1648–60 Polish Jewry, faced by enemies capable of overwhelming the Polish army, employed the options of desperation: flight, participation in armed resistance where there was any, seeking capture by Tatars instead of slaughter by Cossacks and Ukrainians, and for some, conversion in the hope of a later return to Judaism. When all else was impossible, martyrdom meant death in faith and inner dignity.

Perhaps 30,000 Jews died during the spring and summer of 1648. Little is known about captives whom the Tatars brought to the slave market in Salonika and Constantinople, but it is related that funds were raised in many Jewish communities to assist in buying and freeing them.[4]

Chmielnicki was about to continue his onslaught but instead he heeded the demand of Poland's new king Jan Casimir to negotiate. When nothing came of the Cossack hetman's demand for Ukrainian autonomy, in 1651 he resumed the war. When the Polish army decisively defeated him, Chmielnicki had to sign an agreement which included an affirmation of the Jews' right to continue their functions for the Polish ruling nobility. Then and for years to come, such clauses meant little because the Jews had fled the Ukrainian regions for older,

[3] *Megillat Eyfah*, in Y. Halpern (ed.), *Beit Yirael be-Polin* (Jerusalem, 1954), ii. 252.

[4] Israel Halpern, 'Captivity and Redemption in the Ukraine and Lithuania, 1648–1660' (Hebrew), in *Yehudim ve-Yahadut be-Mizrah Ayropah* (Jerusalem, 1969), 212–49.

safer parts of Poland and stayed out of the Ukraine. Chmielnicki returned to the attack and also made the fateful decision to become a Muscovite instead of a Polish vassal, thus involving the Russian state in the uprising and the affairs of Poland. The army of Muscovy, where Jews were not allowed to settle, invaded Poland in 1654, recaptured the once Russian cities of Smolensk, Vitebsk, and Mohilev and slaughtered the Jews they found there. In 1655 a Russian army advanced northwards towards Vilna but joined up instead with Chmielnicki's Cossacks and marched southwards towards Lwow and Lublin.

As in 1648, Lwow with its cosmopolitan merchant population protected the Jews, who again paid heavily to buy off the invader. Lublin, however, submitted and dragged its Jews by force into the Russian camp. At that fearful moment the Lublin Jews' lives were spared, but many died anyhow or were sold into captivity while their quarter was looted and put to the torch.

Rabbi Moses Rivkes (1621–62), a young Talmud scholar, describes the scene of terror in the introduction to his commentary on the *Shulhan Arukh*:

When the enemy approached Vilna on Wednesday, 23 Tammuz, 5615 [= 1655] almost the entire community fled as one man for their lives. Those who prepared horses and wagons for themselves left loaded with their wives, sons and daughters, and a bit of their belongings. Those who did not prepare went on foot with what they had, and their young children on their shoulders. By God's mercy I happened to meet an official's aide with his country wagon, and I sent away my family on it . . . I remained there alone because I did not yet believe the danger. Towards evening I became very frightened, and the next morning, 24 Tammuz, I set out with a staff in my right hand, holding my phylactery bag, and with a book of penitences in my left hand.

Filled with melancholy over the fine home and library he had abandoned, Rivkes caught up with the columns of terrified, weeping refugees. As they approached the Prussian frontier they were accosted by Swedish troops who seized what little remained to them. At last Rivkes and some of his family 'embarked on a ship across the high seas, and we sailed towards Amsterdam'. They and later Polish refugees by ship were received kindly. Vilna, like many other Lithuanian towns, was destroyed by a fire in which hundreds of Jews lost their lives, and others were killed. The tsar complied with the Christian burghers' request and compelled the Jews to resettle across the Niemen river, where they remained until the Poles returned in 1661 and the Jewish community of Vilna could begin its rehabilitation.

As mentioned above, the Swedes also invaded Poland in the summer of 1655, capturing and looting city after city and their Jews. There were no Jews in Sweden, but those in Poland were treated no worse and in some places better by the Swedes than the rest of the population. In the words of a chronicler:

First, the king of Sweden came to the holy community of Posen, city and mother in Israel. Two thousand family heads lived there, and the Swedes dealt kindly with the Jews. But most died of hunger and plague, and only three hundred survived. Then they went on and captured Krotoschin. There were four hundred family heads there and only fifty survived, for the remainder perished by famine and sword. From there he went to the holy community of Lissa where there were four hundred very rich heads of family; everything was devastated and only one hundred survived, who fled to Germany.

Worst of all came to pass in the medieval capital of Cracow, home to Poland's foremost Jewish community. The Swedish siege destroyed the Jewish quarter, and many Jews fled to Bohemia and Moravia. The Swedes conquered the city, but not before the retreating Polish army found and stole the wealth which many Jews had hidden within the fortified city. Although clergy, municipal councillors, and nobles besides Jews collaborated with the Swedes, it was the Jews who were held responsible for Cracow's misery when the Swedes withdrew before the Russian advance. The war came to be perceived as the struggle of Polish Catholicism against Swedish Protestantism, with Jews in treacherous league against the religion of Poland. The Jews suffered severely from Czarniecki's anti-Swedish irregulars, who wreaked numerous massacres on them in 1656–57.

Peace came to Poland's ravaged west and south in 1661, but not before 1667 with Muscovy in the east, after it took all the lands east of the Dnieper. What remained of Poland-Lithuania had undergone immense devastation and even by the end of the eighteenth century the country had not reached its production of the sixteenth century. A Polish historian has estimated that the country's population was reduced by half. In the central province of Mazovia it dropped by 64 per cent; 85 per cent of the land was untilled and 35 per cent of all towns were razed to the ground.[5] The Jews were thus fortunate when they lost 'only' an estimated 20 per cent of their 450,000 people. By no means did wars end in 1667; in the sixty-eight years between 1648 and 1716 Poland was at war for fifty-five years. An unknown number of Jews fled the country, mainly to German and Habsburg lands to the west.

The experiences of a certain Rabbi Jacob, described in his sermon which he published in Venice in 1662,[6] sketch what Polish Jews underwent. Like many others, he fled his native Tomashev to 'safety' in the fortress city of Nemerov:

When I was in Poland, the land of persecution, during the severe, eerie travails of 1648, a consuming fire broke out in the community of Nemerov. The [Ukrainian] enemy, a cruel nation, overcame us . . . My light turned to darkness when they killed my wife and three children. I wandered about until 1655, when many old and new troubles stirred up . . . I was taken captive with my [second?] wife and child to a cruel nation, to a man without compassion for old or young . . . I was beaten and bitterly tormented.

Rabbi Jacob vowed that if he were liberated he would settle in the Holy Land. Other authors also wrote of their sufferings and losses and displacement during those years.

The fortunes of four major Jewish communities exemplify the religious fanaticism and the terror and bewilderment which were the bequest of the years of the Deluge. All the communities were in old, once prosperous but now decaying cities as Polish trade and industry declined. Acutely conscious of their decline, the cities pressed harder to maintain their monopolies and to exclude Jews, and were willing to pay well for the privilege 'not to tolerate Jews' (*de non tolerandis judaeis*) in their midst. Jews of course would pay well to counter such demands. Hardly

---

[5] Jerzy Topolski, 'Economic Decline in Poland from the Sixteenth to the Eighteenth Centuries', in Peter Earle (ed.), *Essays in European Economic History* (Oxford, 1974), 127–42.

[6] Jacob ben Shimon, *Ohel Ya'akov* (Venice, 1662). Nothing further is known of the man.

had the Swedes quit Cracow in 1660 when an anti-Jewish riot after a religious procession had to be suppressed. It was the doing of autonomously governed, frequently riotous university students. In 1662 the accused in a blood libel went free, but next year Dr Matthew Calahora, of a leading family that came from Italy, was barbarously put to death for supposedly writing anti-Christian blasphemy which was 'found' on the altar of a church. Riots followed, as they did in 1664 with the arrival of rioters from Lwow. Belated news of Sabbetai Zvi's conversion to Islam stirred a disturbance in 1670. The aftermath of an epidemic which took the lives of 21,500 Christians and 1,100 Jews was marked by the largest disturbance of all, again led by students. Lwow Jewry underwent attacks in 1664, 1672, 1695, and 1704. In Lublin, the burghers whom the Swedes compelled to admit the Jews to the city proper after their quarter was destroyed, secured royal decrees in 1677 to keep Jewish business out of their city. They finally expelled the Jews from Lublin proper in 1761. Posen suffered severely during the Polish–Swedish war of 1698 and was devastated in 1716. The Posen Jewish community urged its members to build houses on the ruins of what had been a congested Jewish quarter. For the smaller community of Opatow in the Cracow region, Hundert has enumerated a series of accusations against Jews between 1650 and 1720. They included Host desecration and ritualized insults to Christianity. The Jews emerged from these episodes without fatal results but scathed and out of pocket.[7]

On the other hand, what happened in Pinsk in White Russia, a community investigated by M. Nadav,[8] shows that its Jews' relative position under the protection of Polish rulers actually improved. In contrast to Christian inhabitants who remained in Pinsk, the Jews fled *en masse* from two of the city's three foreign occupations, saving their lives and much of their possessions. They were then able to expand their businesses, but the antagonism of the Christian townsmen increased sharply.

[7] Gershon David Hundert, *The Jews in a Polish Private Town: The Case of Opatów in the Eighteenth Century* (Baltimore and London, 1992), 40–2.

[8] *Pinsk: Sefer Edut ve-Zikkaron . . . 1506–1941*, i. *Kerakh Histori*, ed. M. Nadav, 17–50; 'The Jewish Community of Pinsk from the Khmelnitsky Massacres to the Peace of Andruszow' (Hebrew) *Zion*, 31 (1966), 153–96.

The hatred for the Jews which coincided with the disasters of the Polish commonwealth somewhat resembles the hysteria of the assault on the Jews after the Black Death catastrophe of 1348–9. In both cases, there was a search for a scapegoat and the purging upon it of primitive fears. However, Polish Jewry was quite affluent and numerous and was needed, particularly by the nearly omnipotent nobility who protected them. Regional assemblies of the nobility, especially in western Poland, complained about the Jews but no assembly would propose serious measures against them. During these distressful post-Deluge years they increased their prominence in Poland's foreign and domestic trade.[9]

Ottoman Weakening

As the economic decline of Poland already became visible during the 1620s, so did that of the eastern Mediterranean and Turkey. Trade routes between western Europe and the Orient via Poland lost most of their traffic, while the Atlantic economy swelled. Yet the trade of Turkey was still considerable, and much of it was controlled by Jews. Thus, in the narrow, crowded streets of Salonika (Thessalonika today) lived 12,000 Jews in a population later estimated at 60,000. Their autonomous community was active in the city's trade, which was famous for cloth weaving and silk and linen manufacture, important export products.[10] Many Salonikans moved to Smyrna (Izmir) in Asia Minor, which they helped to make 'the preferred port of the Dutch in the Levant'.[11] A modern scholar summarizes that

[9] Hundert, *Opatów*, 30–2.

[10] Felix Beaujour, *Tableau du commerce de la Grèce*, 2 parts (Paris, Year 8 = 1801), 53, a later estimate of a population which changed little; P. M. Coronelli, *Description géographique et historique de la Morée* 2 parts (Paris, 1686), part 1, p. 57; part 2, pp. 121–2; Michel Febvre, *Théâtre de la Turquie* (Paris, 1682), 375–400; Hubert Pernot (ed.), *Voyage en Turquie et en Grece du R.P. Robert de Dreux . . . 1665–1669* (Paris, 1925), 103; Halil Inalcik, 'Capital Formation in the Ottoman Empire', *Journal of Economic History*, 29 (1969), 97–108, 118, 121–2.

[11] Bruce McGowan, *Economic Life in Ottoman Europe: taxation, trade and the struggle for land, 1600–1800* (Cambridge/Paris, 1981), 31.

it was in Constantinople and Thessaloniki particularly that the Jews who, though living in communities in Adrianople, Gallipoli and Smyrna, held an outstanding place. They mainly acted as agents between the Ottoman administration and the merchants of the [British] Levant Company; they levied the taxes on all the vessels that entered the Turkish ports, leased custom houses, served as overseers, watchmen, accountants and money-changers, appraisers.'[12]

Marrano merchants were especially important on account of the capital which they brought to Constantinople. Banking did not exist in the Ottoman empire, but credit institutions, especially the Muslim religious *waqf*, were highly developed. They were better capitalized than the relatively few Jewish moneylenders. As put by a modern scholar:

where the indigenous credit institutions were highly developed, Jewish money-lenders had little room for activity, but in places where these institutions were less highly developed [such as Rhodes and Arab lands], Jewish money-lenders may have found attractive conditions.[13]

Polish Jewry in Straits

Poland's government was unlike those of the west, which aggressively promoted the country's economic interests. It became an economic backwater and by 1700 was practically a colonial market providing grain, timber, cattle, and furs for western countries and importing their luxury articles, textiles, and other manufactured goods. The demand for grain in the west stimulated the growth of huge Polish grain plantations and helped to reduce the Polish peasantry to serfdom. Most of the profits were spent in western Europe.[14] Jews were indispensable as buyers

[12] Paul Cernovodeanu, *England's Trade Policy in the Levant . . . 1660–1714* (Bucharest, 1972), 30.

[13] Haim Gerber, 'Jews and Money-Lending in the Ottoman Empire', *Jewish Quarterly Review*, 72 (1981–82), 100, 105, 107, 117–18.

[14] Hermann Kellenbenz, *The Rise of the European Economy: An Economic History of Continental Europe from the Fifteenth to the Eighteenth Century*, rev. and ed. G. Benecke (London, 1976), 158–9, 230–1.

and sellers, distributors, and financiers and managers of Poland's domestic and international commerce. *En route* to Vienna, Prague, Amsterdam, and the annual Leipzig fair Jewish international trade routes passed through old towns like Posen and Lissa, as well as the newer Brody in Galicia, recently founded by the enlightened magnate Sobieski. Polish Jewry adjusted to the new economic conditions by shifting from the stagnating, hostile cities to the villages and countryside. On the serf-worked estates Jews leased most of the noble owners' unlimited privileges. Further down the economic ladder Jews kept inns, distilled liquor, and collected road tolls. Those higher up were purchasing agents and purveyors to the lords' tastes. On top, they might be stewards for vast estates who employed hundreds of Jewish subordinates, marketing thousands of tons of produce, and purchasing the finished goods which Poland had to import. For their leases the Jews paid heavily. Taxes on Jewish communities and individual Jews were basic to noble and government finance. Polish commerce was in Jewish hands, but the capital for moneylending and banking came mainly from the endowments of the Catholic Church.

The Jews on top were harsh, dynamic men. They had to deal with gentry unfettered by higher authority, who controlled the life and death of masses of peasant serfs and of others who inhabited their lands. Like medieval Jews in western countries, those in Poland were officially subjects of the king, their lord and protector. But after royal power in Poland virtually vanished from 1660, the Jews were subject to the unbridled gentry. The gentry for their part depended on Jews, but concealed their dependence by treating them with contemptuous arbitrariness. The one remaining central power was the Roman Catholic Church. Victorious in its struggle against sectarians and Protestants and successful in encouraging the piety of Poland's kings, the church turned the full force of nationalist religious fervour against the primordial dissenters from Christianity, the Jews.

The Jewish community's ceaseless demands for money from its people and the abuses in assessing and collecting it did much to undermine its authority and moral prestige. Evidence from several *kehillah* budgets shows that 70 to 80 per cent of its income went to externals— taxes, subsidies, and *douceurs*. The latter included paying authorities to bring to justice someone who had killed or robbed a Jew, saving a falsely accused Jew, suppressing an anti-Jewish tract, or preventing university students in Cracow and other places from assaulting Jews. Only the remaining 20 to 30 per cent could be used to maintain the Jewish quarter and to provide poor relief, bridal dowries, salaries to communal employees, and education. Some communities lent money to wealthy members to finance their mercantile operations, and they paid well for the use of the money. It was financially worthwhile for the community even to borrow from Christians in order to lend to Jews. Yet the precedent of mixing private and public accounts led to deplorable extremes. By the close of the seventeenth century, Jewish communities were burdened with mountainous debts owed not only to nobles and church bodies, but also to some of their members. These members, however, constituted the oligarchic governing *kahal* who imposed taxes and disposed of the money as they saw fit. The community also guaranteed the loans its members took. Thus it assumed many of the functions of a bank with the taxes it levied as the source of funds.

What the plain people thought of all this came forth in the sayings of several contemporary preachers who were beginning to function as the voice of opposition. Rebellious persons were said to murmur, 'What do we need a rabbi and *kahal* men for? Only to make us trouble and impoverish us.'[15] A young member of the right family, whether or not worthy and mature, not infrequently was installed by domineering oligarchs in the lucrative and honorific office of community rabbi.[16] Newly rich communal despots were believed to be advising their noble clients how to squeeze more money out of poor Jews, while avoiding their own fair share of communal taxes. 'In our time', it was alleged, the leaders 'authorize themselves . . . to consume [poor Jews'] money, leaving them nothing with which to nourish their infant children. They fleece the mass of people and compel them [to pay] added taxes and assessments, and conduct themselves as rulers of Israel.'[17] In progressively more severe language the *kahal* for its part threatened 'conspirators' and 'gossip

---

[15] Quoted in B. Dinur, 'The Beginnings of Hasidism and its Social and Messianic Bases' (Hebrew) *Be-Mifneh ha-Dorot* (Jerusalem, 1955), 96.

[16] Benjamin Wolf ben Matthew, *Sefer Tohorat Kodesh* (Amsterdam, 1733), part 2, 9a.

[17] Quoted in Dinur, 'The Beginnings of Hasidism', 109.

mongers', usually meaning dissenters, with fines and the ban. With financial needs uppermost, the *kahal* employed its authority to restrict the right of settlement to dependable taxpayers while keeping others out. In order not to create new households which might need aid rather than pay taxes, even the right of the poor to marry was subject in at least one instance to an annual quota. The Lithuanian Council of Lands generously permitted refugees from the disasters of the Deluge to settle tax-free for several years, but afterward they had to pay or move out. Rigorous measures, such as assignments and guarantors, were employed to prevent a member from quitting a community without paying his tax arrears. To be sure, while these abuses were widespread, most communal oligarchies conducted their communities' affairs with reasonable equity.

Houses in the overcrowded Jewish quarter, which was prevented from expanding outwards, were carefully kept under Jewish control although Jews could not own real property. In this and many other spheres vested right (*hazakah*) was recognized. No Jew was permitted by the Jewish community to outbid another's toll-house or distilling concession, nor to attract away another artisan's or shopkeeper's steady customers. *Hazakah* applied not only to the economic sphere but also to house tenancy and to synagogue rights and honours. (The latter remains in many orthodox synagogues today.) *Hazakah* could not hold, however, in Jewish communities in the dynamically growing west European economy.

West European Revival

Those Polish Jews who escaped during the disastrous years by fleeing to western lands hardly realized that they were beginning a migratory movement which continues to the present day. As a contemporary preacher put it, 'Jews left their city and country for a strange land, in flight from the enemy sword which, for our many sins, overcame the other inhabitants of their city.'[18] They fled to other parts of Poland and abroad, as exemplified by biographies such as Rivkes', cited above.

[18] Quoted, ibid., 112.

Another Vilna rabbi, Jacob Ashkenazi, fled into Hungary, where his son Zvi was born in 1660. (This son, one of the foremost rabbis of his era, styled himself 'pure Sefardi' after serving in the Sefardi community of Sarajevo.) Yet another rabbinic refugee from Vilna, one Rabbi Meir, met a violent end in Germany in 1659. Bearing a letter, perhaps one of recommendation, from the rabbi of Worms, he made his way to Wilfsburg *en route* to the Rhine crossing at Germersheim. His final, distant destination was Pressburg, but his body was found nine days later near Wilfsburg. Testimony concerning his death, taken in order to prove him dead and thus to enable his wife to remarry, included the significant statement, 'it is known that no Jew passed that day to the river crossing at Germersheim.'[19] It implies that Jews were recognizable, few, and were frequently seen on the public roads.

From the seventeenth century, Jewish migratory movements responded not only to the 'push' out of eastern Europe but to the 'pull' of western Europe, which was advancing to its centuries of world supremacy. Still, the numerous Bohemian and Alsatian Jewish settlements remained tight-knit little traditional communities. The same was true for those in the Rhineland, Hesse, Franconia, and Bavaria. Jews were still petty merchants, cattle dealers, and moneylenders and their tongue was Yiddish of the west European dialect. Yet not every Jew was cut to the same pattern. An unusual example was a Jew of Worms who drew up briefs for litigants in the public courts. This unofficial lawyer was paid by the scrivener who rendered his briefs into the required Latin.[20]

Important changes were becoming visible in these traditional communities. The tale of Viennese Jewry is suggestive. Vienna's medieval Jews had been expelled or put to death in a mass cremation in 1421, but the community was revived and granted toleration in 1526. It grew slowly to perhaps 500 families or 2,000 persons in the mid-seventeenth century, living autonomously in the *unterwerd* ('lower world') and governed by Jewish law. Their occupations of second-hand goods, pawnbroking, and moneylending led to friction with the poorer artisan class. Emperor Leopold I accepted the municipality's assurances that it would

---

[19] Yair Hayyim Bachrach, *Hut ha-Shani* (Responsa, mainly by the author's father (d. 1670)] and grandfather) (repr. Jerusalem, 1970), no. 72. This responsa is from the father. [20] Ibid., no. 45.

make good the loss of the sizeable Jewish tax revenue and, overriding Jewish pleas and his treasury's objections, expelled the Jews in 1670. Viennese Jews scattered and could be found throughout Germany and Moravia, and in Poland and Lithuania; one, Gerson Ashkenazi, became rabbi of Metz. The third Viennese Jewish community was founded on a different basis in 1676 by one wealthy Jew, Samuel Oppenheimer, who settled there with his retinue of 100 in order to become Imperial War Purveyor. Oppenheimer undertook vast obligations and surpassed all rivals in his ability to deliver necessities to the Austrian army in large quantities thanks to his network of Jewish agents and suppliers. However, he often had difficulty in collecting debts from his imperial master, and his palace was looted by a mob in 1700. Shortly after he died in 1703 Oppenheimer's strained business was forced into bankruptcy by the imperial treasury's avarice.[21] Twenty years later Vienna had seventeen Jewish families, with retinues, totalling about 420 persons.

Like those of Vienna. Berlin Jews had been massacred and expelled two centuries earlier. But when word of the Viennese expulsion of 1670 reached Elector Frederick William of Brandenburg he became interested in receiving some of the exiles. After a year of negotiation fifty families were admitted in 1671 for twenty years, paying a sizeable head tax but enjoying a degree of economic freedom which was rare for Brandenburg. It was Jewish economic venturesomeness and ingenuity that the Elector sought as a prod to the stodgy, exclusive Prussian merchants and guildsmen. It is not surprising that they constantly complained over the Jews.

The new Berlin Jewry constituted a *kehillah*. Its powers included taxation, which was assessed by elders (*parnassim*) who were usually substantial merchants. Later the elders were also granted the right of controlling residence and domicile. No wonder, then, that the Jewish community of Berlin was often the scene of bitter quarrels in which the government had to intervene. Judaism could be practised only in private until the first Berlin synagogue was allowed to open in 1714.

Charters, restricted entrance, and close regulation were the path pursued by the Habsburg and Prussian regimes towards the Jews as towards their other subjects. On the other hand, England, where Jews

[21] Max Grunwald, *Samuel Oppenheimer und sein Kreis* (Vienna, 1913).

began to resettle during the seventeenth century, and the Netherlands followed a course of immigration and settlement without restriction and comparative freedom of economic activity. Still, the Dutch *kehillah* and that of the Sefardim in England wielded far-reaching authority over their constituents.

The dramatic story of the Jews' resettlement in England during the 1650s combines Christian religious fervour, mercantile self-interest, and the exigencies of war.[22] With the expulsion of 1290 still on the books, Jews already in England were called euphemistically 'Spanish merchants' who practised Judaism privately but not secretly. They were not buried as Jews and even years later, when there was a synagogue and a cemetery, quite a few still chose Christian burial. The most striking figure of the Jewish resettlement is the imaginative Amsterdam rabbi, author and printer, Menasseh ben Israel, the son of Marrano refugees and a member of the Amsterdam rabbinic presidium. He has been dubbed 'the first modern rabbi' on account of his preference for Jewish apologetics and religious discussions with learned Christians, especially about eschatology and the millennium to come.[23] Menasseh's awareness of affairs led him to conceive of a formally re-established Jewish community in England, chartered by Lord Protector Oliver Cromwell. Quite likely Menasseh also conceived of himself as rabbi of the new community. The material advantages of resettlement to the Jews and to British overseas commerce were obvious. Publicists of the day linked Dutch commercial success to its tolerant religious policies, which in reality were for foreigners rather than for the Dutch themselves. But in England admitting the Jews was believed to possess transcendental significance besides. The religious merit of allowing Jews to settle originated with the fervid reports of Christian travellers, which persuaded Menasseh and many Christians that the American Indians were really Jews of the Ten Lost Tribes, leaving England supposedly the only country in the world without Jews. Scripture 'proved' to Christian sectarians that once Jews

---

[22] Lucien Wolf, *Menasseh ben Israel's Mission to Oliver Cromwell* (London, 1901), is the classic but outdated account which includes the rabbi's writings; see now David S. Katz, *Philo-Semitism and the Readmission of the Jews to England, 1603–1655* (Oxford, 1982).

[23] Cecil Roth, *A Life of Menasseh ben Israel: Rabbi, Printer, and Diplomat* (Philadelphia, 1934); Yosef Kaplan *et al.* (eds.), *Menasseh ben Israel and his World* (Leiden, 1989).

dwelt in every land they would gain messianic redemption and Jesus would then return. To readmit the Jews to England therefore could be the final requisite for salvation.

This heady mixture of redemption and profits, eschatology and commerce, allured Oliver Cromwell, leader of men, general, far-sighted politician, and deeply religious sectarian. He invited Menasseh to come from Amsterdam to plead his cause. At the Whitehall conference of November 1655 religious, mercantile, and political spokesmen made their respective cases, but no consensus was achieved. The highest legal authorities declared on that occasion that Edward I's expulsion decree of 1290 was no longer in force. In general, vested commercial interests and conservative religious principles opposed readmission, while religious sectarians and 'growth-oriented' politicians favoured it. The contemporary pamphlet debate on the Jews' readmission was the first modern public discussion of the Jews in largely secular terms. However, the 'Spanish merchants' in London preferred to keep their Judaism private. Rabbi Menasseh ben Israel's grand design of a chartered Jewish community repelled them and led to a breach.

Events briefly reconciled Menasseh and his Jewish opponents. The outbreak of war with Spain in 1655 brought an order impounding the property of Spaniards in England. One whose belongings were seized, Antonio Robles, boldly petitioned for the return of his property, declaring himself not a Spanish Catholic but a Portuguese Jew who had fled the Inquisition. Most significant, Robles's petition was granted. Next, Menasseh and six merchants presented the 'Humble Petition of the Hebrews at Present residing in this city of London . . .' Acknowledging the 'many favours and Protection' received from the Lord Protector, they prayed written assurance that they might continue Jewish worship 'without feare of Molestation either to our persons famillys or estates', and that they might acquire land for a burial ground. Cromwell transmitted this petition to his Council of State. To the present day it is unclear what if anything was decided there or whether that body left the matter to Cromwell for his personal, unofficial decision. Yet there is no doubt that the public practice of Judaism was approved by someone in authority, since a synagogue was under construction during 1656, and the new cemetery received its first burial in 1657. That was the year of

Menasseh ben Israel's death, aged 54. Penniless, he had returned home thanks to a grant from Cromwell with the remains of his son who had died in England.

Had Menasseh's project been approved and a charter for the Jews been granted, it would probably have been cancelled together with other enactments of the commonwealth when the monarchy was restored in 1660. The unofficial character of their resettlement saved the Jews from this fate. Charles II rejected suggestions to harass the inconspicuous Jewish community, assuring them of 'the effects of the same favour as formerly they have had, soe long as they demeane themselves peaceably and quietly with due obedience to his M*aties* laws, & without scandall to his Government'. These prosaic words of 1664 were the real charter for the Jews in England. Their numbers grew, reaching about 1,000 at the turn of the eighteenth century, most of them tradesmen and merchants. By 1700 Jews from central and eastern Europe outnumbered the Sefardim.

The mother community of early English Jewry was Amsterdam, whence came many of its people and communal institutions. Amsterdam Jewry's thin upper stratum of wealthy merchants and financiers towered over a mass of impoverished pedlars and day labourers. The 2,500 Sefardim of 1674 hardly increased from then until 1800, while the number of Ashkenazim during the same period went from 5,000 to 21,000. German Jews could be found in the Dutch metropolis from early days, and they founded their community under Sefardic patronage. Its growth, thanks mainly to refugees from Lithuania, was accompanied by internal strife which led to the founding of a second Ashkenazic community. At first the Sefardim backed the east Europeans against the Germans, but they complained to the Council of Four Lands in Poland in 1670 that these newcomers were treating Sefardic piety and liturgy contemptuously. Quite possibly it was Sefardic intercession which brought a command in 1672 from the magistrates to the two Ashkenazic communities to merge. That was one year after a large and costly Ashkenazic synagogue was built. In 1675 the celebrated Sefardic synagogue, standing today, replaced their earlier, modest edifice. By that time, however, the Sefardim were a diminishing minority, fortified in Amsterdam and northern Europe by a proud exclusiveness which became proverbial.

Theirs was the world's foremost commercial city as well as a manufacturing centre for colonial raw materials. Prominent as brokers, speculators and investors, Amsterdam Jews took the lead in making it the world's financial centre even after Amsterdam's commercial decline from 1672. The economic historian H. Kellenbenz has detected a shift of the Jews after the mid-seventeenth century from international trade to finance. Yet Marseilles's commercial crisis of 1729–31 found Amsterdam as well as Venetian Jewish merchants there.[24] Aside from finance, Jews worked in such trades as tobacco, diamonds, silk, sugar, and jewellery, and culturally the most important, printing and publishing. Twenty of Amsterdam's 273 book printers were Jews, and they did not publish only Judaica. The greatest printer was Joseph Athias, who boasted in 1687 that 'for several years I have myself printed more than a million Bibles for England and Scotland. There is not a ploughboy or servant girl without one.' In 1667 the Estates General awarded Athias a gold chain and medal and a fifteen-year monopoly on the printing of English Bibles. One grateful Hebrew author, R. Zvi Ashkenazi, enthused that after several earlier attempts to publish his responsa, which were to attain classic status, 'God brought me to the great city of Amsterdam, centre of world trade, a city of master artisans and men expert in arts and crafts, especially the making of the type forms needed for printing. There is no place like it in the world.'[25] He did not exaggerate. Amsterdam inherited the place formerly held by Constantinople, Venice, and other Italian cities, and was overtaken in turn, though not qualitatively, by eastern Europe. The glory of Amsterdam Hebrew printing lasted into the nineteenth century, and its combination of superior type, printing, and paper has never been surpassed.

Not only Bibles and Talmuds and other Jewish classics poured from the Amsterdam Hebrew printing houses, but also the first Jewish newspapers, the Spanish *Gazeta de Amsterdam* in 1678 and the Yiddish semiweekly *Kurant* in 1687. Works in Spanish were published, which were aimed at the Jewish education of newly Judaized Marranos and the

---

[24] C. Carrière, 'Image du capitalisme hollandais au xviiie siècle: Le miroir marseillais', in M. Aymard (ed.), *Dutch Capitalism and World Capitalism* (Cambridge, 1982), 192–3.

[25] Zvi Ashkenazi, *She'elot u-Teshuvot Hakham Zvi* (Amsterdam 1712, repr. Israel, 1970), intro.

defence of Judaism against Spanish Catholic denigration. A fine specimen is *Las excelencias de los Hebreos*, by the New Christian physician Fernando (Isaac) Cardoso (1604–93), whose life went *From Spanish Court to Italian Ghetto* in Verona, the title of Y. H. Yerushalmi's notable book about him. Amsterdam Jewry had rabbinic scholars, Hebrew and Spanish poets and chroniclers, mystics and heretics. These varied cultural interests were nourished by the finest educational system of its period. But there was significant questioning and dissent from normative Jewish faith and practice, which was emphatically put down by the community. The returned Marrano Uriel da Costa professed a religious faith which has been described as 'normal Marranism . . . an impoverishment of rabbinic Judaism' by rejecting what he could not deduce directly from the Bible.[26] Da Costa recanted and after undergoing public humiliation took his own life in 1640. A few years later the nearly deistic heresies of another returned Amsterdam Marrano, Dr Juan Prado, led him in and out of trouble with the Jewish community. The heresies discussed in Prado's circle were taken up and developed by his young friend and disciple Baruch Spinoza, whose genius was to create a system of pantheism and philosophical deism. Unlike the others in the group, Spinoza accepted his expulsion from the Jewish community in 1656 and never looked back.[27] Opposite trends also carried on within Amsterdam Jewry. A decade after the Spinoza episode 'Dutch Jerusalem' fervently shared in the greatest outburst of messianism ever known, in which old and new Jewish communities in western Europe such as Vienna, Prague, and London fervently joined.

[26] I. S.Revah, 'La Religion d'Uriel da Costa, Marrano de Porto (D'après des documents inédits),' *Revue de l'histoire des religions*, 161 (1962), 74.
[27] I. S. Revah, *Spinoza et le Dr. Juan de Prado* (Paris The Hague, 1959); *idem*, 'Aux origines de la rupture Spinozienne: nouveaux documents', *Revue des études juives*, 123 (1964), 359–431, add important material on the heretical atmosphere among Amsterdam Marranos. The Jewish roots of Spinoza's thought are revealed in the great work of Harry A. Wolfson, *The Philosophy of Spinoza* (2 vols., Cambridge, Mass., 1934).

Messianic Explosion

The world-wide Jewish acclaim in 1665 for Sabbetai Zvi (1626–76) of Izmir as the divinely ordained Messiah, scion of King David and redeemer of Israel, appears unrelated, indeed opposed, to the slowly modernizing Jewish world we have been describing. Perhaps inexplicably, the Sabbatian movement was most fervent in mercantile port cities where Jewish merchants were suffering hard times, and less so among afflicted Polish Jewry, where modernization was still far off. To understand the many peculiarities of the Sabbetai Zvi movement one turns to the penetrating studies of Gershom Scholem (1897–1982) which culminated in his masterwork *Sabbetai Sevi: The Mystical Messiah.*[28] In the view of Scholem and his disciples, the permeation of Judaism, especially that of the Sefardim, for 150 years by doctrines of mystical messianism is the cause of the great outburst. Persecution and socioeconomic factors played no role.

The 'Messiah' came from a prosperous family of merchants which supported him in his erratic, wandering life of Talmudic and mystical studies. He was moderately proficient in both, sang well, and possessed personal charm. Sabbetai's first vision of his messianic identity came in 1648, and he along with a few followers had faith in his destiny. He acted out his conception of his calling with deviant acts. Once he dressed a large live fish as a baby and placed it in a tank 'cradle', probably to symbolize the growth of redemption under the sign of Pisces (fish), and on another occasion he 'married' a Torah scroll under a bridal canopy. Sabbetai was twice married and divorced and exhibited symptoms of sexual disturbance. Suggestive of what was to come, he punned a frequently recited benediction into an antinomian blasphemy,

[28] Princeton, 1973, a translation and revision of the Hebrew original, *Shabbetai Zvi ve-ha-Tenuah ha-Shabtait bi-Yemey Hayyav* (2 vols., Tel Aviv, 1957). Scholem wrote the articles in the *Encyclopedia Judaica* (16 vols., Jerusalem, 1971) on Sabbetai Zvi, Nathan of Gaza, and other Sabbatian and *kabbalah* subjects, and the reader may read his views in summary there. Many facets of Scholem's interpretation have been questioned, such as the 'messiah' as a merely passive instrument largely manipulated by Nathan of Gaza. See e.g. Isaiah Tishby, *Bi-Netivey Emunah u-Minut* (Hebrew; Paths of Faith and Heresy) (Ramat Gan, 1964), 235–77.

'Blessed are You, God, who permits things which are forbidden', reading '*issurim*' for '*assurim*'. Sabbetai was considered mad, and his messianic pretensions as but a sign of his madness. This 'diagnosis' probably saved him from punishments and expulsion from communities.

How could such a person, neither hero nor scholar nor saint, suddenly gain world-wide acclaim and reverence as the Messiah? The answer appears to lie in the constantly wider acceptance of kabbalistic messianism, spreading out from its sixteenth-century centre in Safed. It has recently been argued, however, that Scholem considerably overstated the extent of *kabbalah*'s acceptance. Its seventeenth-century activist version is inseparably connected with the kabbalists R. Isaac Luria and R. Hayyim Vital, who gave a goal, theology, and ritual to what had been abstract speculation concerning the nature of creation and the universe. They conceived that a cosmic disruption in the heavens, called in kabbalistic metaphor the 'breaking of the vessels', had taken place at the Creation. The Divine Presence (*shekhinah*) went into exile. The coordinate on earth was the exile of the Jews. The traditional religious way of life was reinterpreted as a system which would heal the cosmic rupture, a titanic task which would be fulfilled by the devoted performance of religious acts with their specified correct intent. The 'exile' of the Divine Presence would end with the 'healing' of the 'broken vessels', and with it earthly Jewish exile would also end and ultimate redemption arrive. Such a cosmology was unspeakably bold and pious, summoning every Jew to participate in bringing on the messianic era by his religious efforts. The restoration of the Jewish people from exile would be achieved not by patiently waiting for God to act nor by means of secular political endeavour, but through purposive religious devotion. The Messiah was thought of less as a man who would crush the enemies of Israel and inaugurate the age of human bliss, than as the mystical master who could heal the cosmic rift and thereby bring on ultimate redemption.

Remarkably little resistance was encountered by this audacious reinterpretation of sacred tradition. The prayer book incorporated numerous kabbalistic additions, such as invocations beginning 'Hineni mukhan u-mezuman' ('I am ready and prepared') to fulfil some religious precept or recite a prayer as redefined kabbalistically. The Sabbath eve psalms with their *Lekha Dodi* (Come, My Beloved) hymn, the invocations before Sabbath *kiddush*, and the 'third feast' on Sabbath late afternoon furnish examples. Messianic mysticism was permeating the Jewish world until its culmination in the Sabbetai Zvi movement. How would one recognize the Messiah and what manner of man would he be? Judaism's messianic doctrines did not make that clear. Maimonides, the greatest medieval jurist and philosopher, had insisted that the Messiah could not abolish nor even modify Jewish law, and the messianic age would remain within the order of nature. Yet Maimonides' teaching availed little against the flaming ardour of the Sabbatian and other messianic movements. The simplest explanation why it spread like wildfire is that the theological basis had been laid, and the passion for redemption became subject to bandwagon psychology. Even those who felt sceptical about Sabbetai did not wish to appear faithless Jews and accepted him. Scholem's doctrine that Sabbatianism erupted because of internal spiritual developments which ultimately burst forth and cast off all restraints, now holds the field. The last word, however, has by no means been spoken.

Sabbetai Zvi's life oscillated between feverish activity and despondent passivity, characteristic of a manic-depressive person. He showed himself capable of a successful quasi-diplomatic mission to Egyptian Jewry, requesting their intercession for oppressed Jerusalem Jewry. He also issued antinomian declarations buttressed by theological arguments. The fateful moment occurred when Sabbetai stopped in Gaza in May 1665 *en route* back from Egypt, in order to consult the gifted young kabbalist Nathan ben Elisha Hayyim (1644–80), to become known as Nathan of Gaza. Already known as a 'prophet', he was a charismatic who read the inmost heart and prescribed its appropriate healing (*tikkun*), usually fasts, special prayers, and mortification of the flesh. Was this what Sabbetai sought for his own troubled spirit? Nathan, who remembered him from Jersualem, was now convinced that he was indeed the Messiah. In days of intensive discussion he persuaded Sabbetai to accept the role. Or, alternatively, did Sabbetai, inspired by his success in Egypt, stop at Gaza in order to persuade Nathan? At any rate, Nathan spent the rest of his short life as Sabbetai's ideologist and organizer. He won over many from the outset with the argument that acceptance of the Messiah did not depend on his signs and wonders, but rather on faith in his power as saviour of the Jewish people—an echo of Christian faith remarkable especially because there was no known contact with Christians.

Sabbatian messianism captivated the Jewish community of the Holy Land. Yet in Jerusalem Sabbetai had been put under the ban years before on account of his antinomian acts, including the abolition of the fast on 17 Tammuz and consuming forbidden animal fats. Yet the Holy City ban, far from aborting the movement, had no effect as the new Messiah went north to Safed and Damascus *en route* to Aleppo. Enthusiastic recognition spread very rapidly, and by the time he reached his home town of Izmir (Smyrna) Sabbetai Zvi had a large and fervid following. Contrary to the supposed fate of prophets, he quickly won recognition in his native city, and the movement took over the community. The few doubters and scoffers were intimidated and thrust aside. The 'Messiah' won the support of rabbis when he prescribed penitence by prayers, fasts, and mortification of the flesh. Could the messiahship of a pious Jew who called for prayers and penitence be denied? To be sure, uproarious celebrations of the wonderful redemption also went on. One observes the making of the paradox which dogged the Sabbatian movement until its denouement: how must a messiah behave? How and when does redemption once proclaimed express itself?

During Sabbetai's months at Izmir Jewish as well as Christian observers came from far and wide to witness the marvels as word spread in Christian Europe. Epistles from the Sabbatians were dispatched throughout the Jewish world, and reactions came from Persia to Algiers and London. Regardless of their senders' cultural background or social class, the general tone of the letters bespeaks excited hopefulness. Sabbetai, accompanied by the 'chiefs of the twelve tribes of Israel' whom he had appointed, set sail from Izmir on 30 December 1665 for Constantinople. The implications of the 'Messiah' stirred concern in the Sublime Porte. Was his grandiose talk of kingship and restoring God's people to their Holy Land exciting unrest and perhaps sedition? And if his talk was only figurative, the disruption of trade and commerce on account of the excitement among the Jews had to stop.

The Messiah's ship was intercepted in the Dardanelles and Sabbetai and his retinue were taken for trial before the Grand Vizier. Their lives were spared, but Sabbetai was lodged in a filthy gaol until a huge bribe got him removed to the reasonably comfortable fortress of Abydos. The new gaol was interpreted as the Messiah's 'Tower of Strength' (*Migdal Oz*), a characteristic inversion of meaning and plain sense which saturated the movement. At his fortress-gaol the imprisoned Messiah was allowed to receive throngs of visitors who now came from all over the world. Ordinary affairs were in suspense as the élite no less than plain people fervently welcomed the Messiah. Many performed sincere and often painful penance for their sins in order to purify themselves for the great deliverance. A spirit of defiance and confidence pervaded Polish Jews which inspired mob attacks on them. The king commanded the attackers to stop, while telling the Jews to destroy Sabbatian literature.

During the frenzy the antinomianism of the movement became more prominent. The requirements of Jewish law were set aside as followers ate forbidden fats, offered a paschal sacrifice which could not be done without the Temple, turned the fasts of 17 Tammuz and 9 Av into feasts, rewrote prayers, and indulged themselves sexually. Had the Sabbatian movement endured, such acts would have inevitably led to schism and conflict. But the Sabbatian denouement was sudden and shattering.

The undoing began about 1 September 1666, one year after the movement caught fire, with the visit of a Polish mystic and preacher, Nehemiah Cohen. He evidently came to pay homage, but unlike other pilgrims he entered into a doctrinal discussion with the inmate of the Tower of Strength. The discussion turned into three days of stormy debate. Nehemiah challenged Sabbetai's messiahship because it did not follow the course prescribed by mystic and apocalyptic literature; for example, where was the martyr Messiah of the house of Joseph? He had to come before the advent of the ultimate messiah of the house of David, Sabbetai himself. Many years later Nehemiah recounted how he had told Sabbetai he was a 'provocateur and renegade' meriting the biblical penalty of death, and then took a drastic step. Fearing the disasters which the false messiah might bring on the Jews, he rushed from his presence and told the guards that he wanted to become a Muslim. This was promptly done, and he was taken in his new turban to Adrianople where he denounced Sabbetai as a seditious character. Nehemiah quit the scene at once and returned to Judaism and to his wandering life, mainly in Germany. In old age he told his story in Yiddish to a chronicler, Leib ben Ozer.[29]

A few days after Nehemiah's denunciation Sabbetai was brought before the sultan's privy council, among whom was an apostate Jewish physician. Behind a screen sat the sultan. Sabbetai had to choose at once between death by torture or apostasy. He emerged from the momentous session a Muslim with a title, robes of honour and a pension, but Sabbetai Zvi the Messiah was shattered. He seems to have lived in a state of misery and depression at what he had done. He had killed his movement, for an apostate Messiah was inconceivable. His name was reviled, and some communities 'burned all records in which his name appeared so that he might not be spoken of or remembered among them, or be a stumbling block and a source of sin'.[30] Burning the records might eradicate the embarrassing fact that not only the common sort were infatuated with Sabbetai Zvi but also their superiors—rabbis, community leaders, and persons of means.

The mass of Jews dismissed Sabbetai Zvi perhaps with a muttered curse, but some insisted on remaining faithful to him. One might say that they remained faithful to their memory of once feeling free and redeemed. R. Yair Hayyim Bachrach of Worms, no Sabbatian but active in the movement before Sabbetai's conversion, spoke always thereafter of 'Our Master [*Rabbenu*] Sabbetai Zvi', a title reserved for great sages.[31]

After the 'Messiah'

The faith that Sabbetai the apostate was yet the Messiah produced a full-blown mystical theology. What remained of his movement descended into an underground existence which lasted nearly two centuries. Scholem has demonstrated how it long exercised extensive though

---

[29] R. Leib ben R. Ozer, *The Story of Shabbetay Zevi* (Yiddish with Hebrew translation), ed. Zalman Shazar (Jerusalem, 1978).

[30] Samuel Aboab, *Devar Shmuel*, no. 376.

[31] Quoted in *Encyclopedia Judaica*, s.v.

hidden influence within Judaism. Only to the blind faithless had Sabbetai Zvi apostatized, the Sabbatians held. In their own clear sight he had committed an act of self-sacrifice, defiling himself by descending to the netherworld of lost souls in order to bring redemption by assisting scattered 'sparks' to reunite with their 'broken vessels' and be healed. The Lurianic cosmos became the metaphysics of Sabbatianism. Should believers accompany Sabbetai on this journey of the soul? Very few of them entered Islam, not even Nathan of Gaza. However, after Sabbetai's death in 1676 the Zvi family led several hundred to Salonika, where they entered Islam as a distinct sect. Known as the Dönmeh, the Muslim Sabbatians remained socially separate and kept their teachings secret. A shadow of them lingered into the twentieth century. Sabbatian theology, focusing on freedom and redemption, led to the repudiation of Judaism as law in the name of a 'higher' Torah which permitted the forbidden. However, few scholars follow Scholem in seeing Sabbatian antinomianism and its consciousness of spiritual freedom as the inward transition from medieval to modern Judaism.

Sabbatianism had furtive as well as outspoken believers, and it encountered mild as well as militant opponents. One furtive believer was Solomon Ayllon, rabbi [Haham] of the London Sefardim from 1689 to 1700, when he became the honoured Haham in Amsterdam. Ayllon managed to keep away from the bitter conflict which erupted when the Sabbatian theologian and propagandist Nehemiah Hayun came to Amsterdam. For their relentless attacks on Hayun the scholar R. Moses Hagiz and the chief rabbi Zvi Ashkenazi [Haham Zvi] were driven out of the city, yet Ayllon the Sabbatian trimmer enjoyed cordial relations with these colleagues. Such a man as Ayllon could hold on in the decades before controversy was rekindled by the renewed aggressiveness of Sabbatian believers. That in turn spurred opponents' militancy and vigilance. After the Hayun–Hagiz controversy there were no more Sabbatian victories in Jewish communal life.

Post-apostasy Sabbatianism in Poland lasted longer and had more influence than anywhere else. Itinerant Sabbatian preachers who set up cells of their faithful led the Council of Four Lands in 1670 and 1671 to promulgate a ban on Sabbatian believers. They were to be excluded, degraded, fined, and handed over to the public authorities for imprisonment.[32] The effect of this sweeping ban is questionable. The centre of Polish Sabbatianism was the frontier province of Podolia, which was ruled by Turkey between 1672 and 1700. During this period contacts between Poland and the centres of the sect in Ottoman lands could be carried on unhindered. After 1700, wandering preachers of heresy still had freer play in the new Jewish settlements in the sparsely settled stretches of the south-east than in the long-established communities to the north.

A religious type better known in Christianity than in Judaism made his appearance within Sabbatianism at this time, the simple pious man neither learned nor awed by tradition, who spoke as he heard God direct him. Such a man was Heshel Zoref (1633-1700), a silversmith of Vilna and a refugee in Amsterdam when the Sabbatian year transformed him from a workman into a mystical recluse. To Heshel came religious seekers to consult with him. Unlike other Sabbatian 'prophets', he did not lead a wandering life. His extensive manuscript writings did not seem Sabbatian, and they impressed favourably Israel Besht, the father of the Hasidic movement. Only later were they recognized and rejected as Sabbatian.

Another of the type, Hayyim Malakh, fused Talmudic learning and ascetic piety with antinomianism. This 'evil angel', as a hostile pun interpreted his name, was a leader in the ill-fated messianic pilgrimage to the Holy Land led by Judah the Hasid in 1700. There had been expectations of Sabbetai's return, and one Zadok of Grodno made a stir with his prediction of 1695. Judah the Hasid's mostly Sabbatian group went to the Holy Land in 1700, where they aspired to receive Sabbetai as the Messiah. Lacking money and experience, their trip was harrowing; Judah died within a week of arrival aged about 40, and the unhappy group broke up.

Polish Judaism, whose leaders were vigorously anti-messianic after the débâcle of 1666, thus had to confront a palpable religious opposition encamped in its bosom. Sabbatian believers, who included proficient scholars and occupants of rabbinic office, turned more and more to antinomianism and religious nihilism. Scholem has eloquently suggested what troubled their spirit:

---

[32] *Pinkas Va'ad Arba Arazot*, ed. Israel Halpern (Jerusalem, 1945), 495–6.

Was it the self-hatred of men for whom a tradition emptied of meaning had become repulsive? Uprising and rebellion against mechanization by a rational culture, and a secret, nearly satanic pleasure at trampling by both minor and serious mischief everything which had dominated their day to day physical and spiritual lives? Pleasure in showing their mastery over the very Talmudic authority which placed them under its rule, pleasure at destroying it from within . . . ? Or perhaps more positive yearnings were combined here, which had no outlet in that form of life—yearnings for human liberation and redemption which took the guise of the doctrine of liberation from the yoke of the commandments, and a shadowy vision of a fundamental change of values? Could they really not find their way between conscious attachment to the ancient Talmudic culture and the attachment which came from deep faith in the vision of messianic liberty, and they became entwined and sought to serve both masters and to give satisfaction to both urges at the same time? [33]

Deep in the fastness of Jewish orthodoxy, surrounded by Catholic Poland and innocent of modern culture, dissenters held to their faith in the apostate Messiah. We shall see how the tangled windings of that faith brought unpredictable outcomes.

A New Age in Embryo

Towering geniuses in science and philosophy during the seventeenth century pioneered modern science and philosophy and created the intellectual frame of modern man. Contemporary with Sabbatianism they appear to inhabit a different planet. One of this handful was the son of Amsterdam Jewry, Baruch (in his Latin writings, Benedict) Spinoza. When the 24-year-old Spinoza refused to retract his pantheistic views, the lay council of the Jewish community, not its rabbinic court, held a hearing which was attended by various witnesses and by Spinoza himself. The council had 'long since been acquainted with the false opinions and deeds [obras] of Barukh d'Espinosa, and having tried in various ways and by various offers [?] to steer him back to the path of righteousness'

---

[33] Gershom Scholem, 'The Sabbatian Movement in Poland' (Hebrew)', *Beit Yisrael be-Polin*, ed. I. Halpern (2 vols., Jerusalem, 1948, 1953), ii. 60.

but had failed. What Spinoza may have said remains unknown. After the rabbinic authorities joined the deliberations over the evidence, on 27 July 1656 'it was decided that the said Spinoza be cast out of the nation of Israel', and scriptural curses were heaped on him. Proper Jews were forbidden to associate with him until he should submit to the humiliation of public repentance. But Spinoza went on to become one of the founders of modern philosophy.

Spinoza and the ex-Marrano circle from which he emerged rejected traditional religion not because of the new science nor because God's ways in the world were beyond acceptance. Instead, their skill with Scripture showed them flaws, contradictions, and anachronisms in its text which raised doubts about revelation. Their own or their close ancestors' experience with concealing or changing religions made them aware of the common moral and intellectual basis of all religions, or it encouraged them to doubt all religions.

Spinoza's radical step was his alone; he had no Jewish successor. However, the intellectual winds of the late seventeenth century did rustle faintly in European Jewry. D. B. Ruderman has recently identified three groups of scientifically interested Jews. There were converso intellectuals just discussed, a few traditional Jews in places like Prague and Cracow, and Italian medical graduates, mainly from Padua, who were scattered throughout Europe.[34] In a quaint but revealing example from the early eighteenth century R. Zvi Ashkenazi dismissed the assumption made in a query addressed to him, and ruled that there could not have been a chicken without a heart to make the fowl unkosher for eating. Every creature must have a heart, he stated, and this one must have been devoured by the kitchen cat. Thus, the findings of contemporary biology could be absorbed into the halakhic system. To the same rabbi came a more searching issue in 1704. David Nieto (1654-1728), physician, philosopher, and calendric expert had come in 1701 from his native Leghorn to serve as Haham of the Sefardic Jews of London. A year later he lectured to his new community's advanced students concerning God and Nature and declared them identical. To Nieto, Nature (*teva'*) was no more than the term which expressed Divine Providence operating

[34] David B. Ruderman, *Jewish Thought and Scientific Discovery in Early Modern Europe* (New Haven, 1995), 11–13.

regularly to produce rain, clouds, plant growth and all other phenomena of 'nature.' Were God and Nature then identical? To some pious unsophisticated minds, a few of whom had perhaps heard of Spinoza's heresy, this was disturbingly like pantheism. One member who attacked the orthodoxy of the renowned Haham was punished, yet the community was still troubled enough to seek out a rabbi who could tell them whether Nieto's teachings were indeed acceptable. Rabbi Ashkenazi responded with an unqualified approval. He roundly declared Nieto's 'Nature' identical with Divine Providence; did not God cause all things?[35] Condemned in Germany and Poland and distrusted among ex-Marranos, only in Nieto's native Italy did the traditions of Jewish science and philosophy retain any vitality, but rabbis who approved of philosophy at all wanted it studied very little by very few. All agreed that the truth of faith stood above the truth of philosophy and did not require its confirmation.

Medicine was the field in which Jews were prominent. A few Jews showed awareness of the new science and its implications. Some declared that the Torah properly understood contained all science. However, a few scholars showed signs of uneasiness at the inadequacy of rabbinic learning and traditional education in the face of the advance of science.

The basic compatibility between science and Judaism had appeared axiomatic to the early Jewish practitioners of science; to their successors, it was increasingly fraught with difficulties . . . The contest between science and Jewish tradition had left its shattering mark . . . [Yet] by the end of the 17th century, a larger number of Jews knew more about science than ever before, most of them saw a positive value in the acquisition of this knowledge, even though it inevitably created obvious strains for some of them regarding their own fidelity to traditional Judaism.[36]

Nearly a century passed before Moses Mendelssohn became the first significant Jewish contributor to modern intellectual life. Nearly another

[35] *She'elot u-Teshuvot Haham Zvi* [Ashkenazi] (Responsa) (repr. Israel, 1970), nos. 74, 18.
[36] David B. Ruderman, *Science, Medicine, and Jewish Culture in Early Modern Europe*, Spiegel Lectures in European Jewish History, 7 (Tel Aviv, 1987), 19, 21–2. I have rearranged the order of sentences.

century went by before Jews became conspicuous in the cultural realm. On the other hand they played a significant part in the early development of the modern economy, not only in international commerce but also in their unique position as court Jews, meaning bankers, purveyors, and financial agents of German and Austrian rulers. During the age of dynastic absolutism, especially from 1660 to 1730, rulers employed Jews not only to procure luxuries like jewels and exquisite foodstuffs but to perform the vaster task of transporting, equipping, and feeding armies. The court Jews operated within a largely Jewish network of finance and commerce which extended into Holland and Poland.[37]

Monarchs employed court Jews on contract because of their ready connections to sources of credit and to the products of overseas colonies and Polish granaries. They were valuable to monarchs who sought to free themselves from their estates' tax and revenue constraints. Besides raising money on credit court Jews commuted feudal fees into modern taxes, producing more revenue for the monarch who did not have to bargain for it with estate assemblies. Unattached to any estate, the court Jew was completely the monarch's man. Indeed, if he turned Christian he would have lost his class neutrality at home and his status among fellow court Jews abroad.

A court Jew arranged the financing of Emperor Leopold I's war against the Turks, another financed the Duke of Hanover's ambition to become an elector of the Holy Roman Empire, and still another did the same for the Duke of Saxony's desire to wear the crown of Poland. Court Jews could also serve as scapegoats when needed. A celebrated case was the versatile, arrogant man of power Joseph Süss Oppenheimer (1697-1735). His success in satisfying the absolutist ambitions of his master Duke Karl Alexander of Württemberg outraged the estates of the duchy. After the duke died, his 'Jew Süss' was tried and sent to the gallows.[38]

The court Jew's hardest task was to collect debts. Only the need to maintain a modicum of credit for further borrowing compelled some defaulting rulers to pay, at least partially. The difficulties of collecting led to extremes of wealth and penury in the court Jews' lives and even

---

[37] The basic study is Selma Stern, *The Court Jew* (Philadelphia, 1950).

[38] Besides scholarly literature, Oppenheimer was the subject of Lion Feuchtwanger's novel *Power* and the viciously anti-Semitic Nazi film *Jud Süss*.

more so among their heirs, whose inheritance sometimes consisted of uncollectable claims. In their risky business court Jews who flourished lived sumptuously. They and their families in some instances adopted courtly ways, while others adhered to Jewish tradition and even wore beards. But no court Jew could forget nor was allowed to forget he was a Jew. Only within their own Jewish community could they feel completely themselves. Many of them, not always the most pious, became patrons of rabbinic scholars and published their writings. They founded such Jewish communities as Leipzig, Dresden, and Kassel by settling there with their retinues. They often tyrannized over their communities, high-handedly assessing taxes, installing relatives in key positions, closing synagogues in a fit of pique, and deciding whom to admit or keep out. They could also dominate communities which they had not founded, including Berlin and Frankfurt. Periodically there were communal rebellions against them.

Although the German lands were the court Jews' arena, they functioned as financial agents in England and France as well, but in a far reduced role in those economically advanced lands.[39] Economically underdeveloped territories provided a large field of activity for them. When Hungary returned to Habsburg rule after 175 years under the Turks, Jews began to settle in its little inhabited lands, functioning as merchants and as purveyors to local military commanders. They founded the community of Buda.[40] Court Jews' importance declined as the modern state's bureaucratic finance and taxation emerged. While they did much to advance the absolutist state they did not, as some have said, bring about Jewish emancipation. That was an expression of liberalism and equality, not of privilege and absolutism.

The view of the Jew was changing fundamentally but gradually at this time. This was the great age of Christian Hebrew studies, mainly of the Bible but to some extent even of rabbinic literature. Some of these scholars acquired a measure of respect for Judaism. Moreover, the thinking of political leaders and theorists shifted from the theological to a secular

---

[39] P. G. M. Dickson, *The Financial Revolution in England: A Study in the Development of Public Credit* (Oxford, 1956), 34, 222 ff., 259, 263–6, 282–3, 292, 306 and esp. 314.

[40] Anat Peri, 'Jewish Settlement in Hungary under the Habsburgs, 1686–1747' (Hebrew), *Zion*, 63/3 (1998), 319–50.

conception of the state including its Jews. Enhancing state power became the central political concern, and regimes took particular interest in the classes and social groups which could do the most towards that purpose. Religious tolerance had been advocated by such masters as Jean Bodin in sixteenth-century France, Hugo Grotius in Holland and John Locke in England during the seventeenth century. Besides reasons of conscience they observed how religious tolerance aided the peace and prosperity of the realm. Two contemporary rabbis, Simone Luzzato of Venice and the already familiar Menasseh ben Israel provided mercantilist arguments for Jewish toleration, arguing that Jews as skilful merchants would amass large profits which they would reinvest rather than dissipate in luxurious living. Lacking any focus of political loyalty, they would be intensely devoted to the ruler who treated them fairly. The leading statesman of his time, Louis XIV's chief minister Colbert, protected Jewish merchants in port cities against his king's inclination to expel them. On the other hand, Louis XIV did not disturb the substantial Jewish population which he acquired when he annexed Alsace, and even visited one of its synagogues.

We may conclude with a passage from Spinoza. Taking a critical and secular approach to Scripture, the great heretic reflected on the Jews' history and future:

Nay, I could go as far as to believe that if the foundations of their religion had not emasculated their minds they may even, if occasion offers, rouse up their empire afresh, and God may a second time elect them.[41]

Renewal of their land lay far ahead. The Jews were seeking to improve their position in Europe or to retain what they had in eastern Europe, as the eighteenth century flowed ahead.

---

[41] *Theological-Political Tractate*, ch. 2, end; Elwes translation, p. 56.

3

A Rift Opening, 1720–1780

Between 1720 and 1780 the surface of traditional Jewish life changed little, as most 'sacred communities' (*kehillot kedoshot*) appeared solid and continued to be governed autonomously by their holy law (*halakhah*). Cracks began to appear in the structure of community and religious life, but they did not appear about to topple. Neither did the social and economic life of the Jews undergo any basic change except among a small wealthy minority. Yet the undermining of traditional Jewish life by capitalism, Enlightenment, and the modern state had already begun, as we have seen, in the seventeenth century although broad effects were first felt late in the next century. The revolutionary storm in western Europe which started in France in 1789 drew much of its power from a century of critical Enlightenment. Its Jewish version, Haskalah, reached into the Jewish community. These forces of the modern age were subverting traditional Jewish life in the west but hardly existed yet in the east or in oriental Jewry. Instead, creative and controversial Hasidism, although it provoked sharp communal disputes, powerfully strengthened traditional religion in Poland and Russia. However, continued economic backwardness in eastern Europe and oriental lands meant deep poverty which probably aggravated communal splintering.

During the eighteenth century some Jews found their way into select society in western lands. Religious toleration, confined about 1700 to Holland and England, in the course of the eighteenth century became the general opinion of educated persons. Yet Frederick II of Prussia, personally an educated atheist, subordinated religious toleration to his conception of the needs of the state. Toleration for the Jews in any case remained far short of social and political acceptance. It became easier as the pressure of Christian churches and doctrines against Judaism somewhat lessened, except for the implacable papal absolutism in Rome and adjacent states under papal rule. Implacable in a secular fashion was the state-building regime of the Protestant Prussian kings, culminating in Frederick II's 'General Jewish Regulations' of 1750. It codified Prussia's policy of allowing only 'useful' Jews, especially industrial entrepreneurs, to settle, and of extracting from them the maximum revenue and restricting their opportunities to live as Jews. Such 'protected' Jews could bequeath their privilege to only one child, seldom to two. Some Jews without resident rights anywhere in German lands joined bandit gangs, to the scandal of respectable Jews. When they were caught Jewish bandits like others of their ilk ended on the gallows.[1]

Sectarian Continuity

Beneath open Jewish life two groups existed furtively. They were the Marranos, already discussed, and the varieties of Sabbatians with varying degrees of attachment to Judaism and the community. For the attenuated remainder of the Marranos' Jewish identity there was no tolerance. The final onslaught by the Spanish Inquisition occurred after the discovery of a clandestine synagogue in Madrid in 1720. It was the last campaign against judaizing if only because almost no one remained to persecute.[2] The Portuguese Inquisition was stripped of its powers during the 1750s and was abolished soon after. With few Marrano refugees left to arrive in tolerant countries, their tragic, dramatic history virtually expired in the middle of the eighteenth century. Yet family recollections linger to the present day, and in 1917 a community of Marranos was discovered intact in a remote Portuguese village.

Subterranean Judaism of another sort, Sabbatianism, entered the period of its greatest vitality three and four decades after the great eruption

[1] Rudolf Glanz, *Geschichte des niederen jüdischen Volkes in Deutschland* (New York, 1968), and 'Gypsies and Jews', in Carsten Kuther, *Räuber and Gauner in Deutschland* (Göttingen, 1976), 24–7.

[2] I. S. Revah, *Revue des études juives*, 118 (1959–60), 4; Henry Kamen, *The Spanish Inquisition* (New York, 1968), 227–8; on the pressures behind Inquisitorial persecutions see the remarks of P. Chaunu, 'Inquisition et vie quotidienne dans l'Amérique espagnole au xviie siècle,' *Annales*, 11/2 (April–June, 1956), 235; Cecil Roth, *A History of the Marranos* (Philadelphia, 1932), 344–54.

of 1666–7. It too continued at a gradually slackening pace throughout the century. Some Sabbatian believers abandoned Judaism and followed their apostate messiah into Islam, but the majority of Sabbatians appeared proper Jews. They kept their true beliefs furtive and wrote their religious works in code language. Thus the rabbinical brothers Jacob Koppel and Hayyim Lifschitz wrote learned mystical works. Jacob deprecated Sabbatianism, but he was actually a master of Sabbatian code language. His contemporary and fellow townsman R. Israel Baal Shem Tov (Besht), the founder of Hasidism, did not penetrate the code language and praised Lifschitz highly. The younger Lifschitz, on the other hand, was openly heretical. Rabbinical and communal authorities attempted to curb these seemingly pious heretics.[3] Sabbatians were identifiable by such pious habits as frequent citation of the verse, 'Do not bless them and do not curse them' (Numbers 23: 25) and daily recited specified psalms in a fixed order, into which they read Sabbatian meanings.[4] When R. Ezekiel Landau of Prague heard from his Polish home town of Opatow that a Sabbatian was moving to Prague, a centre of the sect, he reacted tersely, 'Should he come to our community I shall harass him properly.' R. Landau's vigilance was far surpassed by the zealotry of his contemporary R. Jacob Emden. Like his father Haham Zvi Ashkenazi an outstanding Talmudist, Emden as a private scholar in Hamburg and Altona spent much of his life ferreting out concealed Sabbatians, and publishing tract upon tract exposing Sabbatian formulas concealed in pious works of learning. Emden's antennae detected Sabbatianism in the works of the eminent Rabbi Jonathan Eybeschuetz of Metz, setting off years of furious controversy. Modern research has upheld Emden's accusation.[5]

One of numerous cases where Orthodox piety and Sabbatianism mingled appears in the life and writings of Moses Hayyim Luzzatto (1707–47) of Padua,[6] a wonder child in poetry, exegesis, philosophy,

---

[3] Ezekiel Landau, *Noda biYhudah*, II, Yoreh Deah, no. 6.

[4] Ibid., II, Hoshen Mishpat, no. 16; I, Yoreh Deah, no. 93, dated 1776.

[5] M.A. Perlmutter, *R. Yehonatan Eibeschutz ve-Yahaso el ha-Shabta'ut* (Hebrew; Rabbi Jonathan Eibeschuetz's Attitude to Sabbatianism) (Jerusalem, 1946).

[6] Isaiah Tishbi, *Netivey Emunah u-Minut* (Hebrew; Paths of Faith and Heresy) (Ramat Gan, 1964), 169–204, and other studies by him.

and mysticism who had an adoring band of disciples. For his poetic dramas Luzzatto has even been credited the first modern Hebrew writer, while his beautiful ethical work, 'The Path of the Just' (*Mesillat Yesharim*) is widely studied to the present day. He believed he was receiving guidance from on high by a heavenly mentor (*maggid*). Luzzatto's mysticism led to messianic speculation, provoking attacks by Emden and other anti-Sabbatian warriors which compelled the already famous young Luzzatto to cease mystical study. He had not taken to heresy but, as appears from recent research by I. Tishbi, his thinking contained undertones of the notorious doctrine of the 'holiness of sin' and an 'understanding' of Sabbetai Zvi's apostasy. Upon his marriage a year later a fresh stream of poetry gushed forth, in which Luzzatto imagined himself the bridegroom messiah. When the brilliant young man backslid in 1735, new antagonists were added to the old ones.

Compared to the talent and personal magnetism of the young Luzzatto the rabbis who pursued him may appear dogmatic and inquisitorial. Yet they were convinced, not without reason, that Sabbatianism was insidiously subverting Judaism and had to be uprooted. Finally, in 1743, Luzzatto and his family moved to the Holy Land, where they perished of the plague in Tiberias four years later. Moses Hayyim Luzzatto's tragic career shows what could befall a brilliantly endowed man who played with Sabbatian fire while he wished to be reckoned a proper Jew. Although his travail took place on the eve of the Jewish Enlightenment, the range of his ideas and the sanctions which were imposed on him belonged to the traditional community.

Sabbatianism existed not only in western Europe, where the small Jewish population would soon be affected towards a different direction by the Enlightenment. Among the Jewish masses in eastern Europe, Sabbatian recluses, ascetics and preachers constituted a distinct, covert sect whose centre was in Podolia, where they carried on without much need for secrecy. Some towns, such as Zolkiev, became known as Sabbatian hotbeds where sectarian teachers and holy men spread doctrines of anarchic religious life and the holiness of sin. They virtually inverted the symbols of Judaism and enveloped their believers in a fervent, secret cult. The believers felt redeemed and superior to other Jews, whom they called heretics (an inversion!). The sense of negating the established order and of furtive redemption by doctrines held in private recans the lure which Communism once had for many of 'the brightest and the best'. Sabbatianism's extent and influence are debatable, but something was amiss when learned Talmudists leading outwardly pious and frequently ascetic lives secretly repudiated their religious principles by such acts as eating on days of fast, consuming leavened foods on Passover, and reciting heretical prayers. The loud accusations of Sabbatianism hurled by men like Emden were documented and, as contemporary research has demonstrated, generally true. The belief that Sabbetai Zvi would reappear soon or that he never died inspired a consciousness which differed from that of the masses of Jews whose ingrained caution about messianism had been tightened by the débâcle of 1666. As decades passed and Sabbetai did not reappear, many believers lost faith. The frustrations continued into a new generation of unchastened believers and finally burst forth in the Frankist movement discussed below, starting in the late 1750s.

Numerical Increase

A striking Jewish population increase began in western Europe during the eighteenth century. The number of Jews was increasing faster than that of the population of Europe. About 1650 there were some 500,000 Jews among 100 million Europeans. One hundred years later there were 140 million Europeans and the Jewish population seems to have doubled, showing that the 'vital revolution' among the Jews had begun. By 1800 there were 188 million Europeans, in 1850 266 million, and 400 million in 1900, while the number of Jews, whose overseas emigration rate was far higher than Europe's during this period, jumped from approximately 1 million to 8.85 million. No sure explanation exists for the Jewish 'vital revolution', but the most widespread is increased food supply, although masses remained hungry. Plagues were almost eliminated, and the famines which periodically decimated Europe's population came less and less often. Even wars were mainly naval and colonial or took place in limited regions of the continent.

Polish Jewry continued to dominate European Jewry numerically. It was counted in the unique Polish census of 1765, even though its Jewish data, while invaluable, also illustrate the pitfalls and shortcomings of census figures. The task of counting the Jews was imposed upon local rabbis and community leaders, who had to swear upon the Torah scroll that they had counted everyone. Just the same a substantial proportion was uncounted. Since the avowed purpose of the undertaking was to levy a per capita tax and, the Jews suspected, also to recruit Jewish boys for the army, many youths and resident servants disappeared on the day of the enumeration. The official Jewish totals were 430,009 for Poland and 157,649 for Lithuania, plus 6.35 per cent added for infants under 1 year old who were not counted. How many were missed is unknown; R. Mahler, who studied the census intensively,[7] suggests about 20 per cent. If so, about 550,000 Jews lived in Poland, including Galicia and the Ukraine, and 200,000 in Lithuania, including White Russia. When this total is compared with the approximately 400,000 Jews living there when the disasters of 1648–60 concluded, Polish and Lithuanian Jewry nearly doubled in a century, unaided by sanitary, medical, or nutritional improvements. Yet peasants who would have found large families economically valuable, unlike traders and craftsmen, did not make the population of Poland increase.[8]

The Jewish population of the Ottoman empire, which in 1650 had been approximately the same as Poland's, was stagnating and perhaps decreasing. Demographic stagnation of the Jewish and general Balkan population was a cause of the empire's economic decline. It has been reckoned with fair reliability that about 0.5 per cent of the 1 million households in European Turkey, whose size was uncertain, were Jewish. Assuming five per household, we find some 25,000 Jews in the Balkans plus the previously mentioned 12,000 in Salonika. In the Anatolian town of Bursa and elsewhere in Turkish lands, Jewish merchants functioned as moneylenders and tax gatherers until their impoverishment late in the seventeenth century. By the mid-eighteenth century the

---

[7] Raphael Mahler, *Yidn in Amolikn Poiln in Likht fun Tsiffern* (2 vols., Warsaw, 1958).

[8] Jacek Kochanowicz, 'The Peasant Family as an Economic Unit in the Polish Feudal Economy of the Eighteenth Century', in R. Wall, J. Robin, and P. Laslett (eds), *Family Forms in Historic Europe* (Cambridge, 1983), 153–66. The chapter on Russia, ibid. 105–26, is appropriately called 'A Large Family: The Peasant's Greatest Wealth'.

Ottoman empire's lag in economic policy and military technique, as well as its cultural immobility, left it a medieval realm overtaken by rapidly modernizing states.[9] Its once proud Jewish communities likewise decayed as they lost the mercantile vigour and cultural and linguistic skills which had made them a valued Ottoman connection to Europe. When Ottoman rule in the Balkans ended and most of it joined the Habsburg realm during the eighteenth century, a new market opened for Balkan Jewry. Their merchants, many of them settled Jews from other Ottoman regions, began to prosper from trade with western Europe.[10]

Long-established German and Bohemian communities posted major increases during the eighteenth century. Prussia, starting its long march to power, had no more than 3,000 Jews about 1720 but ten times that many in 1780. Forty to fifty thousand Jews were scattered among hundreds of Bavarian villages, and an equal number could be found in Bohemia and the rest of Germany. Alsace, which with Lorraine came under French rule in 1689, had 6,800 Jews in 1716, who numbered 13,600 in 1766 and 19,600 on the eve of the revolution in 1789. England and the Netherlands both increased sharply from perhaps 2,000 in 1720 to 6,000 in 1789, and from 7,000 to 20,000 respectively in the same time span. The Jewish increase in Poland just mentioned occurred when the country existed as a republic of almost feudal nobles who elected an almost powerless monarch and ruled a mass of enserfed peasants. Even towns were ruled not by the monarch but by nobles or episcopal nobles. Brody, the largest Jewish community of the time, was chartered in 1699 by the Sobieski magnates, whose power and wealth exceeded kings'. They granted generous privileges to the Jews, whom they wanted in order to build up Brody's commerce. The Jews constituted a majority of its population. However, the cash-starved monarchy was always responsive to pleas and money offers from its subjects for the

---

[9] Hayyim Gerber, 'Jews in the Economic Life of the Anatolian City of Bursa in the 17th century: Comments and Documents' (Hebrew) *Sefunot*, NS 1/16 (1980), 235–72; Norman Itzkowitz, 'Eighteenth Century Ottoman Realities', *Studia Islamica*, 16 (1962), 73–95; Bernard Lewis, 'Some Reflections on the Decline of the Ottoman Empire', ibid. 9 (1958), 111–27.

[10] Traian Stoianovich, 'The Conquering Balkan Orthodox Merchant', *Journal of Economic History*, 20/2 (June, 1960), 234–313, esp. 244–8.

privilege 'of not tolerating the Jews' (*de non tolerandis judaeis*) to live in their midst. Numerous church estates in the region of Cracow, called Little Poland, kept out the Jews. In non-tolerating Warsaw, then a small place, Jews resided in a suburb within a magnate's jurisdiction (*juridika*) and could enter the town on business. This practice went on in some other non-tolerating towns as well. It of course nettled Christian burghers who had paid well to keep Jews out, and led to many a scuffle and endless complaints and lawsuits. Magnates generally wanted Jews and cared nothing for non-toleration demands from their subject towns as long as the Jews paid to remain.

Jews and Polish Magnate Nobility

The grain, timber, and cattle which Poland provided for western Europe were grown on estates which sometimes attained great size and exploited the labour of thousands of serfs. On these plantations, which contained villages and sizeable towns, Jews played a role of singular importance. They lived on the estates in communities, but a noble owner might contract with an individual Jew to manage his affairs. As a group, the Jews could deal in all forms of commerce and crafts, and they paid much higher taxes than Christians. Jewish estate stewards collected dues owed the lord by his servile peasants, as well as the fees for using his monopolies such as distilled whisky and the mill. Jews sold whisky in taverns and manned toll-houses to collect from travellers who used the lord's highway, which had to operate every day. With sources of livelihood poor and limited, experts in *halakhah* had to find means to circumvent its stringent rules against doing business on the Sabbath. This was usually accomplished by some form of partnership with a Christian who worked on Saturdays and received that day's revenue and profit. Jews were also prominent in a more exciting and profitable enterprise as river merchants, accepting produce from estates and convoying it in flotillas down tributaries into the Vistula river for sale at Danzig (Gdansk), like Warsaw a non-tolerating town which Jews could enter to do business. Given the differences, the lore and atmosphere of Polish river traffic somewhat resembles tales of nineteenth-century Mississippi river steamboats. M. J. Rosman's recent study has shown Jewish merchant shippers travelling more often, carrying more kinds of goods, and bringing higher income to the flotillas which they organized. The river fleets took Jewish merchants into account by not loading or embarking on Saturdays. Even more than in river freight Jews were prominent in the overland trade from Poland to Germany, whose focal points were the fairs, especially at Leipzig and Breslau. Jews dealt there with one another and with others who converged from many parts of Germany.[11]

A key position on the magnate's estate was held by the man, virtually always a Jew, who leased the estate as a whole for a fixed period (the *arrenda, arrendator*). Noble owners of several estates usually employed an *arrendator* for each, if only because hardly anyone had sufficient means or credit to undertake one vast *arrenda*. The *arrendator* might then sublease to other Jews parts of his lease, such as taxes and charges on liquor, mills, fishponds, warehouses, and tobacco. He thus controlled the livelihoods of dozens or even hundreds of Jews, but he had to deal with his despotic noble (Polish *pan* or Hebrew *poritz*). The Jews were not serfs but they had to endure the *arrendator* like some tyrannical noble. Some Polish nobles were hard-headed but rational rulers while others, or even the same man, might behave with whimsical generosity or capricious cruelty. Such was the outcome of unfettered, irresponsible noble rule. Life under the tyrant was worse for the serfs, but there are stories of Jewish children held hostage for their fathers' debts and in danger of conversion, Jewish debtors imprisoned in a dungeon, and more. The only recourse was to flee or to invoke the aid of the Jewish community.

Notwithstanding the Jews' autonomous privileges, nobles occasionally interfered in Jewish judicial processes. A noble could force Jews to resort to his manorial court, against the Jewish community's demand that Jews litigate in its own courts. There were instances where the noble intervened in the selection of a community's rabbi. The *kahal* claimed

---

[11] M. J. Rosman, *The Lord's Jews: Magnate–Jewish Relations in the Polish-Lithuanian Commonwealth during the Eighteenth Century* (Cambridge, Mass., 1990); Hermann Kellenbenz, *The Rise of the European Economy: An Economic History of Continental Europe from the Fifteenth to the Eighteenth Century*, rev. and ed. G. Benecke (London, 1976), 158–9.

the right to approve the *arrendator* or at least his sub-lessees and to protect them by granting *hazakah*, tenure, to their sub-leases. The realities were different. Rarely could a magnate be restrained by Jewish community rules from dealing as he wished with whom he wished, and the *arrendator* seldom allowed the *kahal* a voice in his business affairs. In fact, the *arrendator*'s economic power and his closeness to the noble carried over into communal life. He with his family and dependants often took over the community and thwarted its attempts to regulate Jewish economic affairs. They nepotistically installed unfit or immature community rabbis, like medieval and Renaissance potentates who arranged high church offices for their relatives. The Jewish oligarchs levied community taxes and, it was often charged, avoided their fair share and played fast and loose with community funds.

Community Conflicts

The extensive writings of contemporary preachers (*maggidim*) and 'admonishers' (*mokhihim*) describe and lament the state of affairs from the standpoint of pious Jews. Often their complaints against immodesty and impiety and boorishness are stereotyped, but there are also sharp observations concerning the tangible realities of their day. These *maggidim* were not social reformers but mainly mystical pietists who felt moved to protest by the wrongs of Jewish community life. Sometimes they reported what poor, oppressed Jews were heard saying, such as, 'What do we need a *kahal* for? It only makes us miserable and poor.'[12] In 1744 an uprising even occurred in Opatow against the control of the community by the Landau family. The family complained to the lord of the town, who thereupon tried and punished the rebels.[13] One moralist assails 'informers, who always increase in power and number. Any Jew in a lawsuit with another Jew must go with him to the Gentile courts of the noble-judge. This is because the informer promptly tells the noble

[12] Quoted in B. Dinur, 'The Origins of Hasidism and its Social and Messianic Foundations' (Hebrew), *Be-Mifneh ha-Dorot* (Jerusalem, 1955), 96, translated in G. D. Hundert, *Essential Papers on Hasidism* (New York, 1991), 86–225.

[13] Hundert, *Essential Papers*, 124–33.

whatever is happening among the Jews.' Other men of power, 'criminals and rebels', threatened to resort to the non-Jewish court in case the Jewish court's verdict went against them.[14] The 'informer' might have been the *arrendator*, performing an unofficial duty of keeping his lord posted on affairs among the Jews and among the peasantry as well. Repeatedly he was assailed for 'turning over Jewish money to the Gentile nations', probably referring to his role as tax collector. Charity from such a man should be scorned, since 'against every penny of charity he gives there is robbery from hundreds'.[15] Another moralist lamented the debasement of rabbinic office,

the widespread practice in our day by which every rich man having a son or son-in-law even if merely twenty years of age, does his utmost to place him in a rabbinic position at once. It is even more so with the major rabbis of large communities. Without effort but sometimes by coercion they manage to place their sons and sons-in-law in the rabbinate of a community under their jurisdiction . . . The townsmen are unable to protest and must subordinate their wishes to those of the important rabbi because they fear him, and sometimes on account of some flattery or material benefit. There are many such cases.[16]

The forthright R. Berekhiah Berakh denounced these beneficiaries of nepotism as greedy men who kept a yeshiva only to collect tuition fees, lent money to Jews at forbidden interest, and expected gifts from the parties involved before hearing a case at law.[17]

Rabbinic office had always been keenly desired, and influence and money were omnipresent when selections were made. In fragmented eighteenth-century Poland, however, money matters dictated communal affairs to an extent which brought the communal order into disrepute. Central communal bodies, including the Council of Four Lands, sank into impotence. Heavily in debt since the 1650s, the Council had great difficulty in servicing it. Council oligarchs were compelled to 'roll over' debts when they came due, thus increasing the principal. Lords or

[14] Anon., *Tohorat Kodesh* (Holy Purity) (Belazorka, 1806), 22b.

[15] Joseph ben Judah Yudel, *Yesod Yosef* (Homilies), many edns., ch. 36.

[16] *Tohorat Kodesh*, part 2, 9a.

[17] Little is known of him, and his name may be R. Berekhiah Berakh, *Zera Barekh ha-Shelishi* (Frankfurt am Main, 1738), 14b.

monasteries were the creditors, for whom Jewish community loans were a good investment. The reforming Sejm of 1764, acting in the new spirit of ending independent jurisdictions, abolished the Council of Four Lands and divided up its debts among local Jewish communities. Few Jews mourned the Council's demise.

Many rabbis as well as plain people committed to traditional values lamented the low level to which rabbinic culture was said to be sinking in large areas of its east European heartland. From its own negative standpoint the Jewish Enlightenment in western Europe and its successors to the east considered traditional Jewish rabbinic culture desiccated and exhausted. Yet eighteenth-century rabbinic culture boasted representatives as outstanding as those of past centuries. Ethical and responsa literature was notable and prolific, and the nascent Hasidic movement contributed brilliantly to Jewish thought. The difference, then, between traditional culture of the eighteenth and of earlier centuries was not internal but in a changed environment. Jewish traditional culture rested on foundations of faith and revelation which it had in common for centuries with Christianity and Islam. By the eighteenth century, however, science, rationalism, and secularism were far advanced in their victorious struggle for the intellectual domination of the western world. Their victory had to widen greatly the gap between modern western and traditional Jewish cultures. To contemporary and later Jewish critics this cultural gap only demonstrated how antiquated Jewish culture had become.

Two eighteenth-century rabbis of the highest calibre may serve to exemplify the continuing vitality of rabbinic culture within its methods and categories. They are Elijah ben Solomon, called the Gaon (Excellence; abbrev. GR'A) of Vilna (1720–97),[18] and the rabbi of Prague Ezekiel Landau (1713–93). R. Elijah had been a child prodigy, capable at the age of 6 of a Talmudic discourse before a learned congregation. He grew up to be an ascetic Talmudic scholar of heroic diligence and erudition, the culture hero of Talmudic learning, for whom rigorous piety and ceaseless study were the central values. Without a formal position in his community, he was recognized as its religious head. R. Elijah's

[18] A recent study is Immanuel Etkes, *The Gaon of Vilna: The Man and his Image* (Hebrew) (Jerusalem, 1998).

writings are mainly textual notes which display critical acumen before the age of philological scholarship, and biblical commentaries which combine the rational and grammatical with the homiletic and mystical. Solely in the interest of clarifying Talmudic subject matter, he studied basic mathematics and astronomy. He brought renewed attention to the relatively neglected Talmud Yerushalmi, and emphasized the study of the earliest commentators and glossators. The yeshiva in its modern institutional form was founded by his disciples. From his broader circle came settlers in Eretz Yisrael who renewed its Ashkenazic community and moulded its religious image for generations. The Gaon of Vilna was a devoted mystic, but would have no truck with messianic mysticism. It is not surprising that he viewed both Frankism and Hasidism as perversions of religion, and fought them unremittingly from 1772 until his death. So powerful was his influence that Hasidim thought it worth while to fabricate a story that on his deathbed he recanted his opposition to them. Soon after his death the persecutions ceased. The attraction to many Talmud students of Hasidic spirituality was countered in *Nefesh ha-Hayyim* by the Gaon's disciple Rabbi Hayyim of Volozhin. To him, and no doubt to the Gaon, the world's very existence depends on intensive study of sacred texts even more than on prayer.

Unlike his Vilna contemporary, Rabbi Ezekiel Landau of Prague, who came from Poland, where his family dominated the community of Opatow, was the active religious head of Prague's Jewish community, the largest in German-speaking lands. Loyal to the persecuting Maria Theresa and the reforming Joseph II, he was virtually chief rabbi of the Habsburg lands. The Prague rabbi's deepest concern was to retain traditional Jewish life as the basis common to all Jews, and to do so certain compromises were acceptable. In his later years he had to deal with the Jewish Enlightenment which did not yet exist in Vilna of the GR'A. As mentioned elsewhere, he also contended with Sabbatians and Frankists, to whom he gave no quarter. The Hasidic movement, the bane of the Gaon of Vilna, hardly touched Bohemia. R. Landau delivered periodic discourses to his community in a tone which ranged from sternness to endearment. Some of them probably touched sensitive nerves. The offences which he lists include neglecting the study of the Torah for trivial pursuits (but not yet for reading Enlightenment writings). R.

Landau castigated his community for failing to resort to its court (*beth din*), preferring arbitration or the secular courts. He described and denounced the contrivances which were employed to circumvent the stringent prohibition against taking interest from Jews. One may speculate that businessmen immersed in commercial capitalism, constantly lending and borrowing, may have regarded the *halakhah* as too confining, even when the head of the *beth din* was an acknowledged master like R. Landau.[19]

R. Landau's writings contain little if any mystical content, even when their theme was exile and redemption of which he often spoke. If his *beth din* did not receive all the local cases which he thought it should, halakhic queries reached him from all over the Jewish world: 855 responsa constitute his main work, *Noda biYhudah*, one of the pinnacles of responsa literature and much used in rabbinic jurisprudence to the present day.[20] The place held by R. Landau among the greatest rabbis is due not only to his eminence in rabbinics, but also to its combination with resourceful communal leadership.

Frankism

During the prime of the two great rabbis Sabbatianism entered a new and radical phase. In the career of Jacob Frank (1726–91), the nihilistic implications in Sabbatian doctrines were fully acted out. Even the Hasidic movement at its outset, founded by Israel ben Eliezer (1700–60) of Miedzyborz in Podolia, probably contained some Sabbatian residue unknown to itself. Frankism and Hasidism differed fundamentally, but neither possessed any associations outside Judaism. Attempts to link

---

[19] Ezekiel Landau, *Derushey ha-Zelah* (repr. Jerusalem, 1966), no. 8, par. 10, 14, 15.

[20] The two volumes, first published in 1777 and 1790, received the compliment of commentaries and novellae by later rabbis, rare for works of responsa. Its rulings include authorization to shave on the intermediate days of festivals, the first opening towards allowing autopsies to be performed, and a finding that sturgeon was kosher although its scales, the criterion for a kosher fish, fell off when it was out of the water. (The latter ruling did not receive general acceptance, and observant Jews do not consume sturgeon or caviar. But the South African kingklip fish, similar to sturgeon, was recently ruled kosher in that country on the basis of R. Landau's ruling.)

Hasidism with contemporary European pietism or 'enthusiasm' have not gone beyond assertions.

Jacob Frank, of average family background and education, had an adventurous career as a merchant who like many of his kind crossed the Polish–Turkish border back and forth. In Turkey he was drawn to Sabbatian circles and became familiar with their doctrines. Back in Poland during the 1750s, he came forward as the despot and ideologist of the sect which he founded. With cunning magnetism Frank led his followers further than many of them meant to go, binding them to himself by compelling them to avow their faith openly and to take part without concealment in blasphemous sexual and religious rituals. Frank's doctrines were expressed in aphorisms which emphasized his own majesty and grossness and contemptuously rejected the Talmud and Jewish tradition. The God of Israel was placed remotely beyond another deity whose direct emissary was Frank himself. He and a few renegade rabbis co-operated in 1756 with a Catholic Church 'trial' of the Talmud in Lwow for supposed blasphemies. Jewish leaders argued that an attack on the Talmud infringed their right to practise their religion and refused to debate. Many folios of the Talmud were put to the torch.

Worse was to come. After most of them followed their leader into the Catholic Church, the Frankists collaborated with some clergy in a blood libel. This calumny, long repudiated by the papacy itself, brought another public trial of Judaism. Soon after it recessed inconclusively, a blood libel was concocted at a cost of Jewish lives. Frank profited little from all this, since the clergy became suspicious of his Catholic sincerity and had him imprisoned at the pilgrimage town of Czestochowa for twelve years. Perhaps the shrine of Mary at his prison inspired Frank's doctrine of the female semi-deity 'Matron'. If so, it demonstrates his openness to influences from any religion. His teachings were direct, stressing simple motifs for his several thousand followers, above all complete submission to himself:

Everything must be done with total dedication. There will be a day when they will want to make you distant from me and will say to you, 'Go away!' Whoever goes away from me will stay far away and be banished forever, and whoever stays with me will have the privilege of being with me forever . . . Things which are sweet at the start are bitter at the end, and when the beginning is bitter the end is sweet. When I said bitter things to you then you must suffer in silence until you have the privilege of feeling the sweetness . . . If you do in awe and devotion everything I order you, then you will enjoy a great reward. . .[21]

To his followers' wives, submission and acceptance meant subservience to Frank's sexual mastery and taking part in his orgies. He flaunted his libertinism. Not every husband was complaisant, however, and Frank's lust caused departures from his movement. But he always saw great things ahead. In his crude apocalyptic vision, during 'bloodshed in the world . . . we shall find what we have lost and are looking for. Turbid waters are good for catching fish, so when the world fills with bloodshed we shall catch what belongs to us.' Frank and his new heavens and new earth were abhorred by the Jews. Frankists were placed under ban in communities where they did remain within Judaism, but their missionaries spread the word. Jacob Frank died in 1791, succeeded by his daughter Eva until her death in 1816.

The founders' descendants were not Jews nor were they really Christians, but they did become models of propriety who kept the flamboyant indecencies of Frank and his contemporaries closeted by concealing the sect's early writings. The writings surfaced for one historian during the 1890s and disappeared again. Only a few years ago, however, a Polish manuscript 'Chronicle' and 'Sayings of the Master' came to light, and the revealing 'Chronicle' has been published.[22]

Aside from the interest which inheres in the person of Frank and in his sect emerging from late eighteenth-century Polish Jewry, a broader interest exists in Frankism. Nihilism, brazenness, and the glorification of bravery foreshadow a secularized world to be ushered in by the European revolutionary era. Frankist descendants included prominent Polish entrepreneurs and nationalists who knew of their forebears. One Frankist descendant on his mother's side was the great Polish romantic poet Adam Mickiewicz.

---

[21] Alexander Kraushar, *Frank va'Adato* (Hebrew; Frank and his Community) (Warsaw, 1895), 120–1.

[22] Hillel Levine (ed. and trans.), *Ha-Khronika—Te'udah le-Toldot Ya'akov Frank u-Ten'uato* (Eng. title: *The Kronika—On Jacob Frank and the Frankist Movement*) (Jerusalem, 1984).

Hasidism

The Jewish community's outrage over Frankism made it suspicious of another new movement, Hasidism. Actually, the Hasidic movement was altogether different from Frankism. True, it was somewhat critical of religious and communal leaders, it restructured religious authority, and it altered the scale of religious values. Above all, however, the entirety of Jewish law was unquestioningly accepted by Hasidism as sacred and binding. There was no overt sexuality, no contact with other religions, no nihilism, no messianic pretender.[23] Many Hasidic religious ideas were expressed by eighteenth-century Polish Jewish pietists,[24] before they became distinctively Hasidic.[25]

Hasidism began with the appealing figure of Israel ben Eliezer (1699/1700–1760),[26] born to humble, pious parents in Podolia province. As a child he was but a fair pupil who loved stories and nature. By the time Israel attained manhood his parents were dead and he was on his own. He found work as an assistant schoolmaster, leading children to and from the schoolmaster's house in the dark and mud and entertaining

[23] This must be somewhat modified on account of the recent messianic pretensions of the Rebbe of Lubavich who lived in New York City from his arrival in 1940 until his death in 1992. He did not directly lay claim to the status of Messiah, although his followers fervently did without his veto and generated world-wide publicity. No one except the Rebbe's followers accepted him as messiah, and most Orthodox Jews considered the claim scandalous. When the Rebbe of Lubavich died without an heir, the claims were abandoned except by a few who would not even believe that he had gone the way of all flesh.

[24] An invaluable collection of up-to-date studies is Ada Rappaport-Albert (ed), *Hasidism Reappraised* (London, 1996).

[25] As shown fully in Mendel Piekarz, *Bi-ymey Zemihat ha-Hasidut* (Hebrew; When Hasidism Grew) (Jerusalem, 1978). Although outdated and its interpretation of Hasidism as a lower-class social movement is now rejected, Simon Dubnov, *Toldot ha-Hasidut* (first publ. 1930; repr. Tel Aviv, n.d.) remains the only substantial account of the movement before 1815. Important contemporary articles, many translated from Hebrew, are gathered in G. D. Hundert (ed), *Essential Papers on Hasidism* (New York, 1991). Another important collection in translation is Joseph Weiss, *Studies in Eastern European Jewish Mysticism* (Oxford, 1985); of great importance is the same author's 'The Beginning of the Hasidic Way' (Hebrew), *Zion*, 16 (1951), 46–105.

[26] Recent, iconoclastic and authoritative is Moshe Rosman, *Founder of Hasidism: In Quest of the Historical Ba'al Shem Tov* (Berkeley/Los Angeles, 1996).

them with stories and parables. When the time for marriage arrived, a match was arranged with the local rabbi's daughter who was a divorcee and therefore available for a humble teacher to 'marry up'. The rabbi died before the wedding and his son and successor, R. Gerson of Kitov, was incredulous when Israel came to claim his bride. When he proved the match had been made, the status-conscious rabbi, dismayed to have so unsuitable a brother-in-law, persuaded the new couple to move to the Carpathian mountains. There they earned a hard living by hauling clay twice weekly to the local market.

Nothing about Israel's career up to then showed promise of distinction. His socially advantageous marriage did not gain him a place in the local circle of men of the spirit. But the years he spent in the mountains were decisive for his formation. His plentiful spare time was not devoted to Talmud study as tradition recommended, but to mystical study and long contemplative tramps in the forest. His extensive reading included, it appears, the voluminous manuscript writings of the Vilna cobbler Heshel Zoref (1633–1700) who had been 'born again' into Sabbatianism. Unaware of the heresy concealed within them, Israel reportedly thought highly of his works, although Sabbatianism itself left him untouched. He and his wife returned from the mountains about 1736, and he soon made a reputation as an exorcist and folk healer of illnesses, mental depression (the probable meaning of 'melancholy', *marah shehorah*), childlessness and the like by means of mystical prayers and amulets, and by invoking the Divine Name. These gained him the title 'Good Master of the [Divine] Name', Ba'al shem tov or its acronym Besht, by which he is generally known. Yet he did not differ essentially from others who practised them and he did not rank high in the local spiritual circle. Perhaps it was the quest for such recognition which brought Israel to settle in Miedzyborz. For a few years about 1740 he dwelt free in that community's house, which implies that he was well regarded by the powers that were.

During the 1740s Israel intended to visit the Holy Land, perhaps to enhance his spiritual credentials, but he never went. One of the few authentic biographical sources is his letter to his rabbinical brother-in-law, telling of his heavenly vision on Rosh ha-Shanah, 1746. Sinners had entreated Israel to undertake the perilous ascent which would elevate his sanctity and might assist in their forgiveness. He ascended heavenward with his teacher Ahiyah of Shiloh, the biblical seer who foretold and endorsed the splitting of Solomon's kingdom.[27] Israel entered the Messiah's presence, saw him sitting with the sages of the Mishnah and other holy men and enquired, 'When will our Master come?' The Messiah replied that he would appear on earth when his suppliant's 'teachings become known and spread wide in the world, and your fount gushes forth. What I have taught you and you have grasped, they too can.' Mass recitation of mystical prayers and other pious acts would bring the Messiah, meaning that mystical devotion had to leave the circle of the elect. Two years later, also on Rosh ha-Shanah, another vision foretold what had already happened but Israel did not know, the cessation of Haidamak pogroms against Ukrainian Jews due to the spread of a lethal epidemic.

Below the level of these empyrean visions and mystic prescriptions, Israel Besht as Good Master of the Name taught things accessible to ordinary people. Man, placed in God's world, was religiously bound to rejoice in it and in performing the commandments of the Torah which sustained the world. Gloom or asceticism were not proper religious attitudes. A mood of melancholy implied a want of complete trust (*bittahon*) in God's benevolent interest, and could undo the good effects on high of commandments joyfully performed below. The religious ideal was communion with God (*devekut*, lit. adhesion) so intimate that one lost consciousness of self. Prayer recited in such a spirit brought boundless spiritual benefits. Not only prayer but performing any commandment of the Torah could bring about *devekut*. Israel Besht realized that very few Jews, even the most pious and learned, were capable of constant *devekut*, and one should therefore establish a relationship of *devekut* with a man who was capable of it. This man was the *zaddik*—the righteous man or saint. In the perspective of *bittahon*, *devekut*, and the *zaddik*, what was the place of Talmudic erudition, long the source of respect and honour and the major requirement for rabbinic office? Israel Besht said little about this, but the implication of his teaching is evident.

---

[27] See 1 Kings 11: 29–39. Perhaps Israel considered Ahiyah his mentor not on account of the seer's secessionist prophecy but because his name means 'God my brother/comrade'.

The study of the Torah must not be for intellectual accomplishment and honour, but for a deeper purpose. When the Torah's letters, not its words, are studied, lights emanate from which *devekut* is achieved. When the main purpose of study becomes subjective contemplation, it is difficult to understand the Torah's text, but for Israel that is secondary.

The teachings of Israel Besht had precedents reaching back to medieval Spanish and German pietists, Safed mystics, and even to some rabbis of the Talmud. Closer to the age of the Besht were moralists, some of them community rabbis, who wrote on themes similar to Israel's and other early Hasidic masters'. However, the moralists' emphasis was usually ascetic, not joyful. Israel's teachings seemed keyed to the poor, the unlettered and righteous folk unnoticed by men but especially loved by God. He had come from their midst. He taught them that their humble religious ways, when performed with fervour and devout intent, equalled or even surpassed the intellectual feats of the self-regarding scholarly élite. Their pious prayer and fervent singing and even their dancing and drinking could manifest *bittahon* and attain *devekut*. The élite might take offence while the poor embraced his teachings, but Israel was not leading a social revolt. It is even difficult to speak of a movement during his lifetime. He gathered followers who were called by the venerable term *hasidim*, more or less meaning pious persons. Similar groups seem to have existed with their respective leaders. Some of them were prosperous and learned and prominent in their communities. Such is approximately the scholarly consensus on Israel Besht. In Rosman's challenging view, however, he was not only a well-regarded member of his community but more of a scholar than hitherto realized. He attained fame as a healer and exorcist, a shaman in the anthropological term. He did not found a movement nor establish any institutions; those came later.

After Israel Besht died in 1760 the leadership of his Hasidim did not pass to his inconspicuous son or son-in-law, nor to his impressive daughter Adel because female leadership was unthinkable. A community rabbi, Jacob Joseph of Polnoyye (d. 1780), was perhaps the most gifted intellectually but he was evidently a solitary and somewhat irascible man. The successor was Dov Ber of Mezerich (d. 1772), known as the Great Preacher, who presided over the study hall (*beit midrash*) in his town which became the incubator of Hasidism as a movement. Young men, some of them proficient Talmudists, turned away from learning and joined R. Dov Ber's contemplative sessions, where the verses of the Torah were interpreted with great freedom. He drew his inspiration from passive contemplation, trusting that his spontaneous utterances would be wise and meritorious. Among the disciples of R. Dov Ber were R. Levi Isaac of Berdichev (d. 1810) and R. Shneur Zalman of Lyuzny (1743–1812), an accomplished rabbinic scholar and founder of the Lubavich dynasty.

Hasidism as a unified movement ended with R. Dov Ber's demise, and young leaders went forth on their own, mainly to southern Poland and the Ukraine. Especially in view of their bitter experiences of Sabbatianism and Frankism, some local communities attempted to suppress the new movement, which seemed suspiciously similar. Widely circulated bans that were issued in 1772 in Vilna, bastion of rabbinic learning, and in somewhat Germanic and modernizing Brody, referred to the evil forerunners. The bans opened a forty years' combat.[28] They forbade Hasidim to pray separately, where they introduced unacceptable liturgical changes. Other complaints were repeated constantly during the long quarrel. Hasidim neglect prescribed times of prayer and instead spend long periods in contemplation before they pray. They adopt the prayer book in its mystical Lurianic version, and dote on the supposed mystic meaning of every word and letter while crying out in wild fervour. They scoff at Talmud learning and scorn scholars. They defy community regulation of *shehitah* by using only their own specially sharpened knives, thus reducing badly needed income from the community tax on meat.

Rabbi Jacob Joseph, a community rabbi who turned Hasid after hearing Israel Besht speak, was an abrasive critic of his fellow rabbis. He dismissed them as men more interested in money and honour than in modesty and pious reverence. His *Toldot Yaakov Yosef*, published in 1780 as the first Hasidic book, contained many slurring remarks about

---

[28] The sources are presented in Mordecai Wilensky, *Hasidim u-Mitnagdim* (Hebrew; Eng. title *Hasidim and Mitnaggedim: . . . the Controversy . . . 1772–1815* (2 vols., Jerusalem, 1970).

the rabbis of the day and presented a conception of the mystical and pastoral leadership of the *zaddik*. The book confirmed doctrines which for years had circulated only by word of mouth, and aroused opponents' deep anger. *Toldot Yaakov Yosef* was publicly burned in Vilna as fresh bans were issued in 1780, the year of its author's death.[29]

The persecution took place under the direction of the GR'A of Vilna. His religious intellectualism was outraged by the new movement's hostility to his scholarly ideals. He also suspected the presence of Sabbatianism within Hasidism, as stated in the ban of 1772 which he was instrumental in promulgating. The GR'A rebuffed all attempts at rapprochement or reconciliation, and on one occasion left Vilna to avoid a proposed meeting with the Hasidim.

As we have said, Hasidism was not a social revolt.[30] Its early leaders included members of the community establishment such as community rabbis, tax farmers, and estate managers. Neither did the movement necessarily flourish in towns where popular revolts erupted against abusive *kahal* oligarchies. Still, the movement held particular appeal for the poor, unlettered, and country Jews living isolated and too few to constitute a community. They were little noticed or respected when they came to town to celebrate the major holidays. Itinerant Hasidic teachers visited these neglected country Jews and readily won many of them for the new movement. Salo W. Baron has suggested that the rural Jew was especially exposed to the religious influence of his Greek Catholic-Uniate or Greek Orthodox environment, which 'despised learning as the mark of intellectual haughtiness and glorified good deeds performed out of humble, blissful ignorance'.[31] Such an outlook was present in Hasidism.

Faith in the coming of the Messiah was a tenet of Judaism which of course was maintained within the Hasidic movement, but Hasidism was

---

[29] Ibid., i. 101–10 ff.

[30] Made trenchantly by Shmuel Ettinger, 'Hasidic Leadership in the Making' and 'Hasidism and the *Kahal* in Eastern Europe', (Hebrew) in his *On the History of the Jews in Poland and Russia* (Hebrew) (Jerusalem, 1994) and 'The Hasidic Movement: Reality and Ideals', in Hundert, *Essential Papers*, 226–43. Rosman, *Founder of Hasidism*, 173–86 discusses the Besht in this light–see below.

[31] *A Social and Religious History of the Jews* (3 vols., New York, 1937), ii. 154. The great historian held to this idea some fifty years later when he brought the passage to my attention, expressing the hope that this possible influence would be studied more closely.

neither a messianic movement nor a substitute for one, nor was it connected to the remnant of Sabbatianism. Some early *zaddikim* settled in Palestine, mainly at Safed and Tiberias, but the intense redemptionism of Lurianic mysticism, a fount of Hasidic thought, was toned down. The ordinary Hasid would find his spiritual fulfilment in *devekut* and in sanctifying life's pleasures. The Messiah would surely come, and meanwhile the *hasid* would devoutly follow his *zaddik* and the special codes of conduct (*hanhagot yesharot*) which many *zaddikim* devised for their followers.

Hasidism spread almost unchallenged into the Ukraine and Galicia but encountered strong opposition to establishing itself in Lithuania and White Russia. There is no evidence of a serious attempt to introduce Hasidism into western Europe. It is doubtful whether the Hasidic movement which belonged essentially to medieval Judaism could have flourished in the west. Western Jewry from the eighteenth century had to comprehend and cope with a new world outlook which had begun its conquests during the previous century. Capitalism, rationalism, science, and nationalism, the basis of the new political and intellectual order in the west, were antithetical to Hasidism's mystical exegesis, confidence in miraculous redemption, unquestioning religious faith, and attachment to a *zaddik*. Hasidism needed a community immersed in traditional religious faith, remote from modern society and culture.

Enlightenment

As Hasidism was coursing through the spiritual arteries of east European Judaism, the reorientation of west European Jewry to a new political and intellectual order was beginning. The first manifestations, already mentioned, were the court Jews in Germanic lands and the freethinking Amsterdam circle out of which Spinoza emerged. In the mid-eighteenth century, during the full flowering of the European Enlightenment, a Jewish Enlightenment grew forth with its centre in Berlin and spread from there to Bohemia and Galicia and in the nineteenth century to Russia. Unlike the Amsterdam circle and earlier ones in Renaissance Italy, the Jewish Enlightenment of Berlin with its offshoots and successors openly and vigorously sought extensive changes in Jewish life. The movement was called Haskalah, from the Hebrew root *skl*, meaning 'to reason' and connoting 'making reasonable', 'making wise, understanding'. Thus the term, used originally in medieval Jewish philosophy, stressed its rationalism. A devotee of Haskalah was a *maskil*, derived from the same root.

The European Enlightenment, the Haskalah's prototype, seldom dealt with the Jews, but when it did it was in a manner not generous or complimentary. To the English Deists, the Enlightenment's forerunners as rationalist sceptics towards religion, who attacked received Christianity, the Jews were merely one more barbaric tribe of the ancient world. The Deists thought little of Judaism from which Christianity emerged and still less of the biblical and rabbinic laws by which the Jews lived. Moses' and the prophets' rebukes and denunciations were taken to show the Jews 'a very cloudy people . . . [of] stubborn habit and stupid Humor', as Shaftesbury put it.[32] The Jews long adhered to the base beliefs of the Egyptians, Anthony Collins argued in 1724, and the positive moral and monotheistic qualities of Judaism were mere borrowings from Mesopotamian religion.[33] Matthew Tindall went yet further, attacking biblical Jewish morality and its continuation in Christianity. The Deists had to be cautious in denouncing Christianity,[34] but they could assail Judaism, its forebear, without concern. In biblical laws of priestly dues and sacrifices they found the beginning of the clericalism they hated. The harsh later history of the Jews drew little attention or sympathy on the Deists' part. An exception was the cantankerous John Toland, a pioneer advocate of Jewish emancipation, who combined low regard for ancient Jews with friendship towards some London Jews whom he knew.

English Deism remained within small élite circles. The French Enlighteners who inherited Deism from the English, however, made it an influential, widely known current in European thought, accompanied

---

[32] S. Ettinger, 'The Beginnings of the Change in the Attitude of European Society towards the Jews' *Scripta Hierosolymitana*, 7 (1961), 193–219.

[33] Ibid., 70.

[34] S. Ettinger, 'Jews and Judaism as Seen by the English Deists of the Eighteenth Century' (Hebrew) *Zion*, 29 (1964), 182–207.

by fierce hostility to existing religions. They despised religious establishments, especially France's Roman Catholic, and condemned religious persecution, also of the Jews. The French Enlighteners' knowledge
of Judaism and the Jews came from the extensive writings of seventeenth-century Christian Hebraist savants, to which they added their
own sarcastic hostility.[35] French Enlighteners' ideas about the Jews were
decided. They disliked Judaism as drawn from the Bible which they had
rejected, and also as a code of laws devised by fanatical rabbis.

Some Enlighteners had contact with Jews. Montesquieu knew some
Sefardic Jews of Bordeaux where he lived, and cared little for Judaism.
His principled stand for religious liberty, however, included them. But
Voltaire, the prince of the French Enlightenment, combined Deism and
libertarianism while expressing attitudes which qualify as anti-Semitic a
century before the term was invented. He had bad business experiences
with two Jewish financiers in Berlin, but his hostility went far beyond
disagreeable memories. Rather than invoke the ancient hatred of dei-
cides, Voltaire instead reviled the Jews' character, which he regarded as
innate and unchangeable: 'They are, all of them, born with raging
fanaticism in their hearts . . . I would not be in the least bit surprised if
these people would not some day become deadly to the human race.'[36]

---

[35] Not all enlightened persons were Deists in the sense described here. The English
Unitarian and liberal Joseph Priestley, one of the founders of modern chemistry, wrote
conversionist tracts to the Jews and was forcefully answered by David Levi, hatmaker
and apologist. Among the books Priestley bequeathed to the fledgling Dickinson College in Pennsylvania is a set of the Talmud (Amsterdam, 1745) still there in mint condition.

[36] Quoted in Arthur Hertzberg, *The French Enlightenment and the Jews* (New York,
1968), 300; also Miriam Yardeni, 'Jews in French Historiography of the Sixteenth–
Seventeenth Centuries,' *Zion*, 34 (1964), 171–5. On Montesquieu see Robert Badinter,
Libres et égaux . . . : L'émancipation des Juifs (1789–1791) (Paris, 1989), 52–3. Jews and the
French Enlightenment have become a matter of controversy, fuelled by Holocaust memories and the experience of contemporary leftist anti-Semitism. Theodore Besterman's
authoritative *Voltaire* (3rd edn., Chicago, 1976) disregards all his subject's writings on
Jews to reach an apologetic conclusion on p. 24. Peter Gay's argument that 'Voltaire was
content to mouth the accepted clichés' about the Jews does not square with the obsessive bitterness and violence of his statements. Peter Gay, *Voltaire's Politics: The Poet as
Realist* (Princeton, 1959), 351–4. Hertzberg, to the contrary, regards the French Enlightenment and Voltaire above all as a fount of modern secular anti-Semitism; pp. 280–6,
191–313. Frank E. Manuel, *The Changing of the Gods* (Hanover, NH, 1982), 105–29,

The Jews are 'the inevitable result of their laws; they either had to conquer everybody or be hated by the whole human race'.[37] Voltaire's 'Philosophical Dictionary' calls them

the most abominable people on earth . . . [an] ignorant and barbarous people, which has long combined the most sordid greed with the most detestable superstition with the most invincible hatred for all the peoples who tolerate and enrich them. Still, it is not necessary to burn them.[38]

Nothing as venomous came from any French Catholic quarter, which satisfied itself with repeating the ancient condemnation and liturgical vilifications. Voltaire ingeniously substituted for the old religious hostility a conception of the Jews' inherent corruption which remained unaffected by religious conversion. Diderot had only slightly better to say. The Jews

lack accuracy in their ideas, or exactness in their reasoning, or precision in their style . . . only a confused mixture of the principles of reason and of revelation . . . principles that lead to fanaticism . . . an ignorant and superstitious nation.[39]

In the *Encyclopédie*, the summary and quintessence of the French Enlightenment which Diderot edited, some articles such as 'Jews', 'Judaism', and 'Usury' were written in a more liberal but none the less unsympathetic spirit while others, such as 'Messiah', 'Church Fathers', and 'Political Economy' were hostile. The atheist Holbach assailed Christianity in his anonymously published *L'Esprit du judaïsme* while also denouncing Judaism and 'the stupid Hebrews, the frenzied imbeciles'. Rousseau, however, expressed in passing mild sympathy for Jewish sufferings and respect for the virtues which enabled the Jews to

basically agrees on anti-Semitism, but is less trenchant than Hertzberg and emphasizes the Enlightenment's heritage of Christian Hebraism which, to be sure, was not sharply hostile to Judaism. Manuel's *The Broken Staff: Judaism through Christian Eyes* (Cambridge, Mass., 1992), 162–222, continues this standpoint and follows the consequences of the Enlightenment into the twentieth century.

[37] Quoted in Hertzberg, *The French Enlightenment*, 302.

[38] Quoted by F. Delpech in Bernhard Blumenkranz, *Histoire des Juifs en France* (Toulouse, 1972), 270.

[39] Quoted in Arthur M. Wilson, *Diderot* (New York, 1972), 237; compare Hertzberg, *The French Enlightenment* 310–12.

survive in exile, and observed in his *Émile* how little Christians knew about Judaism. He noted that the Jews possessed no means for telling the wide world about Judaism. Their faults were the result of centuries of ill treatment, but Rousseau also demeaned Judaism itself.[40]

To this hostile consensus of the French Enlighteners there was barely a Jewish response. Isaac Pinto (1715–87), economist and sometime community head in Amsterdam, wrote an *Apologie pour la nation juive*. He was also the author of a deistic work, *Précis des Arguments des Matérialistes* (1774). Pinto did not defend the Jews nor quote any Jewish source, but sought merely to persuade Voltaire that he had unjustly maligned the Sefardim. Those of Amsterdam and Bordeaux were following Enlightenment prescriptions and differed from the benighted Ashkenazim who by implication were more fit for attack. However, Moses Mendelssohn, an Ashkenazi, was annoyed to be cited by Pinto as an enlightened philosophical Jew. Voltaire responded with a half-hearted apology to Pinto which he contradicted in private correspondence, but altered nothing in his writings and continued sneering at the Jews.

What did the men of the Enlightenment require of the Jews in order to grant them admittance to enlightened society, where privilege was abolished and equal rights assured? Nowhere were the *philosophes* specific, but having no respect for Jewish culture and tradition, holding a negative view of Judaism, and scornful of contemporary Jews, they hardly considered that anyone could be Jewish and enlightened. The conspicuous example of Mendelssohn notwithstanding, a contradiction between rational enlightenment and being a Jew was taken for granted. Generally, Voltaire's and the French Enlightenment's bequest was disdainful impatience with the Jews and their separateness.

The Enlightenment in Germany, where Haskalah originated, had a different character. As put by Hajo Holborn:

German Enlightenment . . . displayed a more religious and philosophical bent than that of western Europe. The belief in a personal God of supreme wisdom and benevolence, the creator of a perfect world, who had planted in the immortal human soul the power to rise—through moral virtue—to the highest objectives of the universe, was not questioned by any serious German thinker.

[40] Blumenkranz, *Histoire des Juifs* 270–1 (by F. Delpech); Bandinter, *Libres et égaux* 53–4.

Philosophical materialism, which became one of the important schools of thought in France, found no place in Germany.[41]

Religious and philosophical issues dominated the German Enlightenment, with political and social reforms seldom considered. Enlightened monarchs and their civil servants were depended on to introduce the necessary changes. The foremost figures of the German Enlightenment were not much more favourable to the Jews than their French counterparts, but their reflections are usually more suggestive and thoughtful. Goethe grew up in Frankfurt am Main where he saw the Jews in their ghetto and held them in lofty disdain—a widespread attitude. The most significant instance to the contrary is the poet, dramatist, and philosopher Gotthold Ephraim Lessing, who enjoyed a famous friendship with Moses Mendelssohn. His Jewish friend described Lessing as his 'oldest and best friend'. It was commonly known that Mendelssohn was the model for 'Nathan the Wise' in Lessing's classic drama, which expresses the essential moral unity of all religions. There is a respected place for Judaism in his 'Education of the Human Race' in its upward progress under Divine guidance. Biblical Judaism served as the primer for humanity's childhood, and Christianity followed for humanity's adulthood; a yet higher religion would come in time. Christianity is not the ultimate religion, but it stands above Judaism. The later German philosophers who replaced Enlightenment rationalism with nationalist romanticism viewed Judaism even more negatively.

The social basis for Jewish Enlightenment existed in eighteenth-century German Jewry. Although most German Jews remained within traditional Jewish life,[42] contemporary research has shown an increasing number of Jews in Germany fluent in German, educating their children in the arts and sciences, and discarding distinctive Jewish garb. Secular

---

[41] Hajo Holborn, *History of Modern Germany, 1648–1840* (New York, 1964), 310–11; compare the characterizations of Enlightenment by country in Roy Porter and Mikulas Teich (eds), *The Enlightenment in National Context* (Cambridge, 1981).

[42] Cf. the suggestive remarks of Lucien Febvre on the relation of enlightened thinkers to one another and their patrons in a far different time and place in his *The Problem of Unbelief in the Sixteenth Century: The Religion of Rabelais* (Cambridge, Mass. 1982), 23–5. Azriel Shochat, *Im Hillufey Tekufot* (Hebrew; In Changing Eras) (Jerusalem, 1960), shows the considerable extent of modernization before Haskalah.

studies and European culture began to penetrate the Jewish community, creating a new educated class. Many Jewish communities were composed of substantial bankers, generally pious men who were open to the broad cultural world. So it was in the Vienna of Empress Maria Theresa, who 'sincerely' hated Jews and could not bear their sight.[43] Even a few rabbis showed familiarity with modern culture. This growing body of acculturating Jews was ripe for a new formulation of Judaism to fit the widespread ideal of *Bildung*, individual moral and cultural cultivation. True, there had been earlier periods when Jewish cultural life was deeply influenced by the surrounding culture, such as seventeenth-century Amsterdam and Renaissance Italy not to go still further back. In the German Haskalah, however, there is something new: a comprehensive critique of contemporary Jewish life and a programme for the social and cultural reorientation of the Jewish people. Its centre was the fast-growing Prussian capital of Berlin, whose Jewish community was refounded only in 1671 but for many years remained fully traditional. The Jewish merchants of Berlin have been characterized an 'imported economic élite,' of which there were several in the Prussian capital.[44] Berlin was attracting some of the foremost figures of German culture, men who associated with enlightened Jews. The young Wilhelm von Humboldt, the future philosopher-statesman, came and went in a Jewish salon in 1785–7 and carried on 'a sentimental dalliance' with its hostess Henriette Herz.[45]

There were already *maskilim* in the early eighteenth century. Israel of

[43] P. G. M. Dickson, *Finance and Government under Maria Theresa, 1740–1780*, i. *Society and Government* (Oxford, 1987), 140–53. To the empress 'there was no worse plague in the state' than the Jews, and a British observer reported, 'Her aversion to the sight of a Jew was too great to be concealed'. Quoted in ibid. 148 n. 26.

[44] S. Jersch-Wenzel, *Juden und Franzosen in der Wirtschaft des Raumes Berlin/Brandenburg zur Zeit des Mercantilismus* (Berlin, 1978); the massive work of H. Rachel, J. Popritz, and P. Wallich, *Berliner Grosskaufleute und Kapitalisten* (3 vols., Berlin, 1967; originally published as manuscript, 1932–9) is practically a business history of Berlin with Jews in a central position.

[45] Paul R. Sweet, *Wilhelm von Humboldt: A Biography*, i. (Columbus, Ohio, 1978), 16–19. A parallel with Edinburgh and the Scottish Enlightenment is suggestive; Nicholas T. Philipson, '. . . The Case of Edinburgh,' in Laurence Stone (ed.), *The University and Society* (2 vols., Princeton, 1975), i. esp. 407, 423–7. An important recent study is Steven M. Lowenstein, *The Berlin Jewish Community: Enlightenment, Family, and Crisis, 1770–1830* (New York/Oxford, 1994).

Zamosc, Leibniz's associate Avigdor Levi, and several others were not themselves important figures, but their combination of Jewish erudition with self-taught secular learning suggested future directions. Moses Mendelssohn (1729–86) is the central figure of the Berlin Haskalah, indeed of Haskalah everywhere. The story of his life symbolizes Haskalah ideals, has been told many times, and is overlaid with myths. Recently it has been retold masterfully and at length by Alexander Altmann.[46] The child of a poor Hebrew scribe in Dessau, Mendelssohn showed exceptional promise during his completely traditional education. When his mentor, the eminent Rabbi David Frankel, left Dessau to become rabbi of Berlin, the 14-year-old Moses, who was undersized and afflicted with a spinal deformity, followed him. The lad supposedly underwent strict interrogation at one of the city's gates by a gendarme or, more likely, by one of the watchmen whom the Jewish community was required to post lest the 1,943 Berlin Jews illicitly increase. Admitted as part of someone's extended household, he studied in Rabbi Frankel's *beit midrash* and soon began to earn his way as a tutor. The young Mendelssohn studied the Talmud diligently for a decade, and also mastered Maimonides' classic *Guide for the Perplexed* and other works of Jewish philosophy. Later *maskilim* who followed him also were inspired by studying the long-neglected medieval Jewish philosophers.[47] The budding scholar learned Latin from the writings of John Locke, besides Greek and modern languages and mathematics, and with the aid of his new friend Lessing he acquired an admirable writing style in German. These secular studies were not opposed by Rabbi Frankel. By the age of 25 Mendelssohn was not only a proficient Talmudist but also expert in Bible studies, Hebrew language, and Jewish and general philosophy, and had mastered the general culture of his age. For generations no Jew in central or eastern Europe could claim such accomplishments.

Mendelssohn cherished the ambition, unknown for a Jew, to be a

[46] Alexander Altmann, *Moses Mendelssohn: A Biographical Study* (Philadelphia, 1973). The earliest biography, published in *Ha-Meassef* just after his death by one who knew him well, is Isaac Euchel's *Toldot he-Hakham ha-Hoker Elohi Rabbenu Moshe ben Menahem z'ts/l* (Hebrew; Life of the Scholar and Divine Inquirer Our Master Moses ben Menahem o'b'm') (Lemberg, 1860; many edns). It is an important source of facts and likewise of legends.

[47] Amos Funkenstein, *Perceptions of Jewish History* (Berkeley, 1993), 234–47.

philosopher and German writer. During and after his years of study there is no appearance of storm and stress although, in replying to Lavater's public challenge of 1769 to turn Christian, Mendelssohn did remark that he had at a certain time given his religious beliefs systematic thought. His personal synthesis between the secular and the Jewish did not come from wrestling and striving, but was the fruit of harmonious growth. He did not originally intend to concentrate in the Jewish sphere, although his first literary effort was the Hebrew satirical journal, *Kohelet Musar* of 1760,[48] which he soon gave up under community pressure. He sought his true career in general philosophy, assuming that the mere recognition of a Jew as intellectually distinguished would contribute to elevating the Jews' position. He achieved this ambition, for by 1768 he was a metaphysician and philosopher of aesthetics of European fame, on terms of friendship with leading German cultural figures.

Mendelssohn continued to adhere faithfully to the religious requirements of Judaism, and was the pride of the Berlin Jewish community. The honour (and material rewards) of membership in the Prussian Academy of Sciences was proposed, but Frederick II would not grant a Jew this privilege. Herr Moses, as he was respectfully known, made a good living as the manager and then partner in a silk manufacturing firm, a field in which he became an authority. Of sociable temperament and generous disposition, he had many admirers and guests. He prayed with fellow Jews, but intellectual conversation was with gentiles. Unusually for that day, his marriage was not arranged but was the outcome of a courtship. It was a happy one, and produced six children who grew to adulthood. There is more controversy over these children than over Mendelssohn himself, for only two of them did not convert to Christianity. Herr Moses had no Jewish grandchildren. No answer can be given to how their upbringing by the great scholar and philosopher influenced the life of his children.

Mendelssohn became a respected member of 'religiously neutral society', so called thanks to its benevolent neutrality towards all religions. He belonged in the broad stream of general religious enlightenment

---

[48] This and his other Hebrew writings are gathered in *Hebräische Schriften*, i, ed. H. Borodiansky (Bar-Dayan) (repr. Stuttgart, 1972, from the mostly destroyed original of Breslau, 1938).

common to both Catholics and Protestants. They combined religious faith with endorsement of the principles of reason and tolerance and acceptance of modern culture. Cultured Berlin with many such persons seemed to be such a society, as the few Jews possessing modern culture and manners found a place in its midst. But Berlin's cultured society included pietistic Lutheran clergy and others who wondered how a philosopher could profess Judaism. The question burst into the open when the fervently pietist young clergyman Johann Christian Lavater, who had sat at Mendelssohn's table, publicly challenged him in 1769 to convert or explain why not. The enlightened world considered Lavater impertinent but awaited Herr Moses's answer. He, normally equable and uncombative, was deeply angered. Rather than answer fully, Mendelssohn rebuked Lavater in seemingly mild tones for exploiting remarks in private conversation in which he had complimented the moral stature of Jesus the man. He assured the pastor of Zurich that he remained a Jew out of considered conviction, and declined to enter a religious discussion since Judaism did not proselytize but respected the ethical principles of all religions even if their foundations were faulty. Anyhow, he observed pointedly, Jews knew better than to enter uninhibited religious discussion.[49] The cultured world applauded Herr Moses's dignified rejoinder and Lavater apologized. While these universal religious principles were under civil but strained discussion, about 150 miles away Rabbi Dov Ber, isolated from other religions, was expounding mystical exegesis with a small group of disciples.

Things were not the same for Mendelssohn after the Lavater episode. His career took a turn, and he suffered during the sixteen remaining years of his life from a nervous ailment, possibly psychosomatic or psychogenic, which put sustained metaphysical philosophizing beyond his strength. The sage of Berlin devoted himself to Jewish subjects, and became not only the symbol of Enlightenment as he had been but also its active leader. He organized, arranged financing, recruited authors, and saw to completion in 1783 a great Bible project. Called *Biur* ('explana-

---

[49] But religion was discussed at his table in general terms; *Frederik Munter et Mindeskrift,* ed. O. Andreasen (7 vols. in 8, Copenhagen, 1935–44), ii. 37–9, reports such conversation in 1782 with an enlightened young Danish clergyman. See David Sorkin, *Moses Mendelssohn and the Religious Enlightenment* (London, 1996).

tion') after its main component, a rationalist grammatical commentary in elegant Hebrew, Mendelssohn's Bible included a translation into German printed in Hebrew letters, and detailed textual notes (*Masorah*). He did much of the translation and *Biur* himself, and drew the best *maskilic* talent of the day into the work. The erudite grammarian Solomon Dubno composed the *Masorah* until he fell out with Mendelssohn, probably over the excessive length which his contribution reached. The Mendelssohn Bible ran into numerous editions, and became the means by which young men of exclusively traditional education in eastern Europe could acquire a modern language, appreciate rationalist Judaism, and be introduced to modern culture. It was a notable scholarly accomplishment and Haskalah's greatest monument. As will be discussed below, Mendelssohn's Bible stirred extensive criticism.

Berlin *maskilim* also wrote works of imaginative literature. The scholarly *Biur* collaborator Naftali Herz Wessely (1725–1803) composed 'Poems of Glory' (*Shirei Tiferet*) an earnest, long-winded epic poem about Israel's bondage, exodus, and revelation at Mount Sinai, resembling Klopstock's German work. Another member of the Berlin circle, Isaac Satanov (1732–1804), wrote didactic Aesopian fables, *Mishley Assaf*, and pious poems, *Zemirot Assaf*. The latter, published in 1793, contained a rhymed introduction by one Zerahiah ben Mas'ud, an Italian Jew serving in Brabant with the Habsburg army. Haskalah poetry was typically hortatory and didactic. One of the few specimens of true lyric poetry was love poems, *Eleh B'ne ha-N'urim*, by Ephraim (Angelo) Luzzatto, the wayward Italian physician of the London Sefardic community.[50] The bulk of German Haskalah *belles-lettres* hardly contains any good literature. Among other reasons its Hebrew was stiff and limited. However, genres with medieval pedigrees such as textual commentaries and exegesis, philosophy and linguistics stood at a higher intellectual level and were more acceptable to the Jewish community.

Part of the cultural importance of Haskalah lay in its broadening the language of Bible, Talmud, and rabbinic culture to make it that of the arts and sciences and general culture. Today's Hebrew of the Israeli army, bus station, and university takes its start in the Haskalah Hebrew revival. The Haskalah movement itself had rather different goals, the

[50] David Mirsky, *The Life and Work of Ephraim Luzzatto* (New York, 1987).

conversion of the Jews into a people of European culture, readying themselves to acquire rights and citizenship.
Was there a Haskalah in England? The Jewish community was little more than a century old. Jewish access to English culture was unrestricted. Cecil Roth's list of Anglo-Jewish Hebrew writers, none of whom equals those in German lands, does not include any authors who sought to reform Jewish life.[51] Endelman has argued that Haskalah in England was not an intellectual movement but communal modernization. David Ruderman finds there a modest Haskalah not drawn from the intellectuals on the Continent but from 'intellectual currents primarily located on English soil'.[52] Probably one may speak of Haskalah in England but only in the limited sense of communal improvement. Haskalah had many forms but all led towards secular modernizing.

[51] Cecil Roth, 'The Haskalah in England', *Essays Presented to Chief Rabbi Israel Brodie*, ed. H. J. Zimmels, J. Rabbinowitz, and I. Finestein (London, 1967), 365–76.

[52] Todd M. Endelman, *The Jews of Georgian England, 1714–1830* (Philadelphia, 1979), esp. 149–52; David B. Ruderman, 'Was There a Haskalah in England? Reconsidering an Old Question' (Hebrew; English summary) *Zion*, 57/2 (1997), 109–32.

4

Era of Revolution

Haskalah Practical and Radical

The 1780s, when many Haskalah ideas began to reach practical realization, were a stirring decade for the advocates of change. Internal criticism of contemporary Jewish life became more outspoken and former Haskalah suggestions were rephrased as demands. New laws in the spirit of tolerance were enacted and hailed as a gracious benefit to the Jews. *Maskilim* received monarchical backing for projects to make their people 'useful' subjects.

Until he died in 1786 the towering figure of the little Mendelssohn kept the Haskalah movement relatively unified and in peaceable relations with community establishments. The once widespread view that his Bible edition stirred a storm and that prominent rabbis placed it under a ban, has been shown to be greatly exaggerated.[1] No ban was imposed and Mendelssohn's grammatical, rationalist exegesis was little if at all criticized. What controversy there was concerned the German translation. There had been earlier Jewish Bible translations into rudimentary German in order to teach children, but the Mendelssohn version possessed such literary distinction that R. Ezekiel Landau, otherwise not opposed, complained that its merits would distract students from studying the Bible to studying German. The rabbi of Prague touched on one of Haskalah's deepest wishes. Not only would students learn German through the translation, but the *Biur's* fine Hebrew would revive linguistic studies and replace the long prevalent slapdash, ungrammatical Ashkenazic Hebrew rabbinic style. In 1784 *Ha-Meassef* (The Gatherer), the first Hebrew periodical, made its appearance. Written in

---

[1] M. S. Samet, 'Mendelssohn, Weisel and the Rabbis of their Time' (Hebrew; English summary), *Meḥqarim be-Toldot Am Yisrael ve-Erez Yisrael*, i (Haifa, 1970), 233–56.

a didactic, self-consciously literary style, it included morsels of news but mostly essays, poetry, and learned studies. While Mendelssohn lived, *Ha-Meassef*, like Haskalah itself, remained pronouncedly conservative, not criticizing religious customs and avoiding conflict.

During these last years of his life the sage of Berlin produced a final metaphysical work, *Morgenstunden*, and his treatise *Jerusalem: or, On Religious Power and Judaism*, which dealt with Judaism as a faith, its place in society, and religious liberty.[2] Like other works of his it was inspired by a conversionist tract, this one called 'The Search for Light and Truth'.[3] Mendelssohn fully presented in *Jerusalem* the case for religious tolerance. Religion, he argued, dealt only with matters of belief, about which man could not be forced but only persuaded. Therefore, 'neither state nor church would be authorized to assume any right in matters of faith other than the right to teach, any power other than the power to persuade, any discipline other than the discipline of reason and principles.'[4] No religious body, the Jewish body included, could justly exercise coercive power. Mendelssohn claimed quite erroneously that when the Jews ceased their existence as a state their Diaspora communities did not exercise religious coercion. It was the state's duty to protect its subjects which entitled it to employ coercion. Implicit is the case for separation of Church and State. Mendelssohn's argument for toleration for Judaism and all religion harmonized with the ideas of the time. He was, in Randall's words, 'the very embodiment of the Enlightenment drive to make religion rational and to prove its tenets'.[5]

Mendelssohn distinguishes between the revelation of moral laws, perfectly embodied in Judaism which is a religion without dogmas, and re-

---

[2] The 1790 edition of the two works in the British Library (shelfmark C. 43.a.5.) contains marginal comments by the English poet-philosopher Samuel Taylor Coleridge.

[3] Long thought to be the work of the Habsburg statesman and the son of a convert to Catholicism Joseph von Sonnenfels, it has been shown to be the work of a minor writer, A. F. Cranz.

[4] Moses Mendelssohn, *Jerusalem: or On Religious Power and Judaism*, trans. A. Arkush, intro. and comm. A. Altmann (Hanover, NH, 1983), 77. Cf. another translation: *Jerusalem and Other Jewish Writings by Moses Mendelssohn*, trans. and ed. A. Jospe (New York, 1969), 50.

[5] John Herman Randall Jr., *The Career of Philosophy: From the German Enlightenment to the Age of Darwin* (New York, 1965), 146.

vealed 'religious legislation', prescribing the religious life obliging Jews alone. Every rational human mind knew the moral laws, and revelation served only to reinforce them. Revelation was required, however, for 'Divine *legislation*—laws, commandments, ordinances, rules of life, and instruction in the will of God as to how they should conduct themselves in order to attain temporal and eternal felicity'.[6] Here Mendelssohn introduced a momentous dichotomy by driving a wedge between ethical religion held in common by Jews and all humanity, with revelation merely reinforcing its natural acceptance, and the necessity of 'Divine legislation' requiring a distinct Jewish life. Already in his time, fidelity to 'Divine legislation' was weakening among acculturating German Jews. Mendelssohn himself faithfully observed the 'Divine legislation', but his doctrine could be used to justify religious indifference, anti-traditional Judaism, and even conversion to the rational, universal version of the religion of the great majority.

As a man of the world, Mendelssohn for many years was the address for distressed Jewish communities. His discreet intervention with cultivated rulers and senior civil servants who knew and admired him aided communities endangered by expulsion, confiscatory taxes, demands to delay burials, and other oppressive measures. His most significant intervention took place in French Alsace, a province more German than French, where a very poor Jewish population lived in little communities under oppressive conditions as moneylenders and pedlars. They were heavily taxed, besides bribes and attorneys' fees they had to pay. During a violent popular agitation against them, receipts were forged to ruin Jewish lenders by 'proving' the repayment of debts.[7] In the spirit of cautious improvement Alsatian Jewry's leaders, headed by the rich, *maskilic* Herz Cerf-Berr, sought from Louis XVI the elevation of their degraded position and asked the sage of Berlin to write on their behalf. Mendelssohn reckoned that a sympathetic non-Jewish writer would serve the purpose better, and recruited the enlightened Prussian civil servant Christoph Wilhelm Dohm, who produced a comprehensive 'Memorandum on the Condition of the Jews in Alsace'. Its result was the

[6] A. Arkush trans. (n. 4), 90; Jospe trans. (n. 4), 61.

[7] Zosa Szajkowski, *The Economic Status of the Jews in Alsace, Metz and Lorraine* (New York, 1954), 20–2, 66, 68.

abolition of the head tax against bitter opposition from Strasbourg, the bastion of Jewish exclusion.[8] The few hundred Jews of Paris were also allowed a cemetery of their own from 1780, and no longer had to bury their dead at night without ceremony in a garden behind an inn.[9] Count Malesherbes, the enlightened noble whose report had legalized the Protestants' position, was put in 1787 to investigate the Jews' status. After much study he reached the conclusion that persecution had caused the Jews' faults and they should be encouraged to settle on the land. Nothing was done, however, before the great upheaval which began in 1789. [10]

Aided and encouraged by Mendelssohn, the earnest Dohm wrote *On the Civil Improvement of the Jews*, so called because the Old Regime knew nothing of equality and emancipation. Its two parts, published in 1781 and 1783 and translated into French, proposed substantial civic freedom for the Jews within the existing regime of privilege. Like other advocates of the Jewish cause, Dohm allowed that the Jews were repellent, but responsibility for their degraded condition belonged to

the governments which were unable to reduce the friction between the religious principles separating them [from Christians] . . . These were Christian governments, and therefore we cannot deny if we want to be impartial that we have contributed the greater part to the hostile feeling of the two groups . . . If, therefore, those prejudices today prevent the Jew from being a good citizen, a social human being, if he feels antipathy and hatred against the Christian, if he feels himself in his dealings with him not so much bound by his moral code, then all this is our own doing . . . we ourselves are guilty of the crimes we accuse him of.[11]

While Dohm praised Jews' domestic virtues and religious fidelity, he observed their

[8] Zosa Szajkowski, 'The Jewish Problem in Alsace, Metz and Lorraine on the Eve of the Revolution of 1789', *Jewish Quarterly Review*, 44 (1954), part 2.

[9] John McManners, *Death and the Enlightenment: Changing Attitudes to Death among Christians and Unbelievers in Eighteenth-Century France* (Oxford, 1981), 281.

[10] Pierre Grosclaude, *Malesherbes: Témoin et interprète de son temps* (Paris, 1962), 631–49.

[11] C. W. Dohm, *Über der bürgerliche Verbesserung der Juden* (Berlin, 1781, 1783), i. 38–9; trans. Helen Lederer, *Concerning the Amelioration of the Civil Status of the Jews* (Cincinnati, 1957), 20–1.

exaggerated love . . . for every kind of profit, usury, and crooked practice; a fault which is nourished in many by their exclusive religious principles and rabbinic sophistries, and more still by Christian oppression, and the antipathy against other religions which they are taught . . . all these crimes do not stem from the national character of the Jews, but from the oppressed state in which they live.[12]

Mendelssohn did not like Dohm's harsh words about the Jews' character,[13] and dissented from his low opinion of trade which inspired scorn for the Jews as a trading people. Yet Dohm's was the first major statement during a century of debate in many countries concerning Jewish 'amelioration' and then emancipation. Advocates of the Jews generally followed his argument that the faults of the Jews are the guilt of their oppressors. Once oppression ended, the Jews' character might again display the vigorous and straightforward ways of biblical times. Dohm's programme for Jewish 'civil improvement' meant not only legal equality, freedom of occupation and the end of special taxes and insulting forms of discrimination, but also the end of their privilege of charging higher interest on loans made to poor risks. Young Jews might be compelled to take up the occupations of farmers and craftsmen, which were considered morally superior to commerce. The Prussian reformer wanted every branch of the arts and sciences and in time even public office open to Jews. The Jewish community should freely conduct its religious and charitable affairs but in the German tongue and under government supervision, and rabbis could continue to impose the religious ban (*herem*). Dohm's ideas assumed government supervision of a freer Jewish life, a paradox common in Prussia. His proposals were far different from his sponsor Mendelssohn's programme to separate Jewish life from state authority. Yet Dohm's programme was the most generous and comprehensive plan yet seen.

The most important reform before the French Revolution was enacted not in Berlin or Paris but at the Habsburg court in Vienna, where the anti-clerical Emperor Joseph II (1780–90) was decreeing secular enlightenment for his subjects, Jews included. His Patent of Tolerance for Jews was applied to Bohemia and Moravia in 1781, Vienna in 1782, and

---

[12] Ibid., 96–7; Lederer trans., 51.
[13] Alexander Altmann, *Moses Mendelssohn* (Philadelphia, 1973), 457.

finally Galicia in 1789. 'Tolerance' for the Emperor's Jews in the patent consisted of abolishing the body tax and permission to pursue any livelihood except retail business. Jews were encouraged to be craftsmen, although guild opposition ensured that few Jewish youths would serve an apprenticeship and no Jew could become a guild master. Residence in Vienna was allowed only to Jews of means, and in other cities they could not be freemen (*Stadtbürger*). They could lease real estate for a term up to twenty years, and in perpetuity once they converted. As a step to curtail communal autonomy the Jewish courts' jurisdiction was sharply reduced. The most far-reaching clause did not concern the Jews' legal and economic position, which regimes had fixed for centuries, but the internal matter of education, which non-Jewish rulers had never touched. The patents required Jewish children to receive secular instruction either in Christian schools or in Jewish community schools to be established. They were also compelled to provide a quota of youths for fifteen years' military service. The soldiers' religion was to be respected and there was hope that their good service would bring further improvements in Jewish status. Unlike the reaction to Tsar Nicholas I's brutal conscription in 1826, Habsburg Jewry apparently was not much shaken by Joseph II's conscription.

On 12 May 1789 the aged Rabbi Landau headed a Jewish delegation to the military barracks at Prague for an occasion without known precedent. (The Estates General was to open at Versailles two days later.) In words which were reported in *Ha-Me'assef* he addressed twenty-five young Jews who were about to commence military service:

My brothers, for you are and will always be that so long as you act piously and lawfully! God and our most gracious Emperor have desired that you be taken for military service. Accept your fate without grumbling, obey your superiors, be true to your duties and patient in subordination. But do not forget your religion. Do not be ashamed to be Jews among so many Christians. Pray to God daily as soon as you awake. The Emperor is required to pray to God, and all his servants . . . also pray daily to their Creator. Do not be ashamed of the signs of the Jewish religion [at this point he presented each with a packet of fringes, phylacteries, and prayer book]. If you do not have enough time, recite at least the 'Hear, Israel' chapters.

The recruits should do what they could to observe the Sabbath and not eat meat but subsist on eggs, butter, and cheese.

Earn gratitude and honour for yourselves and for our Nation when it is seen that our Nation, oppressed until now, loves its sovereign and its rulers, and in case of need is ready to sacrifice its life. I hope that through you, if you conduct yourselves faithfully and honourably, as every subject should, the shackles which still bind us will be loosened.

A year or two later, when Joseph II was in his grave and nothing was done to loosen the shackles, Landau seems to have regretted his support for Joseph's reforms.

Altogether, there was more glitter than gold to the reforms, which benefited mainly prosperous Jews and their children seeking to acculturate. However, the reception of the emperor's enlightened despotism and compulsory Haskalah was stormy. *Maskilim* were delighted. Increased economic freedom was welcomed, but it was quickly realized that commercial interests would oppose Jewish rights. Changing the language of community records and activity to German occasioned some difficulty. The most controversial was secular studies for Jewish children, with its implication of social and cultural change. To be sure, the need for German led to the founding of a Jewish school in Prague for secular studies under R. Landau's aegis with *maskilim* as the teachers. On the other hand, he took care that they not teach Jewish studies, which remained unchanged in *hadarim*. Modern schools combining Jewish and secular studies had been founded recently by *maskilim* in Berlin, Frankfurt, and Breslau, but they were mostly for poor and orphan children. In England and the North American colonies, secular and Jewish studies went side by side without further ado. Middle-class families everywhere employed private tutors for their children. In support of secular studies a prominent *maskil*, the poet Wessely, published 'Words of Peace and Truth' (*Divrey Shalom ve-Emet*) in 1781 which brought the orthodox man considerable trouble. He argued that knowledge is twofold, human wisdom (*torat ha-adam*), which was prerequisite for the second, Divine wisdom (*torat ha-elohim*). Without the former, the latter is stultified. Invoking Maimonides and other great rabbis of the past who had mastered 'human wisdom', Wessely wrote derogatorily of rabbis who lacked 'human wisdom', which meant most of them. Denunciations and bans flew, and Wessely apologized and explained.[14] His rash remarks helped to make Haskalah a matter of controversy which the far more important Mendelssohn Bible project, in which Wessely took part, had largely escaped.

Moses Mendelssohn died, universally lamented, on 4 January 1786, a few months before his fifty-seventh birthday. His prestige in the Jewish and European cultural worlds, as well as his governmental connections and activity in the Jewish community, made the sage of Berlin a cultural hero in his lifetime, and so he remained throughout the history of emancipated German Jewry. He was the shining example of a poor ghetto boy who rose to fame and honour in secular culture and gentile society while remaining a learned and devoted Jew. No other Jew in German lands ever enjoyed such a status.

It is not clear whether Mendelssohn realized during his last years that the ground was slipping from under his feet. Religious rationalism and cultural cosmopolitanism were giving way to romanticism and nationalism. During the last years of the eighteenth century Haskalah turned from Hebrew to German, just as the Latin and French of educated people were being replaced by German. Mendelssohn's admirer, the philosopher of history and culture Johann Gottfried Herder, exemplifies the new trend. The Jewish philosopher had thought in rational abstractions and was indifferent to history, while Herder was fascinated by the varieties of history and language and national cultures. The title of one of his main works, *The Spirit of Hebrew Poetry*, exemplified his conception that literature reflected the unique qualities of every national group. Herder exalted Moses and the ancient Jews as the authors of the Bible: 'All the laws of Moses evince wonderful reflection: they extend from the greatest to the smallest things, to sway the spirit of the nation in every circumstance of life, and to be, as Moses frequently repeats, an everlasting law'.[15] The ancient Jews lost their original spirit, but 'the writings of

---

[14] Naftali Herz Wessely, *Divrey Shalom ve-Emet* (4 parts, Warsaw, 1886); parts 2, 3, and 4 were responses to his critics and endorsements of reformed education by Italian rabbis.

[15] Johann Gottfried Herder, *Reflections on the Philosophy of the History of Mankind*, ed. F. E. Manuel (Chicago, 1968), 137.

the Hebrews unquestionably have had an advantageous effect on the history of mankind.'[16] Herder scorned the Jews of his own day—'parasitic moneylenders', yet like Spinoza a century earlier he holds they can re-establish their national home and regain honour among the nations.[17] As a founder of modern historical thought, Herder's intellectual world superseded that of Mendelssohn, the non-historical rationalist.

Within the Jewish community, an aggressive and critical approach by the *maskilim* in treating religion replaced their earlier caution. An extreme direction was taken by Mendelssohn's wealthy disciple David Friedlander. He believed that radical religious reform would lead to Jewish regeneration and emancipation. In 1799 he petitioned Pastor Teller, the liberal head of the Berlin Lutheran consistory, to allow a group of Jews to become Christians without accepting Christian dogma. They had cast off the Jewish ceremonial laws and believed that the moral laws which remained were identical for both religions. Teller rebuffed their approach. Men like Friedlander tried to accomplish reform from within Judaism, but most of their children converted.

The death of the granitic Frederick II in 1786 and the accession of the more benevolently disposed Frederick William II seemed promising for the Prussian Jews. Committees studied the Jewish question once again, and in 1790 an ordinance allowed them into schools and, with many exceptions, into occupations as well. Jews had to adopt German family names and record their business and communal affairs in German. Religious services could at last be conducted openly. All this was far from the legal equality which the Jews sought. Individuals and families continued to hold separate rights and privileges. As if to give point to their continued inequality and the variety of Jewish statuses, one rich Jewish family was granted a hereditary title.

Perhaps it was the newness of Berlin that made its barely 3,000 Jews so significant for the making of modern Jewish culture and society. Its Jewish and general population was constantly growing. The laws and

---

[16] Ibid. 141.

[17] Isaiah Berlin, 'Herder and the Enlightenment', in *Aspects of the Enlightenment*, ed. Earl R. Wasserman (Baltimore, 1965), esp. 60–76; Frederick M. Barnard, 'Herder and Israel', *Jewish Social Studies*, 28/1 (Jan. 1966), 25–33.

decrees enacted in Berlin, capital of Prussia which was to dominate Germany, possessed particular importance. The beginning of Reform Judaism, the 'Science of Judaism' and much of their subsequent development took place there. From about 1780 Berlin was the city of the Jewish salons, which also flourished briefly in Vienna a few years afterwards. Well-educated daughters of wealthy families, eager for release from their families' largely traditional life, conducted salons where they found it easy to make connections with Christians. In a society of rigid social distinctions and social classes the salons allowed ready social contact unobstructed by class divisions for writers, intellectuals, artists, clergymen, civil servants, and others who likewise felt stifled by class society. For about twenty years the Jewish salons were places to see and be seen. Even Goethe, Herder, Schleiermacher, and Friedrich Schlegel put in appearances, besides a host of lesser lights. It was considered impolite to speak openly of the Jewishness of the salons, but plenty was said in private. The salon women found their Judaism a meaningless burden. Some of them, like others of their background, divorced their Jewish husbands, converted, and married Prussian nobles whom they had met at a salon. The turn away from cultural cosmopolitanism to Christian Prussian patriotism after 1806 ended the Jewish salons' day. They were overtaken by the significantly named Christian-German Eating Club which excluded Jews.[18]

By the time Joseph II was dead his reforms were beginning to take effect and the Berlin salons were entertaining Prussian luminaries. But when the winds of change started to heave from France with mighty velocity, enlightened measures on the part of the Old Regime quickly halted.

Upheaval

Two opposing points of view which emerged in the discussions of reforming or liberating the Jews foreshadow the terms of Jewish emancipation in revolutionary and Napoleonic France. One view resembled

[18] Deborah Hertz, *Jewish High Society in Old Regime Berlin* (New Haven, 1988); there is deep insight in Hannah Arendt, *Rahel Varnhagen* (London, 1957).

Dohm's, that the end of oppression and a humane policy would lead to Jewish 'regeneration', a term which became common in France. The other view, influenced by the Christian doctrine of the Jews as an accursed stock, maintained that the Jews were incorrigible. They could be bettered only by coercion, the practice of enlightened despots. Both viewpoints agreed that Jewish autonomy had to be abolished and concurred in their disdain for Jewish tradition.

The most significant discussion in France before the revolution took place in an essay contest sponsored by the Royal Academy of Arts and Sciences in Metz, the local society of enlighteners, and sponsored unofficially by Malesherbes. Nine replies were received to the set question, 'Are there means of making the Jews happier and more useful in France?' One came from Thiery, a local lawyer, and another was signed 'Zalkind-Hourwitz, Polish Jew', an anti-rabbinic and anti-Talmud *maskil* who was cataloguer of Hebrew books at the royal library in Paris. Both wrote in terms of coercive reform by enlightened despots. The most significant reply came from a priest of millenarian and predestinarian beliefs, Abbé Henri Grégoire, who foresaw the Jews' conversion as a preliminary to universal salvation. He believed they were likelier to convert once emancipated rather than when oppressed and confined.[19] (The British Philo-Judaeans thought likewise during the 1820s.[20]) Grégoire played a public role well into Napoleonic times, contributing not only to Jewish emancipation but also to the abolition of slavery in the French colonies.

The French Revolution profoundly affected the Jews, as it affected all Europe and much of mankind, far beyond the five years of its duration. The epochal events began with Louis XVI summoning an Estates General to relieve his government's financial distress. Asked to specify their grievances, the king's subjects did so in some 30,000 'notebooks of grievances' (*cahiers de doléances*), of which 307 complained against the Jews. Some of the latter seem to be based on a draft which circulated in

[19] Ruth F. Necheles, 'The Abbé Grégoire and the Jews', *Jewish Social Studies*, 23 (1971), 122–9; Grosclaude, *Malesherbes*, 631. David Feuerwerker, *L'Émancipation des Juifs en France de l'Ancien Régime à la fin du Second Empire* (Paris, 1976), contains some significant new material.

[20] Todd M. Endelman, *The Jews of Georgian England, 1714–1830: Tradition and Change in a Liberal Society* (Philadelphia, 1979), 78–83.

Alsace. Most of these hostile complaints demanded an end to Jewish usury and landholding, or even the expulsion of the Jews from the province. On the other hand, a few *cahiers* displayed a spirit of enlightened tolerance towards the Jews' condition and criticized the poor organization of credit facilities which almost compelled Jewish usury.[21] Not permitted to vote for delegates to the Estates General, the Jews of Alsace and neighbouring Lorraine chose representatives who composed *cahiers* and presented them to the Estates General. The Sefardim of Bordeaux took part in the general election, but saw nothing in their own condition to require a *cahier* or the enactment of a special law. Still, they dispatched a delegation to watch over developments at Versailles, and to combat any attempt to treat all Jews as one body.[22] Altogether, the Jewish issue was a minor one except to some Alsatians and of course to the Jews.

Six weeks after it convened the Estates General became the National Assembly and the revolution commenced. Jewish requests such as reduction of special taxes and freedom of residence and occupation continued to be presented until Grégoire impressed on them that in a time of revolution they should ask for everything. Contrary to the programme of Jewish and Christian reformers the Alsatian Jews requested to 'keep our synagogues, rabbis, and syndics, in the same fashion as it all exists today'.[23] Jewish autonomy remained until it shared the fate of other legal privileges and was abolished in the grant of emancipation in 1791.

Sparked by the 'great fear', the peasant insurrection against noble landlords during the revolutionary summer of 1789 did not spare the Jews. When the peasants rushed to destroy documentary proof of their debts and feudal obligations, an estimated twenty Alsatian Jewish communities were harmed in property and slightly in person. An emigration

---

[21] David Feuerwerker, 'Les Juifs en France. Anatomie de 307 cahiers de doléances de 1789', *Annales*, 20 (1965), 45–61, sharply criticized by Bernhard Blumenkranz, 'A propos des Juifs dans les cahiers de doléances', *Annales historiques de la Révolution française*, 39 (1967), 473–480.

[22] Zosa Szajkowski, 'The Diaries of the Bordeaux Jews to the Malesherbes Commission (1788) and the National Assembly (1790)' (Hebrew; English summary) *Zion*, 18 (1953), 31–79.

[23] *Addresse . . . le 31 août 1789*, in *La Révolution francaise et l'émancipation des juifs* (8 vols, Paris, 1968; facsimile reprints of sources), v, no. 5, 13–14.

followed which was far different from the later exodus of diehard partisans of the Old Regime. Perhaps 250 Jews with children fled, mainly into nearby Switzerland.[24] One local Jew lamented in traditional fashion:

God comfort us for the distress [of Alsace] . . . some eighteen communities were destroyed, two synagogues laid waste and their Torah scrolls torn up for our many sins . . . Jews were expelled from the towns for now, their homes plundered and destroyed together with holy books beyond number. Wonders and miracles beyond number have been performed by God for us and all Jewry in 5549 [1789].[25]

Next year, in 1790, a Jew appealed for a Jeremiah to compose dirges 'over the persecution, devastation, assaults and robbery committed upon our poor despised people'.[26]

The National Assembly explicitly omitted the Jews from the revolutionary legislation of August 1789, but Alsatian Jewish delegates joined many others in loyal addresses:

In the name of the Eternal, author of all justice and truth; in the name of the God who, having given everyone the same rights, has prescribed the same duties for everyone; in the name of humanity outraged so many centuries by the ignominious treatment which the unhappy descendants of the most ancient people have undergone in almost all countries of the world, we come to beseech you kindly to give consideration to their deplorable fate.

Twice the Jewish question was brought before the Assembly and twice postponed. During one of the debates a deputy who favoured the Jews, Count Stanislas de Clermont-Tonnerre, expressed the general view in celebrated words: 'To the Jews as a nation everything is to be denied; everything should be given to them as individuals; they must not constitute a political body nor an order within the State; they must be citizens individually.' The Jewish community as an autonomous body must be dissolved, and the Jews must fit into the new society without legal privilege. If they insist on their autonomy, Clermont-Tonnerre added, they

---

[24] Zosa Szajkowski, 'Jewish Émigrés during the French Revolution', *Jewish Social Studies*, 16/4 (Oct. 1954), app.

[25] Z. Szajkowski, 'Anti-Jewish Riots during the Revolutions of 1789, 1830, and 1848' (Hebrew; English summary) *Zion*, 20 (1955), 82.   [26] Ibid. 83.

must be expelled. The Declaration of Equality and the Rights of Man enacted in August 1789 included the Sefardic Jews of Bordeaux and the south, but the abolition of their special privileges left them worse off than before.[27] Stung into action, they appealed to the National Assembly. After noisy debate and a close vote it granted them the right of active citizenship on 28 January 1790.[28] The fully French Jews of Bordeaux promptly dissolved their autonomous community. When news of Jewish emancipation reached the city a near-riot ensued anyhow.

Alsatian Jewry were admitted to active citizenship twenty months later. Their petition of 28 January 1790, composed by their young Parisian lawyer Jacques Godard, substantially modified the Alsatians' earlier petition to retain communal autonomy. It only said, 'it is necessary for the Jews to have their religious laws; they must have certain internal regulations concerning the execution of these laws.'[29] Godard visited the sixty districts of Paris to urge his clients' case. He was well connected with the radical Paris Commune which provided the Constituent (successor to the National) Assembly physical security. The Commune demanded that the Alsatian Jewish question be brought promptly to the Constituent Assembly floor, which was done. In sharp debate, the delegates of Alsace and Lorraine forcefully opposed Jewish citizenship and equality. Since arguments based on religion were unacceptable in the new regime, the chief Alsatian spokesmen Abbé (later Cardinal) Maury and Reubell argued against the Jews as moneylenders and speculators. Catholics felt it intolerable that their faithful could not conscientiously take the oath of active citizenship while the Jews could. Neither did the recently emancipated Protestants favour Jewish emancipation.

What actually was the Jewish emancipation passed by the Constituent Assembly on 27 September 1791? This first Jewish enfranchisement in modern history allowed Jewish men to take the oath of

---

[27] Z. Szajkowski, 'The Diaries of the Bordeaux Jews', esp. 45–7, 64–79.

[28] This has been interpreted by numerous Jewish historians as a betrayal of oppressed Ashkenazim by privileged Sefardim. However, the two groups had entirely different legal statuses. The Sefardim cared little for the Ashkenazim and saw no likelihood that they would receive rights.

[29] 'Petition des Juifs établis en France . . . le 28 janvier 1790', in *La Révolution française*, v, no. 10; Zosa Szajkowski, 'Jewish Autonomy Debated and Attacked during the French Revolution', *Historia Judaica*, 20 (1958), 31–46.

allegiance and thus enrol as 'active citizens'. Citizen rights were for individuals only, and a Jew's oath of citizenship was 'considered a renun-
ciation of all privileges and exceptions introduced previously in their
favour'. Without the mantle of autonomy, Alsatian Jews were then expected to become French in language, culture, and appearance. Hope-
fully, they would also quit peddling and moneylending.[30]
Jews were inescapably drawn into the revolutionary vortex. Many took
the citizens' oath ceremonially. When twenty-eight Jews were sworn at
Lunéville on 17 January 1792, one of them delivered a speech and took
part in a session of the municipal council. The financier Berr-Isaac Bing
led Jews to be sworn in Nancy, and in a speech asked 'indulgence for his
timid and ignorant coreligionists' who had not come with him. Diehard
Strasbourg for a month refused to swear in Jews as citizens.[31] Hostility to
Jews in Alsace continued high and in February 1792, five months after
the emancipation, rumours of Jewish speculation in the new assignat
currency sparked a mob attack on the Metz ghetto, which General
Lafayette helped to suppress.[32] Jews purchased mainly for resale 'national
property', formerly feudal and church lands, but in nothing like the
amounts reported in tales of vast Jewish speculation.[33]

The Reign of Terror between September 1792 and July 1794 claimed
five known Jewish victims, and others who felt endangered fled or hid.
One who hid was a wealthy Bordeaux Sefardi, Abraham Furtado, an
active Girondist who left a memoir of his experiences.[34] Neither the

---

[30] Metz Jews and their descendants, even those living in other parts of France, were
compelled to pay off that community's long-term debt to a ducal family which had
been granted the privilege in 1720 of collecting a tax from them. Zosa Szajkowski, *Autonomy and Jewish Communal Debts during the French Revolution of 1789* (New York, 1959).
The case dragged on in the courts until 1870!

[31] Robert Anchel, *Napoléon et les juifs* (Paris, 1928), 6–7, 13.

[32] Z. Szajkowski, 'Riots against the Jews in Metz' (Hebrew; English summary) *Zion*, 22
(1957), 76.

[33] Zosa Szajkowski, 'Jewish Participation in the Sale of National Property during
the French Revolution', *Jewish Social Studies*, 14 (1952), 291–316; and *Zion*, 22 (1957), 76.

[34] A copy of its French original has recently been found: Frances Malino, 'Mémoires
d'un patriote proscrite by Abraham Furtado', in *Michael: On the History of the Jews in
the Diaspora*, iv, ed. S. Simonsohn and J. Shatzmiller (Tel Aviv, 1976), 74–162; Zosa
Szajkowski, 'The Sephardic Jews of France during the Revolution of 1789', *Proceedings of
the American Academy for Jewish Research*, 24 (1955), 137–64.

Terror nor the accompanying persecution of religion was anti-Semitic, and Catholics probably suffered more than Jews. When the Religion of Reason briefly reigned in 1794 synagogues yielded up their silver ornaments and closed, and their functionaries made themselves scarce. Circumcision, kosher slaughter, and Sabbath observance were forbidden and cemeteries were violated in the name of the short-lived new religion. In St Esprit near Bayonne, however, the mainly Jewish members of the local Jacobin club kept the synagogue intact while urging it to be patriotic and revolutionary.[35]

Little had been known of one prominent victim of the Terror, 'Junius Frey', an Austrian military volunteer, born a Jew, who became involved in obscure intrigue. Thanks to Scholem's research we now know him as Moses Dobruschka, a near relative and once a possible heir of Jacob Frank. In his youth a Hebrew and German writer, Dobruschka converted to Christianity with the rest of his wealthy family and took the name 'von Schonfeld'. He became the leader of an esoteric mystical branch of Freemasonry before he moved to Strasbourg and then on to Paris as 'Junius Frey', to cast his lot with the Revolution. Dobruschka/von Schonfeld/Frey at his core was a Frankist through all the peregrinations which ended under the guillotine in 1794.[36]

When the conservative Directory took control in 1795 France was embroiled in the wars which ended only in 1815. Jewish religious life struggled back to normal. Compared with what had just ended and what lay ahead under Napoleon, French Jews enjoyed a quiet period. Few Jews sought yet to exploit the opportunities opened by emancipation. However, many freshly emancipated young Jews were attracted to a military career and enlisted in the army, while others resorted to the widely used right of procuring substitutes to be drafted in their place. Hundreds were to serve under Napoleon, the wealthier ones as officers. The number of Jewish soldiers steadily rose to 630 in 1810.[37]

[35] Zosa Szajkowski, 'Synagogues during the French Revolution of 1789–1800', *Jewish Social Studies*, 20 (1958), 215–29.

[36] Gershom Scholem, 'The Career of a Frankist: Moses Dobruschka and his Metamorphoses' (Hebrew; English abstract) *Zion*, 35 (1970), pp. v–viii, 127–8l.

[37] Another report gave 797 in 1808. Zosa Szajkowski, 'French Jews in the Armed Forces during the Revolution of 1789', *Proceedings of the American Academy for Jewish Research*, 26 (1957), 139–52.

Old ways persisted. Complaints went to the authorities over disorder in synagogues, failure to pay the now voluntary community imposts, rabbis' unpaid salaries, a man's allegation that he had been placed under a ban, and the plaint from the rabbi of Worms that since Worms was annexed to France his religious authority had been flouted.[38] One observes the halting steps by which Jews oriented themselves to a new status which their traditions did not anticipate. Republican fervour took hold. The gravestone of Samuel Patto, dead at 24 in Bayonne, was not inscribed with Hebrew or even civil data but read, 'Deceased the 28 Prairal, Year II [16 June 1794] of the one and indivisible French Republic . . . O immortal soul, seek to live free or let me be a good republican.'[39] Paris Jewry, numbering 500 in 1789, increased to 4,000 by 1808, evenly divided between Sefardim and Ashkenazim.[40] Jews were not intermarrying, or not yet, in part because civil marriage did not exist.[41] Even within the deeply traditional Alsatian communities one sees linguistic change from Alsatian Yiddish to French, disaffection from religious and communal rules, and migration to the metropolis. Probably exaggerating the extent of change, the prefect of Meurthe found in 1802 'a noticeable amelioration'. After a decade of emancipation manners were 'more polite in the leisured class' and French was replacing Yiddish and German. Some Jews still sought 'to maintain the rules of discipline which are as much religious as civil', while others found them 'an insufferable yoke'. The prefect proposed that the Jews be 'placed under regulation'.[42]

Jewish life in neighbouring lands likewise underwent revolutionary disruption. The arrival of the French army meant conquest or liberation, and to most Jews it meant liberation. Between 1793 and 1797 the Netherlands, northern Italy, and the German Rhineland came under French rule. In the unstable conditions on France's border banditry evidently became common. A bandit chief proffered as alibi for his deeds that he 'conducted hostilities exclusively against Jews'.[43] On the other

---

[38] Anchel, *Napoléon et les juifs*, 43–54.
[39] Ibid. 30 n. 5, citing earlier literature.   [40] Ibid. 37–8.
[41] Zosa Szajkowski, 'Marriages, Mixed Marriages and Conversions among French Jews during the Revolution of 1789', *Historia Judaica*, 19 (1959), 33–54.
[42] Anchel, *Napoléon et les juifs*, 35–6, 45–6.
[43] T. C. W. Blanning, *Reform and Revolution in Metz, 1743–1803* (Cambridge, 1974), 295–7.

hand, about eighty Jewish robbers and killers known as *la bande juive* operated profitably around the French–Dutch–Spanish Netherlands frontier. Their leaders were a husband and wife who had family members with them. The wife, Dinah Jacob, told of her brother who was also a robber chief. Her bandits had connections with Jewish merchants, reputable or otherwise, from Brussels and Ghent to Paris.[44]

The Jews in Italy suffered assaults when the arrival of the French army was imminent. Papal officials prevented an attack on the Roman ghetto in 1793 but tightened its already stifling regime. Jews in northern Italy welcomed their deliverance from ghetto life by the French. In Venice ghetto gates were taken off their hinges and burnt, and similar scenes were enacted in Padua, Verona, Siena, and Ancona. A bitter price for the brief freedom was exacted, however, when the French army withdrew in 1797 and the old regime was restored. Bloody riots took Jewish lives. In Ancona Jews were burned alive, and murders in Siena reached up to the Torah ark in the synagogue. On the other hand, papal Rome was captured in 1798 and its ghetto regime abolished, the pope exiled, and the ghetto gates destroyed. The Jews of the Italian peninsula were again liberated by French conquest in 1800, this time without disturbance.[45]

Amsterdam Jewry remained the largest urban community in Christendom even after much emigration.[46] Most Dutch Jews had been firmly loyal to the conservative House of Orange during the uprising of the liberal Patriots of the 1780s. After a winter siege they underwent the French conquest without molestation. The general commanding the self-styled 'liberators' of 1796 summoned the Ashkenazic leaders to assure them of his benevolence and to offer his aid. Relieved, they asked and promptly received permission to take their unburied dead with a military escort across the ice to the cemetery out of town. A sweeter moment came when the lofty Sefardim requested the Ashkenazim to show them the ropes with the new rulers and make introductions. Other implications

---

[44] The story is told from Dinah's full confession to the French police in Richard C. Cobb, *Paris and its Provinces, 1792–1802* (London, 1975), 142–93.

[45] Cecil Roth, 'Some Revolutionary Purims', *Hebrew Union College Annual*, 10 (1935), 451–82; 'Supplement', ibid. 12–13 (1938), 679–699.

[46] C. H. Wilson, *Anglo-Dutch Trade and Commerce in the Eighteenth Century* (repr. Cambridge, 1966), index s.v. 'Jews'.

of 'liberation' appeared when the French gave the Jews, like other Amsterdam religious bodies, placards to hang in their houses of worship which proclaimed liberation and the end of Sabbath restrictions such as riding. Jewish representatives, joined by their rabbi, had the awkward task of explaining to the French military rulers that they could not abrogate religious laws prohibiting Sabbath riding.[47]

Signs of internal division appeared when young members of the upper middle class, one-time partisans of the Patriots, established the Felix Libertate society to modernize the community and its religious services. Felix Libertate sought curtailment of community autonomy, with power taken away from rabbis and lay authorities, besides freedom of occupation. The traditional community, including the socially and religiously conservative poor, many of whom depended on community charity, refrained from demands. Nor did traditionalists manifest enthusiasm for complete emancipation by the National Assembly of the Batavian Republic in 1797. They were adhering to the rule which was as old as the community, to stay out of general politics; it was Felix Libertate which broke the rule, followed later by others. French pressure made sure of a unanimous vote for Jewish emancipation. During the extended debate principles of justice and equality were invoked in favour of emancipation, while opponents raised complaints against Jewish business practices and claimed that the Jews were more interested in the Jewish state to be miraculously restored than in the land where they lived. The Dutch debate over emancipation, unlike that in France and later in Germany, contained few expressions of hostility to the Jews. Its tone and motifs somewhat resemble later discussion of emancipation in nineteenth-century Britain. Moreover, Dutch emancipation once enacted was accepted as a settled issue not to be reopened. The Felix Libertate reformers established a separatist Jewish community but had to abandon it in 1809 when the sympathetic monarch, Napoleon's brother Louis, told them he required undivided Jewish support.

The French campaign of 1795 also conquered the west bank of the Rhine. Like most of the German population, the Jews were cautious about siding with the French even when they came as liberators. The

---

[47] This episode is taken from the unpublished protocols of the Ashkenazic community which are chronologically arranged at the municipal archives of Amsterdam.

local Jewish communities stayed loyal to the respective rulers of Mainz, Bonn, and Worms. Mainz had a Jewish history extending back to medieval and even ancient times; the modern community began in the late seventeenth century after centuries of exclusion. Mainz Jewry's favourable conditions made it appear a needless risk to side with the liberators from the other side of the Rhine. To be sure, the local rabbi differed from the clergy in that mainly Catholic town by his adherence to the revolutionary cause.[48] The Jews of Mainz, eighty-seven in 1738, numbered about 1,000 when the French arrived, squeezed into fifty-seven houses containing 250 dwellings. Contrary to general practice Mainz Jews could own land and houses. The Jews were in the early stages of modern life, with general schooling open to their children and the authority of rabbis and community declining. Nearly all Jews were occupied in finance and trade, with twelve of the 227 Jewish householders having incomes in excess of 12,000 florins and no fewer than fifty-seven assessed in the highest two categories of taxpayers. A Jew needed 5,000 florins to be allowed to settle in Mainz.[49] After France annexed the west bank of the Rhine in 1797 and emancipation was enacted, the meaning of the new regime became clearer. Jewish autonomy dissolved as the Mainz Jewish community was forbidden to impose taxes. Two French commissioners sharply threatened the Jews if they did not take the citizen's oath.[50] In Bonn the Jews had a more stirring experience. Led by the young physician and revolutionary Dr Solomon Amschel, on Rosh ha-Shanah, 26 September 1797, they tore down their ghetto gate.[51] Less exciting was the Jews' long, ultimately successful struggle to settle in Cologne,[52] which they could previously enter only on business and then leave.[53]

[48] Joseph Hansen, *Quellen zur Geschichte des Rheinlandes im Zeitalter des französischen Revolution* (4 vols., Bonn, 1931–8), iv. 920 n.

[49] F.-G. Dreyfus, *Sociétés et mentalités à Mayence dans la seconde moitié du XVIIIe siècle* (Paris, 1968), 310–20; Blanning, *Reform and Revolution*, 180, 184–5.

[50] Hansen, *Quellen*, ii. 760 n. 3.; iv. 812 n.   [51] Ibid. iv. 76 n. 3.

[52] Ibid. iii. 410, is an unusual example of non-Jewish support for the Jews' rights.

[53] An admirable study is Shulamit S. Magnus, *Jewish Emancipation in a German City: Cologne, 1798–1871* (Stanford, Calif., 1998).

Jews and the Napoleonic Empire

Napoleon Bonaparte, First Consul from 1799 and emperor from 1804, had a negative attitude to the Jews, as is known from his occasional remarks. The oft-repeated tale that as French commander in the Holy Land in 1799 he issued an invitation to all Jews to resettle in their homeland is no more than a fable. That supposed invitation has never been found or authenticated, and no contemporary Jew mentioned it. Once Napoleon proclaimed himself emperor in 1804, he prepared to formulate a policy for the Jews he ruled as he had done with the Protestant minority and for the Catholic Church of the great majority. Throughout his reign Napoleon's policies for French Jews tended to be arbitrary, but for Jews elsewhere they were generous. French Jews had unhappy memories of their emperor but most French Jewish historians, following the Jacobin tradition which Napoleon appropriated, wrote of him apologetically. Jews elsewhere on the Continent had reason to see him admiringly as their liberator.[54]

The Jews' turn came in 1806. Debtors' difficulties during the financial crisis of 1805–6 stirred bitter complaints that the Jews were the harshest creditors. The actual proportion of Jews among creditors has not been established and may run from 14 to 40 per cent. Hearing these complaints *en route* home through Alsace after his victory at Austerlitz, the emperor gave free rein to his dislike of the Jews, '[A] reviled nation, degraded, capable of every low act . . . the Jews must be considered a nation and not a [religious] sect . . . it is too humiliating for the French nation

---

[54] Just as historians have long argued over Napoleon as the first modern dictator or 'the son of the Revolution' (see Pieter Geyl, *Napoleon for and against* (paperback edn., New Haven, 1967)), so have debates flared over Napoleon's Jewish policies. They are summarized in two articles by François Delpech, 'L'histoire des Juifs en France de 1780 a 1840', in *Les Juifs et la Révolution française*, ed. B. Blumenkranz and A. Soboul (Toulouse, 1976), esp. 24–33, and 'Les Juifs en France et dans l'Empire et la genèse du Grand Sanhedrin,' in Blumenkranz and Soboul (eds.), *Le grand Sanhédrin de Napoléon* (Toulouse, 1979), 16–26. In 'L'histoire', 28–9, Delpech tells an instructive story of the distinguished pro-Jacobin historian Albert Mathiez's verbal and written rage at his pupil Robert Anchel's revision of the accepted adulation of Napoleon. See also Z. S. Pipe, 'Napoleon in Jewish Folklore' (Yiddish), in E. Tcherikower (ed.), *Yidn in Frankraykh* (Yiddish) 2 vols., (New York, 1942) i. 153–89.

to find itself at the mercy of the vilest nation.' If Alsatian Jewry were massacred, he fumed, they would bear the blame themselves.[55] Napoleon was convinced that the position of the Jews had to be regulated and debtors saved not from creditors but from Jewish creditors. A new Jewish policy was in the making, one which set aside their emancipation to appease complaints against Jewish moneylending in Alsace and to give expression to the emperor's prejudices and nationalist wishes to convert the Jews quickly into Frenchmen.

As word spread of Napoleon's intention to deal with the Jews, the first salvo of anti-Jewish, anti-emancipation reaction in Europe was fired. With the argument against giving rights to Jews outdated, the new attack was aimed at the 'error' of having given them. Poujol, a spokesman for Alsatian grievances, denounced Alsatian Jewry in a widely noticed pamphlet, *Some Observations about the Jews in General, and More Particularly Those of Alsace*. In 'On the Jews' Viscount de Bonald, the philosopher of royalist reaction, argued that Jews could never belong as equals to Christian French society and were harmful to it. They would oppress far more than they had been oppressed in the past. Jewish rights endangered the virtue and welfare of the Christian French people, who could lose control of their own country to the ruthless skill of the Jews. Their emancipation should be cancelled.[56] De Bonald's aristocratic young friend Mole 'sold' some of his mentor's ideas to the emperor in Council of State debates over Jewish policy, against the arguments of the majority for maintaining equal rights.

In May 1806 the Emperor Napoleon issued a decree in two parts. The first suspended for one year the execution of judgments against farmers in default to Jewish lenders—not just lenders—in Alsace, the Metz region, and the German west bank of the Rhine. The second part summoned an Assembly of Jewish Notables to be selected by local prefects among the acculturated, wealthy and patriotic Jews of France and northern Italy. The intention was 'to make the Jews useful citizens, to reconcile their beliefs with the duties of Frenchmen'. Notwithstanding

---

[55] Quoted in Anchel, *Napoléon et les juifs*, 90. A briefer, more up to date account is Simon Schwarzfuchs, *Napoleon, the Jews and the Sanhedrin* (London, 1979).

[56] Vicomte de Bonald, 'Sur les Juifs' (1806) in *Œuvres complètes* (2 vols., Paris, 1864), ii, cols. 933–48, esp. conclusion.

the condemnation which was implicit in the moratorium, the gathering was expected to deliberate 'in good spirits' with concern for the public good.[57] In fact, it was a rather discordant event because clashing opinions reigned among the 111 delegates. Abraham Furtado, the one-time fugitive from the Terror who was elected president, represented the outlook of reform and acculturation. The foremost notable, however, was Rabbi David Sinzheim of Strasbourg, an eminent rabbinic scholar of the traditional type who represented the most conservative view tenable within an assembly whose duty was to foster the Gallicization of the Jews. Government representatives soon realized that Sinzheim's views carried more weight with the mass of Jews than anyone else's.

The emperor's commissioners, after admonishing the notables that they were expected to show themselves truly French, then put twelve questions to them for deliberation and response. Two questions enquired about polygamy and the issuance of divorces, and three asked about the appointment of rabbis and the extent of their authority. One queried the permissibility of intermarriage with Christians, and another enquired whether any professions were religiously forbidden to Jews. Two questions called for patriotic responses: whether 'Frenchmen are considered brothers or strangers' and did they 'acknowledge France as their country. Are they bound to defend it? Are they bound to obey its laws?' The final two questions were the touchiest:

11. Does the law of the Jews forbid them to take usury [*neshekh*] from their brethren?

12. Does it forbid them or does it allow them to take usury from strangers?

The questions which raised few if any halakhic problems were those about polygamy, the obligation to obey French law and render military service, and to regard France as their land and Frenchmen as their brothers. The answers were delivered with fervent cheers. However, it was touchier to explain why they would not intermarry even after the parties underwent civil marriage. It was explained that rabbis, like clergy of other religions, could hardly recite Jewish marital blessings for persons of a different religion. Divorce took place among Jews but only after a

---

[57] Letter of 22 July 1806, quoted in Anchel, *Napoléon et les juifs*, 159.

civil divorce. The taking of interest was the touchiest question of all, since the Bible did forbid it from 'your Hebrew brother' and permitted it from the 'stranger'. The assembly, guided by Sinzheim, declared that the Bible's distinction was between loans for personal need and business loans. On personal loans no interest (*ribbit*) was to be taken from Jews or from Frenchmen who were now their brothers, while on business loans it was permissible to take modest interest from a fellow Jew by means of legal fiction.[58]

Napoleon's officials professed themselves satisfied with these answers, but in private they doubted their sincerity. The next step in the emperor's scenario was to convene the renowned Grand Sanhedrin of 1807. Jewish communities throughout Europe were invited to send deputies to a body which would frame a charter for Judaism in the new age. Governments were also apprehensive of Napoleon's revolutionary appeal to their respective Jews, as shown by the edgy reaction of the Habsburg rulers. Conservative Jewish communities outside France similarly distrusted the French proposal. Only Frankfurt Jewry was represented, but that city was under direct French rule. The delegates from Amsterdam were only the reformist Felix Libertate after the official community refused to take part. The small communities of northern Italy were represented and also French Jewry itself.

The Grand Sanhedrin which followed, with almost the same membership as the Assembly of Notables, was opened by the emperor himself and conducted ceremoniously. The Grand Sanhedrin was no more than an exercise in public relations, but it represented itself as the revival of the ancient institution, defunct since Mishnaic times.[59] Few rabbis were present, among whom only David Sinzheim was of note. The Grand Sanhedrin ratified the decisions of the Assembly of Notables and declared, without basis in Jewish law, that they bound all Jews. It proclaimed the glory of French citizenship and the duty of military

---

[58] This resembles John Calvin's doctrine of interest; R. H. Tawney, *Religion and the Rise of Capitalism* (London, 1926), 202–6.

[59] A contrary opinion, upholding in halakhic terms the emperor's authority to call a Sanhedrin, is Charles Touati, 'Le Grand Sanhédrin de 1807 et le Droit rabbinique' in Bernhard Blumenkranz and Albert Soboul (eds.), *Le Grand Sanhédrin de Napoléon* (Toulouse, 1979), 27–48. See also Schwarzfuchs, *Napoleon, the Jews and the Sanhedrin*: 64–114.

service. Everyone felt satisfied: reformers like Furtado saw paths open to modern Judaism, traditionalists led by Sinzheim were relieved that the decisions had not transgressed Jewish law, and all felt that they had pleased the regime. The Grand Sanhedrin adjourned until called again, which never happened.

The regime's further plans had been kept from the Jewish deputies. Eight months later three decrees were issued, allegedly requested by the Jewish deputies, after efforts to modify them from within proved fruitless. Two decrees established a new communal regime. There were to be twelve regional committees, called consistories, whose original members would be selected by local prefects from the prosperous, patriotic, and French Jews of their respective regions. They would direct the practice of Judaism in their districts, including the form of religious worship, a communal census, the appointment of truly French rabbis, and communal taxes. In Paris a Central Consistory with a chief rabbi would rule the system. This oligarchic, compulsory system with its bias towards French acculturation was the first modern communal structure. After democratization and other changes, as a voluntary body it remains the central institution of French Jewry to this day. The consistory system was copied in lands under Napoleonic rule. A minor Napoleonic reform was the requirement that all Jews assume family names, as many had already done, in place of X son/daughter of Y. The scorpion's sting came in the third decree, known as 'the infamous decree' and scheduled to remain in force ten years. While ending the moratorium on repaying debts to Jewish lenders, it made most such debts to Jewish lenders uncollectable even in court. The decree regulated the interest which Jews were allowed to charge, and limited who might borrow from them. In order to deal in commerce Jews in Alsace had to secure an annual licence backed by proof of character and honesty. The 'infamous decree' included many more limitations and caused serious economic deterioration to Alsatian Jewry while it was in force. Unlike other Frenchmen, Jews were forbidden to hire a substitute to do their army service. During the remaining years of his regime Napoleon did not trouble much with the French Jews. Under Louis XVIII the decree expired in 1818.

European Jewry and Napoleon

The dictator Napoleon who curtailed the rights of French Jews was revered and hated in much of Europe as 'the son of the Revolution'. The conquering French army stimulated far-reaching changes in the regimes of the lands it subdued, including western Germany, Prussia, and northern Italy. Monarchs felt apprehensive that their Jews might take part in the Grand Sanhedrin and forbade them to go, but its message reached distant countries. In the satellite Kingdom of Westphalia of north-west Germany an ambitious latter-day court Jew, Israel Jacobson, dominated the new consistory and sponsored religious and educational reform. His proposal to the French emperor in 1805 that a Sanhedrin legislate basic changes for the new era of Judaism may have started that project. In the synagogue which he erected in Seesen Jacobson devised and conducted from 1809 the first services of what later became Reform Judaism.

The free cities of Germany under French rule, including Hamburg, Lübeck, Bremen, and Frankfurt, had Jewish rights thrust upon them. They sought to cancel what the French imposed as soon as the conquerors departed. Prussia moved towards Jewish rights on its own but its path was long and tortuous. Reforming the Jews' status had been discussed endlessly in memoranda circulated within its all-powerful bureaucracy from the death of Frederick II in 1786, but no concrete result emerged before Prussia suffered total defeat by the French and was forced into submission. Prussia then undertook far-reaching reforms between 1807 and 1812, and Jewish subjection and the privileges enjoyed by a few wealthy Jewish families came under consideration. The prevalent Prussian view, which fitted the mind of that absolutist state, held that the Jews must be educated and show they merited improved status. With eloquent clarity the statesman-philosopher Wilhelm von Humboldt advocated in 1809 full, immediate rights:

[A]s a result of gradual abolition the very segregation that it sets out to liquidate is confirmed in all the spheres that it has not yet abolished . . . Though they may admit that there are worthy Jews, no matter how many the people will still not readily change their views about Jews as such. They will always look upon the individuals as exceptions. It is not that the state ought to teach respect for the Jews. What it ought to do is to eradicate the inhumane and prejudiced mentality that judges a human being not by his specific qualities but by his descent and religion . . . This the State can only do by saying loud and clear that it no longer recognizes any difference between Jews and Christians.[60]

Humboldt's brilliance in ministerial office did not overcome the habits of states and individuals. Radical liberals who advocated separation of Church and State and broad civic equality also favoured equal rights for the Jews, expecting in return internal reforms on their part.[61] However, many liberals clung to the idea of only gradually granting rights, while some leaders of reform, including Baron vom Stein of Prussia and Montgelas of Bavaria, not to speak of opposition diehards, opposed equal Jewish rights altogether. However, the sympathetic Prussian chancellor Hardenberg favoured granting rights. As a first step, when towns were empowered in 1808 to elect councils and officials, Jews were granted municipal rights, which a few already had by virtue of their naturalization in German states and in Berlin. In further steps the monopoly privileges of guilds which kept out Jews were revoked, and economic freedom was broadened. The climax came at the end of the era of the 'revolution from above', in the law of 1812 which granted citizenship, equal rights, and freedom of occupation to Prussian Jews. The Act denied to Jews army officership and administrative and judicial posts, saying vaguely, as was the case with reforms in other spheres, that further legislation would extend Jewish rights. Instead, during the post-1815 reaction Jewish rights were whittled down. Even so, patriotism in the rising Jewish generation became fervent and Prussian Jewry long celebrated 11 March 1812 as its day of liberation. Many Jewish volunteers fought Napoleon in the German 'war of liberation' in 1813–14, and their own full liberation was expected soon. However, the ruling classes, again secure in the saddle after the French conqueror's downfall, had opposite intentions towards the Jews and other subordinate classes.

---

[60] Quoted and trans. in Reinhard Rürup, 'Jewish Emancipation and Bourgeois Society', *Leo Baeck Institute Year Book*, 14 (1969), 86.

[61] Fritz Valjavec, *Die Entstehung der politischen Strömungen in Deutschland, 1770–1815* (Munich, 1951), 402–4.

Eastern Europe

But the most drastic change in Jewish status seemed about to take place in Napoleon's creation, the Duchy of Warsaw, fashioned in 1807 mainly from Prussia's Polish lands.[62] Its political life retained some of the spirit of the reform programmes that had been undertaken when Poland was collapsing politically. The men of the Polish Enlightenment had put forth proposals to foster industry and alleviate the wretchedness of the peasantry, while the status of the Jews was the subject of yet other proposals coming mainly from the liberal wing of the gentry. Polish reformers said little if anything about Jewish rights, but spoke much of abolishing Jewish autonomy and ending Jewish distinctiveness in dress and language. The reforming Sejms after 1764 sharply increased Jewish taxes and did away with the once powerful Council of Four Lands. The Council's vast debts were parcelled out among local communities. The Sejm also legislated against Jewish innkeepers, and townspeople pressed for drastic restrictions and expulsions against the Jews. Several Jewish reformers and *maskilim* presented programmes derived from the Haskalah in the west. These laid special emphasis on guiding young Jews away from commerce and into 'productive' occupations in farming and handicrafts. They too said very little about Jewish rights. Traditional Jews, the rabbis, and the *kehillot* opposed all these reforms and nothing came of them during the Four Years Sejm from 1788 to 1792. The Polish revolt of 1794, led by Kosciusko, once a volunteer in the American War of Independence, who spoke in terms of Jewish equality, recruited Jewish volunteers and stirred Jewish enthusiasm, but it was crushed by Russian intervention. That marked the end of independent Poland.

The Duchy of Warsaw contained nearly 400,000 Jews, almost twice as many as all other lands under Napoleonic rule. They petitioned for equal rights in 1808, but reaction was riding high in France. The 'infamous decree' had just been issued, so there was no pressure from France to give rights to Polish Jews. Equal rights were accordingly postponed by decree for ten years, to give the Jews time to 'eradicate their distinguish-

[62] Artur Eisenbach, *The Emancipation of the Jews in Poland, 1780–1870* (Oxford, 1991), 128–48.

ing characteristics, which mark them off so strongly from the rest of the population'. After ten years, in 1818, the Duchy of Warsaw no longer existed and Russia ruled. Emancipation and assimilation in Poland was to run a different course.

The new political reality of Poland began in 1772 with its threefold division into Prussian, Galician Habsburg, and Russian lands. To the Jews of eastern Europe, whose way of life differed broadly from that of western Jewry after 1800, the regime of Napoleon must have appeared an apparition. Indeed, Napoleon was believed by many to be the Jewish Messiah, preparing the way for the Messiah of the House of David. Revolutionary reform and Napoleonic rule left a vivid memory but little lasting effect. The social structure changed little. As long as Polish territorial lords maintained faithful allegiance to tsar, emperor, or king respectively, they were allowed to continue ruling their domains, and Jews continued being subordinate to them. Polish Jews, for centuries a recognized corporate body accustomed to ready access to the ruling powers, now found themselves legally undefined and powerless. The highest authorities in Russia and Prussia were almost inaccessible, and only the provincial governors sent to Galicia by the Catholic Habsburgs were easier to reach. Prussia was Lutheran, while newly Russian Jews became the subjects of tsars who were the pontifical rulers of the hostile Russian Orthodox Church. Polish Jews under Prussian rule found themselves in a tightly regulated regime like that which governed the Jews of Prussia itself. These included strict limitation of population and livelihoods. The old methods of bribing and influencing the Polish gentry had little play with Prussia's centralized bureaucracy. On the other hand, Prussian officials soon learned that the Jews dominated Polish commerce, while Jewish craftsmen could not be easily regulated nor could their number be limited. The Prussian bureaucrats were surprised to find that Polish Jews were more educated than the generally illiterate Poles. Prussian Jewry's emancipation in 1812 did not apply in Prussian Poland, which continued until 1833 under the old regime of severe restrictions.

Jews had been generally forbidden to live in Russia even by the modernizer Peter the Great (1698–1725), although small settlements existed sporadically. The early development of the new Russian Jewish community was unusually liberal even by west European standards, but it ended in reaction. Catherine the Great (1762–96) decreed that, religion notwithstanding, the newly annexed Polish Jews would enrol in one of the six economic classes with its respective privileges. That is, they enjoyed equality with other members of their economic class. Still more remarkable, during the 1780s Jews were elected to municipal councils within a broad Jewish quota. Besides being allowed to own property and sell liquor, they were allowed to preserve their autonomy, although there was much discussion of curtailing or abolishing it. But then came the revolution in France, which frightened reforming monarchs throughout Europe into ceasing their reform projects.

Russia turned to reaction after 1790 and the Jews' legal position slowly worsened. From 1791 they could not buy land and could live and carry on business only in specified provinces which were defined conclusively in 1800. The nobility wanted to drive the Jews off the land, and especially to cut them out of the nobles' profitable monopoly of distilling and selling liquor. Alexander I's Jewish Statute of December 1804, based on the detailed deliberations and elaborate reports of his Committee on the Jewish Question, codified reaction and set the direction of Jewish status until 1917. One of the statute's clauses decreed the expulsion of the Jews from the countryside in three stages, to be completed by 1812.[63] After the first stage the menace of Napoleon came close to Russia, and the regime delayed further expulsions. Loyalism and conservatism inspired the great majority of Jewish religious leaders to support the tsar during Napoleon's invasion in 1812. Besides, they had heard of his regime's policies against Jewish traditions. But the loyalty of the Russian Jews to their tsar was ill rewarded.

The compulsory Enlightenment which the regimes sought to impose stimulated the spread of Haskalah in eastern Europe after 1815. However, not Haskalah was spreading but its polar opposite, the Hasidic movement. Hasidism was opposed by rabbis and communal leaders and

[63] Shmuel Ettinger, 'The Foundations and Tendencies in Russian Government Policies towards the Jews from the Partitions of Poland' (Hebrew) *He-Avar*, 19 (1972), 20–34 and his 'The Statute of 1804' (Hebrew) *He-Avar*, 22 (1977), 87–110, including text of the statute. Both articles emphasize traditional Russian state and Orthodox Church hostility. Richard Pipes, 'Catherine II and the Jews: The Origins of the Pale of Settlement', *Soviet Jewish Affairs*, 5/2 (1975), 504–17, emphasizes the empress's Enlightenment intentions.

also by regimes and suffered persecution in many places. The most intensive persecution was in sizeable communities like Minsk and Vilna and in the regions of Lithuania and White Russia. Their communal regime was more potent than in the south, where Hasidism spread almost unopposed. Hasidism also gained a strong foothold in central Poland. The rejoicing of some Hasidim in Vilna during the Sukkot festival of 1797 despite the death of the revered GR'A, their implacable opponent, inspired angry vows of vengeance. Persecution included forcing Hasidim to leave town, closing their prayer houses, and preventing or destroying Hasidic publications.

Both sides 'played rough'. *Zaddikim* were harried from town to town in Austrian Galicia. In the north, Rabbi Shneur Zalman of Lyady was twice informed on falsely to the Russian government as a traitor and imprisoned. After many weeks of detention and interrogation he was released as a harmless religious leader. Hasidim would eat only meat which had been slaughtered by specially sharpened knives used by their own *shohetim*, thus depriving the community of kashrut income. Communities had to come to terms with Hasidim, and the latter were quite willing. Haskalah, fostering modernization and broadened opportunities and enjoying official encouragement, for many years failed to influence the Jewish masses in eastern Europe. It was Hasidism, despised and persecuted in many quarters, which drew the allegiance of masses of common folk and of some of the wealthy and learned as well. If the movement ever had elements of social revolt, they disappeared by 1800.

Hasidism was above all a religious movement. It endorsed folk religion and sanctified the pleasures of plain people, rejecting asceticism and heightening joy and fervour in religious life. The early generations of *zaddikim* moved among the people unencumbered by local attachments, counselling and blessing them. The supreme potency of the *zaddik*'s prayers and incantations was believed to heal the sick, assure livelihoods, and bring fertility to childless women. There is a treasury of tales of the merits of *zaddikim* and the miracles they wrought. Even to narrate their deeds was believed to confer religious merit. Not only the lowering of Talmud study in the scale of religious values offended the rabbinic and communal establishments, but also the independence of Hasidism from the community. Later, to be sure, Hasidim often succeeded in taking over communities and installing a *zaddik* as local rabbi. As early as 1799 they placed their own people on Vilna's community board.

Hasidism survived and flourished even later when modernity advanced into eastern Europe, but it was essentially rooted in late medieval mystical Judaism. The Hasidic movement made no headway in western Europe. It briefly appeared in Germany, in the Frankfurt community, where a gifted leader, Rabbi Nathan Adler, pursued many ritual practices like those in east European circles. He too underwent severe communal censure, and the movement did not outlast his death in 1800.[64] Late medieval Hasidic practices unrelated to the contemporary movement held on in German Jewry into quite modern times. East European *zaddikim* and their followers were more alien to critical, rational, and scientific modes of thought than those trained in Talmudic rationalism. Hasidim were immersed in a world of legend and miracle and mystery. Biblical and Talmudic texts were understood mainly mystically or homiletically, remote from the rational and grammatical methods of great medieval exegetes or the contemporary Mendelssohn. Judaism in rational, scholastic form could cope with modern life more readily than Hasidism of mystery and miracle. Its contemporary vogue as an antithesis to modernity is a separate story.

Across the Sea

Far from divided east European Jewry and its political and religious struggles a small Jewish community of about 2,000 persons was taking shape in the new American republic. Ashkenazim among them were already preponderant over Sefardim by the time of the Declaration of Independence in 1776. Jews took part in the American Revolution, mainly but not only as adherents of the party of independence, serving in the army and holding minor military and civil positions. Immigration came from Britain, Holland, and Germany, but almost stopped

[64] Rachel Elior, 'Nathan Adler and the Frankfurt Pietists: Pietist Groups of Eastern and Central Europe during the Eighteenth Century' (Hebrew; English summary), *Zion*, 54/1 (1994), 21–64.

during the French revolutionary and Napoleonic wars. The American Jewish population was probably no higher than 4,000 in 1815.

Emancipation and the separation of Church and State were predicates of American Jewish existence from early days. To practise Judaism to any extent or to be a Jew at all were voluntary matters, so that communal and religious life were whatever the Jews wanted to make of them. Most desired affiliation with Judaism, and upheld Jewish tradition to the best of their limited knowledge and inclinations. Elsewhere in the New World, Canadian Jewry barely existed and in Spanish and Portuguese Latin America, even with the Inquisition gone, there still were only minuscule settlements. The flourishing settlements in Dutch Surinam and the West Indies in 1780, prospering from the sugar trade, were badly reduced by 1815.[65] Altogether, Jews in the New World, above all the United States, did not appear before the middle of the nineteenth century as a significant factor in Jewish life.

[65] Robert Cohen, *Jews in Another Environment: Surinam in the Second Half of the Eighteenth Century* (Leiden, 1991).

5

Emancipation in Western Europe, 1815–1870

The Meaning of Emancipation

The peoples of Europe and their rulers sought peace and repose when the stormy generation of revolution and war ended in 1815. The Jews sought improved status as well. The era just ended had taken them far towards equality and rights, but German states and principalities which had been compelled to give these under Napoleonic dictation wished to turn back the clock. For more than a half-century following the French Revolution and Napoleon, obtaining emancipation and acceptance in the general society became the central concern of Jewish life in western and to a lesser extent eastern Europe.

The meaning of Jewish emancipation needs to be clarified. Jewish citizenship and equal rights, as they were originally called, became a contested issue wherever an Old Regime fell or underwent drastic reform. The opposition to Jewish rights had its basis in ancient prejudice and in support for the Old Regime with its official Christianity and established church. Giving equal rights to the Jews implied a secular, de-Christianized state, a prospect detested by the faithful of the Old Regime.[1] Ancient prejudices restated and justified strengthened hostility to the Jews. In opposing Jewish equality upholders of the Old Regime avoided quoting from the many aspersions on the Jews expressed by men of the Enlightenment because these intellectual destroyers of the Old Regime were even more anathema than the Jews. During the nineteenth century, however, religious hostility to the Jews and partiality for the Old Regime gradually receded and were replaced by a new motif, national-

[1] An effective statement is Theodore S. Hamerow, *The Social Foundations of German Unification, 1858–1871: Struggles and Accomplishments* (Princeton, 1972), 77 ff. A stimulating recent collection on emancipation is Pierre Birnbaum and Ira Katznelson (eds.), *Paths of Emancipation: Jews, States, and Citizenship* (Princeton, 1995).

ism. In its name equal Jewish rights were opposed after 1815, in Germany above all. To most German nationalists and to many nationalists in other countries the Jews were always foreigners, strangers to the nation and the national state.

The term emancipation was not yet applied to the Jews in the days of Mendelssohn and Dohm.[2] It was first used for the movement to free black slaves in the European colonies of the West Indies. In the Jews' case, the terms first used for rights were 'citizenship' or 'civic improvement'. These distinctions are not merely verbal. Jews were of course not slaves, and the familiar usage 'discriminated against', which assumes legal equality, is likewise out of place because that did not yet exist. In Old Regime societies Jews like everyone else had their distinct legal status. Most eighteenth-century Jewish communities in western Europe were part of the Old Regime, set in their beliefs and community life and generally accepting its order of things. It was possible for individual Jews to rise in the legal and social scale, and for wealthy Jews to acquire a privileged status for themselves. But when the Jews petitioned for some change it was not for 'civic improvement'. That usually meant compulsory Enlightenment and reduced autonomy with little given in return.

It was the French Revolution's abolition of legal privilege which made Jewish equality possible, indeed necessary. The debates during the revolution show that French Jews acquired equality and citizenship in the revolutionary regime not because they were now regarded with greater affection but on account of the revolution's principles. These principles also compelled them to surrender their autonomy. The grant of citizenship and equality was repeated in the countries which came under revolutionary or Napoleonic rule. To many Jews equality and citizenship were unwanted or unsettling, even though the abolition of heavy Jewish taxes and forms of degradation was doubtless welcome.

Two countries may be mentioned as an exception. In Great Britain Jews had virtual legal equality but, like all who were not of the established Church of England, no political rights. In the newly founded

---

[2] Jacob Katz, 'The Term "Jewish Emancipation": Its Origin and Historical Impact', in Alexander Altmann (ed.), *Studies in Nineteenth Century Jewish Intellectual History* (Cambridge, Mass., 1964), 1–25, first made these distinctions, but his conclusions differ from those here.

United States of America, where about 2,000 Jews lived when the Constitution went into force in 1789, there were equal rights for all white persons. The Constitution did not even mention Jews. Remaining restrictions on political rights in some of the thirteen original states' constitutions were abolished within a few years.

Why the indifference, bewilderment or downright opposition of many Jews in the Napoleonic empire to the new world of equality? The answer appears to lie in the extent of assimilation among them. Contrary to much tendentious usage, assimilation does not mean an end to Jewish identity. It means being or seeking to be similar to the majority society in dress, language, education, and culture. However, it does not mean similarity to the majority, who were still uneducated, impoverished peasants in every European society, but rather acceptance into a more desirable social class within the majority society.

Except for Bordeaux Sefardim and several well-to-do Alsatian enlighteners, few Jews in revolutionary France knew the world they were expected to become part of. They acquired equal rights before they underwent a significant degree of assimilation. This minimal Jewish assimilation irritated Napoleon, who disliked Jews anyhow, and his Jewish policy sought to compel them to become French. A contrast is England, where the thirty years' campaign for political emancipation was carried on from 1829 by a Jewish community which was already quite British. This made demands to assimilate superfluous. Some British Jews, especially the more pious, opposed political emancipation, feeling that it would encourage religious indifference in the Jewish community. In their view the civil rights they already possessed were sufficient. Similarly, many British Christians were also opposed to political rights for Jews, which would permit them to take part in making laws for Christians. They realized that Jewish emancipation meant 'the extension of religious plurality in a non-authoritarian society';[3] Great Britain, they feared, would become a secular society.

---

[3] G. I. T. Machin, *Politics and the Churches in Great Britain, 1832–1868* (Oxford, 1977), 380; Israel Finestein, 'Anglo-Jewish Opinion during the Struggle for Emancipation (1828–1858)', *Jewish Society in Victorian England* (London, 1993), 1–53; David Feldman, *Englishmen and Jews: Social Relations and Political Culture, 1840–1914* (New Haven, 1994), 28–47, 72–89.

It is first possible to speak of a Jewish emancipation movement after the Napoleonic wars in countries where legal equality already existed. When the struggle for emancipation resumed about 1830 after a period of political reaction, it was conducted by the Jews themselves, since their acculturation had advanced considerably. More and more Jews, for example, spoke German and dressed, furnished their homes, read books, and educated their children as Germans. They fervently declared themselves loyal members of the German states where they lived and devoted to Germany as a whole. Yet even when the long emancipation process in western Europe concluded in 1870 German Jewry still lacked full equality. They felt confident, however, that during the age of progress the remaining forms of inequality would in good time be removed.

Nothing like emancipation had ever happened before to Jews. Adjusting to it was an arduous, unprecedented task for the Jewish community. Judaism knew all too much of solace for sorrows and disasters, but many centuries of confined life in most lands did not prepare the Jews for broad personal freedom and mass transgression of religious obligations. Ideologies which altered ancient fundamentals of Jewish life were likewise new. Bereft of autonomy and powers of compulsion even where the law demanded formal community membership, as in Germany and Austria, the emancipated Jewish community had to find a voluntary basis for Jewish religious and cultural life. The effort was difficult, but new and creative expressions of Judaism came forth as a result.

Was emancipation delusive? Even before the catastrophe of European Jewry in the twentieth century, it became common to speak of Jewish emancipation as a delusion which deceived the Jews as to their real position. Open, blatant anti-Semitism in low and high places belied emancipation. There was a sad awakening for those Jews who had supposed that emancipation meant that the era of full Jewish acceptance had arrived, when the limits of emancipation and the strength of anti-Semitism became evident. Most Jews, however, took a practical view of their emancipation. They had only to think of the world their grandfathers had inhabited. The cramped Cannongate main street of Edinburgh, dark and dirty, reminded a visiting German geographer during the 1820s 'that the extreme dirtiness in clothing and appearance has much in common with the Jews' in the ghetto of his native Frankfurt.[4] Emancipation allowed Jews to quit such ghettos for more agreeable neighbourhoods where they could enjoy personal freedom and physical comfort. Emancipated Jews could enter most occupations, dress like others of their social class, educate their children for further success, take part in many areas of public life, and be Jews in the manner and to the extent they desired. That was enough for the German and other Jews to appreciate the benefits of emancipation even while they realized its limitations.

The Aftermath of Revolution and War

The Congress of Vienna, settling Europe's affairs amid gaiety and entertainment, dealt mainly with Germany.[5] The three Jewish representatives sent by the Frankfurt community who appeared at Vienna represented Jews on the international scene for the first time. That city's mercantile oligarchy, back in power, sought to cancel the Jews' new rights and force them back into the ghetto while the Jewish representatives were seeking to preserve and advance what had been gained there and elsewhere in German lands. Other German independent cities and principalities also sought to rid themselves of the Napoleonic bequest of Jewish rights, while Jews and Christian liberals tried hard to save them. The police of Vienna clapped the Frankfurters in gaol for overstaying their permitted time in town. The somewhat sympathetic Austrian chancellor Metternich, the most important man at the congress, had difficulty in getting them freed.

The Congress of Vienna's German Federal Act confirmed for the Jews 'those rights which they have already been granted by the several confederate states'. The 'by' was the sting. That innocuous preposition took in only nominal rights acquired under Acts of individual German principalities. It excluded the broad rights acquired thanks to the French conqueror's will. Only Prussian Jewry was left with the rights Prussia,

---

[4] Heinrich Meidinger, *Reisen durch Grossbritannien und Irland*, ii. (Frankfurt, 1828) II, 11.

[5] Salo Baron, *Die Judenfrage auf dem Wiener Kongress* (Vienna, 1920).

not Napoleon, had given them in the law of 1812. Even there, Prussian Poland and large areas of western Germany given to Prussia at Vienna were excluded for years more. The Napoleonic era which had brought hope and expanded rights to German Jews concluded in despair.

Progress to emancipation went more smoothly in the other countries of western Europe. French Jewry outlasted the ten years of Napoleon's 'infamous decree' of 1808 and regained full rights. Prodded by the restored monarchy, it set itself to 'regeneration'. This was a programme of communal change and educational reform directed by the consistory somewhat in the spirit of earlier Haskalah proposals.[6] Remnants of inequality remained for some time. Not until 1831 were Jewish religious officiants paid by the state like those of other religions, and a demeaning courtroom oath was required until challenged and abolished in 1845. Dutch Jewry also had a consistorial system and enjoyed emancipation under the new constitution of which a Jew, Jonas Daniel Meyer, was one of the main authors. The diverse regimes and territories which composed Italy lived under very varied conditions once Napoleonic rule ended. Napoleon's emancipation was maintained in Tuscany but not in Piedmont, the kingdom out of which united Italy later arose. Northeastern Italy, which included Venice, came under mild Habsburg rule patterned on that of Austria. Rome and the papal states it ruled returned to the ghetto and dark oppression. In Great Britain the revolutionary period on the Continent had driven political life in the contrary direction of reaction. However, British Jews already had civil rights. They had to struggle only for political emancipation, the right to take part in the government of the land. After restrictions were lifted from non-Anglican Protestants in 1828 and Catholics in 1829, the Jews remained for thirty years the sole group disqualified from Parliament on account of religion. In concrete terms, a Jew elected to the House of Commons needed a qualifying Christian oath to take his seat. By the time they were emancipated politically in 1858 British Jews were far advanced socially and economically.

---

[6] Described in detail in Jay R. Berkovitz, *The Shaping of Jewish Identity in Nineteenth-Century France* (Detroit, 1989).

Political Defeat and Spiritual Quest

The quite smooth, gradual progress of British Jews and others towards full emancipation was not the experience of German Jews, as we have mentioned. Troubled times began for them in 1815. After fifty years of an atmosphere of change and improvement, however slow and toilsome, their prospects were reversed. The majority, to be sure, continued to live traditional religious lives in small towns where Yiddish in its German dialect was still widely used. The Jews had been assured in the Prussian Act of 1812 and by legislation in other German states that new laws would reduce the areas of Jewish exclusion. What emerged instead was increased exclusion. New laws forbade Jewish lawyers, teachers, and other areas of livelihood, and officership in the idolized army remained hermetically closed. Young people who had been encouraged to train for various crafts and trades were prevented from practising them in Bavaria by the monopoly power of guilds which would not admit Jews. One available new profession was journalism, and educated young Jews who might have been distributed among other professions often became journalists. The influence which the heavily Jewish press acquired in moulding public opinion became an issue later in the century.

The intimacies of life were invaded by laws intended to inhibit population growth by prohibiting marriage until death or removal made room in a community for a new family. True, this law applied also to poor Christians, who reacted with an illegitimacy rate of 20 per cent; Jews, however, were apparently more scrupulous of the marriage bond and their community's sanctions, so that their illegitimate births were barely 5 per cent.[7]

Germany's intellectual climate changed in the early nineteenth century. Eighteenth century classical ideals of universal reason and humanity as exemplified by Kant, Lessing, and Schiller lost their intellectual dominance before a new wave which started about the 1790s. To an extent it came in reaction to French conquest and the rationalist Enlightenment which France represented. Intellectual Germans now

---

[7] Mack Walker, *Germany and the Emigration, 1816–1885* (Cambridge, Mass., 1964), 54–5, 163–6.

exalted subjective feeling, idolized the history of the German people and its medieval Christian 'organic' society, and found transcendental significance in the German states and monarchies. A fusion of conservatism, romanticism, nationalism, and Christian piety dominated German intellectual and political life by 1815. As had already been done with the Prussian civil service, the Prussian Lutheran hierarchy, controlled by the state, was stocked systematically with prelates imbued with the correct official ideas.[8]

Jews in post-Napoleonic German states thus found political reaction and economic restriction aggravated by cultural exclusion from the 'Christian state'. Besides rejecting them as equals they were considered inherently unable to belong truly to the German culture that they were eagerly absorbing. The growing number of educated and intellectual Jews felt rejection the keenest. The German fatherland would not accept them, they felt, and they would remain aliens in German cultural life. Jews were troubled by a wave of anti-Jewish literature, much of it written by philosophical intellectuals, 'demonstrating' that as adherents of inferior, ossified Judaism they could be only tolerated foreigners in Germany. Most shocking to contemporaries was the chain of small-scale Bavarian pogroms of 1819, mainly by students. The pogroms were called 'hep, hep', mocking the cry to goats when Jews who wore traditional beards were molested.[9] Yet the Jews persevered in their German cultural and political aspirations, believing that in time prejudice would fade and barriers would fall.

What options were open to Jews in post-Napoleonic reactionary Germany? Two were obvious. Thousands of young people mainly from Bavaria and Prussian Poland, frustrated in their occupational and marital prospects, decided to emigrate. The destination of about 150,000 German Jews, like some 5 million Germans who emigrated with them during the century, was mainly the United States of America, where they took a central role in the development of American Jewry.

[8] Robert M. Bigler, *The Politics of German Protestantism: The Rise of the Protestant Church Elite in Prussia, 1815–1848* (Berkeley, 1972); John R. Gillis, *The Prussian Bureaucracy in Crisis, 1848–1860: Origins of an Administrative Ethos* (Stanford, Calif., 1971), chs. 1 and 2.

[9] Jacob Katz, *From Prejudice to Destruction: Anti-Semitism, 1700–1933* (Cambridge, Mass., 1980), 92–104.

for frustrated German Jews was conversion to Chris-
;en between 1800 and 1870 by some 11,000 Jews, an
L57.[10] Mere formal conversion sufficed, since no In-
religious conduct. Yet some converts, like Moses
Mendelssohn's daughters, were moved by religious zeal. The advantages
of conversion were clear. The new Christian was relieved of obstacles to
rights and a career, and could feel fully German.[11] Yet they too could not
overcome the barrier of social exclusion, and in numerous instances
maintained their own social set. 'Conversion was taken seriously, but
did not mean oblivion of the Jewish ancestry and tradition. Yet surrounding society asked these men and women to behave as if they had
no Jewish past, and in general they complied with this requirement . . .
Silence on Judaism was the official line.'[12] The converts' attitude to their
former religion remains unfathomable but their Jewish families often
kept some connection with them. Many justified their conversion by
claiming the moral identity of Judaism and Christianity, making unim-
portant whether one was Jew or Christian. Others felt as did Heinrich
Heine, one of the greatest German poets, who in famous phrases described Judaism as 'not a religion but a misfortune', and a baptismal
certificate as 'a ticket of admission to European culture'. Heine did not
want to remain a Jew but never forgave himself for converting. On the
other hand Friedrich Julius Stahl, born Joel Jolson (or Golson), became
the philosopher and parliamentarian of Christian Prussian conservatism and an opponent of Jewish rights and Judaism. Benjamin Disraeli,
brought by his father (who remained a Jew) to be converted, became a

[10] This figure covers all of Germany. Between 1800 and 1924 21,000 Jews converted
in Prussia alone, an average of 168 annually. The number of converts remains an un-
solved question. Scholars have utilized much exaggerated missionary statistics while attempting to discount them. The figures here have a firmer base. See David Sorkin, *The
Transformation of German Jewry, 1780–1840* (Oxford, 1987), 111 and literature cited,
p. 206 n. 25; S. M. Lowenstein, *The Berlin Jewish Community* (New York and Oxford,
1994), 53.

[11] Racist ideologies of eternally 'impure' Jewish blood came later in the century.

[12] Arnaldo Momigliano, *Essays in Ancient and Modern Historiography* (Oxford, 1977),
318. The author, an eminent ancient historian, suggests that the Jewish origins of the
historian Droysen's wife inhibited him from carrying his great pioneer history of
Hellenism to the point in history when Judaism became important in the Hellenistic
world. This 'would have touched the inmost recesses of his personal life'.

famous British prime minister and sympathetically close to Jews. Karl Marx, converted with his father who turned Christian in order to continue as a lawyer, spewed hateful remarks on Jews. In contrast was the composer Felix Mendelssohn, a convert's son and the philosopher's grandson, who did not heed his father's urging to adopt a less Jewish name and nourished some quasi-Jewish feelings. The majority of converts came from families little attached to Judaism and, one supposes, made the most of the opportunities acquired by conversion while suppressing any feelings of guilt they may have had.

It was in these unpromising years that creative Jewish energies burst forth, leaving achievements more original and enduring even than those of the Haskalah a half-century earlier. Among a few intellectual young Jews in Berlin who questioned the future of Judaism the idea took root that the Jewish heritage was deeper than the surface of contemporary Judaism which repelled them.[13] They had studied German philosophy and literature in university and believed that the central new principle of historical change and development must apply to Judaism, which should be studied closely. The historical principle was also new to Judaism; and fifty years earlier Moses Mendelssohn had only a superficial interest in history. A few *maskilim* grasped the idea of historical development, but the potent influence of German historical thought beginning with Moser and Herder was required to bring the idea to full expression. The young intellectuals set out to explore the vastness of Jewish literature. It was axiomatic that Judaism had basic concepts (*Ideen*) which were timeless, but developments over thousands of years must have produced endless variety in Jewish life and literature. Judaism was far broader than the narrow limits of its present. Scholars could recover and comprehend this buried past by applying the methods of

---

[13] For what follows see Michael A. Meyer. *The Origins of the Modern Jew* (Detroit, 1967); Nahum N. Glatzer, 'The Beginnings of Modern Jewish Studies', in Altmann, *Studies in Nineteenth Century Jewish Intellectual History* 27–45; Fritz Bamberger, 'Zunz's Conception of Jewish History', *Proceedings of the American Academy for Jewish Research*, 10 (1941), 1–25; Ismar Schorsch, 'From Wolfenbuttel to Wissenschaft—The Divergent Paths of Isaak Markus Jost and Leopold Zunz', and 'The Emergence of Historical Consciousness in Modern Judaism,' *Leo Baeck Institute Year Book*, 22 (1977), 109–28; 27 (1983), 413–37, repr. in his *From Text to Context: The Turn to History in Modern Judaism* (Hanover, NH, and London, 1994).

modern philology which they had learned at university. It assumed that knowing a literature meant knowing the people who created it and their times.

The young intellectuals established an association to further the *Wissenschaft des Judentums*, Science of Judaism, meaning its neutral, scientific study. The association lasted about five years, until 1825. Two members, Heine and the legal philosopher Gans, converted and others emigrated or entered careers. Only one, Leopold Zunz, remained constant to the idea while earning his living for years as a journalist. After a few early essays the Science of Judaism displayed its full possibilities with Zunz's masterpiece of 1832, 'The Sermons of the Jews in their Historic Evolution'. The work implies that sermons in German, which the Prussian government forbade as a 'change', were but the renewal of the ancient practice of vernacular preaching in the synagogue. The young Zunz himself delivered such sermons in the pioneer reform congregation in Berlin. His book's title suggests aridity, and contemporaries were indifferent, to judge from the 600 copies it sold in twenty years.

Had the antiquity of the vernacular synagogue sermon been the book's full scope, its significance would be limited. But Zunz's work broke new ground by presenting a method for studying and dating the vast midrashic literature,[14] and Jewish literature in general. He showed that much of *midrash* was fragments of ancient sermons from which much could be learned about a millennium and a half of Jewish religious life. Such a method, his book implied, was applicable to the immense Jewish literature. It further implied that the true way to understand Judaism was through its historical development, to which the key was Jewish literature. From Zunz's works a school of Science of Judaism scholars took their inspiration, including Solomon J. L. Rapoport in Galicia and Prague who began somewhat earlier,[15] Samuel David Luzzatto in Italy, Salomon Munk in France, and Zacharias Frankel, Abraham Geiger, Moritz Steinschneider, and Heinrich Graetz in Germany, to mention scholars of the first rank. None received a university appoint-

---

[14] Free exegesis by the ancient rabbis on the biblical books. Some *midrash* collections do not follow books of the Bible.

[15] His pioneer, extremely erudite biographies of early rabbinic scholars are gathered in *Toldot* (2 vols., Warsaw, 1913; repr. Jerusalem, 1969).

ment, but a few held positions in the newly founded rabbinical schools or other Jewish schools or as librarians. The Science of Judaism meant to show the place of Judaism in civilization, but no German university took notice of it.

German Jewry led the Jewish communities of western Europe in cultural accomplishment. In addition to the men of the *Wissenschaft*, representatives of traditional learning as well as significant philosophers of Judaism were active. Some writers and musicians became noteworthy, particularly composers in France like Meyerbeer, the son of a wealthy Berlin Jew, Offenbach, and Jacques Halévy, grandson of a synagogue choirmaster. As the son of a convert, Felix Mendelssohn can hardly be included despite some Jewish feelings he articulated. Major cultural achievements by Jews lay in the future.

From Germany also came new religious movements which recast nineteenth-century Jewish religious life. A trend to orderly and decorous synagogue services spread throughout western Europe as many communities even enacted codes of conduct which prescribed how and when to enter, sit, and leave the synagogue, sing in unison and pray decorously rather than with loud fervour, and so forth.[16] Newly printed prayer books included vernacular translations facing the Hebrew text. Bigger, more impressive synagogues were built, especially in growing cities, reflecting the larger size of communities and the ampler purse of their members. Their architectural style was often 'Moorish' Spanish, out of keeping with the surroundings but expressing the freedom and greatness of medieval Spanish Jewry which emancipated Jewry wanted to emulate. Many old chants were replaced with music in European style composed by men like Salomon Sulzer of Vienna, also a great cantor, and Louis Lewandowski of Berlin, and were sung by trained cantors and choirs. The synagogue of 1860 had come far from that of 1800, although in the small communities in rural regions of Bavaria, Alsace, Holland and Bohemia the old ways continued with little change. While the new demand for decorum stirred some discomfort and nostalgia for the old

---

[16] See Steven M. Lowenstein, 'The 1840s and the Creation of the German-Jewish Religious Reform Movement', in Werner E. Mosse *et al.*, (eds.), *Revolution and Evolution: 1848 in German-Jewish History* (Tübingen, 1981), esp. 260–3 and table IV, pp. 286–97. For the quite different French case see Berkovitz, *The Shaping of Jewish Identity*, 127–209.

ways it aroused no real controversy. The new Reform Judaism, however, was the subject of bitter dispute which has lasted to the present day. Reform Judaism built upon the manifest desire for change,[17] but its changes went much beyond orderly worship and fine religious edifices. Moving with contemporary intellectual currents, it maintained that Judaism had a spiritual, eternal core which came from revelation. On the other hand, specific religious observances, often difficult to keep and regarded unsympathetically by contemporary German Jews, were merely the product of changing historical circumstances. The demonstration of change within Judaism and how religious forms, as observances were called, had come and gone supported one of Reform's central ideas, that Judaism constantly accommodated the needs of its time. Taking a concept from German idealist philosophy, it held that religious observances were changeable, and thus inferior to spiritual concepts which would never change. Reform Judaism also derived much from Haskalah, which bequeathed the endorsement of secular learning and the antagonism to old-fashioned Judaism as expressed by *maskilim* in the generation after Mendelssohn. Reform drew especially on the 'Science of Judaism', to legitimate the religious reforms which it believed were essential to maintain Judaism under emancipation. The critique of religious tradition was initiated by Reform's greatest leader, Abraham Geiger, a brilliant exponent of the Science of Judaism. To be sure, few 'Science' scholars were allied with Reform. Zunz took part only in Reform's early years and then left it, while Rapoport, Luzzatto, Frankel, and later Graetz were steadfast opponents.

The first winds of Reform Judaism blew between 1814 and 1823 in Berlin and Hamburg. One of the several congregations in the Prussian capital turned to Reform under the leadership of Israel Jacobson who, we recall, had conducted the first such services as a court Jew in Seesen from 1809. Relative peace in Berlin Jewry was kept until the government forbade the slightest change in the Orthodox worship, and commanded the worshippers to return to the old synagogue. But when that synagogue

---

[17] Michael A. Meyer, *Response to Modernity: A History of the Reform Movement in Judaism* (New York and Oxford, 1988), is now the standard work. A useful collection of documents is W. Gunther Plaut, *The Rise of Reform Judaism: A Sourcebook of its European Origins* (New York, 1963).

had to close for repairs it divided into three small congregations; those inclining to Reform as well as many Orthodox went back to the home of the rich pro-Reform Jacob Herz Beer.[18] A struggle ensued between Beer's reformers and traditionalist arrivals, and an inconsistent religious service was the outcome. Looming behind the dispute was the highly conservative Prussian government, which might allow or forbid forms of Jewish worship on the basis of its principled hostility to any religious change, Jewish or Christian. Reformers and their opponents both turned to the government, which distrusted religious reform as a species of change and reformers as subversive liberals. It was alarmed that Christians, including clergy, were visiting Reform Jewish services. Jews who sought genuine religious change should better become Christians, the regime held, although a few officials maintained the contrary, that the reform of Judaism would elevate the Jews' moral level. Until approximately 1860 Jewish religious life had to reckon with German governments' inclinations for or against religious change. When the young rabbi Abraham Wolf arrived in Copenhagen in 1828 to begin more than sixty years' service, the Danish government compelled the little congregations to merge into the new large synagogue, where Wolf introduced a more Danish, but not Reform, form of worship.

The first serious contest between reform and tradition came in Hamburg. In 1817 a group of educated Hamburg Jews, dissatisfied with the languishing state of religious life, turned their worship group into the first openly Reform congregation. They had a preacher, as early Reform called its spiritual leaders, and at least two scholarly lay leaders. Men and women sat separately. The liturgy, traditional and almost all in Hebrew, subtly altered or softened some theological principles. For example, the faith in messianic restoration to the Holy Land became low-key. The 'flash point' over Hamburg Reform was the organ, played by a Christian during services. The newly built temple, not synagogue, sought in traditional fashion to validate its practices in Jewish law by means of publishing letters of endorsement from rabbis. In reply came a sizeable volume by many other rabbis, some of the first rank, prohibiting the organ and declaring the Hamburg temple unfit for proper Jewish worship. Unlike the Prussian government, Hamburg's municipal authorities

[18] Father of the composer Giacomo Meyerbeer.

stayed out of the fight, which almost tore apart the Jewish community. A settlement of sorts was reached with the appointment of the modern and Orthodox [19] Isaac Bernays as community rabbi. He agreed not to attack the Reform congregation and a *modus vivendi* was reached.

Reform Judaism remained relatively quiescent until the late 1830s, when it began a vigorous expansion which lasted until about 1860. Already by 1835 there were thousands of Germanized Jews, including young 'rabbis doctor' who had gone to university besides their traditional Jewish education. The new rabbis avoided the halakhic questions dealt with by traditional rabbis and saw themselves as teachers and preachers who also conducted wedding and burial ceremonies. They taught in community schools and preached at the novel Saturday devotional meetings. The modern profession of congregational rabbi originated with them before they used the title. The intellectual task of early Reform rabbis, however, was to justify Reform in Jewish law and tradition. Some laymen, however, regarded this effort indifferently and were interested only in a religious platform suitable for themselves as acculturated German Jews. They founded radical Reform congregations in Frankfurt and Berlin. A few rabbis shared their convictions, notably the one-time yeshiva student Samuel Holdheim, who accepted only Jewish moral law and considered the state's supremacy to transcend any religious requirement. Radical Reform Judaism did not flourish in Germany but did in America where it was brought.

The official religion of the Jewish community in France, Britain, and Holland was moderate and decorous orthodoxy, which took most of the wind out of Reform sails in those countries. However, when Gallicized rabbis of the French Consistoire, supported by the bourgeois lay leaders, sought in 1856 to introduce mild religious changes for the entire community, they encountered tenacious opposition in extremely traditional Alsace, led by Rabbi Salomon Klein, which compelled them to retreat.[20] Reform failed to take root in France and barely did so in Hol-

[19] The term itself did not exist before the challenge from Reform Judaism. Orthodoxy, literally 'correct belief', is the continuation of divinely ordained halakhic Judaism without conscious or deliberate change.

[20] Berkovitz, *The Shaping of Jewish Identity*, 203–28; generally, Phyllis Cohen Albert, *The Modernization of French Jewry: Consistory and Community in the Nineteenth Century* (Hanover, NH, 1977).

land but established itself in England, where the issues at stake were quite different from those in Germany. Reform's West London Synagogue of British Jews, composed of Sefardim and Ashkenazim, owed its beginning in 1840 to the unyielding attitude of religious leaders, headed by the aged Chief Rabbi Hirschell, to improving order and decorum. Sefardi religious leaders would not permit services to be held outside their City synagogue even though most members resided at a distance. The West London Synagogue ceased observing the second day of holidays and altered liturgical Bible readings, but held to faith in messianic restoration. British Reform Judaism did not bring forth a comprehensive conception of Judaism as did Reform in Germany. It was founded on biblicism, and did not accept as obligatory what was laid down by the Talmud and later rabbis. The West London Synagogue included prominent and wealthy men and had only two Reform counterparts in Britain. Hirschell placed the congregation and its members under a ban which his more modern successor, Rabbi Nathan Adler, held to until 1849. It remained sedate and conservative but unrecognized in the communal framework.

As Reform penetrated the established German communities a struggle began between Reformers and traditionalists over membership on community boards, the rabbi to be elected, the character of services at the official synagogue, and control of communal money and institutions. Since there could be only one community in a locality and its institutions and services required support, there was deep reluctance to split a community over religious issues, which most German states would not allow anyhow. A test came with the decision of the Breslau community's board in 1840 to elect Abraham Geiger as coadjutor and in due time successor to their aged Orthodox Rabbi Ticktin. A long, bitter fight ensued. Against Geiger it was argued that he could not judge in Jewish law because he personally violated it. As a Frankfurter he was not a Prussian citizen and could not serve in Breslau until citizenship was finally granted him. Geiger served until 1863 in Breslau, where like most community rabbis he circumspectly subordinated some principles for the sake of peace and unity. In the eyes of the Orthodox, however, Reform denied fundamentals of Judaism. Its refusal to accept *halakhah* as sacred and binding, denial of the authority of the Talmud, abrogation of laws which they found in conflict with the conceptions and duties of modern patriotic German Jews, and the repudiation of the messianic faith and ultimate return to the Holy Land, disqualified Reform religiously in Orthodox eyes. Most German communities, however, especially the larger ones, nevertheless came under Reform control. In divided communities the Orthodox maintained a synagogue and a school of their own, and sometimes a *beit midrash*. Both sides collaborated in cemetery upkeep and charitable efforts.

Reform came closest to organizing as a movement at three conferences of rabbis in different cities in 1844, 1845, and 1846. Permission had to be received from each city to hold the conference and each rabbi had to receive his government's permission to attend; one, to be sure, was commanded to go. At these conferences a Reform platform without binding authority was hammered out. The 1845 conference was jarred by the walkout of the eminent rabbi of Dresden, Zacharias Frankel, traditionalist and man of Science of Judaism who founded modern Talmudic study. He had been amenable to moderate change but the conference's merely permissive attitude to Hebrew as the language of public worship was the last straw and he withdrew completely from Reform attachments. Frankel's widely noticed statement of withdrawal set forth his own platform of 'positive-historical' Judaism. It argued that Judaism had to be guided by the historic experience of the Jewish people, sanctioning only changes which were in accord with Jewish law and the collective Jewish consciousness of past and present. Frankel's and his colleagues' writings and works of scholarship expressed a widespread middle-of-the-road viewpoint but did not found a movement. However, they laid the ideological basis for later Conservative Judaism in the United States.

German Orthodoxy was long a rearguard, remote from the intellectual life of its time and handicapped by identification with ghetto ways and beliefs. It was concentrated in small Bavarian towns and the German borderlands of Bohemia, Slovakia, and Prussian Posen. Two rabbis of the first rank, Akiva Eger of Posen and Moses Sofer-Schreiber of Pressburg (Bratislava), led the Orthodox.[21] R. Sofer, widely known as Hatam

---

[21] Eger was Sofer's father-in-law by the latter's second marriage. A basic study is by Jacob Katz, 'Contributions towards a Biography of R. Moses Sofer' (Hebrew), in *Studies in Mysticism and Religion presented to Gershom G. Scholem* (Hebrew and other langs.), 115–48.

Sofer after one of his works, a native of Frankfurt who had an uncompromising religious style, was an important traditional scholar who combined practicality with charisma. Quite indifferent to emancipation, he forcefully opposed every manifestation of modernity including Mendelssohn's Bible translation and his philosophic works as well as the works of all *maskilim*, general education for children, and the application of philosophic reason to Judaism. For a Jew only unconditional faith and reliance on tradition could be allowed. Not only Jewish law but all customs were obligatory and unchangeable, including clothing and synagogue practices. Hatam Sofer's ethical testament to his descendants admonished them to refuse all association with men and books of the Jewish Enlightenment.[22] Sofer insisted on separation from religiously unobservant Jews, thereby fostering a form of Orthodox sectarianism. Obviously his outlook differed from the more accommodating R. Ezekiel Landau a half-century earlier. From the many disciples of R. Sofer in his Pressburg yeshiva came forth a new breed of authoritarian community rabbis in their master's spirit, who set the tone for Moravian and Hungarian Orthodoxy. The Orthodoxy of Sofer and other leaders as well as Frankel's conservatism reasserted themselves especially when Reform's pace slowed after 1860. Rabbis Samson Raphael Hirsch in Frankfurt and Esriel Hildesheimer in Berlin founded acculturated Orthodoxy, strictly observant of Jewish law while endorsing secular studies and employing the German language. Late in his career Hirsch led his Orthodox followers in withdrawing from the Jewish community to avoid any co-operation with Reformers who governed the community. They founded a separate Orthodox community after the Prussian law was changed to allow two communities. Few Orthodox Jews followed Hirsch's precedent; Hatam Sofer's Pressburg community needed no separation because it was entirely Orthodox.

---

[22] Of many editions, I used [Moses Sofer], *Zava'at Moshe* (with Yiddish trans.) (Jerusalem, 1924) *Igrot Soferim*, ed. Shlomo Sofer (Vienna, 1933; repr. Jerusalem, 1970), section 2, nos. 54–9, 63, 64, 76.

Religion and Community in Western Europe

German Jewry dominated the Jewish scene in western Europe, but it was organized only at a local level. The small Jewish community of Italy was likewise composed of local units. Those of Holland, France, and Britain, however, were centralized. The respective capital cities of Amsterdam, Paris, and London were their foremost communities. Berlin acquired the leading role in German Jewry only towards the end of the nineteenth century. The French Jewish community establishment was controlled by well-to-do Gallicized Jews with the aid of a narrow voting franchise. Its consistory in Paris was remote from the majority of its people, who still lived in Alsace in traditional Jewish manner. Dutch Jewry also was controlled by a consistory. Of all these countries only in Germany was Reform Judaism a powerful presence.

The end of Jewish autonomy, for centuries the basis of community life, required communities in emancipated countries to redefine their tasks and overhaul structures. Alongside the demands made by Reform and other religious trends, the community itself underwent reconstruction. The new structure for the Jews of France and the Netherlands was ordained by Napoleon's consistorial decrees of 1808. The emperor also commanded the consistories to work at acculturating their 'backward' brethren. The British Jews' communal structure, on the other hand, developed without government intervention. It grew out of the original London synagogues of the seventeenth century, Shaar Hashamayim (known as Bevis Marks after its street) of the Sefardim and the nearby Great Synagogue of the Ashkenazim in Dukes Place. The rabbi of each congregation gradually became recognized as rabbi of all congregations in their respective 'communions', as they were called. Thus emerged the Haham of the Sefardim as well as the Chief Rabbi of the Ashkenazim, who in time was accepted as chief rabbi of Great Britain and the British empire. The Board of Deputies, a name taken from the Protestant Dissenters' representative body, spoke for the British Jews through congregational representatives.

Since Reform Judaism and the Jewish emancipation movement were contemporaneous, the question arises what if any connection subsisted between the two. The Reformers sought to mould Judaism not only to be decorous and aesthetically attractive but also to harmonize with nineteenth-century culture and philosophy, particularly in Germany. German Reformers made much of their patriotism, and believed that their movement promoted emancipation by displaying Jewish improvement and Germanness. However, they did not claim that Reform would show the German Jews to be worthy of emancipation, nor argue that Reform was a necessary stepping-stone to emancipation. In the United States the Jews needed no emancipation and Reform Judaism flourished, emphasizing that Judaism in a free society must remove religious obstacles from ghetto days which restricted free access to general society. France's acculturated Jews outside Alsace accepted the Consistoire's adaptation of tradition. 'Regenerated' French Judaism underwent significant changes but remained officially Orthodox. Likewise in Britain, Reform's beginnings were undercut by improvements in official Orthodoxy which were enacted by Chief Rabbi Adler in collaboration with Anglicized ministers and lay leaders.

From Congregation of Israel to Jewish People

In the middle of the nineteenth century emancipated European Jews took the first steps towards converting the intangible religious conception of 'community of Israel' (*knesset Yisrael*) into the tangible reality of international Jewish organization. This transition was possible thanks to modern transportation and communication. Railroads and steamships from the first decades of the nineteenth century and the telegraph and mail service soon after allowed fast travel and quick correspondence. Still more important was mass printing by rotary press, which enabled the Jewish press to grow with explosive speed, as did the popular press. The *Allgemeine Zeitung des Judenthums* in Leipzig from 1837, the *Archives Israélites* in Paris from 1840, and the *Jewish Chronicle* in London from 1841 were the first of many Jewish newspapers, mainly weeklies. Beginning with local notices and religious discourses, the newspapers broadened to include news about Jews elsewhere, including the barely known Jews of eastern Europe and the Orient. The Jewish press set the stage for world-wide Jewish connections, thus stimulating philanthropic effort aimed at helping and modernizing oriental Jewry in particular.

Emancipated Jewry first acted on a wider scene during the Damascus affair of 1840,[23] when eight Damascus Jews were arrested and brutally mistreated for supposedly murdering a Catholic priest and using his blood for ritual purposes. The belief in ritual murder was still current in Europe. Exceptions were allowed for civilized European Jews, but supposedly it was still practised in the barbarous Orient. Ratti-Menton, the consul of France in Damascus whose influence was predominant in Syria, promoted the persecution. Two arrested Jews died under torture and two others converted to be spared. Jews of France and Britain protested along with Christian humanitarians, and were joined by Jews of Holland and the distant United States, which appeared for the first time on the wider Jewish scene. A visit to Damascus by Adolphe Crémieux of France and Moses Montefiore of Britain brought the release of the battered survivors of the blood libel. This was the first of Montefiore's many visits of intercession, in which he had the potent support of Foreign Secretary Palmerston. The reaction of Thiers, the French premier, was quite different. No doubt irked at having French dominance in Syria undercut, he rebuked a Jewish member of the Chamber of Deputies for supposedly putting Jewish interests before French interests and deplored the power of the Jews in European capitals.[24] A long thread of anti-Semitic argument thus began which strengthened the widespread Jewish feeling that much hostility remained notwithstanding emancipation. Montefiore (from 1851 Sir Moses, the first Jewish knight) became the Jewish world's symbolic hero and knight errant. The triumphant outcome of the Damascus affair inspired many Jews to thoughts of secular Jewish unity and action. One of them, the pioneer socialist Moses Hess, then an alienated Jew, recalled that Jewish efforts during the Damascus affair inspired the turn in his life that made him a forerunner of Zionism.

During the twenty years following the Damascus affair there were fur-

[23] The definitive account is now Jonathan Frankel, *The Damascus Affair: 'Ritual Murder', Politics and the Jews in 1840* (Cambridge, 1997).

[24] David H. Pinkney, *Decisive Years in France, 1840–1847* (Princeton, 1986), 134.

ther interventions to aid oppressed fellow Jews. Efforts to aid Moroccan and Persian Jewries and those in Palestine enjoyed some success thanks to British support. However, attempts to ease the conditions of Russian Jewry failed despite the adulation heaped on Montefiore by Russian Jews during his visits. Russia was not dominated by a great power, but was itself a great power whose policies could not be swayed by intervention.

After these rather sporadic efforts the first international Jewish organization, the Alliance Israélite Universelle, was founded in 1860 by French Jews.[25] Its founders had only a peripheral connection to the official Jewish community and took little interest in its parochial affairs. However, the idea of a world-wide Jewish organization led by French Jews excited their imagination. It would advance France's 'civilizing mission' among Jews mainly in oriental countries. The Alliance Israélite Universelle established branches in many western countries. In pre-modern lands it aimed to bring modern life and modernized Judaism through a network of schools. For the first decade of its existence the Alliance was genuinely world-wide. After France's defeat in the Franco-Prussian War of 1870 similar Jewish bodies sprang up in other emancipated lands and the Alliance became almost exclusively French. Its activities aided the spread of French influence in oriental countries with the blessing and support of the French government.

Jewish Demography and Place in the Western Economy

Whether fully or partly emancipated, Jews found their place in the economy of western Europe during its era of world supremacy. The Jewish population in the western half of the continent, like the population in general, vastly increased, requiring a broader range of livelihoods. We may note population growth in three major countries. The 1816 population of what would become Germany stood at 22,377,000, and that of its Jews in the early 1820s at about 223,000. German Jewry's highest proportion to the general population came about 1860, and thereafter

[25] Michael Graetz, *Les Juifs en France au 19-e siècle: de la Révolution française à l'Alliance Israélite Universelle* (Paris, 1989).

slowly declined. When the German empire was proclaimed in 1871 472,000 Jews were included among 41,059,000 Germans. France tells a somewhat different story. There were 29,107,000 Frenchmen in 1806, of whom in 1808–9 approximately 47,000 were Jews, while in 1866 the respective numbers were 38,067,000 and 89,000. Soon, however, came the loss of Alsace and Lorraine to Germany with about 2 million Frenchmen, 40,000 of them Jews.[26] Great Britain's 11,970,000 inhabitants in 1811 reached 26,072,00 in 1871, while its Jews, perhaps 12,000 at the earlier date, numbered about 45,000 in 1868. Thus the Jewish increase in each country outran the general population's. The reason for the Jewish advantage does not lie in a higher Jewish birth rate, which in fact was lower than the general population's, but in lower Jewish infant mortality and to a slighter extent longer Jewish life expectancy. General mortality was gradually declining, but the Jews kept a lead. The fundamental reason for the general improvement was a higher standard of life and, later, better sanitation.[27] During the nineteenth century the number of children per French Jewish family was actually in steady decline, dropping from 3.37 about 1808 to 2.04 in 1872. Even in pious and traditional Alsace, where Yiddish was still widely spoken, families were becoming smaller and men tended not to marry until they had the capital needed to start a business.[28] In equally traditional Bavaria, Jewish men generally married past the age of 30, yet couples averaged over four children before 1870. There was evidently some form of birth control, because births tended to stop abruptly after children were born close together.[29] In larger towns where the impact of emancipation and the modern

---

[26] Zosa Szajkowski, 'The Growth of the Jewish Population in France', *Jewish Social Studies*, 8/3 and 4 (July and Oct 1946), esp. 186–9; Jacob Toury, *Beyn Makpekhah Reaktsiah ve-Emantsipatsiah* (English title: *Revolution, Reaction and Emancipation: A Social and Political History of the Jews in Germany in the Years 1847–1871*) (Tel Aviv, 1978), 3–9.

[27] We generalize from T. G. McKeown and R. G. Record, 'Reasons for the Decline of Mortality in England and Wales during the Nineteenth Century', in M. W. Flinn and T. C. Smout (eds.), *Essays in Social History* (Oxford, 1974), 218–50, esp. p. 247.

[28] Paula Hyman, 'Jewish Fertility in Nineteenth Century France', in Paul Ritterband (ed.), *Modern Jewish Fertility* (Leiden, 1981), 78–93 P. Hyman, *The Emancipation of the Jews of Alsace: Acculturation and Tradition in the Nineteenth Century* (New Haven, 1991); Toury, *Revolution, Reaction and Emancipation*, 9–13.

[29] Steven M. Lowenstein, 'Voluntary and Involuntary Limitation of Fertility in Nineteenth-Century Bavarian Jewry', in Ritterband, *Modern Jewish Fertility*, 94–111.

economy were felt women's role generally changed. Women quit the realm of business and stayed at home, where they ran the domestic hearth with the aid of servants, usually not Jews. Bringing up children preoccupied them, and to an increasing extent they became the bearers of Judaism, as the man of the house frequently dropped away from Judaism owing to the pressure to prosper in business and extensive contact with the non-Jewish world. Matching, and negotiating a suitable marriage settlement, was a largely maternal occupation; offspring's independent choice of mates came slowly.[30]

Especially in small towns the Jewish birth rate continued to be robust until the last third of the nineteenth century—slightly over 30 births per 1,000 population.[31] Small-town Jewish population nevertheless failed to rise because restless and ambitious young people, compelled to wait long in order to marry, emigrated to growing German cities or to America. Bavarian Jewry remained fixed about 50,000 in its villages and little towns, and continued a traditional way of life into the twentieth century. On the other hand Berlin's Jews, 3,700 in 1817, numbered 11,835 in 1852 and kept increasing fast, as Breslau went only from 7,631 to 12,967 in the same period.[32] Other fast-growing towns drew much of their increase from Bavaria and similar rural and village areas. Jews from small places in Alsace and the Rhine valley as well as Bavaria helped to swell Paris Jewry.

About 1870 signs of Jewish population stagnation began to appear as the Jewish birth rate dropped. In France stagnation affected Jews along with the general population, which reached 40 million and then stayed for many decades at that figure. Matters differed in Germany. The demographer John E. Knodel has shown that the commercial and professional middle class which German Jews were mainly entering began a long demographic slide in the 1860s and the Jews did likewise.[33] There

[30] Marion Kaplan, *The Making of the Jewish Middle Class: Women, Family and Identity in Imperial Germany* (New York, 1991); Paula Hyman, *Gender and Assimilation in Modern Jewish History* (Seattle, 1995).

[31] Steven M. Lowenstein, 'The Pace of Modernization in German Jewry in the Nineteenth Century', *Leo Baeck Institute Year Book*, 21 (1976), 41–56.

[32] Heinrich Silbergleit, *Die Bevölkerungs- und Berufsverhältnisse der Juden im deutschen Reich*, i [no more publ.] (Berlin, 1930), 18, table 8.

[33] John E. Knodel, *The Decline of Fertility in Germany, 1871–1939* (Princeton, 1982), 4–5, 43, 52, 70–1, 104, 109, 136–41, 170–1.

is no reliable demographic evidence for nineteenth-century British Jewry, where a steady flow of immigration concealed any demographic decline by native Jews.

Commercial and industrial development did not do away with the old economy. For example in Britain of 1881, a century after the Industrial Revolution began, the most numerous occupational group was not in industrial labour or commerce but servants. The transition from handicrafts to industry, the growth of banks and of large-scale commerce were bitterly resented by those who made their living in traditional ways, nowhere more than in Germany. The Jews were blamed, and their accusers had a point—Jews were highly prominent in the new economic order.[34] Yet emancipation did not break down the distinct Jewish economic structure. There were some shifts but they did not change the Jewish occupational structure. From earlier days there were still numerous Jewish itinerants, occasionally labourers but mostly beggars. Most Jews who made a living in handicrafts and commerce led hard lives. A small class of brilliantly successful merchants and financiers were the prime Jewish beneficiaries of western Europe's ecoonomic advance.

In France moneylending in its traditional form continued in Alsace but was unknown elsewhere in rural France.[35] The mass of Jews continued in trade, a great many as lowly country pedlars and street hawkers buying and selling second-hand garments. Further up the scale were shopkeepers selling consumer articles like clothing and jewellery, besides kosher foodstuffs to Jews such as bread and meat. Beyond shopkeeping one comes to wholesale importing and exporting, occupations enlarged by the new economy. Commerce offered more mobility opportunity than artisanship, which also engaged a sizeable group of Jews. There were numerous Jewish tailors decades before ready-made clothing and Jew and tailoring became nearly synonymous. Other consumer goods such as cigars, jewellery, artificial flowers, and millinery likewise provided livelihoods for Jewish artisans. Frequently they toiled long

---

[34] Some German complaints are quoted in Hamerow, *Social Foundations of German Unification*, 77, 79, 81–2.

[35] Eugen Weber, *Peasants into Frenchmen: The Modernization of Rural France* (London, 1977), 39–40.

hours at home or in small workshops—rarely in factories—in dirty, crowded conditions which were later called sweatshops. Jews in these occupations were usually poor, frequently sick and neglected, and lived meanly with hunger and unemployment their lot. This was the economic picture for most Jews not only in France but generally in western Europe. A group which presented special problems were the Jewish vagrants who wandered among the countries of western Europe.[36] The efforts of Jewish institutions to draw young Jews away from commerce and vagrancy into artisan trades, such as those specified here as well as carpentry and printing, met modest success. No efforts were made to draw Jews into factory labour.

Far removed from these humble folk, connected with them only by charity, was bourgeois Jewry, whose uppermost level lived palatially. This was the class which made its fortune from the new economy. There were Jewish industrialists and also merchants on a grand scale, but most of the conspicuously wealthy Jews founded or inherited family businesses as merchant bankers, so called because they often began as merchants or brokers whose funds provided credit to other merchants. Where they got starting capital early in the century is not certain. Neither capital amassed by court Jews nor profits of currency exchange seem to be the source. It was probably merchants', jobbers', and commodity brokers' accumulated profits. These lenders gradually quit as merchants, although their main clients continued to be merchants, and became financial agents of governments and new enterprises especially railroads.[37] Merchant bankers' affairs were private and their dealings confidential, an advantage much desired by borrowers. Merchant banks practically controlled public and private finance until the unwelcome coming of joint stock and savings banks late in the nineteenth century. The Rothschilds and several others foiled for a time the establishment of corporate banks, but most other bankers co-operated in projects with these usually non-Jewish rivals.

[36] Aharon Bornstein, *Ha-Kabzanim* (Hebrew; The Beggars: A Chapter in the History of German Jewry) (Jerusalem, 1992).
[37] Very helpful is David Landes, 'The Old Bank and the New: The Financial Revolution of the Nineteenth Century', in *Essays in European Economic History, 1789–1914*, ed. F. Crouzet, W. H. Chaloner, and W. M. Stern (New York, 1969), 112–27.

For much of the nineteenth century Jews and banking were nearly synonymous. Jewish bankers gained their fame—some thought it notoriety—by dominating merchant banking. Their basic function was to raise capital by selling government or private obligations, and advising bond flotations on the suitable rate of interest from knowledge of risk and financial market conditions. Bankers sometimes combined in syndicates to provide funds and share financial risks. They made tremendous profits from their percentage on transactions, but the risks could be great. Their special risk lay in underwriting, the responsibility for selling all the securities in a flotation and taking the unsold on themselves. It was Jewish finance which enabled rail kilometres to increase from 43 in 1825, all in Britain, to the 1870 figures of 15,544 in France, 18,876 in Germany, 21,558 (1871) in Britain, and 10,731 in Russia.[38]

There are some clear reasons for Jewish domination of nineteenth-century European banking, and the history of the Rothschilds of London, Paris, Vienna, and Frankfurt, the greatest banking family of the time and probably of any time, illustrates a few of them. They had long experience in the money trade in their home town of Frankfurt, and carefully kept their capital liquid. Aided by their agents and international connections, often within the family, they obtained intimate knowledge not only of market conditions and customers, essential for business but hard to come by, but also of political affairs. These connections could be used to help one another and sometimes fellow bankers in tight spots. The Rothschilds often married within their large family or with another Jewish banking family. European banking in its earlier phases was often in the hands of such close-knit, self-segregated minorities as Russian Old Believers, French Protestants, and English Quakers, and Jews obviously belonged in that category. Few if any Jewish bankers converted to Christianity, if only because their membership in the 'club' could have been forfeited.

A risk which could not be figured on the balance sheet was widespread resentment when Jewish bankers appeared to back the policies of reactionary regimes whose securities they underwrote. Actually the financiers avoided political involvement. They were almost solely interested

---

[38] B. R. Mitchell, *European Historical Statistics, 1750–1975*, 2nd rev. edn. (New York, 1980), table G1, pp. 609 ff.

in political stability, meaning whether regimes could dependably pay interest and principal. Still less refutable was the belief that the Jewish bankers, and by extension the Jews, were the hidden power behind the policies of governments. Just the title of Toussenel's French book of 1845, 'The Jews, Rulers of the Age' (*Les Juifs rois de l'époque*) expressed a conviction which no facts could break down. More generally, social classes and intellectuals who were devoted to traditional agrarian and artisan life observed its stagnation and decline with dismay, and placed the responsibility on the transactions of high finance under 'Jewish domination'.

Revolutions in 1848

The revolutions which broke out spontaneously in 1848 [39] found the Jews in a far different position from where they stood six decades earlier at the start of the French Revolution. They not only had achieved emancipation or measurable improvement in their status throughout western Europe, but they played an active political role unthinkable in the world of 1789. The 1848 revolutions, although separate and local, shared a common liberal ideology. Nationalism was joined to liberalism, as liberal Germans sought national unification but denounced the nationalist rebellion of the Poles in Prussia. Austrian Germans confronted Czech, Hungarian, and Polish movements within the Habsburg realms. The liberal writer and politician Ignaz Kuranda, a Czech Jew by origin yet an Austrian delegate in the German parliament of Frankfurt, aroused anti-Jewish hostility in Bohemia because he exemplified Jewish partiality to Habsburg Germanism.[40] Socialism also emerged on the scene in 1848. A few Jews were socialists but there was no distinct Jewish socialism.

[39] See the stimulating study of E. Labrousse, '1848–1830–1789: How Revolutions are Born', in Crouzet *et al.*, *Essays in European Economic History*, 1–14. On the Rothschilds there is now the comprehensive, outstanding Niall Ferguson, *The World's Banker: The History of the House of Rothschild* (London, 1998).

[40] Francis L. Loewenheim, 'German Liberalism and the Czech Renaissance: Ignaz Kuranda, *Die Grenzboten*, and Developments in Bohemia, 1845–1849', in *The Czech Renascence of the Nineteenth Century: Essays Presented to Otakar Odlozilik*, ed. P. Brock and H. G. Skilling (Toronto, 1970), 146–75.

Jewish national sentiment also found occasional expression during the revolutionary year. However, emancipation from what remained of the Old Regime stood highest on the liberal revolutionary agenda and dominated the parliaments of the revolution. Many Jews and others held that a separate Jewish effort for emancipation was wrong in principle, since it was bound to come with general political emancipation in the new liberal order. The Frankfurt assembly's abortive constitution for a united Germany included Jewish legal equality, but liberal Germany and its paper constitution were swept away. Jewish emancipation was almost achieved in revolutionary Vienna also, but Habsburg reaction regained control and dissolved the assembly. For French Jewry, possessing emancipation, the demands were internal: a democratic franchise and popular control of Jewish community affairs, in which the Orthodox majority would predominate. The demands were gained but within a few years most of the old ways crept back.[41]

Jewish representatives sat in the revolutionary assemblies in Paris, Vienna and Frankfurt. Isaac-Adolphe Crémieux, a lawyer and leader in the Jewish community, was minister of justice in the new French republican regime, while German Jewry's foremost voice for emancipation, Gabriel Riesser of Hamburg, also a lawyer, was elected a vice-president of the national assembly at Frankfurt. There were Jewish leaders of the revolution in Vienna, especially Adolf Fischof and Josef Goldmark, physician and chemist respectively, as well as the community's preacher, Isaac Noah Mannheimer. Two young Jews were among the revolutionists who were executed after a Viennese revolutionary uprising against the reaction; one was Hermann Jellinek, brother of a famous and respectable Vienna rabbi. The Jewishness of all these men was open and not made an issue. The scholars of the Wissenschaft des Judentums were strongly pro-revolution. Such men as Zunz, Geiger, Steinschneider, Graetz, and especially Luzzatto in Italy, were filled with revolutionary enthusiasm, but they and their successors later became politically passive. However, the administration of the Jewish communities was thrown into confusion by the revolution. Dues and taxes could not be collected and there was widespread feeling that compared with the revolution the community's affairs were of little importance. There was

[41] Phyllis Cohen Albert, *The Modernization of French Jewry*, 77–85.

another side, however. Revolutionary political changes also involved the political status of the Jewish community. Thinking about the position of emancipated Jewry in the modern state did not end when the reaction restored the previous regimes.

There is another face to the events of 1848–9 which raised questions over the Jews and the revolution. At the very time the revolution broke out and Jews collaborated with other revolutionary citizens in the large cities, a chain of anti-Jewish riots broke out in the small towns and villages of Alsace, south-west Germany, and Bohemia. On the other hand there were no attacks on Jews in revolutionary Italy nor in rebellious Polish Galicia and Posen. Where riots occurred, the rioters were satisfied with destroying and looting Jewish and other property but hardly any physical injury and no killing. Thirty Jewish communities are known to have been affected in south-west Germany alone, and probably an equal number in Alsace. The cause of the riots above all was the debts the peasants could not meet, which they blamed on remote Jewish bankers, as well as the low prices for their produce, supposedly the fault of local Jewish dealers. These riots dampened the enthusiasm of many Jews for the revolution and awakened a feeling that emancipation did not mean ultimate security. Liberals, however, widely believed that attacks on the Jews were a function of lingering prejudice and social backwardness.

Jews in the Habsburg lands endured the most violence. A wave of riots came with the proposal to grant suffrage to prosperous Jews in Hungary, and a bloody attack almost erupted in Pressburg (Bratislava). In many places Jews were kept from serving in the 'National Guard' of the revolution which protected the peace or were forced to quit it. Outside Pressburg attacks on Jews in Prague and small Slovakian and Hungarian places were minor, put in objective terms. But Jews were tense and frightened, and thousands fled to safer locations. Arguably the wave of post-revolutionary emigration overseas had its origin as much in these assaults as in the less tangible failure of emancipation by revolution.[42]

---

[42] Jacob Toury, *Turmoil and Confusion in the Revolution of 1848: The Anti-Jewish Riots in the 'Year of Freedom' and their Influence on Modern Anti-Semitism* (Hebrew, English title; Tel Aviv, 1968), views the riots as the basic fact of the revolution *vis à vis* the Jews. Salo W. Baron published a series of articles on 1848 in a more optimistic spirit: 'The Impact

The revolutions of 1848 suggested the direction of Jewish history in central and western Europe for the remainder of the century. Jewish emancipation was not won through revolutionary movements, and where that occurred it was cancelled by reactionary restorations. It was monarchs back on their thrones after 1848 who granted Jewish emancipation, just as they bestowed constitutions. After a few years of reaction, Jews found themselves in prospering Europe.

Liberal High Tide

The years between 1850 and 1870 mark the fullness of the liberal tide which began with the French Revolution. Emancipation was achieved or almost so, and it appeared to be the grand answer to all Jewish needs. The vehemence of internal Jewish debates died down. Compared with the storms of the generations between 1789 and 1848, 1850 to 1870 can even be called a monotonous time. Great Britain, untouched by revolution in 1848 although its rulers shuddered, and France, the Netherlands, and Italy after unification in 1860, were open to Jewish talent and ambition. Jews could also take part in public life. From Vienna to Galicia Habsburg Jews professed loyalty to Austrian German domination under Emperor Franz Josef. Between 1850 and 1870 they still took little note of the subject nationalities of the empire among whom they lived. One who did take note was the widely respected Adolf Fischof, erstwhile revolutionary leader, who until he died in 1893 urged a federative empire.

of the Revolution of 1848 on Jewish Emancipation', *Jewish Social Studies*, 11/3 (July 1949), 195–248; 'Aspects of the Jewish Communal Crisis in 1848', *Jewish Social Studies*, 14/2 (April 1952), 99–144; 'The Revolution of 1848 and Jewish Scholarship', *Proceedings of the American Academy for Jewish Research*, 18 (1949), 1–66, and 20 (1951), 1–100; 'Church and State Debates in the Jewish Community of 1848', *Mordecai M. Kaplan Jubilee Volume* (New York, 1953), 49–72; 'Samuel David Luzzato and the Revolution of 1848' (Hebrew) *Sefer Assaf* (Jerusalem, 1953), 40–63. Baron sees the revolution in a basically favourable light. Reinhard Rürup, 'The European Revolutions of 1848 and Jewish Emancipation', in W. E. Mosse *et al.*, *Revolution and Evolution*, 1–53 (comments by R. Kosseleck, pp. 55–62), is a fine summary. Istvan Deak, *The Lawful Revolution: Louis Kossuth and the Hungarians, 1848–1849* (New York, 1979), *passim*, contains data on Hungarian Jews.

But his voice went unheeded, and Jews were perhaps the most faithful Habsburgers of all.

German Jews entered a period of twenty years' equipoise while continuing to live in a still restrictive society. The arts and sciences and public employment, including law and universities, opened for them in 1858. Except for lawyers in private practice, however, abandoning Judaism was usually an unwritten requirement for entry or advancement in these fields. German Jews nevertheless continued their steady acculturation and quiet progress towards full emancipation, and above all their economic advance.

Urbanization in western Europe, which accompanied economic advance, had Jews among its leaders. The Jewish population of small towns flowed towards the metropolitan centres. We have mentioned movement from Alsace to Paris, besides from provincial towns to London, and from Bavaria to Frankfurt, Hamburg, and Cologne. Viennese Jewry, where a negligible 1 per cent of its adult Jews had been born, is perhaps the most striking example. It grew from about 4,000 legally resident Jews in 1848 but many more unofficially, to 175,000 unrestricted residents in 1910 among the 2,031,000 Viennese. Vienna's Jews came mainly from Moravia, Hungary, Slovakia, and eastern Austria, and a few from Bohemia. Galicians among Viennese Jews became numerous late in the century. These Jewish immigrants to the big city did not furnish its apprentices and manual labourers as did Christian immigrants, but the salesmen and petty traders.[43]

When the German lands underwent years of reaction and economic depression after 1848, the United States received its largest arrival of German immigrants, almost 30,000 of whom were Jews. Jews who remained in the 'fatherland' were repeatedly told to redistribute themselves in 'productive occupations' as proof that they merited emancipation. However, Jews asking for what they lacked in full emancipation now did so not as humble petitioners but in terms of their rights as Germans. Yet the political scene was gradually moving rightwards.

[43] Peter Schmidtbauer, 'Households and Household Forms of Viennese Jews in 1857', *Journal of Family History* (winter 1980), esp. 371–8; Marcia L. Rozenblit, *The Jews of Vienna, 1867–1914: Assimilation and Identity* (Albany, NY, 1983), tables 2.1, p. 17, 2.5, p. 22, and pp. 13–34, dealing mostly with a later period.

University student associations turned anti-Semitic during this period, and excluded Jews from membership.[44]

As more young Jews attended secondary schools which fitted them for white-collar and technical work or university, the Jewish community practically ceased training its youth for 'productive' occupations. In industrializing Germany Jews became entrepreneurs in such fields as textiles, clothing, food and drink, and some luxury products. Gathering and selling scrap metal, once derided, became a respected, useful occupation. Such was also the case with one-time travelling merchants, now commercial travellers and commission salesmen who played a recognized role in distributing the products of industry. Jews were also prominent as brokers, bankers, factors, and financial intermediaries. German conservatives, hostile to the developing industrial society, found in the Jews' modern economic activities another reason to detest them. On the other hand, social relations between Jews and Germans began to flourish modestly, and there was a small degree of hitherto unknown concord between Judaism and some Christian sects, although not with the dominant Lutherans. Reform Judaism slackened, Orthodoxy in large cities revived, and graduates of the new Breslau rabbinical school headed by Zacharias Frankel began to serve communities in his 'positive-historical' spirit. Jewish authors, musicians, and writers both on Jewish and general German themes became prominent. Scientists and scholars, however, needed an institutional base, and had the bitter choice between being blocked professionally or converting. Still, the quarter-century after the revolution of 1848 was German Jewry's most hopeful generation.

British Jewry at last acquired political emancipation in 1858 when Lionel de Rothschild, who had been repeatedly elected to the House of Commons, could be sworn in. The House of Lords finally accepted that the oath to sit in the House of Commons might omit the words 'on the true faith of a Christian'. Minor in substance, the admission to parliament was still a step away from a Christian toward a secular state and had long been resisted by Christian traditionalists. British Jews remained a mainly mercantile group, and entered comparatively slowly

[44] Konrad H. Jarausch, *Students, Society, and Politics in Imperial Germany* (Princeton, 1982), 96–100, 271–4, 351–66.

into British public life. Cultural contributions were much fewer than in France and Germany. Their well-organized community, acting through its Boards of Guardians in every community, was quite effective not only in relieving want but also in start-up loans to small business and in apprenticing boys. The Jewish community sought to draw Jews away from street trades and peddling and to discourage entry into the tailoring trade. The long-range policy was to foster a class of self-supporting skilled workers. The children of families receiving relief were required to attend a few years of school. At any rate, dependence on charity noticeably decreased as the lower classes' conditions bettered.

Seldom if ever was a transformation of Jewish life as comprehensive as in western Europe during the half-century after the Napoleonic era. Not only did social and political status rise far higher, but languages and cultural life changed drastically as the Jews adopted those of their surroundings. They became much more prosperous, even though many poor remained. Their communities' structure and function were reorganized on a basically voluntary basis. While a sizeable number remained attached to the old ways, there appeared no question which way the current of Jewish life was flowing. It was in eastern Europe that basic questions of the direction of Jewish life existed.

6

Travail in Eastern Europe, 1815–1881

The rift between west and east in European Jewry widened during the nineteenth and early twentieth centuries. While the Jews in western Europe moved decisively towards emancipation and acculturation, those of eastern Europe lived under tsarist autocracy without personal liberty. Jews like others in Russia did not possess rights in general but lived instead under special laws which confined or deprived them in some way. A small minority of Jews received privileges which were doled out for meeting governmental requirements regarding wealth, military service, or Russian education. The most significant privilege was that of residing outside the Pale of Settlement, which consisted of the fifteen western provinces of Russia besides Poland. However, about 95 per cent of the Jews had to live within the Pale.

The status of the Jews in the Kingdom of Poland, successor to Napoleon's Duchy of Warsaw, also called Congress (of Vienna) Poland, and now under the rule of the tsar, differed significantly from that of Russian Jewry proper. Poland remained as it had been under the French. Polish Jews under Russian rule possessed few civil or political rights, but Tsar Nicholas I's edicts did not include them.[1] Far more than in Russia, the Jewish question in Congress Poland was a frequent subject of public discussion. For decades Polish writers and politicians, sometimes with Jewish collaborators, proposed laws which would require the Jews to modernize their ways in return for very limited rights. Nothing came of any of this.[2] Polonized Jews and Jewish university students took part enthusiastically in the failed uprising of 1830–1 against Russian rule, even establishing a Jewish National Guard in Warsaw during the rebellion. Like the majority of Poles, however, most Jews looked on the

---

[1] Artur Eisenbach, *The Emancipation of the Jews in Poland, 1780–1870* (Oxford, 1991), 153–7.　　[2] Ibid., 158–96.

uprising passively, although they were promised rights in return for joining in. Probably they were aware that alongside such promises, strident anti-Jewish voices were accusing them of exploiting the Polish people.[3]

Waves of autocratic reaction and liberal reform came and went in Russia, deeply affecting Jewish privileges. What was given could be taken away summarily and arbitrarily. The close of the era in 1881 found Russian as well as Polish Jewry far more numerous, but so restricted in their residence and occupation that they were unable to participate fully and enjoy the benefits of Russia's economic growth. As a group they may have been poorer at the close of the era than they had been at its outset.

Russian Jewry's intense Judaism, wholly Orthodox around 1815, acquired variety in the course of the century as a secular Jewish dimension developed. Religious reform, however, failed to take root. Together with religious and cultural abundance Russian Jewry carried on an active communal life even after communal autonomy was officially abolished in 1844. Despite governmental prohibition the organized Jewish community continued to exist quite openly but unofficially. Its power could be felt especially in smaller cities and towns where Jewish public opinion was still potent. Curiously, power in such local communities was wielded by the managers of the burial society (*hevra kadisha*), who had to arrange burials and had the authority to assign cemetery places. Stingy or disreputable persons and their families might be disgraced by the burial society's decisions, which could be announced while the person yet lived and might feel moved to return to proper conduct. The burial societies' activities were in some cases conducted with corrupt extortion.

The Jews of Galicia (Austrian Poland) were east European Jews within a central European monarchy. They resembled those of Russia socially and culturally, but Galician Jews had their distinct political history under Habsburg rule. Until 1848 they were heavily taxed in order to advance their compulsory 'improvement' in Enlightenment style. A minimum of taxed Sabbath and holiday candles had to be bought, and

---

[3] N. M. Gelber (ed.), *Ha-Yehudim veha-Mered ha-Polani: Zikhronotav shel Yaakov ha-Levi Levin* (Hebrew; The Jews and the Polish Revolt . . . The Memoirs of Yaakov ha-Levi Levin) (Jerusalem, 1953), introduction.

kosher meat (but not fowl) was also taxed by the pound. The tax collectors were Jews and they ruled their communities. Galician Jews made meagre livings from distilling and selling liquor and from trades and crafts. They were little drawn to Enlightenment or to modern schools but rather to Hasidism. Until the revolution of 1848 briefly overturned the Old Regime, they lived under highly restrictive rule. The emancipation which they owed to the revolution was brief, since it was cancelled in 1851 along with the rest of revolutionary legislation, not to be renewed until 1859 by the restored emperor. When emancipation came conclusively to Galicia and the rest of Habsburg Jewry in 1867, as in Great Britain it did not include universal equal franchise. Yet what Galician Jewry secured was far better than the lot of the Jews in the tsarist empire.[4]

Probably the most remarkable development within east European Jewry went practically unnoticed or at least unmentioned at the time. This was its immense, century-long population increase. It exemplifies a vastly important latent historical process of whose existence contemporaries were barely if at all aware. Russian Jewry lacked statisticians and political economists before the 1880s and distrusted those of the government. The only reasonably accurate and comprehensive Russian statistics came late, in the unique census of 1897, when 5,216,000 Jews were enumerated. But even without censuses or social science methods, alert contemporaries might well have observed a great many newly founded Jewish communities, old-established communities bursting their bounds, and larger families than in earlier days. To be sure there are fair population estimates for the period before 1897. The Jewish subjects of the tsars numbered approximately 1.6 million in 1820, of whom 212,000 lived in Russian Poland in 1816. They increased to 2.4 million in 1851, 564,000 of them in Russian Poland, and to some 4 million by 1880, of whom 1,004,000 were in Russian Poland. The sizeable increase in the total population of Russia in the same period, from 46 million to 86 million, was still proportionately much less than the Jews' increase. Russia's Jewish population continued to climb until the early twentieth

[4] Raphael Mahler, *Divrey Yemey Yisrael, Dorot Aharonim*, part 2 vol. 1: *Mizrah Ayropah . . . (1815–1848)* (Hebrew; History of the Jewish People in Modern Times . . . Eastern Europe) (Merhavia, 1970), 241–66.

century, when the huge emigration overseas offset natural increase. Outside Russian rule Galician Jewry, about 225,000 in 1800, numbered 449,000 in the 1857 census and 686,000 in that of 1880, regularly constituting about 10 per cent of Galicia's population.[5] The huge increase of east European Jewry becomes still harder to explain when one realizes that Jewish women were gradually marrying at a later age. Improvements in health and sanitation were meagre. On the other hand, major epidemics no longer decimated large regions' Jewish and general population after the typhus epidemic of 1848. However, data concerning Jewish sexual habits, such as occasional references in rabbinic responsa, is too sparse to generalize from.

The main portion of east European Jewry dwelt of course in the Russian empire. Tsarist policy was based on the axioms that Judaism was a degraded religion, Jewish economic activity harmed the Russian people, and Jewish occupations, commerce in particular, were unproductive. The policy of the tsars and their bureaucracy was so-called enlightened absolutism, which aimed to 'reform' the Jews by compulsory methods. The reform most desired of them, however, was conversion to Christianity. This ill-concealed wish was clear enough to the Jews to make them suspicious of all reforms. Between 1796 and 1825 a series of high-ranking officials and committees all concluded that Jewish reform under government order was necessary. They also agreed essentially on the direction it ought to take. Two high officials, I. G. Frizel, a general and former governor of Lithuania, and the conservative nobleman and noted poet G. R. Derzhavin presented reports on the Jews in 1800. The ex-general's report was in places sympathetic while the poet was consistently hostile. Both wished to banish the Jews from the liquor trade, abolish their autonomy, and require them to change their traditional garb as well as the education of their children. Derzhavin even credited

---

[5] Jacob Lestschinsky, *Dos Idishe Folk in Tsiffern* (Yiddish; Berlin, 1922), chs. 4 and 5 and *passim*, which contains the faults and inaccuracies of a pioneer; John Doyle Klier, *Russia Gathers her Jews: The Origins of the 'Jewish Question' in Russia, 1772–1825* (DeKalb, Ill., 1986), 19, 55–6, 81; Salo W. Baron, *The Russian Jew under Tsars and Soviets* (New York, 1964). 76–84; Mahler, *Divrey Yemey Yisrael*, 16–18, estimates 1 m. Russian Jews in 1818 and 1.75 m. in 1851, besides Poland. Michael Stanislawski, *Tsar Nicholas I and the Jews: The Transformation of Jewish Society in Russia, 1825–1855* (Philadelphia, 1983), 160–70, stresses the difficulties of obtaining reliable figures.

the blood libel, blaming it on individual fanatics whom the Jewish community allegedly shielded. Perhaps influenced by physiocratic doctrines, he advocated that the Jewish population be divided into fixed proportions of farmers, merchants, and craftsmen. Derzhavin and Frizel proposed to make Jews productive by encouraging craftsmen and by colonizing them as farmers in underpopulated southern areas. Innkeepers, distillers, and petty traders, a 'useless' and 'harmful' sector of the Jewish population, were to be forced or encouraged to change occupations.[6] Major reforms were embodied in the decree of 1804, which barred Jews from leasing land, keeping inns, or selling liquor. This policy, with halts and pauses, in the long term succeeded in driving the Jews out of the countryside, with the exception of Jewish rural colonists who had settled with government endorsement.

Significant for future co-operation between the Russian regime and Jewish enlighteners, Derzhavin enjoyed the collaboration of two pioneer Russian *maskilim*, Nota Notkin and a physician, Dr Ilya Frank, in drawing up his report. They endorsed much of his critique of Jewish life and proposed some of the reforms which Derzhavin put in his programme, mainly in education.[7] Their critique of Russian Jewish life and reform proposals was in the spirit of the Berlin Haskalah and western enlightened absolutism. In Russia's serf society, Haskalah conceptions imported from the west were to be applied to a deeply traditional Jewish community which was unready for change. When Haskalah ideas were taken up by the government, they were applied in an arbitrary and often ruthless manner which indifferently disregarded Jewish opinion.

Arbitrariness also characterized the proposals of tsarist Russia's first liberal movement, the secret, ill-fated Decembrist group of young army officers, formed about 1816. They conceived of rights and equality within a unitary Russian state where all ethnic and national minorities would have to assimilate completely. Like everyone else the Jews too would receive rights and their autonomous cultural and communal life

[6] Klier, *Russia Gathers her Jews*; S. Ettinger, 'The Statute of 1804' (Hebrew) *Beyn Russiya u-Polin* (Hebrew; Eng. title: *On the History of the Jews in Poland and Russia*) (Jerusalem, 1994), 234–56, including a translation of the statute; M. Minc, 'A Long Marginal Note on the Derzhavin Report in 1800' (Hebrew), *Israel and the Nations: Essays Presented in Honor of Shmuel Ettinger* (Hebrew; English title) (Jerusalem, 1987), 103–12.

[7] Klier, *Russia Gathers her Jews*, 86–115.

would be abolished. The Decembrists also endorsed a Jewish state in Asia Minor, perhaps for those who could not accept their drastic version of liberalism. But the movement, which included in its ranks one converted Jew, was crushed brutally by the newly enthroned Tsar Nicholas I.[8]

Sadness and Oppression under Nicholas I

A folk song, one of probably many, expressed tersely what the new tsar meant to the Jews:

> When Nicolas Pavlovich became tsar
> Jewish hearts filled with sadness . . . (*umetik gevoren*)[9]

A long train of edicts issued from this arch-autocratic militarist. They were supposed to reform the Jews and, unmentioned but suspected, to lure or drive them to the baptismal font of Russian Orthodoxy. For a start, Nicholas I expelled the Jews from one rural area in Lithuania, continued to bar Jews from Kiev, and limited the growth of Kurland Jewry in the Baltics. However, it was the edict of military conscription in 1827 which set the tone for the Jews under Nicholas I's regime. Military service itself was not new for Jews. They had been conscripts or volunteers in the French revolutionary armies and the Habsburg regime had applied conscription to them from the 1780s, without enthusiasm or outrage on their part. Russian conscription, however, was far more onerous than in other lands. There were widespread exemptions among the general population but numerical shortages were compensated for by serfs whom their lord drafted. The Jewish quota resembled the general population's, between four and eight per thousand taxed persons, but it was raised sharply during the tsar's last years and the Crimean War in

[8] Saul M. Ginsburg, 'Di Dekabristen un Iden', *Historishe Verk*, (3 vols., New York, 1937), i. 3–16; Hugh Seton-Watson, *The Russian Empire, 1801–1917* (Oxford, 1967), 183–98, on the movement generally.

[9] Quoted in Elias Tcherikover, 'The Jewish Masses, the *Maskilim* and the Regime in the Era of Nicholas I' (Hebrew), *Yehudim be-Itot Mahpekhah* (Hebrew; Jews in Revolutionary Times) (Tel Aviv, 1957), 107–26.

1854–5. There were exemptions for rabbis, members of merchant guilds, and pupils as well as graduates of Russian educational institutions. Volunteer substitutes were allowed, but practically no one volunteered. The term of service was twenty-five years from the age of 18, but thousands of adolescents or even children were conscripted, serving as 'cantonists' until their years of service began to count when they turned 18. Jewish soldiers were always sent far away from their families and communities, and were prevented from practising Judaism notwithstanding the religious freedom promised in the edict. As his private statements show, Nicholas I aimed explicitly at converting Jewish conscripts. The recruits had to take a formidable oath of absolute obedience to their superiors up to the tsar, and then swear that they took the oath with no mental reservations.[10] As soldiers they were plied with inducements or coerced to turn Christian. Most did so sooner or later, although there are also instances of youthful martyrdom.

Jewish parents employed every means to protect their children. Mutilation was practised, like amputating a finger or toes, or youngsters were enrolled in schools which would gain them exemption. Some crossed the border out of Russia. What outraged Jews nearly as much as conscription itself was *kahal* complicity in gathering recruits. Like their imperial master the *kahal* regarded conscription as a form of social control. Children from 'good' families well connected with the *kahal* were not taken, but the defenceless poor or nonconformist, 'undesirables', and juvenile delinquents in today's term, were taken. Without volunteers to go, the *kahal* had problems in finding manpower. The activities of many a *kahal* left undying bitterness among the Jewish masses. During the panic of Nicholas I's last years and the Crimean War Jewish *khappers* (literally, grabbers) were employed to seize youngsters and spirit them away. Streets and whole towns emptied when word came that *khappers* were on the prowl.

There are fair approximations but few exact figures of conscription. The large Minsk community together with several small ones nearby offered seventy potential conscripts in 1828. As summarized by Michael Stanislawski:

[10] The Hebrew text is in Hayyim Lieberman, *Ohel Raḥ'el*, iii (New York, 1984), 652–3. Its authorship is unknown.

Of these seventy, forty-one were over eighteen, but forty-four were either unmarried or living alone; thirty had no occupation, thirteen were listed as servants, three as beggars, three as unskilled laborers, and fourteen as tailors, tradesmen, or cobblers; forty-nine of the seventy were registered as living in the city, twelve were vagabonds, and eight were living in nearby villages.[11] Since most of the seventy possessed exemptions or fled, a new list of fifty-two was composed:

almost half were under eighteen, but only twenty-three lived alone; their occupational distribution was roughly the same as their predecessors, but now only twenty-four were listed as city dwellers, while the remaining twenty-eight were living in villages or were vagabonds.[12]

There and elsewhere the pattern of recruitment was clearly biased towards taking the poor, unmarried, and village Jews and vagabonds. Dreadful scenes were enacted. The Hebrew writer Judah Leib Levin, himself a privileged child, recalled how a young child was dragged from his house by six *khappers*, followed by his screaming mother who was roughly thrown aside, and trundled off in a carriage. He also recalled the departure by horse-drawn carriage of youngsters who had been conscripted:

[S]oldiers took the children out of the house one after the other and put them into the carriage until . . . they were squeezed and crammed like fish in a barrel. All around stood mothers and fathers and a great mass of people . . . Mothers and fathers were wailing bitterly, one of them giving a child a psalm book, another giving phylacteries, and so forth, 'Be a Jew!', 'Whatever happens, be a Jew!' Outcries like this and tears and groans are heard on every side.[13]

Stories of the fate of conscripted Jewish children are numerous in Hebrew and Yiddish literature. A few true instances are known where courageous men forcibly freed Jewish children awaiting transportation. Such a highly dangerous act won admiration but few imitators.[14]

[11] Stanislawski, *Tsar Nicholas I and the Jews*, 28–9.   [12] Ibid. 29.

[13] Yehuda Leib Levin, 'The Seized' Hebrew, 1904, in *Zikhronot ve-Hegyonot* (Hebrew: Memories and Reflections), ed. Y. Slutzky (Jerusalem, 1971), 30–5; quotation, p. 35.

[14] E. Tcherikover, 'The Jewish Masses', 111–14.

The most careful estimate is 70,000 Jewish conscripts from 1827 to 1854, after which the system was discontinued under the new Tsar Alexander II. Of these 50,000 were minors beneath 18. The majority of conscripts apparently became Christians. Very few survived a quarter-century as Russian soldiers and Jews, and few families ever saw their conscripted children again.[15] Conscription scarcely damaged Russian Jewry demographically since population was rising rapidly, but it left a lasting scar of communal class conflict and bitterness against the tsarist regime. Many other instances are known of *kahal* graft, cooked accounts or refusal to render accounts at all, and no satisfaction could be obtained from Russian officials.[16]

The tsar tightened the censorship of Hebrew and Yiddish books by commanding that they be printed nowhere but Zhitomir and Vilna, where the censors sat. Further laws fixed the definitive boundaries of the Pale of Settlement and the privileges of merchants of the first class. Jews were forced out of distilling and dispensing liquor in rural inns. Thousands who made this their living were expelled piecemeal from the countryside. The Jews were even required to change their traditional garb. Concerned over the problem of Jewish smuggling, the tsar ordered in 1843 the mass expulsion of Jews within 50 versts (33 miles) of the western border. Tens of thousands of Jews would have lost homes and livelihoods had the imperial command been enforced.

In the absence of substantial economic data, we may cite a memorandum on the disastrous effects of decades of these policies presented by Vilna Jewry to Sir Moses Montefiore when he visited in 1846. Although thirty-nine trades and crafts were listed which Jews practised, they could not make a living because they were driven out of one employment after another and had long-established dwellings taken from them on legal pretexts.

After these distractions came famine, with its massive harm. It touched every corner of the city and shook loose the last coin. Householders lost their businesses and gave up on trade. They hug themselves and consume their own flesh. The destitute poor who until now could eat the bread of charity now lie

---

[15] Ibid. 25, 194–95, no. 51, 52. This estimate appears better based than Baron's (*The Russian Jew*, 37). [16] Mahler, *Divrey Yemey Yisrael*, 116–22.

at street corners and plead for bread with no one to give it to them. They wait for death but it is long in coming. . . . Wherever one goes one sees dreadful sights of poverty and famine.[17]

The poverty of the Jews in a poor country was deepened by government policies. At the same time, several provincial governors reported the Jews too poor to pay any taxes, not to speak of repaying communal debts. A Polish noble describes abysmal Jewish poverty in his country during the early 1840s:

There is really no more miserable race under the sun than the Jewish people who live in our villages. It is sufficient to visit some of them . . . most of [the Jews] live twelve in a small room infected with pestilential air, dirty, half-naked, sleeping in beds suspended one above the other, struggling almost ceaselessly with hunger, sickness, and often with death, without any hope or salvation in this world except the faith deep in their hearts despite every misfortune.

The impoverished Polish peasant, he adds, at least has some food stored away and a few domestic animals, but the Jews have not even that.[18]

With a view to reforming the Jews, Nicholas I's regime continued Jewish agricultural colonization in the Ukraine (New Russia) which had begun under his predecessor from 1804 until 1810. Colonization also began in Siberia but was scuttled on Nicholas I's command after its opponents in the bureaucracy warned him that the Jews would infect that vast territory. Jewish colonists already in Siberia were transferred to the Ukraine. Government policy thereupon ceased encouraging colonization and instead ignored it. The first colonists between 1804 and 1811 had come unprepared and inexperienced, and lived in hunger under primitive conditions. They were given land and burdened with debt to pay for it, but received no training or aid. The 9,757 colonists of 1811 numbered only 3,657 in 1818 after perhaps 1,000 quit and 5,000 died of their hardships. The colonists of the 1820s had to accept the lowly status of peasant and could not employ Christian workers. During the 1830s

---

[17] 'Memorial of Vilna Community Leaders to Moses Montefiore' (Hebrew), in Ginsburg, *Historishe Verk*, ii. 293–8.

[18] Quoted in Mahler, *Divrey Yemey Yisrael*, 183; many more examples are given on 43–8.

and 1840s more Jews turned again to agriculture in the south, and still larger numbers settled when Jewish colonization was allowed in White Russia. True to the tsar's principles, the colonies' regime was one of implacable discipline. Jews were ordered about in military fashion, could not leave, and might be flogged for laziness or disobedience at the whim of their supervisors, who were former army officers. On the other hand, the Jewish peasants and their sons were exempt from conscription. In 1860 the number of Jewish colonists stood at 32,000 in White Russia and 28,000 in the Ukraine, besides a few thousand in Poland. In general the Jewish farms were too small to support a family at a minimal standard and material conditions were miserable. The colonies' population growth lagged far behind that of the Jewish population as a whole.

Settling the barely inhabited Ukraine was not the only purpose of the agricultural project. Russian officials and *maskilim* were certain that making Jews tillers of the soil would reform them fundamentally. Belief in the moral virtue of working the soil has a continuous history extending from the early Haskalah to Zionist colonization. The tsarist project was a link in this chain, one distinguished for its habitual brutality and disregard of colonists' basic needs. Russian Jewry, including the ardently favourable *maskilim*, took little notice of the Jewish farmers, who in any case lived in remote and barely accessible places.[19]

After the despotic rule of conscription and quotas and conversion, the emphasis in the second half of Nicholas I's reign changed from force to persuasion and extensive use of carrot and stick—privileges for individuals in return for their Russification. The tsar became persuaded by Count Kiselev's report that the Jews, who had withstood centuries of oppression, were not being reformed by the severe measures taken to date. From 1840 approximately the regime turned to reforming Jewish life from within. A new, relatively milder policy proposed to refashion Jewish children's education in collaboration with Jews who realized the need for it, namely *maskilim*. Thus came about the momentous link between the tsarist regime and the Russian Haskalah, the Jewish Enlightenment.

[19] Stanislawski, *Tsar Nicholas I and the Jews*, 39–40, 166–7; a general account is Mordechai (Marcus) Levin, *'Erkhey Hevrah ve-Kalkalah shel Tekufat ha-Haskalah* (Hebrew; Social and Economic Values during the Haskalah Era) (Jerusalem, 1975), 187–256.

Russian and Polish Jewish Enlightenment

The central ideas which guided the Russian Haskalah had been shaped a half-century earlier in Mendelssohn's Berlin and then in Galicia. The long-lived Haskalah in the Habsburg province of Galicia began a quarter-century later than in German lands. Major intellectual talents appeared there, notably the philosopher of Jewish history Nachman Krochmal, the only *maskil* of intellectual stature comparable to Mendelssohn, and his disciple Rabbi Solomon J. L Rapoport, at first a Hebrew writer and then a great scholar in the Science of Judaism. The literary efforts of the Galician *maskilim* specialized in satire, with the Hasidic life and practices of the majority of Galician Jews the target of Joseph Perl, Isaac Erter, and others. Modern culture in eastern European Jewry arrived indirectly via the German Haskalah and Galicia. Many early Russian *maskilim* studied in Germany or lived for a while in Galicia and imbibed Haskalah at its centres in Brody, Tarnopol, and Lemberg (Lwow). The Galician and later Russian Haskalah were also heavily indebted to earlier Jewish sources, such as the then forgotten or inaccessible medieval and Renaissance Hebrew poets and the rationalist philosophers, whom the Science of Judaism scholars were then unearthing.

The Russian Jewish community differed in fundamental ways from the west and the Russian Haskalah differed accordingly.[20] The number of Jews ruled by the tsars was vastly larger than in Germany or Galicia. The oppressive regime and *kahal* authority made individuals careful of what they said and wrote. Russian Jews lived outside Russian culture and society without non-Jewish cultural stimuli or intellectual links until later in the nineteenth century. Polish Jews, however, were less enclosed, and even before the end of the eighteenth century some of them,

---

[20] Most writing on the Russian Haskalah has treated it in literary terms. Exceptions are Stanislawski, *Tsar Nicholas I and the Jews*, chs. 3 and 4; Steven J. Zipperstein, *The Jews of Odessa: A Cultural History, 1794–1881* (Stanford, Calif., 1985), chs., 2, 3, 4; Raphael Mahler, *Hasidism and the Jewish Enlightenment* (Philadelphia, 1985); Eli Lederhendler, *The Road to Modern Jewish Politics: Political Tradition and Political Reconstruction in the Jewish Community of Tsarist Russia* (New York, 1989), chs. 4 and 5.

mainly among the new bourgeoisie in Warsaw, were immersed in Polish culture. Decades before the issue of schools arose in Russia, several Polish Jewish schools were established by private initiative, first in Warsaw in 1806 and later in Lublin and elsewhere in Congress Poland.[21] Although Polish Jewish schools were not opened in smaller cities and villages, their development illustrates the freer field of operation of Haskalah in Russian Poland when compared with Russia. The new Polish Jewish schools taught at first in German and followed the German pattern, teaching only morsels of the biblical text and no Talmud. The schools' sponsors sought to replace German with Polish, but after 1839 they were pressured into Russification instead. The schools earned the opposition of the Orthodox, who held fast to their *hadarim*. During the 1830s, thanks to moderate *maskilim*, a compromise with the Orthodox was reached in 1835 by which the schools began to teach Bible texts and cultivated a religious atmosphere. However, outside Warsaw and even within it the masses continued to send their children to *hadarim*, where they had teachers who avoided government teachers' tests which they probably could not pass. The Orthodox masses and their leaders resisted the new education with greater vigour than they had in Germany, where their numbers were much fewer.

The Russian Haskalah's programme was stated with the extreme caution required for dealing with the intensely traditionalist Russian Jewish community. Thus the justification for secular study, which was the foremost demand, was originally put in terms of its value for sacred purposes. *Maskilim* argued that secular study brought better understanding of the sacred literature. In fact numerous Jews including rabbis, especially in Lithuania, dabbled in secular studies for such reasons. The *maskilim*, however, had deeper interest in secular study than using it as a tool of rabbinic studies. Another argument of the *maskilim* was that the nations looked down on the Jews as intellectually debased. Mastery of the modern arts and sciences was needed in order to redeem Jewish honour. Actually the *maskilim* desired to refashion the Jews as a modern

[21] Jacob Shatzky, *Yidishe Bildungs-politik in Poyln fun 1806 biz 1866* (New York, 1943), is the standard study; also Sabina Levin, *Chapters in the History of Jewish Education in Poland: In the Nineteenth and Early Twentieth Centuries* (Hebrew; English abstract) (Tel Aviv, 1997).

European people, and to have Judaism become a recognized European culture.

The few *maskilim* in Russia before the 1840s felt oppressed by their isolation in the towns where they were scattered. The foremost early *maskil*, Isaac Ber Levinsohn, lived and studied among Galician *maskilim* but spent his adult years in his native town of Kamerets-Podolsk in the south, sick and lonely. Levinsohn set forth the tenets of Russian Haskalah with constant reference to precedents in the Talmud and the lives of rabbinic sages, in order to show that the ways of Haskalah were historically and religiously valid. Thus his argument for learning Russian and Polish draws on the record of the ancient Jews. Even after they ceased speaking Hebrew, they spoke and composed religious literature in the languages of their surroundings, such as Greek. Contemporary Jews should therefore abandon Yiddish, in the Haskalah view a debased dialect, and use proper Russian or Polish. As to profane studies, Levinsohn readily demonstrated with extensive citations that the sages of the past, including the authors of the Talmud, mastered natural sciences, mathematics, and medicine: 'You should know, dear reader, that every body of knowledge on earth, great or small, is very necessary and essential to man. Therefore he should endeavour to learn and to know them, since there is no wisdom or knowledge for which there is not some use.' One should not be satisfied only with the knowledge that even the greatest forerunners possessed: 'Our ancestors were vast in knowledge, meaning as far as knowledge went in those days. Even though we must not be satisfied only with that, we have mentioned it everywhere for a certain reason, and the thoughtful person will understand', presumably, that the achievements of past sages were being cited in order to persuade the pious. Contemporary inquiry, however, should range beyond what they had studied. Levinsohn showed that the ancients avoided commerce, practised crafts, and lived on the land, obviously meaning that their ways should set the example for Russian Jews. He waxed lyrical when advocating agricultural life for Jews. Haskalah ideology, however, took no notice of weighty economic and social factors which made their proposals pointless.[22]

---

[22] The quotations are from Levinsohn's *Te'udah be-Yisrael* (1828), cited in Israel Zinberg, *Toldot Sifrut Yisrael* (Hebrew; History of Jewish Literature), vi (Tel Aviv, 1960), 173–5.

Only in Vilna and Berdichev were there even small concentrations of *maskilim*. Their demonstrative loyalty to the regime was not simply traditional Jewish fidelity to the ruler but stemmed from their confidence that the Russian government's goal of reforming and enlightening the Jews resembled their own. Backing by the regime would empower the *maskilim* to override community opposition and carry out their programme. Thus they found little fault with conscription, seeing in it a praiseworthy means of integrating the Jews into Russian life which would lead to equality.[23] Isaac Ber Levinsohn was the exception. He saw what conscription really meant, realized the oppressiveness of the *kahal* regime which enforced it, and wrote an indignant, anonymous work about it in Yiddish, *Hefker Velt* (Wanton World).

Secular studies and gaining a place for Judaism in European culture did not exhaust Haskalah interests. The most fervent ardour was bestowed upon the Hebrew language, not only as the language of the holy books but as an object of study itself. The great medieval language scholars were restudied as Hebrew grammatical correctness and elegant, often stilted diction became *maskilic* hallmarks. Out of Haskalah Hebraism a galaxy of Hebrew writers created modern Hebrew literature, while from the Yiddish stories and tracts which *maskilim* produced for common people came modern Yiddish literature. Literary efforts were expressed in the new Hebrew press, which began in 1841 with the short-lived *Pirhei Tsafon* (Flowers of the North). The stable Hebrew press began in 1856 with the weekly *Ha-Maggid*, published just over the border in Lyck, East Prussia. Notwithstanding this uncensored location it was a very conservative journal, more so than its contemporary *Ha-Meliz*, published in Odessa and later St Petersburg three times weekly. In Warsaw *Ha-Zefirah* was a sometimes daily third journal. Its publisher, Hayyim Zelig Slonimsky, was a long-lived, self-taught mathematician and astronomer of original accomplishments who remained a fully Orthodox Jew and enjoyed the admiration of the Orthodox public. When the Russified Jewish public grew large enough, a series of noteworthy Jewish journals began to appear in Russian, beginning in 1860 with *Raszvet* (The Dawn) in 1860–1 and continuing with *Den'* (The Day)

[23] e.g. I. M. Dick, in Mahler, *Hasidism and the Jewish Enlightenment*, Suppl. C, 283–4; generally, E. Tcherikower, 'The Jewish Masses', 107–27.

in Odessa a decade later.[24] These periodicals provided a platform for discussion, circumspect though it had to be, from which an active Jewish public opinion grew up in eastern Europe.

Before the late 1860s the *maskilim* in Russia, unlike the Galician Haskalah satirists, cautiously limited their criticism of religious life to deprecating the lack of synagogue decorum and the prevalence of customs of dubious or kabbalistic origin. Well aware of the Jewish masses' fervent Orthodoxy and anxious not to antagonize unduly the rabbinical leaders, the *maskilim* long avoided the subject of religious change. In Vilna they had a 'model' congregation of their own which was not notable for its members' piety. Opponents of the Haskalah held the Berlin Haskalah responsible for contemporary German Jewish assimilation and Reform Judaism. Russian Haskalah uncurbed would lead to the same result, they warned.

Educational reform was the great ambition of *maskilim*. They yearned to banish the shabby *hadarim* in the teachers' dwellings and replace them with graded elementary schools where Bible and Hebrew language, but not Talmud, would be prominent in the curriculum. Still more important, arithmetic and a foreign language—German at first but later Russian—would be taught. The teachers should not be incompetent *heder* schoolmasters, the butt of *maskilic* ridicule, but proper teachers. Many poverty-stricken *maskilim* desired employment as these modern teachers, and some succeeded. A few modern Jewish schools existed in Russia before 1840, notably in Odessa and Vilna.

The Regime and the Reform of Jewish Education

The entrance of the Russian regime into the sphere of Jewish education excited the *maskilim*. Its lack of interest in educating the illiterate Russian masses might have made the regime's concern with educating the

[24] Yehuda Slutzky, *Ha-Itonut ha-Yehudit-Russit ba-Me'ah ha-Tesha `Esreh* (Hebrew: The Russian Jewish Press in the Nineteenth Century) (Jerusalem, 1970) is comprehensive; Alexander Orbach, *New Voices of Russian Jewry* (Leiden, 1980) deals with Odessa, a major publishing centre; Moshe Perlmann, '*Razsvet* 1860–61: the Origin of the Russian-Jewish Press', *Jewish Social Studies*, 24 (1962), 162–82.

Jews, who possessed a comparatively high literacy rate, appear all the more suspect. Many pious Jews saw the project as another conversionist device. Conversion to Christianity was welcomed by the regime, to be sure, but the main purpose was to Russify the Jews by teaching them the Russian language and secular studies. Studying the Talmud, regarded as the source of Jewish 'superstition' and separatism, was strongly discouraged. The reforming project was undertaken seriously under the direction of Uvarov, the minister of education, who stood for enlightenment joined to autocracy. As he put it, 'the education of our people [must] be conducted, according to the Supreme intention of our August Monarch, in the joint spirit of Orthodoxy, autocracy and nationality.'[25] Realizing nevertheless that he needed Jewish collaborators, Uvarov turned to the *maskilim*, whose educational ideas had much in common with those of the government but without its conversionist bias. Educational reform under government sponsorship transformed the *maskilim*, who alone could do little to advance their programme, from a powerless group into an important force. Uvarov's central Jewish figure, however, was not a Russian *maskil* but a modern orthodox German rabbi aged 26, Max Lilienthal.[26] He was heading a reformed Jewish school in Riga, a modern, Germanic Jewish community in Latvia within Russia, when he was brought to St Petersburg by Uvarov. Thus there was some recognition of Jewish public opinion even under the autocracy. Lilienthal's task was to explain to the Jews the need and religious legitimacy of the government's programme to establish modern schools for their children. They would be financed by a Jewish tax on Sabbath candles.

Lilienthal made two trips to meet Russian Jews and their leaders. On the first he spoke to audiences in Vilna and Minsk. The Vilna leaders were polite and cautious, but neither they nor later audiences were much impressed by the young rabbi, whom they regarded as naïve and lacking the learning of a true rabbi. The reception in Minsk was disorderly, led by the *heder* teachers whose livelihoods were at stake. In

---

[25] Quoted in Nicholas V. Riasanovsky, *A Parting of the Ways: Government and the Educated Public in Russia* (Oxford, 1976), 107–8.

[26] Excellent accounts are Stanislawski, *Tsar Nicholas I and the Jews*, 59–96 and *passim*; E. Etkes, '"Compulsory Enlightenment" as a Crossroads in the History of the Haskalah Movement in Russia' (Hebrew; English summary), *Zion*, 63 (1978), 264–313.

both places crowds of plain people met him with cries, 'We don't want schools!', employing the Russian *shkole* to emphasize what they meant. The newcomer produced a tract, *Maggid Yeshuah* (Proclaiming Salvation), which a prominent *maskil*, Sh. J. Fin, translated into Hebrew. There Lilienthal reiterated his arguments for secular education: the tsar genuinely sought the Jews' welfare, secular education was economically advantageous, and no religious harm would come of it. Less amiably, he cautioned that the government would proceed with its educational plans and would brook no opposition nor insults to himself. Severe punishment awaited hostile words or acts. His journeys were meant only to explain, not to convince nor to gain approval. Lilienthal made a second swing through eighteen larger communities in 1842, escorted by police whose presence no doubt muffled open opposition. Uvarov established an Imperial Commission for the Education of the Jews of Russia for the 'swift implementation of the goals of the government'. Supposedly a commission of rabbis, its Jewish members included also a *maskilic* educator, a traditionalist financier, Lilienthal, and two distinguished rabbis. They were the Hasidic rebbe of the Lubavich dynasty, opposed to any change, and Rabbi Yizhak of the Volozhin yeshiva, a recognized rabbinic leader of Lithuanian Jewry. His attitude to secular studies was believed to be moderate, especially after Lilienthal reportedly warned him privately that Nicholas I would act with great severity, perhaps employing mass expulsions, if the Jews opposed his educational policy. Little of the proceedings of the commission in 1843 is known and the 'Imperial Commission' never came into existence. It is clear, however, that the rabbis were unable to prevent the reform which was decreed in the law of 1844. Under its terms there was to be a network of Jewish primary and secondary schools and a rabbinical seminary, all supported by special taxes on the Jews. The *heder* and its teachers had to be licensed and supervised by government inspectors. The educational code's opening struck at the heart of Jewish life and faith: 'The goal of the education of the Jews consists in their gradual rapprochement with the Christian population and in the eradication of the superstitions and harmful prejudices instilled by the study of the Talmud.' The curriculum of the schools, including the rabbinical seminaries, contained literary, scientific, and technical studies which Christians could also teach.

The directors of the system had to be Christians. Pupils and graduates received prolonged draft exemptions.

Hardly had the law been placed on the books when Lilienthal abruptly left Russia, returned to Germany, and soon left for America with his bride. There he presently left Orthodoxy and became a prominent Reform rabbi. Lilienthal left behind few admirers in Russia among either traditionalists or *maskilim*, but the schools which he promoted blossomed. By the close of Nicholas I's reign in 1855 their estimated number ranged from 62 to 103; Stanislawski lists 71 known schools with 3,300 to 3,700 pupils, apparently all boys. This was the onset of Russian culture among the mass of Jews of Russia.

Continuity of Traditional Life

The policy of outright coercion was by no means abandoned. Jewish autonomy and the *kahal* which exemplified it were abolished in 1844. After *kahal* collaboration with conscription and its oligarchs' use of tax powers to their private advantage, few mourned the *kahal*'s demise. Yet Jewish autonomy continued to a significant extent but under the closer control of local Russian officials. Jewish taxes continued to be a collective obligation, but after 1844 their collection was placed in the hands of a *sborshchik*, usually a wealthy and aggressive Jew recognized by the government, with his Jewish assistants. They were widely disliked for using their practically unlimited power unjustly. The *sborshchik*'s authority was implied by the widespread application to him of the traditional title *Rosh ha-Kahal*, head of the community. Even more detested was the 'starosta' who controlled the selection of Jewish conscripts and, as noted above, was less than scrupulous in his selections. The abuses of this post-autonomy regime were pilloried in contemporary Hebrew and Yiddish fiction, notably by Mendele Mokher Seforim.

Unlike community administration, rabbinic tribunals (*batei din*) had a reputation for fairness and promptness. Besides Jews who resorted to them, many Russians preferred *batei din* to their civil courts. Within the Jewish communities, mainly in Lithuania and White Russia, elected 'deputaty' gave some appearance of popular control, but their actual authority was slight. Yet important new communities like Odessa and St Petersburg conducted their affairs without an oligarchic cabal or 'deputaty'. Only a few of the wide variations in communal governance have been investigated. What finally curbed local Jewish potentates was the reform of 1863 which ended collective responsibility for Jewish tax payments, and the conscription act of 1874 which made young men individually responsible.[27]

The age of Nicholas I was still a period, indeed the last, when traditional religious life went on without serious challenge from dissenting voices within the Jewish community. Except for the fear they aroused the Russian regime's decrees and its heavy-handed support of Russifying and modernizing trends had little effect on traditional religious life. Rabbinic culture maintained a high level of development. Many of the rabbis who served local communities achieved renown by producing notable works of learning, while other rabbinic scholars were private persons not holding official positions. Compared with the richness and inbred assurance of traditional rabbinic literature, the *maskilic* voice of dissent was still tentative and ambivalent. The various genres of rabbinic literature, such as responsa, commentaries, and novellae, flourished. There were rabbis like Joseph Saul Nathanson of Lemberg and Isaac Elhanan Spektor of Kovno who produced responsa which attained classic status as solutions to knotty halakhic problems. Of special interest was the Lithuanian school of editors and commentators on the long neglected Palestinian Talmud (Talmud Yerushalmi), inspired by the precedent of the Gaon of Vilna.[28] Bible commentary, like the Bible itself not much emphasized in eastern Europe, was nevertheless represented by the rationalist, grammatical, and voluminous *Ha-Torah veha-Mizvah*, composed by Meir Leibush Malbim. One of his express purposes was to refute Reform Judaism's teachings on the Bible. Naftali Zvi Yehudah Berlin as head of the Volozhin yeshiva (see below) delivered discourses on each week's Pentateuch reading, out of which his valuable commentary, *Ha'amek Davan*, emerged in addition to more customary rabbinic works.

---

[27] A survey is Azriel Shochat, 'Leadership of the Jewish Communities in Russia after the Abolition of the "Kahal"' (Hebrew) *Zion*, 42 (1977), 143–233.

[28] Louis Ginzberg, *A Commentary on the Palestinian Talmud* (Hebrew), (3 vols., New York, 1941), i., pp. lv–lxiv, 124–32 (Hebrew and English introductions).

In the eyes of the regime these traditional rabbis were merely the assistant rabbis of their communities, since the government wanted rabbis with Russian education to function as registrars of vital records and even to report on unrest within their communities. No rabbi qualified and none desired such a position. When governmentally sponsored rabbinical schools opened in 1844 in Vilna and Zhitomir, their directors and teachers of general studies were Christians, while *maskilim* were the little respected instructors in sacred literature. The government insisted on recognizing only these seminaries' graduates as 'Crown rabbis'. The Jewish communities, however, avoided them as lacking piety and learning and would not consider them true rabbis. Some later 'Crown rabbis', however, were devoted spokesmen for Jewish interests, but the schools failed of their purpose. The students were drawn from the poorest classes and were more interested in studying Russian and qualifying for university admission than rabbinical education. In Warsaw there was also a privately maintained rabbinical seminary. Its graduates were likewise unacceptable as rabbis to Jewish communities, but in any case most of them used their education to obtain white-collar positions in Warsaw's fast-growing commercial sector. The Russian authorities found they were really training Russian Jewish intellectuals and from the late 1860s, nests of revolutionary activists. In 1873 the government abruptly closed down the rabbinical seminaries.[29]

An important and altogether different educational framework was the yeshiva, supported by small donations throughout the Pale of Settlement.[30] The first yeshiva at Volozhin near Kovno opened in 1803. The term 'yeshiva' is ancient, but Volozhin was a new model since it was not a transient group of one local rabbi's students, as European yeshivot had long been, but a self-perpetuating school. Volozhin's enrolment of about 300 older adolescents and young men occupied themselves solely with intensive study of the Talmud. Individual study and even the student's own selection of the tractate he would study were the essence

[29] Azriel Shochat, *The 'Crown Rabbinate' in Russia: A Chapter in the Cultural Struggle between Orthodox Jews and 'Maskilim'* (English title; Hebrew with English summary) (Haifa, 1978).
[30] An important study is Saul Stampfer, *Ha-Yeshiva ha-Litaït be-Hithavutah* (Hebrew; The Development of the Lithuanian Yeshiva) (Jerusalem, 1995).

of the yeshiva's system. Great rabbis taught at the Volozhin yeshiva, including the founder Hayyim of Volozhin, Naftali Zvi Judah Berlin, its head for forty years, and Joseph Baer Soloveichik and his son Hayyim. The *élan* of the yeshiva was seen in its student body's pride in the world eminence of many of the rabbis who taught them, and the awareness that studying at Volozhin was a recognized distinction. The students were able to keep out or even hounded out of the yeshiva rabbis who they felt did not measure up to these standards. Yet the rabbis' lectures did not require attendance! Volozhin and later yeshivot neither trained professional rabbis nor conferred ordination but existed only for Talmud study which, to be sure, was the basic requirement for a rabbi. Sabbaths and holidays and daily prayers were of course observed at Volozhin, but even they were less emphasized than Talmud study. To acquire rabbinic ordination a student presented himself to one of Volozhin's rabbis, or a rabbi elsewhere, who tested and certified him privately. It was highly informal.

Changes came about in the yeshiva world, particularly under the influence of Rabbi Israel Salanter's *mussar* ethical movement.[31] A distinguished, individualistic Lithuanian scholar, Salanter sought to make the systematic study of ethical literature and ethical reflection subjects for adult Jewish laymen. To many *mussar* advocates, including Salanter himself, this study was the antidote to Haskalah and a corrective for moral shortcomings in communities. However, very few laymen took an interest in *mussar* study. It made headway only in some yeshivot later in the century, and even there often encountered strong resistance. The self-absorbed, unworldly 'mussarnik' was widely regarded with disapproval in pious circles. Salanter's own writings included astonishing, almost Freudian insights into the unconscious forces which controlled human behaviour. He lived for many years in Germany and France and was received respectfully wherever he went, but the *mussar* movement which he founded remained confined to eastern Europe, largely in yeshivot.

---

[31] The best work is Immanuel Etkes, *Rabbi Israel Salanter and the Mussar Movement: Seeking the Torah of Truth* (Philadelphia and Jerusalem, 1993); also Hillel Goldberg, *Israel Salanter* (New York, 1982). Still useful is the essay of 1906 by the great Talmud scholar Louis Ginzberg, who grew up in the *mussar* atmosphere: 'Rabbi Israel Salanter', *Students, Scholars, and Saints* (Philadelphia, 1928), 145–94.

Haskalah before the 1860s reached only inquiring students and an educated middle class, while Hasidism, which the *maskilim* detested, attracted the masses of all social levels. Hasidic Judaism continued to make substantial gains, especially in central and southern Poland and the Ukraine. Yeshivot and *mussar* were for the élite, but the masses, especially Galician, Podolian, and Ukrainian Jewry, sought guidance and inspiration from Hasidic *zaddikim*. The majority of Jews in those areas turned to Hasidic life. For Hasidism this was mainly a period of institutionalization. New houses of *zaddikim* were springing up while others withered or died out. After the first two generations of Hasidism, the principle of dynastic succession was accepted over that of selecting a suitable successor to the *zaddik* by elders among his followers. Yet the practice in central Poland of continuing to choose the successor to a *zaddik* by consensus of elders rather than by inheritance probably gave Hasidism in that region a more dynamic character. Dynastic succession did not necessarily avoid quarrels, since several sons frequently fought among themselves. It was quite usual for each of several sons to set up as a *zaddik*.[32]

As the Hasidic movement spread rapidly into Poland and the Ukraine, to a limited degree it developed regional characteristics.[33] Working among the relatively unlettered Jews of the Ukraine, *zaddikim* and their followers used aggressive methods, such as getting control of kosher meat income and installing religious functionaries loyal to them, in order to take over communities and advance their interests. These rebbes were men of comparatively little learning but were often supple and dynamic, aiding Jews and acquiring their allegiance. Some 'specialized' in working wonders, such as healing the sick and aiding infertile couples. The *zaddikim* settled in small towns, to which their followers in pre-railroad times might have to travel for days in order to spend holidays in their 'court'. Some rebbes, like that of Sadigora in Bukovina, lived regally to the dismay of *zaddikim* of the older generation, justifying their lifestyle as a foretaste of the messianic times to come. Some other

---

[32] Ada Rapoport-Albert, 'The Hasidic Movement after 1772: Structural Change and Continuity' (Hebrew; English summary) *Zion*, 55/2 (1990), 183–245.

[33] A. Z. Eshkoli, 'Ha-Hasidut be-Polin', *Beit Yisrael be-Polin*, ed. I. Halpern, ii (Jerusalem, 1954), 86–141.

zaddikim, however, led a threadbare existence.[34] Hasidism after approximately 1830 continued to boast arresting personalities, but its religious originality declined just when vast numbers of Jews, particularly from rural and village surroundings, became attracted to the movement. In Poland such men as R. Simha Bunim of Przysucha and R. Jacob Isaac the 'Seer' of Lublin and their intellectual heirs, who included the tragic recluse R. Mendel of Kotzk and R. Isaac Meir of Warsaw-Ger, led in new directions, characteristically expressed in striking aphorisms supported by rabbinic learning. R. Hayyim Halberstam of Sandz-Klausenberg in Galicia was a Talmudic scholar ranking with the foremost. Rabbis of communities in Hasidic territory, such as Solomon Kluger of Brody, usually got on with Hasidic rebbes who frequently consulted them on halakhic questions. In time many Hasidic courts established a yeshiva on their premises, in which traditional study was combined with closeness to the *zaddik*. Hasidism became ultra-conservative in all things. As such it was unready to cope with the social and intellectual currents which gained momentum under the new tsar of the 'great reforms'.

Reform and Reaction under Alexander II

It is reported that when Nicholas I died 'there was light and joy amongst the Jews; they gathered secretly and drank toasts to life, to joy, be happy, be happy!'[35] Gone was the conception of Russia confronting revolutionary Europe and the stifling post-1848 censorship and political atmosphere.[36] Now opened the age of the Great Reforms. They were enacted during the first decade of the reign of Tsar Alexander II, who succeeded to the throne in 1855, in an atmosphere very different from his predecessor's. The new tsar's reforms gave Russia a judicial system, some local

[34] A very full picture of one of the most influential rebbes is David Assaf, *The Regal Way: The Life and Times of R. Israel of Ruzhin* (English title; in Hebrew) (Jerusalem, 1997). The techniques of Hasidic expansion and dynastic 'imperialism' are set forth in the author's ' "The Causeless Hatred is Ongoing": The Struggle against Bratslav Hasidism in the 1860s', *Zion*, 54/4 (1994), 465–506.

[35] A. Liessin, cited in Tcherikower, 'The Jewish Masses', 116.

[36] Riasanovsky, *A Parting of the Ways*, 124, quoting the poet Tyutchev; Hugh Seton-Watson, *The Russian Empire, 1801–1917* (Oxford, 1967), 274–9.

self-government, and above all emancipated the mass of serfs in 1861. Each of these momentous changes was accomplished peacefully under autocracy, just when the similar issue of slavery brought upon the American democracy 'the mighty scourge of war', in Lincoln's phrase. The Russian Jews were not serfs and they could take part in local government (*zemstvo*) as employees and council members. Only a comparatively small number of Russian Jews benefited directly from the reforms. What was given them is puny when compared with the giant steps taken in Russian society at large.

Undoubtedly the change most welcomed by the Jews was the cessation in 1856 of the notorious Jewish conscription. Jewish youths were taken thenceforth in the same way as Russians, and from 1874 collective Jewish responsibility for supplying recruits ended. The government's conversionist policies were also toned down so that, for example, children under 14 could no longer convert without their parents' consent, and outright rewards for baptism ceased. Other changes mainly benefited the thin stratum of so-called 'useful' Russified middle-class Jews. Between 1859 and 1867 a series of decrees allowed substantial merchants ('of the first guild'), former soldiers, and holders of professional degrees the privilege of residing outside the Pale of Settlement. However, there were arbitrary legal interpretations, and if a privileged Jew changed his occupation he could be sent back to the Pale. The same could be done to the family of an ex-soldier when he died. The privileges thus carried little security except what a bribe could obtain.

Yet Alexander II's reign was a time of hope after the dark years of Nicholas I with their stream of persecuting edicts. Although the actual liberalization was small enough, the Jewish community became so confident of its future that there was serious talk of equality. Some liberal public figures favoured it, but the general view expressed even in the left-wing Russian press was not favourable. Although the Jews still bore their 'undesirable' hereditary and religious characteristics,[37] the class of Jews classified as 'useful' grew rapidly. The number of Jewish pupils

---

[37] This impression emerges from two Hebrew studies by S. Ettinger: 'The Ideological Background of Russian Antisemitic Literature' and 'The Image of the Jews in Russian Public Opinion until the 1880s', *Ha-Antishemiyut ba-Et ha-Hadashah* (Hebrew; Modern Anti-Semitism) (Tel Aviv, 1978), 99–144, 145–68.

receiving Russian education reached 8,000 in 1880, while Jewish university students, whose access was still unlimited, numbered about 600 by that time. Universities were staffed by liberal professors, among them some scientists of great distinction, who believed deeply that the advance of science was bound to liberalize the regime. For its part, the regime was anxious to keep out dangerous ideas and prescribed a heavily classical education. The universities, originally intended for the sons of privilege, produced a constantly growing number of rebels and radicals, some of whom were Jews.[38]

The Jewish proportion in secondary school enrolment, merely about 1 per cent in 1853, jumped to more than 13 per cent twenty years later, much higher than the Jewish proportion in the population. While the absolute figures were far less than those of Jews receiving traditional education or (more often than now realized) receiving no education at all, they were portents of coming times and recognized as such by contemporaries.

The economic development of Russia of course affected the Jews, but not always favourably. Rural overpopulation, especially after the emancipation of 1861, brought to the cities a constant flow of people who became servants and menial labourers.[39] Jews were among the first industrial entrepreneurs in textiles during the early nineteenth century, and later were prominent sugar, tea, and tobacco entrepreneurs. Even petroleum, which developed later, had Jewish entrepreneurs. Russia's railroads, requiring vast investment before any return could be realized, needed large imports of capital from western Europe. They were built mainly by Jewish contractors who borrowed from the western Jewish bankers. Samuel Poliakov typified Russia's Jewish railroad entrepreneurs, while three generations of Ginzburgs were major bankers as well as philanthropists who stood at the head of Russian Jewry. Yet the great majority of Russian Jews, like the Russian people, remained poor. Of the new industries only textiles employed Jewish workers in any numbers.

---

[38] Daniel R. Brower, *Training the Nihilists: Education and Radicalism in Tsarist Russia* (Ithaca, NY, 1975), 62–4, 113–14, 229 and *passim*; James C. McClelland, *Autocrats and Academics: Education, Culture and Society in Tsarist Russia* (Chicago/London, 1979).

[39] R. H. Rowland in Michael F. Hamm (ed.), *The City in Russian History* (Lexington, Ky., 1976), 119–21.

A very partial survey of 1851 showed that 91 per cent of the Jews were urban, a category which included small villages, and only 3.2 per cent worked the land. The respective proportions for the general population were the reverse: 6.8 per cent urban and 89.3 per cent on the land. Zhitomir, a larger town where the Jews constituted about one-quarter of the population, showed 39 per cent of the Jews as innkeepers and keepers of taverns, 25 per cent tradesmen and shopkeepers, 21 per cent craftsmen, 7 per cent servants, and 8 per cent simply destitute. Berdichev, another southerly city, was the centre of Jewish banking for a large surrounding area. Its 'Golden Street' was so called because it was lined with Jewish banks. Jewish dealers and merchants bought and sold agricultural produce, while craftsmen were mainly makers of garments and footwear. As very small producers they had poor training if any, and worked by unchanging, backward methods. Jewish masters seldom employed more than two workers. Jewish innkeepers and taverners, as we have seen, were being squeezed out by government policy.[40] The outlook was discouraging for the masses of petty Jewish tradesmen and craftsmen.

As a significant parallel to the Russian intellectual scene, the Haskalah in the 1860s became more radical. Institutions were unsparingly criticized as their usefulness and pragmatic value in improving the lot of the impoverished became the sole criteria of worth. Values of beauty and artistic merit were shunted aside by Russian intellectuals who turned their attention to the plight of the masses. A powerful current wished to feel at one with the common people, in their slogan 'going to the people' and sharing their lives and hardships. The Russified Jewish intelligentsia did not look to their own people but joined the movement out to the peasant villages. However, like their Russian comrades they were rejected by the peasants, frequently with curses on them as Jews. This new Jewish intelligentsia, educated in a Russian Jewish school and a Russian secondary school, numbered thousands by 1870. Their language was Russian and their Jewish education was minimal. They had

---

[40] A good summary is Benjamin Pinkus, *Yehudei Russiyah u-Berit ha-Mo'etsot: Toldot Mi'ut Le'umi* (Eng. title: *Russian and Soviet Jews: Annals of a National Minority* (Kiryat Sdeh Boker, 1986), 72–9; Baron, *The Russian Jew*, 97–118; Arcadius Kahan, 'Notes on Jewish Entrepreneurship in Tsarist Russia', *Essays in Jewish Economic and Social History* (Chicago, 1986), 82–100.

gone far beyond the original Haskalah programme of learning Russian and acquiring secular knowledge while remaining Hebraic modern Jews. That programme no longer meant anything to them. The new generation of intellectuals originating in the Haskalah divided into two extremes. There were Russifiers who besides despising Yiddish—a view common to *maskilim* of all kinds—also saw no reason to foster a Hebrew culture. To Russifiers, Haskalah Hebraism was merely a preparation for entry in Russian culture and, so they hoped, Russian society. A different Haskalah extreme was professed by Hebraist radicals who were sharply critical of traditional Jewish life, especially that of the small towns. Their religious critique verged on secularism. This group included men of a somewhat earlier period, like the poets 'Adam ha-Kohen' Levinson and his son Micah Joseph who died aged 24, and the writer A. B. Gottlober. The central figures were Judah Leib (Leon) Gordon, the foremost Haskalah poet, whose Hebrew poetry expressed stinging, ironic hostility to traditional Jewish life, and Peretz Smolenskin, who moved to Vienna where he published his much-read radical journal *Ha-Shahar* (The Dawn) and viewed Russian Jewish life negatively. Moshe Leib Lilienblum, who remained in Russia, bitterly critcized the education which had led him as a Talmud prodigy to a dead end, unable to find a place in general society. He demanded extensive religious and educational reforms. Gordon, Lilienblum, and especially Smolenskin, observing during the late 1870s the erosion of old and new Jewish culture and values by Russification, questioned the viability of Hebrew letters and the entire Haskalah programme. Gordon put his views in verse, while Lilienblum and Smolenskin wrote influential articles. Once enthusiastic for the enlightened Russian Jewish life which seemed to be forming during the 1860s, they now reversed themselves. Smolenskin condemned Haskalah and even its revered hero Moses Mendelssohn. For men like him the path to Jewish nationalism lay open.[41]

There were not only literary and ideological reasons for the changes in Haskalah mood. By the later 1860s the years of reform were over. The

---

[41] Michael Stanislawski, *For Whom Do I Toil? Judah Leib Gordon and the Crisis of Russian Jewry* (New York, 1988), is an excellent discussion; chapters in *Ha-Dat veha-Hayyim* (Hebrew; The East European Jewish Enlightenment), ed. I. Etkes (Jerusalem, 1993), are useful.

Polish rebellion of 1863, in which but few Jews took part, stimulated autocratic and Russifying reaction. Polish Jewish schools in Warsaw and elsewhere were compelled to switch to Russian. Articulate trends in Russian public opinion showed that they feared rather than welcomed a large number of Jews immersed in Russian culture, since they considered the Jews aliens who could never really be Russians. The regime was dissatisfied that its favours to the Jews had not led to their complete Russification, while the Jews realized that their earlier optimistic expectations of steady progress towards equality were an illusion. Russian reaction and Jewish social and ideological ferment after 1881 were the consequences of the impossibility of reconciling reform with autocracy, and of fostering hope and then thwarting it.

7

Outposts

Up to this point in chronology—about the 1870s—our study has been dominated by European Jewry. This should not be surprising. Well before the 1870s Europe, mainly western Europe, exercised world-wide economic and political domination. Also during this period the number of European Ashkenazim, who constituted about half the Jewish people about 1650, multiplied especially in eastern Europe. They became numerically predominant by far and continued to increase until the Holocaust. While most of the New World's original Jewish settlers were of Sefardic origin, Ashkenazim also took part in founding these distant Jewish settlements which spread European influence. Their majority in the New World increased steadily, especially in North America. By the middle of the nineteenth century Jewish outposts existed in what had been wild or unsettled territories not long before not only in the Americas but also in southern Africa and Australia. By the beginning of the twentieth century the outposts' geographic isolation was ending as telegraphy and steamships drew the New World into world commerce and international affairs. The old Jewish world began to hear more from the new as it moved from the margin into the centre of world as well as Jewish affairs, with the United States of America obviously taking the leading role. Oriental lands on the eastern Mediterranean coast benefited similarly from modern transport and communication. Landlocked territories, however, deep in the Balkans or east of the Mediterranean basin, took still longer to shed their isolation.

At the same time as these new outposts were being established the parity of oriental and Ashkenazic Jews at the onset of modern times slipped away. Sefardic and oriental Jewry's distinguished, colourful culture added little new lustre. Their numbers remained almost stationary and their economic functions diminished within the almost static economies of the countries where they lived. For example, they were no longer the commercial go-betweens and interpreters between Ottoman lands and Europe as they had been until approximately 1700. That role was taken over mainly by Greeks and Armenians. However, when the European powers' political and economic influence in oriental countries steadily increased from the early nineteenth century, oriental Jews began to come under the protection and patronage of emancipated western Jewry, but the absence of an Enlightenment and substantial development in the arts and sciences in their countries denied them the sort of cultural opportunities which western Jewry profitably exploited.

The Jews of the Ottoman empire, including Greece before it became independent in 1830, numbered 150,000 in the middle of the nineteenth century. An eloquent, detailed report on their contemporary condition came from the Viennese physician, poet, and community leader Ludwig August Frankl after his lengthy tour in Greece, Turkey, and Palestine in 1852. He found the Jews impoverished, culturally far beneath what they had once been. Like other religious and ethnic minorities they lived within the *millet* system, exercising autonomy under the governance of their religious leaders. Frequently, however, some rich, well-connected notable functioned as a local despot. In the blood-stained Ottoman palace putsch of 1826 when the domineering military corps of janissaries was abolished, the dominant Jewish family which was closely connected with them was put to death and its wealth confiscated. Security of life was subject to the whims of a sultan or pasha. Elsewhere in the sultan's capital city its 38,400 Jews lived in abject poverty in four neighbourhoods, besides probably several hundred foreign Jewish subjects and about 250 Karaites. Constantinople Jewry had numerous synagogues, some of them centuries old and reflecting the grandeur of better times. The livelihoods of most Constantinople Jews in the nineteenth century came mostly from an assortment of crafts, somewhat oddly distributed, including 1,000 bookbinders, 500 each of musicians, physicians, and tailors, 200 distillers, 180 dyers, and ten rope dancers. There were two Jewish courts and chief rabbis to preside over each. Besides keeping vital and tax records the chief rabbis possessed the power to impose punishments. As to the community itself, revenue came from the kosher meat tax, in addition to a tax of 0.5 per cent on dowries, real estate purchases and the estates of childless persons. Deficits were covered by a special levy (*'arikha*) as needed.[1] Constantinople Jewry also took responsibility for the Jews of Jerusalem. After assuming the holy city's debts early in the eighteenth century it established the Committee of Officials for Eretz Israel in 1727 (or 1737), which received funds from the Diaspora and remitted them to Jerusalem. The Constantinople committee also intervened with the Sublime Porte on occasion. Obviously they had a decisive voice in many of Jerusalem Jewry's affairs until well into the nineteenth century when emancipated western Jewry assumed the lead.[2]

There were smaller Ottoman Jewish communities of 3,500 families, or about 20,000 persons, in Edirne (now Adrianople), Smyrna (Izmir) and Bursa, the first of them in Europe and the others in Asia Minor. Brussa (Bursa), with 1,542 souls in 376 families, dwelt in 204 houses. It boasted many craftsmen, especially silk spinners and weavers. The community had a chief rabbi, twelve Jews entitled 'sages' (*hakhamim*), and four community presidents. All this was destroyed by an earthquake in 1855, and Bursa did not return to its relative prosperity.[3] A community with a notable history under the Ottomans was Salonika with its 16,000 Jews. It constituted a large proportion of the city's total population but as elsewhere they were miserably poor and uneducated. They were reported to marry young and to suffer legal insecurity, not being allowed to bequeath possessions to their children.[4] The only truly Greek Jewish community was Chalcis on the island of Euboea, where there were 300 very poor descendants of Spanish exiles. The islands were in general the main habitation of Greek Jewry. Corfu had 4,000 Jews and Zante 2,000. Suggestive of Corfu's political orientation, its Jewish school taught boys Hebrew, Greek, and Italian.[5] On the other hand, the fidelity of the Greek Jews to Turkey during the Greek war of independence cost them dear. Many were killed in 1821 by Greek rebels.[6]

[1] Ludwig August Frankl, *The Jews in the East* (London, 1859; repr. 2 vols., London, 1975), 140 ff., 152 ff.

[2] Jacob Barnay, *The Jews in Palestine in the Eighteenth Century* (Tuscaloosa, Ala, 1976), 81–105.

[3] Frankl, *The Jews in the East*, i. 185 ff.

[4] Ibid. 188–9.   [5] Ibid. 5, 99–101.   [6] Ibid. 78.

A new age in the Ottoman empire began with the Tanzimat, the reform movement in government and society, which addressed itself also to the Jews' status. They were given equality in decrees of 1839 and 1856. The empire began to become a modern state when equality was enacted for all, as confirmed by the decree of 1869 which declared the equality of all persons regardless of religion. However, Turkey did not go down the road towards democracy until the Ottoman sultanate was finally deposed in 1909 and the empire began to break up. As a result of these profound changes all that remained after 1856 of Ottoman Jewish autonomy, the *millet*, was the continuance of Jewish courts for such family matters as inheritance and divorce. In terms resembling traditional Jewish leaders in other countries, one of the chief rabbis expressed to the Viennese visitor Dr Frankl his doubts over the recent emancipation. He was apprehensive of religious decay and neglect of religious observance. In Turkey, however, this happened far slower than in the west. The other progressive development was a modern school system conducted in French, established and maintained by the Alliance Israélite Universelle in Paris. Modern education had been urged ever since Crémieux's visit of 1840 in connection with the Damascus affair. Until the advent of Alliance schools children were educated under generally bad physical conditions by old-fashioned teachers, and the little they learned was Jewish studies exclusively. Very few advanced beyond mechanical reading and daily prayers. Turkish Jewry had to draw its rabbis from Palestine, and its modern intelligentsia was puny. In later years there were already Jewish medical students in Constantinople with special religious arrangements, and an excellent modern school under a French director.[7] French, not Turkish, became the tongue of educated Jews in place of Jewish languages until the 1920s approximately.

There were Jewish communities still further away from the Mediterranean hub. The most distant larger Jewish community was that of Iran, where an estimated 30,000 Jews lived at the opening of the nineteenth century and 50,000 at its end. Classified as ritually unclean and treated with constant contempt under Shia' rule, nineteenth-century Iranian Jewry, in the words of its recent historian, was 'an uninterrupted

[7] Ibid. 170–1.

sequence of persecution and oppression'.[8] The repeated interventions of emancipated Jewry and of benevolent diplomats had very little effect, but the founding of modern schools by the Alliance Israélite Universelle began to improve the cultural position of this ill-treated community. On the other hand, old Jewish communities on both shores of the Persian Gulf, many of them involved in maritime commerce, lived under more favourable conditions.[9] The same may be said of the approximately 30,000 Jews of Kurdistan, of whom there is but fragmentary knowledge.[10] Yemenite Jewry lived no less isolated in the south-west corner of the Arabian peninsula, possessing a unique Jewish culture and literature. They were mainly pedlars and small craftsmen. Only late in the nineteenth century did scholarly Jewish travellers bring their distinctive life to wider notice.

One oriental land, Palestine or for Jews Eretz Israel, retained everlasting meaning, even during its centuries of poverty and oppression which lasted until the late nineteenth century. The eighteenth century was the nadir of Palestine's fortunes, despite the heroic obstinacy of its few thousand Jewish inhabitants. In 1792 the French consul in Acre lamented, 'This good, lovely land is now in a most deplorable condition', and an Arab source of that time reported 'a state of utter desolation'. The depredations of a piratical ruler in Galilee drove the inhabitants out, many of them southwards to Jerusalem.[11] After continued population decline in the first half of the eighteenth century the number of Jews about 1772 stood no higher than 3,000 or 4,000. From that point it gradually ascended, thanks in some measure to the movement of Jews, like other subjects, within the far-flung Ottoman empire. Thus, thousands of Jews preferred living under Ottoman rule rather than in its territories newly annexed by Russia or in the new, intolerant Balkan states recently carved out of Ottoman lands, and migrated to

[8] Walter J. Fischel, 'The Jews of Persia, 1795–1940', *Jewish Social Studies*, 12/1 (April, 1950), 119–60; the quotation is on p. 121.

[9] Idem, 'The Region of the Persian Gulf and its Jewish Settlements in Islamic Times', *Alexander Marx Jubilee Volume* (New York, 1950), 203–30.

[10] Idem, 'The Jews of Kurdistan a Hundred Years Ago', *Jewish Social Studies*, 6/3 (July, 1944), 195–226.

[11] Quoted in Amnon Cohen, *Palestine in the Eighteenth Century: Patterns of Government and Administration* (Jerusalem, 1973), 325, 326.

them.[12] Jewish settlement in the Holy Land concentrated in the four towns esteemed sacred: Hebron, Tiberias, Safed, and especially Jerusalem, the holy city par excellence. Its Jewish population reached perhaps 6,000 in 1800, declined to perhaps 3,000 about 1840, and ascended to 14,000 in 1877. By that time Jews constituted the majority of its population. Jewish settlement overflowed the walled city as new neighbourhoods were founded. The pace of population growth increased with the onset of Zionist colonization in the 1880s. Although Zionist settlers showed little interest in ultra-traditional Jerusalem, its population rose to 18,000 in 1895. By that date Ashkenazi preponderance had replaced that of the Sefardim.[13] The country's general population, mostly Muslim Arabs, was about 100,000 throughout this period.

Birth and death data for Palestine are lacking, but infant mortality was known to be very high, so that natural increase was low. Public health conditions were very poor, and recurring epidemics wrought havoc on all sectors of the population. Jerusalem Jews living in filthy conditions were decimated by cholera in 1833 and 1837, and in the latter year thousands died in an earthquake which devastated Safed, Tiberias, and other places in Galilee. In the recent balanced judgment of a demographer:

Devotion to ideals and self-sacrifice on the one hand, and on the other hand the wastage of human lives and health, abject poverty, idleness, alms-seeking, unreadiness for self-help, fanaticism, and apparently the absence of high standards of religious scholarship—all this formed part of the life of the Jews in Jerusalem in the middle of the nineteenth century.[14]

[12] An important but perhaps overdrawn Hebrew article is Kemal H. Karpat, 'Jewish Migration within the Ottoman Empire in the late Nineteenth Century', *Cathedra*, 51 (April 1989), 78–92; I have not seen the English version, if published.

[13] Amnon Cohen, *Palestine in the Eighteenth Century*, 173, table 1A; Svi Karagila, *The Jewish Community in Palestine ('Yishuv') during the Egyptian Rule (1831–1840)* (Hebrew; Tel Aviv, 1990), 17; Tudor Parfitt, *The Jews in Palestine 1800–1882* (London, 1987), 126 (with abundant population data); O. Schmelz, 'Development of the Jewish Population of Jerusalem during the Last Hundred Years', *Jewish Journal of Sociology*, 2/1 (June, 1960), 56–73; *Ha-Historiyah shel Eretz-Yisrael* (Eng. title: *The History of Eretz Israel*) viii. *Shilhey ha-Tekufah ha-Otomanit (1799–1917)*, ed. Y. Ben-Arieh and Y. Bartal (Jerusalem, 1983), 204–9 (by Y. Bartal).

[14] Schmelz, 'Development', 59.

The insecurity of the Jews' life was increased by assaults during periods of unrest, such as Bonaparte's invasion in 1799, Mehemet Ali's from Egypt in 1834, and even the distant Crimean War in 1853. Even when there was no emergency the Jews suffered chronic maltreatment and verbal abuse. As the first British consul in Jerusalem reported to his superiors during the comparative security of Egyptian rule:

What the Jew has to endure, at all hands, is not to be told. Like the miserable dog without an owner he is kicked by one because he crosses his path, and cuffed by another because he cried out—to seek redress he is afraid, lest it bring worse upon him; he thinks it better to endure than to live in the expectation of his complaint being revenged upon him. Brought up from infancy to look upon his civil disabilities everywhere as a sign of degradation, his heart becomes the cradle of fear and suspicion—he finds he is trusted by none—and therefore he lives himself without confidence in any.[15]

Turkish soldiers and officials could beat or even kill Jews or seize their possessions for not speaking with due subservience. Such an offence could even be classified as blasphemy, a capital crime. Jews constantly suffered the openly expressed contempt of Muslims as well as Christians. Visitors and foreign residents regularly mentioned the filthy state of Jerusalem's Jewish quarter: 'Most of the streets are desolate, badly paved, narrow, and disgustingly filthy,' reported one missionary, while a travel writer warned his readers that 'If the traveller have the courage to inhale the infected air of its close alleys, reeking with putrid filth, he will soon hasten out of them.'[16]

Palestine's upward curve began during the middle of the nineteenth century. Its Egyptian conqueror Mehemet Ali, after freeing his own country from Turkish rule, invaded Palestine as well as Syria in 1834 and ruled until western pressure compelled him to withdraw in 1841. The land began to stir from its stagnation and western, primarily British and French and Dutch Jewries, began to devise improved living conditions and education for the country.

[15] W. T. Young to Lord Palmerston, 25 May 1839, quoted in Parfitt, *The Jews in Palestine*, 23–4.

[16] F. C. Ewald, *Journey of Missionary Labours in the City of Jerusalem during the Years 1842-3-4* (2nd edn., London, 1846), 42–3; W. H. Bartlett, *Walks about the City and Environs of Jerusalem* (2nd edn., London, n.d. [late 1840s]), 80.

Outside Jerusalem fewer than a thousand Jews dwelled in the holy, barely accessible town of Hebron, while Tiberias, another town regarded as holy, had about 1,500 when its population began to increase after 1877. Although it suffered disastrously from the earthquake of 1837 and from physical attacks and epidemics, Safed, the holy town in the Galilean hills, had a larger population. It was the home of perhaps 4,000 Jews before its population too began increasing in 1877. Palestine as Eretz Israel was proverbially the land where pious Jews went to live out their years in sacred study and prayer, to die and be buried. Yet its population, even for Jerusalem, the holy city *par excellence*, does not show an unduly elderly age distribution. Mid-nineteenth century samples reveal that 32 per cent of heads of house in the four holy cities were aged 45 or over, but 38 per cent were boys and girls, aged probably 13 or under.[17] Population increase included noticeable immigration from north Africa and Ottoman lands, a growing proportion of whom settled in seacoast towns. From the late eighteenth century there was an east European immigration consisting of Hasidim and Lithuanian disciples of the GR'A of Vilna. They laid the foundations of a new Ashkenazic community.[18]

Sanitation and public health were a chronic problem in the country. Visitors from the west, including Benjamin Disraeli and Mark Twain, reported a settlement sunk in poverty and lacking elementary sanitation. The worst conditions, it appears, prevailed in Jerusalem, where water was in short supply, streets were mired in filth, and competent medical attention was lacking. The city's only hospital before western Jews took up the matter was a British hospital conducted by missionaries where the patients were plied with the Christian message. The Jerusalem rabbinate for its part would not allow a Jew who died there to be buried in the Jewish cemetery. Still, Jerusalem remained by far the largest Jewish community in the Holy Land. Its Jewish population gyrated widely and was subject to greatly conflicting estimates. Reasonable estimates suggest merely 2,000 about 1800, climbing to about 7,000 in 1853–4 after a smallpox epidemic reduced it from some 10,000. At the close of

---

[17] Parfitt, *The Jews in Palestine*, 124.

[18] Parfitt, *The Jews in Palestine*, provides extensive if not fully critical population data, *passim*; Barnay, *The Jews in Palestine*, 27–49.

the period covered here, Jerusalem Jewry amounted to 15,000–20,000 in 1882, which was a majority of the city's population.[19]

The Jewish situation began to improve from the middle of the nineteenth century. Life and limb became noticeably more secure when many Jews came under the legal protection of foreign powers, themselves anxious to extend their influence in the fragmenting Ottoman empire. The French sought political influence mainly by backing the Catholic Church's claim to control Christian holy sites. The Prussian government could interfere on behalf of pious Lutherans who came from Prussia to found long-lived colonies. Even Russia took steps out of the same self-interest. It protected Russian Jews in Palestine even while realizing that some of them had come there to avoid the notorious conscription in Russia.[20] Protestant Great Britain, in addition to the numerous missionaries and other Englishmen in the Holy Land it protected, took a large number of Jews under its wing. In 1841 Foreign Secretary Palmerston instructed British consuls thoughout the Ottoman empire including Palestine that

whenever any cause is brought to your knowledge in which Jews resident within your district shall have been subject to oppression or injustice, you will make a diligent inquiry into the circumstances of the case and will report fully thereon to Her Majesty's Ambassador at Constantinople . . . you are not authorized to interfere officially with the local Authorities, except in favour of those Jews who may be entitled to British protection. But nevertheless you will, upon any suitable occasion, make known to the local Authorities that the British Government feels an interest in the welfare of the Jews in general, and is anxious that they should be protected from oppression, and that the Porte has promised to afford them protection . . . and will listen attentively to British representations.[21]

Needless to say, besides humanitarianism the British government was concerned to extend its influence. Interests in common is a more solid basis than one-sided benevolence. Great Britain, then at the acme of its world power, was starting on the path which led to the Balfour

[19] Parfitt, *The Jews in Palestine*, 29–38.
[20] Parfitt, *The Jews in Palestine*, 65, 66, 129.
[21] Palmerston to Lord Ponsonby, 21 April 1841, ibid. 132–3.

Declaration of 1917, to be discussed below. The political events of 1840 also inspired the hopes of Christian restorationists, who sought a renewal of Jewish settlement in the Holy Land as a stage of the Christian faith in the second coming of Jesus.

Another long-range factor of change was the development of the country's two natural harbours, at Jaffa and Haifa. The latter took the place of Acre, which was a risky place after it suffered ruinously from the earthquake of 1837 and a heavy naval bombardment in 1840. New means of access to the wide world opened, which encouraged the coastal towns to grow into significant Jewish communities. Except for these coastal communities Palestine's Jewish population lacked productive employment and training in any skill or vocation. Very few worked the land. The sizeable number whose occupation was pious study subsisted on small stipends from funds sent by overseas philanthropists to local *kollelim*. These were institutions for providing aid which were named after the places whence they drew most of their support, for example *kollel Varsha* (Warsaw) and *kollel America*. Beneficiaries had to follow their *kollel's* religious and sometimes political line or forfeit support. To nascent Zionism this *halukkah* (disbursement or division) exemplified living by refined begging, opposed to all they sought to build in the homeland.

Central to these factors was the unique status of Palestine in the Jewish consciousness. As we have seen, the land's physical conditions were generally miserable, even for that region of the world. Although its inhabitants were mostly pious Jews, the land was not intellectually important. Except for mystical contemplatives who had come during the eighteenth century, often in connection with Sabbatianism, there was no field of Jewish learning where Palestine had high standing. Its rabbis ranked far behind the commanding figures of central and eastern Europe or Baghdad and Syria. The general arts and sciences hardly existed. The pride of its Jews was that they lived in the Holy Land, that it would one day revive, and that the Messiah would come there. World Jewry was obliged to support them in need, besides the dole which pious bodies extended to aged Torah students. In the age of western emancipation thoughts stirred overseas towards finding a new, solid basis for the Holy Land's Jewish inhabitants.

As emancipated western Jewish communities became more deeply involved in the problems of Palestine Jewry, practical plans were in the air for its expansion and for placing it on a sound material footing. The greatest obstacle was the indifference, when not opposition, of the beneficiaries to these plans. Yet Anglo-Jewish philanthropy led by Montefiore combined with an unexpected bequest from the New Orleans merchant Judah Touro enabled a Jewish hospital to be built in Jerusalem with a Jewish physician on the premises.[22] The founding of a school for girls with secular studies in 1855, also at Montefiore's initiative, was a fighting issue. Pious souls in Jerusalem believed a girls' school would bring dread modern secularism and Reform Judaism. Notwithstanding talk of a ban (*herem*), the school duly opened. In 1871 an agricultural school, Mikveh Israel, opened near Jaffa. In the gathering spirit of the times a group of Jerusalem Jews banded together to establish an agricultural town, Petah Tikvah, but it did not last long in its original form. Altogether, around 1880 the abjectly poor and devotedly pious Jewish community still conducted itself as it had fifty or a hundred years earlier, but epochal change was in the making.

America

The extreme contrast to these oriental outposts of Jewry were the thriving new communities in the New World. Jews had come there in recent times. There were no Jewish settlements extending back into the mists of antiquity, as was true in countries near the homeland and along the Mediterranean. Jews in the New World settled in the relatively tolerant British and Dutch Protestant empires, whereas Catholic France in the New World forbade Jews in its territories and the Spanish and Portuguese empires imported the Inquisition. When the Portuguese conquered Dutch Brazil in 1653, the active Jewish community of Recife, largely composed of Judaizers—former Catholics who had returned to their ancestral Judaism—shut down at once. In mortal danger, most

[22] There was rivalry between French and English Jews to build it. See A. Schischa, 'The Saga of 1855: A Study in Depth', in *The Century of Moses Montefiore*, ed. Sonia Lipman and V. D. Lipman (Oxford, 1985), 269–346.

Recife Jews went back to Holland or to Dutch Surinam on the northern coast of the continent.[23] However, a celebrated group of twenty-three tried their fortune in another Dutch colony far to the north, New Amsterdam, where they arrived by ship in September 1654. The efforts of its intolerant governor Peter Stuyvesant to keep them out were overruled by the directors of the ruling body, the Dutch West India Company in Amsterdam. When the English seized New Amsterdam in 1664 and changed its name to New York the Jews' status was hardly affected. With persistent effort they gradually acquired civic rights, and so did Jews in the other North American British colonies.[24] Jewish communities in Latin America, however, were not securely founded until the latter half of the nineteenth century, well after independence from Spain and Portugal was secured.

When the European wars ended in 1815 transatlantic immigration became safe again, at least by the standards of sailing ship days. Even during the war decades a few hundred Jews had come to the United States from the sugar-growing West Indies, convulsed by slave revolts and debilitated by the loss of European markets. After a decade of renewed European immigration the number of Jews in the United States in 1826 was approximately 6,000. Unrestricted entrance to the United States and the development of rail and steamship travel were keys to the increasing immigration. A spreading network of aggressive travel agents throughout Europe also stimulated emigration, which came mainly from German lands, especially Bavaria and Polish Posen under Prussian rule. Emigrating Polish Jews before 1870 approximately were often uprooted individuals, whereas Bavarian Jewish emigration to a great extent resembled a folk movement. Families, groups of families, and

---

[23] Documents unearthed and published by Arnold Wiznitzer have made the dramatic story clear: *Records of the Earliest Jewish Community in the New World* (New York, 1954); *Jews in Colonial Brazil* (New York, 1960).

[24] The early history of United States Jewry is treated in full, authoritative manner in Jacob R. Marcus, *The Colonial American Jew* (3 vols., Detroit, 1976). On Canada, Sheldon J. Godfrey and Judith C. Godfrey, *Search Out the Land: The Jews and the Growth of Equality in British Colonial America 1740–1867* (Montreal and Kingston, 1995), is primarily legal and political, while Gerald Tulchinsky, *Taking Root: The Origins of the Canadian Jewish Community* (Hanover, NH, 1993) is broader but deals summarily with the colonial period.

fellow townsmen voyaged together, intending to settle in common.[25] Few of the brave plans for group settlement in America materialized, but chain migration, where family members drew each other overseas in succession, was common.

One dramatic report, from the little town of Ichenhausen in Wüerttemberg in 1839, can stand for many:

Today was the day of deepest sadness . . . Six families . . . all told 44 persons of the Mosaic faith, left home to find a new fatherland in far-off America. Not an eye remained dry, not a soul unmoved, when the bitter hour of parting struck. Such departures leave a visible void in the local community, from whose midst 100 persons have left so far, and have already or will settle in the free United States of America.[26]

Two other reports portrayed general conditions:

They are emigrating, indeed. We have young men who have completed their apprenticeship and journeymen's year of travel just as precisely anyone of another faith, who can legally prove possession of no inconsiderable fortune, who can meet all requirements that can be made of them, and yet cannot obtain letters of protection and domicile.[27]

Two hundred *Bavarian* Jews embarked here [Mainz] last week, to seek a new fatherland in North America. They drew a very dismal picture of the situation of the Jews in Bavaria, where nothing is left but to suffer or to emigrate.[28]

When these accounts were published in 1839, the number of Jews in the United States had risen from the 6,000 reported in 1826 to approximately 15,000 among 17,069,000 Americans. After the immigration 'take-off' commenced around 1840, there were by 1848 an estimated 100,000 Jews in the United States population of 22,018,000, and when the Civil War erupted in 1861 the number of Jews stood at about 150,000 in the population of 32,351,000. This was more Jews than in

[25] For an example of group emigration to a common destination see Lloyd P. Gartner, *History of the Jews in Cleveland* (2nd edn., Cleveland, 1987), 8–10.

[26] *Allgemeine Zeitung des Judentums*, 20 July 1839, in Rudolf Glanz, 'Source Material on the History of Jewish Immigration to the United States, 1800–1880', *Studies in Judaica Americana* (New York, 1970), no. 36, p. 40.

[27] Ibid, 9 September 1837, no. 25, p. 36   [28] Ibid, 1845, p. 346, no. 39, p. 41.

France and Britain combined. After the break in immigration caused by the war, the American Jewish population continued to rise, reaching perhaps 260,000 in 1880. The sharp increase was due not only to immigrants but to their very numerous offspring, Americans by birth.[29]

Of the Jewish immigrants the Bavarians were the most Germanized. Most of the Poles were east Europeans in culture with Yiddish as their tongue. Yet in America most of them adapted to German. Russian Jews were already coming to the United States but still in small numbers. The Bavarians were mainstays of the active secular German culture in the United States. They cherished and preserved that language and were prominent in the German press, politics, theatre, music, and German American education. Jews were German journalists, editors, musicians, and actors, and there were rabbis who took a prominent role in American Germanism. German Jews in America desired that their children learn German and sent them to schools where it was taught. However, alongside the German cultural milieu there were spheres of German American social life, including sports, which were inhospitable to Jews.[30] Growing assimilation into American life late in the nineteenth century and the ubiquity of the English language sapped the vitality of American Germanism and the Jewish role within it dwindled.

Emancipation, the subject of a century's weary debate in Germany, was achieved in America by merely setting foot in the land. Freedom in the vast, open land exhilarated immigrants, who became fervent American patriots. They took part in politics,[31] mostly within the German ethnic enclave and usually as loyal voters of the Republican Party except in New York, where they were generally Democrats. In the debate which preceded the Civil War whether slavery was religiously justified Jewish

---

[29] Gartner, *History of the Jews in Cleveland* 14–15. Children under 14 comprised 40% of Milwaukee Jewry in 1874, another indication of reproductive fertility. Louis J. Swichkow and Lloyd P. Gartner, *History of the Jews of Milwaukee* (Philadelphia, 1963), 66–7. Population figures are from US Bureau of the Census, *Historical Statistics of the United States: Colonial Times to 1970* (2 vols., Washington, 1975), i, series A, 1–5, 6–8, p. 8.

[30] Rudolf Glanz, 'Jews in Relation to the Cultural Milieu of the Germans in America up to the Eighteen Eighties', *Studies in Judaica Americana*, 203–55.

[31] Diner, *A Time for Gathering: The Second Migration 1820–1880*, The Jewish People in America, 2 (Baltimore, 1992) 142–56, where the approach differs from Swichkow and Gartner, *Milwaukee*, 140–47.

opinions were forcefully expressed. They did not feel the inhibitions they had felt in Europe about openly expressing opinions on public issues. Most Jews neither justified slavery nor demanded its abolition, although there were indeed such views. Their American patriotism went much further than expressing opinions. In the Civil War perhaps 10,000 Jews served as soldiers between 1861 and 1865, nearly always as soldiers for the regions where they lived, 7,000 for the northern Union and 3,000 for the southern Confederacy; over 500 lost their lives.[32]

The German Jewish immigrants' fervour for their new land influenced their Judaism as well.[33] The great majority had been reared in traditional Judaism in Germany and were generally quite Orthodox (a term of later vintage) when they arrived in America. The synagogues which they founded followed at first the Orthodox form of worship. However, nearly all the new German congregations turned to Reform Judaism within ten to twenty years. Such a speedy change appears due in large measure to the harmony of Reform Judaism with the American environment, so different from its German land of origin. American Reform Judaism was nourished by the growing conviction among immigrant Jews that in free America, where their centuries of inferior status disappeared, no need or justification existed to observe religious laws which kept them apart from Christian neighbours. Reform's driving impulse was not the hope for emancipation, as in Germany, but to draw the consequences of all legal restrictions on Jews having vanished. Unlike its German forebear, Reform Judaism in America did not trouble greatly with theology or philosophy, despite the presence of such Reform rabbinic intellectuals as David Einhorn and Samuel Hirsch who came to America possessing notable accomplishments in those fields. It was rather the homely moderate, untheological Reform of Isaac Mayer

[32] The basic work is Bertram W. Korn, *American Jewry and the Civil War* (Philadelphia, 1951), supplemented by Diner, *A Time for Gathering*, 80–1, 156–60, 198–9. Practically every local Jewish history deals with the Civil War's impact upon the community.

[33] Michael A. Meyer, *Response to Modernity: A History of the Reform Movement in Judaism* (New York and Oxford, 1988), 225–96, is the standard account, with an emphasis somewhat different from the present one. A good selection of sources is W. Gunther Plaut, *The Growth of Reform Judaism: American and European Sources until 1948* (New York, 1965). Naomi W. Cohen, *Encounter with Emancipation: The German Jews in the United States, 1830–1914* (Philadelphia, 1984), is thorough and reliable.

Wise, the organizer and spokesman, that carried the day. A native of Bohemia, Wise came to the United States in 1846 when he was 25, un-burdened by weighty rabbinic learning and probably without formal ordination. He felt American, he said, even before he quit Europe. The reality of America inspired him to bring about changes in Judaism with his own Cincinnati synagogue as a model. Besides weekly newspapers which he published in German and English, books he wrote, and tireless travels, he founded Hebrew Union College for training rabbis. The title of Wise's revised prayer book of 1855, *Minhag America*, American rite, provided the guiding idea of his work. In Wise's conception America, like other Jewish communities of the past, required its distinctive form of Judaism. American Judaism would be reverent of biblical revelation while freed from the legal prescriptions of the Talmud and its commen-tators and jurists, which were merely the work of men. Judaism would take its equal place among the religions of the land.

Reform drew far-reaching conclusions from the Jews' new situation in America. The Exile (*galut*) had ended, and Jews in the hospitable United States could cast off the restrictions mandated by Jewish tradition. It was time to discard the faith in ultimate redemption in the Holy Land, and some Reform leaders like Einhorn and Hirsch viewed America as the land of messianic fulfilment. Upholders of religious tradition inter-preted American freedom differently from the Reformers. Such men as Isaac Leeser and Sabato Morais argued that in a free society Jews could observe unaltered traditional Judaism in its fullness without fear or con-straint. What became Conservative Judaism in the twentieth century existed in the nineteenth with a limited following and not clearly defined as a movement distinct from the even more limited number of Orthodox.[34]

It was not religion or culture, however, which preoccupied Jewish immigrants. Like other immigrants, they came to America to make a living in freedom. The famous term 'golden land' (*goldene medineh*) probably originated after the California gold rush of 1848–9, but belief in the United States' promise of abundance for all went back further. Young Bavarian Jews had been trained in crafts by government fiat but

---

[34] Moshe Davis, *The Emergence of Conservative Judaism: The Historical School in 19th Century America* (Philadelphia, 1963).

very few practised them in America. Instead they went to commercial occupations for which their new country provided a plentiful field. The most promising beginning for young men was rural peddling. It was hard labour, because the pedlar had to carry everything on his back for long distances; after a while, he usually progressed to a horse and wagon and in time to a store in some town. Since rural folk lived far from stores, they welcomed itinerant 'Jew pedlars' as they had the 'Yankee pedlars' of earlier days. An immigrant of 1852, recalling early experiences in his old age of wealth and esteem, spoke of peddling dry goods taken on consignment from one of the wholesale stores which specialized in supplying pedlars:

Started out Euclid Avenue [Cleveland] way and travelled many miles in the course of the next six weeks. Then I sold my pack boxes and all, clearing about $100.00. Did not like the business but made lots of friends among the people I stopped with over night . . . and they later traded where I was clerking. I would help with the chores wherever I stayed, help milk the cows or feed the stock, and go to church with them on Sundays.[35]

At the age of 19 he was blending contentedly into his new Ohio environment. Many like him gladly adapted to the ways of 'the land of the dollar'. Not so the immigrant of 1840 who implored Divine forgiveness for having unavoidably travelled on the Sabbath. He sadly reflected on other Jewish pedlars: 'Thousands of peddlers . . . forget completely their Creator. They no longer put on the phylacteries; they pray neither on working day nor on the Sabbath. In truth they have given up their religion for the pack which is on their backs'.[36]

The opposition between the craving for material success and a critical view of the acquisitive society remained a permanent tension in American Jewish life. The critical view had the endorsement of Jewish tradition, but the unprecedented possibilities of America for self-enrichment gave the search for material success the upper hand.

Quite a few pedlars remained religiously observant, avoiding peddling on the Sabbath when they returned home if possible, and observing

---

[35] Quoted in Gartner, *Cleveland*, 17.

[36] A. V. Goodman, 'A Jewish Peddler's Diary, 1842–3', *American Jewish Archives*, 3/3 (June 1951), 81–111 (quotation is on p. 99).

dietary laws on the road as best they could. They were founders and members of synagogues all over the country. To these congregations and the hard-working, slightly educated businessmen who managed them Reform Judaism meant the religious adjustment to good relations with gentiles and to the requirements of life, not the subtleties of *halakhah* and theology. They did not want to give up all the traditions in which they were raised in the old country, but their children a generation later, perhaps after 1870, were more ready to do so.

Thanks to Jewish pedlars who became shopkeepers in many distant small towns, American Jews during the 1870s and 1880s were more dispersed than ever before or after. Even before the Civil War vast regions of the middle west, the Mississippi river shores, and the deep south and northern California were dotted with little Jewish communities, and their synagogues and cemeteries. The United States was not yet a country of large cities, but sizeable urban Jewish communities already existed in New York, Cincinnati, San Francisco, Philadelphia, Baltimore, and Chicago in that order of size. American Jewry was a community largely of merchants who spoke with a German accent. A few Jews could boast accomplishments in the arts and sciences, especially medicine, but real cultural distinction lay in the future.

This picture appears idyllic by comparison with Jewish status in the Old World, where even emancipated Jewries were conscious of a long heritage of hostility which equal rights could never completely overcome. What there was of anti-Semitism did not threaten the Jews' security nor their rights, but rather their acceptance in American society. There is a string of separate incidents such as expressions of hostility during an 1826 debate on Jewish rights in the Maryland legislature, belittling remarks to Jewish children in school especially around Easter, a hostile speech in 1854 in the California legislature, invidious statements by lawyers when their adversary in court was a Jew, and bitter attacks on Jews all over the Confederacy during its time of shortages and approaching defeat. The most notorious episode of all came from the Union side, when General Ulysses Grant's General Order no. 11 expelled specifically Jews from territories under his military control, mainly Kentucky and Tennessee, because they were supposedly smugglers of contraband cotton. Grant's order was promptly revoked by

President Lincoln when it was brought to his attention. As a rule verbal assaults on Jews received sharp replies not only by Jews, as contrary to the spirit of American life and religious liberty. One finds a current of hostility, but popular reverence for the Constitution and its guarantees provided a more powerful counter-current. When the rich banker Joseph Seligman was turned away in 1877 from the fashionable Grand Union Hotel in Saratoga expressly because he was a Jew, public condemnation was widespread. However, this was the beginning of upper-class social exclusion of Jews which became common within two or three decades.[37]

Judaism in America was the religion of a small minority. If any religion was to be recognized officially in the public sector it would not be Judaism. The Jews had to contend with prolonged efforts to proclaim America officially Christian, actually Protestant, the denomination of the vast majority. Bible readings and prayers in the public schools, Christian phraseology in public proclamations, and Sabbath blue laws were steps toward attaining the goal of official recognition. These were resisted by the Jews, even though advocates of the sectarian goal generally did not propose to curtail the Jews' constitutional equality. The Jews believed, however, that in an officially Christian country they would be relegated to second-class citizenship, despite their equal rights.

The Jews also confronted tireless missionary efforts to convert them. Some efforts were based on the 'necessity' of converting the Jews in order to bring on the Second Coming. Conversion was believed by some Christians to be the prelude to the Chosen People's return to the Holy Land. Another, simpler missionary motive was the special desire to see the Jews, as the first people who rejected Jesus, accept 'Christian truth'. Missionary preaching and literature was answered by the Jews, most prominently by Isaac Mayer Wise, with an aggressiveness they would not have dared to express in Europe. It is very difficult to reckon the number of Jewish converts, because Jews were reluctant to speak of them while no credence can be given to the missionaries' grossly

---

[37] Diner, *A Time for Gathering*, 173–85. In the large, contentious literature on anti-Semitism two important studies by John Higham stand out: 'Ideological Anti-Semitism in the Gilded Age' and 'Social Discrimination against Jews, 1830–1930' rev. and repr. in his *Send These to Me: Jews and Other Immigrants in Urban America* (New York, 1975).

exaggerated claims. The number of converts before 1880 was probably a few thousand, the majority of whom became Christian less from religious fervour than from worldly ambition or from living in a completely Christian environment. Few, however, needed conversion to open the door to careers, as was widespread in Germany, since there were very few barriers in the United States. On the other hand, one must also reckon in a few dozen known Christian converts to Judaism.

American Jews held that their religious freedom required strict separation of Church and State and the removal of religion from the public realm. They insisted that America was a Christian country only in the sense that the vast majority were Christians but government was, or had to be made, religiously neutral. To be sure, many Christian denominations such as Baptists, not to mention the Catholic Church, were of like opinion concerning religion in the public sphere.[38] Jewish devotion to religious neutrality in the governmental sector was exemplified in the far from abstract matter of their children's schools. Jewish children did not enrol in the new public schools while they carried on in a Protestant spirit with Christian prayers and Bible readings. Instead Jewish children attended Jewish schools usually established by local congregations, which also possessed the advantage of teaching German. However, when the public schools more or less discarded sectarianism between 1850 and 1870 and also began in many places to teach German, the Jewish schools soon closed and Jewish children joined other children in the public schools. Public school education fast became a symbol of equal Jewish status in American society and was accepted as an article of Jewish ideology. At the same time vigilant efforts were devoted to keeping religious exercises out of public schools.[39]

Jewish life in the United States was conducted at the local level. Thus, congregations adopting Reform did so on their own without central organization or direction. Visits from the much-travelled rabbinical leaders Isaac M. Wise and Isaac Leeser were the closest substitute to

---

[38] Naomi W. Cohen, *Jews in Christian America: The Pursuit of Religious Equality* (New York, 1992).

[39] Lloyd P. Gartner, 'Temples of Liberty Unpolluted: American Jews and Public Schools 1840–1875', in *A Bicentennial Festschrift for Jacob Rader Marcus*, ed. B. W. Korn (Waltham, Mass., 1976), 157–92.

leadership in remote communities. The traditional communal activity of charity was required for the local needy and a few itinerant mendicants. It did not become a preoccupation of American Jewry until the mass arrival of east European Jews. Aid to Jews overseas, such as donations for Palestine or protests during the Damascus affair of 1840, took place by newspaper solicitations and the appeals of the much-admired Moses Montefiore, besides itinerant emissaries.

An important factor in American Jewish life were weekly and monthly Jewish newspapers, which began in the 1830s and became numerous in the 1850s. They connected communities when transportation was slow and difficult and the telegraph was for messages rather than communication. Very few Jewish organizations existed beyond the local level. There were Reform Jewry's Union of American Hebrew Congregations from 1873 and the benevolent order of B'nai B'rith, founded in 1843. B'nai B'rith maintained the large Jewish Orphan Asylum in Cleveland from 1869, which accepted children from a wide region of the west. There was a none too active Board of Delegates of American Israelites,[40] founded in 1859, whose name suggested its British inspiration from the Board of Deputies of British Jews. The American Board followed the British system of synagogue constituences, but Reform congregations felt alienated from its Orthodox leadership and stayed out. The Board concerned itself mainly with promoting Jewish rights in unemancipated foreign lands, and it functioned as Moses Montefiore's American connection. There were local Jewish notables but no recognized national leaders, although Isaac Mayer Wise as editor, author, lecturer, and Reform rabbi, and Isaac Leeser of Philadelphia, also editor and rabbi but of the traditionalists, are possible exceptions. The age of national organizations and leaders, and above all mass immigration from eastern Europe, transformed American Jewry of 1880 with its 260,000 Jews. American Jewry ceased to be a remote outpost. The steamship and the European family connections of more than a million immigrant Jews in the new land made it a distant suburb.

There were other Jewish communities in the Americas which were still very small. Canada's Jews arrived with the British in 1759, but the

---

[40] Allan Tarshish, 'The Board of Delegates of American Israelites, (1859–1878)', *Publications of the American Jewish Historical Society*, 49/1 (Oct. 1959), 16–32.

acquisition of political rights did not occur until the 1820s. The Jewish community was composed almost exclusively of merchants concentrated in Montreal with connections which reached the Pacific coast. Canadian Jewry grew very slowly, and there were only 2,443 Jews in Canada in 1881. After the end of their wealth from sugar the West Indies stagnated. Many islands were abandoned and nowhere did their Jewish population number more than the low hundreds. In Latin America, only Argentina had a Jewish population of any size, possibly amounting to 2,000 in 1880. A small Jewish community existed in Australia, some of whose early members arrived as transported criminals and political offenders from Great Britain. A few Jews settled in the southern end of Africa under its original Dutch rule, but since Protestant religion was required they were probably converts. Religious freedom was granted by the Dutch republican regime in 1803, just before the British conquest of what became the Cape Colony in 1805. There was hardly any growth before the mid-nineteenth century and very little thereafter. All these places had the colonial characteristics of mobile merchants, shaky community life, vast unsettled lands, and a native population to be put to labour. The seeds of permanent tension existed with French–British friction in Canada and Dutch Boer–British rivalry in the Cape Colony. The Jews took their place among the British in both cases. These lands were ripe for massive Jewish settlement when the great age of Jewish migration opened in 1880.

8

Age of Migration and Ideologies

From the later 1870s we can see distantly but perceptibly the outlines of an era in the Jewish world which concluded about 1950. It is marked by the most concentrated change, achievement, and horror in the Jewish people's entire history. All-encompassing ideologies interpreted what was happening or predicted what was to come intuitively or, as ideologists claimed, scientifically. The vast scope of what did happen is suggested by a simple fact: few Jews in the world of 1950 lived in the city or country where their grandparents had lived in 1880, let alone the enormous annihilation of generations during the Holocaust. But one cannot simply search the past only in order to find the one path leading to a future which itself is now past and known to historians and their readers. One result of this too frequent procedure of selecting the sole path is to assume falsely that all that happened was inevitable. The course of Jewish history, as much or more than the course of history in general, offers far too many points of choice and chance.

The Rise of Anti-Semitism

About 1875, as the severe depression that had begun in 1873 continued, racist and nationalist anti-Semitism, then a new term, began its assault against the Jews in many countries. The depression in emancipated countries, worst in the new German empire, interrupted the Jews' enjoyment of the fruits of their freedom and their conspicuous economic and cultural successes. The collapse of stock market promotions, many of them fraudulent, involved a high proportion of Jews. The economic conditions which prevailed during the long depression of

1873–96 fostered the emergence of anti-Semitism.[1] At about the same time the ideology of Zionism took form, and in 1897 the World Zionist Organization was founded by Theodor Herzl. This was also the period when distinctive Jewish trade unionism and socialism likewise appeared in eastern Europe and its emigrant offshoots. New organizational forms came into being to express these ideologies in action, including Jewish trade unions and Palestine settlement societies. With little if any ideology Jewish population increase continued after 1875, and the pressures it generated now had an outlet in international emigration. Vast new Jewish communities arose overseas, in the United States particularly but also in other New World countries. A flow of newcomers from eastern Europe also invigorated west European Jewry.

None of these vast movements was new. Hostility to the Jews, by whatever name it is called, is ancient. The hope for restoration to the Land of Israel is as old as the exile from it. Migration is likewise a permanent feature of Jewish history. But what marked these movements after 1875 was not only their intensity and their simultaneity but also their intimate links with contemporary world history—Zionism with contemporary minority nationalism, for example.

There is no doubt that the prolonged world-wide economic depres-

---

[1] The interpretation in Hans Rosenberg, *Grosse Depression und Bismarckzeit* (Berlin, 1967), 88–117, has been widely accepted. There is a vast but mostly indifferent literature on anti-Semitism. A few of the better works include two excellent studies by Werner Jochmann: 'Struktur und Funktion des deutschen Antisemitismus', in Werner E. Mosse (ed.), *Juden in Wilhelminischen Deutschland 1890–1914* (Tübingen, 1976), 389–477, and its continuation, 'Die Ausbreitung des Antisemitismus', in Werner E. Mosse (ed.), *Deutsches Judentum in Krieg und Revolution, 1916–1923* (Tübingen, 1971) 409–510. Rosenberg's and Jochmann's works deserve English translation. See also the older, discerning study by Paul W. Massing, *Rehearsal for Destruction: A Study of Political Anti-Semitism in Imperial Germany* (New York, 1949), and the recent valuable survey by Peter Pulzer, *The Rise of Political Anti-Semitism in Germany and Austria* (rev. edn., London, 1988); Uriel Tal, *Christians and Jews in Germany: Religion, Politics and Ideology in the Second Reich, 1870–1914* (trans. from Hebrew, Ithaca, NY, 1975), and Jacob Katz, *From Prejudice to Destruction: Anti-Semitism, 1700–1933* (Cambridge, Mass., 1980), deal mainly with anti-Semitic ideas. Bruce F. Pauley, *From Prejudice to Destruction: A History of Austrian Anti-Semitism* (Chapel Hill, NC, 1992) concerns mostly the period after 1918. There are some relevant chapters in Jehuda Reinharz (ed.), *Living with Antisemitism: Modern Jewish Responses* (Hanover, NH, 1987). A fine general history which pays substantial attention to anti-Semitism is Gordon A. Craig, *Germany 1866–1945* (Oxford, 1981).

sion contributed to the rise and spread of the new anti-Semitism. But was it not the old hatred, merely cloaked in new, ideological garments? What if anything about it was new? Unlike what had gone before, the Jews now were not only hated for religious or economic reasons but were held responsible for all that was wrong in the world—'the cause of world unrest', as anti-Semitism's sometime American propagator Henry Ford put it later. Since evil and racial inferiority were rooted in their nature or blood or race, or in the genes as might be said today, Jews could not escape by religious conversion nor by any degree of assimilation. These movements of anti-Semitism, emigration, Zionism and socialism grew and flourished in the four decades before the First World War. Largely thanks to them the Jewish world began to regain the unity of destiny it had lost a century earlier.

Jewish Numbers and Movement

Besides the Jewish people's continued increase in numbers, their distribution around the world altered sharply. There were about 7 million Jews in the world in 1875 and in 1910 the number stood at 12,075,000, a vast increase in a short time.[2] As before, eastern Europe, principally the Russian empire, was the main population centre, but a major demographic change was under way. About 4 million lived under the rule of the tsar in 1880, and the unique Russian census, taken in 1897, counted 5,216,000. When we add 800,000 for Galicia and perhaps 700,000 for eastern Hungary and Romania, we find perhaps 6.7 million east European Jews at the turn of the twentieth century. East European Jewish fecundity after this date continued but numbers did not rise, owing to the huge emigration which was siphoning off the increase. East European Jewry was functioning as biological reservoir for the entire Jewish people. From that reservoir came United States Jewry's ascent from 260,000 in 1880 to 1,704,000 in 1907 and 3,197,000 in 1915.[3] These

---

[2] Arthur Ruppin, *Soziologie der Juden* (2 vols., Berlin, 1930), i. 75–86.

[3] There are other estimates. Another one for 1915 is 3,777,000. The source quoted in the text gives 3,389,000 for 1918. Since on account of the war there was practically no immigration, the increase of 192,000 in one year is due to natural increase alone. See the full account by H. S. Linfield in *American Jewish Year Book*, 42 (1940–1), 215 ff.

estimates, based on immigration statistics, clearly show where the east European population increase went. The much smaller but proportionately as great increase in other countries in the Americas likewise illustrates where the Russian Jewish population increase flowed.

Population growth was accompanied by urbanization on a grand scale, especially to metropolitan centres and capital cities. Urbanization was the trend of the age, and the Jews took to it avidly. Large cities offered varied and extensive economic opportunities as well as a wide range of cultural activity and schools of every description. Cities such as Lodz or Philadelphia, not to mention even larger places, had vast Jewish neighbourhoods but weak communal controls. A Jew who so desired—and great numbers did—resided among Jews while subject to little if any pressure or discipline from the Jewish community. Numbers tell much of the story. Of four major east European communities—Warsaw, Lodz, Vilna and Odessa—only Vilna had any size in 1800, and the four together amounted to merely 5,000. At the end of the nineteenth century their collective total was 505,000. Long-established communities like Minsk, Lublin, or Lwow increased fourfold or fivefold during the century to 48,000, 24,000, and 57,000 respectively. The same was taking place in western Europe. Jews flocked to capital cities such as Vienna, 72,000 in 1880 to 175,000 in 1910, Amsterdam, 20,000 in 1800 and 90,000 at the close of the century, with minimal east European immigration, and Paris, where the 8,000 in 1808 reached 60,000 in 1900. In the short space between 1880 and 1914 east European immigration raised London Jewry's numbers from 40,000 to 200,000. Vienna's east Europeans came mainly from Galicia within the Habsburg realm while Paris and Amsterdam gathered in Jews especially from small places in their own countries. Alsace had supplied much of the Jewish population of Paris, and after Germany annexed it in 1870 many Alsatian Jews shunned life under German rule, mild though it was in Alsace and Lorraine, and moved to the French capital.[4] Dutch Jewry quit its dozens of small towns, familiarly called the *medineh* (country), and settled in Amsterdam, known among them as the *mokom* (the place).[5]

[4] Vicki Caron, *Between France and Germany: The Jews of Alsace-Lorraine, 1871–1918* (Stanford, Calif., 1988), 71–95.

[5] This was a play on ancient terms, when Jerusalem was called the 'place' and the rest of Eretz Israel the 'country'. It also shows the exalted regard for the 'Dutch Jerusalem'.

An enormous change in numbers and urban concentration took place in the United States. An example on an immense scale was New York City. Its Jews, no more than 60,000 in 1880, numbered 1,500,000 in 1915, 40 per cent of American Jews and one-quarter of the metropolis' population. The vast majority in 1915 were immigrants and their children. New York City far outran historic Jewish communities to become within one generation the largest urban Jewish community ever known. American Jews also dwelt in the country's other big cities, notably Chicago with 250,000 at the end of our period, and descending numerically to Philadelphia, Baltimore, Cleveland, Detroit, and Boston. To take other examples, the Jews of Detroit, rapidly becoming the automobile manufacturing centre, shot up from merely 1,000 in 1880 to about 34,000 in 1914, while Cleveland, another industrial city, saw its Jewish population leap from about 3,000 in 1880 to 75,000 in 1915. While it is true that the general population of all these American cities multiplied, the Jewish rate of increase was far higher. Montreal in Canada and Buenos Aires in Argentina also exemplified the primacy of metropolitan cities. By the time the First World War broke out world Jewry had become a city people. Less than one century earlier they had been town and village dwellers who did not live on the land in significant numbers. The Jewish people presented a radically different demographic picture in 1914 from 1875 and continued changes were in the offing.

The Anti-Semitic Threat

The liberalism of European political life during the middle of the nineteenth century was superseded after 1870 by a combination of hard-shelled nationalism, aggressive imperialism, social Darwinist materialism and, from a different source, socialism and trade unionism. A conspicuous place in this new set of ideas was taken by the revived hatred of the Jews in a new mode called anti-Semitism. It appeared in every country of western Europe, in each with a different social background. In France, Germany, and the Austrian empire anti-Semitism became a central feature of the political scene and deeply affected

Jewish life. Other countries had anti-Semitic movements contemporary with Germany's, but attention inevitably focuses there not only because of Germany's catastrophic history but also because German anti-Semitism was the most extensive and philosophically elaborated.

Nowhere was the change to the new mode of secular or pagan anti-Semitism more visible than in the German empire, while the religious hostility to Jews of the state Lutheran church did not abate. German liberalism resisted the new trend only weakly. Liberalism in Germany and Austria was not a world outlook transcending class interests, as it became in Britain and France, but remained a class ideology congenial especially to bourgeois Jews. However, most liberals embraced Otto von Bismarck's anti-liberal nationalism of 'blood and iron'. German and Austrian liberalism's class-specific character, its failure to become a national consensus, greatly handicapped the Jewish response to anti-Semitism in those countries.

Under Junker rule personified by Bismarck, imperial Germany's military agrarian ruling class effectively resisted basic political and social change until the downfall of 1918. German classes, religions, and regions existed in profound, unresolved antagonism. Not very different was tsarist Russia, which was about to re-enter a period of uncompromising absolutism after some years of liberal reform. After two decades of partial Jewish integration into German social and political life, idyllic in comparison with what had been and with what came afterwards, a wave of the new anti-Semitism began in the mid-1870s. Austrian, Russian, and German anti-Semitism was not politically marginal but played a significant role in those countries' political life. Anti-Semitism's first German expression in the gathering cultural pessimism of the age came from the journalist Wilhelm Marr, who wrote despairingly in racial terms 'The Victory of Judaism over Teutonism', the title of his tract of 1873. It stirred the German public with its proclamation that 'Finis Germaniae' was approaching because the talented, resilient Jews' racial endowment was inevitably overcoming the simple German stock. A more prominent person than Marr was the eloquent Adolf Stoecker, Kaiser Wilhelm I's Lutheran court preacher. A man of humble background with fixed traditional beliefs, Stoecker was disturbed at the alienation of Berlin's rapidly increasing industrial working class from the church. He founded a Christian Social movement to counter the rising Social Democrats. It sought a proletarian following and circumspectly urged social reforms while remaining patriotically loyal to Church and State. Stoecker's party, however, enjoyed no success with proletarians and in 1879 the court preacher's message was 'adjusted' to its membership of clerks, salesmen, and white-collar employees by adopting anti-Semitism. Such upsetting new phenomena as the press, department stores, stock market, and banks were blamed on the Jews. Germany had given them equality and they now figured conspicuously in the new, hated economic order. Jewish economic success, Stoecker charged, came from impoverishing true Germans, but the Jews would bring disaster upon themselves with their arrogance and boastfulness. His eloquently delivered messages drew audiences up to 3,000. A popular movement, especially on the conservative side, in the German capital generated lively interest as the debate over anti-Semitism dominated the political life of Berlin for three years. Influential Jews pleaded with the emperor and Bismarck to silence their court preacher and quash the anti-Semitic movement, but the chancellor found Stoecker useful for smiting his liberal opponents, while the old emperor thought the Jews had become 'insolent' (*frech*) and deserved to be taken down a few pegs. Neither of these highest authorities considered Germany's emancipated Jews part of the German people.

Stoecker's first anti-Semitic speech set forth the views he advocated for years to come.[6] Everywhere he saw the decline of religion and the German spirit. It outraged him that rabbis and Jewish writers dared to exalt 'inferior' Judaism which had been superseded long before by Christianity, boasting of its moral superiority and world mission. Stoecker charged that the press under Jewish control was mocking and deriding the church and Christianity and eagerly reporting its internal conflicts, while avoiding all mention of anything embarrassing in Judaism. In the Jews of the press he saw a force leading toward secularism. The complaint that the Jews promoted secularism was not unique to Germany. Abraham Kuyper, the great Dutch neo-Calvinist and political leader, denounced the Jews in 1878–9 for being prominent as secular liberals, his bugbear. Yet Kuyper, who was a major figure in Dutch

---

[6] Reprinted in Massing, *Rehearsal for Destruction*, 278–87; quotations from pp. 284–7.

politics and religion, thereupon desisted permanently.[7] Stoecker's nationalist and social arguments became the stock in trade of anti-Semitism:

The Jews are and remain a people within a people, a state within a state, a separate tribe within a foreign race. All immigrants are eventually absorbed by the people among whom they live—all except the Jews. They pit their rigid cult of law or their hatred of Christians against Christianity . . . [The Jews] control the arteries of money, banking and trade; they dominate the press and are flooding the institutions of higher learning . . . We are moving toward the point where public opinion will be completely dominated and labor completely exploited by the Jews . . . More than ever, they cultivate those trades where they can get rich quickly and easily . . . they do not enjoy work and . . . do not believe in the German concept of the dignity of labor.

If modern Jewry continues to use the power of capital and the power of the press to bring misfortune to the nation, a final catastrophe is unavoidable. Israel must renounce its ambition to become the master of Germany.

Stoecker's message profited from his prestige as court preacher.[8] In the same year of 1879, another voice of commanding prestige held forth on modern Jewry, Professor Heinrich von Treitschke, one of Germany's foremost historians. He had started as a liberal nationalist but like many of his stripe he went over to Bismarck's Prussian conservative nationalism. Treitschke's deepest desire was a socially and culturally unified German nation, and in his view the Jews were holding back from complete integration. As he put it in *Ein Wort über unser Judentum* (A Word about Our Jewry) published in his influential *Preussischer Jahrbücher*, many Jews were hardly Germans:

The only way out is for our Jewish fellow-citizens to make up their minds without reservations to be Germans, as many of them have done already long ago . . . There will always be Jews who are nothing else but German speaking

---

[7] Ivo Schoffer, 'Abraham Kuyper and the Jews', in *Dutch Jewish History*, ed. J. Michman (Jerusalem, 1984), 237–59.

[8] On the Kaiser's and Bismarck's avoidance of any disavowal or reproof to their preacher, see Fritz Stern, *Gold and Iron: Bismarck, Bleichröder, and the Building of the German Empire* (New York, 1977), 510–31.

orientals . . . the Jews, who talk so much about tolerance, [should] become truly tolerant themselves and show some respect for the faith, the customs, and the feelings of the German people which has long ago atoned for old injustice and given them human and civil rights.

While endorsing the Jews' emancipation Treitschke, like Stoecker, warned them against their new 'arrogance'. He meant not merely parvenu Jewish upstarts, but his contemporary Heinrich Graetz, the foremost Jewish historian. Graetz's great *Geschichte der Juden* (History of the Jews) spoke repeatedly of Germany in unflattering terms.[9] The words of the centrally positioned clergyman Stoecker and the leading historian and nationalist intellectual Treitschke marked a long step towards making anti-Semitism respectable.

A timorous Jewish reply to Treitschke came from the medieval historian Harry Bresslau, who humbly enquired of his colleague what the Jews had yet to do in order to attain full Germanness. A different reply came from the historian of Rome and liberal intellectual Theodor Mommsen, one of the greatest historians ever, whose *Auch ein Wort über unser Judentum* (Another Word about Our Jewry) defended the Jews in terms of the liberal anti-Bismarck tradition of which he was a lifelong adherent. In his great work *The Provinces of the Roman Empire* Mommsen had praised the Jews in the Roman empire as 'a true fermenting element of cosmopolitanism and national decomposition', forerunners of detribalized culture. His compliment was not fortunately worded, for it became grist to the anti-Semitic mill, proof that the Jews would not become Germans. Like Treitschke, Mommsen too wanted the Jews to become thoroughly German. He urged them to dissolve as a community and give up all Jewish associations except synagogal ones. Privately, he wished to see them adopt Christianity. Mommsen threw up his hands at the futility of dealing in terms of reason with the anti-Semites, because anti-Semitism defied reason.[10]

---

[9] I have used the translation in Heinrich von Treitschke, *A Word about Our Jewry*, trans. Helen Lederer, Readings in Modern Jewish History (Cincinnati, 1958), 7. The attack on Graetz recurs throughout. Note G. A. Craig's astute remarks on Treitschke in his *Germany, 1866–1945*, 48–9, 204–5.

[10] Hans Liebeschutz, 'Treitschke and Mommsen on Jewry and Judaism', *Leo Baeck Institute Year Book*, 7 (1962), 153–82.

The development of racist secular anti-Semitism can be read in the writings of Eugen Dühring, a social philosopher and economist. He found the Jews harmful and racially inferior, their immutable racial and moral characteristics already visible in the Bible. The anti-Semitic programme of Heinrich Class (pseud. Daniel Frymann) in his work of 1912, 'If I Were the Kaiser' was not far from that of the Nazis. Houston Stewart Chamberlain, British by birth but the fully Germanized son-in-law of Richard Wagner, published in 1899 the 'masterpiece' of racist myth, *The Foundations of the Nineteenth Century*. What Marr started with the division between 'Semitism' and Germanism was taken over by the racist and imperialist Pan-German League, which promoted this cause energetically.[11]

This resounding beginning made anti-Semitism in Germany part of the public agenda. In Berlin several anti-Semitic mass meetings were held, and one of them ended in attacks on Jewish shops. Disturbances were repressed, but regional agitators could appeal continually to the anxieties of local audiences. Thus, Otto Boeckel, folklorist and librarian, stirred up the peasantry in south-west Germany against Jewish moneylenders who foreclosed for unpaid debts as the cause of all their woes.[12]

Indeed, a petition to Bismarck in 1880 to prohibit Jewish immigration, conduct a special Jewish census, and exclude Jews from positions of governmental authority and as teachers drew 250,000 signatures. But the chancellor refused, although some of the petition's other demands were gradually met.

Anti-Semitism moved into the political sphere as anti-Semitic parties won five seats in the Reichstag of 1890. They reached their peak in 1893 when they gathered 264,000 votes and gained sixteen seats in the Reichstag, mainly from Saxony. In 1898 they were down to ten seats and continued declining to six in 1912. Repeated attempts to establish stable anti-Semitic parties and to achieve a unified anti-Semitic voice failed, to an extent because the anti-Semitic leaders were erratic, unstable persons and one-issue political parties attracted few voters. The anti-Semitic

[11] Massing, *Rehearsal for Destruction*, 246–7.

[12] For the reaction of a Jewish village teacher to these Jews see the memoirs of Johanna Harris née Brandes in Monika Richarz (ed.), *Jewish Life in Germany: Memoirs from Three Centuries* (Bloomington, Ind., 1991), 218–19.

parties had no accomplishment or influence in Germany's parliament and also did poorly in provincial legislatures.[13]

More insidious than the futile efforts of the anti-Semitic parties was the spread of anti-Semitism into central institutions of German life. In 1892 the Conservative party advocating hoary Prussian values supplemented its principles of 'rever[ing] Christianity, monarchy and fatherland, protect[ing] and encourag[ing] all honest work' with a pledge to 'fight the multifarious and obtrusive Jewish influence that decomposes our people's life'.[14] Although the party did not actively promote anti-Semitism, such a resolution from the party closest to the regime took a long step towards making anti-Semitism respectable. The Agrarian League (Bund der Landwirte) of large Prussian agricultural interests and the Federation of Commercial Employees were explicitly anti-Semitic. Numerous professional organizations refused to take in Jewish members and so did athletic and mountaineering clubs. Besides the long-standing discrimination against Jewish academic appointments at universities, Jewish students were kept out of openly anti-Semitic fraternities and other student organizations. The future classical and Judaic scholar Isaak Heinemann found about 1895 as a Göttingen student that the student classics club would not invite him to membership, contrary to accepted practice. His mentor, the renowned Wilamowitz-Moellendorff, would not exert personal influence on his behalf because he believed 'Jewish pride' and 'separatism', especially of the religiously observant Heinemann, had to cause anti-Semitism. Heinemann finally went home to Frankfurt and studied there.[15] A rising number of Jews were once finding places in public appointments and political life, but these became virtually closed to Jews after the 1880s. They were also closed, for different reasons, to Social Democrats and even to Liberals. An army reserve commission was out of the question to Jews and the new navy, although socially less élite than the army, sought to be no less

---

[13] Richard S. Levy, *The Downfall of the Anti-Semitic Political Parties in Imperial Germany* (New Haven, 1975), index s.v. 'Elections' and *passim*.

[14] Massing, *Rehearsal for Destruction*, 66.

[15] The episode is presented in Christhard Hoffmann, 'Antiker Volkerhass und moderner Rassenhass: Heinemann und Wilamowitz', *Quaderni di storia*, 25 (Jan.–June, 1987), 145–57. I thank the author for bringing his study to my attention.

exclusive and anti-Semitic.[16] Jews constituted no more than 0.4 per cent of public employees at all levels. Only three Jews were allowed into the diplomatic service, and converts apparently were treated no better.[17] There was a social gulf between Jews, including baptized Jews, and others even at high levels of German economic life. This array of discriminations demonstrates how deeply exclusion of the Jews pervaded German life by the early twentieth century, above all at governmental and semi-official levels. It also strengthened the Jews' tendency to seek their careers in independent business and professions, where market forces and individual merit and not official policies played the decisive role.[18]

German parties of the Catholic centre and the left generally kept a distance from anti-Semitism, but only the Social Democrats rejected it with any vigour. Repeatedly they heaped contempt upon the anti-Semitic leaders. The party interpreted anti-Semitism in terms of the Marxian social analysis it had officially adopted in 1891. It held that anti-Semitism was the vain resistance of declining social classes to their inevitable fate. Misguided people were persuaded by lying demagogues serving the cause of capitalism and reaction that the Jews were the cause of their misfortunes. In the words of Engels in 1890:

Anti-Semitism, therefore, is nothing but the reaction of the medieval, decadent strata of society against modern society . . . under a mask of apparent socialism it therefore serves only reactionary ends . . . If it is possible in a country, that is a sign that there is not yet enough capital in that country.[19]

Some socialists held that anti-Semitism, although objectionable, served the socialist cause as a movement of protest whose futility would in-

---

[16] Holger H. Herwig, *The German Naval Officer Corps: A Social and Political History, 1890–1918* (New York, 1971), 42 ff., 94 ff.

[17] Lamar Cecil, *The German Diplomatic Service, 1871–1914* (Princeton, 1976), 97–103.

[18] Two books illustrate discrimination at the economic and political levels: W. E. Mosse, *The German-Jewish Economic Élite, 1820–1935* (Oxford, 1989) esp. 332–45, and Peter Pulzer, *Jews and the German State: The Political History of a Minority, 1848–1933* (Oxford, 1992), 108–47.

[19] Quoted in Robert S. Wistrich, *Socialism and the Jews: The Dilemmas of Assimilation in Germany and Austria-Hungary* (Rutherford, NJ, 1982), 128; Pulzer, *Jews and the German State*, 148–67.

evitably be realized by the masses. They would inevitably turn to socialism when they realized that capitalism, not Jews or Jewish capitalism, was the real enemy. Along with their rejection of anti-Semitism, however, the socialists disavowed 'philo-Semitism', by which they meant variously sympathy with the Jews and recognition of their collective existence and aspirations, such as Zionism. Opposition to anti-Semitism was not stated in terms of justice but in the framework of the party's official Marxism.[20]

Social Democracy fights anti-Semitism as a movement which is directed against the natural development of society but which, despite its reactionary character and against its will, must ultimately become revolutionary. This is bound to happen because the petty bourgeois and peasant strata, which are being whipped up by anti-Semitism against the Jewish capitalists, will finally realize that not merely the Jewish capitalists, but the capitalist class as a whole is the enemy.[21]

The party's Marxist, determinist interpretation of anti-Semitism in terms of lagging economic development was belied by later history, which showed that anti-Semitism could flourish in the most economically advanced countries. Jews were prominent among Social Democratic leaders as intellectuals, writers and technical experts, few of whom maintained any connection with the Jewish community. Although there was practically no Jewish industrial proletariat to provide rank-and-file members, the party nominated numerous Jews for the Reichstag. On the other hand, its leaders desired and expected the dissolution of the Jewish people once they were liberated from oppression. Following the Marxian practice of finding social processes inevitable, they followed their theoretical pontiff Karl Kautsky's doctrine, based on Marx, that the Jews survived only because they served economic functions. These, however, were passing and so 'inevitably' would the Jews. Socialist revisionists, however, led by their theorist Eduard Bernstein, reached the conclusion that the Jews' history and tradition qualified them as a nationality. Bernstein and many revisionists showed sympathy for Zionism after the Balfour Declaration of 1917.

[20] Wistrich, *Socialism and the Jews*, 101–16.   [21] Quoted ibid. 133.

The Catholic party kept a distance from anti-Semitism, partly because of their own persecution by Bismarck but especially on account of racist anti-Semitism's paganism. Its denial that Jews could become true Christians contravened church doctrine. The Lutheran state church, on the other hand, was susceptible to invocations of the German people's Christianity against Judaism. Judaism was treated with disdain, shut out of German scholarship and public and intellectual life. Rabbis were never invited to take part in public ceremonies as were Christian representatives, no rabbi could serve Jewish soldiers as Christian clergymen did theirs, and no university taught Jewish history or literature. The Bible was taught Christologically, as if living Jews had nothing to do with it except for their theological guilt as the crucifiers of Jesus. Germany, like Britain, was a religious country and the motifs and beliefs of Christianity weighed heavily in its life, but in Germany they were expressed in a strongly anti-Jewish when not fully anti-Semitic tone.[22]

How did German Jewry, emancipated and economically flourishing and proud of its *Deutschtum* (Germanness), react to this attack on its political and social status? Many, such as the successful and respected novelist Berthold Auerbach, were deeply disillusioned by the return of ideas which they thought had disappeared forever in the age of enlightened progress. For a decade it was widely believed that anti-Semitism would fade away and was best ignored, and no concerted action was attempted. Only the congregational union Deutsch-Israelitischer Gemeindebund, founded in 1869, responded by appeals for government action and by refuting canards. However, it became clear by the 1890s that the government would not restrain anti-Semitism, nor would judges and prosecutors act on Jewish complaints. Ismar Schorsch summarizes German Jewry's weakness in its initial confrontation with anti-Semitism:

For nearly a century Jews had labored to win German citizenship by diminishing their differences. As late as 1890 they were still consciously suppressing every conspicuous and distinctive Jewish trait . . . In the process of 'self-improvement' Jews had become emotionally and ideologically incapable of defending their 'Jewish persuasion,' the last remaining objective difference

---

[22] There is a discerning discussion in Uriel Tal, *Christians and Jews in Germany*.

[from Christians] . . . the first wave of anti-Semitism to sweep the Empire failed to compel the Jews to abandon their traditional reliance upon accommodation, silence, and Christian intervention.[23]

But this Jewish policy was bound to change. In 1891 the Verein zur Abwehr des Antisemitismus (Association for Defence against Anti-Semitism) was founded by non-Jewish German liberals. Its roster of members included few Jews and many illustrious men of letters and scholars. The association's tactics were apologetic literature and legal assistance in defamed Jews' lawsuits. While the Jews were appreciative of this support, the association's implicit demand that they minimize their separateness was disturbing to many.[24] The main organization in the field was the Centralverein deutscher Staatsbüerger jüdischen Glaubens (Central Association of German Citizens of the Jewish Faith), which adopted a relatively aggressive approach of combating anti-Semitism by literature and legal defence, and denouncing anti-Semites. Founded in 1893, by 1914 the Centralverein was the foremost Jewish membership organization and implicitly professed a view of German Jewish life which resembled that of Liberal Judaism. At its peak during the 1920s the Centralverein had 60,000 members. It avoided conflict with the Zionists, then a small minority in German Jewry, until they adopted a radical position in 1912 which questioned Jewish emancipation itself. The Zionists thought little of the Centralverein's efforts since they regarded anti-Semitism as inevitable in *galut*.[25]

Realizing the corrosive effect of anti-Semitism upon Jewish identity and self-respect, the Centralverein undertook education in Judaism and deepening Jewish identity, which had not formed part of its original programme. The goad of anti-Semitism and a growing sense of Jewish isolation inspired the founding of an array of German Jewish religious, cultural, and welfare organizations at the opening of the twentieth century. The ultimate tragedy of Centralverein efforts was not due to their

[23] Ismar Schorsch, *Jewish Reactions to German Anti-Semitism, 1870–1914* (New York, 1972), 66, 68.   [24] Ibid. 79–102.

[25] Jehuda Reinharz, *Fatherland or Promised Land? The Dilemma of the German Jew, 1893–1914* (Ann Arbor, 1975), 107–11, 144–6, and examples, beginning in 1885, in idem (ed.), *Dokumente zur Geschichte des deutschen Zionismus 1882–1933* (Tübingen, 1981), index s.v. 'Anti-Semitismus'.

inadequacy but to hostility or indifference on the part of government, churches, universities, and much of German society in which the Centralverein functioned. Although Austria was German in language, the Austrian anti-Semitic movement had different sources. Austria of the Habsburgs faced a rising challenge by the Habsburg empire's nationalities to German dominance. Moreover the empire was for the most part still a society of peasants and nobles. Only a few, a high proportion of them Jews, pursued capitalist enterprise. To oppose capitalism practically meant opposition to the Jews. Austrian Germans' liberal ideology rested on a narrow class basis. Liberalism was a secular, pro-capitalist *laissez-faire* ideology largely identified with the business and professional middle class, again including a large proportion of Jews, which held little or no appeal for others. Austrian German liberals began to emphasize the defence of German dominance in the Habsburg empire and also anti-Semitism, leaving Jewish liberals isolated and disillusioned. Out of disputes and factions in Austrian Germandom grew potent racial anti-Semitism which took its place alongside Catholic anti-Jewishness. The dwindling Liberal Party's Linz programme demanded social legislation and the preservation of German supremacy within the Habsburg realm, and added in 1885 that 'the removal of Jewish influence from all sections of public life is indispensable for carrying out the reforms aimed at.' After this 'Point Twelve' Jews and others left the Liberals. The eccentric, doctrinaire, vehemently anti-Catholic Georg von Schönerer exemplified the shift away from liberalism. He was stripped of his title of nobility and served a term in gaol for violently attacking a newspaper office, and then joined the racist Pan-Germans, who sought the annexation of Austrian Germans to Germany. As a racist anticlerical Schönerer achieved little in his parliamentary career of anti-Semitism.[26] Populist anti-Semites, including Karl Lueger, who quit the Liberals found their place in the

[26] Besides literature cited above, see the pioneer study by Oskar Karbach, 'The Founder of Modern Political Antisemitism: Georg von Schönerer', *Jewish Social Studies*, 7/1 (Jan. 1945), 3–30; Menachem Z. Rosensaft, 'Jews and Antisemites in Austria at the End of the Nineteenth Century', *Leo Baeck Institute Year Book*, 21 (1976), 57–86, who is charitable when comparing Lueger with more rabid anti-Semites. An important study is John W. Boyer, *Political Radicalism in Late Imperial Vienna: Origins of the Christian Social Movement 1848–1897* (Chicago, 1981), supplemented by his 'Karl Lueger and the Viennese Jews', *Leo Baeck Institute Year Book*, 26 (1981), 125–41.

Catholics' Christian Social Party. Heinrich Friedjung, a Jew who also left the Liberals, became a great historian, while the baptized Victor Adler and his friend the non-Jew Pernerstorfer left to found and lead the Social Democrats.

Austria's Social Democrats were more ambivalent about anti-Semitism and the Jews than their German comrades. Irritated by the close connection between Austrian capitalism and Jewish capitalists, they balanced anti-Semitism with 'philo-Semitism', the defence of liberalism or the Jews, and condemned both. When a delegation of Russian immigrant Jews coming from America asked the international socialist congress of 1891 to condemn anti-Semitism Victor Adler, the leader of Austrian socialism, successfully moved to include a condemnation of 'philo-Semitism'. Contemptuous as they were of anti-Semitic agitation the socialist *Arbeiterzeitung*, edited by Adler, nevertheless avowed that 'nothing is more alien to social democracy than to carry on a ridiculous fight against anti-Semitism side by side with the [liberal] arch-enemies of political freedom and socio-political progress.' Altogether, the Austrian Social Democrats' opposition to anti-Semitism before 1914 was decidedly ambivalent. Nevertheless, by the beginning of the twentieth century Viennese Jews had begun turning to them as the sole party opposing anti-Semitism.[27]

The Jewish issue did not readily leave the socialists' agenda. Recognizing the enduring importance of nationalities within the Habsburg empire, the party theorists Karl Renner and Otto Bauer, a Jew, led the Social Democrats in advocating the empire's reconstruction as a multinational federation. The party gave autonomy within its ranks to the Czechs, Poles, and others but not to the Jews. They were not accepted as a nationality although it was finally realized that, contrary to Marxist doctrine, they were not doomed to disappear.[28] In Habsburg Galicia, however, the Polish Socialist Party (PPS) demanded Polonization of the Jews and had no tolerance for Jewish national aspirations in that deeply traditional Jewish society.

[27] Wistrich, *Socialism and the Jews*, 143, 242–70; quotation on p. 253: Walter B. Simon, 'The Jewish Vote in Austria', *Leo Baeck Institute Year Book*, 16 (1971), 97–123.

[28] Wistrich, *Socialism and the Jews*, 262–71, 299–348. The Social Democrats' national minorities doctrine was transferred to Russia, where Jewish intellectuals adapted it to east European Jewish reality.

At the opposite end of Austria's political spectrum, Schöenerer's former movement made its peace with the Catholic church and joined the Christian Social Party to form the United Christians. The anti-Semitic party alliance rode to victory in Vienna under the leadership of Karl Lueger, the most personally impressive and successful anti-Semite in Europe and probably the one most opportunistic about his anti-Semitism. In 1890, years before he became mayor of Vienna, Lueger pronounced his anti-Semitism 'something higher[!], which does not direct itself against the poor Jew or Jewess . . . we do not hate anything except the oppressive big business that finds itself in the hands of the Jews.'[29] Elected mayor several times before he was reluctantly confirmed by the emperor in 1897 and could take office, Lueger crushed the Liberals and dominated Vienna's politics until he died in 1910. Under him there was, in Pulzer's words, 'a decline in sectarian fanaticism and in the vehemence of anti-Semitic propaganda, combined with the widespread acceptance of mild, almost incidental, anti-Semitic opinions.'[30] The mayor's anti-Semitism was above all rhetorical, and his concrete policies consisted mainly of excluding Jews from public employment and municipal contracts. To improve his beloved city physically Lueger dealt openly with Jewish financiers. He willingly associated with Jews, even socially, and with cynical nonchalance told fellow anti-Semites who objected, 'I decide who is a Jew.'

The young Adolf Hitler, living rootlessly in Vienna at the time, later expressed admiration for *der schöne Karl*, as Lueger was popularly known, who supposedly taught him the principles of anti-Semitism. Lueger forged a politically effective mass movement by the unscrupulous exploitation of hatred, even if he did not share it, and skilfully employed slogans and demagogic oratory. This was surely Hitler's debt to the mayor of Vienna.

Even while under attack in the Habsburg capital Viennese Jewry's numbers greatly increased to 175,000 in 1910 thanks to immigration from Moravia, Hungary, and Galicia. Their proportion in the city's population, 8.63 per cent in 1910, was the highest in any west European city. Viennese Jews, like those of Germany, were stunned by the first anti-Semitic wave of the 1870s and they too did not present an organ-

[29] Quoted in Rosensaft, 'Jews and Antisemites in Austria', 72.
[30] Pulzer, *The Rise of Political Anti-Semitism*, 185.

ized response. The official Israelitische Kultusgemeinde, which was controlled by a small wealthy élite elected under a restrictive voting franchise, would not touch the sensitive subject. Since the emperor openly detested anti-Semitism, the Jewish bourgeoisie was convinced that their security lay in dynastic patriotism. Jewish replies to the anti-Semites came mostly from the community's famously eloquent spiritual leader and scholar Rabbi Adolf Jellinek, and slightly later from his successor Rabbi Moritz Guedemann, a distinguished historian. Virtually excluded from their city's public life, middle- and upper-class Viennese Jews invested their frustrated political impulses in the musical affairs of the Vienna Opera and the Vienna Philharmonic. Few took an interest in the politics of the Kultusgemeinde, at least not until Zionists challenged its oligarchy.

The passivity of Viennese Jewry's leaders in the face of attack was challenged by the activities of the rabbi of the industrial suburb of Florisdorf, Joseph Samuel Bloch. The son of a poor family, Bloch was born and educated in Galicia and moved west, where he went to university and mastered German to become a formidable orator and polemicist. When the oligarchs of the Kultusgemeinde forced him out of his congregation, he moved into Vienna and ceased functioning as a rabbi. Unhesitating in taking on anti-Semitic agitators, Bloch first won fame in 1884 by exposing in court the charlatan 'expert' on the Talmud August Rohling. Besides sitting in the Reichsrat for a Galician constituency from 1883 where he spoke vigorously for Jewish interests, Bloch published the weekly *Oesterreichische Wochenschrift*. He founded the Austrian Israelite Union in 1886 to enhance Jewish self-respect and knowledge of Judaism, and it gradually entered the fray against anti-Semitism. The Union was favoured especially by Jewish students of the University of Vienna, the city's hotbed of anti-Semitic insult and violence. It obviously paralleled the German Centralverein, but the latter's philosophy was closer to Reform Judaism than the Orthodox Rabbi Bloch's Union and more cautious about taking sides in general politics. The Israelite Union became the leading Jewish organization in Vienna, the focus of Jewish cultural activity and struggle against anti-Semites.[31]

The Viennese Jewry described here seems utterly remote from the

---

[31] Jacob Toury, 'Defense Activities of the Osterreichisch-Israelitische Union before 1914', in Reinharz, *Living with Antisemitism*, 167–92.

Vienna of Mahler, Schnitzler, Freud, and other contemporary luminaries who were Jews. Yet they and other outstanding contemporaries in the arts who grappled with the irrational found that it secured a firm foothold in the glittering cultural life of the metropolis. Vienna exemplifies especially in its anti-Semitism the decline of the rational and liberal in the face of mass political movements' appeal to the emotions with slogans and pageantry. The appeal of Viennese art and of politics to unconscious drives were not so far apart. One historian has argued that Zionism as conceived by the adopted Viennese Theodor Herzl possessed some of this character. Some of the externals important to Herzl also departed from rationalist liberalism, but the Zionist movement which he founded was imaginatively rational and far-sighted.[32]

Still, it was not in Germany or Austria that European anti-Semitism first attained world notoriety.[33] That distinction, such as it is, belongs to France, owing of course to the Dreyfus affair which began in 1894. To be sure there was a long record of hostility, beginning early in the nineteenth century, to France's emancipated Jews as symbols of its new political and economic order. A long series of anti-Jewish novels appeared, and such masters as Alphonse Daudet and even Émile Zola, later celebrated as the defender of Dreyfus, employed anti-Jewish stereotypes. Alfred de Vigny, romantic poet and aristocrat, repeatedly expressed bitter hatred of the Jews. Unlike the left wing in Germany the French left aspired to perpetuate France of the small producer and the independent peasant. Consequently they were even more negative towards the Jews, who were undoing that France, than the right. Proudhon, Fourier, and Leroux, early anarchists and social planners, detested the Jews whereas Saint-Simon, as a pioneer prophet of modern industry, was surrounded by a coterie of young Jews. The domination of France by Jews, subverting its traditions and cultural glory, was a pervasive theme

---

[32] Carl E. Schorske, 'Politics in a New Key: An Austrian Triptych', *Journal of Modern History*, 39/4 (Dec. 1967), 343–86.

[33] Of the vast literature see esp. the older but useful Robert F. Byrnes, *Antisemitism in Modern France, i. The Prologue to the Dreyfus Affair* (New Brunswick, NJ, 1950) (no more published); the massive Stephen Wilson, *Ideology and Experience: Antisemitism in France at the Time of the Dreyfus Affair* (Rutherford, NJ, and London, 1982); Michael R. Marrus, *The Politics of Assimilation: A Study of the French Jewish Community at the Time of the Dreyfus Affair* (Oxford, 1971), concentrates on French Jewry during the affair.

of French anti-Semitism. Alphonse Toussenel's comprehensive attack of 1845, *Les Juifs rois de l'époque* (The Jews, Kings of the Age), was not expressed in primarily religious terms. Rather, he denounced them as the anti-Christian masters of 'financial feudalism'. Racism also took its literary start in France with the four-volume work of a disgruntled aristocrat, Count de Gobineau, *Essai sur l'inégalité des races humaines* (Essay on the Inequality of Human Races, 1853–5). His object was to glorify the 'pure' Aryanism and natural superiority of the French aristocracy against the masses of Frenchmen, 'degenerate products', and their abominable democracy. Gobineau's work drew very little attention in France, but German racist anti-Semites read and admired it and transmitted its message of racial purity and immutable racial characteristics. Of greater influence in nineteenth-century France was the flow of religious attacks on the Jew from conservative Catholic sources, written in the spirit of disaffection from contemporary secular France. The theme of this literature was Jewish responsibility for anti-Catholicism and Freemasonry. The great 'hit' of anti-Semitic literature, however, was the journalist Édouard Drumont's best-selling work of 1886 in two large volumes, *La France juive*. This lively compendium of gossip and canards and history sold 100,000 copies in the year of its publication and became the talk of the town for years. Thanks to Drumont Jews replaced Masons as the scapegoats for France's ills.

With all the hostility, there were yet fundamental differences between France and Germany in the effect of anti-Semitism. Basic French liberties were preserved and governments gave no countenance to the anti-Semitic agitation. Jews moved ahead socially and economically and attained positions which were out of the question in Germany—military commissions despite an unfriendly atmosphere in the officer corps, academic appointments, and political office. They were able to circulate in high society, as immortalized by Marcel Proust, the son of a Jewish father, in his *Remembrance of Things Past*.

French anti-Semitism reached its climax in the 1890s. There had been the scandalous collapse of the Union Générale bank in 1882. Bontoux, a disgruntled Rothschild ex-employee, attracted Catholic depositors by emphasizing the Union Générale's Catholic character. Its collapse was blamed on the great Jewish banker. It shortly became clear, however, that blame for the collapse and the depositors' losses lay with the irresponsible Bontoux himself. Much worse came with the Panama scandal, where the responsibility of some Jews was patently true. The collapse in 1889 of the financial scheme for digging the Panama Canal became known in sensational fashion in 1892. The anti-Semitic press gleefully trumpeted that crooked Jewish fixers had bribed French newspapers and politicians.

With a segment of the literary world, the church, army, and a rabid anti-Semitic press eager to pounce on any incident, the way was clear to label the Jews traitors when Captain Alfred Dreyfus of the General Staff was tried and convicted by court martial behind closed doors of betraying France by selling its military secrets to Germany. There had at first been some figment of evidence incriminating Dreyfus which was found to be baseless in advance of the court martial, but it was used secretly against him anyhow. After a dreadful ceremony of public degradation to the accompaniment of shouts, 'Death to the Jews!' Dreyfus was packed off to Devil's Island for life. For three years the case was regarded as settled and little was heard except for a few persons' efforts, headed by brother Mathieu Dreyfus and the maverick socialist Bernard Lazare. After the weight of contrary evidence mounted, the army stonewalled rather than reopen the case, and new 'evidence' was forged.

The unfortunate Dreyfus languished on Devil's Island as his case became the Affair, the central political issue which penetrated the core of French life and divided families. It became world famous especially after Émile Zola's renowned 'J'accuse' appeared in 1898 and a new military trial was held at Rennes. The forger of evidence Lieutenant Colonel Henry was exposed and committed suicide. The 25,000 subscriptions, mostly in small sums, to a fund for his widow's benefit and the attached letters suggest the depth of anti-Semitic sentiment. There were sixty-nine known anti-Semitic riots which occurred in January and February 1898, evidently sparked by the trial of Zola for insulting the French army, and they provide still more incisive evidence of anti-Semitic feeling. They have been little mentioned by historians, although in severity they are comparable to the well-known Russian pogroms of 1881–2. Up to a thousand people took part in some of the French riots, which attacked mainly Jewish businesses and property. Jews were occasionally manhandled but there were no fatalities as the local authorities merely looked on.[34] Dreyfus's retrial again found him guilty but with 'extenuating circumstances', an absurd verdict, and in 1900 he was pardoned. The affair dragged on to 1906, when Dreyfus was at last exonerated, reinstated in the army and promoted. The real culprit, named by Zola, was Major Walsin-Esterhazy, who had been tried and found not guilty. He fled France and never returned. Colonel Picquart, the officer who courageously 'blew the whistle' on the false evidence and was brought to trial for leaking military secrets, returned to France from the desert outpost to which he had been consigned.

The Dreyfus Affair possesses a broader context than the Jewish one. France's political structure and even families were bitterly split. As to the French Jews, the affair was a deep shock. During the years when Dreyfus's guilt was assumed they avoided even speaking of it, but with later revelations the great majority became Dreyfusards. Their reaction to the case resembled their view of anti-Semitism generally: dependence on government action in cases of illegality and injustice, and reliance on liberal public opinion. The institutions of the Jewish community, led by the Consistoire, kept a discreet distance from Dreyfus, while the Alliance Israélite Universelle kept a completely different agenda. Behind the scenes, however, French Jewry's distinguished Chief Rabbi Zadok Kahn was very active in Dreyfus's cause. The Jewish defence organization, although not labelled Jewish, was the left liberal, anticlerical League for the Defence of the Rights of Man and the Citizen (Ligue pour la Défense des Droits de l'Homme et du Citoyen), founded in 1898, which evolved into a general liberal, humanitarian body. Jewish protest demonstrations for Dreyfus and against anti-Semitism were frowned upon by French Jewry's leaders, and were resorted to only by east European immigrant groups.

The triumphant end of the Dreyfus Affair brought a halcyon decade of prosperity and self-confidence to French Jewry. The traditional faith in emancipation was invigorated and there was no noticeable growth of Zionism, which questioned emancipation. Rather, an invigoration of Jewish identity by a number of Jewish authors occurred, notably the poets and essayists André Spire and Édmond Fleg. Spire recalled that

[34] Wilson, *Ideology and Experience*, 106–24.

during the period of the affair and after, 'Jews who had lost all contact with Jewish life, who were ignorant of virtually all of Jewish history, began to study them with fervor. Instead of hiding their Jewish souls . . . [they published] Jewish poems, Jewish novels, Jewish dramas and comedies.'[35] The actual content of the renewed Jewish identity of Spire and Fleg, both polished Frenchmen and senior civil servants, was apparently a keen sense of ancestry and sympathy with Zionism.

This antebellum decade, the *belle époque*, was in Paula Hyman's words 'the last act of the French Jewish synthesis of the nineteenth century. While the seeds of future social problems had already been sown both within the Jewish community and the larger society, they were not to sprout until the conclusion of World War I.'[36] Thanks in part to its anti-Dreyfusard political record, the Catholic Church was disestablished together with other religions, including Judaism. The Jewish community needed only a year or two to adjust to complete self-support. Anti-Semitism was at low ebb after Dreyfus's exoneration, although the young ruffian followers of Charles Maurras's Action Française, called the *Camelots du roi*, were a nuisance.

In Britain there was some hostility to Jews as non-Christian and different, but this did not produce an anti-Semitic movement.[37] Indeed, the themes which were played on by Continental anti-Semitism made little headway in Britain. The Jews were not held responsible for the industrial and commercial revolutions which had engulfed England when few Jews lived there. Jewish private banking, its potency symbolized by Rothschild, did attract fear and dislike, but British banking did not originate with Jews and was accepted anyhow as indispensable to the economic order which placed England at the head of the world's economy. However, the anti-Semitic conception that the Jew was a traitor manipulating the nation's destinies for alien Jewish purposes appeared during the Balkan crisis of 1875–8 and again during the Boer War of

---

[35] Quoted in Paula Hyman, *From Dreyfus to Vichy: The Remaking of French Jewry, 1906–1939* (New York, 1979), 46. See Aron Rodrigue, 'Rearticulations of French Jewish Identities after the Dreyfus Affair', *Jewish Social Studies*, NS 2/3 (spring/summer 1996), 1–24.   [36] Hyman, *From Dreyfus to Vichy*, 34.

[37] See Colin Homes, *Anti-Semitism in British Society, 1876–1939* (London, 1979), and David Feldman, *Englishmen and Jews: Social Relations and Political Culture, 1840–1914* (New Haven and London, 1994).

1900 to 1902. The culprit in the Balkan crisis was the prime minister, Benjamin Disraeli, regarded everywhere and sometimes by himself as a Jew despite his baptism as a boy. He was accused of betraying England's true interests by supporting Turkey against Russia in the Balkans despite Turkey's anti-Christian deeds, because of Russia's maltreatment of the Jews. E. A. Freeman, historian and anti-Semite, said that 'blood is stronger than water, and Hebrew rule [i.e. Disraeli] is sure to lead to a Hebrew policy.'[38] Disraeli's famous rival, the great Liberal leader William E. Gladstone, wrote that he 'always had occasion to admire English Jews in the discharge of their civil duties, but I deeply deplore the manner in which what I may call Judaic sympathies, beyond as well as within the circle of professed Judaism [i.e. the convert Disraeli], are now acting on the question of the East.'[39] And Gladstone had supported Jewish emancipation and as prime minister had appointed Jews to high office. Later, Britain's war on the Boer republic was blamed on Jewish mining magnates in South Africa who supposedly planned it. Yet British Jews reached high society and were received as guests in aristocratic country houses. King Edward VII's mostly Jewish social circle provoked negative comments, and there was noticeable satisfaction when it dispersed with the king's death in 1910. At the other extreme of the social scale, about 120,000 east European Jews settled in Britain at the same time, and a much larger number spent various periods of time there as they passed through *en route* to other countries. This Jewish immigration aroused nativist antagonism, but most anti-aliens insisted they were not anti-Semites.

The division of anti-Semitism by country is true to its essential character. Anti-Semites had fervent nationalism in common, a sentiment obviously discouraging to cross-national connections. Attempts to hold international anti-Semitic congresses had little success. Anti-Semites in Britain and the United States had independent agendas, and did not seek connections in other lands. Theoretically, racist anti-Semitism should have crossed national boundaries, but that hardly happened.[40] The core of anti-Semitism in each country was national, and the specific

---

[38] Quoted in Feldman, *Englishmen and Jews*, 101. [39] Quoted ibid. 102–3.
[40] For the example of the United States see John Higham, *Strangers in the Land: Patterns of American Nativism, 1860–1925* (paperback edn., New York, 1970), 140–57.

political and social culture of every country defined its extent and forms of expression. To suggest an example, Dreyfus would never have been freed in Germany, where the army's prestige was invincible, public opinion was nebulous, and citizens' rights had little chance against the power of the state.

In 1914 no political party specifically devoted to anti-Semitism existed in western Europe and the status of west European Jewry appeared more secure than it had been for a century. Their wealthy lived in unabashed opulence and often enjoyed access to high social spheres. Anti-Semitism was marginal in electoral terms and unseemly to express openly, but it seeped into society at large. However German and Austrian political parties adopted anti-Semitism, as we have seen, and only the Social Democrats definitely rejected it, even then with some ambivalence. In political and cultural life and in the press Jews were regularly labelled as such and nasty jests and witticisms were constantly traded. In the arts and professions and the universities Jews were kept out or at arm's length. To estimate the force and success of anti-Semitism its strength has to be measured against its liberal, democratic opposition. It was that liberal, democratic opposition which freed and finally exonerated Dreyfus in France and kept anti-Semitism down in Britain, while in Germany and Austria the weakness of opposition forces allowed anti-Semites easy successes.

Year of Crisis: 1881

If a year is to be reckoned as setting the direction of contemporary Jewish history, it must be 1881. Aside from the anti-Semitism which was bursting forth, the massive immigration from eastern Europe which began then caused the number of Jews in western Europe to increase steadily notwithstanding a falling birth rate. The migration which always went on was most intense during the forty years which ended in 1914. It went from east to west, from eastern Europe to western Europe and the Americas, above all the United States. Anti-Semitism in western countries apparently did not inhibit Jews from going there, but Russian anti-Semitic violence and government policies had much to do with

Jews leaving. Throughout the nineteenth century the tsarist empire kept the Jews in a position inferior to Russian subjects and after 1881 the Jews' status worsened further.

The change in Russia and particularly for its Jews in 1881 was dramatic. Tsar Alexander II, *en route* to announce a form of constitution on 1 March 1881, was torn to pieces by a bomb flung by one of an anarchist group. His son and successor Alexander III rejected the option of a modern Russian state and set Russia on the road to an absolutist police state. Six weeks after his father's demise a pogrom erupted in Elizavetgrad, the first in a chain which lasted into 1883. While figures are uncertain at least forty Jews were killed and and hundreds were injured, mutilated, or raped, besides 9 to 10 million roubles in damage inflicted on impoverished Jews in 169 recorded pogroms. About 20,000 homes were destroyed.[41] The ill-paid, understaffed police generally allowed pogromists to carry on uninterrupted for a few days before soldiers appeared and the perpetrators promptly fled. But there were exceptions. In the White Russian town of Nezhin near the Ukraine soldiers came promptly and killed some pogromists, while no Jews were injured. In the majority of cases, however, a few pogromists were arrested and punished lightly if at all.

High officials at first viewed the pogroms with comparative indifference until it appeared that they might menace the regime's stability. The new tsar detested Jews and penned a marginal note expressing satisfaction at their beating, but added that pogroms disturbed public order and could not be tolerated. It was long accepted that the pogroms were governmentally inspired, but this view has been reconsidered. The pogroms actually surprised the regime, which at first believed them to be the doing of revolutionary agitators. Some revolutionists for their part imagined that the pogroms showed revolutionary spirit stirring among the people, but they too were soon disabused.[42] Altogether it

[41] Of the many conflicting estimates I follow that of Hans Rogger in John D. Klier and Shlomo Lambroza (eds.), *Pogroms: Anti-Jewish Violence in Modern Russian History* (Cambridge, 1992), 328. A list of places affected is provided in the pamphlet *The Persecution of the Jews in Russia* (London, 1882).

[42] There is a striking parallel with the belief of many western socialists that anti-Semitism, although undesirable, indicated a commendable spirit of anti-capitalist rebelliousness.

appears likely that the pogroms were outbreaks which local officials welcomed or at least tolerated. However, when Count Tolstoy (not the writer), no lover of Jews, replaced the slippery, crooked Ignatiev as minister of the interior, he announced that he would not tolerate pogroms and would hold local officials directly accountable to himself. The pogrom movement dwindled and before long ceased.

Who were the pogromists? It has been persuasively argued that they were roving bands of workers from Moscow and St Petersburg who had lost their factory jobs in the depression which had just begun. They did not find their usual seasonal agricultural work in the Ukraine because of crop failures. These unemployed proletarians rode the rails from town to town where they were joined by railroad workers and local riffraff in beating and robbing the Jews. The chronology of the pogroms even follows the railroad lines. One Russian historian holds that the pogroms, which took place in southern Russia, were 'a part of the fight against the Jewish village bourgeoisie (tavern owners, shopkeepers, and creditors) . . . local officials encouraged the anti-Semitic movement. Most *pogromshchiki* were drawn from the lumpenproletariat.'[43] In the rapidly developing Ukraine, most of which was open to Jewish settlement, rivalries between mobile social classes jockeying for advantage exploded during hard times. Consequently it was in the Ukraine that national rivalries and anti-Semitism burst forth. Although until Poland became independent in 1918 there were practically no pogroms there, a small pogrom erupted in Warsaw in 1881.[44]

The pogroms could not be openly reported in the press. They had to be called 'the southern tempests' (*ha-sufot ba-negev*), and are still known in Hebrew by this euphemism. Only when a report was smuggled out of Russia by Rabbi Isaac Elhanan Spektor of Kovno to Nathaniel Rothschild in London and printed in *The Times* of London in January 1882 did the

[43] Peter A. Zaionchkovsky, *The Russian Autocracy in Crisis, 1878–1882* (Gulf Breeze, Fla., 1979), 265; I. Michael Aronson, 'Geographical and Socioeconomic Factors in the 1881 Anti-Jewish Pogroms in Russia', *Russian Review*, 34/1 (Jan. 1980), 18–31; the author extends his argument in Klier and Lambroza, *Pogroms*, 16–25, and *Troubled Waters: The Origins of the 1881 Anti-Jewish Pogroms in Russia* (Pittsburgh, 1990). See also Yehuda Slutzky, 'The Geography of the Pogroms' (Hebrew) *He-Avar*, 9 (1962), 16–25.

[44] Michael Ochs, 'Tsarist Officialdom and anti-Jewish Pogroms in Poland', in Klier and Lambroza, *Pogroms*, 164–89.

public learn what was happening.[45] There was shock in the west at such events occurring in an enlightened age. A wave of protest meetings in major western cities took place, and unprecedented sums were raised for Russian Jewish relief. The plight of Russian Jewry and steps of protest and alleviation set the international Jewish agenda for years to come. For foreign consumption the tsarist regime presented these and later pogroms as the Russian people expressing anger at Jewish cheating and exploitation. When Ignatiev appointed provincial commissions to recommend measures for dealing with the Jewish problem, he prejudged their task by instructing them to seek means of preventing the continued 'exploitation' of the Russian people. These were not the only commissions during the 1880s, and none of them recommended further restrictions on the Jews. At the highest level the Pahlen commission, reporting from 1884 to 1888, recommended steps towards opening the Pale of Settlement and easing restrictions on the Jews. Neither did the tsar's Council of State assent to new decrees against the Jews.

Liberal opinion still loyal to autocratic rule existed at high levels, especially in financial and business circles, which desired to end or at least to limit anti-Jewish laws. This fitted their vision of the Russian empire becoming a modern state. But Tsar Alexander III and his son Nicholas II, the last tsar, adhered unswervingly to absolutism and continued to oppress the Jews, vetoing measures presented in the aftermath of the 1905 revolution for slight relaxation of restrictions. Alexander III employed his autocrat's power to enact 'temporary laws' without Council of State ratification. These, the May Laws of 1882, remained in force until the end of tsardom in 1917. Further limitations were placed on the privilege of living outside the Pale and on Sunday trading by Jews who already did not trade on their Sabbath, and access to higher education was subjected to even more stringent quotas. Buying land and building new houses in rural areas were forbidden, even within the Pale. Jews were driven out of the rural liquor trade. Even within the Pale of Settlement

---

[45] The tale of the rabbi and the border smugglers is presented in Israel Oppenheim, 'The Kovno Circle of Rabbi Isaac Elhanan Spector: Organizing Western Public Opinion over Pogroms in the 1880's', (Hebrew) in Benjamin Pinkus and Ilan Troen (eds.), *National Jewish Solidarity in the Modern Period* (Hebrew; Ben-Gurion University, 1988), 85–115.

in cities such as Kiev new Jewish settlers were forbidden without special permits. Jews served in the army like other Russians, but officers' commissions were almost impossible to earn. All these rules were subject to the arbitrary whims of the local police, softened only by frequent bribes.

Pogroms and tsarist policy from 1881 made it clear that for Jews in Russia there would be no improvement, and they would remain a separate, inferior class. A far-reaching change occurred in Jewish thinking. The belief in gradual progress towards emancipation on the western model withered, and was replaced by Jewish answers to their version of the Russian reformists' oft-repeated question, 'What is to be done?' To be sure east European Jewry to a large extent continued its traditional political passivity and held devotedly to religious tradition while hoping and praying for better days. But after 1881 masses of Jews came to believe that there were new options to their deteriorating situation in Russia. There might be major change in Russia, but only a small minority, mostly Warsaw and St Petersburg Jewish bourgeois, believed it would come by liberal constitutionalism.

The wealthy St Petersburg leaders held three conferences in 1881 and 1882 at the mansion of Baron Ginzburg, the foremost Jewish banker. One conference was improvised and two were more formal, with invited participants from the provinces. Lengthy deliberations merely produced a fervent declaration of loyalty to the tsar and another decrying emigration as disloyal to the 'fatherland'. The participants gave little of the money which was raised for relief. One of them, the railway contractor Poliakov, took it on himself at a time when a mass eastward expulsion was feared to discuss with the notorious Ignatiev the possibility of a large-scale transfer of Jews to western Siberia. The conferences showed that except for Ginzburg and his son after him, Russian Jewry was not to have a bourgeois leadership in the style of western Jewry.[46] Their weak-kneed reaction to events lost the men of St Petersburg credibility and leadership among the Jewish masses. New, younger men and a few women took the magnates' place as leaders.

[46] B. Dinur, 'Ignatiev's "Programs" for Solving the Jewish Question and the Assemblies of Jewish Community Representatives 1881–1882' (Hebrew) *He-Avar*, 10 (May 1963), 5–82. The best study of the crisis year is Jonathan Frankel, *Prophecy and Politics: Socialism, Nationalism, and the Russian Jews, 1862–1917* (Cambridge, 1981), 49–132.

The Parting of Ways, 1881–1914

Among Russian possibilities in 1881 a liberating revolution was dangerous even to mention. However, an increasing number, especially young proletarian Jews and students, put their faith in revolution, risking and sometimes giving their lives to bring it about. They had a virtually mystical faith in the Russian peasant's revolutionary potential. When revolutionists vainly undertook in 1874 the gigantic task of arousing the peasantry, some young Russified Jews, having almost no Jewish peasantry, also went out to Russian peasant villages but were scornfully ejected. During the pogroms of 1881 at least two revolutionary circles circulated manifestos among peasants which encouraged pogroms against 'Jewish exploiters' as a step towards revolution. Issued without authorization, they outraged not only the Jewish members and were withdrawn. The young revolutionists soon learned the real meaning of pogroms.[47] Instead, during the 1880s and 1890s they turned to organizing revolution among Russia's new industrial proletariat. A similar effort also began among Jewish proletarians.

The establishment of Jewish socialism was the work of the Algemayne Bund fun Yidishe Arbeter in Rusland Poyln un Lite (General Association of Jewish Workers in Russia, Poland, and Lithuania) to cite its full name, always called just Bund.[48] Its goal was not as much trade unionism as aggressive labour action to mould a revolutionary force. Many Bund activists came from underground revolutionary ranks, brought back to their Jewish origins by pogroms and persecutions and by the realization

[47] Moshe Mishkinsky, '"Black Repartition" and the pogroms of 1881–1882', and Erich Haberer, 'Cosmopolitanism, Antisemitism and Populism: A Reappraisal of the Russian and Jewish Response to the Pogroms of 1881–1882', in Klier and Lambroza, *Pogroms*, 98–134.

[48] Frankel, *Prophecy and Politics*; Ezra Mendelsohn, *Class Struggle in the Pale: The Formative Years of the Jewish Workers' Movement in Russia* (Cambridge, 1970); Henry J. Tobias, *The Jewish Bund in Russia: From its Origins to 1905* (Stanford, Calif., 1972); Moshe Mishkinsky, *Reshit Tenu'at ha-Po'alim ha-Yehudit be-Russiah* (English title *The Emergence of the Jewish Labour Movement in Russia*) (Tel Aviv, 1981). A remarkable Yiddish study is Abraham Menes, 'Di Yidishe Arbeter-Bavegung in Rusland fun Onhayb 70er bizn Sof 90er Yorn,' *YIVO Historishe Shriftn*, iii. *Di Yidishe Sotsialistishe Bavegung biz der Grindung fun 'Bund'* (Vilna/Paris, 1939), 1–60.

that the growing Jewish proletariat could be organized only in their own Yiddish language. Some activists first had to learn Yiddish in order to communicate with Jewish workers. The Bundists dismissed Jewish and all nationalisms while affirming the Jews as a distinct national group. As they struggled to build a Jewish division of the army of revolution the Bundists educated promising workers to become organizers and intelligentsia. A noteworthy activity in many cities was the Bund's "Fighting Division" (*Kamf Obtaylung*) and 'Self-Defense' (*Zelbstshuts*), which suffered casualties from battling pogromists especially in 1905–6.[49] Funds for self-defence were donated mainly by an arch-capitalist Jew, Jacob H. Schiff of New York. The Bund's success in organizing Jewish workers inspired the sincere flattery by imitation of the secret police's Zubatov, who sponsored unrevolutionary trade unionism from 1900. Furiously attacked by the Bund and other revolutionary organizations and also rejected by tsarist reactionaries, the Zubatov movement's relative independence recruited a few genuine Jewish organizers. It enjoyed some success but the inherent contradiction in such a movement led to its demise in 1903.

Revolutionists 'possess an overflow of moral powers. They live quickly and die young,' wrote Vladimir Medem, a Bund leader and early opponent of Lenin who died in America aged 44. Very few could carry into mature years the life of hiding and evasion, or establish a family. Some went to the gallows, but many were exiled to Siberian villages to live and frequently die in privation. Medem, the son of a physician who converted to Russian Lutheranism, returned to the Jewish people but not to Judaism. After the failure of the revolution of 1905 many fled Russia to the United States, where they were important in building the American Jewish labour movement towards practical goals. A handful turned to socialist Zionism and settled in Palestine. Bundists who survived to retire from revolutionary activity were generally let alone by the tsarist police.

---

[49] The battered bodies of fighters were laid out on display before burial and photographed, often with banners and surrounded by surviving comrades. More or less the same was done, although less ceremoniously, in the case of pogrom victims after 1881. I do not know the source of this practice, which contravenes Jewish sensibilities and religious practice.

In its early years the Bund had no defined Jewish goal. It was emphatically secularist but did not engage in anti-religious activity, and it strenuously opposed Zionism, which it regarded as delusive bourgeois utopianism. The Bund's Jewish identity was definite if vague, and its language was Yiddish at least until the Jewish workers could carry on their affairs in Russian, as the Bund wanted. Years later it put forward a programme for secular Yiddish cultural life and education. The Bund's main activity, of course, was labour action. To organize workers was itself an act against the hated tsarist regime. There had been strikes of Jewish workers, of which perhaps the most dramatic was the pious *tallit* weavers of Kolomea in Galicia in 1893. Strikes were dramatic affairs, with processions, demonstrations, and ardent speeches to hundreds of workers. They took place in large towns such as Minsk and Vilna and enjoyed some notable successes. As a demonstration of proletarian unity for the dignity of the worker and against oppression the strike was more important than the tangible gains it achieved. The struggles of the Bund brought impressive accomplishments. Of 50,000 organized workers in Russia in 1903 30,000 were Jews, a proportion which encouraged the Bund not to accept ideological dictation from the Bolshevik wing of the Marxist Social Democrats led by Lenin. To him Bundism was the first proscribed ideology. Bundist sympathies lay more with the Mensheviks, led by Iulii Martov, himself a Jew.

The forces of tsarist reaction and of those seeking change, peaceful or revolutionary, both reached their climax in the dramatic events of 1903–7. Whether they took part as individuals or were victimized as a group Jews were drawn into the revolutionary storm. Violent agitation against them was carried on in the newspaper *Bessarabets*, published in Kishinev, the capital of Bessarabia (today Moldova), and subsidized by the government. Its calls for a 'Crusade against the Hated Race!' together with the heated atmosphere of Easter after the discovery of a child's body, quickly believed to be murdered by the Jews to use his blood in *mazzot*, brought on the notorious Kishinev pogrom of 19–20 April 1903. In the city of 147,000 where about 50,000 Jews lived, heated mobs roamed the Jewish areas undisturbed by police or soldiers, beating and murdering savagely while not forgetting to plunder. The provincial governor and chief of police had hundreds of police and thousands of soldiers at their disposal but did nothing. The toll was 47 Jews murdered, 424 wounded, 700 houses burned, 600 shops looted. There are photographs of butchered bodies awaiting burial and of groups of wounded victims. Few pogromists were apprehended and the few brought to trial were lightly punished. Government propaganda blamed the Jews for the disaster.

Cries of horror and outrage came from Russian liberal circles and throughout the world in reaction to this bloodiest pogrom yet. The government was accused of planning the Kishinev pogrom, especially the powerful minister of the interior, the arch-reactionary and anti-Semite Plehve. This was probably not so, but they did nothing to prevent or stop it and hardly anything to punish the perpetrators. They clearly had no interest in the lives of Jews and not even for public order as in earlier days. Money for relief and rehabilitation flowed in to Kishinev Jewry, and the moral reputation of Russian autocracy sank to zero.[50]

There was also a new sort of Jewish reaction to the pogrom. A few efforts at self-defence had been made in Kishinev, but it was believed that the Jews in the town only cowered and hid. The brilliant young poet Hayyim Nahman Bialik, who had gone there as a member of a Jewish commission of inquiry, wrote 'In the City of Slaughter',[51] one of the most famous modern Hebrew poems, which heaped scorn on the alleged cravenness of the attacked Jews. The poem had vast influence, fitting well into the Jewish mood of the day. Socialist and Bundist rebelliousness against autocracy and Zionist rejection of *galut* life and its passivity fused. When the next pogrom struck, at Gomel in September 1903, armed Jewish defence functioned vigorously, and continued during the severe disturbances throughout Russia which lay ahead. How many

---

[50] There is a sizeable literature on Kishinev. All the histories of Russian Jewry, cited elsewhere, deal with it. For the sixtieth anniversary, the World Federation of Bessarabian Jews published *Ha-Pogrom be-Kishinev* (Tel Aviv, 1963). Contemporary treatments are S. Lambroza in Klier and Lambroza, *Pogroms*, 195–207, and Edward H. Judge, *Easter in Kishinev: Anatomy of a Pogrom* (New York, 1992). Judge's *Plehve: Repression and Reform in Imperial Russia* (Syracuse, NY, 1983) regards Plehve as guilty not of first degree murder but of 'negligent homicide'.

[51] Russian censorship compelled it to be entitled originally 'The Vision of Nemirov', supposedly about a massacre during the Cossack rising of 1648. Everyone understood the real subject.

Jews' lives were saved by self-defence cannot be known, but it raised Jewish morale and made pogromists think twice before attacking. On the other hand, armed resistance may have encouraged Russian soldiers and police to join the attack. Many pogroms turned into battles.

While Russia was undergoing an economic depression in 1903–6, late in 1904 it went to war with Japan. Thousands of young Jews hastily emigrated to avoid serving the tsar in Manchuria, but many did go and witnessed Russia's disastrous conduct of the war. Most of the forty-three pogroms in 1904 were the doing of men mobilized for the unpopular war who hung restlessly around stations waiting to be dispatched. There was a wave of pogroms in the spring of 1905, and then a tremendous wave when the tsar's Manifesto granted the equivalent of a constitution in November 1905. In 1905 and until September 1906, 657 pogroms occurred, in which 3,103 Jews were murdered and tens of thousands injured.[52] The provinces of the Ukraine and adjacent Chernigov were the main centres, and hundreds were killed in the cities of Zhitomir, Bialystok, and Odessa. Extreme reactionary bands, known as the Black Hundreds, were at work during the pogroms with the blessing of the tsar, who accepted honorary membership in their parent body, the Union of the Russian People.[53] For the first time in history a government was organizing attacks on the Jews. Thus, it was found that anti-Semitic placards calling for pogroms were being written and printed inside police headquarters.

Jews were not mentioned in the tsar's Manifesto. They took for granted the right to vote and to be elected to the newly established Duma, and thousands signed a dignified demand for equal rights 'as men who, despite everything are conscious of their human dignity . . . [and]

[52] The figures of wounded are not reliable, since many did not go to the police or to hospitals. They suffered silently or were treated privately.

[53] Klier and Lambroza, *Pogroms*, 211–47, and Robert Weinberg, 'The Pogrom of 1905 in Odessa: A Case Study', ibid., 248–89. A voluminous contemporary report is A. Linden (ed.; pseud. of Leo Motzkin), *Die Judenpogrome in Russland* (2 vols., Cologne/Leipzig, 1910), giving figures slightly higher than Lambroza's. Abraham Ascher, *The Revolution of 1905* (2 vols., Stanford, Calif., 1988, 1992) is a full account, with vol. i, pp. 130–1 and 253–62 and vol ii, pp. 145–54 on pogroms; on reactionary politics, Hans Rogger, *Jewish Policies and Right-Wing Politics in Imperial Russia* (Berkeley and Los Angeles, 1986), 188–232; in general, Hugh Seton-Watson, *The Russian Empire, 1801–1917* (Oxford, 1967), 598–627.

as a matter of honour and justice'. Jews generally voted for liberals and moderate socialists, and twelve Jews were elected to the Duma. The Duma benefited Jews little. Its report denouncing the officials who countenanced the Bialystok pogrom gave the tsar, who detested the idea of a parliament, cause to dissolve the body and reduce its authority.[54] The three succeeding Dumas had little power, a very restrictive franchise, and few Jewish members. With revolution suppressed Russia returned to autocracy under the able conservative reformer Stolypin. He sought some improvement in Jewish status, but Nicholas II vetoed any change. The laws and decrees which practically imprisoned the Jews remained intact, and in 1911 the regime undertook a grotesque prosecution of Mendel Beiliss, a brick factory employee in Kiev, on a ritual murder canard. The prosecution and trial, which provoked world-wide protests, ended with Beiliss's exoneration, but the case demonstrated further the bankruptcy of tsarism on the eve of the war which brought its demise. To be sure the Beiliss trial also showed that an independent judiciary existed.[55] But Russia's path was set until revolution struck in 1917.

Towards Zion

The eventful year of 1881 brought the everlasting hope for Zion its first modern expressions in urgent and persuasive writings and action.[56] As we have seen, Haskalah writers and several rabbis and scholars in central and eastern Europe had for decades been urging settlement in the Holy Land and the purchase of its land to become the property of the Jewish people. Palestine was a country of bad government, ravaged soil, and

[54] Besides works just cited see Sidney S. Harcave, 'The Jewish Question in the First Russian Duma', *Jewish Social Studies*, 6/2 (April 1944), 155–76.

[55] A dramatic account is Maurice Samuel, *Blood Accusation: The Strange History of the Beiliss Case* (Philadelphia, 1966).

[56] The most sophisticated work in English of a vast literature is David Vital, *The Origins of Zionism* (Oxford, 1975). Two definitive Hebrew works by Shulamit Laskov are *Ha-Biluyim* (Jerusalem, 1979) and her much expanded edition of A. Druyanov's earlier documentary collection, *Ketavim le-Toldot Hibbat Zion ve-Yishuv Erets Yisrael* (6 vols., Tel Aviv, 1982–8).

almost no natural resources. The material position of its Jews had improved and their population increased after 1840, but no larger goals came to expression in the Holy Land itself other than those of piety and the religious merit of living and being buried in the Holy Land.

The new goals were articulated from 1881 by European writers and intellectuals. One was Moshe Leib Lilienblum of Odessa, a classic *maskil*: as an advanced Talmud student he rejected the piety of his upbringing in Lithuania and moved to Odessa, a new community where he unsuccessfully sought general education and a modern career. For many years Lilienblum wrote wrathfully against traditional religious ways. The events of 1881 brought him to the realization that his Haskalah reform programme was irrelevant and the surrounding world he had wanted to join was hostile. The source of the Jews' woes was not social or cultural backwardness but their homelessness as strangers everywhere. To remedy this, assimilation *en masse* was impossible and unworthy and emigration, even to the fortunate land of America, would still leave the Jews vulnerable strangers. The solution had to be a home, which could only be in Palestine. Leon Pinsker, a respected Russified physician in Odessa who had personally achieved what Lilienblum could only dream of, like him underwent a dramatic change of heart in 1881. His passionate German pamphlet *Autoemancipation* reached the same conclusion as Lilienblum in a somewhat different way.[57] The Jews, Pinsker argued, are an uncanny, homeless ghost nation wandering among the established nations, feared in the way humans fear ghosts. Out of the ghost nation's wanderings has come irrational Judaeophobia, the term Pinsker employed. The successes of individual Jews do not mitigate the Jewish people's homelessness with its Judaeophobic consequences. There must be some territory to become a Jewish homeland; Pinsker did not specify where.

Pinsker, a rather withdrawn bachelor, and Lilienblum became active leaders of the new Lovers of Zion (*Hovevei Zion*; the abstract noun is *Hibbat Zion*) movement which arose just after the pogroms. It quickly sprouted hundreds of uncoordinated branches in Russia and many parts

---

[57] A valuable collection of Zionist texts with discerning introductions is Arthur Hertzberg (ed.), *The Zionist Idea* (New York, 1959). Gideon Shimoni, *The Zionist Ideology* (Hanover, NH, 1995), is an excellent discussion.

of the Jewish world. As a country-wide membership organization Russian *Hovevei Zion* was beset with problems, starting with obtaining the necessary permission from the government. It was finally licensed in 1890 as a charitable society to aid settlers in Palestine. That, in fact, became its central dilemma as the fervour of 1881–2 gradually faded. The thirty delegates to the first *Hovevei Zion* conference, held at Katowice outside Russia in 1884, prudently devoted themselves to organizational and fund-raising matters. *Hibbat Zion*'s support included some rabbis of high standing.[58] To pious Jews it was sufficient to cite the authority of Rabbis Isaac Elhanan Spektor of Kovno, Samuel Mohilever of Bialystok, and Naftali Zvi Judah Berlin ('Nezib') who headed the Volozhin yeshiva. As *Hibbat Zion* supporters they expected the new colonists to live and to till the land in conformity with the *halakhah*, a demand which provoked friction between the religious and the irreligious. The colonists conformed, many with open reluctance.

Linked to *Hibbat Zion* was the first settlement movement, known by its acronym as *Bilu* (Beit Yaacov lekhu ve-nelkhah = House of Jacob, let us go; Isaiah 2: 5). Settling Palestine meant agricultural settlement. The restoration of the wasted land would be accomplished by a new class of Jews, not the stereotypical Jewish merchants, brokers, pedlars, and shopkeepers but sturdy farmers free of 'ghetto mentality'. The land had to be 'redeemed'—a telling term—an emphasis which continued well past the establishment of the state of Israel in 1948. Characteristic of *Bilu* members was their youth and a Haskalah or assimilated Russian background. Few if any came directly out of the Orthodox life of the masses. Their backgrounds differed little from those of Bund activists. Most *Bilu*ists were middle-class students, but the pogroms of 1881 turned them inward. On the basis of an ideology which owed much to the Russian revolutionary 'Land and Labour', they decided they would settle on the land and work it. *Bilu* went without money, substantial support, or agricultural training. Only about sixty arrived in Eretz Israel between 1882 and 1884 and a mere twenty-seven remained, far from the

---

[58] Relations between religion and Zionism are studied in two good books: Ehud Luz, *Parallels Meet: Religion and Nationalism in the Early Zionist Movement (1882–1904)* (Philadelphia, 1987); Yosef Salmon, *Dat ve-Zionut: 'Imutim Rishonim* (Hebrew; English title *Religion and Zionism: First Encounters*) (Jerusalem, 1990).

mass movement dreamed of. They succeeded only in founding the colony of Gedera, while independent individuals established Rishon le-Zion and Romanian *Hovevei Zion* founded Zikhron Yaakov and Rosh Pinah. Petah Tikvah had been founded in 1878 by a Jerusalem group and abandoned, to be refounded in 1884.

Poverty and illness enervated the settlers and their prospects were bleak. It was not *Hovevei Zion's* small donations which saved them but the vast largesse of Edmond de Rothschild of the banking family's Paris branch. While he did not share their nationalist enthusiasm a deep chord of sympathy existed, and 'the well-known benefactor' (*ha-nadiv ha-yadua*) so called in deference to his wish to remain officially anonymous, poured in £1.5 million between 1884 and 1899 (in today's money about twenty times as much). But there was a price. Rothschild took over the land in trusteeship and ruled the colonies he subsidized through a staff of domineering officials, paying periodic visits in regal style. Most of his overseers were unsympathetic to the colonists. There were uprisings, occasional dismissals of officials, and a few intractable farmers were expelled. The knowledgeable overseers realized that wheat and other grains were not suitable crops for the soil of Palestine and supervised the transition to more profitable vineyards and orchards. The Rothschild regime lasted until 1899, when 'the well-known benefactor' transferred his interests to the new Palestine Jewish Colonization Association (PICA) but without ending his benevolent interest. *Bilu's* time was past by 1890, the year *Hovevei Zion* was legalized by the Russian government. But *Hovevei Zion* was stagnating, raising little money and unable to make nationalism and Palestine the central idea in Jewish life. Under Russian autocracy and considering the character of Turkish rule in Palestine it dared not air political demands.

The hopes of 1881–2 were at a dead end when the Viennese journalist and playwright Theodor Herzl suddenly appeared on the scene. One of the most arresting and dramatic figures in all of Jewish history, his life has been the subject of extensive research, yet the man's aura retains some mystery. A native of Budapest whose prosperous family was German in its culture, with a grandfather who had known early proto-Zionist leaders, Herzl grew up in a conventionally liberal Jewish atmosphere with little Judaic knowledge. He first became a lawyer before succeeding as a playwright and as feature editor and feuilleton writer for Vienna's famous liberal newspaper, the *Neue Freie Presse*. From his student days in the 1880s Herzl knew Viennese anti-Semitism, and he also witnessed Dreyfus's public degradation in Paris. Repeatedly he was drawn to the Jewish question. He wrote his play *The New Ghetto* in white heat while imagining 'solutions' for the Jews like their mass public conversion at Vienna's St Stephen's Cathedral. He never abandoned dramatic and ceremonial trappings in his political life. Serious consideration of the Jewish question began in 1895, when he put forward proposals in conversations with Jewish literati, a fruitless meeting with Maurice de Hirsch, and a long letter, unanswered, to the Rothschilds. These ideas were written into *Der Judenstaat* (The Jews' State), published in 1896. Eight years of feverish activity ensued, ending only in Herzl's death of a heart ailment in 1904, aged 44. *Der Judenstaat* argued the inevitability of anti-Semitism wherever Jews dwelt in large numbers. A few years later, in 1898, Herzl stated the paradoxical connection between Zionism and emancipation. Here as in many other places he speaks of collective will as the force which achieves the goal:

It could not have been the historical intent of emancipation that we should cease to be Jews, for when we tried to mingle with the others we were rebuffed. Rather, the historical intent of emancipation must have been that we were to create a homeland for our liberated nation. We would not have been able to do this earlier. We can do it now, if we desire it with all our might.[59]

To remove anti-Semitism, concentrating the Jews in a state of their own was necessary. It was in the interest of enlightened governments to aid the Jews to establish this state which would be conducted on liberal, secular lines. Herzl's analysis of anti-Semitism and Jewish homelessness was not original, but he did not know what Pinsker, Lilienblum, and others had written in Russia. He did not originate an ideology but established a method, an organization, and a political goal. Moving the solution to the Jewish problem from settlement and colonization to international politics was new. The Zionist [60] goal was an internationally

[59] Quoted in David Vital, *Zionism: The Formative Years* (Oxford, 1982), 65.
[60] The term was coined in 1892 or 1893 by the nationalist ideologist Nathan Birnbaum.

guaranteed charter for large-scale Jewish settlement and economic development in Palestine, which would lead to a Jewish state. Most of *Der Judenstaat* deals with means and procedures, to the extent of discussing labour conditions and workers' housing in the state to come. To acquire the Jewish state there would be a 'Society of Jews' to manage political affairs, while a well-financed 'Jewish Company', chartered in England, would become responsible for the European Jewish exodus and resettlement. (Oriental Jewry was not mentioned in these plans.) No such daring scheme had yet been proposed. To carry it off Herzl depended on enlightened statesmen, apprehensive of destructive anti-Semitism in their own lands, and on benevolent Jewish financiers, weary of philanthropy and fearful for personal reasons. They would arrange the international loan to refinance Turkey's huge debt, and in return Turkey would allow the 'Jewish Company' to take control of Palestine. Before the charter was received there should not be further Jewish settlement in Palestine, which was puny in scale and could only irritate the Turkish rulers.

In more than a year of meetings and comings and goings, Herzl attracted interest but no firm, influential support. Edmond de Rothschild and the rest of his family would have no part of the scheme, nor would Hirsch or any other major Jewish financier, although one or two toyed with it. German and British statesmen were interested but remote. Turkey was unreachable as well as venal, uninterested before seeing the promised financial aid. Only Herzl's charm and boldness and his reputation as an influential journalist enabled him to negotiate, although he represented no one but himself.

Herzl had only slightly greater success in the Jewish sphere. Of all the Jewish men of letters he approached, only the social philosopher and essayist Max Nordau was converted and became a close confidant and a major asset to the movement. More typical, however, was the response of the Danish Jewish author and critic Georg Brandes, that his interests were universal and Jewish matters were but parochial. As we have seen, the socialist response was also negative. The Jewish communal establishments and religious movements in different countries were unfavourable, although Chief Rabbi Zadok Kahn in France and the Rabbis Hildesheimer of Berlin, father and son, at first showed interest. Young dissenters and old mavericks endorsed Herzl, such as the aged Reform Rabbi Bernard Felsenthal in Chicago and Rabbi Simeon Singer in London. Unable to win over financial, cultural, or communal élites in western Europe, Herzl finally turned to the Jewish masses, and received a rapturous reception from an immigrant audience at the Jewish Working Men's Club in London for his first speech to a popular audience. (He spoke a Judaized German somewhat equivalent to Yiddish.) Early in 1897 he concluded that he had to call a general assembly of Zionists.

Jewish wealth and political influence were found in western Europe but Jewish masses, intensity of Judaism, and *Hovevei Zion* had their home in eastern Europe. Why did *Hovevei Zion*, veterans of struggle and adversity, quickly accept the newcomer Herzl as their leader? Probably because they felt nearly at the end of their tether, doomed to little more than petty fund-raising. They were stung by the trenchant criticisms written in superlative Hebrew prose by a man most of them greatly esteemed, 'One of the People' (Ahad ha-Am, the *nom de plume* of Asher Ginzberg). The tide of support which led to Herzl's leadership swelled. *Hovevei Zion* knew he lacked Jewish depth, but he was a man of the great world and western society, an entrée which they sorely missed. In sociological terms, Herzl was a leader from the periphery, the first of many in the Zionist movement.

Herzl's Zionist assembly, planned for Munich, was not held there owing to its Jewish community's opposition. Other protests against Zionism came, one from a group of German rabbis dubbed the 'Protest-rabbiner'. The planned assembly moved to Switzerland, but not to Zurich because the Russian regime regarded it as the hotbed of refugee revolutionists. So it was at Basle that the gathering, named the World Zionist Congress, assembled in August 1897. Most Zionist groups took part, thereby acknowledging the man from Vienna as leader.[61] Herzl, who planned the Congress in fine detail, succeeded in making the event formal, parliamentary and widely publicized. From the three days' meeting emerged the World Zionist Organization (WZO), the 'Basle Programme' of the Zionst movement, and plans for the Jewish Colonial Trust (today's Bank Leumi). The programme announced:

---

[61] The Bund's founding meeting was held by coincidence at the same time, furtively in a house on the outskirts of Vilna.

Zionism aims for the creation of a home for the Jewish people in Palestine to be secured by public law. To that end the Congress envisages:

1. The purposeful advancement of the settlement of Palestine with Jewish farmers, artisans, and tradesmen. . . .

3. The strengthening of Jewish national feeling and consciousness. . . .

The history of the Zionist movement until the end of Herzl's short life revolves about his efforts. The support of a great power was essential, so Herzl worked first on Germany without success before turning to Great Britain with its vast colonial empire. The imperialist colonial secretary Joseph Chamberlain broached in 1902 the idea of a settlement in El Arish in the Sinai peninsula, but it was vetoed by Lord Cromer, Britain's proconsul in Egypt. In 1903 came a problematic sort of recognition of Zionism with the British offer of autonomous settlement in the almost unoccupied uplands of Uganda, deep in Africa. Although Herzl called Uganda a mere 'night asylum' for needy Jews until Palestine was secured, the offer split the Zionist movement. A powerful group, mainly east Europeans, opposed any destination but Palestine. Ironically, some religious Zionists led by Rabbi Reines were willing to accept Uganda, not of course as the Holy Land but to show religious opponents that Zionism with its irreligious leaders was only secular philanthropy without religious meaning.

A commission was sent to investigate Uganda. Herzl died in the meantime, and a negative report ended that bitter episode. After Uganda was rejected a Jewish Territorial Organization (ITO), led by the novelist Israel Zangwill, sprang up to seek an autonomous Jewish territory anywhere, but it met with no success. The indispensable Herzl was gone, and during the Russian revolution and pogroms of 1905–6 the Zionist movement could do nothing to aid Russian Jewry. Like many other ideological movements after 1905, it entered a depressed period. Under the conscientious but uninspiring David Wolffsohn the WZO departed from Herzl's policy and established a Palestine Office to promote what was called *Gegenwartsarbeit* (work of the present).

Zionist ideological differences, muted in Herzl's day, became prominent. Even in his lifetime many of the movement's able people, steeped in Jewish religion and culture and in the political trends of the time, sought to enrich the content of Zionism beyond the founder's rather bare political platform. At the Zionist Congress of 1901 the Democratic Fraction made its appearance.[62] It was composed mainly of young men from eastern Europe, many of them studying in western universities, with the young chemist Chaim Weizmann as a leader. They were strongly influenced by the doctrine of Herzl's critic Ahad ha-Am that the Jews required cultural rebirth in a Hebraist, mostly secular mode before they were ready for a state.[63] They also questioned Herzl's single-handed control. He placated the Democratic Fraction, which did not break with him. It dissolved in 1904 but its cultural goals became part of the Zionist programme. The adoption of cultural and educational work by the WZO antagonized the religious Zionists, who regarded Jewish culture as essentially religious. They declared that Zionist sponsorship of secular Jewish culture would compromise their loyalty to the movement. Religious Zionists were an embattled minority within orthodoxy, since the large majority of rabbinical leaders, even many once favourable to *Hibbat Zion*, opposed Herzl's Zionism.[64] The religious Zionists' opposition to the Zionist cultural programme prompted them to establish in 1902 the orthodox Mizrachi Zionist organization led by Rabbi Reines, the head of a modernist yeshiva at Lida in Lithuania.

Far from the religious scene socialist Zionism also arose, starting with Nachman Syrkin's German pamphlet of 1898, *The Jewish Question* and the socialist *Jews' State*.[65] To be sure socialist Zionist thought extended back to Moses Hess's almost forgotten *Rome and Jerusalem* of 1862. Faithful to class struggle ideology, socialist Zionists declined for years to take part in the bourgeois Zionist congresses. The first socialist Zionist groups in Russia originated about 1898, and their Poale Zion organization

---

[62] On this group see Jehuda Reinharz, *Chaim Weizmann: The Making of a Zionist Leader* (New York, 1985), 70–125, 195–8.

[63] On this extremely influential philosopher and ideologist see Steven J. Zipperstein, *Elusive Prophet: Ahad Ha'am and the Origins of Zionism* (London, 1993).

[64] Yosef Salmon, *Dat ve-Zionut: Imutim Rishonim* (Jerusalem, 1990) is the standard account.

[65] *Die Judenfrage und der sozialistische Judenstaat*, translated partly in Hertzberg, *The Zionist Idea*, 333–50. Fine discussions of socialist Zionist thought are Frankel, *Prophecy and Politics*, 288–453 (before 1917) and Shimoni, *The Zionist Ideology*, 166–235.

was founded in 1905. It drew many of its members from disillusioned revolutionists after the revolution of 1905. Poale Zion's main branches were in Minsk and Poltava, with Vilna and other Lithuanian towns also represented, and it blossomed in the freer conditions of Habsburg Galicia and among immigrants in the United States and Britain. Ideology was central. Contrary to the doctrines of Marx and international socialism, Poale Zion ideology set out to demonstrate the Jewish people's collective existence and future. It fought against the doctrine that Jews in the labour movement were only Russians or Poles. Utopianism and class collaboration were common accusations against socialist Zionists, who replied through their own able ideologists. Its first great theoretician, Nachman Syrkin, often quoted Marx but was no Marxist and denied immutable laws of social development. He pressed the Jewish proletariat to organize socialist settlement in Palestine and self-defence in the Diaspora. Rejecting the connection made between capitalism and anti-Semitism which the coming revolution would sever, Syrkin insisted on the permanence of anti-Semitism in the Diaspora and the need for a mass exodus to a Jewish land built on socialist principles. Ber Borochov was a more influential ideologist than Syrkin, besides being a Yiddish linguistic scholar, because he performed the intellectual feat of synthesizing the regnant Marxism with Zionism.[66] He introduced the concept of relations of production into his analysis, which required Marxists to consider seriously the needs of national groups such as the Jews no less than those of economic classes. Borochov also 'proved' that Palestine was the only possible land for Jewish colonization, not for religious or sentimental reasons which he disregarded but because nowhere else could the Jewish proletariat grow without anti-Semitic discrimination and participate in the world-wide class struggle. Borochov even argued that the Jewish proletariat would be drawn to Palestine by an automatic ('stychic') social process. Syrkin, on the other hand, drew more than Borochov on Jewish tradition yet was willing to consider any suitable

[66] Selections from Borochov in translation have appeared as *Nationalism and the Class Struggle*, ed. A. G. Duker (New York, 1937, repr. 1972) and *Class Struggle and the Jewish Nation*, ed. Mitchell Cohen (New Brunswick, NJ, 1984). M. Minc has published extensively in Hebrew on Borochov: *Igrot . . . 1897–1917* (Letters) (Tel Aviv, 1989); *Ha-ma'gal ha-Rishon 1900–1906* (Life, 1900–1906) (Tel Aviv, 1977); *Zmanim Hadashim . . . 1914–1917* (Life, 1914–1917) (Tel Aviv, 1988).

territory for Jewish needs. One may read Borochov's 'scientific' doctrines as mainly apologetics which squared Jewish nationalism with the Marxism which then dominated the socialist movement. Its 'scientific' forecast is really myth, and Borochov seems to have given up Marxism in the last years of his short life.

International Migration

The generation before 1914 was rich in leftist and Zionist ideologies. However, the great Jewish mass migration proceeded without ideology, since the quest for lands of freedom and economic opportunity hardly qualifies as ideology. The ideologists who held that migration to Palestine would be 'stychic' on account of political and economic pressures driving Jews to emigrate might better have said this of mass emigration westward.[67] However, with the exception of Poale Zion, the leaders of communities, ideological movements, and religious life urged east European Jews not to emigrate overseas. Jewish leaders in the United States and other lands of immigration expressed themselves likewise. There were altruistic as well as self-interested reasons for their opposition: anti-Semitism was universal, and emigrants would only exchange woes in one country for woes in another; capitalist oppression and disastrous economic fluctuations reigned everywhere; emancipated countries were religiously dissolute and missionaries were ubiquitous; a revolution would come and transform conditions in Russia, an argument abandoned after the failed revolution of 1905. In the receiving countries there was the desire to avoid the burden and embarrassment of poor relations and to avoid a probable surge of anti-Semitism inspired by masses of Jewish foreigners. We cannot know how many Jews heeded warnings and remained in eastern Europe, but 2,400,000 did cross international frontiers between 1881 and 1914. Approximately 80 per cent went to the United States of America, where they constituted a net proportion of 11 per cent approximately of the 22,000,000 European

[67] See generally, Lloyd P. Gartner, 'The Great Jewish Migration—the East European Background', *Tel-Aviver Jahrbuch für deutsche Geschichte*, 27 (1998), 107–33.

immigrants who arrived between 1880 and the virtual cessation of im-migration in 1914.[68]

For poor emigrants, meaning the vast majority, without knowledge of any larger environment or a foreign language, the voyage was especially perilous. While leaving Russia was illegal, it was overcome by large-scale bribery of border guards on the part of smugglers who guided Jews across for a price. Russian passports were expensive, slow to secure, required bribes, and Germany, which emigrants had to cross *en route* to seaports, did not demand them. After 1907, thanks to the efforts of the Jewish Colonization Association (ICA), emigration from Russia was legalized and passports became more easily obtainable. The ICA in turn obliged the Russian regime by urging emigrants to acquire passports and to embark on vessels which sailed from the Latvian port of Libau and called at Rotterdam before crossing the Atlantic. Border smugglers also operated at Libau and passports were not essential even there. However, Russian ships out of Libau did not afford a 'prosperous voyage', the trip was circuitous, and probably many emigrants wanted to leave things Russian behind them. At the German border, officials required of emi-grants wishing to cross Germany tickets for German ships, usually the Hamburg-America (HAPAG) line from Hamburg, or they would be com-pelled to buy them on the spot. This policy was meant to benefit Ger-man shipping interests, which were headed by the Kaiser's friend and head of HAPAG Albert Ballin, himself a Jew who had made his start in the emigration trade. For reasons of mutuality, tickets in hand for British lines were also accepted. Besides Hamburg, Bremen and Rotter-dam were frequent Continental ports of embarkation for Jews, but only Hamburg had a large emigrant compound where travellers were held

---

[68] An authoritative study is Simon Kuznets, 'Immigration of Jews to the United States: Background and Structure', *Perspectives in American History*, 9 (1975), 35–125. Jews consti-tuted 9% of gross immigration, and after returning immigrants are deducted 11% of net immigration. Unlike the Jews and Irish, a high proportion of other nationalities came to the United States for limited periods, often to make enough money to buy land back home. Brief statements are Lloyd P. Gartner, 'Immigration and the Formation of Ameri-can Jewry, 1840–1925', *Journal of World History*, 11/1–2 (1968), 297–312 and his 'Jewish Migrants en Route from Europe to North America: Traditions and Realities', *Jewish History*, 1/2 (Fall 1986), 49–66. The larger picture of European emigration is placed in Philip Taylor, *The Distant Magnet: European Emigration to the U.S.A.* (New York, 1971).

until they sailed. Then a band escorted them with their baggage to the ship. Many sailed only as far as England where a ticket for America was substantially cheaper than at Hamburg, and they then sailed from Liverpool. Less than 10 per cent of transmigrants arriving in England remained there, which was enough to produce a settlement of perhaps 120,000 east European immigrant Jews.[69] Germany like England bestrode the emigrants' travel routes, and perhaps 80,000 foreign Jews lived there despite insecurity of status and the extreme difficulty of naturalization for them and their German-born children. In France, away from travel routes, about 40,000 east European Jews settled before 1914, nearly all in Paris.[70]

The ocean voyage to America was uncomfortable and often sickening but practically all ships reached their destination. It was a widely copied innovation of Albert Ballin for ships to carry emigrants in their steerage in place of the heavy freight which had gone the other way. The ships, displacing about 5,000 tons and carrying 500 to 1,000 persons each, made port, generally New York, in seven to ten days. Big ships also carried emigrants in steerage; they were among those who went down with the *Titanic* in 1912. Arriving steerage, immigrants had to pass inspection at the Ellis Island immigration depot in New York harbour, a place which, in John Higham's words, 'will be remembered as long as the story of the immigrants survives' and where 1 to 2 per cent were disqualified.[71] In Britain immigrants could debark and go their way no differently from getting off a bus, until strict inspection of immigrants' ability to support themselves was prescribed by the Aliens Act of 1905.

To these large outlines of the history of Jewish migration westward many additions may be made. The process of immigration and the pro-

---

[69] Lloyd P. Gartner, *The Jewish Immigrant in England, 1870–1914* (2nd edn., London, 1973), 24–56.

[70] Jack Wertheimer, *Unwelcome Strangers: East European Jews in Imperial Germany* (New York, 1987); Paula Hyman, *From Dreyfus to Vichy*.

[71] John Higham, *Stranger in the Land*, 99. Ellis Island functioned from 1892, when it replaced Castle Garden at the foot of Manhattan, to 1964. Reasons for rejection were contagious disease, or manifest inability to support oneself or to have a spouse or parent who could do so. Prostitutes and anarchists were excluded, but obviously could not be readily identified. There is much folklore about Ellis Island, which today is a museum of immigration history.

tection of immigrants was a major concern of Jewish communities. Thus, German Jewish organizations placed welfare workers at railway terminals and at the Russo-German border crossings, where they evidently made little impact in the hectic, turbulent atmosphere which reigned there. Indeed, there is evidence that emigrants started to avoid the rough treatment prevailing at the German–Russian border stations and travelled instead via Austria, Switzerland and France to Dutch and Belgian ports. Treatment at the border stations thereupon improved. At the dockside in London, Poor Jews Temporary Shelter representatives met arriving immigrants, keeping waterfront crooks away and also providing temporary lodging as well as guidance for travellers to provincial destinations. Similar work was performed exemplarily from 1903 by the Hebrew Sheltering and Immigrant Aid Society (HIAS),[72] in New York and other United States port cities, and by the Baron de Hirsch Institute in Montreal. Immigration authorities accepted HIAS as guarantors in cases when one sick member of a family group was not admitted to the United States. HIAS saw to the person until he or she recovered and could be admitted. It often appealed, sometimes successfully, on behalf of excluded arrivals. The activity of the Jewish Association for the Protection of Girls and Women in meeting unaccompanied girls at London's dockside testifies to the existence of a slimy Jewish traffic in prostitution. Men in the traffic lured girls in east European towns and even on board ship to go with them to 'fine positions' in western countries. They even went through with marriage, but when the girls reached the destination they were forced into prostitution if they did not do so voluntarily. To reach South Africa or Argentina, favourite destinations for the traffic in prostitution, it was necessary to pass through London, itself a favoured destination, where the Jewish Association's representatives warned off often unsuspecting girls and when possible had the men in the trade arrested and prosecuted. The traffic was also carried on in the United States, but apparently girls were not imported because the local supply was sufficient.[73]

[72] Unconnected to the Hebrew Emigrant Aid Society which functioned from 1881 to 1884.

[73] Lloyd P. Gartner, 'Anglo-Jewry and the Jewish International Traffic in Prostitution', *AJS Review*, 7–8 (1982–3), 129–78.

An intensive effort was made in the United States to draw immigrants away from the densely crowded eastern cities, above all New York. This was done by the Industrial Removal Office, administered by B'nai B'rith, which found jobs for immigrant workers in western cities and helped them to move there with their families. Perhaps 75,000 immigrants became removal clients, and successful cases attracted others to follow them.[74] More ambitious but less successful was the Galveston movement, financed by the banker-philanthropist Jacob H. Schiff. From 1907 to 1914 Jews were recruited in eastern Europe for the long voyage to the Texas port of Galveston, to be dispersed from there in the lightly populated south-western United States.[75] Numerous attempts to make farmers of the Jewish immigrants enjoyed little success. There was a grandiose but ultimately disappointing agricultural project during the 1890s of Baron de Hirsch's Jewish Colonization Association (ICA) in Argentina. ICA also tried similarly in Brazil and Canada with modest results.[76] Besides, Canada and Argentina each received a sizeable number of immigrants from eastern Europe, who settled mainly in Montreal and Buenos Aires as pedlars and small tradesmen as well as clothing workers. Between 1900 and 1920, 98,000 Jews came to Canada, 10,000 of them from the United States, and 87,000 came to Argentina by the end of 1914.

The Jewish communities' greatest effort in the countries of immigration was invested in the urban slums where the great majority of immigrants dwelt. The extensive charitable and educational aid of native Jews had the underlying intention of making the immigrants Americans, British, and so forth, as well as Jews in the style these benefactors thought proper. In the era before public relief Jewish charities assisted widows, orphans, the handicapped and unemployed, while attempting by means of social casework to ameliorate their condition more basically. Existing

---

[74] Robert A. Rockaway, *Words of the Uprooted: Jewish Immigrants in Early Twentieth-Century America* (Ithaca, NY, 1998). Many histories of American Jewish communities include discussions of local IRO activities.

[75] Bernard Marinbach, *Galveston: Ellis Island of the West* (Albany, NY, 1983).

[76] Haim Avni, *Argentina 'H-Aretz ha-Ye'udah: Mif'al ha-Hityashvut shel Baron de Hirsch be-Argentina* (Hebrew; Argentina 'The Promised Land'; Baron de Hirsch's Colonization Project) (Jerusalem, 1973); Arthur Goren, 'Mother Rosie Hertz, the Social Evil, and the New York Kehillah', in *Michael: On the History of the Jews in the Diaspora*, iii, ed. Lloyd P. Gartner (Tel Aviv, 1975), 188–210.

hospitals and orphan homes were expanded and new ones founded, notably sanatoriums for victims of tuberculosis, the widespread immigrant workers' disease. Employment agencies, vocational training, hospitals, summer camps, free personal and business loans, recreation facilities, and community centres were established in every sizeable city. Thanks to the generosity of 'uptown Jews' the downtowners received more help than any other immigrant group, and the Jewish welfare institutions ranked among the best of their kind. The foundations of modern social work were laid in philanthropic efforts to aid immigrants and their offspring.

This impressive Jewish philanthropy was not without controversy. Relations between immigrants and their benefactors were often far from harmonious. The benefactors might consider their beneficiaries insolent, demanding, and ungrateful, too much given to old-fashioned Orthodoxy or to doubtful ideologies such as Zionism or socialist radicalism. It was disturbing that some immigrant children turned to crime. The immigrants too had complaints. In their eyes the Jewish patricians were ashamed to be Jews, aloof and domineering and lacking kindness and sympathy, and their vaunted 'scientific' charities were stern and cold. There was a measure of justice on each side, yet the patricians provided the model of American (or English or French) Jew, the image of Jewish success, and functioned as sponsors and protectors in the wider society. Even more important than their philanthropies, Jewish leaders upheld free immigration and were critically important in holding back for years the advent of severe immigration restriction. And by vastly enlarging the size of the Jewish community, the immigrants gave its leaders greater public standing than they would otherwise have had. Many leaders and native Jews were impressed by the immigrants' Jewish fervour, whether it was for traditional religion or a modern secular movement. They brought a previously unknown enthusiasm, intensity, and intellectualism into the rather pale Jewish life of their new countries. The immigrants established welfare and educational institutions of their own, often financed with difficulty but more personal in manner than the patricians' philanthropies. The basis was laid for collaboration between the native and immigrant wings of the Jewish communities.[77]

[77] Patrician aloofness is exemplified in the Jewish Board of Guardians in London; Gartner, *England*, *passim*. The gradual shift in American Jewish communities from

East European Jewish immigration had distinctive trades and occupations. As a rule the immigrants were occupied in making consumer goods, and toiled in jobs which required relatively little skill in workshops rather than factories. Small production units and low overheads opened the way to entrepreneurship which was eagerly desired by many Jewish workers. By far the foremost immigrant trade was the making of ready-to-wear clothing, built primarily by east European Jewish entrepreneurs and workers into a vast industry whose American centre was New York City and London in Great Britain. Tens of millions of American and British men, women and children wore well crafted, fashionable, ready-made garments made by immigrant producers and bought at low prices. Ready-made clothing, which was also an important export industry, was high-risk and speculative, teeming with activity and subject to the whims of fashion and seasonal fluctuations. Fortunes were often made and unmade, and workers easily became entrepreneurs and vice versa. At the peak of Jewish participation in the ready-made clothing industry about 1915, an estimated 250,000 Jews in the United States, practically all immigrants and some of their children, found livelihoods in it. Hardly less common as an immigrant occupation was commerce at all its levels. Jewish pedlars roamed in neighbourhoods when shops were few, alongside street hawkers, pushcart owners occupying fixed places in street markets, and customer pedlars who filled orders taken from customers in their homes. Many advanced to shopkeeping and some came to own large stores and wholesale firms. Very few immigrants could enter white-collar or professional occupations such as law, pharmacy, bookkeeping, accountancy, or teaching because they arrived at too mature an age to acquire the necessary education and language mastery. These became vocational goals for the next generation, who had to cope with considerable anti-Semitism in non-immigrant spheres of employment.[78]

aloofness to collaboration is found in Gartner, *History of the Jews in Cleveland* (Cleveland, 1978), 209–64; Arthur A. Goren, *New York Jews and the Quest for Community: The Kehillah Experiment, 1908–1922* (New York, 1970); Jeffrey S. Gurock, *When Harlem Was Jewish, 1870–1930* (New York, 1979).

[78] Every American Jewish local community history discusses these matters. For the Jewish immigrant economy in New York City, the largest community by far, see Moses

Hebrew and Yiddish literature of that era in eastern Europe depicted the Jews, of whom the vast majority were poor, as gaunt and pinched from hunger. The few well-to-do were identified conspicuously by their ample paunches. These portrayals expressed the central reality: poverty meant hunger and prosperity meant eating. Immigrant consumption in America began with more and better food, and as incomes rose the quantity and quality of what they ate likewise improved. A unique study by researchers of the British Board of Trade in 1910 studied intensively a sample of 758 Jewish working men's families, which comprised 4,452 persons of whom 2,216 were children, looking closely into their diet like that of other immigrants in many cities. The bulk of immigrants had weekly incomes between £2 and £5 ($10 and $25). Few wives worked, for income from that source was merely a few shillings weekly, and the main source of higher income was the contribution made by working children. Families once better off could retain 45 per cent of their income after paying for food and rent, and used this surplus to shop and spend in what had been the dream world of consumer goods. Higher consumption, however, began at the table. A Jewish immigrant family in the middle of the income scale—about £4 ($20) a week—consumed twenty-eight eggs, ten pounds of beef, and 8.51 quarts of milk weekly. As the British researchers put it: 'The most noticeable peculiarities of the Jewish dietary . . . are the total abstinence from pig's meat, the large quantity of poultry, fresh milk, eggs and rye bread consumed, and the comparatively small consumption of flour, potatoes, sausage, lard, suet and dripping and condensed milk.' From eating eggs and beef to a piano in the front room to a country vacation, the hard work of immigrants yielded its rewards. [79]

Revolutionary changes occurred in the forty years which were cut

Rischin, *The Promised City: New York's Jews, 1870–1914* (Cambridge, Mass., 1962), and for the later period Deborah Dash Moore, *At Home in America: Second Generation New York Jews* (New York, 1981). A large mid-western Jewish community is discussed in Lloyd P. Gartner, *Cleveland.*

[79] Great Britain, Board of Trade, *Working Class Rents, Housing and Retail Prices . . . Rates of Wages in the Principal Towns of the United States of America* (Cd. 5609, 1911), pp. lxxxviii, 419. Consumption of fresh fruits and vegetables in the diet is not mentioned. See also Andrew R. Heinze, *Adapting to Abundance: Jewish Immigrants, Mass Consumption and the Search for American Identity* (New York, 1990).

short by the outbreak of war in 1914. More than 2.5 million Jews underwent the fundamental change of settling in a new country. The new Palestine Jewry and the Zionist movement which fostered it secured a firm foothold in the Jewish world. Anti-Semitism, Zionism and mass migration were symptoms that European Jewry's century of emancipation and growth was imperilled. The European continent and its 7 million Jews stood on the brink of disastrous developments.

9

From War to War, 1914–1939

The catastrophic wars from 1914 to 1945 which practically destroyed Europe came on unexpectedly. There was ample warning of the advent of the Second World War in 1939 to all who would see, but the European peoples before 1914 had little or no inkling of the explosion to come, and of course neither had the Jews. Only a few sophisticated diplomatic observers had forebodings. The murder of the Austrian Archduke Ferdinand, heir to the Habsburg throne, in Serbia on 28 June 1914 did not at first indicate that the continent would be aflame five weeks later. The soldiers marched off in August to enthusiastic cheers ringing in their ears, confident that the war would be over by the year's end. With the exception of minorities among the German Social Democrats and the British Labour Party, the European socialists abandoned international labour solidarity as they too gave their support to the war. As the war dragged on some German socialists began to oppose it. Opposition to the United States' entry in the war in 1917 came not only from socialists but also from native pacifists and German Americans. This socialist opposition, particularly in Germany, included many Jews. But by 1917 opposition came too late to halt the war; in Germany it only served to establish the stab-in-the-back alibi when Germany had to surrender a year later.

The vast majority of Jews pledged support to their respective countries, although it was a disturbing thought that Jew might fight Jew in opposite armies. In the west British and French Jews endorsed the wartime slogan of *Union sacrée*, proclaiming that national unity replaced political partisanship for the war's duration. When Kaiser Wilhelm II declared, 'I know only Germans, but no parties,' German Jews gladly assumed that civil peace (*Bürgfrieden*) meant that anti-Semitism would cease. Notwithstanding official American neutrality, most American Jews, especially immigrants from eastern Europe, tended to favour the German-Austrian side out of hatred for its Russian enemy. Yet in Russia thousands of Jews rushed to enlist and some Russian Jewish students abroad returned home to serve in the tsar's army. Even the anti-Semitic newspaper *Novoye Vremya* praised Jewish patriotism. For Jews the decisive front was in the east, where millions lived and hundreds of thousands performed military duty. Far more than what happened on the western front, the end of the German, Austrian, Turkish, and Russian empires in the east on account of the war had vast consequences for the Jews and the world.

As the war ground on with no end in sight and the killing mounted and food and other shortages grew, civilian populations became restive. *Bürgfrieden* crumbled and the Jews soon felt the consequences. The end of civil peace brought trouble to Jews even in Great Britain. With volunteering practised until 1916 and compulsory service in effect only from then, an estimated 41,500 British Jews served, of whom 2,000 lost their lives. On the other hand, thousands of unnaturalized Jews qualified for exemption as foreign, that is, Russian, subjects. A section of the public called the Jews 'shirkers', overlooking the creditable Jewish military record as they saw exempt Jewish aliens carrying on civilian life. In Leeds and in London's East End there were riots against immigrant Jews in June and September 1917. However, the fall of tsardom earlier in 1917 enabled a treaty to be negotiated which offered conscription in Britain or deportation to serve in Russia. About 4,000 Jews were returned to Russia, where few served but still fewer ever could get back to Britain.[1] The 186,000 Jews of France and Algeria contributed 46,000 soldiers, of whom 6,500 fell. In the German army there were 85,000 Jews, 12,000 of whom lost their lives.[2] The figure of 600,000 has been cited as the number of Jews who served in the Russian army. However Russian figures are far from certain, and it cannot be determined how many Russian Jews fell in the line of duty. During the United States' nineteen months in the war, 250,000 Jews served and 3,500 were killed.

The German military occupation of Russian Poland brought a stream of Polish Jews into Germany. Widely accused of being dangerous foreigners, many of the approximately 35,000 were actually prisoners of

---

[1] V. D. Lipman, *A History of the Jews in Britain since 1858* (Leicester, 1990), 143–7; Colin Holmes, *Anti-Semitism in British Society, 1876–1939* (London, 1979), 121–40.

[2] Bernhard Blumenkranz (ed.), *Histoire des Juifs en France* (Toulouse, 1972), 373.

war taken to Germany as workers.[3] Many never returned to war-torn Russia. At the beginning of the war the German high command had proclaimed to 'Jews in Poland' that they should welcome the German armies which were liberating them from Russian tyranny.[4] In German plans for a post-war restoration of Poland under German domination the Jews were counted on as allies and German Jewish organizations working among Polish Jews, such as the Komitee für den Osten and the orthodox Agudath Israel, enjoyed government favour.

The idyll of *Bürgfrieden* did not last long. German efforts to secure Polish Jewish support did not inhibit anti-Semitic fabrications, which became common currency as the war lengthened and German youth was killed wholesale. Jews, it was alleged, were avoiding danger by bribery or other methods of serving far from the front. They supposedly engaged in hoarding and profiteering. Anti-Semites had collaborators among some senior army commanders in spreading such tales as a means of deflecting unprecedented, nettling questions about the high command's infallibility and rising demands for far-reaching political and social reform. The War Minister accommodated the defamers by ordering a census of Jews in the armed forces, particularly comparing the proportion of front-line with rear-echelon Jewish soldiers. Anti-Semitic officers tampered with the census returns, such as counting wounded front-line soldiers in a hospital as rear echelons. The results showed 27,515 front-line Jewish soldiers in November 1916, 4,782 in the rear and 30,005 in the armies of occupation. This proportion of combat soldiers equalled or surpassed that of non-Jews. The results were never published. The census itself implied doubts of Jewish patriotism. As ever, truth did not silence the anti-Semites and wartime anti-Semitism flourished. Its bitter residue exploded when Germany unexpectedly lost the war despite optimistic communiqués almost to the end, and someone had to be blamed.[5]

---

[3] Werner Jochmann, 'Die Ausbreitung des Antisemitismus', in *Deutsches Judentum in Krieg und Revolution 1916–1923*, ed. Werner E. Mosse (Tübingen, 1971), 414 n.14; S. Adler-Rudel, *Ostjuden in Deutschland 1880–1940* (Tübingen, 1959), 34–7.

[4] One of several similar versions is published in Adler-Rudel, *Ostjuden*, 156–7.

[5] Only an anti-Semitic writer was given access to the census results, which he distorted. Some figures are given in *Judisches Lexicon*, iii, cols. 460–1. See Jochmann, 'Ausbreitung', 414–31; Werner T. Angress, 'The German Army's "Judenzahlung" of 1916', *Leo Baeck Institute Year Book*. 22 (1978), 117–35.

In Russia Jewish 'spying' was used to explain the great retreat of the ill-equipped, barely trained Russian army under often incompetent commanders. Masses of Galician Jews fled west before the Russian invasion in 1915, crowding into Budapest, Vienna, and other western cities, while the Russian occupiers decreed mass expulsion of those who remained. The German counter-offensive into Russia in 1915 allowed many to return to their homes, but the see-saw ruined the lives and destroyed the property of hundreds of thousands. The most drastic step was taken on 28 April 1915, when the Russian military ordered the prompt expulsion of the Jews from most of Lithuania. Tragic scenes were enacted as several hundred thousand Jews (only an approximation is possible), left practically all their possessions and wandered on foot or wagon or by train seeking a place to stay. Expelled Lithuanian Jews broke through the hitherto sacrosanct Pale of Settlement boundaries.[6] There was heavy loss of life owing to disease and hunger besides violence and robbery, and pogroms against village Jews who were allowed to remain. The Lithuanian expulsion was not the last, and hunger and epidemic disease were everywhere rampant.

The greatest Jewish relief effort ever undertaken began at this time. The St Petersburg Jewish leaders proved inadequate to the task of mass relief and grass-roots organizations sprang up, itself a step towards the democratization of Russian Jewry. In the west, especially the United States, nearly every small organization, home town society, synagogue, and Jewish trade union collected for the stricken Russian Jews. Their efforts combined with those of native American Jews in 1914 into the American Jewish Joint Distribution Committee. Representatives of the Joint, as it was familiarly known, distributed funds usually through the local east European Jewish communities. Despite many disagreements and frictions, the Joint performed remarkably in war-torn eastern Europe and elsewhere, organizing local communities in many places in order to distribute relief. Its work continues to the present day.

Beyond the war's vale of tears and blood, political developments of

---

[6] Louis Stein, 'The Exile of the Lithuanian Jews in the Conflagration of the First World War' (Yiddish), *Lite (Lithuania)*, ed. M. Sudarsky *et al.*, i (New York, 1951), cols. 89–118 [written in 1941]); Salo W. Baron, *The Russian Jew under Tsars and Soviets* (New York, 1964), 187–98.

the deepest importance to the Jewish future were taking place. Here the fundamental difference between the Jewish position in the two world wars is evident. In the Second World War from 1939 to 1945 the Jews were friendless and powerless in the face of a fiendish enemy. Nazi Germany's foes had no need to court the Jews, and the Holocaust proceeded with pitifully little rescue aid from those who were supposedly the Jewish people's allies. Nor was there any concern for the post-war fate of the Jews. During the First World War the Jewish people, although far poorer materially in many of their lands of settlement than they were in 1939, were treated as a force in world affairs, and both sides anxiously sought Jewish support. Almost in the manner of anti-Semites, statesmen operated from assumptions about world Jewish power. The future of Palestine and the oppressed condition of Russian Jewry were the stakes in bidding for Jewish support. Jewish communities in neutral countries, including the United States until April 1917, and the governments of Great Britain and France pressed their Russian ally to emancipate the Jews or at least to treat them better and thus avert Jewish hostility. Jacob H. Schiff, the foremost international banker in the United States, kept his firm, Kuhn & Loeb, from floating Russian bonds on account of their treatment of his people. But Nicholas II and his regime remained impervious until their downfall in March 1917, an event joyfully greeted around the democratic world. The end of tsarism enabled President Woodrow Wilson to lead the United States into war as Russia's ally one month later in the name of democracy. The new, republican Russia, which lasted seven months until the Bolshevik coup, speedily emancipated Russian Jewry along with other oppressed minorities, a far cry from the long debates during the French Revolution and the revolutions of 1848–9. Although ravaged by the war, Russian Jewry entered a short period of flourishing community activity.

Jews everywhere emphatically desired Jewish emancipation in Russia and wherever else it was needed. However, opinions were divided over two additional demands: those made by Zionists and national minority rights.[7] The latter ideology originated among Austrian intellectuals,

---

[7] The best general study remains Oscar I. Janowsky, *The Jews and Minority Rights (1898–1919)* (New York, 1933); see also Simon Dubnow, *Nationalism and History: Essays on Old and New Judaism*, ed. with intro. by Koppel S. Pinson (Philadelphia, 1958) (the

many of them Jews, pondering the future of the multinational Habsburg realm. They proposed that it become a federation of nationalities. Each would enjoy autonomy and state financial support in its cultural and educational affairs and be allowed to use their national language in public life, including parliaments and the courts. However, most minority rights theorists refused to recognize the Jews as a nationality eligible for autonomy, mainly because they had no territory. Lenin, who was conversant with these theories, similarly refused to view Russian Jews as a nationality. The idea of national minority rights for the Jews received full exposition from the historian and publicist Simon Dubnow and the Yiddishist Chaim Zhitlovsky, and the socialist Zionists of Poale Zion as well as the Bund gave organizational backing. Gradually the Jews too were recognized as a national minority. A congress in Moscow of newly emancipated Russian Jewry also demanded minority rights. Jewish community leaders in Great Britain, but not in France, somewhat reluctantly endorsed Jewish minority rights.[8] In the United States a popularly elected American Jewish Congress in May 1917 endorsed what was cautiously rephrased as group rights, and the patrician leaders of the American Jewish community were won over to the idea. British and American Jewry disclaimed minority rights for themselves, specifying that they were meant solely for the multinational Habsburg empire or its successor states, and for Russia.

The Zionist movement, mostly in the doldrums since the split over the Uganda project and Herzl's death in 1904, came to renewed life during the war. It carefully asserted neutrality by moving its headquarters from Berlin to Copenhagen. At the same time, Zionists in the warring powers urged their respective governments to win Jewish support in the United States and other neutral countries, and that of Russian Jewry even while tsarist oppression continued, by declaring in favour of a

fullest edition is in French by Renée Poznanski, *Lettres sur le judaisme ancien et nouveau* (Paris, 1989)); on Lenin, Solomon M. Schwarz, *The Jews in the Soviet Union* (Syracuse, NY, 1951), 46–58; and for the Bund, Henry J. Tobias, *The Jewish Bund in Russia: From its Origins to 1905* (Stanford, Calif., 1972), 105–10, 160–75.

[8] Mark Levene, *War, Jews, and the New Europe: The Diplomacy of Lucien Wolf, 1914–1919* (Oxford, 1992), treats the activity of the leading Jewish diplomat, an opponent of Zionism.

Jewish national home. German Zionists secured an encouraging statement from the German foreign office on 22 November 1915 that Jews who settled in 'Turkey' (Palestine was not mentioned) and were not Germans would find 'as a general principle, that the German Government is favourable towards their aspirations, and is prepared to act on this favourable attitude' provided it did not conflict with 'legitimate Turkish state interests'. However, the German government required this lukewarm if friendly declaration to remain confidential, and it could not stir pro-German sympathy.[9] Germany's pro-Zionist gesture was far outdistanced by Great Britain's Balfour Declaration, issued two years later. By early 1917 the British government, in Vital's words, 'resolved . . . that with the military occupation of Palestine impending, the attempt should be made to evade those terms of the 1916 [Sykes–Picot] agreement which applied to that country'.[10]

The Zionists' main diplomatic effort during the war was directed at Great Britain, for a century the main prop of Turkey and its decaying empire. The complex negotiations which produced the British government's endorsement of the Jewish national home were closely connected with inter-Allied diplomacy and Britain's desire to gain Jewish support, and with the war against Turkey. After Prime Minister Asquith publicly warned the Turks in 1914 that by joining the German side they could forfeit their Asian empire and they did so anyhow, Great Britain and France began to plan the disposition of Turkish lands, including Palestine. Britain made clear its interest in taking over Palestine, especially its coast. They and the French struck a deal, the Sykes–Picot agreement, which divided the Middle East between themselves and the Arab state to be established, with Palestine under joint rule. Its northern boundaries were to prove a source of trouble a few years later. As to the 'Arab state', a letter from Sir Henry McMahon, high commissioner in

[9] Isaiah Friedman, *Germany, Turkey and Zionism, 1897–1918* (Oxford, 1977), 277.

[10] David Vital, *Zionism: The Crucial Phase* (Oxford, 1987). Of the large literature on what became the Balfour Declaration, I cite four other books in English: Leonard Stein, *The Balfour Declaration* (London, 1961); Isaiah Friedman, *The Question of Palestine, 1914–1918: British–Jewish–Arab Relations* (London, 1973); Ronald Sanders, *The High Walls of Jericho* (New York, 1983): Jehuda Reinharz, *Chaim Weizmann: The Making of a Statesman* (New York, 1993), vol. ii of the standard biography and covering 1914–1922, also treats the Balfour Declaration in full detail.

Egypt, to Sharif Hussein of Mecca, had already offered British support for a sizeable Arab state under his family's rule after the Arabs rose in revolt against Turkish rule. Palestine lay outside this future Arab state. Practically nothing came of the Arab revolt, but much trouble did come from the interpretation of 'Arab state' and the ambitions of Sharif Hussein's family. Zionism was not mentioned in all this diplomacy except for a reference in Sykes–Picot to Jewish religious interest in Jerusalem, along with other religions. But with partition of the entire Middle East in prospect Zionist hopes became a serious proposition in Britain and diplomatic activity became more intense. The senior Zionist in Great Britain, the polymath and publicist Nahum Sokolow, was favourably received in French diplomatic circles when he visited on behalf of the cause, and even the Vatican was sympathetic. Pope Pius X had flatly rejected Herzl's programme during the Zionist leader's audience in 1903, but now no objection was raised to the Jewish return to the homeland.[11]

The diplomatic art of the Russian immigrant chemist Chaim Weizmann was highly important during these critical years. He was well and favourably known for his important scientific contribution to wartime munitions manufacturing. The Polish Nahum Sokolow, senior to Weizmann in the movement, also played a vital role and both men often took counsel with the astute, prudent essayist and philosopher Ahad Ha-Am.[12] The British government realized that despite his relatively junior position Weizmann was more dependable to deal with than senior British Zionists, some of whom became quite jealous of him. Besides, he could speak more persuasively than they for his fellow Russian Jews, whose sympathy with the Allied side was important for Britain to secure.

The negotiations which produced the declaration of British support for the Jewish national home began early in 1915. It is obvious why the Zionists wanted the ancient homeland, but what was Great Britain's interest? It was concerned to keep Germany, now allied with Turkey, out of the Middle East. Palestine was a strategic crossroads, and naval power

[11] Friedman, *Germany, Turkey and Zionism*, 246–9.
[12] It is of course a legend, originating in Prime Minister Lloyd George's memoirs, that Palestine was given to the Jews as a reward for Weizmann's services. If a personal reward was intended he could have become Sir Chaim and been presented a cash purse.

based in the harbours of Jaffa and especially Haifa with a sympathetic Jewish hinterland could protect the Suez Canal and safeguard thereby Britain's route to India and the east. One cannot dismiss British sympathy with the Jews and a desire to do them justice, along with biblical prophecies of the return to Zion on which many British statemen, including Lloyd George, had been brought up. Perhaps there was a sense that settling Palestine could stabilize the position of the Jewish people in the world, thus reducing the plague of anti-Semitism.

Wealthy and prominent British Jews, the sort of men whom the Foreign Office would normally listen to, strongly opposed Zionism and acted to counter it. The Jewish élite's instrument was the Conjoint Foreign Committee of the Jewish Board of Deputies and the Anglo-Jewish Association, and their spokesman was the influential journalist and historian Lucien Wolf, who spoke and wrote against Zionism. Wolf and his colleagues did favour the development of a large, autonomous Jewish community in Palestine but they tirelessly opposed terms like 'national' in any declaration to be issued. Their fear was not over Palestine but over themselves: to speak of Jewish nationality, they insisted, would compromise them as Englishmen and give aid and comfort to anti-Semitic charges that Jews were foreigners. The bitterest anti-Zionist was Edwin Montagu, an extremely reluctant Jew detached from the Jewish community, close to Asquith and a member of his Cabinet. The scholar and philanthopist Claude G. Montefiore also carried weight. Yet the British government rejected Wolf and his colleagues' views and decided to support the Zionist programme. It disregarded Montagu's vehement objections, especially after Lloyd George became Prime Minister in December 1916. To be sure there were pro-Zionist exceptions among the Jewish élite, notably the second Lord Rothschild, who inherited the title in 1915. Attempts at compromise or rapprochement with the Zionists came to naught. The anti-Zionists' critical error was to publish in May 1917 a declaration in *The Times* in the name of the Conjoint Foreign Committee's parent bodies whom they did not ask. Especially because it was issued to the general British public, their statement provoked an angry reaction in the Jewish community against the 'grand dukes', as they were sarcastically called, a rebuke by the Jewish Board of Deputies, and the dissolution of the Conjoint Committee.

By 1917 the die was cast, and the year was spent mostly in testing formulas for the British government's statement. Several significant changes were made in the text, and there was a final canvass of leading British Jews on the acceptability of Zionism. As a sop to anti-Zionist fears of 'dual allegiance' and Montagu's last-ditch opposition two clauses were added to the sentence of endorsement. The final version, issued over the signature of Foreign Secretary Arthur J. Balfour,[13] read:

His Majesty's Government view with favour the establishment in Palestine of a national home for the Jewish people,[14] and will use its best endeavours to facilitate the achievement of this object, it being clearly understood that nothing shall be done which may prejudice the civil and religious rights of existing non-Jewish communities in Palestine, or the rights and political status enjoyed by Jews in any other country.

This was the celebrated Balfour Declaration, the supreme political achievement of the Zionist movement before the founding of the state of Israel in 1948. Zionism, intellectually fertile but in tangible terms merely a shaky settlement movement and an organization of mostly poor Jews and some intelligentsia, now acquired standing in public law. The great empire bestowed its favour and promised to help. Many disappointments were to come and the Balfour Declaration was virtually revoked by the White Paper of 1939, but the Zionist movement acquired a political basis on which it could build towns and settlements, found a self-governing community, and deal forthrightly with the British regime in Palestine.

In the New World

As they determined Palestine's future the British spoke at times of arranging a joint trusteeship with the United States if President Wilson

---

[13] His role in the Declaration was slight until the later stages. The leading British figures were Lloyd George, Mark Sykes, Lord Robert Cecil, Sir Ronald Graham, and Lord Milner in the War Cabinet.

[14] Not 'of Palestine as', a distinction of phrase which invited interpretative trouble, especially as it concerned non-Jewish inhabitants of Palestine. The last clause was added as a sop to Edwin Montagu's arguments over 'dual loyalty'.

agreed. The subject was never pursued and nothing came of it, but the idea itself illustrates the influence in world affairs which the United States was acquiring. Efforts by France and Great Britain as well as Germany to aid Jews in Russia, then the native land of most American Jews, and to encourage the Zionists testify to the place American Jewry was attaining in American and world Jewish affairs. For the basic fact about American Jewry, as well as Jewish communities elsewhere in the western hemisphere, was its immense population increase after 1880 and particularly after 1900. There were about 1 million Jews in the United States in 1900, nearly four times as many as had been there twenty years earlier. The 1,450,000 who entered the country during the following fourteen years,[15] constituted altogether about 10 per cent of net[16] immigration to the United States. After deducting for mortality and the 7–8 per cent who returned to Europe, about 3,197,000 Jews were in America in 1915, overwhelmingly immigrants and their American-born progeny. Although largely from small towns and villages in the Russian Pale of Settlement besides Poland and Galicia, in America they became an urban people who made their homes in the largest cities. New York City, the New World's metropolis, rapidly became the largest urban Jewish community ever as its Jews increased from about 135,000 in 1890 to 600,000 in 1900 and close to 2 million in 1925, over a quarter of the city's population. In descending order Chicago, Philadelphia, Baltimore, St Louis, Cleveland, Boston, and Detroit each had 75,000 to 250,000 Jews. Even the smallest of these outnumbered all but six or seven of the world's largest Jewish communities.

Intending emigrants sought to know what they could expect in America, and a flow of transatlantic personal correspondence helped to enlighten them. Other sources of information, including the Yiddish press and the bulletins of the Jewish Colonization Association also reached many before they journeyed. But deep in countless hearts, even of those

---

[15] The number could be larger, because these were solely persons entered as 'Hebrews' at immigration stations. 'Hebrews' who did not declare or appear outwardly so could be omitted, like those appearing, say, British or German. Immigrants who did not sail in steerage were exempt from the Ellis Island inspection and might not have been classified as 'Hebrews'.

[16] i.e. after returning immigrants are reckoned in. Jewish return immigration was far below the average, which was above 25%, and ran at about 8%.

who armed themselves with the best information they could get, was the legend of America—streets paved with gold, trees bearing golden fruit, and the like. Such fables symbolized the many immigrants who had come with nothing and risen to wealth. Besides tales of rags to riches which fired immigrants they heard of a far greater number, not the stuff of legends but often members of their own families, who were making a satisfactory living. Newcomers realized that America meant very hard work, but it brought its reward. There was another side to the reports on America—bouts of hard times and unemployment which the correspondence and the press reported. The freedom of America included the freedom to maintain Judaism as they knew it and also to leave or adapt it, and to be rid of the pressures of the small-town Jewish community. All these attitudes to Judaism came to expression in the intensive social and cultural life of American Jewry under the impact of immigration.

After an economic recession at the beginning of the First World War which included the painful collapse of several banks where immigrants deposited their savings, years of prosperity followed. The war years were also the peak of American Jewish immigrant life. Thanks to the urgent desire for news particularly from the eastern front, the Yiddish newspapers' daily circulation increased to approximately 300,000 purchasers and perhaps 600,000 readers. Their reports were fuller than those of the general press concerning Jewish wartime distress. There were several local editions for readers away from New York City. A corps of journalists including some distinguished Yiddish writers made their living from these newspapers. The Yiddish theatre, which appealed to the same audience as the Yiddish press, flourished during the 1910s and 1920s. In 1927 there were twenty-eight Yiddish theatres in the United States, where eighty-five plays received 645 performances. Some of these plays were of high literary and artistic quality. A Yiddish afternoon school network also existed, as did a social, cultural, and fraternal organization, the Workmen's Circle (Arbeiter Ring), whose membership reached 80,000 at its maximum during the 1920s. Impressive as are these numbers and the cultural vitality they evidenced, the entire milieu was short-lived, hardly lasting longer than the immigrant generation. It shrivelled by the 1940s if not sooner.

The immigrants' foremost accomplishment was their labour movement. Of traditional character, sometimes resembling guilds, were Jewish craft unions of carpenters, printers, Hebrew teachers, house painters, kosher slaughterers (*shohetim*) and butchers, soda water deliverers, and other trades. Most of them professed rather conservative goals. On the other hand the huge unions which encompassed the garment trades defined themselves in their early years as revolutionary socialist, 'cosmopolitan' or 'international' but not Jewish. With years the Jewish labour movement became more receptive to a Jewish definition, but their Jewish membership was in decline by the time the unions emphasized their Jewishness.

The Jewish labour movement's success in the decade before the First World War came after years of unsuccessful starts. Workshops became larger and stabler and thus easier to organize. Out of a series of victorious strikes two powerful unions, the Amalgamated Clothing Workers and the International Ladies Garment Workers, as well as smaller ones, emerged in the ready-made men's and women's garment industry. With hundreds of thousands of members, contracts with employers and sizeable assets, utopian and revolutionary ideals were modified into progressive or moderate socialist politics aiming to improve the workers' lot within existing capitalist society. By 1920 the Jewish unions were respected constituents of the American labour movement, widely esteemed for their innovative labour contracts, extensive educational and other services to members, and generous aid to striking unions in other industries. The majority of members before 1920 and practically all the leaders were east European immigrant Jews, almost all speaking Yiddish while gradually acquiring English. A significant, growing place was occupied by Italian immigrant workers, mainly women. A vigorous attack by employers during the 1920s and intra-union civil war with Communists undermined the proud movement, which recovered much of its strength during the 1930s thanks only to the New Deal. Unsuccessful, indeed destructive, in the unions, the Communists successfully established organizations which rivalled those of their reformist socialist antagonists. They had a Yiddish newspaper, theatre, and literature, a fraternal organization, and Yiddish schools, and were active in politics. However, it was all controlled by a Communist apparatus which in turn was under Moscow's thumb. Meanwhile many Jewish trade unionists became small businessmen or turned to other occupations, while ageing members were seldom replaced at the workbench or in union ranks by their children.

If trade unionism and secular Yiddish represented immigrant modernity, then the congregations which attempted to reproduce the religious life left behind in Russia and Poland showed the immigrants' conservative side. There were probably over a thousand little immigrant synagogues, mostly founded on the basis of an east European home town. They were always Orthodox even when many of their members were not. Rabbis from Europe, often men of distinction in the traditional Talmudic sphere, served these synagogues but had much difficulty in adjusting to their changing environment. Immigrants gradually left these synagogues and their immigrant neighbourhood atmosphere for better neighbourhoods with larger, more modern Orthodox congregations which might boast a fine cantor (*hazan*). The majority of immigrants were partially observant at best, yet most were Orthodox in their affiliation. Neither the anti-traditional ideology nor the cold formality of worship in Reform Judaism held attraction. Conservative Judaism, whose ideology was formed by the 'positive historical' school of Zacharias Frankel in nineteenth-century Germany, also came to America with the distinguished scholar Solomon Schechter and the Jewish Theological Seminary in New York City. Despite a strong organizational basis, notable scholarship, and financial sponsorship by the Jewish patricians, it too grew slowly. Those who had passed the immigrant experience were often attracted to Reform or Conservative Judaism, but that usually occurred only with the succeeding generation. The feeling of social and cultural distance from longer-established middle-class Jews also affected east European Jewish immigrants in Great Britain and France, who did not join the affluent, Anglicized United Synagogue nor Gallicized Consistoire congregations, officially Orthodox though these were. During the age of the great immigration most immigrants and many of their children found fulfilment instead in the secular Yiddish left and in the reproduction of east European Judaism.

A Fractured Jewish World, 1917–1929

Eastern Europe, whence came these immigrant masses, was in upheaval as the First World War drew to its close. The Habsburg empire broke up as its nationalities established their own states. In November 1917 the Bolsheviks under Lenin seized power in Russia. There were Jews among them, but Jews were more prominent among their Menshevik rivals, which was close to the Bund and whose leader Martov (Zederbaum) was Jewish. Lenin's mother's father was a Jewish physician converted to Christianity, facts which the handful who knew carefully concealed.[17] The ubiquitous orator and organizer Trotsky né Bronstein, second to Lenin, was fully Jewish but like the other Jewish Bolsheviks he was wholly alienated from Judaism.[18] Bolshevism had an articulate, negative position on Judaism and all religion and condemned national or religious expressions of Judaism as bourgeois, clerical, and counter-revolutionary. They won much Jewish support anyhow during the pogrom years by their unequivocal opposition to pogroms and anti-Semitism.[19] Their old Bundist adversaries were also reckoned Jewish nationalists. A storm of cultural destruction rained down on Russian Jewry. During the period of War Communism, 1917–21, the new regime established 'Jewish Commissions' which dissolved Jewish communities and closed synagogues and schools, and forbade the activities of rabbis, teachers, and others connected with Judaism. Many were subjected to a show trial or other public humiliation.[20] Yet the Red Army generally

[17] Orlando Figes, *A People's Tragedy: The Russian Revolution, 1891–1924* (London, 1996), 142–3, quoting D. A. Volkogonov, *Lenin: Life and Legacy* (London, 1994), 6, 8–9.

[18] Joseph Nedava, *Trotsky and the Jews* (Philadelphia, 1972), documents this. Trotsky found (pp. 202 ff.) some interest in Zionism during his Mexican exile. A sort of Jewish apologia at the party congress of 1924 has lately been unearthed: Figes, *A People's Tragedy*, 802–4.

[19] Lenin recorded speeches on phonograph to be played in the days before radio, one of which denounced anti-Semitism. They were reissued in Soviet Russia in 1961 with the exception of that speech.

[20] Lenin's doctrines on nationalism, including Jewish nationalism, have been widely discussed. See Richard Pipes, *The Formation of the Soviet Union: Communism and Nationalism, 1917–1923* (Cambridge, Mass., paperback edn., 1968), 29–50, 276–93, and Schwarz, *The Jews in the Soviet Union*, 24–58. On harassment of the Jewish community,

protected the Jews from pogroms, although some units, often deserters from other Russian armies, committed outrages for which they were punished.

An entirely different regime confronted Polish Jewry. Extinct since 1795, Poland was gradually reconstituted during complex negotiations between Germans, Austrians, and the Poles themselves during the wartime German occupation of most of Congress (Russian) Poland. On 11 November 1918, the day the war ended, the Polish republic was proclaimed. However, its eastern boundary remained unsettled for several years, leaving the future of several hundred thousand Jews in the air. Poland, which had 2,845,364 Jews in 1921, was the most important target of the national minority rights movement, but the Poles would have none of it. The goal of all Polish parties, supported among the Jews by a small but wealthy and influential Polonizing class, was a Polish national state even though a third of its population belonged to some national or religious minority. As a result ethnic conflict never ceased.

Polish Jewry, which had been emancipated after a fashion even under Russian rule, looked forward to the new state in the making during the First World War. Their optimism was shattered by a series of pogroms and attacks which the new government did nothing to halt, much less punish. They were not perpetrated by Ukrainians on Polish soil, but by Poles in Galicia and Congress Poland after the Germans and Austrians withdrew. By 1919 Jews were assaulted in 106 places in Poland, especially in Galicia, including the industrial centre of Lodz. On the other hand effective Jewish self-defence was reported in many places. Repeatedly, gallant soldiers of the new Polish army picked out Jews travelling the railroads and beat them, cut their beards, and threw them out of moving trains. When Lwow was taken by the Polish army the most savage pogrom of all occurred, in which a reported seventy Jews were killed besides hundreds wounded and their property destroyed. Long

Zvi Y. Gitelman, *Jewish Nationality and Soviet Politics: The Jewish Sections of the CPSU, 1917–1930* (Princeton, 1972), 69–148; M. Altshuler, *Ha-Yevsektzia be-Berit ha-Mo'ezot, 1918–1930* (Hebrew: The Yevsektzia in the Soviet Union, 1918–1930) (Tel Aviv, 1980); an early documentation of the persecution of Zionism is L. Tsentsiper, *Eser Shnot Redifot* (Hebrew: Ten Years of Persecution) (Tel Aviv, 1930).

repressed Polish chauvinism was blamed for these outrages, but right-wing nationalists charged the Jews with 'arrogance'. It was clear that full Jewish equality in the Polish state was deemed unacceptable, much less minority rights.[21]

Much worse happened during Russia's civil war, which lasted until 1921 with the Ukraine as the scene of the greatest Jewish suffering.[22] Between the official policies of the newly autonomous Ukraine, which functioned *de facto* from 1917, and the conduct in the field of its armies, consisting mainly of Ukrainian soldiers who had deserted the collapsing Russian army, there was a wide gap. On one hand, in the sphere of policy the Ukraine state granted national minority rights to the Jews and others in addition to the emancipation already enacted throughout Russian lands. This combination surpassed anything existing in a western country. There was a reputable minister for Jewish affairs, M. Zilberfarb, and Jews were represented in the Central Rada or council. But the government in Kiev had hardly any control over its military. The Ukraine underwent German occupation between March 1918 and the armistice of November 1918 under the terms of the Russo-German peace treaty, and with their departure the land descended into bloody

---

[21] Ezra Mendelsohn, *Zionism in Poland: The Formative Years, 1915–1926* (New Haven, 1981), 88–91, and in L. Chasanowitsch (ed.), *Les Pogromes Anti-Juifs en Pologne et Galicie en novembre et décembre 1918* (Stockholm, 1919).

[22] Even while the pogroms were claiming thousands of Jewish lives the committee to aid the victims established a commission to gather full documentation. Its archives came to include even films of pogroms as they happened. Elias Tcherikower (Tcherikover) was the moving spirit of this early version of the later, massive Yad Vashem which documented the Holocaust. The project moved to Berlin, where one of the projected seven volumes was published in Yiddish in 1923: E. Tcherikover, *Antisemitizm un Pogromen in Ukraine, 1917–1918* (pp. 17–177 were published in a Hebrew volume of Tcherikover's writings: *Yehudim be-Ttot Mahpekhah* (Jews in Revolutionary Times) (Tel Aviv, 1958)). Its introduction gives an account of the project. A Russian edition also appeared. An important fragment, cited below, is N. Gergel, 'Zur Statistik der judischen Pogromen in der Ukraine' (Yiddish), *Shriftn far Ekonomik un Statiktik*, i, ed. J. Lestschinsky (Berlin, 1928), 106–13. Tcherikover wrote the second volume *Di Ukrainer Pogromen in Yor 1919* during the 1930s which appeared in 1965, long after he died in New York in 1943. It contains Z. Szajkowski's afterword on the outcome of the project. The movement of the pogrom archives suggests Jewish fate: Kiev to Berlin to Paris to Vilna to storehouse to New York, where only a fragment remains. A brief contemporary account is L. Chasanowitsch, *Der Idisher Kurbn in Ukrayne* (Yiddish) (Berlin, 1920).

anarchy. Groups of deserting soldiers criss-crossed the country looting and killing, with the eager aid of peasants. Complaints began flowing in to Kiev from small towns late in 1917 of robbery and assaults, accompanied by requests for military protection. One such from Sudlikov, of a type received almost daily, wrote that the Bolshevik soldiers in town were useless and apathetic. 'We beg for help. If possible, send us about ten soldiers, the sort one can depend on, and it will be possible to make order. The community will assume the expense of paying the soldiers.'[23] One of the first reports, from Rashkov on 10 January 1918, reported Cossacks riding through the town shooting wildly.[24] During the repeated changes in the Ukrainian regime,[25] the Jews in hundreds of nearly all-Jewish towns and villages were accused of spying or of alliance with the Bolsheviks, and warring bands asked no questions as they looted, raped, burned and killed. The Ukrainian peasants had stayed out of pogrom movements in 1905–6, but now rose violently against the Jews, who were the mercantile class in a time of shortages and forced food requisitions.

Some groups of Jewish soldiers from the former Russian army volunteered for Jewish self-defence, but leading Jews dissuaded them, claiming that this would only provoke pogroms. Only in Odessa did the Jewish soldiers disregard such well-meant but deluded advice, and it was probably thanks to self-defence that Odessa Jewry passed through the years of slaughter almost unharmed.[26] The killings in the Ukraine were perpetrated in barbarous style, with stabbing, burning, mutilation, and the rape of women and girls accompanying murder. Hundreds of thousands of homes were robbed and burned to the ground. The most notorious pogrom occurred in Proskurov, about half of whose 50,000 inhabitants were Jews, one Sabbath afternoon in February 1919. About 300 Cossacks refrained from using firearms and moved quietly instead from house to house, killing about 1,500 unsuspecting Jews in three hours because they supposedly assisted the Bolsheviks in seizing the

[23] The letter is dated 13 Dec. 1917; Tcherikover, *Antisemitizm*, 189–90.

[24] Ibid. 195–6; idem, *Yehudim*, 476.

[25] An authoritative brief account is Richard Pipes, *The Formation of the Soviet Union*, 50–75, 114–50, 263–6; supplemented by Figes, *A People's Tragedy*, 376–8, 702–8.

[26] Ibid. 477–87.

railroad station. Inspired by 'religious' fervour the Cossacks did not rob or accept money desperately offered to avoid slaughter. Bodies lay piled in Proskurov's streets as the Cossacks next passed through nearby Miedzyborz without harming its Jews. Two days later they committed a major pogrom in the smaller town of Felstin, again slaughtering hundreds of Jews.[27] The small town of Tetiev endured a similar bloodbath in the following year. Besides those murdered on the spot in the Ukraine, a nearly equal number died later of their injuries, and others were maimed for life. From survivors' accounts Kenez has described 'a typical pogrom':

Troops of the Volunteer Army, usually Cossacks, entered a little town. They immediately divided themselves into groups of five or ten, often including officers. These groups attacked Jews on the street, beat them and sometimes stripped them. Then they entered Jewish houses, demanding money and other valuables. The frightened victims handed over everything they owned without the slightest resistance. The pogromists then searched and destroyed the interior of the house. The destruction was frequently followed by rape. . . . The population usually, but not always, joined the looting . . . After several days of unrestrained murder and looting, the local commander would issue an order blaming the Jews for Russia's troubles and therefore for their own misfortune, but promising that henceforth measures would be taken to preserve order . . . at this point the pogrom would either stop or turn into a 'quiet pogrom'. depending on the soldiers' perception of their superiors' attitude.[28]

The counter-revolutionary armies of Denikin, Kolchak and Wrangel murdered thousands. Semion Petlura, minister of defence and army commander in the Ukrainian government, was considered especially

---

[27] Tcherikover, *Antisemitizin*, 118–162 (1919). A prominent priest in Proskurov who pleaded with the Cossacks to desist and tried to shield two Jews was stabbed to death. Mr Charles Bick, then a young child whose father was rabbi of Miedzyborz, recalled to me the march through his town. His father related that they had learned of the pogrom from two Christians who fled Proskurov. Next day they sent wagons of bread baked for the survivors by the Jewish housewives of Miedzyborz. On Felstin see First Felshteener Benevolent Association, *Felshteen* (Yiddish) (New York, 1937), 26–237.

[28] Peter Kenez, 'Pogroms and White Ideology in the Russian Civil War,' in *Pogroms and Anti-Jewish Violence in Modern Russian History*, ed. John D. Klier and Shlomo Lambroza (Cambridge, 1992), 298–9.

responsible. Neither he nor any Ukrainian general actually ordered the killings, but they sanctioned them as necessary to satisfy the bloodlust of their troops, doing nothing to stop them nor to punish killers.[29] There are great differences in the estimates of victims. A member of Tcherikover's contemporary documentation project, N. Gergel, arrived at a minimum of 31,071 killed in 887 pogroms and 570 more in 349 'excesses'. About two-thirds were men aged 17 to 50.[30] Other scholars hold that 150,000 or more were killed, in addition to the injured, leaving hundreds of thousands of children orphaned. Homes and property were destroyed and many Jewish communities were wiped out. The prominence of some Jews in the Bolshevik leadership was given as a justification for the pogroms or as an excuse for not condemning them even verbally. The Jews were told they had to compel other Jews to leave Bolshevik ranks. This was demanded by the Russian Orthodox Church in the Ukraine and, incredibly, by the Kadet party, the banner of Russian liberalism, on the eve of its dissolution.[31]

The Ukrainian pogroms of 1917–20 were the bloodiest mass killings of Jews in history until then. They cast a long shadow on Jewish life. Their savagery and mindlessness registered in Hebrew literature, inspiring such works as Saul Tchernikhovsky's virtuoso sonnet cycle, 'On the Blood' and Isaac Lamdan's impassioned 'Masada'. The slaughter, in addition to attacks in Poland, elsewhere in Russia, and in other countries, made immediate what had been until then the abstract Zionist doctrine of *shlilat ha-golah*, the negation of the Diaspora. Jews were in danger, it was now held, not of disappearance by assimilation as in the west, but by assault on their lives. The only way out was the Jewish homeland. To others, however, safety lay in identification with the forces of progress and world revolution, specifically the Communist movement directed from Moscow.

Slowly the Jews of central and eastern Europe found their way to

---

[29] Petlura was assassinated in Paris in 1927 as an act of vengeance by Sholom Schwartzbard, a refugee from the pogroms. His trial and merely nominal conviction drew world-wide interest. Petlura's responsibility remains an issue to the present day. See the exchange between Taras Hunczak and Zosa Szajkowski in *Jewish Social Studies*, 31/3 (July 1969), 163–213, and trailing off in subsequent issues. Baron, *The Russian Jew*, 182–6.

[30] Gergel, 'Zur Statistik'.   [31] Kenez, 'Pogroms and White Ideology', 306–7.

stability under new regimes. No longer under the rule of tsar, Kaiser, and emperor, they lived in national republics where democracy was much spoken of but little practised. With the exception of Czechoslovakia and Lithuania, the new states observed the minority rights treaties only nominally if at all. They were determined to be nation-states, and centuries-old minorities in their midst were expected to accept a subordinate position. They resisted, and in the ceaseless friction this created lay, as mentioned above, one of the origins of the Second World War.

The European Jewish population showed remarkable resiliency in the decades between the two great wars. Despite losses due to war and pogroms, benign loss by mass emigration, and the decline of births, the 7,362,000 Jews of eastern Europe of 1900 increased to 7,618,000 in 1925. During the same period the Jews of central and western Europe, unaffected by pogroms but suffering heavy losses from military combat and birth rate decline, increased thanks mainly to immigration from eastern Europe from 1,328,500 to 1,677,000. The main Jewish communities were in Poland, where the 2,845,000 Jews in 1921 constituted 10.4 per cent of the population; post-revolutionary European Russia with 2,570,000 in 1926 (of whom 1,574,000 lived in the Ukraine after the pogroms) and 109,000 more in Asian Russia; Romania, much enlarged after 1918, 834,000; Czechoslovakia, 354,000; Hungary, after losing most of its territory to Czechoslovakia and Romania, 473,000; Germany within narrower boundaries than 1914, 564,000; post-Habsburg Austria, 230,000. The new Baltic states of Latvia, Lithuania, and Estonia had 95,000, 155,000, and 4,600 Jews respectively. The Netherlands numbered 115,000 Jews, France with Alsace and Lorraine restored had 150,000, and the United Kingdom, 303,000.[32] From the 1920s, however, the factors which for a century had governed Jewish population trends began to shift. The outlet of emigration was closed off as the United States and other countries drastically curtailed immigration and the Jewish birth rate fell sharply. This new trend was first seen in western Europe. By 1930 deaths exceeded births in Germany and Italy and

---

[32] Arthur Ruppin, *Soziologie der Juden* (2 vols., Berlin, 1930), i. 89–91, tables III and IV. Except for Russia, whose census was taken in 1926, the figures are from censuses of 1919–21. The population of the European countries generally paralleled the Jewish increases.

there is evidence of declining Jewish family size there and in Great Britain.[33] Slowly European and American Jewries accustomed themselves to the world after the war. Besides Communist Russia [34] and the new European states, and German Jewry under the republican Weimar constitution, there was revived Palestine. Under British rule, with the Balfour Declaration's terms written into the League of Nations mandate which conferred that rule, Palestine inspired hope and devotion. Shining accomplishments outweighed deep disappointments, and hope 'sprang eternal'. Indeed, one reason for the widely advertised Communist project of a Jewish autonomous region on the remote Mongolian border was to rival the lure of Zionism. Not that all Jews were Zionists, but the rebuilding of Palestine stirred deep sympathy in broad strata of the Jewish people.

The First World War, civil war, pogroms, and privation combined with War Communism, the wholesale confiscation and requisitioning of trades and commerce, to shatter the economic life of Russian Jewry. The New Economic Policy (NEP), lasting from 1921 to about 1928, re-established private commerce and some manufacturing and allowed the Jews to recoup their position. But when planned industrialization and government control of the entire economy went into operation in 1927 and 1928 the Jewish position again became critical. Jewish trades and crafts were eliminated and there were also social and linguistic barriers to Jewish integration into factory work and the planned economy. Agricultural settlement appeared a viable option, and the Crimea became the centre of a Jewish settlement movement. Biro-Bidzhan was warmly commended for settlement, but most settlers could not endure the hardships and took the long journey back. The 'Jewish Autonomous Region'

---

[33] Ibid. 282–8; Heinrich Silbergleit, *Die Bevolkerungs- und Berufsverhältnisse der Juden im deutschen Reich*, i (Berlin, 1930), 39, table 16; Hannah Neustatter, 'Demographic and Other Statistical Aspects of Anglo-Jewry', in *A Minority in Britain*, ed. M. Freedman (London, 1955), 68–77.

[34] The vast changes in what was the USSR have dated much of the literature about its Communist era and the Jews, yet many works retain value. Besides books by Baron, Schwarz, Gitelman, and Altschuler already cited, one should add Lionel Kochan (ed.), *The Jews in Soviet Russia since 1917* (2nd edn., London, 1972). The antiquity of Jacob Lestschinsky, *Dos Sovetishe Yidntum* (New York, 1941) (Yiddish), makes it valuable.

had some 17,000 Jews by the end of the 1930s, slightly less than a quarter of its total population, and a modestly functioning Yiddish cultural life. These projects show Russian Jewry being recognized as a distinct group with economic problems of its own. To be sure, the 220,000 agrarian Jews in 1928, 175,000 in 1939 when oriental Jews were counted separately, were hardly the solution to a mass problem.[35] Meanwhile, the Communist regime relentlessly persecuted Jewish religious life. Persecution and expulsion were no novelties for Jews, but there never was a combination of emancipation and opportunity with an assault on their heritage led by Jews who were Communists. Lacking territorial concentration, the Jews were not considered a nationality in the full sense while their religion was denied. Besides suppressing religious life by closing synagogues, molesting persons connected with religious life, dissolving organized communities (*kehillot*) and confiscating their assets, shutting yeshivot and houses of study, and carrying on blistering anti-religious campaigns, the regime forbade religious education. The teachers, like rabbis and other religious personnel, were categorized as 'unproductive' and if they sought to respond or to debate with their defamers the dangerous label of 'counter-revolutionary' could be pinned on them.

The Communists' main adversary in Jewish life, however, was not religion but Jewish ideological movements, especially Zionism and left-wing movements like the Bund and Poalei Zion. The connection of the Hebrew language with Zionism, even more than its 'clerical' and 'bourgeois' religious links, 'justified' the forbidding of its study, unlike any other language of the USSR. Although Zionism itself was not declared illegal, persecutions and local arrests of Zionists began in 1919 and became massive from 1922. Their largest organization, the socialist *Zeirei Zion* (Youth of Zion), went underground. When their secret conference was discovered its participants were imprisoned. Many Zionists were allowed to leave for Palestine, but others languished in prison for many years for unspecified offences. *Hechalutz*, training young agricultural pioneers for Palestine, was left alone until its turn came in 1926. Al-

---

[35] Schwarz, *The Jews in the Soviet Union* 164–6, 174–94; Baron, *The Russian Jew*, 201; a full account is Jacob Levavi (Babitzky), *The Jewish Colonization in Birobijan* (Hebrew; English title) (Jerusalem, 1965).

together, Russian Zionism was crushed by 1930. The persecution of the Jewish religion and Zionism was zealously promoted by the Jewish Section of the Communist Party, known as the *Yevsektsiia*, which was composed mainly of ex-Bundists and other leftist Jewish groups. Yet for all the *Yevsektsiia*'s radical, anti-religious assimilationism it was suspected anyhow of Jewish nationalism and was dissolved in 1930. Mere association for a Jewish purpose aroused suspicions, and *Yevsektsiia* leaders were imprisoned or put to death in the purges of 1936–8.[36]

Notwithstanding such constant denigration, traditional Jewish life persisted for some time, especially in small cities. Rabbi Yehezkel Abramsky of Slutsk, writing in 1928 to Chief Rabbi Kook of Palestine for help to leave Russia, reported his own religious life secure in the midst of numerous religious Jews in his White Russian town, but his children would come under the influence of their atheist communist surroundings.[37] The serious risk in not going to work on Sabbaths and holidays, the absence of such necessities as Passover *mazzot* and kosher meat, and above all the sterility of a future without Jewish education, placed in grave question Soviet Russian Judaism's capacity for continuity. Here and there young men substituted for yeshiva study private Talmud study under one of the distinguished rabbis who remained in Russia.[38] Followers of Rabbi Joseph I. Schneerson, the Hasidic rabbi of Lubavich who withstood persecution in Russia until he left for Poland in 1932, organized producers' co-operatives (*artel*) which provided some economic autonomy, enabling them to observe the Sabbath and holidays.

While religion and Zionism were ridiculed and denounced and the remaining Hebrew writers and rabbis found it nearly impossible to express themselves or to publish, secular Yiddish modernism flourished for some twenty years.[39] The government established schools which taught in Yiddish with Jewish content carefully omitted. Parents, however, dis-

---

[36] An excellent account is Zvi Y. Gitelman, *Jewish Nationality and Soviet Politics*.

[37] Rabbi Abramsky emigrated to England in 1931 and to Israel in 1952, and had a distinguished career. Not all his children were allowed to leave Russia with him.

[38] Rabbi Alter Hilewitz (1905–94), whose applications to emigrate were refused many times until he was allowed to emigrate in 1935, reminisced to me of his private study with eminent rabbis in Russia.

[39] Ch. Schmeruk, 'Yiddish Literature in the U.S.S.R.' in Kochan, *The Jews in Soviet Russia*, 232–68 is a penetrating discussion, as is that by Y. A. Gilboa on Hebrew, ibid. 216–31.

played little interest; Russian was preferred for general education and the Yiddish schools did not last. Literary freedom for Yiddish writers was absent as the conception of artistic autonomy was repudiated. Art had to serve 'the masses', meaning in practice Communist ideology, and dissenters could place themselves in physical danger. That ideology, which carried earlier literary doctrines to an extreme, opposed symbolism and expressionism in Yiddish, for example, and prevented the publication of such works. Attachment to the Jewish people or sympathy even for its vanished traditions was another taboo. Major writers like David Bergelson and Der Nister ('The Hidden One', pseud. P. Kaganovitch) struggled with themselves to make the required transition to 'proletarian realism'. Even within these stringent limits and menaced by severe criticism from Yiddish Communist functionaries, works of real merit were produced. Some prominent Yiddish authors who had emigrated saw the possibility of a broad reading public and state support and returned to Russia, to their later cost. In addition there were Jewish authors of *belles-lettres* in Russian, of whom the best known is Isaac Babel, a purge victim in 1941. Jewish scholarship was fostered for a time, and focused on the social history of the Jews in Russia. It was also possible for Sergei Zinberg, by profession a chemist, to compose a splendid *Geshikhte fun der Literatur bey Yidn* [40] since the Middle Ages in many volumes, which has had Hebrew and English translations. Zinberg's death in Siberian exile in 1941 suggests the fate of others well before the final murder of the Yiddish writers on 12 August 1952 and the liquidation of what remained of Jewish culture.

Communism was believed devoutly to be the wave of the future in Russia, now called the Union of Soviet Socialist Republics. Opposition or active dissent was 'counter-revolutionary', a capital crime. Commu-

The definitive bibliography in Hebrew, *Jewish Publications in the Soviet Union, 1917–1960*, ed. Ch. Shmeruk *et al.* (Jerusalem, 1961), lists in detail 4,154 items and includes the editor's noteworthy study of Yiddish and Y. Slutzki's on Hebrew. A companion Hebrew bibliography is *Recent Publications on Jews and Judaism in the Soviet Union*, ed. M. Altschuler *et al.* (Jerusalem, 1970), with the editor's excellent introduction.

[40] A History of Literature among the Jews, and not the simpler but 'bourgeois nationalist' 'History of Jewish Literature'. The titles of the Hebrew and English versions do not have such inhibitions.

nism ruled thanks less to Leninism and its contorted Marxism than to its abolition of tsarism and aristocracy and the opening of opportunity to the excluded lower classes; 'bourgeois' was no less a taint than aristocracy. A great number of small Jewish shopkeepers and merchants were thus categorized and deprived of livelihoods, and their children's chances for careers were seriously handicapped. No one had more reason to welcome the 'career open to talents' under Communism than the Jews, provided their ancestry was untainted and they minimized their identity as Jews. They could quit the one-time Pale of Settlement for the vast reaches of Russia and gain a place in its new society under construction. Most were willing to abandon Jewish particularity and traditions, which masses of contemporary Jews were doing under conditions of freedom in western countries. Population trends are symptomatic. In the industrializing Ukraine, Jewish population held steady at 1,574,000 in 1926, only 100,000 less than it had been in 1897 despite massive pogroms and emigration in the interim. White Russia, however, not much stricken by pogroms but economically backward, dropped from 472,000 in 1897 to 375,000 in 1926. Russia proper outside the Pale had fewer than 200,000 Jews in 1897 but nearly 600,000 in 1926 and 948,000 in 1939.

Jews not only moved out of the Pale, but away from towns and villages to big cities. The Jews in Moscow in 1897 numbered 8,100, but in 1926 there were 132,000 and in 1939 the number stood at about 286,000. [41] Leningrad had 17,000 in 1897 and Kiev 32,800. By 1926 they had increased to 132,000 and 84,000 respectively, numbers which kept increasing to approximately 200,000 and 175,000 at the outbreak of the Second World War. Kharkov, the centre of heavy industry in the Ukraine, went from 11,000 in 1897 to 115,000 in 1935. In addition there were Jews in new industrial cities such as Magnitogorsk, and continuity of settlement in relatively stationary cities like Odessa. [42]

Jewish talent enjoyed its opportunities during the first twenty years of Communist rule. With education and commercial and administrative

---

[41] Mordechai Altshuler, *Soviet Jewry Today* (Hebrew; English title), 76–7.

[42] Since these four cities were outside the Pale of Settlement, the 1897 figures undoubtedly omit thousands of Jews who avoided the census. Baron, *The Russian Jew*, 207; Altschuler, *Soviet Jewry* 76–7.

skills well above the Russian average, they were disproportionately represented in the then élite ranks of the Communist Party and its apparatus including the secret police, and also in government and clerical positions where education was similarly necessary. About 17 per cent of the delegates to the Communist Party congress of 1917 declared themselves Jews, but increased membership in the ruling party lowered its Jewish proportion to 4 or 5 per cent during the 1920s and 1930s. Jewish students were numerous in the universities and achieved previously unattainable professorships and membership in scientific academies. It may never be possible to know precisely, but Russian Jewry apparently favoured the regime which opened such opportunities and repressed anti-Semitism. It could call on a large reserve of idealism. However, there is evidence of a decision at the highest level in the late 1930s to reduce the proportion of Jews in the Communist political élite.[43]

Russian Communism was observed with keen interest throughout the world by Jews and others from viewpoints which ranged from ardent sympathy to vehement hostility. Jews had been relatively prominent in the Bolshevik party, and a significant number in many countries eagerly anticipated the expected Communist world revolution as a secular messianic deliverance. Since the large majority of Jews in western countries were recent immigrants from tsarist Russia, they were easy targets for the anti-Semites' charges of Communist allegiance. In the bitter, heated atmosphere after the First World War the prominence of Jews in the early years of Russian Communism provided additional inspiration for world-wide anti-Semitism, which proclaimed Russian Communism as Jewish. 'Judaism is Bolshevism', bellowed the rising Nazi Party, and the 'discovery' of the fake *Protocols of the Elders of Zion* fitted well the anti-Semitic mood.

The Russian regime controlled a world-wide network of spies, obedient Communist parties, and sympathetic organizations which also raised money for Soviet causes, including Biro-Bidzhan and Crimean colonization. Communists were a small proportion of all Jews but a high proportion of Communists and their sympathizers. When capitalism in

[43] Baron, *The Russian Jew*, 202–4, 285; Benjamin Pinkus, *Russian and Soviet Jews: Annals of a National Minority* (Hebrew; English title) (Sdeh Boker, 1986), 182–6, 313–15; Leonard Schapiro, *The Communist Party of the Soviet Union* (New York, 1960), 171, 475.

the west appeared near collapse during the 1930s and the democracies did not resist Nazism, Communist Russia offered hope and assurance. Jews in particular appreciated Russia's propaganda of bread for all, the prohibition of anti-Semitism, and the call for collective security against the Nazi threat. Most sympathizers' pro-Communist idyll ended with the Hitler–Stalin pact of August 1939 as a preliminary to the Second World War which broke out a few days later.

The Habsburg Successors

Vastly different conditions prevailed among the 5,150,000 Jews who lived in the new states of east central Europe which succeeded the fallen Habsburg and Romanov empires.[44] These were gradually modernizing, strongly nationalist states. All except Hungary and Lithuania had large and varied national minorities in addition to the Jews. Nationalism, which was emphasized by the cityward movement of the native peasantry, displaced the Jews from the dominant position in commerce and the professions which they had long held. Increasingly severe anti-Semitism sharpened these ideological and social trends.

Hungary was not a new state but half of the former Habsburg Austro-Hungary, drastically reduced. Its large population of extremely Orthodox, mainly Hasidic, Jews had been shifted by border changes into Romania and Czechoslovakia, and the redrawn Hungary had 444,000 patriotic Magyarized Jews in 1930 who constituted 5.1 per cent of the country's population. The other new states were in reality multinational, with minorities which had lived enclosed within their own languages, cultures, and religions for centuries. The 155,126 Jews of Lithuania in 1923, Litvaks in Jewish parlance, constituted 7.6 per cent of the little country's population. They contrasted strikingly with Hungarian Jewry by being strong Jewish nationalists and quite unacculturated to Lithuania and its language. Since earlier days Lithuanian

---

[44] These figures and those which follow are taken from Ruppin, *Soziologie der Juden*, ii. 30–1, table II. They apply mainly to 1930–1. I have not used Ruppin's estimates for 1938 which reckon with apparently excessive natural increase, slight emigration, as well as border changes compelled by Nazi German pressure.

Jewry's languages, besides Yiddish and Hebrew, were Russian or German but rarely Lithuanian, a peasant language. Together with Czechoslovakia, Lithuania was also the exception in respecting its obligations under the minority rights treaties, which the other successor states—Poland, Romania, Latvia—ignored or avoided. Unlike the other minorities the Jews had no territorial concentration but were scattered throughout the countries. The minorities' grievances against their frequently oppressive governments were a source of permanent friction between the wars. The German minority's grievances, such as they were, were exploited by Nazi Germany as a major provocation for the Second World War.

Poland was the prime example of a multinational state in reality which was determined to act as a national state. The widespread slogan 'Poland for the Poles', meant that the national minorities which constituted one-third of Poland's population would occupy only a marginal or inferior position in Polish life. Unlike other Polish minorities the Jews lacked a neighbouring state solicitous of their interests—such as Germany even before Nazi rule for the 3 million Polish Germans. Very few Jews remained in formerly Prussian Poland as most of them resettled in Germany after 1918. In Poland of 1921 there were 2,845,364 Jews, 10.5 per cent of its population, and 3,113,900 in 1931, 9.8 per cent of its population. On the eve of the Second World War there were an estimated 3,325,000 Polish Jews.[45] Unlike Jewish communities in western Europe and America or nearby Hungary, Polish Jewry was was not concentrated in large cities although the number of Jews along with the general population was increasing there. The Jews of Warsaw, Poland's political, cultural, and commercial capital and by far its largest city, increased from 310,000 to 352,000 between 1921 and 1931, yet declined from 33.1 to 30.1 per cent of its population. During the same decade the Jews of Lodz increased from 156,000 (34.6%) to 202,000 (33.5%), Lwow from 76,000 (33.5%) to 99,000 (31.9%), Cracow from 46,000 (24.6%) to 56,000 (25.8%) and Vilna from 46,000 (36.1%) to 55,000 (28.2%).[46] These five

---

[45] These are census figures, enumerated by religion. Figures for Jews by nationality are substantially lower—2,110,448 in 1921 and 2,732,584 in 1931.

[46] Raphael Mahler, *Yehudey Polin beyn shtey Milhamot 'Olam* (Hebrew; Jews in Poland between the Two World Wars) (Tel Aviv, 1968), 35, table 4.

largest cities' 634,822 Jews of 1921 and 766,272 of 1931 went from 22 to 24 per cent of Polish Jewry in the respective years, but the Jewish metropolitan concentration still remained far lower than in Hungary and western countries. To be sure, approximately three-quarters of the Polish Jews lived in urban places, including the five just mentioned, and the remainder in small towns and villages. This was just the reverse of Poland's mainly rural general population. Polish Jewry constituted a majority of the inhabitants of many towns in that largely peasant land.[47] Jewish occupations also pointed to urban life. In 1931 merely 4 per cent of the Jews worked the land, while 42.2 per cent lived from industry and (negligibly) mining, and 36.6 per cent from the varieties of commerce.

A sign of official hostility to the Jews was the continuation of tsarist Russian limitations in Polish areas which had once been part of the old Pale of Settlement. Not until 1931 after a decade of struggle were they abolished. Even while subject to crass discrimination and denied many rights, Polish Jewry enjoyed broad political rights, including male suffrage and the right to sit in the Sejm (parliament). Fully-fledged Jewish politics were carried on, if with meagre results, by Jewish political parties actively participating in political life. United action among them was never attained. Ironically, the voting franchise was broader than in Jewish communal elections, where the minimum age was 25 and voting was weighted to favour larger taxpayers.[48]

During independent Poland's first years the minority rights treaties were flouted and sharp antagonism existed between its rightist governments and the Jews. Before the general elections of 1922 Isaac Gruenbaum, the foremost Jewish political leader until he left for Palestine in 1935, brought together a 'Minorities Bloc' which briefly held a balance of power. Polish nationalists were outraged at this 'Jewish domination', and when the newly elected president attained office thanks to minorities bloc votes in the Sejm he was murdered. However, when Poland urgently needed foreign loans and had to improve its poor reputation

[47] Ibid. 24. The author, however, does not define the dimensions of urban and rural.
[48] For the example of Warsaw see Alexander Guterman, *Yehudey Varsha beyn Shtey Milhamot ha-'Olam* (Hebrew; English title *The Warsaw Jewish Community between the Two World Wars* (Tel Aviv University, 1997), 174–5, 263–4.

abroad due to the treatment of its minorities, the government and Jewish interests reached an 'agreement' (*ugoda*) in May 1925. The *ugoda's* clauses spoke of concord and Jewish support of the government while other clauses, kept confidential because public opinion would be hostile to them, included a commitment to respect specified Jewish minority rights. The government soon failed to honour its pledges. The Jewish representatives, headed by the moderate Leon Reich who negotiated the deal while the more militant Gruenbaum who opposed it was out of the country, realized that the *ugoda* was dead and revealed its terms. They evidently also knew of the *coup d'etat* that was about to transform Polish politics.[49]

In May 1926 Jozef Pilsudski, one-time socialist, war hero, and first president, seized power and established an authoritarian regime which lasted until he died in 1935. Pilsudski in power pleased most Jews since he was not an anti-Semite and was expected to respect Jewish and minority rights and enforce order.[50] His regime was indeed less hostile than its predecessors and far less so than its successors. The government of the colonels, as it was called, who succeeded their old chief was openly anti-Semitic. To cope with the ravages of the great depression they pursued a nationalist anti-Semitic programme of replacing the Jews in the Polish economy with native Poles. They endorsed the boycott of Jewish business, required Sunday closing of businesses besides the Sabbath closing which most Jews observed besides a *numerus clausus* in universities. They also promulgated legislation to restrict *shehitah* and only half-heartedly deplored the wave of pogroms in 1936–7. Some openly admired and sought to emulate Nazism which seemed to be unifying Germany and bringing prosperity while beating down the Jews; Germany's emerging designs on Poland were little considered. During these last years before catastrophe, the number of Jews who believed in a Jewish future in Poland decreased steadily, and the regime verbally en-

[49] P. Korzec, 'The Agreement between V. Grabski's Ministry and the Jewish Representation' (Hebrew) *Gal-Ed*, 1 (1973), 175–201; Ezra Mendelsohn, 'Reflections on the "Ugoda" ', *Sefer Raphael Mahler* (Merhavya, 1974), 87–102 (English section).

[50] M. Landa, 'The May *Coup d'État* (1926): Jewish Expectations for a Political Change and the Subsequent Disillusionment' (Hebrew), *Gal-Ed*, 2 (1975), 237–86; Joseph Rothschild, *Pilsudski's Coup d'État* (New York, 1966).

couraged Jews to emigrate. But where could even a fraction of 3 million Jews go? Only Palestine's doors were even partially open. Non-Zionist socialists, however, headed by the Bund, stuck to the policy of *doikayt* ('hereness'), that Polish Jewry would solve its problems in Poland. The title *A People at Bay*, Oscar Janowsky's contemporary report on the situation, aptly expresses conditions during the late 1930s.

The depression of the 1930s hit Poland hard and Polish Jews harder. Jews had played a major role in the Polish economy as estate managers and stewards, financiers, merchants, shopkeepers, and craftsmen. In 1931 they constituted 58.7 per cent of the country's commercial and insurance class, 21.3 per cent of those occupied in industry and mining, and 21.3 per cent of its educational and cultural personnel. Jews built the textile industry, which was centred in Lodz. But their economic standing as well as their legal status came under gathering attack.[51] As part of its trappings of a national state Poland excluded Jews from public life as foreigners.[52] There were no Jewish judges or public officials nor Jewish parliamentarians except in Jewish political parties. Jews could not secure public employment nor army officerships except as physicians, and hold-overs from earlier times were pensioned off. The railroads and post offices would not hire Jews, and when trades such as tobacco became government monopolies Jews were forced out. Discriminatory taxes and prohibitive licence fees in Jewish trades were other means for ruining the Jews but brought no prosperity to Poles who wanted their places.[53] The country's political parties, including the Polish Socialist Party (PPS) and the left wing of the peasants' party were at best neutral towards the Jews and avoided open anti-Semitism. The

[51] There are many studies of anti-Semitism in Poland. An early comparative study is Jacob Lestschinsky, 'The Anti-Jewish Program: Tsarist Russia, the Third Reich and Independent Poland,' *Jewish Social Studies*, 3/2 (April 1941), 141–58. See Raphael Mahler, 'Antisemitism in Poland', in *Essays on Antisemitism*, ed. K. S. Pinson (New York, 1947), 145–72. To these pioneer studies one may add studies by Y. Gutman, A. Polonsky, and E. Melzer in *The Jews of Poland between Two World Wars*, ed. Y. Gutman, E. Mendelsohn, J. Reinharz, and Ch. Shmeruk (Hanover, NH, 1989), 97–137.

[52] Raphael Mahler, 'Jews in Public Service and the Liberal Professions in Poland, 1918–39', *Jewish Social Studies*, 6/4 (Oct. 1944), 291–350.

[53] These policies are summarized in Abraham G. Duker's pamphlet, *The Situation of the Jews in Poland* (Conference on Jewish Relations, New York, April 1936).

right-wing National Democrats (Endek), the largest party and the one most frequently in office, were avowedly anti-Semitic. Under their leader and ideologist Roman Dmowski they denied a future for Jews in national Poland, and came close to racist ideology in asserting that, no matter how assimilated, Jews could not truly be Poles. Reinforcing anti-Semitic policies was the traditional, deep-rooted hostility of the Roman Catholic Church, virtually the national religion of the Poles, which strengthened anti-Semitism. To be sure the church did not accept racism—a Jew who converted became a Christian and therefore a true Pole. Churchmen deplored violence, but supported economic boycotts and discrimination in employment. Distinctly Catholic was the condemnation of the Jews as the source of atheism, revolutionism, pornography, and other ills of modern society. One form of violence was attacks on Jews for supposedly insulting or mocking religious processions or desecrating religious symbols. The universities were another centre of anti-Semitism as Jewish students were sometimes physically attacked and in the later 1930s compelled to occupy segregated 'ghetto benches' at lectures. Many stood rather than sit in them and were joined by a few liberal lecturers. Rare were Jewish faculty appointments. The number of impoverished and destitute Jews increased all the time, and so did suicides. An active programme of vocational training led to few jobs, and young Jews without prospects faced a bleak future. Many turned to leftist radicalism or to emigration to Palestine.

Polish Jewry had centuries of rich cultural traditions in which Lithuanian and White Russian Jewry essentially shared. Political and economic conditions hindered but did not ruin Jewish internal life. Indeed, exclusion from public life probably intensified Jewish communal life, the only sphere where Jews could function freely, although they did so in an atmosphere of strife and uncompromising divisiveness. Whatever may be claimed in terms of an argumentative Jewish temperament, these bitter divisions reflected the genuine, painful transition taking place from traditional social and religious life to modern ideologies of socialism, Zionism, secularism, Yiddishism, and embattled Orthodoxy in a country rife with anti-Semitism and beset with problems of economic backwardness and self-government. Each Jewish ideology was advocated not by one but by two or more political parties. The basic party divisions were the socialist Bund, which could do little as a trade union but was deeply involved in culture and politics; Agudas Yisroel (Agudat Yisrael in Israel today), militantly orthodox and internally oriented, favoured by the Polish regime because its avoidance of modern life made the minimal demands; and the Zionists, who could contribute little political or financial support to the Jewish national home but presented a nationalist view in Polish Jewish life. The parties and their many splinters campaigned in community and general elections. In 1931 the government rewrote the Jewish community law to favour the undemanding Agudas Yisroel. Its five-year reign in Warsaw was marked by a large number of inside deals and corruption. The Bund next took over Warsaw Jewry as the Jewish position deteriorated. An unyielding problem was money for an array of activities in a poor community without significant government aid. Aid from the Joint Distribution Committee and *landsmanshaftn* (home town societies) overseas made up some of the deficit. The Jewish budget of Polish Jews was approximately £800,000 ($4 million) in 1929 and, to judge from available Warsaw figures, the sum of £871,000 ($4,355,000) for 1938. The *per capita* expenditure was thus about 6 shillings ($1.30). (These figures should be multiplied about tenfold to reach today's values.) The larger the community the higher the proportion of income devoted to education and welfare, while smaller communities devoted a greater proportion to religious needs. The latter provided the main source of income in the form of *shehitah* fees and cemetery payments.[54]

Polish Jewry, together with Russian Jewry once the biological reservoir of world Jewry, had an unparalleled record in rabbinic learning and central importance in modern Jewish movements and literature. In fact Jews could also be found prominently in Polish cultural life, and there would probably have been more if hostility had not been intense. There were Jewish mathematicians, historians, musicians, and poets. Of poets, Julian Tuwim and the baptized Antoni Slonimski were major figures, and the historians Szymon Askenazy and Marcel Handelsman were eminent

[54] Based on Jacob Lestschinsky's pioneer study, 'Economic Aspects of Jewish Community Organization in Independent Poland,' *Jewish Social Studies*, 9/4 (Oct. 1947), 319–38. He had figures for 599 communities in which 82% of Polish Jews lived, and interpolated his own estimates for the missing 18%.

scholars. However, the obstacles to Jewish participation were formidable, and Jewish intellectual life remained mostly within the framework of Jewish studies. Even though orthodoxy was no longer the common culture of Polish Jewry it was deeply influential. The *mussar* (ethical reflection) trend expanded, yeshivot developed, and a new and innovative one opened, the Yeshiva of the Sages of Lublin (*Yeshivat Hakhmey Lublin*). Within orthodoxy, Zionism and a current of social radicalism found expression in religious labour Zionism (Hapoel Hamizrachi) and in a wing of ultra-conservative Agudas Yisroel (Poalei [Workers of] Agudas Yisroel). One must mention the fine Yiddish theatre and the Jewish press in several languages, besides the accomplishments in the Jewish social sciences and humanities of the Yiddish Scientific Institute (YIVO) in Vilna and other scholars.[55] Moses Schorr, rabbi, Assyriologist, and historian, as well as Mayer Balaban and Ignaz (Yitzhak) Schipper led historical research and had guided a new generation by the 1930s.

Education likewise underwent a period of innovation. Besides the remaining *hadarim* mainly in small towns there were the very Orthodox schools of the Horev network and most interesting, the beginning of Orthodox girls' schooling in the Bais Yaakov schools founded by Sarah Schnirer. The ideology of secular, leftist Yiddishism was the basis of the small Tsisho (abbreviation for Central Yiddish School Organization) schools, while Zionist secular Hebraism was represented by the more numerous Tarbut schools. Yavneh was Zionist and Orthodox. On the other hand, about 80 per cent of Jewish children went to Polish schools either from their parents' lack of conviction in any ideology or because they could not afford the Jewish schools' tuition. Some afternoon Jewish schools were conducted for these children. Thus a Jew could lead a full modern or traditional life entirely within Jewish confines. He or she was educated for such a life in an impressive range of educational networks tied to ideological outlooks.[56]

[55] Salo W. Baron (ed.), *Bibliography of Jewish Social Studies, 1938–39* (New York, 1941) has world-wide scope, and its listings for Poland show the intellectual vigour of beleaguered Polish Jewry on the brink of destruction.

[56] Nathan Eck, 'The Educational Institutions of Polish Jewry (1921–1939)' *Jewish Social Studies*, 9/1 (Jan. 1947), 3–32; Miriam Eisenstein, *Jewish Schools in Poland* (New York, 1950). Professor Ezra Mendelsohn believes (in oral communication) that the proportion in public schools was about 65%.

Other Successor States

Almost 2 million Jews lived in new states to Poland's south and north-east, among whom Czechoslovakia and Hungary were the most westernized. As mentioned above, the 444,000 Jews of Hungary in 1930 were fervently Hungarian. They had long been allied with the landed aristocracy which ruled the country and carried the torch of Magyarization for them. They were Hungary's commercial and professional class, concentrated in Budapest where 204,000 Jews lived in 1930. Their Judaism was 'Neolog', somewhat resembling Conservative Judaism of America, with Orthodoxy quite weak after the post-war territorial cessions to Romania and Czechoslovakia which had been forced on Hungary. As great a shock was the short-lived seizure of power in 1919 by Bela Kun's Communist revolutionary junta. Kun was a Jew, as were most of his collaborators, although they were wholly detached from Judaism, which gave a sharp stimulus to anti-Semitism. His downfall was followed by counter-revolutionary terror in which Jews were the main target. Hungarian Jewry could not stay immune to the political and social forces which swept across Europe. The old alliance between the ruling Hungarian aristocracy and the Jews ended when the government bureaucracy and the army officer corps became closed to Jews and a *numerus clausus* at universities and in numerous professional fields was enacted in 1938. Radical right governments aligned themselves with Nazi Germany, which arranged for Hungary to receive back from defunct Czechoslovakia the territories in Slovakia and Carpatho-Ruthenia it had lost in 1919, bringing 150,000 more Jews within its boundaries. Zionism and other ideological movements which flourished in Poland were little seen in Hungary.

Czechoslovakia, the model democratic state of central Europe, and its Jews were extraordinarily diverse, stretching like the country itself from west to east. The 117,000 Jews of Bohemia and Moravia were fully westernized and quite assimilated to Czech culture. By the time the republic was established they had abandoned their earlier German cultural orientation. Prague's eminence in Jewish religious culture was a past glory and its once Germanic culture was now Czech. Anti-Semitism existed but not in force, while most Jews voted for Jewish national parties and declared themselves Jews by nationality as well as religion. The further east in Czechoslovakia one went, the less acculturated its Jews and the more they lived in small towns and occupied themselves with crafts and petty trade. There were 136,000 Jews in less developed, poorer Slovakia than in its Czech partner, and 102,000 more lived in Subcarpathian Ruthenia where they constituted 14 per cent of that backward region's population. In Subcarpathian Rus there was a significant number of Jewish peasants and labourers. Orthodoxy was strong in Slovakia with its centre in Bratislava since R. Moses Sofer's times, while the Hasidic variety was dominant in Subcarpathian Ruthenia. The latter was fiercely anti-Zionist, but otherwise the Jewish national movement had a considerable following in Czechoslovakia.[57]

The three Baltic states of Lithuania, Latvia and Estonia were the home of 253,000 Jews in 1930.[58] The last-named, with fewer than 5,000 Jews, was a small Protestant country oriented more to Scandinavian Jewry. Lithuania on the other hand carried on the traditions of 'Litvak' Jewry with Talmudic learning and noted yeshivot as well as Jewish school systems like those of Poland, already described. At first Jewish cultural and political life enjoyed state recognition of minority rights. But dictatorial regimes took control from 1926 and grand programmes of political autonomy and communal organization were discarded.[59] However, Jewish schools like those of Poland flourished and the state steadily provided support. Most Lithuanian Jewish children attended them.

Small towns prevailed in Lithuania and Jews made a meagre living in petty commerce and crafts. However, government policy and a rapidly growing class of native Lithuanian merchants and professionals combined to end the Jews' preponderance in these spheres. Thousands lost their livelihoods and were reduced to poverty. Economic rivalry

---

[57] Ezra Mendelsohn, *The Jews of East Central Europe between the World Wars* (Bloomington, Ind., 1983), 131–70; *The Jews of Czechoslovakia: Historical Studies and Surveys* (2 vols., Philadelphia, 1968, 1971).

[58] Mendelsohn, *The Jews of East Central Europe* 213–54.

[59] Samuel Gringauz, 'Jewish National Autonomy in Independent Lithuania (1918–1925),' *Jewish Social Studies*, 14/3 (July 1952), 225–46.

spearheaded active and often violent anti-Semitism.[60] As to Latvia, most of it, including its main city of Riga, was quite western in society and economy. Part of the country, however, typified eastern Europe. As in Lithuania, most Jews knew nothing of the Latvian language and culture and preferred Yiddish, while the government supported Jewish schools although they had no minorities treaty obligations. Zionism and the socialist Bund were powerful until 1934 when a right-wing Latvian dictatorship put Jewish affairs under Agudas Yisroel control. Romania in the south was vastly expanded by the war's boundary changes, which gave it Bukovina, the Banat, and Transylvania from Austria-Hungary and Bessarabia out of Russia.

Germany at the Centre

It was Germany, however, which became the focus of Jewish anxiety with the rise and rule of Nazism.[61] German Jews had served patriotically in the war and were faithful to the Kaiser's regime, but after defeat they and other 'outsiders' of imperial Germany hoped that the new democratic republic would bring them the equality they merited.[62] The new German constitution framed at Weimar, which was to a large extent the work of the liberal Jewish legal scholar Hugo Preuss, did give Jews and others full equality. This new regime and its constitution were despised by most conservatives, not to mention the radical right, as the illegitimate child of defeat. That unexpected defeat caused deep bitterness among the German people. After being gulled by optimistic com-

---

[60] Jacob Lestschinsky, 'The Economic Struggle of the Jews in Independent Lithuania,' *Jewish Social Studies*, 8/4 (Oct. 1946), 267–96; on nationalist anti-Semitism in 1918–1920, Azriel Shohat, 'The Beginnings of Anti-Semitism in Independent Lithuania', *Yad Vashem Studies*, 2 (1958), 7–48.

[61] Of the immeasurable literature on twentieth-century Germany I have found most useful Hajo Holborn, *A History of Modern Germany, 1840–1945* (New York, 1969), although it tends to scant the anti-Semitic dimension of Nazism; Koppel S. Pinson, *Modern Germany* (2nd edn., New York, 1966) and Gordon A. Craig, *Germany, 1866–1945* (Oxford, 1981).

[62] A useful survey, somewhat biased against German Zionism, is Donald L. Niewyk, *The Jews in Weimar Germany* (Manchester, 1980).

muniqués from the high command, they were unprepared to lose the war. Many maintained that the 'invincible' German army had not been defeated in battle but was 'stabbed in the back' by conspirators plotting world revolution and by 'November [1918] criminals' who surrendered. Needless to say, the Jews played a central role in these fantasies. *The Protocols of the Elders of Zion* began its career as an anti-Semitic fabrication at this time as an exposé of the 'Jewish plot'. Originally composed in French during the 1860s as a political satire, it was revised about 1903 by the tsarist secret police into an anti-Semitic tract. The *Protocols* 'took off' by explaining the post-First World War revolutions as the doing of 'elders of Zion' who assembled in 1897 (referring to the first Zionist congress) to plot revolution and world domination. The *Protocols* gained a hearing in Britain and the United States, where anti-Semitism rose to previously unreached heights.

German Jewry, especially its war veterans, for their part wanted simply to return to normal life. A Zionist project for a German Jewish congress did not interest them, but the unprecedented intensity of anti-Semitism was highly disturbing. It rose to an extent never before experienced, with Jews from eastern Europe the special target. In 1923 there was even a short pogrom in the Berlin neighbourhood where they were concentrated.[63] Jewish participants figured prominently in the revolutions which toppled the Hohenzollern dynasty and gave birth to Communist republics in Bavaria and other German states. The Bavarian republic came briefly under the rule of Kurt Eisner, Georg Landauer, and other anarcho-socialists before Eisner was murdered and the revolution repressed in blood. These revolutionists had severed their Jewish links but they still caused acute embarrassment to the Jewish community, which repeatedly disavowed them publicly. Jews were also prominent in the German revolutionary governments which succeeded the monarchy. Two cabinet ministers, three cabinet department heads, and three of their deputies were Jews—positions previously beyond Jewish aspiration. The new municipal government of Berlin included many Jews, who also figured in new state governments and as senior adminis-

---

[63] Jochmann, 'Die Ausbreitung des Antisemitismus' (n. 3 above); an excellent account is Norman Cohn, *Warrant for Genocide: The Myth of the Jewish World Conspiracy and the 'Protocols of the Elders of Zion'* (New York, 1966).

trators.[64] Enemies of the republic and of Jews made capital of the Jews' prominence, linking it to Jews in Lenin's regime and Bela Kun's in Hungary.

Most of the parties in the Weimar republic continued earlier political patterns, and the Jews could participate fully in the parties which would have them.[65] The Social Democrats, the most hospitable to Jews, split during the war with most of the anti-war Independent Social Democratic faction going to the Spartacus League in 1918. The leaders of the League's disastrous uprising early in 1919, Karl Liebknecht and the Polish Jewess Rosa Luxemburg, were arrested and murdered. The Communist Party (KPD) emerged from the Spartacus League. It had few Jewish members and was not anti-Semitic, but did not disdain occasional flings at 'Jewish capitalists'.[66] As anti-Semitism rose the Communists went with the tide and Jews vanished from their list of candidates. The largest party, the Social Democrats, however, which remained tragically inactive against the Nazi threat, emphatically repudiated anti-Semitism and compelled anti-Semites to leave the party. Jewish leaders and candidates were quite common. Some prominent Jewish members, conspicuously its distinguished intellectual and parliamentarian Eduard Bernstein, drew closer to Jewish life and became interested in socialist Zionism. In the last years before Nazi rule the Social Democrats and the Central Verein quietly co-operated to fight the Nazis. The German Democratic Party (DDP), founded in 1919, briefly bore the banner of German liberalism and was the Jews' favourite party, but its fortunes sank as politics polarized in the late 1920s. With the DDP's decline most Jewish voters moved to the Social Democrats. The moderate rightist German People's Party (DVP) was touched with anti-Semitism despite the efforts of its leader Gustav Stresemann and the presence of Jews in its ranks. The extreme right-wing German National People's Party (DNVP) was avowedly anti-Semitic, especially when the publishing magnate Alfred Hugenberg assumed control. Finally, the Catholic Centre rejected contemporary

[64] Peter Pulzer, *Jews and the German State: The Political History of a Minority, 1848–1933* (Oxford, 1992), 207–14.   [65] Ibid. 214–70.

[66] Its newspaper *Rote Fahne* published serially the quite anti-Semitic novel *Haunch, Paunch and Jowl* by the American Jewish novelist Samuel Ornitz, whose protagonist is a Jewish political fixer. Lecture by Ms Laura Browder, Cincinnati, June 1998.

German anti-Semitism but professed traditional Christian hostility to Judaism, often condemning Jews as promoters of secularism. The centre and right parties' platforms show that they regarded Jews as a problem within German life on which they had to take a stand. Germany did not readily comprehend ethnic and religious differences, even those as slight as those of a half million fully Germanized, patriotic Jews.

Beyond respectable politics were small parties of the extreme right whose ideologies included the use of violence to realize their dream of restoring Germany to its pre-war greatness. Many of their followers were war veterans at loose ends and former army officers whom German disarmament had displaced. All were bitterly anti-Semitic. From their ranks came the assassins of Kurt Eisner, the anti-war socialist leader Hugo Haase in 1919, and the intellectual industrialist and foreign minister Walter Rathenau in 1922, all Jews. One of these little parties took the grandiose name of National Socialist German Workers Party (NSDAP), known in infamy as Nazi, led by the Austrian agitator and war veteran Adolf Hitler. The NSDAP professed a vague socialism, fanatical nationalism, and extreme racist anti-Semitism under its omnipotent Leader (*Führer*). To Hitler and the Nazis mankind was divided into races fixed to eternity not only physically but also in moral and intellectual attributes. Races, they held, are in everlasting warfare to the death with one another. The German people of the Aryan race, superior in mind and body, were locked in conflict with the inferior Semitic race, meaning the Jews, who were physically degenerate, deceitful, and exploiters of Aryan achievements. Aryan Germany had been robbed and betrayed by the Jews. Their character was racially fixed, so that religious conversion or assimilation could never change them. Indeed these increased the danger that Jews would pollute the pure Aryan race and defile Aryan maidenhood. All these doctrines, collectively a vast lie, were not original with Hitler.[67] He picked them up from various pamphleteers and agitators during his pre-war years in Vienna and from their foremost theorist, the Germanized Englishman Houston Stewart Chamberlain. Nazi violence scorned the rule of law and Nazi storm troopers came gradually to dominate the streets. They were not deterred that most

[67] On racism and the related *volkisch* movement see George L. Mosse, *The Crisis of German Ideology: Intellectual Origins of the Third Reich* (New York, 1964).

judges, a markedly conservative group, dealt fairly and sometimes sternly with the acts of violence and slanderous abuse of the 'patriots'.[68] The Nazis enjoyed scant success at the polls before their great leap in the 1930 and 1932 elections. Many Germans deplored their violent ways and thought little of Hitler but expressed admiration for fervent Nazi nationalism, regarding it as a necessary if excessive reaction to the terms of the Versailles treaty and to modernist Weimar culture, despised as 'cultural Bolshevism'.[69]

It was during these years of the republic that German Jewry enjoyed a remarkable Jewish cultural development. This came in addition to the exceptional distinction of Jews in German literature, scholarship, music, and the sciences. The outstanding, almost symbolic figure was Albert Einstein, a political dissenter and pro-Zionist, whose epoch-making contributions in mathematical physics remade man's understanding of the natural world. Paralleling similar developments in the culture of the 1920s, the focus of interest shifted to expressions within Judaism of personalist, mystical thought. New forms of Jewish expression blossomed in music, dance, drama, art, book production, and synagogue architecture. Unlike the conservative German nationalists' visceral opposition to the new Weimar culture, the Jewish renaissance was generally welcomed by staid German Jewry. Local Jewish communities became more active under democratized regimes, and the Jewish People's Party of Zionists, Orthodox, and poorer east European Jews— the community's former outsiders to power—attained some success in turning the formal *Religionsgemeinde* into a people's *Volksgemeinde*. The Hebraic cultural renaissance which was part of Zionism also played a role as Hebrew intellectuals and authors among Germany's east European Jews provided cultural stimulus. Under the inspired leadership of the brilliant young philosopher and scholar Franz Rosenzweig, who had earlier almost converted to Christianity, the *Lehrhaus* movement for intensive study of the Jewish classics spread widely. He and Martin Buber

[68] Donald L. Niewyk, 'Jews and the Courts in Weimar Gemany,' *Jewish Social Studies*, 37/2 (spring 1975), 99–113.

[69] Such was the view, privately expressed, even of Max M. Warburg, the foremost German Jewish banker, in 1932. Quoted from MS in Pulzer, *Jews and the German State*, 233.

were the central figures in the movement, and they collaborated in a new translation of the Bible. In the homeland of the Science of Judaism large projects of scholarly synthesis and collaboration were undertaken, notably the encyclopedic *Jüdisches Lexicon* in five stout volumes (Berlin, 1928–30) and ten volumes of the superb *Encyclopedia Judaica* which reached M when it was halted by the Nazis in 1934. One volume of the Hebrew encyclopedia *Eshkol* appeared at the same time. All were artistically bound and illustrated.[70]

On 30 January 1933 Adolf Hitler was legally appointed German chancellor, and on 24 March 1933 the Enabling Act conferred unlimited power on him.[71] Shortly he discarded his DNVP and other coalition partners and embarked on twelve appalling years of tyranny. Nearly seventy years after the Nazi regime began the rational mind finds nearly beyond understanding how this happened in the nation which led the world in science, scholarship, music, philosophy, and medicine and was eminent in practically every sphere of human endeavour. Men with advanced education were appointed to practise sadism on a vast scale, culture and its institutions including universities yielded with little if any resistance to the dictates of party masters, policies of barbarity were accepted as the products of science, stern censorship and shrieking propaganda replaced discussion and criticism—all this strains belief to the present day. Christian churches accommodated themselves with few voices of question or protest. A nation in the heart of civilized Europe adoring and obeying a coarse, morally vacant, megalomaniacal man as its omnipotent *Führer* must give pause to any observer of human behaviour. The Nazi regime meted out savage treatment in newly established concentration camps to dissenters and opponents and especially to Jews. Nothing like the Nazi regime had ever been seen in a modern society and Jews were at the centre of its attention.

Jews viewed with understandable alarm the Nazis' rise to power.

[70] An excellent study is Michael Brenner, *The Renaissance of Jewish Culture in Weimar Germany* (New Haven, 1996).

[71] Here too the quantity of literature is overwhelming. I found most useful the excellent study by the German scholar Karl Dietrich Bracher, *The German Dictatorship* (paperback edn., Harmondsworth, 1978). An important recent survey of the Jewish side is Saul Friedlander, *Nazi Germany and the Jews* i. *The Years of Persecution, 1933–1939* (New York, 1997).

However, there were circles which entertained the belief that they could reach some understanding with the new rulers. The League of German Nationalist Jews, an extreme right-wing association which disclaimed any connection with Jews elsewhere and denounced the Jewish community as insufficiently German, believed so. They professed radical German nationalism and even sympathized with much of the Nazi programme. Their and kindred youth groups' overtures to the Nazi government were disregarded, and in 1935 they were ordered to dissolve.[72] The Zionists' relation to the new regime was more complex. They had long refused to combat anti-Semitism, considering it not a Jewish but a gentile problem unavoidable in the *galut*. By 1929, however, they could no longer ignore the Nazi menace. One Zionist intellectual writing in 1932 saw Nazism as 'new German nationalism' with lines of similarity between its supposedly less extreme version and 'new Zionist nationalism', in their common emphasis on 'historic destiny'. But he concluded that Nazism's brutal anti-Semitism and its repudiation of common humanity made it mortally dangerous. The foremost German Zionist, Kurt Blumenfeld, rejected any link between Zionism and Nazism, intolerant of all difference and passionately anti-Semitic. The Nazi regime displayed more tolerance to the Zionist organizations than to other Jewish groups which insisted on the Jews as Germans, because the Zionists planned emigration and the Nazis wanted Germany without Jews. This made dealing between German Zionism and the Nazi government possible, indeed necessary, in order to organize Jewish emigration. Blumenfeld secretly proposed to Hitler himself in 1933 that the Jews be permitted to maintain a segregated group existence in Germany. But the Fuhrer would not see him.[73] Relative favour to Zionism diminished sharply when a Jewish state appeared possible thanks to the British government's Peel Commission report on Palestine in 1937. A Jewish state as it recommended was not tolerable to Nazi thinking.

[72] Carl J. Rheins, 'The Verband nationaldeutscher Juden, 1921–1933,' *Leo Baeck Institute Year Book*, 25 (1980), 243–68.

[73] Jehuda Reinharz, *Dokumente zur Geschichte des deutschen Zionismus, 1882–1933* (Tübingen, 1981), 530–42; Daniel Frankel, *'Al Pi Tehom* (Hebrew; English title: *On the Edge of the Abyss: Zionist Policy and the Plight of the German Jews*) (Jerusalem, 1994), 36–8, 81–6.

It is a matter of dispute at what point the Nazis considered seriously the annihilation of the Jews: at the outset of their movement, the ascent to power in 1933, the massive *Kristallnacht* pogrom of 1938, or at some stage of preparation for war or during the war. Was annihilation 'intentionalist', an intention in existence from early in Hitler's career, or 'functionalist', a programme arrived at by internal rivalries and bureaucratic problems? If annihilating the Jews was 'functionalist', no amount of bureaucratic problems could have initiated such a monstrosity and an earlier intention had to exist.[74] The idea of annihilation was spoken of several times by Hitler in limited groups and was clearly expressed in his threat which he called a 'prophecy', on 30 January 1939: 'If the Jewish international financiers inside and outside Europe succeed in involving the nations in another war, the result will not be world bolshevism and therefore a victory for Judaism; it will be the end[75] of the Jews in Europe.'[76] German Jewry had endured exactly six years under the Nazi heel when these words were spoken. In November 1941 Hitler referred in the presence of Himmler and Heydrich to murdering the Jews, and press representatives were told two months later that 'special treatment' (*Sonderbehandlung*) explicitly meant killing.[77] The recently discovered daybook of Himmler shows that he and Hitler met frequently and often spoke of Jews. There and elsewhere the tyrant did not necessarily issue signed orders but just expressed his desire that something be done. Himmler and others in his retinue understood and took the necessary steps. Thus there is no written order to carry out genocide but Hitler's staff acted on his express wishes.

While storm troopers celebrated in 1933 by parading and brawling and beating, Nazi authorities began more deliberate action by forbidding

[74] The conception is the British historian Tim Mason's, sketched in Charles S. Maier, *The Unmasterable Past: History, the Holocaust, and German National Identity* (Cambridge, Mass., 1988), 66–99. To be sure, no 'functionalist' questions that the Holocaust occurred.

[75] *Vernichtung* = annihilation, destruction.

[76] I have followed the translation by Sarah Gordon, *Hitler, Germans and the 'Jewish Question'* (Princeton, 1984), p. 145, with alternative translations for the critical word 'Vernichtung'.

[77] Gerhard L. Weinberg, *A World at Arms: A Global History of World War II* (Cambridge, 1994), 301, 1014 nn. 138 and 140.

violent deeds unauthorized from above.[78] In 1933 German Jewry as well as Jews and humane opinion throughout the world were stunned by events in Germany. However, most still regarded Nazism as the latest and worst outburst of anti-Semitism but not fundamentally different from what had gone before. Early in 1933 Jews were dismissed from the civil service, discharged as teachers and university lecturers and removed from membership in learned bodies, forbidden to perform for German audiences, forced out of positions of prominence, and banned from army service. At the insistence of President Hindenburg Jewish war veterans and children of fallen soldiers were exempted from dismissal, but that held only until the aged president died a year later. Segregated Jewish cultural activity flourished under these conditions of stress, as fine theatrical and musical performances drew large Jewish audiences. Enrolment in Jewish schools boomed because Jewish children in German schools often met with abuse before they were finally excluded in November 1938. On the other hand the boycott of Jewish business was shortened to one day, 1 April 1933, and had little success. Germans continued to buy and sell from Jews and Jewish economic activity continued for years longer. Anti-Semitism was bureaucratized in the sinister Gestapo and Security Service (SD), which also was responsible for torture, humiliation, and murder in the concentration camps. Although the storm troopers spoiled for violent action, the regime allowed only the violence sponsored by itself. Except for some local beatings and killings these thugs had to wait more than five years until November 1938.

After the first onslaught in 1933 the Jewish situation became relatively stable until late 1935, with the Jews excluded from German life outside the economic sphere. In September 1935 the Nuremberg laws, personally proclaimed by Hitler at the annual party congress held in that city, enacted Nazi racism. They were less the product of deliberations than of the dictator's command that a law be prepared instantly to excite the party congress. Bureaucrats from the Ministry of the Interior

[78] Cogent accounts are Karl A. Schleunes, *The Twisted Road to Auschwitz: Nazi Policy toward German Jews, 1933–1939* (Urbana, Ill., 1970) and Friedlander, *Nazi Germany and the Jews*, 113–211. Nazi laws affecting Jews are collected in Joseph Walk (ed.), *Die Sonderrecht für die Juden im NS-Staat* (Heidelberg, 1981).

hastened to obey. The man responsible for legislation on Jews, Lösener, was furtively a disillusioned Nazi who with extreme caution sought to soften the law's application to part-Jews and not to deprive the Jews of citizenship. The law Hitler proclaimed to the roaring masses bore a title of Nazi grandiosity—Law for the Protection of German Blood and Honour. It forbade marriages or sexual relations between Jews and Germans, and a German housemaid could not work for a Jew until she reached the age of 45. Prison terms awaited offenders. The citizenship law conferred upon Aryans alone an elevated but meaningless status denied to Jews. More consequentially, the definition of Jew was fixed in supplementary decrees. As summarized by Karl Schleunes:

the half-Jew (one with two Aryan and two Jewish grandparents) . . . was considered Jewish if: he was an adherent of the Jewish faith, he was married to a Jew, he was the child of a marriage with one Jewish partner, or if he was the offspring of an illegitimate union between a Jew and an Aryan. Someone with two Jewish grandparents, if he was not legally Jewish on the basis of these four conditions, was legally a 'Jewish *Mischling*.'[79] . . . An individual with only one Jewish grandparent was still legally Jewish if he was a member of the Jewish religious community. Anyone with less than one-quarter Jewish blood was considered to be of 'German or closely related origins'.[80]

Germans married to Jews were pressured to divorce them. If the wife was Jewish the husband was still an Aryan, but a Jewish husband made the Aryan wife a Jew. Still finer definitions and exceptions kept the bureaucratic machine occupied for years. After the Nuremberg laws officially excluded Jews from German life, many Jews believed that now they could exist in Germany in an inferior but clearly stated status and better days would somehow come. Germans also appeared satisfied with the exclusion of Jews from the country's life. To many Jews and others in and out of Germany the Nazi regime with its leader, wild and brutal in a civilized country, appeared bound to fall. Matters existed in this fashion for perhaps a year and a half. During the Olympic games of 1936 in

---

[79] The term is hard to translate and means approximately 'mixed blood'.
[80] Schleunes, *The Twisted Road*, 128–9; 120–32 on the Nuremberg laws; Friedlander, *Nazi Germany and the Jews*, 145–62.

Berlin the face of anti-Semitism was covered; Olympic rules enabled German Jewish athletes to compete.[81]

German Jewry amounted to slightly less than 500,000 at the advent of the Nazis, and 150,000 to 200,000 more had Jewish identification forced on them by Nazi laws. Thanks to a local initiative the long split Jewish community came together in September 1933 to establish the *Reichsvertretung der deutschen Juden* (National Representation of German Jews; in 1935 *deutschen Juden* became *Juden in Deutschland* (Jews in Germany)). With representatives of local communities and organizations in its ranks, the *Reichsvertretung* was riddled by political and ideological disputes.[82] Yet it courageously represented German Jewry before the Nazi rulers and maintained social and welfare services for an increasingly impoverished community. Funds came from the Central British Fund for German Jewry and the Joint Distribution Committee in the United States.

The overriding concern of German Jewry was emigration, and it was primarily this which attracted masses of Jews to Zionism and softened the anti-Zionism of the Central Verein and other organizations. Vocational training was set up and *He-Haluz*, before 1933 a little group, and the still smaller Orthodox *Bachad* (*Brit Halutzim Datiyim* = Alliance of Religious Pioneers) enrolled thousands of Jewish youth to train for Palestine agricultural work. Fewer than 1,300 Jews from Germany settled there between 1919 and 1933, but the number in *He-Haluz* multiplied to 15,000 in 1933. Most of them were more committed to personal survival than to the Zionist vision. On the other hand the leaders of the *yishuv* and even of the German Zionist organization wanted only young manpower which had undergone lengthy training for Palestine, preferring not to consider the homeland for mass refuge.[83] Settlement there was no easy matter, although anyone with £1,000 could settle freely, and a large proportion of German Jews, unlike those of eastern Europe, possessed such means. For others the Jewish Agency received a mere 1,500 immi-

---

[81] However they were provided no place to practice.

[82] Jacob Boas, 'German-Jewish Internal Politics under Hitler, 1933–1938,' *Leo Baeck Institute Year Book*, 29 (1984), 3–25.

[83] The tension between Palestine as a refuge and the desire for trained young pioneers is a main theme in Frankel, *'Al Pi Tehom* (n. 73 above).

gration certificates monthly, and distributing them among many lands was a touchy matter. Some German Jews entered as tourists and forgot to go home, and others were smuggled in illegally. Nazi imposts on departing Jews rose steadily, but the *Ha'avara* (transfer) agreements made possible the exchange of marks into sterling without prohibitive charges. Under its terms, Jews could deposit their funds with Paltreu, a bank set up for the purpose, which would use them to buy German goods and ship them for sale in Palestine. The emigrant would receive the proceeds less charges. The German economy benefited accordingly and German marks were saved. This was not an official Zionist–German deal, but leading figures were 'unofficially' involved. *Ha'avara* drew severe criticism, especially because most of the Jewish world was boycotting German goods and the moral aspects of the deal were in dispute. It functioned quite smoothly until 1936, by which time there were more Jewish marks on deposit than there were goods that could be sold in Palestine and nearby countries. *Ha'avara* continued until late in 1938, aiding as many as 50,000 Jews to settle in Palestine. An estimated £8.1 million flowed into the homeland through *Ha'avara*, of the £54.2 million which entered the country between 1933 and 1939.[84]

Jews crossed the border from Germany into France, the Netherlands and Czechoslovakia, only to be caught there a few years later by German conquest. Great Britain's strict rules almost completely prevented immigration until the gates were opened in the crisis year of 1938–9. In the United States, the classic land of refuge and opportunity, the immigration law which fixed national quotas gave Germany a large quota. In 1930, however, a new rule known as 'likely to become a public charge' came into force by which the US consuls who granted immigrant visas had to be satisfied that the applicant would be able to make a living in depression-stricken America. These all-powerful consuls, who were not under the authority of the sympathetic US ambassador Dodd, were generally unsympathetic and in some cases anti-Semitic. As a result of their interpretations, the German quotas were never filled and thousands of

---

[84] Ibid. 126–7; Avraham Barkai, 'German Interests in the Haavara-Transfer Agreement 1933–1939,' *Leo Baeck Institute Year Book*, 35 (1990), 145–66; Shaul Esh, 'Ha-Ha'avara' (Hebrew), *Iyyunim be-Heker ha-Shoah ve-Yahadut Zemanenu* (Hebrew; English title *Studies in the Holocaust and Contemporary Jewry*) (Jerusalem, 1973), 33–106.

Jews could not reach American refuge. There was no chance of relaxing immigration laws, since the US Congress was hostile to immigration and even had bills before it to forbid immigration during the economic depression.

In 1937 steps were taken towards radical Nazi persecution. The Jewish community was deprived of legal standing, and early in the following year Jews were defined 'in all cases as enemies of the state'.[85] They had to submit full statements of their assets, an obvious preparation for confiscation, and Jewish businesses began to be 'Aryanized'—sold for a song to good Nazis. Besides, several large synagogues were razed. The control of Jewish affairs was taken from the government bureaucracy and vested in the SD (Security Service) and Gestapo. They demonstrated their methods when Nazi Germany annexed Austria (*Anschluss*) in March 1938. Its 191,000 Jews, the vast majority living in Vienna, were subjected at once to Nazi laws and, unlike those in Germany, were terrorized and beaten on the streets, by enthusiastic Austrians. A Gestapo staff headed by the hitherto anonymous Adolf Eichmann set up in the Rothschild mansion, where Jews passed through a series of offices to be stripped of citizenship and property. They emerged with passports which they had to use within two weeks or be sent to a concentration camp. In October thousands of unnaturalized or denaturalized Polish Jews in Germany were seized and expelled to Poland, which refused to admit them. They lingered for weeks in no man's land under severe conditions.

The greatest blow fell on 9–10 November 1938. The pogrom was named the Night of Broken Glass (*Kristallnacht*) after the shattered windows of hundreds of synagogues which were put to the torch.[86] In addition 30,000 Jews were seized and taken to concentration camps and thousands were brutally beaten and their homes vandalized by Nazi hoodlums who at last could demonstrate their valour and patriotism. Just before the 'spontaneous' actions began the Gestapo ordered that

---

[85] Walk, *Die Sonderrecht*, 215.

[86] Research in progress at the University of Duisberg shows the widely accepted figure of 270 synagogues to be a gross underestimate. In the state of North Rhine Westphalia alone over 300 synagogues were destroyed or ruined, and the number for all Germany may reach 2,000.

they not be interfered with, and authorized 'most severe measures', meaning killing, against any Jews who resisted. Jews could be thrown out of their houses.[87] This enormous pogrom lasted two days and was represented as the German people's righteous anger over the killing by a young Jew, the son of deported Polish Jews, of a German diplomat in Paris.[88] During *Kristallnacht* 267 synagogues were destroyed, 7,500 Jewish businesses were vandalized, and 91 Jews were killed besides hundreds of suicides and deaths owing to concentration camp abuse of the men taken there.

The world reaction was strongly negative, and President Roosevelt called the US ambassador home. Within Germany, the observant Gestapo reported that the passive German people were disturbed by the sights, especially the destruction of hundreds of houses of God. A tremendous fine, tantamount to robbery, was levied on German Jewry, a further series of prohibitions was inflicted on them, and nearly all Jewish education and communal activity was forbidden. Even the most hopeful and patriotic German Jews realized that they had to flee. And so they did; between November 1938 and the outbreak of war less than a year later 70,000 Jews left lands under Nazi rule, which included Czechoslovakia from March 1939. German Jewry, by then an impoverished, shattered community of 225,000 mostly older persons, descended into a shadowy existence until deportations 'to the East' were decreed in 1942.

Few places in the world were interested in receiving refugees from Nazism. Western Europe and North America did not want them, although Great Britain relaxed its hitherto strict limits and admitted 40,000 after the Kristallnacht. All this became clear at the Évian conference, called by President Roosevelt, in 1938. More than twenty countries attended, and the representative of each expressed in turn his country's sympathy with 'political refugees' and its inability to take any

[87] Walk, *Die Sonderrecht*, 249. The same orders directed that synagogue archives be saved, specifically in Cologne which supposedly contained important historical material. Such orders probably originated with the Nazi research institutes for studying the Jewish past.

[88] It was all planned in advance; the death of vom Rath, the diplomat, was a useful pretext. One year earlier a young Jew killed the leader of the Swiss Nazi Party but no 'righteous anger' had been permitted.

more. A few South American countries and the international zone of Shanghai drew thousands of desperate Jews. Great Britain, as the ruler of Palestine, kept to stringent quotas there.

The Second World War began on 1 September 1939. By the summer of 1941 Germany had crushed Poland, Norway, Denmark, Belgium, the Netherlands, France, Yugoslavia, and Greece in that order, and the great assault on Soviet Russia was progressing rapidly. Other European countries were German allies or benevolently neutral. On 20 May 1941, at the height of German power and one month before the invasion of Russia, the SD ordered restrictions on Jewish emigration 'in view of the very imminent final solution of the Jewish problem'.[89] Two months afterwards, on 31 July 1941, Hermann Goering as head of the Nazi four-year plan passed the command to Reinhard Heydrich, second to Himmler in the Gestapo and SD, to take 'every necessary preparation of a practical and material sort for a general solution of the Jewish question in European areas under German influence'.[90] This was the command to prepare the mass murder, known in Nazi euphemism as the Final Solution and by other names. The command to Heydrich was made more comprehensive by the prohibition of emigration out of Nazi countries from 23 October 1941.[91] Nazified Europe was made ready for the systematic murder of its Jews.

---

[89] Walk, *Die Sonderrecht*, 341, 345.   [90] Ibid. 345.   [91] Ibid. 353.

10

Havens and National Home

As anti-Semitism engulfed the Jews of central and eastern Europe they realized that the coming of war would bring even worse to them. None yet imagined, however, what its full extent would be. Europe was still the cultural and population centre of world Jewry, but the centres of Jewish life beyond the European continent were bound to become ever more important as the European situation darkened. On the edge of Europe was Great Britain, and overseas were countries of the British Commonwealth, North and South America, and above all the United States. In a unique class was the fast-developing Jewish national home. The problems which beset them all paled in comparison with the condition of the Jews who had to endure the expanding Nazi rule.

British and French Jewry

Offshore from the Continent lay Great Britain with its class-stratified liberal democracy.[1] The number of British Jews slowly climbed to an estimated 385,000 in 1940 thanks to modest natural increase and refugee immigration. With stringent limits on immigration about 30,000 refugees from Nazi Germany were in the country by the end of 1938. The severe German persecutions of 1938–9 led to the easing of immigration restrictions, so that by 1940 Britain had about 73,000 German and Austrian refugees, not all of them Jews. Subtracting those who went on to other countries, the net addition to British Jewry was about 55,000. Almost 10,000 of them were the so-called *kindertransport*, children without

---

[1] Contrasting works are V. D. Lipman, *A History of the Jews in Britain since 1858* (Leicester, 1990), and Geoffrey Alderman, *Modern British Jewry* (Oxford, 1992).

parents rescued from Nazi lands in 1938–9 and boarded with Jewish and non-Jewish families.[2] The British government admitted such large numbers after accepting a few influential Jews' personal guarantee that no refugee would become a public charge. The Central British Fund for German Jewry raised the money from 1933 to make good the guarantee, and the Council for German Jewry funded refugee resettlement overseas from 1936.

The main Jewish communal institutions dated several generations back and continued on their well-worn paths—the Board of Deputies for representation, the Anglo-Jewish Association in foreign affairs, local Boards of Guardians for welfare, the moderate orthodox Chief Rabbinate and in London the United Synagogue in religious matters. The Zionist movement was active. Many immigrants from eastern Europe who reached middle-class status and more so their British children began to contest the long dominance of the Jewish community by a 'cousinhood' of old wealth, above all the Rothschilds. The social and economic ascent of the east European immigrants' second generation was slower than in America, and a large proportion remained in petty trade and proletarian occupations, especially tailoring. Still, a class of successful merchants and professionals emerged among the immigrants' children, and some made distinguished careers in law and politics and as judges, artists, scholars, musicians, and scientists.

Jewish politics also changed. After long voting mostly Liberal the Jews turned leftwards to Labour especially in proletarian districts, or further left to the Communists, who then had the image of idealistic radicals. Anti-Semitism became much stronger during these inter-war years. *The Protocols of the Elders of Zion* was circulated and believed widely. Besides upper-class social anti-Semitism a fascist movement grew to menacing proportions under the magnetic leadership of the frustrated politician Oswald Mosley. Their inability to confront vigorously the anti-Semitic movement lost the official Jewish communal leaders much credibility,

---

[2] Lipman, *Jews in Britain*, 191, 204, 232–3; A. J. Sherman, *Island Refuge: Britain and Refugees from the Third Reich, 1933–1939* (Berkeley, 1973), appendix I, who comments on the unreliability of figures. Louise London, 'Jewish Refugees, Anglo-Jewry and British Government Policy', in *The Making of Modern Anglo-Jewry*, ed. David Cesarani (Oxford, 1990), 163–90.

especially in the proletarian Jewish East End of London where Mosley's movement was loud and active. Britain bitterly disappointed most Jews by its Palestine policy and its disastrous foreign policy of appeasing Nazi Germany. The strength of fascism was disturbing, but several Christian organizations resolutely combated it along with anti-Semitism. Anti-Semitism was a force but Great Britain remained a free society when it went to war against Nazism.

Across the English Channel, French Jewry increased sharply in numbers from the 120,000 who lived there in 1914, about 40,000 of whom were immigrants from eastern Europe. Alsace and Lorraine with 30,000 Jews was returned to France after the war. A steady flow from eastern Europe followed by refugees from Nazi Germany brought French Jewry's numbers to approximately 300,000 in 1939. Of the numerous Jews who distinguished themselves as scientists, scholars, and writers, some came from such immigrant stock.

France knew nothing of significant cultural variety, much less cultural pluralism. Native French Jewry's cultural assimilationism and its fervent national patriotism were sorely tried from within and without. The Yiddish language with its articulate press, as well as the conspicuous neighbourhoods and leftist politics of the immigrants, who by now constituted a majority of Paris Jews, disturbed and often angered the French natives. They demanded and did all they could to assimilate the newcomers who, they felt sure, were the cause of the rising tide of anti-Semitism. However, the cloud of fascistic anti-Semitism grew heavier in a country conscious of its declining world position and economic stagnation. To see the socialist Jew Léon Blum as Popular Front premier in 1936-7 infuriated anti-Semites as well as many nativists who could not accept that a 'foreigner' (actually of Alsatian origin many generations in France) should govern the country. Blum on principle turned aside pleas from native Jewish leaders not to head the government. The rigorous anti-alien law of 1938, unopposed by official French Jewry, unintentionally prepared the way for the separation between natives and foreigners which marked the Holocaust in France.

The core organization of French Jewry, the Consistoire Centrale and its local branches, devoted itself almost exclusively to religious affairs under firm lay domination. An array of new organizations expressed broader interests. Yiddish secular culture, Communist societies, Zionism, and lively youth movements made for a more active Jewish community.[3]

American Jewry: Immigrants Coming to Power

The United States went through extreme ups and downs in its economy between 1914 and entering the Second World War in 1941. These exerted powerful influence in shaping American political leadership, social policies, and world outlook.[4] The fading of Progressivism and the negative reaction to American participation in international affairs in the wake of the First World War brought to power the native white, conservative, business-oriented Republicans until the Great Depression turned them out. These were not comfortable years for the status of Jews in American life. Nativism rode high during the 1920s and racism was chronic. The quirky Henry Ford, whose resources were practically unlimited from manufacturing the cheap automobiles which made him a hero to many Americans, became the foremost sponsor of anti-Semitic propaganda. In his case it was a hatred of bankers and money powers which led him to publish 'The Cause of World Distress', meaning the Jews, and a weekly anti-Semitic sheet. Ford had to beat a retreat when a libel suit pushed him to the wall, and in 1926 he caved in and apologized in humiliating terms for his seven years' agitation. The Ku Klux Klan, a nation-wide movement of men professing racism and anti-Semitism who strutted in parades covered with bedsheets and indulged in violence, collapsed in scandal after early political successes.

The influence of nativism and racism was manifest in the Johnson Act which put an end to mass immigration by means of a system of national

[3] Bernard Blumenkranz (ed.), *Histoire des Juifs en France* (Toulouse, 1972), 363–89 (W. Rabi); E. Tcherikower (ed.), *Yidn in Frankraykh* (2 vols., New York, 1942), ii. 207–63; Paula Hyman, *From Dreyfus to Vichy: The Remaking of French Jewry, 1906–1939* (New York, 1977), 115–236; David H. Weinberg, *A Community on Trial: The Jews of Paris in the 1930s* (Chicago/London, 1977); Richard Millman, *La Question juive entre les deux guerres: Ligues de droite et antisémitisme en France* (Paris, 1992).

[4] A general account is Henry L. Feingold, 'A Time for Searching: Entering the Mainstream, 1920–1945', *The Jewish People in America*, 4 (Baltimore/London, 1992).

quotas based on racist doctrines. National quotas had begun with the immigration law of 1921, and the Johnson Act sharpened them to favour racially 'superior' Nordics born in the British Isles, Ireland, Germany, and Scandinavia at the expense of racially 'inferior' Slavic and Mediterranean races from the continent's south and east. Millions of Italians, for example, had entered the United States and more wanted to come, but the quota for 'racially inferior' Italians was set about 4,000 yearly, while that for 'racially inferior' Poles was about 6,000. Jews belonged to the respective quotas of their countries of birth. The quotas for 'Nordic' countries were never filled, but the law prohibited the transfer of unused quotas from one country to another. Moreover, a person was always reckoned by his land of birth. Immigration within the Western Hemisphere was unrestricted, and passage from Canada to the United States was quite common. Naturalized immigrants could bring in members of their immediate family outside the quota.[5] As we shall see, other limitations were attached to the act by executive order. The Johnson Act came to full application only in 1929 and governed immigration until 1965. Each of its provisions, which were rigorously enforced, was decisively important in granting or denying desperately desired visas to emigrate to the United States.

The Johnson Act's first visible effect was a slowdown in Jewish population increase. Soon after mass immigration stopped, there were about 4,228,000 Jews among 119,000,000 Americans, or 3.5%, and 4,831,000 (3.6%) among 132 million Americans in 1937. The effects showed later, when of 204 million enumerated in 1970 the Jewish population failed to keep pace, amounting to 5,869,000 (2.8%).[6] The proportion of Jews

---

[5] A masterly account of the social and intellectual basis of opposition to immigration is John Higham, *Strangers in the Land: Patterns of American Nativism, 1860–1925* (2nd edn., New York, 1963). The quota system in the 1921 law was based on the census figures of 'national origins' of the American population in 1910. 3% of each national origin constituted a given year's immigration quota, e.g. 6 m. Germans (a hypothetical figure) yield a German quota of 180,000. The Act of 1925 reduced the proportion to 2% and changed the base year from 1910 to 1890, when the bugaboo of the act, the 'new immigration' from southern and eastern Europe, had just begun.

[6] As stated earlier, American Jewish population estimates are only educated guesses. Figures for 1937 and earlier are drawn from the report of Harry S. Linfield in *American Jewish Year Book*, 42 (1940–1), 215 ff.

in the population of the United States thus decreased considerably. Yiddish cultural life began to dry up when there were too few new arrivals from Europe to make up for losses to American cultural assimilation.

During this inter-war period the vast cohort of east European immigrants' children and immigrants who had come as young children sought their place in American life and remade the American Jewish community.[7] Great economic changes occurred and new, largely Jewish neighbourhoods were built in big cities, frequently by speculative Jewish builders. As the new generation matured the immigrant trades declined. Peddling and street selling, the starting point for multitudes of newcomers, dwindled although they were renewed by many unemployed as a desperate expedient during the depression. In better times most pedlars became shopkeepers and a few grew to be substantial merchants. While many immigrant tailors and dressmakers, men and women, stuck to that trade, the once dominant role of ready-made tailoring among immigrant Jews diminished as most tailors' sons and daughters turned to other occupations. The seemingly solid Jewish trade unions, the pride of immigrant achievement, lost the Jewish majority among their members by the early 1920s, although the leaders remained almost all Jews. The unions conducted a remarkable gamut of activity for members, including workers' pensions in pre-Social Security days, health clinics, adult education, vacation resorts, a bank, and excellent co-operative housing. The Amalgamated Clothing Workers lent money to strapped businesses to save them from bankruptcy and thereby their workers' jobs. In the early 1920s the Jewish unions turned back a concerted attack by employers. It was followed, however, by a virtual civil war within the ranks of the International Ladies Garment Workers Union (ILGWU) between the established leadership and the aggressive, disruptive Trade Union Educational League of Communist insurgents. With a following composed mostly of newcomers to the trade, they plunged into a disastrous general strike in 1926 which ended in Communist defeat and wrecked the ILGWU, once the largest and

---

[7] Valuable surveys for this period are Henry L. Feingold, *A Time for Searching*, and Deborah Dash Moore, *At Home in America: Second Generation New York Jews* (New York, 1981).

wealthiest garment union. Other Jewish unions were more peaceable internally, but all were severely struck by the Great Depression. They revived during the depression itself thanks to the pro-union legislation of President Roosevelt's New Deal.[8]

The occupations which young Jews sought were in white-collar work or the professions. A large number became teachers, accountants, book-keepers, salesmen, and independent businessmen, as well as the respected professions of lawyers, dentists, and physicians. Academic and scientific positions, however, were few. There had been little employment discrimination when Jews stuck to their immigrant trades, but when they sought white-collar, managerial, or professional careers in the general employment market their opportunities became restricted. Large companies, except Jewish ones (and then not always), usually would not hire Jews. They could not find employment in banks, law firms, insurance companies (except as agents to drum up Jewish clients), hospitals, or universities. Élite private colleges set quotas on the number of Jewish students. Medicine was flagrantly discriminatory, as medical schools imposed drastic quotas on Jewish students they would admit regardless of merit, while hospitals excluded Jewish physicians from their staffs.[9] Many young men determined to be physicians went abroad to study, especially to Scotland. German Jewish refugee physicians in the 1930s, some of whom had gained international distinction, faced obstacles to practising. Newly minted lawyers found that many local bar associations erected barriers to licensing and law firms would not employ them.[10] Social discrimination in élite clubs was rampant, and homes or flats in many expensive neighbourhoods could not be bought or rented by Jews. As the fastest-rising immigrant group during the 1920s Jews were the first to feel the resistance of prejudice to their advance, but they were not the only victims. Anti-Semitism played the central role, but Italians, Poles, and others of the 'new immigration'

[8] Joseph Brandes, 'From Sweatshop to Stability: Jewish Labor between Two World Wars', in *Essays on the American Jewish Labor Movement*, ed. Ezra Mendelsohn (YIVO Annual of Jewish Social Science, 16 (1976)), 1–149.

[9] Jacob A. Goldberg, 'Jews in the Medical Profession: A National Survey', *Jewish Social Studies*, 1/3 (July 1939), 327–36.

[10] Jerold S. Auerbach, *Unequal Justice: Lawyers and Social Change in Modern America* (New York, 1976).

experienced similar obstacles to their progress, and racism against Blacks was all-embracing.

During the 1920s the east European immigrant stock began to foster an American style of Judaism. Americanized immigrants and their children who left New York's Lower East Side and immigrant districts in other cities for more attractive urban areas sought modern synagogues instead of immigrant *hevrot*. Enough foreign-born Jews joined the temples of Reform Judaism to give even that long-established and still Germanic movement an east European-born majority. Within the Reform movement they were a force for the return of some traditional ceremonial.[11] At the same time a large number of modernized Orthodox congregations came into existence, where English replaced Yiddish. But many Jews came to Orthodox synagogues less for a rabbi or Talmudic scholar than to hear a virtuoso *hazan* who filled the synagogue's seats especially on holidays. An American Orthodox rabbinate gradually developed, whose members were usually ordained at the Rabbi Isaac Elhanan yeshiva (RIETS). Alongside this traditional yeshiva, which copied a Lithuanian prototype, Yeshiva College (later University) opened in 1928 under Orthodox direction. Its founder Bernard Revel evolved a philosophy of 'Torah and Science' (*Torah u-Madda*) which attempted to synthesize the two elements.[12] Colleges of Orthodox character had no precedent, and many Orthodox Jews found Yeshiva College religiously unacceptable because it combined the sacred with the profane; other American Jews considered it an academic ghetto. For some twenty years Yeshiva College led an impoverished existence until it reached better days.

Denominational lines were fluid before the 1950s, and Orthodoxy shaded into the still small Conservative movement based at the Jewish Theological Seminary. The movement emphasized a decorous service and in most of their synagogues men and women were seated together, but the Conservatives had deeper ideas as well. They asserted fidelity to *halakhah* while claiming it could be adjusted and interpreted to meet the

---

[11] Michael A. Meyer, *Response to Modernity: A History of the Reform Movement in Judaism* (New York, 1988), 297–8, 306; Arthur L. Reinhart, *The Voice of the Jewish Laity* (Cincinnati, 1928).

[12] Jeffrey S. Gurock, *The Men and Women of Yeshiva* (New York, 1988), 82–120; Aaron Rothkoff, *Bernard Revel: Builder of American Jewish Orthodoxy* (Philadelphia, 1972).

needs of the times, as had been done by sages of the past. However, scholars at the Seminary, led by the great Talmudist Louis Ginzberg, were extremely cautious about interpreting Jewish law. In Conservative congregations worship continued to waver between quasi-Orthodoxy and imitation of Reform until the movement found its own way.[13] All these movements were governed and led by men, both as rabbis and laymen. However, the Jewish education of girls on the same level as boys became widespread among the Orthodox as well as Conservative and Reform. The boys' Bar Mitzvah at age 13 assumed an importance it had never had in Europe and gradually Bat (feminine form) Mitzvah for girls also became common. Women as rabbis and synagogue egalitarianism (except among the Orthodox) lay in the future, once women's work in the kitchen and in raising children became less exacting and women's careers became widespread.

Zionism surmounted denominational lines. Orthodox Judaism, unlike most of its leaders in Europe, was largely pro-Zionist. The Conservatives were probably the most Zionist denomination, although the Jewish Theological Seminary's presidents and monied supporters were not. As a movement Reform Judaism, which included eminent Zionist figures among its rabbis, gravitated towards pro-Zionism especially during the 1930s. Yet American Zionism itself was weak between the days of Brandeis's leadership and the Second World War. However, Hadassah, the women's Zionist organization founded by Henrietta Szold, developed impressively. Staying away from Zionist politics, as befitted contemporary women, it supported health and social welfare in Palestine and during the 1930s undertook Miss Szold's project of Youth Aliyah, bringing children from Germany to Palestine. Otherwise Zionist membership was small and it raised relatively little money even during the flush 1920s. Its political efforts, including those made after the Palestine riots of 1929 (see below), were hesitant. Altogether American Jewry was not much interested in distant Palestine, and probably felt more direct concern for immediate families living in Russia, Poland, and elsewhere in eastern Europe. Many continued to regard Zionism as an undesirable diversion from universalist goals, whether religious or political.

[13] Marshall Sklare, *Conservative Judaism: An American Religious Movement* (2nd edn. New York, 1972).

Nearly all Jewish scholarship in America was concentrated in rabbinical schools, since with two important exceptions the universities disregarded it. The chess term 'international grand master,' may perhaps be used to designate five scholars: Ginzberg the great Talmudist, Israel Davidson in medieval Hebrew literature, Alexander Marx the bibliographer, Harry A. Wolfson in Jewish philosophy at an endowed chair at Harvard, and Salo W. Baron in Jewish history at Columbia, also at a newly endowed chair. There were also several Orthodox Talmudic scholars of high distinction whose American careers 'took off' slightly later, especially Joseph B. Soloveichik and Moses Feinstein. Other reputable, productive scholars were active but the American Jewish community and the academic world hardly took an interest, and they worked almost in isolation. Most students in Jewish studies were rabbinical, since academic careers were practically inaccessible. Magnificent Jewish libraries of world renown were built up at the Jewish Theological Seminary, Hebrew Union College, New York Public Library, and Columbia and Harvard Universities.

The great economic depression which struck in 1929 and worsened yearly caused severe suffering throughout the country.[14] The depression took its toll in the collapse of thousands of banks and the loss of savings and investments. Prolonged mass unemployment meant millions of malnourished children. Jews shared in this suffering. A Jewish charitable agency in a large community reported that its applicants included

the small merchant, the builder and real estate dealer. In fact a new clientele is being created—the so-called 'white collar' class . . . Increased unemployment and the reduction or discontinuance of income for many families have slowly exhausted the self-maintaining resources of ever-widening groups of our Jewish population . . . [this] period takes its toll in various forms of physical illnesses, particularly that of undernourished children, to say nothing of mental conflict and mental illness, depression and despondency and the increasing number of problems of delinquency.[15]

[14] Beth S. Wenger, *New York Jews and the Great Depression* (New Haven, 1996); Lloyd P. Gartner, *The Midpassage of American Jewry, 1929–1945* (Cincinnati, 1982).

[15] Report of Cleveland Jewish Social Service Bureau, 28 March 1931, quoted in Lloyd P. Gartner, *History of the Jews of Cleveland* (2nd edn., Cleveland, 1987), 291.

Jewish unemployment was slightly below the national average of approximately 25 per cent. The movement for public unemployment insurance was begun in those days by two prominent Jews, the pioneer Hadassah physician Dr Isaac M. Rubinow and the Zionist leader and orator Rabbi Abba Hillel Silver. Jews had few farms to be foreclosed but thousands lost their homes. A bankrupted businessman, a category where Jews were heavily represented, found it harder to reopen than a worker to start on a job he found. One employment opportunity was service in the expanding Federal and local bureaucracies created by New Deal legislation. But the occupational and residential mobility of American Jews was dealt a severe setback by the depression and resumed, but on a grand scale, only after the Second World War.

The anti-Semitism which flourished during the 1920s became virulent during the 1930s. Radical right social and political programmes flourished during the depression years. Nazi Germany subsidized some anti-Semitic and pro-Nazi movements, especially the German American Bund. Even though the vast majority of Americans opposed Nazi policy towards the Jews, nativism continued in the form of hostility to refugees and other immigrants who supposedly took jobs away from Americans. Movements such as William Dudley Pelley's Silver Shirts, to abolish democracy and replace it with an élite dictatorship, also won a following. The rabble-rousing Gerald L. K. Smith, after starting as a Protestant minister and a satellite of the powerful Louisiana demagogue Huey Long, who was not an anti-Semite, put anti-Semitism at the centre of a long career from the late 1930s. However, the most dangerous anti-Semite of the period was not an American fascist like Pelley but Charles E. Coughlin, the Roman Catholic 'radio priest'. Like some other anti-Semitic agitators he started with populist appeals to masses suffering from the depression, attacks on 'international bankers', and a grandiose programme which he called 'social justice', but by 1935 he had advanced to open anti-Semitism. Besides the threadbare 'international Jew' and 'elders of Zion' conspiratorial themes, 'Jewish moneylenders' and bankers were blamed for the depression. Thus, Paul Warburg, of a distinguished banking family and a member of the Federal Reserve Board, was held responsible for the Wall Street crash when he actually had been warning against ruinous stock market speculation. Coughlin, a Detroit priest, denounced Communism and Roosevelt along with the Jews at the huge parish church which he built, and drew millions who listened to his eloquence on the radio. Catholics especially respected him as a priest, and his brogue won many Irish hearts. Coughlin sponsored the Christian Front, which distributed his publications and held inflammatory street meetings in large cities with overtones of violence. When the country entered the Second World War Coughlin was silenced by his Church and his Christian Front, like other movements mentioned here, was suppressed. Yet Jews were affected by discrimination in employment and education more than by this agitation.[16]

Jewish communal organizations debated what strategy could counter these lies and slanders.[17] It was usually futile to engage in refutations, although that was done for the record. Picketing, heckling, and protest meetings led to disturbances and near-riots which pleased anti-Semites. There was minor sabotage such as spoiling the anti-Semites' propaganda sheets and obstructing their rental of halls. The basic Jewish tactic was to emphasize that propagating anti-Semitism and other group prejudices was unpatriotic, false to the principles of the Founding Fathers and the Constitution. Organizations like the American Jewish Committee and the Anti-Defamation League of B'nai B'rith played on this theme, which was widely recognized by principled Americans of good will. Unlike the tragic experience in Germany and other Continental states, in the worst of the depression the extremes of right and left in the United States did not crush the centre. In fact the opposite happened. Both major parties, despite sharp differences on public issues, remained within the democratic centre and President Roosevelt's towering presence upheld liberal democracy with unique force. Under the presidency of this scion of old American aristocracy the 'new immigration', which included most of the Jews, came politically into its own. Scorning warnings over anti-Semitic reactions, he appointed Jews to high office,

[16] A survey is Leonard Dinnerstein, *Antisemitism in America* (New York, 1994); Seymour Martin Lipset and Earl Rabb, *The Politics of Unreason: Right-Wing Extremism in America, 1790–1970* (New York, 1970), 150–208 is oriented to sociological theory; David A. Gerber (ed.), *Anti-Semitism in American History* (Urbana, Ill., 1987).

[17] Naomi W. Cohen, *Not Free to Desist: A History of the American Jewish Committee, 1906–1966* (Philadelphia, 1972), 154–227.

such as Henry Morgenthau Jr. as Secretary of the Treasury and Felix Frankfurter, a foreign-born liberal, to the Supreme Court as Brandeis's successor in 1939 even after influential, worried Jews urged him not to do so. Governors Herbert H. Lehman of New York and Henry Horner of Illinois, both Jews, were elected on New Deal platforms and other Jews were elected or appointed to office. The president's own political intimates included many Jews.

Roosevelt's New Deal reforms 'stole' and enacted many planks of the socialist platform and took away most of the radical left's voters. The Jewish labour movement, long a pillar of the socialist movement, also moved towards the New Deal. Yet many Jews did continue to support the socialist and communist movements, and were sympathetic or at least tolerant to leftist radicalism. Frustrated Jewish writers, lawyers, and teachers constituted much of the leftist intelligentsia, whose 'foot soldiers' were often Jewish college students.[18] But the American people voted four times for Roosevelt and his liberal capitalist New Deal reforms. He was overwhelmingly the choice of American Jews, who voted for him four times in percentages between 80 and 90.

After their long control of the Jewish community, the power of the patricians, mostly of German descent, dwindled. Some lost their fortunes in the depression, or when they aged and died their children were often too assimilated or too little interested in Jewish life to inherit their fathers' position. Perhaps most important, the children of the immigrant generation were now in a position to challenge the traditional leaders. The newcomers had the numbers, and the basis of their conquest was the democracy of numbers, since they constituted 80 to 90 per cent of American Jewry. However, although they had the numbers they did not yet have the money, so that the New Deal in American politics could not be readily paralleled in the Jewish community, which depended not on taxes but on voluntary contributions. In the allocation of funds for overseas and Palestine and for use at home the men of wealth had the upper hand over the Jewish masses. Local Jewish Com-

---

[18] The literature on these extremely articulate people includes Daniel Aaron, *Writers on the Left* (New York, 1961); Alan M. Wald, *The New York Intellectuals* (Chapel Hill, NC, 1987), informative and tendentious; Alexander Bloom, *Prodigal Sons: The New York Intellectuals and their World* (New York, 1986).

munity Councils of little power and the American Jewish Congress, re-established by Stephen S. Wise in 1930, sought to express this democratic drive. It reached fuller expression in the changed picture after the Second World War, when the masses also had money.

The universally abhorred Nazi regime made necessary not only monetary relief to Jews in Germany and efforts to help them to leave but some reaction to the regime itself. This came in the form of mass anti-Nazi rallies and the boycott movement of German goods, which was not economically significant but enabled American Jews to express their detestation of the Nazi regime. The boycott movement opposed the *ha'avara* agreement (discussed above) and was contrary to wishes expressed by German Jews. However, it was much more difficult to bring Jews from Germany to the United States. In addition to the Johnson Act, at the beginning of the depression a presidential directive to the United States consuls who were empowered to grant visas instructed them not to issue any to persons 'likely to become a public charge'. Under worldwide depression conditions any person could be so classified, and the consuls in Germany employed their authority severely on desperate Jews. As a result, a mere 27,000 Jews entered the United States from Germany from 1933 until 1 July 1938, less than Britain or Palestine. American Jews did not dare promote any bill to ease immigration restrictions, which had no chance in Congress and would have generated counter-proposals to restrict immigration still further or prohibit it on account of economic conditions. However, the extreme persecutions in Germany and annexed Austria from late 1938 until the outbreak of war had the effect of easing restrictions, and about 43,000 more Jews reached the United States from Germany, Austria, and Czechoslovakia before 1 September 1939. Many came outside the quota thanks to affidavits sent by their American relatives guaranteeing to support them, a serious undertaking in a time of widespread need.[19] Academic and religious institutions could also issue affidavits, but only Hebrew Union College did so. The refugees' early years were hard, since they arrived during the depression, becoming a 'public charge' was grounds for deportation and

---

[19] The successful playwright George S. Kaufman, of German Jewish ancestry, unasked, sent over a hundred to relatives in Germany whom he did not know. This appeared in the *New York Times,* which I did not note.

charitable aid was limited.[20] Professional men found it difficult and lawyers virtually impossible to re-establish themselves. On the other hand famous refugees—scientists, scholars, and musicians—made the transition relatively successfully. They contributed vastly to their adopted country's cultural and scientific life, including the theoretical research which produced atomic weapons during the Second World War.

A National Movement and a National Home

A haven altogether different from that of the United States or anywhere else was the Jewish national home being built in Palestine. Zionists did not intend Palestine just as a haven or a refuge but as the unforgotten home to which the Jewish people were returning after centuries of exile. Zionism meant 'the ingathering of the exiles' to the spiritual centre of the Jewish people. The Jewish national home inspired enthusiasm and self-sacrifice which, Zionists emphasized, were being at last invested in a Jewish and not an alien cause. Non-Zionists readily acknowledged the inspiration of Palestine and responded to philanthropic appeals but did not accept its centrality in Jewish life or the goal of a Jewish state. Zionists who wanted to leave behind demeaning begging habits of the *galut* squirmed at calls to 'help the Jews [even "the poor Jews"] in Palestine'. Non-Zionists, led by the American Jewish lawyer and community leader Louis Marshall, entered into formal partnership in 1929 to found the internationally recognized Jewish Agency for Palestine, to direct the development of Jewish Palestine.[21] The Jewish Agency was recognized as Palestine Jewry's representative, but there was little financial benefit from the partnership with non-Zionists. Marshall's death and the Great Depression struck shortly after the Agency was founded.

Besides non-Zionists there were several categories of anti-Zionist. Many Orthodox Jews in and outside Palestine denied the legitimacy of a

[20] It does not appear that anyone was actually deported.
[21] *Louis Marshall Champion of Liberty: Selected Papers and Addresses*, ed. Charles Reznikoff (2 vols., Philadelphia, 1957), ii. 702–92. On American Zionism see the concise Naomi W. Cohen, *American Jews and the Zionist Idea* (n.p., 1975), and the ampler Melvin I. Urofsky, *American Zionism from Herzl to the Holocaust* (Garden City, NY, 1975).

Jewish movement led by irreligious Jews and rejected the idea of a Jewish state before the Messiah. However, settlement on the holy soil was considered meritorious. As conditions in the east European Orthodox heartland worsened and Palestine flourished, this opposition to Zionism lessened. There were significant Zionist organizations of Orthodox Jews, Mizrachi (abbreviation of 'cultural centre') and the labourite Hapoel Hamizrachi. At the opposite pole to anti-Zionist Orthodoxy stood Jewish Communists who as always followed the Soviet Russian line and denounced Zionism as a 'tool of British imperialism'. The Zionist movement itself was deemed a device of the Jewish bourgeoisie to blind Jewish workers to class consciousness. Some communists 'proved scientifically' in Marxist terms that Jewish existence was bound to end and Zionism was therefore a delusion. As mentioned elsewhere, Soviet Russia allowed some prominent Zionists to leave for Palestine, but Zionist activity was forbidden and Zionists were exiled to Siberia. Neither Communist nor Orthodox were the Jews in western countries who trusted in liberalism and emancipation as the sufficient cure for Jewish problems and held that Zionism was defeatist, a pernicious nationalism. Many liberal and socialist anti-Zionists argued that the solution for Jews did not lie in Zionism but in joining the world struggle against political reaction and anti-Semitism, which transcended religious and national boundaries. To be sure, many liberals and socialists were pro-Zionist. A shrinking majority of Reform Jews held to Reform's original ideology that the national era of Judaism was past and the Jews, now only a religious body, formed an ethical leavening in the nations among whom they lived. These anti-Zionist philosophies steadily lost ground.

The most influential factors in softening all this hostility to Zionism were implacable, growing anti-Semitism and the remarkable development of the *yishuv* which took in persecuted Jews when other countries were closed. Zionist emissaries toured the Jewish world to raise money and to 'gain souls' for the movement, especially young people who could be *halutzim* (pioneers) on the land. The emissaries' task was made easier by the unusual homogeneity of the Jewish people between the two wars thanks to the great emigration from eastern Europe. One could leave from Warsaw or Berlin and deliver in Yiddish almost the same message in Paris and London, then south in Johannesburg, across the Atlantic to Buenos Aires and north to New York and Montreal. Socialist Zionist emissaries also concentrated on converting socialist leaders, and rejoiced in the endorsement of Zionism by such distinguished personages as Eduard Bernstein and Léon Blum. They were inspired especially by *yishuv* institutions which embodied socialism. The exiled pioneer of Russian Marxism, Pavel Axelrod, expressed sympathy. Orthodox Zionist spokesmen worked among the religious masses, particularly in eastern Europe, and some eminent rabbis were won over. Much effort had to be devoted to justifying Orthodox participation in a secular political movement with irreligious leaders. On the other hand, imaginative orthodox rabbis such as Hirschenson, Kook, and Amiel worked out an Orthodox political theory, and the short-lived S. H. Landau sought to synthesize religious Zionism with socialism.[22] While there is no statistical reckoning, before the Second World War Zionism had apparently won over only a minority of the Jewish people although a majority expressed a sentimental interest in Palestine.

The Zionist movement had to struggle to enlarge Palestine's share of money raised in combined appeals for overseas needs. If it did not conquer Jewish communities, it influenced them more subtly. Like many national movements Zionism had begun with cultural expression: Hebrew linguistic revival, the study of the national past, and literature. Hebrew songs, dances, and dramas from Palestine entered and gradually dominated popular Jewish culture the world over. 'Muscular Judaism' advocated by Max Nordau at an early Zionist congress took the form of the Zionist or Zionist-inspired athletic organizations such as Maccabi. It attracted thousands of young Jews, providing a new Jewish ideal of strength and valour. The image of the sturdy, confident *halutz* became an object of admiration, and respect for Palestine Jewry's vigorous self-defence superseded traditional reverence for religious martyrs. The new Hebrew literature was itself one of the factors which created Zionism, and its very existence supported the Zionist idea. This was not true, however, of most Yiddish literature especially that created in Soviet Russia. Yiddish itself, slowly declining but still the tongue of the Jewish

[22] An excellent general discussion is Gideon Shimoni, *The Zionist Ideology* (Hanover, NH, and London, 1995).

masses and widely used within the Zionist movement, was viewed with hostility in Palestine as the language of exile and the ghetto. Higher Jewish culture is less easily labelled as Zionist but much of it acquired a Zionist impress. Under the influence of Jewish nationalism Jewish scholarship drew away from its rationalist, emancipationist Germanic origins, for example by devoting new attention to messianism, mysticism, community structure, popular movements, and the history of Palestine. The Jewish cultural revival in Weimar Germany, already discussed, showed Zionist influences. Few Jews outside Palestine were conversant with the new Hebrew spoken there but it acquired great influence in Jewish education. Some of the pious looked askance, however, at turning the Holy Tongue (*leshon ha-kodesh*) into a language of everyday life. Most, however, saw glory in the ancient sacred language becoming a lively language of ordinary life.

All this cultural expansion required the physical growth of Jewish Palestine. This depended in turn on numerical increase within a political framework which carried out the Balfour Declaration's promise to 'facilitate' the building of the Jewish national home. Yet the political history of the country under British rule may be summarized as the vain attempt to reach a satisfactory balance between British rule, Jewish aspirations, and Arab resistance to them. The Jewish aspirations were the dynamic factor which from the start the Arabs and ultimately the British refused to accept.[23] Within twenty years the original British support for Zionism became support for Arab anti-Zionist demands.

When the conquest of Palestine from the Turks was completed in 1918 the country was divided between the British and French under the existing Sykes–Picot agreement, on a line which gave the French the north of the country. After lengthy negotiations over boundaries and who would rule the Arab state which was to rise despite the fiasco of the Arab revolt against the Turks,[24] the northern boundary between British Palestine and French Syria was fixed in 1920. It endures to the

---

[23] A full, balanced account is ESCO Foundation for Palestine, *Palestine: A Study of Jewish, Arab and British Policies* (2 vols., New Haven, 1947).

[24] The literary gifts of the authorized promoter of that revolt, the British officer and romantic T. E. Lawrence, in his *Seven Pillars of Wisdom*, magnified its promise and muffled its failure.

present.[25] A Zionist Commission consisting mostly of British Jews went to Palestine to take charge of Jewish affairs. It was headed by Chaim Weizmann of Balfour Declaration fame, who was becoming the recognized head of the Zionist movement. The Zionist Commission found only 66,000 Jews in the country compared with some 100,000 on the eve of the war, who were a mere 10 per cent of the country's population. The commission had to work with British administrators, by no means pro-Zionist, and with the elected Vaad Leumi (National Council) of Palestine Jews, which did not always have a clear view of political forces. Within two years a competent British civil administration replaced military rule and the first high commissioner, Herbert Samuel, a pro-Zionist Jew who had been a Liberal Party member of the British government, took office. The British administration regarded its duty as the maintenance of law and order and building such facilities as roads and the post office, but the Balfour Declaration's implication that Great Britain would aid directly in building the Jewish national home was set aside.

It soon became clear that the Arabs were vehemently hostile to all that Zionism meant.[26] The minuscule Arab political class of clergy, landowners and journalists, who when they desired could inflame a mostly illiterate peasantry by means of sermons in mosques, opposed the Balfour Declaration from its issuance and refused to co-operate with the British administration. Zionists who believed that the Arabs would appreciate the benefits that a flourishing Jewish Palestine would bring them were slow to realize the depth of Arab hostility. Along with repeated Jewish declarations of good will there were individual projects for promoting harmony and understanding. None enjoyed even slight success; Arab insistence on the cessation of Jewish immigration and acceptance of permanent minority status were impossible terms to Zionists. The deadliness of the opposition became manifest in April 1920 when Arab bands in Jerusalem murdered four Jews and wounded more than a hundred. Vladimir Jabotinsky, who organized Jewish self-defence, was sentenced to fifteen years in prison and nineteen others to

[25] Its basis was the boundaries given in a noted work of scholarship, George Adam Smith's *Historical Geography of the Holy Land*, first published in 1894.

[26] Neil Caplan, *Palestine Jewry and the Arab Question, 1917–1925* (London, 1978).

three years for illegal possession of arms.[27] Weizmann reacted bitterly to the British failure to maintain law and order. On the other hand Winston Churchill as Colonial Secretary visited the country in March 1921 and vigorously reaffirmed to protesting Arab delegations the British commitment to the Balfour Declaration. In May 1921 serious rioting broke out, and British troops had to be summoned from Cyprus to quell attacks in Jaffa and on the Petah Tikvah colony by countryside Arabs armed with knives and sticks. They had been summoned to defend Islam against supposed Jewish assailants. The forty to fifty Jews killed and over a hundred injured were mainly children, women, and the aged.

The cause of Jewish anger was not only murder and mutilation and the inadequate British response but the sense that pogroms like those of tsarist Russia could be repeated in the Jewish homeland. When high commissioner Samuel sought to appease Arab hostility by restricting Jewish immigration and other measures, there was deep disappointment that he was in effect compelling the Jews to pay for having been attacked. The Vaad Leumi reiterated Jewish rights, but confidence in British rule was jolted never to be fully restored. The Jewish Legion of the First World War had been demobilized and all but a few of its members returned to their native lands, and an illicit Hagana (self-defence) had to be organized. During the 1920s British proposals for a Legislative Council and then an Advisory Council with specified powers were rejected and high commissioners ruled directly. Relations with the Arabs, whose majority was slowly decreasing, remained a central, intractable problem. Zionists felt that British support was shifting from themselves to the Arab side.

The building of the Jewish national home was the business of the World Zionist Organization until Palestinian Jewry gradually took over, mainly during the 1930s. Their 66,000 Jews of 1918 amounted to 121,000 in 1925, a large increase but still only 14 per cent of the population. The number reached 175,000 in 1930, 17 per cent of the population. The Jewish birth rate was lower than the Arabs', but the Arab death rate was higher than that of the Jews. With Jewish natural increase slightly lower than the Arabs', the increase in the Jewish proportion of

---

[27] The sentences were commuted after a year. Jabotinsky was required to leave Palestine never to return.

the population was due largely to immigration. To be sure there was also an unchecked influx of Arabs from adjacent countries.

Socially and culturally the Jews were very heterogeneous. Drawn from many lands, they included veteran and new Zionist agricultural settlers, shopkeepers and craftsmen, old-line pietists often living on charitable pensions (*halukkah*) from abroad, and oriental Jews of old stock. Democracy was a new conception and political cohesiveness did not come easily, but the Jews drew one basis of democracy, a vigorous sense of individual rights and equity, from Judaism itself. A liberal capitalist outlook hardly existed in Palestine of the 1920s, and the most influential social idea was socialism, as brought from eastern Europe by *halutzim*. The Zionist Commission organized the autonomous community along Zionist and democratic lines. Many Jews of the old settlement entered the Zionist camp. Voting was introduced, and the inclusion of women's suffrage was at first a matter of religious dispute. Paralleling arrangements in the other religious communities, a chief rabbinate for Ashkenazim and another for Sefardim were set up with authority over personal status. Thus for Sefardim alone polygamy was still permitted although rare.[28] The remarkable Ashkenazi chief rabbi, Abraham Isaac Kook, as a Zionist and religious philosopher, brought Orthodox Judaism and Zionism closer together. The varieties of Orthodoxy ranged from adherence to an east European or oriental model or to the decorous bourgeois Judaism of western Europe. Reform or Conservative Judaism did not exist outside a small circle of German refugees during the 1930s, and the choice lay between some form of Orthodoxy or secularism. To be sure, a large number, perhaps the majority, were respectful of religious tradition and religiously observant in selective fashion.

The world Zionist movement underwent serious strains as it was achieving international recognition and wide Jewish support. The affairs of Palestine Jewry, which was still limited and lacking resources, were largely in the hands of Zionist congresses and functionaries abroad. As the head of the movement from 1920 Chaim Weizmann was *de facto* head of Palestine Jewry, although he resided in London. In eastern Europe, war, pogroms, and Bolshevism undermined the

[28] In a rare instance of public law entering the sphere of marital relations it was prohibited soon after the founding of the state.

movement while motivating Zionist youth organizations to negate the possibility of secure Jewish life in the *galut* and to train their members to settle in Palestine. In the west British Zionism, not itself strong but important on account of Britain's role in Palestine, and American Zionism, risen to strength thanks to the war, American Jewry's numbers and the masterful leadership of Louis D. Brandeis and his circle, became the foremost centres of the movement during the war and for several years following. After President Wilson appointed Brandeis in 1916 to the Supreme Court, the highest position in America yet attained by a Jew, he directed American Zionism by remote control through lieutenants, a method which undermined his dominance.[29] He and Weizmann collaborated in the Balfour Declaration and securing Wilson's delayed endorsement of it. The American was uninterested in the cultural aspects of Zionism and believed its political problems settled by Balfour; Palestine would now be a question of prudent investment and planned economic development. Brandeis's conception of non-political, economically efficient development by small investors was a doubtful programme for Palestine. It was defeated by the conception of a nationally controlled pattern of growth. This found supporters among the socialist Zionists of Poale Zion and Zeirei Zion who desired a planned, centralized Jewish economy.

Weizmann resigned his University of Manchester lectureship and many Zionist leaders in Europe left careers to devote full time to Zionism, but Brandeis would not consider Weizmann's probably insincere proposal that he leave the Supreme Court in order to head the world movement. Neither did any of the Justice's circle quit their careers, mostly as successful lawyers.[30] The open clash, fraught with long-range consequences, came when the Brandeis Zionists opposed the new general-purpose Keren Hayesod (Palestine Foundation Fund) as uneconomic and politically controlled and refused to campaign for it. Weizmann himself toured the United States for Keren Hayesod in 1921, bringing with him a celebrated new convert, Albert Einstein. Weiz-

---

[29] A stimulating study focusing on Brandeis is Yonathan Shapiro, *Leadership of the American Zionist Organization, 1897–1930* (Urbana, Ill., 1971).

[30] Two of Weizmann's closest collaborators, Israel Sieff and Simon Marks, remained in England to build up their prodigiously successful Marks and Spencer retail chain.

mann's people, headed by Louis Lipsky, won control of the Zionist Organization of America, but it and American Zionism steadily declined during the 1920s. Keren Hayesod and other Zionist funds during those years raised less than the Joint Distribution Committee and less even than Russian Jewish colonization. Brandeis withdrew from Zionist affairs but remained a major background influence and unobtrusively the largest Zionist donor.

While the Zionist movement underwent conflicts in the 1920s, these were institutionally formative years for Palestine Jewry. As the autonomous Jewish population rose to 175,000 in 1930, an array of new social forms and political parties was created. Agricultural settlement was largely collective, starting with the *moshav* and *moshava*. These were settlements which combined collective production with private family lives. In addition there was the unique, fully collective *kibbutz* or *kvutza*. This form of settlement originated about 1910 when small groups of young pioneers, nearly all men, pooled their practically non-existent resources to live and work together. The women performed the same labour as the men, but in time most undertook more 'feminine' work in the kitchen and with children. The *kibbutz* developed especially in Jezreel valley, around the Sea of Galilee and the Jordan river headwaters during the 1920s. *Kibbutz* people coped with hardships by tireless, almost religiously inspired (although they were militantly secularist) toil to build attractive, prosperous collective villages. The sixty-eight *kvutzot* and *kibbutzim* of 1938 with their 15,000 members were outnumbered by the private agricultural sector, but the *kibbutz* way of life was the most unusual. Its most striking feature was their collective life not only in the equal division of labour and income but in family life as well. Children were brought up together in children's houses, although parental ties were recognized. *Kibbutz* collectivism in bringing up children and in social and economic life, originally a matter of necessity, became an ideology which made *kibbutzim* highly influential in the Zionist left. Many of them professed Marxism for their ideology while making ingenious adjustments drawn from Borochov, and followed Freud as they understood him for bringing up children. Moreover, the east European founders rejected the *galut* as they fused western culture with secular Judaism. Not peddling or dealing but living and toiling and drawing strength from the land, not tame piety but confident encounter be-tween man and nature would forge a new Jew in Zionist *kibbutzim*, strong, self-reliant, sure of himself, and intellectually rooted. A small characteristic which suggested the anti-*galut* attitude was the wide-spread substitution of Hebraic family names for those of the *galut* (Green to Ben-Gurion and Shimshelevitz to Ben Zvi, for example) and the preference for given names taken from nature or lesser known per-sonalities of the Bible (for example, Ilan and Ilana or Yoram and Hagar). The *kibbutz* as a new way of life attracted world-wide attention and fascinated sociologists and psychologists. An important variant was the religious *kibbutz* (*kibbutz dati*) movement, which combined the *kibbutz* way of life with religious orthodoxy. They stayed faithful to religious tradition while they conducted a 'sacred rebellion' (*mered kadosh*) against much of its character as *galut* life had shaped it.

To the world of progressive opinion *kibbutzim* demonstrated that Palestine was generating new, utopian social forms. Another new form was the General Federation of Jewish Labour, the Histadrut for short, which advocated the cause of Jewish labour (*'avodah 'ivrit*) in building the country. Its efforts at a separate organization for Arab workers did not succeed. Histadrut trade unionism was less significant than its entrepreneurial activities which included building, shipping, transport, and banking. In the relative absence of private capital investment they built a labour-controlled economy. Through the Histadrut Jews had medical insurance, read a daily newspaper and books which the Hista-drut published, participated in sports, took vacations, and were encour-aged to look upon the labour federation as their second home. The Histadrut and the labour parties, especially Mapai (*Mifleget Poalei Eretz Yisrael* = Palestine Labour Party), the largest, controlled all these institu-tions, which provided the basis for their long domination of Palestinian and then Israeli politics which they first won in 1933.

Party membership was not a simple political affiliation but a way of life whose participants often found employment in one of their party's manifold projects and departments. Minority parties sought to emulate the labour parties' comprehensive way of life, notably Mizrachi and Hapoel Hamizrachi, whose common basis was religious orthodoxy. Out of German refugee organizations grew the General Zionist party. On the other hand, the Revisionists under their ideologist and leader Vladimir Jabotinsky were virtually excluded from political life. During the 1920s Jabotinsky, a magnetic orator and gifted writer, opposed Weizmann's policy of co-operation with Great Britain which had the support of labour Zionists. His following, which included numerous persons of Polish petty bourgeois background, demanded that the Palestine Mandate apply to both sides of the Jordan and that Arab attackers receive an aggressive response. Opposing socialist Zionism in the name of 'monist' Zionism and private enterprise, the Revisionists came into physical conflict with their opponents. They cultivated a military style, wore uniforms for occasions and carried themselves with 'splendour' (*hadar*, a favourite term). There was more than a hint of Polish aristocratic style, and accusations were made of fascism. During the disturbances which began in 1936 they rejected the policy of restraint and retaliated indiscriminately. Some members of Revisionist armed squads paid with their lives on the gallows.

British rule in Palestine was confirmed by the mandate issued by the League of Nations in 1920, whose text incorporated the words of the Balfour Declaration. However, the British obligation to Zionism was unenforceable, as Zionists learned to their sorrow. The World Zionist Organization was recognized in the mandate as the representative Jewish agency for developing Palestine until it 'could secure the co-operation of all Jews who are willing to assist in the establishment of the Jewish national home'. Weizmann as president had to undertake what had been expected of the Brandeis group, raising money and seeking rich and prominent Jews, almost none of whom was a Zionist, as equal partners in a comprehensive Jewish Agency for Palestine. A long and complex courtship lasted six years, which was disrupted by non-Zionist campaigns including Jewish agricultural colonization in Soviet Russia, and by much internal Zionist opposition to having non-Zionists as equal and, they feared, perhaps dominant partners. Finally in August 1929 the deal was consummated and the Jewish Agency for Palestine was founded in a festive atmosphere. Its membership of 224 was half Zionist and half non-Zionist with the incumbent president of the WZO as *ex officio* president.

Troubles promptly began which dashed the high hopes. A dispute which began in 1928 over Jewish prayer at the Western ('Wailing') Wall erupted in August 1929 into a series of murderous attacks on Palestinian Jewry, with some Jewish counter-attacks. Assaults on Jewish neighbour-hoods in and near Jerusalem culminated in the massacre of forty-two students and teachers at the yeshiva of Hebron, a branch of the famed Slobodka yeshiva which had relocated from Lithuania. Safed, another old city, suffered forty-five Jewish victims, and several *kibbutzim* were attacked and destroyed. British troops had to be summoned from Egypt and naval assistance came from Malta to maintain order and safety. These bloody events brought two British official investigations, the Shaw Commission and the Simpson Report, and concluded with a new state-ment of policy issued by the Labour intellectual Colonial Secretary, Lord Passfield (Sidney Webb). It virtually reversed the Balfour Declaration by staking the country's future on the progress of the Arab peasantry and by finding hardly any capacity to absorb further Jewish immigration or land to sell. The Passfield White Paper aroused world-wide Jewish protests and strong voices of British dissent, and Chaim Weizmann resigned the presidency of the Zionist Organization in protest.[31] The Passfield White Paper was virtually cancelled by a letter from Prime Minister MacDonald in February 1931, but it was clear that the new trend of British policy was against the Zionists and favoured the Arabs. What had been the primary obligation to help establish the Jewish national home was reformulated as a 'dual obligation' to Jews and Arabs.[32]

Palestine of the 1930s scarcely felt the world depression. This was thanks largely to the 216,000 immigrants who entered from 1930 to 1939, including about 50,000 refugees from Germany and Austria, mak-ing the population of the Jewish national home grow to 475,000 in 1939, or 31 per cent of the country's population.[33] Many refugees came

---

[31] A moving study of the labour sector in terms of a moral and intellectual leader is Anita Shapira, *Berl: The Biography of a Socialist Zionist* (Cambridge, 1984), abridged from its original Hebrew.

[32] The American and Jewish Agency reaction is presented in Naomi W. Cohen, *The Year after the Riots: American Responses to the Palestine Crisis of 1929–30* (Detroit, 1930).

[33] The British figure was 445,000 Jews, while that given here is the Jewish Agency's which counts in 'illegal' immigrants. The difference of 30,000 suggests the extent of such immigration, which the British did all they could to combat. Arabs had only to smuggle across a land border, and their illegal arrivals were possibly more numerous than the Jews'.

as 'persons of independent means' thanks to the *ha'avara* arrangement, under the immigration ordinance of 1933. A large group, however, were Jews from Poland including *halutzim* sent by Zionist youth movements, who constituted about two-fifths of Jewish immigration and were usually people of little means.[34] The German and Austrian refugees' capital as well as the business and professional experience of these often ridiculed *yekkes* (German Jews), extensively altered the country, especially its cities. They elevated the quality of retail trade and provided many *kibbutz* members as well as students and academic staff for the small Hebrew University, along with musicians for the new Palestine Symphony Orchestra (today's Israel Philharmonic Orchestra). Germany's contemporary *bauhaus* architecture became a widely used urban style.

As the *yishuv* expanded its economy and population, Arab antagonism became more radical. Influenced by the disappearance of democracy and the fervid nationalism which prevailed in the Middle East's former mandates, and inspired by Italian fascism, Arab politicians carried on increasingly violent agitation against Palestine Jewry. A fresh round of violence broke out in April 1936, beginning with a country-wide Arab general strike which lasted six months with little success. There were attacks on individual Jews but no massacres, thanks to the Haganah and the effectiveness this time of the British army and police. The Jewish policy of *havlagah* (restraint) in avoiding indiscriminate counter-attacks was rigorously kept to, except for the independent Revisionist policy already mentioned. By 1939 the Arab attacks had been quelled.

His Majesty's Government appointed in 1936 a Royal Commission headed by Lord Peel which examined the entire subject of Palestine with great thoroughness. It heard the Jewish spokesmen headed by Weizmann, again the head of the Zionist Organization after 1935, and David Ben Gurion, chairman of the Jewish Agency Executive and head of Mapai and the Histadrut. In 1937 the commission produced its principal recommendation—that Palestine be partitioned into Jewish and Arab states with an international zone to include Jerusalem and a belt of

[34] An important study is Ezra Mendelsohn, *Zionism in Poland: The Formative Years, 1915–1926* (New Haven, 1981).

land thence to the Mediterranean. The Jewish state would take in Galilee and the coast south to Ashkelon. The Arabs, who received the rest, as usual rejected all compromise or recognition of the Zionists. An agitated debate over partition took place within the Zionist movement, and the Zionist Congress of 1937 by a divided vote rejected the Peel Commission's boundary proposals but offered to negotiate upon them. Opponents of partition included Hashomer Hatazair, the most leftist *kibbutz* federation, who wished to collaborate with the Arab proletariat, and Dr Judah L. Magnes, president of the Hebrew University, who did not desire a state opposed by the Arabs. The real possibility of a Jewish state frightened some Diaspora non-Zionists, who shifted to an extreme anti-Zionist position. The British, however, sent yet another commission which concluded that satisfactory boundaries could not be arrived at and the Peel proposals were unworkable. The British government withdrew from partition and thereupon set the stage for the reversal of the Balfour Declaration's and the League of Nations Mandate's commitment.

A tragically farcical conference went on for six weeks at St James Palace in London, during which Arabs refused even to meet with the Jews. The terms of the forthcoming British policy were made clear, and in May 1939 it was published in a new White Paper. The British Government had abandoned its appeasement policy two months earlier when Germany occupied what remained of Czechoslovakia, but with war drawing near it appeased Arab demands with the White Paper to ensure their support. Hardly any of Palestine now could be bought by Jews under land transfer regulations, and Jewish immigration was limited to 15,000 yearly for five years more. Then a Palestine state, clearly Arab, would be set up. Jewish opinion everywhere sharply and unanimously rejected this new policy. Typical was the dramatic gesture of Chief Rabbi Isaac Herzog, who publicly tore it up. The Jews were prepared to fight it when the greater tragedy of the Second World War was about to break out.

11

Catastrophe, Recovery, and Triumph

During the greatest, most destructive war of all ages there occurred the most immense disaster in Jewish history, in Winston Churchill's words, 'the greatest and most horrible crime ever committed in the whole history of the world'.[1] The Jews were marked out for annihilation as a German war aim, and the millions who were killed and their institutions and communities that were destroyed made the Second World War a Jewish defeat even though the Jews fought on the winning side. The beginnings of Jewish recovery from the mass murder coincided with Europe's gradual rehabilitation. Most of the survivors, however, quit Europe for overseas destinations or resettled in the new Jewish state of Israel which provided a consoling sense of home if not of safety for years to come. All these vast events took place in the decade which opened with the German invasion of Poland, the home of 3,330,000 Jews, on 1 September 1939 and closed with the truce of 1949 between the new Jewish state and its Arab invaders during the mass arrival there of European survivors.

Fighters from Free Countries

At the centre of the struggle against Nazi Germany stood Great Britain which fought the war, joined by its dominions, for six years from beginning to end. Britain's Jews contributed some 60,000 men and women soldiers to the struggle, of whom 1,200 fell. The trials of war disrupted Jewish community life. Evacuation *en masse* from London and

---

[1] He was referring specifically to the slaughter of Hungarian Jewry. Letter to Anthony Eden, Foreign Secretary, 11 July 1944, in his *The Second World War*, vi. *Triumph and Tragedy* (Boston, 1953), 693.

other big cities mainly of children was disruptive of family life and Jewish education.[2] The East End of London, near London's strategic port and for generations the centre of proletarian and immigrant Jewish life, was heavily bombed during the aerial blitz of 1940–1.

Almost 10,000 soldiers were recently arrived Jewish refugees from Nazism. They participated despite various forms of military discrimination, especially during grave anxiety over a German invasion in 1940 and for a time after. During that period thousands of refugees, the great majority technically German and Austrian enemy aliens, were rounded up and interned. Many were shipped in prison boats to camps in Canada and Australia, where they were kept for years. In Great Britain anti-Semitism surged, and the government avoided acting against it on the dubious theory that the mention of anti-Semitism would only arouse it.[3] Jews of France and the Low Countries also fought until the collapse of June 1940, when many escaped abroad. Jews were numerous in Charles de Gaulle's Free France movement and its military arm.

The United States passed from sending aid to making war when Japan attacked Pearl Harbor on 7 December 1941 and Nazi Germany declared war four days later. Until then nation-wide debate raged over the extent of intervention. The great majority of Jews favoured maximum assistance to Great Britain despite bitterness over its Palestine policy and hostility on the left to British imperialism. Jews also favoured aid to Russia after it was invaded in June 1941. However, they tended to hold back from the public debate for fear of encouraging charges of 'Jewish warmongering' which were in the air. Restraint ended with entrance into the war and the commencement of mass induction into the armed forces. A total of 550,000 American Jews served, of whom 11,000 lost their lives. Refugees in uniform were compensated with speedy naturalization in addition to the extensive benefits bestowed upon discharged soldiers. The territory of the United States was untouched by the war, and Jewish communal life was carried on in somewhat depleted form and with a changed agenda. Education, social welfare, and aid to the

---

[2] Bernard Steinberg, 'Jewish Education in Great Britain during World War', *Jewish Social Studies* 29/1 (Jan. 1967), 27–63.

[3] Tony Kushner, *The Persistence of Prejudice: Antisemitism in British Society during the Second World War* (Manchester, 1989).

needy continued, but now the Palestine issue and overseas aid claimed first place. Overshadowing all in free countries was the fate of European Jewry.

The Holocaust: Preliminaries

The fundamental subject of the murder of European Jewry, now termed the Holocaust,[4] cannot be other than the mass murder itself and how the Germans carried it out.[5] Rescue efforts, Jewish resistance, religious and philosophical interpretations, the diplomacy and policies of other governments, and the reactions of Jews outside German control are significant but of secondary or tertiary importance. An American historian more than a half-century later cites the Holocaust's enduring influence:

The Holocaust has become our era's ghastly icon for fiendishness. The memory of it quivers in the world's imagination, chastening the certainties of philosophers, challenging the pieties of churches, shadowing art and literature, chilling the souls of all who contemplate it . . . recollections of the Holocaust also dictate the policies of governments and even shape relations among nations.[6]

[4] This has now become an accepted meaning of the word. *The Oxford English Dictionary*'s 1993 edition defines it generally as 'a complete or wholesale destruction, esp. by fire', specifically the mass murder of the Jews. This usage began about 1960. The term previously in most general use was 'Jewish catastrophe'.

[5] An excellent brief history with a useful short bibliography is Michael R. Marrus, *The Holocaust in History* (London, 1987), which holds with the 'functionalist' school described below. Also useful is Yehuda Bauer, *A History of the Holocaust* (New York, 1982) tending toward the 'intentional' view. It gives a long historical background to the mass murder. Lucy S. Dawidowicz, *The War against the Jews 1933–1945* (New York/Philadelphia, 1975), as its title suggests, is an emphatically 'intentionalist' survey. It uses Yiddish sources fully. No better studies of the Holocaust have been written than those by a survivor and the founder of the field Philip Friedman (1901–60), gathered in his *Roads to Extinction: Essays on the Holocaust* (New York/Philadelphia, 1980). Friedman's *Guide to Jewish History under Nazi Impact* (with Jacob Robinson) (New York, 1960), the 1st volume in the Yad Vashem Bibliographical Series, first laid out the contours of the field although its large bibliography is now out of date. A major work about the German machinery of destruction is Raul Hilberg, *The Destruction of the European Jews* (Chicago, 1961), which appeared in a 'revised and definitive edition' in three volumes (New York, 1985).

[6] David M. Kennedy, reviewing Iris Chang, *The Rape of Nanking, Atlantic Monthly* (April 1998), 110.

The historian who deals with the Holocaust cannot, as a matter of human decency, look upon it with professional neutrality nor regard it only as a deplorable event. It is too massively evil, beyond the furthest calculation of the most vicious human deeds. Yet it is also impossible to consider the Holocaust as incomprehensible, too awesome to be spoken of, and leave it to philosophers and imaginative writers. The historian is required to examine these immense crimes which were committed by human persons within a tangible social and political reality. That is our task here. The German perpetrators wanted their deeds to remain secret, and preferred to employ such now familiar code words as 'final solution', 'special treatment', and 'resettlement'. There is a vast quantity of German archival evidence of the Holocaust, perhaps exceeding any other German deed, and more is constantly coming to light, such as what recently opened Russian archives reveal. Most Jewish records, however, were destroyed together with the Jews.

The Germans crushed Poland within three weeks and began to work their will on its Jews. About 32,000 Polish Jewish soldiers were killed and 61,000 taken prisoner, nearly all of whom were also killed.[7] As the German army cut a swath through Poland thousands of Jews were tortured, shot singly or in groups, or cremated within buildings such as synagogues which were set on fire. Before the German–Russian border was sealed in November 1939, about 300,000 Jews fled from German rule eastward to Russia's newly occupied Poland lands, and often still deeper into Russia proper. Tens of thousands fled into pro-German but still neutral Hungary and the Baltic states, from which many found their way to distant places, including Palestine. They included the foremost leaders of Jewish organizations, leaving the Jewish community of Poland nearly without experienced leaders. This was one reason why youth movements assumed leadership roles beyond their years. Their youth probably made it possible for them to realize sooner than their seniors that the impossible was actually happening.

Western Poland was incorporated into Germany and thoroughly germanized, with the use of Polish forbidden. Its approximately 330,000 Jews were expelled with brutal speed into the General Gouvernement

---

[7] There is no record of such action by the Germans against Jewish prisoners of war from the British, American, or Canadian armies.

(the German name given to Poland) except for the important community of Lodz, renamed Litzmannstaft after a German general. Poles were also expelled. For approximately 1.7 million Jews who remained in the General Gouvernement random violence such as shootings, torturing and killing refugees caught in flight, indiscriminate robbery, and the burning of homes and synagogues marked only the beginning of German occupation. Germans looted abandoned Jewish homes and helped themselves to whatever they wanted in Jewish stores. Besides such acts, which cost the lives of perhaps 100,000 Jews, the major step of German policy was the compelling of Jews on the shortest notice to leave their homes and belongings and move into vast ghettos.[8] These were old, shabby neighbourhoods in large cities where two or three dozen people of a few families were crammed into small unheated flats with little electricity and barely fit for one family. In Lwow (Lemberg), for example, decrepit huts and cabins were put to use, 'housing' 150,000 to 160,000 Jews in 1940. Warsaw, the foremost Jewish community and Poland's leading city, held between 420,000 and 500,000 Jews. One by one the ghettos were walled, for which the Jews had to pay, and sealed off. That of Warsaw was sealed on 15 November 1940, and no one was allowed in or out without a pass. When the Lodz ghetto was sealed off on 6 June 1940, there were 163,000 Jews within. During the succeeding seven and a half months 7,383 Jews died. In the 'average' month of April 1942, 1,888 died. On the other hand, the number of births was minuscule, about twenty-five in a month. Marriages continued to take place, including that of the flamboyant ghetto dictator Rumkowski, when a holiday was declared.[9]

New shipments of Jews expelled from small Polish towns were constantly replenishing the ghettos' population. In 1941 and 1942 they were joined by Jews from central and western Europe who were transported there. Mainly from Prague, 19,883 were sent to Lodz alone, raising its population to its already mentioned peak of 163,000 on 1 December

---

[8] Philip Friedman, 'The Jewish Ghettos of the Nazi Era', in *Roads to Extinction*, 60–87, is concise and authoritative.

[9] Lucjan Dobroszycjki, *The Chronicle of the Lodz Ghetto 1941–1944* (New Haven, 1984), pp. xxxix, 139, 153–60. A penetrating portrait is Solomon F. Bloom, 'Dictator of the Lodz Ghetto', in *A Liberal in Two Worlds* (Washington, DC, 1968), 148–67.

1941. They included 110 Polish Christians, probably converts from Judaism, and some 250 converts who had just arrived from western Europe.[10] The arrivals from the west were particularly bewildered and bitter over what was happening to them, and the social and cultural differences between them and the east Europeans led to frequent misunderstandings during their time together.

Jews in the ghettos had to live on rations which were far from sufficient for anyone, especially adults who had to work for the Germans long hours under barely human conditions. Rations, mostly bread and potatoes, were steadily reduced and came to approximately 1,400 calories per diem for workers and 700 for others; the average person needs about 3,000 calories, so that Jews in the ghettos were at the threshold of starvation. Life in the ghettos was a ceaseless struggle for food, supplemented somewhat by the black market in food smuggled in, and for minimal clothing in cold weather. Social work and medical treatment were dispensed against impossible odds, including the absence of medicines. On 14 October 1941, Adam Czerniakow, the chairman of the Jewish council in Warsaw, recorded in his diary in his usual dispassionate style on a hospital visit:

Later I inspected the hospitals. Corpses in the corridors and three patients in each bed. I visited in turn all the wards, typhus, scarlet fever, surgery, etc. In one of the sickrooms I gave assistance to a policeman Jakub Katz whose head was clubbed by some smuggler.[11]

Such conditions reached their inevitable conclusion in funeral figures for October and November 1941. In Warsaw there had been 379 and 413 funerals in October and November of 1938, which multiplied to 4,716 and 4,801 for the same months of 1941.[12] Hunger, disease, overwork, and hopelessness also found their reflection in the frequent suicides that the *Chronicle of the Lodz Ghetto* reported.

There was some cultural activity such as lectures, religious worship, and study, and in some ghettos such as Vilna, there were concerts and even cabaret and theatre. In Warsaw, Vilna, and elsewhere some

[10] Dobroszycki, *Chronicle of the Lodz Ghetto* 39–40, 84–5, 93, 100–1 n.

[11] *The Warsaw Diary of Adam Czerniakow: Prelude to Doom*, ed. R. Hilberg, S. Staron, and J. Kermisz (New York, 1979), 288.   [12] Ibid. 310.

cultural and religious life was carried on, but the German rulers in Lwow prohibited every such form of expression. Schooling was also prohibited later in the ghettos' short history. In Warsaw, where over 400,000 Jews were squeezed into 1.55 square miles, about twenty-five to a room,[13] the gifted young historian and community worker Emmanuel Ringelblum established the 'Oneg Shabbat' (Sabbath Pleasure) group, a front for his project of documenting Jewish life under Nazi domination.[14] A large part of the archive it assembled was buried in the ghetto's ruins and found after the war. The Germans buried in caves in Germany a huge quantity of Jewish books, as well as Torah scrolls and ritual objects, looted from synagogues, Jewish libraries, and individuals in Poland and throughout Europe.[15]

The terrible reality appears in photographs, often taken by German soldiers who proudly sent home specimens of their heroic service. They show pinched, hungry faces, emaciated limbs, and staring eyes, individuals lying listless in the street, and other marks of the starvation and illness which caused mass mortality. Jews were forbidden to change addresses, had to wear a yellow star, and could be severely beaten or summarily shot not only for attempting to leave the ghetto but for resisting, for possessing more food than their rations allowed, for retaining warm clothing which had been called for confiscation, for questioning a command, for listening to short-wave radio news, or for not complying with dozens of new German orders which were regularly posted in the ghetto. Needless to say, death was the punishment for violations. Everything was at the whim of sadistic German masters. Several hundred thousand Jews died of untreated diseases, overwork, and starvation besides outright killing.

As the implementation of the 'final solution'[16] drew near, unknown to the victims but suspected by many of them, the question debated

---

[13] Ibid. 396–7 (report of Heinz Auerswald, German ghetto commissioner).

[14] Ringelblum is the Levinson of John Hersey's *The Wall*, perhaps the finest novel set in the Holocaust.

[15] The pioneer, still unsurpassed study is by Joshua Starr, 'Jewish Cultural Property under Nazi Control', *Jewish Social Studies*, 12/1 (1950).

[16] This by now familiar term is a specimen of German perversions of meaning. It means of course mass murder. Similarly, 'special treatment' means killing in a death camp.

nowadays of Nazi 'intentionality' or 'functionality' arises. In common speech, was killing all Jews an intention of Hitler and the Nazis from before the war or even further back? Or was it the outcome of bureaucratic confusion and the inability to get rid of the Jews, which Hitler was determined to do, by any other means?[17] The Germans had briefly concentrated the Jews in a reservation near Lublin and considered exiling them *en masse* to the island of Madagascar, which would be taken from France and utilized as a lethal tropical ghetto.[18] Although reputable historians argue for 'functionality', the weight of evidence supports 'intentionality', beyond belief as such a policy seems to any civilized person. As mentioned above, Hitler spoke of this in several speeches, most frankly to inner groups of Nazi officials. At any rate there is no doubt that the methods of systematic mass murder were decided on no later than the spring or summer of 1941, shortly before or early in the invasion of Russia, after infernal brutality and killings had been going on for nearly two years. The staff conference of Nazi 'Jewish experts', held on 20 January 1942 at a Wannsee villa in suburban Berlin and presided over by Reinhard Heydrich, discussed amicably with touches of humour the means to achieve the 'final solution'. A rehearsal for genocide had already been held. From September 1939 'special treatment' was meted out to about 75,000 mentally ill, feeble-minded, and very handicapped Germans, including children, who lived a 'life without value' (*lebensunwerten Lebens*). They constituted an obstacle to German eugenic purity and so were killed by gas. As they lived in institutions and were not allowed visitors, their killing was to be kept secret, but word got out. A wave of muffled protest arose from aggrieved relatives and Christian

---

[17] Although some of them question Hitler's direct responsibility, 'functionality' advocates are not to be confused with the mendacious anti-Semitic deniers that the Holocaust occurred. Two important arguments are Tim Mason, 'Intention and Explanation: A Current Controversy about the Interpretation of National Socialism', *Nazism, Fascism and the Working Class* (Cambridge, 1995), 212–30, and Hans Mommsen, 'The Realization of the Unthinkable: The "Final Solution of the Jewish Question" in the Third Reich', in *From Weimar to Auschwitz* (Oxford, 1991), 224–53. Intentionality is forcefully put in Eberhard Jackel, *Hitler in History* (Hanover, NH, 1984), 44–65, and Gerald Fleming, *Hitler and the Final Solution* (Berkeley, 1982).

[18] Philip Friedman, 'The Lublin Reservation and the Madagascar Plan: Two Aspects of Nazi Jewish Policy during the Second World War', in *Roads to Extinction*, 34–58.

churches. 'Eugenic' killing stopped in late 1941, but valuable lessons in method were learned and experienced staff became available for the grand plans ahead.[19] Like the killing of the handicapped, the Holocaust was not publicized but was widely known while in progress. Many in the army, including generals, saw it being committed, and so did civilians who carried on much of the work. Neighbours of Jews who disappeared drew conclusions.[20]

Another preparation for the coming mass murder was the concentration camps that were built in 1941–2 to function as death camps at central sites within the General Gouvernement at Belzec, Sobibor, and Treblinka, replacing the less efficient gas vans.[21] In Silesia, within Wartheland and near Cracow and several rail lines, a former Polish army camp, then a German prison camp called Auschwitz (Oswiecim in Polish)-Birkenau was built as the largest death camp ever. It started to function early in 1943, and about 90 per cent of its victims were Jews.[22] To be sure there were concentration camps in Germany itself as well as labour camps all over German Europe and in all of them people died of their sufferings or were killed.

No Polish government was allowed to exist in the General Gouvernement. Promptly with the conquest of Poland, however, Heydrich ordered the Jews in each town to establish a council (Judenrat) to manage Jewish affairs, which meant executing German orders.[23] Some councils were chosen almost at random by the Germans and others were pre-war Jewish community councils. In some cases prominent local Jews constituted themselves a Judenrat which the Germans approved. There were a few regional super-councils but these did not function

---

[19] A full account is Henry Friedlander, *The Origins of Nazi Genocide: From Euthanasia to the Final Solution* (Chapel Hill, NC, 1995).

[20] Hans-Heinrich Wilhelm, 'Wie geheim war die "Endlösung"?', *Miscellanea: Festschrift für Helmut Krausnick* (Stuttgart, 1980), 131–48.

[21] Hilberg, *Destruction of the European Jews*, iii. 873–80.

[22] Ibid. 880–94; Michael R. Marrus, 'Auschwitz: New Perspectives on the Final Solution', *Studies in Contemporary Jewry*, 13 ed. Jonathan Frankel (1997), 74–83; Franciszek Piper, 'The Number of Victims', in Yrsrael Gutman and Michael Berenbaum (eds.), *Anatomy of the Auschwitz Death Camp* (Bloomington, Ind., 1994).

[23] The standard work is Isaiah Trunk, *Judenrat: The Jewish Councils in Eastern Europe under Nazi Occupation* (New York, 1972).

long. As tools of the Germans the Judenrat possessed the power to enforce their orders and had a staff of Jewish police. The Judenrat and particularly its police, called Order Service, are a subject of bitter controversy to the present day, especially among ageing survivors.[24] The Judenrat did what it could to ease inhuman living conditions. The authority it possessed to distribute work and food tickets was a decision for life or death until all were later sent to their death. Council members and Jewish policemen often enjoyed privileges such as more food and exemption from the yellow star and compulsory labour, and the dishonest took bribes and helped themselves to abandoned Jewish property. It fell to the Judenrat to select Jews to go to work, and after 1941 to prepare lists of Jews for 'resettlement', one of the German terms for deportation to death camps. Many refused to prepare lists, but the Judenrat leaders who did so claimed that if they did not prepare the required lists the Germans would do so themselves far more brutally and in yet larger numbers.

Some councils such as Bialystok and Minsk furtively encouraged rebellion and even aided people to join Jewish resistance bands in the forests. On the other hand, most councils strongly discouraged resistance movements, as in Vilna. The reprisal for one German soldier they killed or even wounded could endanger the life of an entire community. A Judenrat might co-operate obediently with the Germans out of a blind sense of order and discipline or in the belief that the only way for the Jews to survive was as a submissive, productive workforce. In a long harangue Rumkowski, the dictator in Lodz, expressed this view:

The plan is work, work and more work! I will strive with an iron will so that work will be found for everyone in the ghetto . . . In carrying out the general program, I will be able to demonstrate, on the basis of irrefutable statistics, that the Jews in the ghetto constitute a productive element, and that they are, perforce, needed . . . [This] will make it possible for you to lead a more tranquil life.[25]

---

[24] After the war many surviving Judenrat members and policemen were put on trial before a Jewish court with judicial procedure in the Displaced Persons camps and in Israel. The Amsterdam Judenrat heads, an egregious case of co-operation, were tried in their country.

[25] Spoken on 4 Jan. 1942, before deportations began. Dobroszycki, *Chronicle on the Lodz Ghetto*, 115.

Each Judenrat possessed its distinct character, with some pliant and nearly treacherous to Jewish interests and others finding excuses to moderate or at least postpone German demands. Many members withdrew rather than assume any responsibility. But council members who refused or sabotaged German orders could be summarily shot, and in some instances an entire Judenrat was put to death. Altogether the Judenrat had the impossible task of reconciling Jewish needs—there can be no talk of rights—with German demands, and the pressures upon them and the moral dilemmas they endured drove many Judenrat leaders to suicide. This happened especially when the Germans ordered them to deliver a fixed number of Jews for forced labour or for 'resettlement'. Adam Czerniakow in Warsaw took his life when deportations began. Who would live and who would die was a moral dilemma beyond solution. A few notorious Judenrat heads, like Rumkowski in Lodz, became infatuated with a messianic conception of their role—their people's hard work would save them and the Jewish leader would be recognized as the redeemer.[26] Gradually the Judenrat level fell as its worthier leaders gave up or were shot, and ineffective or simply venal leaders took their place. The 'grudging consent and sardonic contempt' (Dawidowicz's phrase) of the mass of Jews for the Judenrat turned to bitter hatred as its personal level declined and its duties became mainly preparing Jews for mass murder.[27] A like fate befell them all as they were shipped to be killed.

The Killing

At the end of 1940 the Nazi machine had taken 100,000 Jewish lives in addition to the immeasurable suffering it inflicted. To the masters in Berlin this was far less decrease of the Jews than they desired, and at that

[26] Dobroszycki, *The Chronicle of the Lodz Ghetto*, as an accessible publication, is replete with his Rumkowski's activities. These reports were written with required praise or necessary caution. Friedman, *Roads to Extinction*, 333–81 gives further examples. A valuable discussion in Hebrew of the role of the Judenrat is by Raul Hilberg, 'The Judenrat as a Form of Government', and Yehuda Bauer, 'The Reactions of the Jewish Leadership to Nazi Policy', in *Yalkut Moreshet*, 20 (Dec. 1975), 89–126.

[27] Dawidowicz, *The War against the Jews*, 237–41.

rate the removal of the Jews would take many years. In mid-1941 the leap to mass murder was taken when the German army invading Soviet Russia was accompanied by four regional 'task forces' (*Einsatzgruppen*) which conducted 'mobile killing operations' (Hilberg's term) or systematic massacres.[28] Jews along with Communists were to be wiped out. As the German army drove powerfully over ineffective Russian opposition in the summer and autumn of 1941 the *Einsatzgruppen* moved from one newly conquered city or area to the next. There were wholesale killings in the streets, but the preferred method was to round up the Jews and transport them to some obscure site not far away and mow them down with machine-guns. Only a tiny number escaped to tell the tale, or horrified passers-by who observed from concealed places. Often the victims were first compelled to dig the mass grave into which they fell. SS men moved among the bodies to finish off any wounded survivors. The next group was mowed down and fell into the grave in a layer on top of the first. In Kiev tens of thousands of Jews were taken to the Babi Yar ravine just outside the city and done to death there. There are reports of moans heard from within the earth and blood squirting up after the killing. About 1.5 million Jews were murdered by *Einsatzgruppen* in the first year and few months of the invasion of Russia.

Post-war defenders of the 'honour' of Hitler's army have claimed that this slaughter was performed by Nazi killing squads exclusively and that the army stayed away. However, it has been determined that the army assisted in the killings to a greater or lesser extent as dictated by circumstances and by the commanders' inclinations. It has been suggested there was some muttered, futile objection within the army to the carnage.[29]

As a result of the policy of mass murder 1.1 million Jews died in 1941, perhaps 750,000 of whom were *Einsatzgruppen* victims.[30] The conditions of war in Russia prevented the establishment of concentration camps, but in Poland and elsewhere in Nazi Europe the Jews were rounded up,

---

[28] Hilberg, *Destruction of the European Jews*, i. 286–370.

[29] Gerhard L. Weinberg. *A World at Arms: A Global History of World War II* (Cambridge, 1994), 301–3.

[30] These figures and those which follow are taken from Hilberg, *Destruction of the European Jews*, iii. 1202–20.

often from prepared lists, and packed tight in freight cars for the journey to such camps. To the last moment the pretence was maintained that they were bound for 'resettlement' or 'labour service' under good conditions. A Gestapo officer reported that the 44,056 deportees from Lodz in the first three months of 1942 were living and working in a labour camp of 100,000 people. Some of the west Europeans, whose turn came next, were more than willing to leave the misery of the ghetto for the better environment they expected. It was all a lie; there was no labour camp and all the Lodz deportees had been killed.[31] Everything in Lodz and throughout Poland, including the 'resettlement' of young children and the aged and feeble in labour camps, gave the lie to this pretence. But human beings grasp at straws when the reality is too horrible to accept.

In April 1942 the death camps began their operation, starting with the Jews of the Warsaw ghetto. Even before German 'actions' commenced, terrifying rumours of their intentions circulated, as the head of the ghetto Judenrat, Adam Czernaikow, recorded in his diary. The German officials in the ghetto whom he and Judenrat leaders elsewhere questioned, replied with flat denials or said they did not know, or issued reassuring lies that resettlement meant labour camps and easier conditions.[32] The German rail system was paid 5 pfennigs as fare for each passenger squeezed into a cattle car to Treblinka, a camp whose sole purpose was murder. Upon arrival the Jews were pushed along a fenced road by dogs and whips. They had to undress completely and enter a 'shower room', actually a gas chamber. Gas pellets were dropped in and within a few minutes up to 500 people were dead. Then a *Sonderkommando* of Jews dragged out the fresh corpses for mass burial; incineration came later, when burial proved nauseous and insanitary. Treblinka itself was razed to the ground, but in similar camps mounds of clothing, hairpieces, shoes, eyeglasses, and children's toys are on display to the present day.[33] The victims' gold jewellery and their gold teeth were taken. It was melted into gold ingots and entered the European banking system as German gold assets, mainly through Switzerland. Here was the mass production

[31] Dobroszycki, *Chronicle of the Lodz Ghetto*, 15, 153–60.
[32] *Warsaw Diary of Czernaikow*, 326, 335, 339, 354, 355, 360, 378, 381–3, 384.
[33] Treblinka itself was razed to the ground by the Germans.

of death by the factory system.[34] The Auschwitz camp included a section for medical 'experiments' whose victims were put to exquisite tortures by its head Dr Josef Mengele, a man whose scientific training interested him in twins. Sterilization was also practised in the crudest form. Most victims of experiments died and the others were maimed for life, and the results were published in German scientific journals with their place of origin thoughtfully omitted. They are of little or no scientific value, not to mention their utter violation of scientific ethics. Parts of human bodies from the same source went to university laboratories in Vienna and elsewhere.

Starting in July 1942 the Jewish ghettos of Lublin and western Galicia were sent to their death. On 1 April 1942 15,000 Lwow Jews were seized and deported and on 23 August 1942 50,000 more were sent off to die.[35] Warsaw Jewry had been the largest community. After months of panicky rumours and German denials its deportation *en masse* to the Treblinka death camp began on 23 July 1942 and proceeded at a frightful rate. By 5 September only 70,000 Jews remained in Warsaw, half of them in hiding. The keen observer Emmanuel Ringelblum recorded:

Whomever you talk to, the cry: the resettlement should never have been permitted. We should have run out into the street, have set fire to everything in sight, have torn down the walls and escaped to the Other Side. The Germans would have taken their revenge. It would have cost thousands of lives but not 300,000. Now we are ashamed of ourselves, disgraced in our own eyes and in the eyes of the world, when our docility earned us nothing.[36]

Most survivors were aged 20 to 39, and they at last established a comprehensive Jewish Fighting Organization. Warsaw Jewry's desperate rebellion broke out on 19 April 1943. That famous uprising was largely the doing of Jewish youth movements, whose young people did not expect to save Polish Jewry but aspired to a fighting, heroic death. Without aid

[34] There was widespread belief during the time of the killings and ever since that human fats were made into soap. Although alleged bars exist, unequivocal proof of such a practice is lacking.
[35] Friedman, 'The Destruction of the Jews of Lwow, 1941–1944', in *Roads to Extinction*, 244–321.
[36] *Notes from the Warsaw Ghetto: The Journal of Emmanuel Ringelblum*, ed. and trans. Jacob Sloan (New York, 1958), 326; undated but autumn 1942.

from the Polish underground and armed with nothing but pistols smuggled into the ghetto and home-made Molotov cocktails, they held off overwhelming German military power and materiel until 15 May and killed or wounded a handful of the 2,000 to 3,000 German soldiers. Of the 56,000 Jews who surrendered, about half were shot on the spot or sent to death camps and the other half went to labour camps.[37] The Warsaw ghetto's uprising was the most famous, but there were other cases of doomed heroism at Lwow, Bialystok, and elsewhere. There were also several rebellions and mass escapes from concentration camps, all of which were ferociously suppressed by the Germans.

The year 1942 saw the peak of murder, with 2,700,000 Jews killed, the vast majority of them Polish Jews. The last ghetto was Lodz. Its diligent work for the German army did not save Lodz Jewry, whose population steadily decreased owing to deportations to the Chelmno killing centre not far away. The final deportation, by then to Auschwitz, came in August 1944. The previous year of 1943 had been the turn of the Jews of western Europe.

West of the Rhine, South of the Danube

German domination covered most of continental Europe and the plans for killing the Jews also went that far. The completeness of German mass murder varied in many countries. It depended on the geography of the country, having adjacent neutral countries for escape, and the attitude of the native population and of Germany's allies. Thus, Hitler inclined to friendliness to the Norwegians as fellow Nordics while he sought anyhow to kill the 2,000 Jews of Norway. But the Norwegian people flatly rejected Nazism and paid for it with severe oppression. They helped the Jews to hide and then escape over the border to neutral Sweden in 1943, but several hundred Norwegian Jews were caught and deported to their death. Finland, although allied with Germany against Russia, emphatically refused to deport its Jews. Likewise, at the other end of Europe King

---

[37] Philip Friedman, *Martyrs and Fighters: The Epic of the Warsaw Ghetto* (New York, 1954).

Boris of Bulgaria, surrounded though he was by German conquests and German allies, resolutely refused to surrender his approximately 50,000 Jews. Denmark, the largest Scandinavian Jewish community with 6,000 Jews, refused to enact Nazi decrees. The most remarkable and successful case of rescue during the Holocaust occurred when SS soldiers prepared in September 1943 to seize and deport Danish Jewry *en masse*. A furtive movement of the Danish people at first hid the Jews and then ferried them in small vessels across the straits to safety in Sweden; the Copenhagen main synagogue's Torah scrolls were hidden in a nearby Lutheran church.

The most devious role was that of Hitler's Italian ally. Italy's entry into the war with minimal military participation brought none of the territorial loot that Mussolini expected. Despite the anti-Semitic laws of 1938 which owed much to German 'inspiration', the Italians declined to take part in the German mass murder, which was to begin with Italy itself. Until the Germans took over Greece and Croatia from the Italians there was no Holocaust project in those lands. Italian diplomats were active in protecting as much as they could Italian Jewish citizens in countries under Nazi rule. The crucial change in Italy occurred when it surrendered to the Allies and withdrew from the war in 1943. German troops at once occupied the country and the murder machinery commenced operations. From the windows of the Vatican he could see Jews being rounded up and taken away, but Pope Pius XII did not intervene. On the other hand, he instructed the Vatican premises and Catholic monasteries and convents in Rome to shelter all Jews who came for refuge, and 4,715 Jews did so. [38]

Unlike Italy, the slaughter in the Netherlands was almost as thorough as in Poland. Why could the German occupiers kill some 80,000 of the 110,000 Dutch Jews despite a generally friendly Dutch population? The Netherlands was a flat country, lacking forests and mountains where Jews could hide. It bordered Germany and countries under German control. The North Sea was too wide and rough for escape in small boats to England. The famous case of Anne Frank shows

---

[38] Besides Carpi cited below (n. 41), see Meir Michaelis, *Mussolini and the Jews: German–Italian Relations and the Jewish Question in Italy, 1922–1945* (Oxford, 1978), esp. 364–5.

where hiding had to take place.[39] After early internal disputes the Jewish council of the Netherlands adopted a policy of dutiful compliance with German demands, including lists for deportation to Westerbork, the Dutch transit camp to death camps in Poland. The council feared that if drawn up by the Germans the lists would be yet worse. In neighbouring Belgium some 45,000 of its 90,000 Jews hid or fled into France. Comparatively few were from the small minority of native Belgian Jews, who to a large extent succeeded in fleeing from deportation. From Belgium 40,000 Jews were killed.[40]

The most complex case was that of France, the first home of Jewish emancipation. The terms of its 1940 surrender divided it between the occupied zone under the Germans which included Paris and the Atlantic coastline, and the quasi-Fascist, anti-Semitic Vichy regime in the south headed by Marshal Pétain. Vichy also ruled Algeria, Morocco, and Tunisia, the French possessions in North Africa.[41] Tens of thousands of Jews like millions of Frenchmen fled from the occupied north to the unoccupied south and also into Nice, which the Italians had taken from France. Jews in flight included thousands from venerable communities in Alsace and Lorraine, expelled when the provinces were annexed to Germany. The 5,000 Jews who had lived in Vichy's zone before the war became almost 150,000 in 1940, about equal to the Jewish population of the north. The Germans' Italian allies generally let the Jews of Nice alone after enacting anti-Semitic legislation in obedience to German demands. Matters changed drastically for the Jews of Nice after the Germans occupied it and southern France in November 1942.

The Vichy regime decreed the anti-Semitic Law concerning Jews (*Statut des Juifs*) in October 1940 even before the Germans demanded it, and another decree was issued in the following year. They implemented the rightist programme to reduce or eliminate Jewish influence in France.

---

[39] I know, however, of a Jewish family which passed the war hidden almost undisturbed with a friendly family in a remote farmhouse. From a distance they could see the approach of anyone suspicious and take refuge under the floor.

[40] Dawidowicz, *The War against the Jews*, 364–5.

[41] An important study is Michael R. Marrus and Robert O. Paxton, *Vichy France and the Jews* (New York, 1981). See also Michel Abitbol, *The Jews of North Africa during the Second World War* (Detroit, 1989), and on Tunisia, Daniel Carpi, *The Italian Authorities and the Jews of France during the Second World War* (Hebrew) (Jerusalem, 1993).

Jews were removed from the French civil service and from teaching, expelled from the toothless national assembly, retired as army officers, and subjected to stringent quotas as university students and in the professions. The second *Statut* defined Jews in racial terms, classifying converts by the Jewishness of their parents or two grandparents. The laws did not restrict intermarriage or adoption and did not prevent Jews from appearing in public. France had no anti-Semitic riots nor window-smashing, and most anti-Semitic propaganda was dismissed as coming from the Germans. An attempt to introduce the Jewish badge failed. What was widely accepted was this 'state [i.e. official] anti-Semitism'. The Germans occupying the north appreciated having their policies enacted in French law which also applied in their zone. The Vatican, to which the Jews were the fount of secularism, regarded the new laws with approval. French Catholicism with rare exceptions like Archbishop Saliège of Toulouse firmly supported the Pétain regime. They expressed reservations only over the racial definition of Jew but did not make it an issue. On the other hand Pastor Marc Boegner, the Protestant leader, opposed the persecution at every step.

Foreign and refugee Jews, including those naturalized, were particular targets in France. They constituted the majority of Paris Jewry. Native French Jewry had for decades felt sorely embarrassed by the foreign Jews' mannerisms, their Yiddish, and their leftist politics, and many held the foreigners responsible for causing anti-Semitism. The thousands of foreign Jews who volunteered enthusiastically when the war started were assigned to the Foreign Legion and sent later to internment camps. Vichy leaders reassured native Jews that only foreign Jews would be affected by persecution, which had begun before the war with severe anti-immigration laws in 1938. However, when Jewish bank accounts, businesses, and real estate began to be 'aryanized' in 1941, it became clear that all Jews were in peril. By early 1942 several thousand Jews were imprisoned indefinitely without trial at the pleasure of German or Vichy authorities in a string of camps established by Vichy. The physical conditions may have been even worse than those of German camps, except that torture and killing were not practised. But filth, starvation, and disease were the rule for foreign or 'suspicious' Jews. The Union générale des Israélites de France, representing all French Jewry, was established after much intra-Jewish politicking late in 1941 under German pressure, in order to provide welfare aid for interned and other Jews. Reluctantly it was drawn into dealing with the Germans.[42]

The critical change came in the summer of 1942, when round-ups of Jews for deportation began in both parts of France. It was also the time when vast shipments of Polish Jews to death camps commenced. Heydrich, Eichmann, and their staff visited France with instructions from Himmler to arrange for the deportation of all French Jews. Not only foreign Jews and their young children, but long-established French Jews, war veterans, and other previously exempt categories were included. With merely 2,000 German soldiers in the country the work of rounding up the Jews was managed by the efficient French police under German SS oversight, aided by their vast, detailed card index of 150,000 Jews in the unoccupied zone. Only in France did the German makers of the Holocaust entrust its execution to local police, who controlled deportation until trains bound east left French territory. In 1942 over 42,000 were dispatched to the east on scheduled freight trains for which they were made to wait at the wretched Drancy camp near Paris. The Vichy rulers agreed to the deportation of foreign Jews and looked away when native Jews were deported afterwards, while the Commissariat-General for Jewish Affairs continued to carry on 'state anti-Semitism'. After a slowdown in 1943 deportations resumed in 1944, now aided by the *milice* of French Jew-hunters. Altogether 75,000 to 78,000 Jews were murdered by deportation, and an uncounted number died in France by privations.

In a distinct category was French North Africa, including Morocco, Algeria, and Tunisia. The Vichy laws against Jews were applied and the Crémieux decree of 1870, which granted the Jews citizenship, was revoked by the anti-Semitic French administration. Liberation should have come with the Allied invasion of November 1942 and the campaign which lasted until May 1943. However, the Americans through ambassador Robert Murphy thought it a military necessity to permit the tainted French regime to continue in office with its laws in effect. Even after a statement by President Roosevelt requesting revocation of the

[42] Richard I. Cohen, *The Burden of Conscience: French Jewish Leadership during the Holocaust* (Bloomington, Ind., 1987) is a valuable account.

anti-Semitic laws they were not revoked, and the Crémieux decree was not restored, for a full year and after a vigorous campaign by American Jewry. In contrast, when General de Gaulle assumed power in newly liberated France in August 1944 he at once abolished the Vichy regime, or what remained of it, and all its laws. After losing Algeria and Morocco the Germans held out for seven months in Tunisia, where they began their well-known programme for Jews. Some 5,000 of the 60,000 Tunisian Jews were conscripted for hard labour, working under brutal conditions until the liberation. Time was too short for the Germans to proceed with the 'final solution'.

Other major *Aktionen* must be added to this terrible chronicle. After Germany took over Czechoslovakia in March 1939 the professedly Catholic, Nazi satellite state of Slovakia was founded from its remains and headed by Tiso, a Catholic priest. Several thousand Jews from Slovakia succeeded in emigrating abroad, but thousands of others entered as refugees from Poland.[43] The Slovakian regime was wholeheartedly in favour of deporting all its Jews. At first the Germans sought 20,000 able-bodied Jewish workers, but the pro-Nazi regime persuaded their masters instead to deport all 90,000 Jews of Slovakia. Early in 1942 Slovakian police began to collaborate with the Germans in sending Jews to be killed. Urgent appeals to the Vatican produced no more than a protest to President Father Tiso and the Catholic state against the separation of families during deportation. Later protests were more emphatic. After 57,000 Jews had been deported, other foreign interventions, and bribes and delaying actions, kept the Holocaust machinery at bay for almost a year for the remaining 25,000 Slovakian Jews. But the Joint Distribution Committee and private sources had great difficulty in finding funds, and even greater difficulty in transferring them to Nazi hands. Through Wisliceny the Jews—Slovakian and international— were at one point offered a grandiose and doubtless fraudulent 'Europa Plan' to cease deportations from most of Europe for money. The whole tortuous negotiation process was dropped by the Nazis early in September 1944. The Slovak rebellion in September and October 1944 in which

---

[43] Livia Rotkirchen, *The Destruction of Slovak Jewry: A Documentary History* (Jerusalem, 1961), has documents in Hebrew and an introduction in Hebrew and English. It remains the standard account.

the surviving Jews participated brought the end to Slovak Jewry. Of the 20,000 remaining Slovak Jews, a strongly Orthodox group, most were sent to be killed except only those who hid in the mountains. Of 136,000 Jews within Slovakia's pre-war boundaries only 25,000 survived.[44] The second *Aktion* took place at the foot of the Balkans. When Germany took over Greece from the militarily incapable Italians the same Wisliceny oversaw the deportation to Auschwitz in the spring of 1943 of nearly all the 50,000 Jews of the storied community of Salonika. This was the only large Sefardic group killed in the Holocaust.

Large slices of Romania were turned over to Hungary at Hitler's bidding in 1940. The fate of the Jews in these territories under Hungary will be treated shortly, and that of the 307,000 who lived in Bukovina and Bessarabia. Bessarabia and part of Bukovina were ceded to Russia in1940 upon its ultimatum. Bessarabia quickly fell to Germany in 1941 and its Jews underwent the murderous attentions of the *Einsatzgruppen*. The Old Kingdom, the Regat, of the original Romania had about 300,000 Jews against whom a series of anti-Semitic laws of the familiar type were enacted. The local fascists of the Iron Guard conducted a pogrom against Bucharest Jewry before the new dictator Ion Antonescu crushed them, and 8,000 Jews were butchered by the army in a dreadful pogrom in Jassy. Strange to say, Jews could conduct activities and protest to the dictator Antonescu even while deportations were under way. The leader of Romanian Jewry Wilhelm Filderman, an able lawyer, and chief rabbi Safran protested with bravery and significant success. About 150,000 Jews, mainly from Bukovina, were deported to Transistria in conquered Russia adjoining Bessarabia, where two-thirds lost their lives. Shipments to death camps, supposed to take place in 1942, were delayed and finally cancelled. As a result, most Jews of the Regat were saved by the time Romania quit the war in September 1944.[45]

[44] Ibid., p. 1; Yehuda Bauer, *American Jewry and the Holocaust: The American Jewish Joint Distribution Committee, 1939–1945* (Detroit, 1981) 356–9, 447–9. This is the fullest account of relief and rescue efforts during the Holocaust. Another rescue organization was the American Va'ad Ha-Hatzalah, supported principally by Orthodox Jews and devoted to rescuing rabbis and yeshiva students. Its full history has yet to be written.

[45] Bauer, *American Jewry and the Holocaust*, 335–55; the Hebrew *Pinkas Hakehillot: Rumania*, i, ed. T. Lavi (Jerusalem, 1970), proceeds town by town with a general discussion in part one, pp. 141–205.

Hungary adopted 'moderate' anti-Semitic laws from the 1930s and went to war as a Nazi ally. However, about 14,000 alien, very Orthodox Jews, the type Horthy detested, living in territories Hitler took from Czechoslovakia and presented to Hungary, were deported in Galicia in 1941 and massacred. Beginning in 1939 younger Jews were drafted into the national labour service. At first they were treated relatively well, but gradually the treatment became brutal, inflicting hunger, overwork, and sadistic beatings and punishments upon them. This happened especially to those serving Axis armies in the Ukraine; comparative safety lay in being a Russian prisoner of war. Of some 42,000 Hungarian Jewish labour servicemen about half returned alive.

Yet Hungary was also a land of refuge from the Polish horrors, and an active rescue committee functioned in Budapest. Most Hungarian Jews considered the military alliance with Nazi Germany but an opportunistic necessity and thought themselves secure under the regime of the conservative nobility with Admiral Horthy as regent. Horthy wanted no part of the 'final solution' that the Germans and native Nazis urged on him, but what he had of sympathy was exclusively with assimilated Hungarian Jews. He had not objected to the massacre of alien Jews in 1941. From 1943 the Hungarian share in the German war effort declined after its army suffered shattering defeats in Russia and the regime sought to detach itself from Germany and to bring soldiers home to defend the country. The Germans, knowing that Hungary would change sides as Allied victories mounted and the Russian army advanced westward, occupied the country on 19 March 1944. They installed a pro-Nazi government and the Holocaust commenced immediately, directed by an experienced staff headed by Adolf Eichmann.[46] On 29 March Horthy gave his pro-Nazi ministry a free hand in dealing with the Jews.

The national Jewish council of patriotic Hungarian Jewish bourgeois knew but evidently learned little from the events in nearby countries. They did not tell Hungarian Jewry the true meaning of deportation, although most Jews realized it anyhow. Before the German occupation they had carried on petitions, appeals, and protests to the regime and continued doing so with the Germans, who listened while they deported

---

[46] The standard study, on which the account here draws extensively, is Randolph L. Braham, *The Politics of Genocide: The Holocaust of Hungary* (2 vols., New York, 1981).

trainloads of Jews. The council's admonitions to the Jews to remain calm, disciplined, and law-abiding under Nazi rule were far from what was needed. Thus the council provided detailed instructions on sewing on the newly decreed yellow star, although experienced outsiders had openly warned Hungarian Jews that labelling themselves publicly was a prelude to destruction. Knowledge of the destruction under way in neighbouring Poland and Slovakia was widespread among Hungarian Jews, but the Jewish council itself issued no warning. The months it spent on the details of its reorganization present a pitiful contrast to the packed trains *en route* at that very time to Auschwitz.

The steps towards the Holocaust were taken rapidly. Jewish property was expropriated, but rich Jews were able to trade theirs as the price for escape. Jews were driven out of public and cultural life. Almost 10,000 prominent Jews were arrested. The Jews were compelled to move into ghettos throughout the country, which was divided into ten districts. After a short stay there, they were loaded directly on freight trains to Auschwitz. The trains began to roll on 15 May 1944, district by district, starting with those given by Hitler to Hungary from Czechoslovakia and Romania. The deportations thus began from Carpatho-Ruthenia with its extremely Orthodox population and moved across Hungary towards Budapest. The Jews in the capital were required to concentrate in speci-fied 'Yellow star houses', marked outwardly as such in preparation for the deportations which commenced on 6 July 1944. The train journey to the camps with their gas chambers took three days at a warm time of year, with people packed like sardines without food or water or toilet facilities except a bucket for a car. Upon reaching Auschwitz the dazed, exhausted passengers who survived the trip—many did not—were sorted on the spot into those fit and, the majority, unfit for work. The unfit majority was led directly to the gas chambers, while the fit were subjected to humiliation and beating in the transition to slave labour. Most did not survive the conditions of work, and those who took sick and could not work were sent to be gassed. Auschwitz reached its peak of horrific efficiency in the Hungarian spring of 1944, when it devoured 10,000 daily victims. When the deportation reached the out-lying areas of Budapest, Horthy heeded pleas from many sources and intervened. On 8 July 1944 he ordered the deportations to stop. But 147 trains from 55 ghettos or concentration centres had transported 434,351 (or 437,402) Jews to Auschwitz, where most were promptly put to death.[47] The killings continued as Eichmann succeeded in sending more trainloads to the death camp and Nazi-style Nyilas killers stalked the streets of Budapest and other towns in western Hungary. When liberation came to Hungary in February and March 1945, 501,000 of the 725,000 Jews in the country (324,000 from the annexed areas) besides 100,000 converts to Christianity who were treated as Jews had been killed.[48]

Resistance and Diplomacy

Three million Russian prisoners of war were mistreated and starved but these vigorous young men, not encumbered by families, did not rebel against their captors.[49] What then could the Jews do against the German war machine, whose tremendous power could fight the British, Russians, and Americans for years, when it concentrated on them? Jews were weak from starvation, had no arms or military training, and had to think of wives, children, and the elderly. The Judenrat cautioned against resistance; if the Jews rebelled the Germans would shoot hundreds of hostages and destroy the ghettos. Since the Germans' object was to kill all Jews under their control, Jewish efforts to fight or to escape, or simply to stay alive may be considered resistance. Indeed the first problem of the Jews and of Jewish resistance was to realize that they confronted an enemy who intended to kill them all.[50] Oppression was understood, but for several years no one spoke of annihilation.

There is no evidence that anyone in the German government, including senior generals who commanded armed power, spoke or acted in

[47] Braham, *The Politics of Genocide*, ii. 607, table 19.1.

[48] Ibid. 1144, table 32.1.

[49] To be sure, neither did prisoners of war of western countries, but in general they were treated properly. The Jews among them and members of the Jewish Brigade from Palestine, it appears, were not mistreated. To be sure, the British and Americans held masses of German prisoners who could have been subject to reprisals.

[50] Yisrael Gutman, *Ba-'Alatah uva-Ma'avak* (Hebrew; *Struggles in Darkness*) (Jerusalem, 1985), contains searching essays on the subject.

dissent from murdering all Jews. A few churchmen did speak out. Against them were ranged Gestapo threats and the vast Nazi propaganda machine's ceaseless vilification of Jews and their sympathizers. Even the conspirators who aimed in 1944 to kill Hitler and sue for peace and were equally dismayed by Nazi crimes and the prospect of a disastrous German defeat, did not mention this greatest Nazi crime in their secret discussions or in the declarations they drew up. Some of the conspirators were nationalist conservatives, a type also represented in the Nazi regime, who would have continued a regime of racial separatism without repealing all anti-Semitic legislation. Only thoroughly assimilated German Jews were tolerable to these men.[51]

The Jews were all alone. Jews who escaped or those who could send letters in coded language, journalists and diplomats from neutral countries including the United States until it entered the war in December 1941, and a few sympathetic, well-informed Germans provided Jewish representatives in neutral countries with detailed reports. With rising intensity they spoke of a tremendous death roll from starvation and disease, and of massive killings. By early 1942 reports made clear that deportations to the east in crowded freight trains meant not labour camps but death, although the existence of vast murder camps was not yet known. Since the deportations followed a schedule to the same destinations, it was clear that there was a unified German programme. Gerhart Riegner, the World Jewish Congress's man in Geneva, played a central role in conveying the information to sceptical governments. Based on the reports of a well-connected, reliable German informant (kept confidential to the present day but believed to be the industrialist Eduard Schulte), Riegner's report of a programme of genocide[52] convinced the British and American governments. They and the Russians issued a solemn denunciation in November 1942 and warned of postwar retribution, but thereafter they did hardly anything.

In terms of armed resistance the Jews lacked nearly everything—

---

[51] Hans Mommsen, *From Weimar to Auschwitz* (Oxford, 1991), 315, 333–4. And Mommsen is a prominent 'functionalist'.

[52] The term originated in the 1950s. David S. Wyman, *The Abandonment of the Jews: America and the Holocaust, 1941–1942* (New York, 1984); Monty Noam Penkower, *The Jews Were Expendable: Free World Diplomacy and the Jews* (Urbana, Ill., 1983).

arms, ammunition, and a sympathetic population which would risk death to support them; the ghettos were shut behind walls and had nothing to give a resistance movement. Most partisan bands in eastern Europe refused to accept Jews into their ranks, but there were Jewish partisan bands in Russia and Lithuania, as well as France.[53] In Hungary virtually the only resistance was the activity of young Zionist *halutz* groups in rescuing and smuggling out Jews. Partisans in forests could not save fellow Jews in urban ghettos, and few of them ultimately survived the constant hunt by German forces. The Germans would kill dozens of Jewish hostages for one of their own slain by Jewish partisans. Armed resistance was, as it had to be, the doing of younger people who came mostly from Zionist youth movements.

Hiding and escape were the main means of survival. From surviving accounts we know that Jews of 'Aryan' appearance passed as Germans or other people with the help of forged documents. Passing was possible only for more or less assimilated Jews whose language and personal style would not give them away.[54] Perhaps the most numerous category of survivors was those who simply hid. It could have been in a remote village among sympathetic people, like one Protestant town in France, in a city apartment, in a convent or monastery school for children. While the papacy held aloof from the Holocaust, Roman Catholic institutions, especially in France and Italy, saved many Jews. Hiding was easier in a country with forests and mountains such as France, and more difficult in the flat, unforested Low Countries. Escape meant crossing a border into a neutral country which would let them in, and a country under Nazi rule needed an adjacent neutral country for escape. Thus Franco's Spain, for all its fascist dictatorship and friendliness to Hitler, allowed Jews to enter from France after the perilous Pyrenees crossing by foot. There also had to be a sympathetic native population in Germany

[53] A full description is Dov Levin, *Lohamim ve-'Omdim 'al Nafsham* (Hebrew; *They Fought Back: Lithuanian Jewry's Armed Resistance to the Nazis, 1941–1945*) (Jerusalem, 1974).

[54] I heard from a woman whose father hid through the war in Berlin that Reichswehr deserters from the Russian front declared themselves Jews when caught. As deserters they would be shot on the spot, while as 'Jews' they were sent to a concentration camp where they had at least a chance of surviving. I have not seen this confirmed in any source.

itself or an occupied country not on the lookout for Jews to betray, although there were persons anywhere who would do so for money. Sweden and Turkey took in fleeing Jews, while Switzerland both accepted and rejected. Finland, Germany's ally only in the war against Russia, rejected German suggestions of action against the small Jewish community. As mentioned above, at the beginning of the war hundreds of thousands of Polish Jews fled into the Soviet Union, where many spent the war years under harsh conditions in Siberia. Lithuanian Jews in Russia enlisted or were conscripted into a largely Jewish combat division.[55]

Slovakia, discussed above, and Hungary provide the important cases of serious attempts to save Jews by dealing with the Nazis. The episode of Joel Brand is the most striking. Active in the Budapest rescue *Va'ada*, he and a shady double (or quadruple) agent called Andor Grosz were picked by Eichmann to meet Jewish representatives in a neutral country and negotiate for 10,000 trucks for the eastern front in return for a million Jews to be saved from the slaughter. The disreputable Grosz, probably with the approval of Himmler, was to try to start peace negotiations! He was rejected and held in custody, but Brand's mission was taken seriously by Jewish leaders. He reached Zionist leaders but was held by the British, and the honesty of the German offer he conveyed was disbelieved and likewise rejected. The German demand for trucks was likely to alienate the Russian ally, with unforeseeable consequences for the war and after. From these discussions emerged the urgent proposal to bomb the Auschwitz death camp or the rail lines leading to it. In retrospect there are significant doubts that even effective bombing, which was technically possible, could have saved many Jews. Gas chambers and rail lines would have been speedily restored. However, the manner in which the bombing proposal was passed around, especially by the British, even with Prime Minister Churchill's approval, leaves the impression of bureaucratized heartlessness.

Meanwhile, Eichmann told a prominent Hungarian Zionist and *Va'ada* functionary, Reszoe (Israel) Kasztner, that as a gesture of Nazi sincerity in negotiations he could select a few thousand—the number constantly changed—family, friends, Jewish leaders, and holders of Palestine immigration certificates for a special train which would be

[55] Levin, *Lohamim ve-'Omdim* 47–104.

sent to safety in neutral Spain. Furthermore, 20,000 Jews from western Hungary were deported not to death but for war work near Vienna under tolerable conditions. The 1,684 persons on the final passenger list of Kasztner's train contained his family and 388 persons from his native Koloszvar, Orthodox and Neolog Jews from separate lists, refugees from other countries, holders of Palestine certificates, and persons who simply paid for the life-saving trip including the fiercely anti-Zionist Hasidic *rebbe* of Satmar. They were transported on 30 June 1944 to privileged safety and were kept within the Bergen-Belsen concentration camp until they were allowed into Switzerland in December. Kasztner's train and his dealings with the Nazis aroused bitter controversy and generated a case which reached Israel's High Court ten years later. He was slain, unquestionably over the issue.

When the Germans commenced Holocaust operations Hungary was open to foreign visitors and the meaning of deportations was well known. As Germany's power declined and some executioners of the Holocaust sought to strike a deal which might save them from retribution, intervention from neutral and Allied sources to save Jews became more active than in earlier phases of the war. But this is not to say much, and most of the victims were already dead by then. The International Committee of the Red Cross had declined to lend its aid to the Jews as 'civilian internees', which consisted of inspecting their physical conditions and forwarding mail and food packages. The Red Cross accepted the German position that the Jews were 'civilian detainees', meaning criminals, and ineligible for Red Cross help. Repeated efforts by the World Jewish Congress and others failed to make the Red Cross redefine the Jews as 'civilian internees'. Only during the arrival in Budapest late in 1944 of the 'final solution' did the august body protect 'foreign' children and adults in the city.[56]

The efforts of the Jews of Britain and America seeking to rescue Jews during the war and those of the *yishuv* in Palestine were tragically insufficient.[57] The main American Jewish effort came through the Joint, with

[56] Penkower, *The Jews Were Expendable*, 223–46; his discussion of the IRC in Hungary is corrected in Braham, *The Politics of Genocide*, ii. 1057–64.

[57] Dina Porat, *The Blue and the Yellow Stars: The Zionist Leadership and the Holocaust* (Cambridge, Mass., 1970).

the American Jewish Congress and the Vaad Hatzalah also active. The Joint worked through representatives in endangered communities, some of whom lost their lives. Rescue efforts were impeded by a sense of hopelessness and the belief that only victory would save the Jews—those still alive. Besides, money was very limited. Palestine Jewry became absorbed in its military effort and in its political struggle with British rulers, leaving its rescue attempts underfinanced and almost sidetracked. As to the American government, it long employed rhetorical eloquence against Nazi killings but little more. A swelling chorus of demands for rescue effort led to the convening of the Anglo-American conference on refugees, held in April 1943 for ten days in pleasant seclusion on the island of Bermuda. After much bureaucratic shuffling it was agreed and announced by a well-prepared British and an ill-prepared American delegation that nothing could really be done to rescue Jews.[58] The public reaction to the Bermuda conference was markedly hostile. Finally, in early 1944 Secretary of the Treasury Morgenthau, a Jew, stimulated by three vigorous young aides who were not Jews, went to President Roosevelt with a full report on his colleagues in the State Department. That department was already notorious for its stonewalling on visas and, as was revealed later, its avoidance of diplomatic reporting about the Holocaust. The President, who probably had domestic political consequences in mind as well as humanitarian aid, was prodded into establishing the War Refugee Board in January 1944 with sweeping powers to aid and save Nazi victims. Most of its money came from the Joint Distribution Committee, which throughout the war had been labouring for Holocaust rescue with sadly limited funds and against legal limitations on their transfer abroad. The War Refugee Board played an important role against the Holocaust as it neared Budapest. As usual Pope Pius XII spoke in guarded terms against all killing of civilians, but some Catholic prelates in countries ruled by Germany, such as France, denounced the murder of Jews. The strongest Catholic opposition was to the racial classification of Jewish converts as Jews. Other countries spoke through diplomatic channels. The most remarkable effort came from Sweden. It dispatched Raoul Wallenberg,

---

[58] Bernard Wasserstein, *Britain and the Jews of Europe 1939–1945* (Oxford, 1979), 188–205.

a young man of an influential family, in a minor diplomatic post, with instructions to do whatever he could to save Jews and others in Budapest. He carried out his mission with zeal and effectiveness unparalleled by anyone in the Holocaust years, granting safety by diplomatic status to perhaps 10,000 people and setting up feeding and housing arrangements for an even larger number. Wallenberg was called to meet the Russians when they liberated Budapest and was never heard from again.

After the End of Nazism

As they saw their end approaching the Germans sought to conceal their monstrosities and some, notably Himmler, sought to make deals to save their skin. They extinguished the fires of Auschwitz in November 1944 and razed a number of concentration camps to the ground. They also took perhaps 50,000 inmates of their camps in Poland on mad marches through Germany with no destination except another concentration camp further west or capture by British and Americans rather than Russians. Hardly clad in freezing weather and lacking minimal food and sanitation, the victims were forced along and shot if they lagged behind or fell in exhaustion. Even the rare German who tossed them food out of pity was beaten. Relief came only when their guards tired or when advancing armies freed them.

As final unconditional surrender drew near, diplomatic efforts were exerted to keep the Germans from carrying out their reported intention of killing all camp prisoners. Some camps were liberated by advancing armies before the war ended. The Russians liberated Lublin (Majdanek) in the summer of 1944 and photographs showed furnaces with skeletons within. Auschwitz was liberated in January 1945. British, Canadian, and American soldiers rushed into the camps within Germany and liberated them. 'It is my duty to report a sight beyond the imagination of mankind,' solemnly wrote a British reporter with the troops who liberated Bergen-Belsen and were horrified by the heaps of grotesquely emaciated corpses lying unburied and thousands of nearly dead prisoners. In spite of devoted efforts by physicians lacking experience in treating such victims, about 10,000 died after liberation of typhoid and complications of starvation. American soldiers who liberated Buchenwald and Dachau were stunned by similar sights, and outraged soldiers assigned to guard concentration camp guards in Dachau shot sixty to seventy of them.[59] General Eisenhower and other military 'brass' as well as delegations of the American Congress and the British Parliament came to behold the horrors, which newsreel reporting showed to the shocked world. Earlier, cautiously doubtful reports of Nazi atrocities were now verified and believed.

How many Jews died in the Holocaust? The Nuremberg trials of Nazi criminals in 1945 estimated 5.7 million. An exact count is impossible, but the number calculated by Raul Hilberg reaches around 5.6 million, somewhat short of the mythic 'Six Million'. About 1 million were children under 15. In the round numbers given by Hilberg about 3.5 million were killed in concentration camps and 1.3 million by *Einsatzgruppen* and other public shootings. About 800,000 were lost by disease, starvation, and ghettoization.[60] Lucy Dawidowicz's figure is 5,933,000.[61] This was one-third of the Jewish people, and struck disproportionately the Jews of eastern Europe which for centuries had been the people's biological and intellectual centre, and also the centre of their impoverishment.

In August 1945, soon after the war's end, there were 50,000 survivors of the camps and a few thousand hidden Jews who survived in Germany and Austria. The original number of survivors in Poland was also about 50,000 but was constantly supplemented by Jews returning from the Soviet Union. Of concentration camp survivors surveyed in November 1945, 85 per cent were aged 18 to 40, about 60 per cent of them male. This age disproportion declined a few months later, probably on account of new arrivals who had a slightly more normal age distribution; everywhere young children were absent. The large majority of those counted

---

[59] Oral testimony in Robert H. Abzug, *Inside the Vicious Heart: Americans and the Liberation of Nazi Concentration Camps* (New York, 1985), 93. An Israeli survivor of Dachau, Dr Shlomo Shaffir, has told me that he witnessed the shootings, which took place the day the camp was liberated.

[60] Taken from Hilberg, *Destruction of the European Jews*, iii. 1219. However, his figures for Hungary are too low and have been corrected here.

[61] Dawidowicz, *The War against the Jews*, 402–3.

were the sole survivors of their immediate family and close relatives. By the end of 1947, when the displaced person (DP) Jewish population was at its peak, there were 170,000 in Germany, the vast majority in the American zone, 23,000 in Austria, and 15,000 in Italy. The bulk of those in Austria and Italy were *en route* elsewhere. About 15,000 DPs somehow made their way into France and Belgium, and 36,600 left French and Italian ports as illegal immigrants into Palestine. Between 1945 and 1948 almost 13,000 were admitted to the United States and 29,000 to Latin America, Australia, and Canada. This rough total of 300,000 represents the surviving remnant of the great slaughter,[62] who became an obstinate pressure group for a new home in Palestine.

Thousands of former concentration camp inmates needed hospital or sanatorium treatment to recover, as much as they could, from what the Germans did to them. They were in many cases disturbed by symptoms like nightmares and anxiety, but their psychological condition after enduring Nazi bestiality was better than was widely expected. They abounded in energy and ambition. One expression was the groups some survivors organized to hunt for Nazi guards who had fled the camps they had tyrannized. Once found they were seized and told that they would now receive justice in the name of the Jewish people, and were summarily put to death. Apparently several hundred fugitive Nazi killers were dealt with in this way.

The surest evidence of Jewish determination for continuity and to re-establish themselves lies in the rate of marriage and reproduction by the unmarried and widowed under the unfavourable conditions of DP camps. Despite the absence of privacy restoration of marriage ties and family life occurred on a massive scale.[63] The Jewish DPs were credited with an amazing birth rate of 75 to 100 per 1,000, the highest recorded in the world. It gradually declined to a level of about 32 per 1,000,

---

[62] I follow the summary in Yehuda Bauer, *Flight and Rescue: Brichah* (New York, 1970), 319–20. Koppel S. Pinson. 'Jewish Life in Liberated Germany', *Jewish Social Studies*, 9/2 (April 1947), 101–26, observes (p. 103 n. 2) that '[p]opulation figures for Displaced Jews are to be treated with a great deal of reserve and caution', and estimates their number at the close of 1946 at 200,000. Pinson, a notable historian, served the Joint in the camps in 1945–6. His sensitive, authoritative article is the best of its kind.

[63] Women generally recovered from amenorrhoea but nothing could be done for thousands of men and women who had been brutally sterilized.

on the eve of quitting the camps. Starting in 1945 practically without little children, in 1948 the proportion of infants less than 1 year old to the entire DP camp population was four times higher than that proportion in the population of 'baby booming' America.[64]

Perhaps it was the shock of discovery, and certainly the difficulties of transport, that caused a hiatus of months before relief on a large scale began to arrive, mainly from the Joint, which also sent staff. The Jewish survivors were thrilled to meet soldiers of the Jewish Brigade from Palestine who had fought mainly in Italy and now helped them generously after hostilities ended. From Palestine came a considerable group of teachers and organizers of the flight by all possible means from eastern Europe into the American zone of Germany. That zone was to be a staging post for 'illegal' emigration to Palestine.

Most striking was the survivors' capacity to organize themselves within weeks of their liberation into the Central Committee of Liberated Jews. It proved itself a resourceful, articulate body with several leaders of outstanding ability. Tenacious and not always dealt with easily, the Central Committee and its constituency depended completely on the aid they were receiving from the American army and the Joint. The army's Jewish chaplains played an estimable role, especially in securing supplies and explaining Jewish needs to American officers who controlled well-stocked warehouses.[65] The American army had initially lacked understanding for the special position of Jewish victims. This was exemplified by the combat hero and anti-Semite General George Patton's contemptuous, rough attempt to force survivors back to camps. Complaints over the condition and treatment of DPs reached the ear of President Truman, who dispatched Earl G. Harrison in the summer of 1945 to report on the state of affairs of DPs in Germany. Harrison's report was scorching. He even alleged that American treatment of

---

[64] Leo W. Schwarz, *The Redeemers: A Saga of the Years 1945–1952* (New York, 1953), 308, quoting the DP newspaper *Dos Vort*, 10 Jan. 1950. I have seen the figure of 89 per 1,000 but I cannot recall the source. Once in Israel the survivors' birth rate was twice as high as that of the native Jewish population. Irit Keynan, *Lo Nirga ha-Ra'av* (Hebrew: *Holocaust Survivors and the Emissaries from Eretz-Israel* (Tel Aviv, 1996), 37, 78–80, 213.

[65] Schwarz, *The Redeemers*, relates in dramatic fashion the Central Committee's work with the assistance of extensive archives and oral interviews.

liberated Jews differed little from Nazi treatment except that they were not being killed, but they were hungry and still in many cases residing in former concentration camps behind barbed wire. Truman's personal interest and Eisenhower's sharp commands brought prompt improvement in food, housing, and general attitude. His successors in Germany, Generals McNarney[66] and Clay, were friendly, and in the new position of Adviser on Jewish Affairs to the American army in Germany, Judge Simon Rifkind, Rabbi Philip Bernstein, and their successors provided valuable guidance and advice to both sides. In October 1946 the American army of occupation recognized the Central Committee of Liberated Jews as the official representative of the survivors.

All these steps constituted a considerable improvement, but did not settle the question of the DPs' ultimate destination. In the United States a special immigration act was so framed as to exclude all but a few Jews, and was not changed until 1949. And the British held tenaciously to the virtual cessation of Jewish immigration to the Jewish national home under the White Paper of 1939, still in force. However, hundreds of Jewish child survivors were taken to Britain and resettled there by Rabbi Solomon Schonfeld and Leonard G. Montefiore at their personal expense, over the opposition of DP leaders. The remaining DP community was a solid Zionist bloc, repeating tirelessly their insistence on going to Palestine. Had immigration to America been freer, a higher proportion would probably have opted to go there. But Palestine was the sole accepted goal. Groups of young survivors organized training *kibbutzim* on confiscated German farms, preparing themselves for emigration to Palestine where they would live in real *kibbutzim* and work the land.

Yet the victorious nations did not know what to do about the survivors. Return to lands of origin was favoured especially by the British, who sought to avoid refugee pressure to emigrate to Palestine. The idea was furiously rejected by east European Jews, the large majority, for whom the term 'displaced persons', DPs, originated. Surviving French, Dutch, and Belgian Jews generally returned to their former homes where

---

[66] A remarkable expression of appreciation to McNarney was the dedication to him personally of an edition of the Talmud in nineteen folio volumes, published in Germany in 1951.

few, however, succeeded in reclaiming their property.[67] Many Polish Jews did return to seek lost relatives and reclaim property if they could, and some hoped to rebuild their lives in Poland. In addition thousands of Jews who had survived the war in Russia came back west, mainly to Poland. A wave of anti-Semitism greeted them. They encountered the hostility of former neighbours who had themselves suffered heavily during the war and had appropriated abandoned Jewish property. Moreover, the Communist regime installed in Poland by the Russians included many Jews, which did not endear it or them to the Poles. Matters came to a series of pogroms in 1946 which culminated at Kielce, where forty-two Holocaust survivors were killed. This gave the signal for the mass movement called *Brichah* (flight) out of Poland to the American zone of Germany.[68] Particularly disturbing was the case of several thousand Jewish youngsters saved by Christian families who hid and nurtured them as well as others sheltered in Christian institutions, who had become orphans. There were tragic disputes between surviving relatives of the children alongside Jewish communal organizations who sought to reclaim them as Jews, and sheltering Christian institutions and individual, loving families.

Much of the DPs' bitterness and restlessness came from being in the enemy land of Germany which they wanted to quit in order to begin, or resume, a normal life elsewhere, above all in Palestine. Their indefinite future led to friction with American soldiers guarding the camps, while their attempts at petty business brought accusations of black marketeering and quarrels with Germans nearby. They refused to work for Germans, and would accept only the United Nations Relief and Rehabilitation Administration (UNRRA) or Jewish organizations as employers. American Jewish organizations and their leaders feared that the DPs' spreading demoralization in 1947 after two years of temporary dwelling in camps or expropriated German houses (often of Nazi officials) and institutions would end in a revolt and riots involving American soldiers.

[67] Indifference or apathy to returning Jewish survivors even in these democratic countries is described in Pieter Lagrou, 'Victims of Genocide and National Memory: Belgium, France and the Netherlands, 1945–1965', *Past & Present*, 154 (Feb. 1997), 181–223.

[68] David Engel, *Beyn Shihrur li-Berihah* (Hebrew; *Between Liberation and Flight: Holocaust Survivors in Poland and the Struggle for Leadership, 1944–1946* (Tel Aviv, 1996).

Such thoughts weighed on leaders who were far from Zionism yet saw no place but Palestine for displaced Jews. The gates of America were barely open.

The fate of Jewish cultural property looted by the Germans was better. It was found concentrated in vast depots, mainly in Czechoslovakia and Germany, which the American army expropriated. A vast project of sorting and disposing of hundreds of thousands of stolen books and ritual objects was undertaken, at first by American soldiers who were usually men with substantial Jewish knowledge. In 1947 world Jewish organizations collaborated to establish Jewish Cultural Reconstruction to take over this task under the presidency of Salo W. Baron. After their identifiable property had been returned to the few individuals found alive, the vast collection was distributed among Jewish institutions of learning according to fixed criteria. Most was sent to the United States and Palestine, and the rest went to Jewish institutions in many countries.[69]

The experience of the Holocaust inflicted a permanent psychic scar on the entire Jewish people, not only on those personally affected. Besides the immense loss of lives the cold, sadistic deliberateness with which the vast murder was carried out, and the absence of serious concern among Germany's foes and their impatience with Jewish pleas for rescue aid, could not be forgotten. Democratic governments had let the Jews down disastrously and their reassuring words of comfort meant far less than once. The lustre of 150 years of enlightenment and emancipation was dim indeed. This was probably the lowest point in the Jewish people's collective fortunes. They were not represented as such at the San Francisco conference of April–May 1945 which founded the United Nations nor did they appear on the agenda of any post-Second World War conference. Jews would invest no more in great schemes of social salvation, and would look out for their needs themselves and accept help from whoever would give it.

---

[69] The executive secretary, Joshua Starr, was also a historian and Hannah Arendt was on the staff. One fortunate case was the recovery of most of the YIVO library and archives of Vilna and its return to YIVO in New York. No study yet exists of this organization, which concluded its task in 1951.

National Home to State

Most of the *yishuv* was of recent European origin, and the fate of European Jewry was an issue of the deepest moral and personal meaning. Appalling rumours began to reach the *yishuv* in mid-1942. Confirmation came in the autumn of that year with the eyewitness testimony of a group of Palestinian Jews stranded in Nazi Europe who were exchanged for German subjects in Palestine. The mass murder plainly meant that Zionist settlers' immediate families were being killed. Days of fasting and prayer were called. The Jewish Agency for Palestine set up a committee on rescue headed by the veteran leader of Polish Jewry, Yizhak Gruenebaum, who had settled in Palestine in 1935. As in other countries, they faced the problem of rescue—how were Jews to be saved? A remarkable rescue was that of 900 Jewish children in 1943 through Iran. However, the main method was already in use before the war—taking Jews out of Nazi Europe to Palestine. The preferred route was a steamboat down the Danube to a Romanian port, then another vessel through the Black Sea to a Turkish port, and finally by sea to Palestine. The entire procedure was illegal and very risky. It meant buying or renting a usually decrepit ship from a dealer, often of dubious reputation, and bribes to sail it down the Danube through hostile countries or those allied with Germany. There was often a wait of weeks at a Romanian Black Sea port, while the Turks allowed the vessels the briefest stay at their ports. And when the boats neared Palestine they were usually taken in tow by the British navy, which interned the passengers for the duration of the war in the Athlit camp near Haifa or more often in a British dependency in Africa, Cyprus, or the remote island of Mauritius. About sixty vessels and 35,000 refugees came by this means between 1938 and the end of 1944; two ships sank with large loss of life.[70] One of these, the *Struma*, was refused admission to Palestine and forced out of Istanbul. It sank off Turkish shores in February 1942 with the loss of 767 refugee lives, to world-wide indignation. With great effort Colonial Secretary Lord Cranborne persuaded the cabinet to allow into Palestine

---

[70] Dalia Ofer, *Derekh ba-Yam* (Hebrew: *Illegal Immigration during the Holocaust*) (Jerusalem, 1988), esp. appendix, pp. 474–6.

within the White Paper quotas refugees who did succeed in reaching its shores.[71] It was argued there might be spies amongst them. Neither Arab sympathy with the Axis, which included a cordial meeting of the exiled Mufti of Jerusalem with Hitler, nor the Jewish plight altered British White Paper policy.[72] The British government announced that long-term decisions must wait until peace came. Irritated by insistent American Zionist agitation, the British tried but failed to persuade the American government to join in a declaration that the agitation was harmful to the conduct of the war.

At the war's end, confronted with several hundred thousand bitter, insistent Jewish survivors, outspoken American Jewry, impatient President Truman, and Palestinian Jewry ready to go to all lengths in opposing its policy, the British government had to decide on its course in Palestine. Control of Zionist affairs had meanwhile shifted from London headquarters to Palestine, or in personal terms from Chaim Weizmann to David Ben-Gurion. In the largest sense Zionist diplomacy, led by Weizmann for a quarter century and oriented to Great Britain, moved under Ben-Gurion's direction to the United States. He was confident that the United States could be brought to favour Zionist aims if American Jewry pressed with determination. Answering the British freeze on Palestine until the war's end, the Zionist movement staked its post-war claims at the 'Extraordinary Zionist Conference' held at the Biltmore Hotel in New York in May 1942. Central to the 'Biltmore Programme' were unrestricted Jewish immigration to Palestine under Jewish Agency control and the development of the country, which would lead to Palestine as a Jewish Commonwealth after the war. Flaccid, sporadically active American Zionism came to life during the war years under a new, vigorous leadership and built a highly effective political machine. A public relations campaign of unprecedented scope and vigour was initiated under Rabbi Abba Hillel Silver, an able political tactician and a superlative orator. The Zionist campaign was directed especially at members of Congress, and the press, churches, trade unions, and uni-

---

[71] Ibid. 266–72. The Palestine government finally agreed to take seventy children off the *Struma*, but word of this concession came after the ship went down with but one survivor.

[72] *The Israel–Arab Reader: A Documentary History*, ed. W. Laqueur and B. Rubin, 79–85.

versities. It won over almost all Senators and Representatives, and gained the broad support of American public opinion. This was a highly important struggle which the British lost to the Zionists.

While carrying on its political struggle the *yishuv* prospered during the war. The needs of the British military brought good business, and British servicemen on leave were everywhere to be seen, spending freely. The Jewish population increased from 475,000 in 1939 to 600,000 in 1945, despite the severe limits on immigration. The *kibbutzim* reached their maximum, with more than 40,000, or 7 per cent of the Jews, living there. Strict collectivism and ideological uniformity were the rule in each of the several *kibbutz* movements, and a remarkable degree of self-sacrifice existed under their still spartan conditions of life. The politically dominant Palestine Labour Party (*Mapai*), led by Ben-Gurion, contended with considerable doctrinaire factionalism in and around its ranks. *Hashomer Hatzair*, primarily a *kibbutz* movement, also constituted a pro-Soviet Russia party which combined Zionism with a preference for a bi-national rather than a Jewish state in Palestine. Between *Hashomer Hatzair* and *Mapai* stood 'Faction B' (*Siyya Bet*), also a *kibbutz* movement primarily. There were religious Zionist parties, the middle-class *Mizrachi* and the labourite *Hapoel Hamizrachi*, besides the non-Zionist *Agudath Israel*. Liberalism in politics and economics was represented by two parties designated as General Zionist A and B. Zionist Revisionism was represented by two illicit armies with far-right principles, who were detested and practically driven out of political life by the dominant Zionist left.

A current of high tension ran through the relations between the *yishuv* and its British rulers. Contrary to most peoples in British imperial domains the Palestine Jews and their leaders were neither humble nor suppliant, and their articulate self-confidence and ready citation of legal rights and demands did not endear them to British officials. Early in 1940 land transfer rules forecast in the White Paper were imposed, forbidding Jewish land purchases in 95 per cent of the country. This would throttle Jewish agricultural development, a further sign of Britain's intention to halt the Jewish national home's growth. Hidden Hagana arms disturbed the country's rulers, who did not 'buy' the explanation that the arms they sometimes found merely served local, defensive needs. The arrival of *aliyah beth* boats also angered the British, but on this issue the Jews offered no excuses and refused to yield—they considered immigration to their homeland their legal and moral right. The war came dangerously close in 1942, when the advance of General Rommel's Afrika Korps close to Alexandria frightened the *yishuv*. One or two large steps further would bring German troops into Palestine. Desperate plans were made for a retreat into a Carmel Mountains redoubt, but fortunately the menace was removed by the British victory at El Alamein which secured north Africa.

The Jews of Palestine wanted to take part in the war against Nazi Germany not merely as individual soldiers under the British flag but as a Palestinian Jewish division. The British government withstood worldwide pressure to form a Jewish army unit. It wanted Arab and Jewish soldiers in equal numbers, but the Arabs' Axis sympathies were patent and enlistments were few. British and Zionists both knew but did not express openly the real reason for the delay—the Jews wanted trained, experienced soldiers in Jewish units for the anticipated post-war struggle over Palestine, while the British did not want a wartime Jewish fighting force superior to what the Arabs could put in the field. A Jewish combat unit, called the Jewish Brigade, was at last organized late in 1943, four years into the war. It fought gallantly in Italy and, as has been mentioned, after the war its soldiers aided Jewish DPs until the Brigade was demobilized in April 1946. As much as possible they brought home their weapons, and many returned to Europe as civilians to aid in *Brichah* and furtive *aliyah*, called *aliyah beth*.

Did the British government feel some degree of moral responsibility over the Holocaust? They were sorry for its victims, but Great Britain had sacrificed much and suffered heavily and was almost bankrupt. Vast, prospering, victorious America, its soil untouched by the war, barely opened its gates to Jewish refugees, and instead indulged in free advice and admonitions over Palestine to its British ally. But world opinion did not accept resentful British reactions to Zionist and humanitarian demands for survivor immigration. Thus, France and Italy as well as the Americans in their zone of Germany did not act to prevent *aliyah beth* despite British protests.

When Labour took office in July 1945 and the war in the Pacific finally ended the next month, the new British government was expected to implement its party platform for free immigration and the full development of the Jewish national home. But Labour in power soon bitterly disappointed those who trusted its platform. Foreign Secretary Ernest Bevin, a power in the party, 'saw the light' as shown to him by pro-Arab Foreign Office officials, and reiterated established policy in Parliamentary speeches which were punctuated by anti-Jewish slurs. From Bevin's policy it became clear that the Jewish political and diplomatic struggle for Palestine would be hard. It was to be accompanied by action against the British army of some 100,000 soldiers as well as a campaign of settlement in defiance of land regulations.

The struggle began in earnest in the autumn of 1945, when Haganah, meaning simply 'defence', destroyed several strategically important Jordan river bridges. Haganah's history reached back to the 1920s and even earlier, to self-defence against Russian pogroms. It was under the control of the Jewish Agency and especially the Labour leadership. Yet the Jewish Agency insisted to the disbelieving British, to whom the matter was important and abrasive, that they knew nothing of this clandestine army. Haganah's members were young people as well as employed adults on call. There was also a full-time combat élite called Palmah (abbreviation for *Plugot Mahatz*, shock forces) of young men and women who lived and trained at *kibbutzim*. Outside the Haganah framework and refusing to accept its discipline were the Revisionist *Etzel* (abbreviation for *Irgun Zvai Leumi*, National Military Organization) and the Stern gang (officially, *Lohamei Herut Yisrael*, Fighters for the Freedom of Israel). Haganah tactics were circumspect, carefully avoiding civilian and non-military targets. *Etzel*, with less arms and far fewer members, many of them oriental with religious backgrounds, was not as restrained and the Sternists even less so. They were quite willing to resort to terror, and the Sternists toyed with theories which glorified political violence.

As a first post-war political step the British established the Anglo-American Commission of Inquiry. Its composition of six British and six Americans with an American judge as chairman signalled Britain's wish to involve the Americans in their policy. This would be more important to them than yet another official inquiry. The commission's recommendation of 100,000 visas to Jews at once and steps toward a bi-national state was accepted in part by the Jews and rejected by the Arabs. It was also rejected by the British, who demanded that Haganah first disarm in the full knowledge that it would not do so. As to the goal of United States involvement, it would take no part in British rule in Palestine.

In 1946 and 1947 the Palestine situation descended towards anarchy. Every step the British took failed to settle anything. They fortified themselves in urban compounds, sarcastically called Bevingrad, and arrested most of the Jewish leadership on 30 June 1946 with the important exception of Ben-Gurion who was out of the country. Finally they released them. The land transfer rules were defied by the overnight founding of eleven new settlements in the Negev under cover of darkness. They all claimed the next day that they had existed there for years. In 1946 and 1947 over forty new settlements were established, mainly in places which would anticipate the expected partition boundaries. Above all, boatloads of 'illegal' immigrants, mainly Holocaust survivors, implicitly denied the legality of White Paper restrictions by sailing for Palestine before the eyes of the world. These boats usually fell foul of Britain's naval blockade and were seized, frequently after a pitched battle between British sailors and 'illegals', and the passengers were transported to an internment camp in Cyprus. The climax of 'illegal' immigration came in the summer of 1947, when the ship *Exodus 1947* set sail from a French port with approximately 4,500 passengers and crew. Its journey was trailed by British aircraft and naval vessels until it was stopped and boarded near the Palestine coast, setting off a pitched battle that cost several lives. The immigrants were forced off the ship at Haifa, accompanied by scenes before the shocked gaze of the democratic world and seen by several members of the United Nations Special Committee on Palestine (discussed below). The destination of *Exodus 1947*, it was decreed, was not to be Cyprus but back to Germany. Great Britain suffered a deep moral defeat in its dealings with the ships. But for Bevin's political power and his party's strict discipline there would have been a rebellion within its parliamentary ranks.

Even worse was to come. Dov Gruner, an *Etzel* member, was hanged early in May 1947 for the possession of firearms contrary to emergency regulations, and other *Etzel* members were hanged for terrorist killings or flogged for other offences. Besides the death sentences the humiliation of flogging caused bitter resentment, and *Etzel* seized two British sergeants and hanged them in retaliation, an act repudiated by the Jewish authorities. The exasperated Colonial Office demanded of High Commissioner MacMichael why with 100,000 British troops he could not maintain order in Palestine. He replied that every public facility, school, post office, and seemingly innocuous place in the country was a centre of hostility and rebellion. Great Britain had no friends or supporters in Palestine. Only a massive pogrom with hundreds killed could restore British rule; he would have nothing to do with such an act and was sure that neither would the British government nor the British people.[73]

It is difficult to discern what goal Ernest Bevin was pursuing, for his considerable pique and fury with the intractable Jews could not serve as a policy.[74] British policy, not stated but inferred, evidently aimed at an Arab state in Palestine with a permanent Jewish minority, which the Jews would never accept. Britain toyed with other plans, such as the Morrison–Grady for the 'cantonization' of the country under British control, but there was no means by which Britain could maintain stable rule while its fundamental policies remained unchanged. Avowing itself powerless under the Mandate to determine the future of Palestine, the British government announced on 14 February 1947 that it had 'reached the conclusion that the only course open to us is to submit the problem to the judgment of the United Nations'. As Abba Eban later recalled, 'the United Nations seemed to matter very much to the world in those days. It was still regarded as the central arena in which the destiny

[73] The High Commissioner's reply is on display at Acre Prison, and I paraphrase from memory. The letter makes clear the content of the letter to which it replied.

[74] Harold Wilson, who was in a position to know as a junior member of the government from 1947 and later prime minister, maintained that Bevin aimed at a federation of independent Arab states under British patronage. They would acquire stability by elevating living standards and curtailing the Jewish national home. Wilson claimed that Bevin was not hostile to Holocaust survivors, but could feel deep sympathy only with the British working class from which he sprang. Harold Wilson, *The Chariot of Israel: Britain, America and the State of Israel* (London, 1981). None of this is borne out in the authoritative Alan Bullock, *Ernest Bevin: Foreign Secretary, 1945–1951*. He too does not state clearly Bevin's Palestine policy.

of mankind would be determined.[75] The British government studiously abstained thereafter from United Nations endeavours on Palestine, but its hostility to the Jewish cause was manifest. It continued to rule Palestine until finally leaving on 14 May 1948. Great Britain divested itself of its empire during the decade following the Second World War, but quit no dependency with as much bitter feeling as the small land it had begun to rule under promising auspices thirty years before.

In 1947 a political solution was inescapable, and the possibilities were few and well known. All Palestine west of the Jordan river as a Jewish state or an Arab state was impossible, and a bi-national state of fixed equality between the two sides was a pipe dream of earnest intellectuals without backing. With no Arab voice speaking for the slightest compromise, partition of the country into two states remained the only solution. The proposal for partition went back to the Peel Commission of 1937, when a Zionist Congress endorsed it. Still, partition was a divisive idea to Zionists, although the World Zionist Congress in 1946 endorsed a 'viable' partition proposal if made. Some Zionist diplomats, the rather self-propelled Nahum Goldmann in particular, began to work unofficially towards that goal in London and Washington. When Britain turned over the problem to the United Nations, it appointed a Special Committee on Palestine (UNSCOP) of thirteen member nations uninvolved in the conflict which studied the subject for months before issuing recommendations. The Arabs boycotted UNSCOP, thereby easing the way for Jewish liaison diplomats, one of whom was the newcomer Aubrey (Abba) Eban. UNSCOP returned a majority of ten for partition into two states and three for a federal state with autonomous Arab and Jewish sections. However, constant immovable Arab opposition to co-operation with the Jews again ruled out any political or other collaboration between the two sides. For its part the Jewish Agency Executive decided to back the UNSCOP partition proposal despite dissatisfaction with its limited borders and the international status which it proposed for Jerusalem as a holy city despite its Jewish majority.

Between 1 September 1947 when the UNSCOP report was presented and the United Nations vote on 29 November 1947 exhaustive efforts were invested in securing the needed two-thirds vote for the majority

[75] Abba Eban, *An Autobiography* (Jerusalem, 1977), 90.

report. Altogether unexpected support came from the Soviet Union, whose delegate Andrei Gromyko spoke in almost Zionist terms of the Jews' hopes and their need for a national home after their wartime suffering. Gromyko's declaration was worth at least seven of the needed votes. More subtle was the support given by the Roman Catholic Church, a weighty influence in many countries. According to Moshe Shertok (later Sharett), the Political Secretary who headed Zionist diplomatic activity, Pope Pius XII decided to set aside his church's historic opposition to the Jews regaining the land they had 'forfeited' as the penalty for the crucifixion. Overruling theological opponents of a Jewish state in the Holy Land, he gave his church's support to a Jewish state as a bulwark against communism, the great enemy of the time, taking root in the Middle East. On the other hand the church pressed for the internationalization of all Jerusalem, not only its holy places. As to the United States, its vote for partition was sure but it had to be urged to exert its influence on other countries for their votes. The historic vote on 29 November 1947 was 33 to 13 in favour of separate Jewish and Arab states when Great Britain quit Palestine on 14 May 1948. After that vote there were attempts to change the decision. The United States presented a proposal in March 1948, apparently without President Truman's approval, for an international trusteeship over the country. The Palestine issue continued to be debated at the United Nations until the State of Israel was proclaimed.

News of the partition decision made Jews dance in the streets of Jerusalem, while David Ben-Gurion as head of the *yishuv* brooded in his office on the expected Arab invasion and how to meet it. An extraordinary period began with attacks by Palestinian Arabs on Jewish persons and places, answered in full by the Jewish forces. At the same time, Britain's withdrawal in stages from departments of Palestine government was countered by the detailed plans of the Jewish Agency, as the recognized representative body, for establishing a democratic Jewish state. In order to create a temporary governing structure, the Jewish Agency was dispatched to London to carry on its work there and the *Va'ad Leumi* and *Asefat Nivharim* were abolished. In their place a provisional 'people's parliament', *minhelet ha-am*, of thirty-seven members arose representing the different parties. Mapai continued its dominance and the Revisionists and communists were kept out. Palestine Jews already had schools and hospitals and some social services, and now such functions as post offices and even a meteorological service commenced operations according to plan or by continuing those of the British.

The main Jewish effort of course had to be invested in defence against Arab determination to prevent the state's establishment. The Jews had been stockpiling weapons for years, besides those brought home by demobilized Second World War soldiers. They made desperate efforts to secure more arms from America and, at this juncture, from Czechoslovakia. A massive conscription of able-bodied males raised Haganah's ranks from 12,000 to 22,000, organized in ten brigades with a suitable command structure. Besides, about 20,000 Jewish volunteers came from abroad, many of them Second World War veterans with important technical skills. To be sure, much about Haganah was hasty and improvised, but its fighting spirit was indomitable. Palestinian Arabs recruited no more than 12,000, a rather ill-disciplined ragtag group, many from neighbouring countries. Vast was the contrast between the vigorous, well-directed Jewish steps to establish a state and the negligible efforts of the Palestine Arabs. While the British still ruled, Arab armies from neighbouring states had to stay out and Palestine Jewry readily overcame Arab attacks by April 1948. By that time there was a sizeable Arab exodus, mainly of urban and middle-class people.

The great historic moment arrived on 14 May 1948. On that day the British flag was finally lowered and all British personnel, headed by the last High Commissioner, Sir Alan Cunningham, boarded ship at Haifa and left the country. In Tel Aviv the 'people's parliament' and representative figures assembled at the Tel Aviv Museum on Rothschild Boulevard to hear David Ben-Gurion read the 'scroll of independence', and then affixed their signatures. The document itself recited the Zionist understanding of Jewish history, as a people which always hoped and believed it would return to its historic homeland. On the strength of the Jewish people's 'national and intrinsic right' and the United Nations resolution the Jewish state was proclaimed and named Israel. The scroll of independence was a secular document. Objections that there was no religious reference were satisfied by mentioning faith in the 'Rock of Israel'.

This was the Jewish state, the goal of Zionism and the millenial hope of the Jewish people in secular garb. The remainder of the twentieth century would be spent in elaborating its religious and cultural meaning, encouraging immigration of Jews from all parts of the world ('Ingathering of the Exiles'), fructifying its soil, developing its economy despite puny natural resources, training its considerable intellectual power, making it a recognized member of the community of nations, and above all from the first day of its existence, defending it. Israel was founded contrary to the wishes of the men who planned and directed the foreign policies of Great Britain and the United States. They thought in hard, logical terms of avoiding Arab hostility, preventing Soviet Russia from entering the region, and ensuring the supply of oil. A Jewish state could disturb all these objects. The Jews' historical and emotional demands, especially after the Holocaust, won over public opinion, most members of the United States Congress, President Harry Truman, and politicians who understood the force of emotion. They prevailed in setting the policies of governments. The American State Department and its distinguished Secretaries of State George C. Marshall followed by Dean Acheson were not favourable to a Jewish state, but they loyally followed the president's wishes. However, the British Foreign Office after Bevin's departure long remained adamantly negative to the new state. When essential it even tried to communicate with 'the Jewish authorities in Tel Aviv' rather than recognize Israel, but Eban as Israel's representative declined to recognize such an address.

The cause of the Palestinian Arabs, politically and militarily ineffective, was taken over by the Arab states which invaded the new state the day after it was proclaimed, or more exactly the day after the British left. The armies of Egypt, Syria, Iraq, and Lebanon, expected to be saviours of the Palestinian Arab cause, showed themselves ineffective. Only the 7,400 troops of Transjordan's King Abdullah, trained and equipped by the British, performed with military competence. Abdullah had a confidential but widely suspected understanding with the Zionists not to use his army, and the Zionists in return would have no objection if he took over the unorganized Arab state—nor would his British sponsors. But the king invaded anyhow. His forces besieged Jerusalem and forced the Old City with its defenders to surrender after months of privations. The other Arab armies were driven off with heavy losses. The Syrians who came from the north were defeated in mid-1948, and after an armistice in May and June 1948 the invading Egyptian army was thrown back from the points it occupied south of Jerusalem and in the Negev. But the War of Independence also exacted a bitter toll from the Jews, who lost some 6,000 people, proportionately the costliest price in lives of any of the wars which followed.

Numerous attempts at conciliation and armistice were made, especially by committees of the United Nations. The side which was winning scorned a cease-fire, and that which was losing sought it. The most important such attempt was made by the Swede Count Folke Bernadotte as United Nations mediator, who presented two plans during 1948. The first plan barely recognized the existence of the Jewish state, while the second, which was drafted in collaboration with the British, would have taken the Negev from Israel. Both plans were unacceptable to the Jews. Bernadotte himself was assassinated by the Stern gang in September 1948. His assassins were never brought to trial.

The Jewish effort brought a costly victory, but the Palestinian Arabs lost not only lives but almost all else. Their leadership, small and limited as it was, fled the country when hostilities started and could not return, leaving their people without spokesmen or recognized representatives. The great majority of the Arabs also departed, creating the refugee problem which endures to the present day. There was no Jewish master plan at the beginning of the war to expel the Arabs, nor did the 'Arab Higher Committee' urge them to leave. About 70,000 left by February 1948, and 380,000 were gone by 15 May 1948 in many cases by expulsion and also by flight. The number of Arab refugees may have reached 750,000 by the end of the war. Most of them vegetated in camps and lived on United Nations refugee rations, while the Arab governments did virtually nothing to aid them, holding them as counters against the Israelis. The borders of Israel were expanded by the results of war, and they remained unchanged until another war, that of 1967, changed them again.

Triumphant Israel in 1949 set about tasks without precedent in Jewish history. They were exacting enough to draw world-wide interest and general sympathy. Around the globe Jewish communities were eagerly drawn into the endeavours of the new state. Few of the military volunteers remained, but vast sums of money were donated by Jews all over the world. The huge constructive work in Israel was felt as a reward after the weary duties of Second World War refugee rehabilitation. Israel ended the Jewish refugee problem.

12

A New Jewish World, 1950–1980

Seventy years of demographic transformation, Holocaust disaster, building a homeland, and founding a state, ended in 1950. A new era in the Jewish world opened. The era that had ended was one of passionate ideologies, primarily nationalist and socialist. By 1950 they lost their fire, and the new era ran its course without fervent new ideologies. Jews had achieved political, scientific, and cultural prominence in many countries during the years after 1880, but in countries not shattered by the Holocaust their cultural, political, and economic distinction after 1950 became extraordinary. The communal and socio-economic structure of the Jewish people, like their demography, was also entirely different in 1950 from what it had been in 1880. Post-Second World War prosperity mitigated or ended poverty for many and improved material life, and remorse or guilt over the Holocaust silenced most anti-Semitism.

The founding of the state of Israel, its growth and achievements, appeared a miracle in 1950. Nothing like it had ever happened in Jewish history and even in the history of the nations a parallel could not be found. For example a mother country planting colonies in distant places was quite usual, but colonies recreating the mother country had no precedent. For the long scattered and much suffering Jewish people to erect a modern state in its ancient land was breathtaking. Not only religious Jews believed this to be the beginning of the Messiah's coming.

The overwhelming disaster in Europe meant in cold terms that the Jews were no longer a mainly European people. In like terms the Holocaust destroyed the European centres of Jewish poverty and Jews were now concentrated in rich, flourishing North America and in the rapidly developing Jewish state. There and in other free countries emancipation was neither a shining hope nor a profound disappointment but something taken for granted. The homeless Jewish refugee, that all too familiar figure, disappeared when Israel took in every Jew who would come. Anti-Semitism from 1950 was no longer the menace, whether nagging or frightful, it had been during the preceding generations. But if no longer the chronic danger or worse which had set limits to Jewish life and dominated the agenda of Jewish communities, anti-Semitism by no means vanished. It was subdued in America and other liberal countries and unknown in the Jewish state. Active in some South American countries and in the Soviet Union, anti-Semitism was unofficially sanctioned and found propaganda employment under several code names. In some quarters anti-Zionism was its code name.

Judaism and its culture expanded to broader spheres than ever as Christianity and the intellectual world displayed unprecedented interest in studying Jewish thinkers and learning Jewish concepts and history. Remarkable was the change in the Roman Catholic Church, that ancient antagonist, which fundamentally reconsidered its policies towards the Jews. It started with the epoch-making Vatican Council II in 1962, in which the church's 2,000 bishops and equivalent ranks participated. Pope John XXIII, who had acted to save Jews while posted in Turkey during the war, summoned the Council and indicated that he wished to revise his church's doctrine on Judaism. Its last official word was thoroughly negative and delivered by the Council of Trent's decrees in the mid-16th century. The harshly oppressive papal rule over Roman Jewry in its ghetto until 1870 exemplified the church's ideal expressed at Trent for dealing with the Jews. The new pope named his friend Cardinal Bea to head a commission of Vatican Council II to revise doctrines on Catholic relations with other religions, especially Judaism. As an earnest of intentions the prayer to convert 'the unbelieving Jews' was stricken from the Good Friday liturgy and Catholic missionizing to Jews was discontinued, although a Jew who came on his own to be converted could be accepted. As Jewish consultants to his commission Bea asked for philosophers and scholars rather than the community leaders and public relations specialists who were proposed. Rabbis Solomon B. Freehof, Abraham J. Heschel, and Joseph B. Soloveichik constituted the panel at first, but Soloveichik soon withdrew on principle and Heschel became the principal consultant.[1]

Opposition to the new decrees on the Jews came from very conservative prelates and from bishops of Near Eastern dioceses wary of anything possibly favourable to Israel. Various drafts wound their way through the council's committees and sessions, continuing after the death of John XXIII into the pontificate of Paul VI. The new pope was less favourable to the project but by then it had a momentum of its own.[2] Attempts were made by some bishops to erase the exoneration of the Jews from the ancient charge of deicide and the request for forgiveness for past persecutions, and to insert a missionary note. Heschel reacted with deep anger, but a council plenum improved the statement substantially.

Two decrees, *Lumen gentium* (Light of the peoples) and *Nostra aetate* (In our time), both of 1965, contain the key texts of revised Catholic doctrine concerning the Jews.[3] The first document speaks of ancient Israel as the original Church of God, 'that people to which the covenant and promises were made, and from which Christ was born according to the flesh: they are a people most dear for the sake of the fathers, for the gifts of God are without repentance,' that is, are never cancelled. Ancient Israel's 'more intimate life with God [is] an event which the Church recognizes as a certain prefiguration of Christian salvation.'[4] This essentially restated traditional theology, but in a new tone of respect for Judaism and without claiming that the Jews' rejection of Jesus had caused them to forfeit the divine covenant which was theirs. *In nostra aetate* broke important new ground. Recalling Christianity's 'nourish-

---

[1] The forthcoming second volume of E. K. Kaplan and S. H. Dresner's biography of Heschel will contain important material. Some of the conclusions have kindly been conveyed to me by Rabbi Dresner.

[2] As Monsignor Montini in the Vatican curia he had endorsed Vichy legislation, including its *Statut des juifs*, which was promulgated in 1940 even before German urgings for anti-Semitic laws began. Michael R. Marrus and Robert O. Paxton, *Vichy France and the Jews* (New York, 1981), 202.

[3] Texts here are taken from the authoritative collection *Vatican Council II: The Conciliar and Post-Conciliar Documents*, ed. Austin Flannery (Boston, 1975). Another source is *The Documents of Vatican II*, ed. Walter M. Abbott (London, 1966), with observations by various commentators.   [4] Flannery, *Vatican Council II*, 359, 657.

ment' from the Hebrew Bible of the Jews and the Jewishness of Jesus and his disciples, it declared that the church

wishes to encourage further mutual understanding . . . by way of biblical and theological enquiry and friendly discussions.

Even though the Jewish authorities and those who followed their lead pressed for the death of Christ, neither all Jews indiscriminately at that time, nor Jews today, can be connected with the crimes committed during his passion. . . . the Jews should not be spoken of as rejected or accursed as if this followed from holy scripture.

[The church] reproves every form of persecution . . . [and] [r]emembering, then, her common heritage with the Jews and moved not by any political consideration, but solely by the religious motivation of Christian charity, she deplores all hatreds, persecutions, displays of antisemitism leveled at any time and from any source against the Jews.[5]

These very carefully measured words repudiated deicide and deplored anti-Semitism, linking it with persecution of all sorts but not with church doctrines. There is no request for forgiveness on account of past persecutions nor any reference to the Holocaust. The state of Israel, also unmentioned, presented the theological problem that Jews restored to their homeland in a sovereign state contradicted church doctrine.[6]

The Vatican II documents were not the final word on the Jews, since a group of devoted Catholic theologians and scholars pressed ahead with improving Catholic attitudes to the Jews. The 'Guidelines on Religious Relations with the Jews' of 1974 emphasized dialogue, which required knowledge, respect, understanding, and sensitivity to each other. Judaism, said the Guidelines, 'did not end with the destruction of Jerusalem . . . it is still nevertheless rich in religious values.'[7]

By 1980 revolutionary changes had taken place in Catholic–Jewish relations, with more in the offing. The church did away with the ancient accusation of deicide and denounced anti-Semitism. It purged such ref-

[5] Ibid. 738 ff.

[6] The theological problem became more acute in 1967, when Israel captured and annexed the Old City of Jerusalem including the remnants of the Temple, contrary to the dire prophecies in the New Testament.

[7] Abbott, *Documents of Vatican II*, 743–9.

erences from its schoolbooks, and replaced the venerable 'teaching of contempt,' (the title of Jules Isaac's influential French book) with unprecedented respect for Judaism and study of its teachings. Serious issues remained, however, notably the church's role during the Holocaust and recognition of the state of Israel. By 1980, however, the Roman Catholic Church's reconciliation with the Jews had advanced far beyond what Protestants in the World Council of Churches had done.

The phenomenon of the state of Israel excited Jews everywhere and fascinated much of the Christian world. Armed Jews fighting with fierce effectiveness to defend their country against threats to its existence phrased in genocidal rhetoric gave many Jews some psychological recompense for the helplessness of Holocaust years. Israel's defence and development concerned Jews throughout the world. As its population and power swelled, it became a factor in world affairs, receiving attention of a different sort from the sympathy or acts of kindnesss to Jews which great powers had granted or withheld in earlier decades. Israel as the tangible centre of Jewish loyalty also transformed the tone of Jewish life. Jews, including many without emotional ties to the Jewish state, began to assert a confident and sometimes aggressive Jewishness.

Demographic recovery from the Holocaust catastrophe was slow. In 1950 there were 11 million Jews in the world, of whom about 5 million lived in the United States and 900,000 in Israel. The total number of Jews in Israel continued to rise sharply but elsewhere it stagnated or decreased. In the Soviet Union, within whose borders of 1939 3,020,000 Jews lived, the Holocaust as well as Soviet annexation of large areas of eastern Europe resulted in a census count of 2,267,000 Jews in 1959 but only 1,811,000 in 1979.[8] The remainder of the Jewish people lived mainly in western Europe and Latin America. Oriental Jewry, fewer than 10 per cent of all Jews before the war, became more significant in the post-war decades. They were relatively little affected by the Holocaust and their mass emigration to Israel after 1948 where better health conditions prevailed allowed their prolific births to survive nearly intact into adulthood. The other main source of population increase was the high birth rate of ultra-Orthodox Jews. On the other hand, more than

[8] Mordechai Altshuler, *Soviet Jewry since the Second World War: Population and Social Structure* (New York, 1987), 3, 74.

conversion or complete assimilation, a low birth rate was the cause of population stagnation in other Jewish communities. World Jewish population in 1980 was estimated at 12,259,000.

The overwhelming fact of the Holocaust reached deeper than statistical facts. Before 1960 approximately, what had happened was not yet spoken of freely, perhaps because the wound was too raw and recent. As early as 1949 one observer in America feared that its memory was fading away.[9] The survivors devoted their full mental and physical energy to reconstructing their lives, which most of them accomplished impressively at least at the conscious level. To their children they said little if anything about the catastrophe and only in their later years, about 1980 and thereafter, did many of them unlock their memories and recall orally or in writing what had happened to them.[10]

After years of subdued intensity and scholarly memorial projects, the memory of the Holocaust returned with shattering force when Israeli agents located one of its main perpetrators, Adolf Eichmann. He was abducted to Israel in 1957 from Argentinian hiding for trial under an Israeli law of 1950 for the punishment of Nazi persecutors and their collaborators.[11] Not Eichmann's guilt, which was assumed, but the trial's validity aroused controversy. Argentina's protest at the abduction was settled by an apology from Israel. Ben-Gurion's declaration that Israel was trying Eichmann in the name of the Jewish people disturbed some, especially American non-Zionists. Proposals were made to bring him before some international or German court but the Germans refused, no international court could be constituted, it was unacceptable to let Eichmann go free, and so he came to judgment before three judges in the Jerusalem District Court early in 1961. As he sat in a bulletproof glass booth the chronicle of the Holocaust was unrolled before an attentive Israeli and world audience through the testimony of dozens of

---

[9] Abraham G. Duker, 'Comments,' made at Conference on Problems of Research in the Study of the Jewish Catastrophe [the term then used], 3 April 1949, *Jewish Social Studies*, 12/1 (Jan. 1950), 79–82. This was perhaps the first such event, and the papers presented there are models of scholarship.

[10] A sensitive account is William B. Helmreich, *Against All Odds: Holocaust Survivors and the Successful Lives They Made in America* (New York, 1982).

[11] A full popular account is Moshe Pearlman, *The Capture and Trial of Adolf Eichmann* (New York, 1963).

expert witnesses and victims. Ben-Gurion wanted Israelis, especially youth, to hear it all, as they could on radio. The world audience and legal opinion were satisfied that a proper trial took place. Eichmann was found guilty, sentenced to death, and after appeal was denied he was hanged on 2 May 1962. (This is Israel's only capital punishment to the present day.) Through the case the Holocaust entered Jewish public discourse and also inspired the expansion of research on the Holocaust. The trial granted many survivors psychic release to speak at last of their experiences.

Lives could never be recovered, but the enormous damage inflicted by Nazi Germany on Jews' health and careers, not to mention their property, could in some measure be compensated. The robbery or destruction of Jewish communities' property, including synagogues, schools, and libraries as well as money, hospitals, and cemeteries, demanded reparations where restitution was impossible.[12] Chaim Weizmann presented the original request to the allied powers in 1945, and Moshe Sharett, foreign minister of Israel, subsequently submitted a demand for $1,500 million (£357 million) to be paid by Germany, reckoning a cost of $3,000 (£714) for each of the 500,000 refugees received in Israel. In September 1951 Chancellor Konrad Adenauer of the recently founded (1949) Federal Republic of Germany, after reaching an understanding with Nahum Goldmann, co-chairman of the Jewish Agency and president of the World Jewish Congress, and with the approval of all parties in the Bundestag, offered to negotiate on reparations with representatives of Israel and the Jewish people. Adenauer carefully declared that 'unspeakable crimes have been committed in the name of [not *by*] the German people calling for moral and material indemnity, both with regard to the individual harm done to Jews and to the Jewish property for which no legitimate claimants still exist.'[13] Israel's claims on behalf of its refugees were represented by the Jewish Agency, and those of Diaspora Jewry for $500 million (£119 million) were spoken for by the

[12] A concise account is Ronald W. Zweig, *German Reparations and the Jewish World: A History of the Claims Conference* (Boulder, Colo., 1987). The exchange rate at the time was $4.20 = £1.

[13] Ibid. 9. Of the total sum, the communist German Democratic Republic was asked to pay $500 million. It ignored this request, disclaimed responsibility for the Nazi past, and never paid any reparations.

Conference on Jewish Material Claims established by twenty-two major Jewish organizations shortly after Adenauer spoke. The use of 'material' meant to emphasize that for immeasurable moral damage there could be no reparation. It was on moral grounds, however, that there was continuous, bitter Jewish opposition to all dealings with Germany, however it disavowed its Nazi past. When the proposal to negotiate with Germany came before Israel's Knesset for approval in January 1952, the then opposition leader Menachem Begin denounced it to a demonstration outside the Knesset building in terms which incited a physical assault on that body.

After Knesset approval the negotiations were carried on in Luxembourg in an atmosphere of studied reserve. The Diaspora's Jewish negotiators were Goldmann, the oil magnate Jacob Blaustein who headed the American Jewish Committee, and the Joint Distribution Committee's executive head Moses Leavitt. Felix Shinar with Giora Josephthal represented the Jewish Agency. The cosmopolitan Goldmann's suppleness and political skill made him the central figure in the entire, often tortuous negotiation process even though he lacked patience for the endless details. It was agreed to negotiate reparations to Israel separately from those to Diaspora Jewry, and that two-thirds would go to Israel and one-third to the Diaspora. A separate, additional matter was the lifetime pensions paid by the German government to persons harmed in the Holocaust. They had to be applied for by victims, who could have the help of lawyers arranged by the United Restitution Organization. Many survivors, however, refused to apply for German money. The total agreed upon in the group negotiations was DM 450 million or $110 million (£26 million) for the Diaspora, far less than the requested $500 million (£119 million), while Israel was to receive $845 million (£203 million). There were strict rules concerning payment and accounting for money spent, which were carefully adhered to. For example, money paid to kibbutz members could not follow the usual *kibbutz* rules but had to remain individual property, given to the member if he quit the *kibbutz*. On the other hand, the Israel–Diaspora financial ratio was adjusted internally.

Since the Germans were unable to pay in foreign currency, instead an Israeli purchasing mission resided in Germany which ordered German products, especially of capital goods, for shipment home. Despite the bitter protests just mentioned German reparations gave huge assistance to the struggling Israeli economy. Most reparations money for the Diaspora went to aid Holocaust refugees in many countries, and to reconstruct Jewish communities stricken by Nazi Germany. Claims Conference relief funds were administered by the Joint Distribution Committee on account of its unequalled experience in world-wide Jewish relief. Some of the money, however, was earmarked for cultural projects undertaken by scholarly survivors and organizations. The Conference on Jewish Material Claims was deeply interested in commemorating the Holocaust, and hence it subsidized the erection of monuments in several countries. It also made sizeable grants to the scholarly Yad Vashem, established in Israel in 1953 as the institution for Holocaust history and for education about the history of that dread period.

Regions of Diaspora

In the Soviet Union and the United States, which were locked in the cold war from the end of the Second World War until the Soviet Union began its collapse in the late 1980s, Jewish communities lived under very different conditions. Yet there were suggestive similarities in the respective social development of these, the two largest Jewish communities in the post-war world. Both were leaving their Jewish language, Yiddish, and adopting Russian and English respectively. Russian and American Jews were enrolling in higher education *en masse* as a means to social and economic advancement. To a great extent they sought careers in the professions. American and Soviet Russian Jews settled in the largest cities of their countries where their birth rate and population growth declined and intermarriage grew.

About 1.6 million Soviet Jews were lost to Nazi genocide, 200,000 died as Russian soldiers including prisoners of war who were murdered, and an uncounted number succumbed to wartime conditions of disease and starvation besides natural causes. The greatest Holocaust losses came in the small cities of western Russia, the Ukraine, and the annexed Baltic states, where much of traditional Jewish life still survived. The open assertion of Jewishness which was allowed during the Second World War had encouraged the expectation of better post-war times for Jewish cultural and communal life. These were sharply negated as the cold war set in and Soviet Russia adopted exclusive Great Russian nationalism, persecuting the slightest suspicion of dissent. The Jewish Anti-Fascist Committee was abruptly shut down, most of its members were arrested, and its leader, the noted actor Solomon Mikhoels, died in a staged 'accident'. Jewish institutions and all things Yiddish also ceased; Hebrew and Zionism were long since proscribed. A few synagogues were allowed to function, with their officials often serving as informers.

Russian aid and sympathy for the new Israel continued until 1954 but had no reflection within Russia. In fact, the mass of Jews who happily but silently surrounded Israel's first ambassador, Golda Meir, in a Moscow street (there is a photograph of the scene) provoked anger and suspicion in the Kremlin. The Soviet Union's east European satellites behaved similarly. In 1952 satellite Czechoslovakia tried the pro-Communist Israeli Zionist Mordecai Oren for 'spying' under the auspices of the comdemned American Jewish Joint Distribution Committee. He was imprisoned and Rudolf Slansky, a party leader and a Jew without Jewish affiliation, was hanged as a 'spy'. Starting in 1948 the Soviet regime expressed the anti-Semitism it supposedly rejected by constantly assailing 'cosmopolitans', often expanded to 'rootless cosmopolitans', the recognized code term for Jews. Satirical as well as serious articles appeared in the press exposing the 'cosmopolitans' as crooks, exploiters, and evaders of military service during the war. Even in Birobidzhan, officially the Jewish Autonomous Territory, Yiddish was largely suppressed and Jewish officials, labelled 'cosmopolitans', were replaced with Russian functionaries. At the peak of the campaign other nationalities underwent similar repression. The Communist Party line was enforced in cultural and scientific fields, such as the domination of genetics by the charlatan Lysenko or the disgrace of the composers Prokofiev and Shostakovich. In his last years the ageing dictator Stalin, the object of hysterical adulation by Communist masses and their sympathizers, reached directly into Jewish life with the arrest and killing of twelve prominent Yiddish writers in August 1952. There is also evidence that

Stalin was planning mass expulsion of Russian Jews into Siberia. Early in 1953 nine physicians were arrested, six of whom were Jews, and accused of killing the party boss Zhdanov in 1948 and of plotting to kill Stalin himself. The Jewish physicians were charged with being 'Zionist spies'. They were saved, as was Russian Jewry, by Stalin's death in March 1953 and were exonerated soon after. Oren was not released until 1956.[14]

Stalin's successor Khrushchev, after the short interlude of Malenkov, was against Jews in a traditional, 'popular' way without Stalin's ideological trappings. He spoke of 'good' and 'bad' Jews, of some of his best friends being Jews, and of Jews married into his immediate family. Articulate Jewish consciousness was a form of dissent which the Soviet regime and its satellites would still not tolerate and sought to crush. Zionism was declared dead, but the obsessive regularity of denunciations suggested there was life in it. Soviet Russia, to be sure, unlike the Nazi regime, did not aim at all Jews. Russian Jews who conformed and did not identify with Jewish life were able to advance despite quotas on their admission to higher education, exclusion from upper-level party and government positions, and other forms of discrimination. There were rich prizes for the talented as long as they conformed politically. Some Jewish physicists, technicians, and engineers were recognized among the country's leading scientists. They enjoyed a privileged status and superior living conditions. But even David Oistrakh, Russia's greatest violinist and a Yiddish-speaking Jew, had to perform where and when musical bureaucrats dictated. Writers, whose art was in words and not in mathematical abstractions or musical tones, had a more complicated life, while serious historians preferred to study subjects where a party line did not dictate their research. Jews could be found in disproportionate numbers in all these intellectual fields.

Ordinary Jews, like Russians in general, lived a much humbler life than conforming artists and intellectuals or party bigwigs. Especially after the annihilation of the rural Crimean Jews by the Nazis the Soviet Jews became an almost entirely urban people, with a mere 1 per cent in agriculture. The Soviet Union's largest cities were also the main urban

---

[14] He thereupon wrote a memoir, *Zikhronot 'Assir Prag* (Memories of a Prague Prisoner) (Merhavyah, 1958), which still professes faith in the Communist system and blames those who 'distorted' it (Introduction).

Jewish communities: Moscow (239,000 (4.70% of total population) in 1959 and 251,000 (3.56%) in 1970), Leningrad/St. Petersburg (168,000 (5.08%) in 1959 and 162,000 (4.12%) in 1970), Kiev (153,000 (13.89%) in 1959 and 152,000 (9.32%) in 1970), and Odessa (116,000 (13%) in 1970).[15] Jewish urban population in absolute numbers declined somewhat while non-Jews continued to flow into the cities. There was no Jewish community life but it was noticed that Jews tended to concentrate in specific neighbourhoods and even, it has been reported, in particular apartment houses. They went zealously for education as the key to advancement, and advanced education could have as its reward acquiring the status of 'scientific workers'. Such persons might ascend from better-paid technicians to membership in the highly élite Academy of Sciences. In 1970 about 33% of economically active Jews had completed a university education and 38% secondary school, far more than the general population. Merely 7% of the Jews had only primary school and 14% incomplete secondary school education.[16] There were also numerous Jews in skilled occupations such as tailoring. Before the 1950s Jews generally married other Jews, but the rate of intermarriage rose steadily, especially in the Russian Republic, to more than half of marriages in which one partner was a Jew. Only a small minority of the intermarried declared their nationality to be Jewish. Direct evidence on the Jewish birth rate is lacking, but the social classes to which Jews belonged had the lowest rates of any occupational group. This was also true of the regions Jews were concentrated in. One finds accordingly a Jewish birth rate below the replacement rate as Jewish households outside oriental Russia were uniformly below 4.0 in mean size.[17]

Jewish cultural life barely existed. Research institutes, libraries, Yiddish theatre, and periodicals were closed down between 1949 and 1952. An occasional Yiddish book or a prayer book was printed in small editions. The only forbidden language in Soviet Russia was Hebrew, while Yiddish, once encouraged as the people's tongue, was also in

---

[15] Altshuler, *Soviet Jewry*, 88; Benjamin Pinkus, *The Jews of the Soviet Union: The History of a National Minority* (Cambridge, 1988), 264. There is no figure for the city of Odessa in 1959, only for its entire region. [16] Altshuler, *Soviet Jewry*, 144, table 6.3.
[17] Ibid, *Soviet Jewry*, 24–31, 37–45, presents tables of detailed statistics with skilful interpretations.

decline. Regions outside the Soviet Union before the Second World War as well as White Russia and the Ukraine were areas where the Jewish language nevertheless lasted the longest. Religious necessities such as kosher food, Passover *mazzot*, and *tallitot* (prayer shawls) were almost unobtainable. Although Jews abroad sent or brought them to Russia, they were often confiscated upon arrival. Of long-term significance was the absence of any Jewish education and the virtual impossibility of abstaining from work on Sabbaths and Jewish holidays. Quite on their own, limited groups of Habad Hasidim, loyalists of the Lubavicher rebbe, maintained Orthodox Judaism furtively.

Against this grey, oppressive background the revival of Jewish national consciousness seems almost miraculous.[18] The openly expressed euphoria of 1948 was severely repressed during the 'black years' until Stalin's death in 1953. During 'the thaw' under his successor Khrushchev there were tentative expressions and small Zionist groups which carried on underground. These activities blossomed from 1958 to 1967. There were study groups of Judaism, an international youth festival in which far-leftist Israeli youth took part, Israeli athletic teams in Russia, furtive Jewish publishing (in *samizdat*), and synagogue attendance or congregating *en masse* in the street outside on Jewish holidays. In the years until 1967 6,934 emigration permits were issued, all of eighteen before 1953.

After the late 1960s a serious Jewish national movement, mainly but not exclusively Zionist, attained high visibility. The Soviet Jewish national movement remained separate from the movement of Russian dissent in which there were Jewish participants, but both shared common sources and mutual sympathy. Fifty years of ceaseless propaganda, suppression, and frequent and brutal persecution produced conformity but also its opposite—the alienation of many from the Soviet system. Jewish awareness of discrimination, anti-Semitism and officially sanctioned anti-Semitic publications, besides the unforgettable trauma of the Holocaust, inspired a desire to emigrate or at least to express oneself openly as a Jew.

The Russian Jewish movement cautiously fostered contacts with the outside world and links with Jewish communities abroad, often by

---

[18] Yaacov Roi, *The Struggle for Soviet Jewish Emigration, 1948–1967* (Cambridge, 1991), is a full account.

means of visitors who came to teach Judaism to private groups for brief periods. Above all there was Israel, which invited applications from prospective Russian immigrants. Overseas Jewish communities and persons of good will pressed the Soviet regime loudly and relentlessly to release Jews who wanted to leave.[19] From 1954 to 1964 a mere 1,452 Jews were permitted to emigrate to Israel, but from 1968 to 1982 some 163,000 braved dismissal from work and long delays which applications to leave the Soviet Union meant. About 10,000 Jewish applicants were refused but may have been released later. Clearly the Russian regime, while still heavily repressive, ceased mass terror and was somewhat responsive to pressures from within and without. Thousands of petitions were presented to the rulers of the Soviet Union and even some street demonstrations were ventured. Despite police action and imprisonment, the Jewish movement gave evidence of the decline of Soviet power although practically no one supposed in 1980 that the Soviet Union would collapse eleven years later.

The 'Golden Exile'

Jewish communities of western Europe such as the Netherlands, Denmark, France and Italy began slowly to rebuild themselves. Much help came from the Claims Conference through the Joint Distribution Committee, assisting them to return to self-reliance, a process completed by 1955 approximately. A particularly problematic country was Germany, whose Jews included a small number of surviving native Jews, some DPs who settled there, returning German Jews, and adventurous Jews attracted by German prosperity. The new west German Federal Republic, highly sensitive to Germany's foul reputation in the world, acted energetically to suppress anti-Semitism, although not a few of its officials had Nazi records which they claimed to disavow. The new German regime treated the Jewish community generously, aiding it to rebuild synagogues and other destroyed institutions besides the vast programme of pensions and reparations.

[19] Pinkus, *Jews of the Soviet Union* 251, 315.

Victorious Great Britain, bankrupted by the war and about to give up its empire, likewise needed years to recover, simply to clear the rubble of bombings and erect new buildings. On the other hand, the fruits of post-war prosperity, finally coming after the era of strict food rationing and austerity, were distributed more equitably than in earlier times. This meant that the average Jew, like his or her fellow Briton, lived better than before the war. The Jewish community of Britain was no longer dominated by a few affluent old families. New wealth, mainly of recent east European immigrant descendants with deeper Jewish commitment than most of the old ruling circle, largely took over the Jewish community. The traditional institutions of the community continued, with the addition of strong Zionist or pro-Israel activity. There was some immigration to Britain but substantial emigration, mostly to Commonwealth countries and the United States for greater economic opportunities, and to Israel. Besides, a low birth rate and considerable intermarriage helped to lower the Jewish population of Britain from about 450,000 just after the Second World War[20] to perhaps 350,000 in 1980.[21] London was by far the dominant local community, and its proportion of the country's Jewish population continued to increase. The Anglo-Jewish tradition of lax but official communal orthodoxy was challenged from two sides—a rising movement towards stricter Orthodoxy and the increasing strength of Liberal and Reform Judaism. The Jewish community, partly out of concern with defections and intermarriage, began to pay serious attention to Jewish education. Anti-Semitism in Britain existed, but it was associated in public opinion with hated, defeated Nazism. It did not hold back the distinguished careers enjoyed by many Jews in politics, business, law, literature, and the arts and sciences.

The most striking development in European Jewry was that of French Jewry, which numbered about 225,000 in 1950 after losing about 75,000 in the Holocaust and gaining some immigrant displaced persons. The loss in the Holocaust, demoralizing in itself, was made more so for

[20] Hannah Neustatter, 'Demographic and Other Statistical Aspects of Anglo-Jewry', in Maurice Freedman (ed.), *A Minority in Britain: Social Studies of the Anglo-Jewish Community* (London, 1955), 55–79.

[21] Authoritative surveys mainly by B. A. Kosmin, quoted in Geoffrey Alderman, *Modern British Jewry* (Oxford, 1992), 321–2.

having been efficiently organized by French, not German, police in the land of the revolutionary tradition where Jewish emancipation had once begun. Thousands of assimilated French Jews changed names and left the Jewish community after the war. The change in the bleak picture came with the arrival during the late 1950s and 1960s of Jews expelled from Egypt and those who were French citizens and left France's former dependencies in north Africa for France. By 1980 there were 700,000 Jews in France, the large majority Sefardic and oriental in the country where Ashkenazic Jewry had originated early in the Middle Ages. The government, which granted aid to them as 'repatriates', distributed these Jews throughout France. Marseilles, Lyons, Nice, Strasbourg, and Toulouse became major communities and the number of Jewish localities rose from 128 to 293. Despite the policy of avoiding the placing of 'repatriates' in Paris, thousands moved there. These Jews from Tunisia, Algeria, and Morocco included many professionals but were largely a Jewish proletariat, following the one-time proletariat of east European immigrants.

The new French Jewry was far more assertive as Jews than its predecessors, even employing a once unthinkable 'Jewish vote'. New synagogues and community centres were opened for them by the native Jewish community in many places, and to accommodate them some synagogues' form of worship changed from Ashkenazic to Sefardic. Jewish study became popular, and courses on Jews and Judaism entered the curriculum of French universities. France was warmly pro-Israel from the mid-1950s, but a gradual turn towards the Arabs took place under the regime of Charles de Gaulle from 1958 to 1968. His praise of Israel after the Six Days War as a 'warrior determined to expand' and of the Jewish people as 'an élite people, self-confident and dominating' seemed to suggest anti-Semitism and stirred a great storm. The kingly president, who very rarely troubled to explain himself, did so somewhat apologetically to the chief rabbi.[22] The French New Left turned violently against Israel in the name of Arabs but general public opinion favoured Israel.

In shining contrast, the decades from 1950 to 1980 were fine years for

[22] De Gaulle's ill-considered praise was meant genuinely. In his writings he speaks in precisely those terms of his own France during her finest hours.

the Jews of the United States. Their numbers increased from approximately 5 million to 5.8 million thanks more to larger family size than to limited post-war immigration. Directly after the war, President Truman's executive order gave displaced persons preference in the unused quotas of their native lands. This well-meaning order became enmeshed in bureaucracy and helped little and it was superseded by legislation. However, the first Immigration Act, passed in 1948, was covertly anti-Semitic. It specifically favoured *Volksdeutsche*—Germans from east European countries, among whom were Nazis—and minimized the number of Jews eligible to immigrate by setting the eligibility deadline at a date before most Jewish displaced persons entered the American zone of Germany. Truman signed the Act reluctantly while denouncing its discriminatory character. After his victory in the 1948 presidential election, a new law passed in 1950 treated Jews fairly by altering the deadline to a later date. Altogether some 200,000 Jewish displaced persons entered the United States under these Acts.[23] Other Jewish immigration to the United States was relatively small, consisting mainly of arrivals from Israel, Cuba, and some from Russia. In 1957 there was a surge of Hungarian immigration after the failure of the Hungarian uprising of November 1956. Unlike the earlier era of mass immigration, post-war immigrant influence on American Judaism extended only to the Orthodox, especially the ultra-Orthodox and Hasidic sector who came from Hungary.

The 1950s were a decade of falling discriminatory barriers as discrimination in employment declined sharply. The American economy's need for labour encouraged prejudice in the workplace against Jews and other minority groups to be discarded. Jews continued to be lawyers, accountants, civil servants, and teachers. Now, however, they could secure jobs in banks, business corporations, insurance companies, large law firms, and many hospitals which had been virtually shut to them. No less important in ending employment discrimination was a series of state and federal laws and court decisions, and a broad change in public opinion which opened the gates for Jews and other formerly excluded minorities. Jewish community organizations led the struggle for fair

---

[23] A full account is Leonard Dinnerstein, *America and the Survivors of the Holocaust* (New York, 1982).

employment practices not only for Jews but for Americans generally. Even more than Jews the most noteworthy gainers were Blacks, who long suffered the severest discrimination. Universities and professional schools abandoned quotas on Jewish admissions. Besides, the vast expansion of higher education required a great increase in staff. Appointments to university faculties, long rare for Jews, became common as the foremost universities appointed Jewish scholars and scientists in recognizable numbers.

After a full post-war generation of general prosperity and careers open to talents, American Jews were employed approximately one-third in professional occupations, one-third as businessmen (categorized statistically as managers and proprietors), and others, including skilled labour, clerks and salesmen who constituted the final third. Jews were about 20 per cent of American lawyers, physicians, and dentists, far beyond their proportion of hardly 3 per cent in the American population, and were nearly as prominent among accountants and independent businessmen. Altogether Jews were the most prosperous ethnic or religious group in America. But there also was a stratum of poor Jews—sick, handicapped, ill-trained, or just unfortunate.

American Jews gained a remarkable place in American cultural life. The rosters of symphony orchestras showed about a third to half their musicians bearing Jewish names. Solo performers of serious music were also considerably Jewish. The proportion of Jewish opera singers was lower—this was a famous Italian speciality. The composers of classical music included Aaron Copeland and the protean Leonard Bernstein, celebrated as a popular and classical composer, pianist, conductor, and musical educator. In the new popular music such as rap and rock, Jews were less conspicuous than they had been in one-time Tin Pan Alley. The American stage was also extensively Jewish. Impresarios of every sort were mostly Jewish, and so were playwrights and the composers of musical theatre. Producers of films were so disproportionately Jewish that defence against allegations of Jews in control of American films became a concern before the Second World War, but Jewish prominence in the post-war television industry made no waves. Journalism, not markedly Jewish, also had Jewish representation, especially in such newspapers of world influence as the *New York Times* and the *Washington*

Post. When one turns to the arts and sciences the number and importance of Jewish writers and critics is striking. The Jewish genre entered American literature, particularly that derived from the immigrant experience, alongside regional or other ethnic genres. Writers like Saul Bellow, awarded the Nobel prize and many other honours, Bernard Malamud and Philip Roth exemplified this trend. The Yiddish writer I. B. Singer in English translation became an outstanding American literary figure; he too won a Nobel prize. The leaders of literary criticism were Jews, especially those coming from the so-called New York intellectuals— Lionel Trilling, Alfred Kazin, Clement Greenberg, and Irving Howe. Characteristically they were preoccupied with the connections between literature and social and political issues. Jews were also prominent in the social sciences and humanities, particularly as sociologists and economists and to a lesser extent as historians. On the other hand, Hebrew and Yiddish literary creativity faded away owing to linguistic assimilation in the case of Yiddish and the virtual monopoly of Israel on the Hebrew reading market. Turning to sports we find few Jewish athletes, but Jews were the owners of many professional teams in various sports. It was American Blacks who held the prominent position in sports that Jews had in the arts and sciences.

During the 1960s the little populated field of Jewish studies was long dominated by a few giant figures. A few endowed university chairs existed, but only from the 1960s did Jewish studies begin to take root in American universities. The foremost Talmudist was Saul Lieberman, who came from Israel in 1940 to the Jewish Theological Seminary as the successor to Louis Ginzberg. Lieberman uniquely combined mastery of both textual analysis and classical culture which he showed was reflected in the world of the Talmud. Harry A. Wolfson at Harvard was foremost in the study of Jewish philosophy including its relation to the development of Christian thought, and as the source of the medieval synthesis of faith and reason. At Columbia Salo W. Baron's voluminous studies in Jewish history focused on the interlocking influences of Jewish society and religion, and of Jews with their non-Jewish environment. Shlomo D. Goitein, an arrival of 1950 from Israel, cultivated Judaeo-Arabic studies in works of vast scope. They and other scholars in Jewish studies no longer worked in isolation from American scholarship. Those who followed them were mostly native Americans who had some notable achievements but did not attain their predecessors' monumental accomplishments. Jewish scholarship in Great Britain before 1980 focused on Anglo-Jewish history and ancient Judaism, while that in France, after wartime ravages, resumed the study of French Jewish history in a much more critical spirit than yesteryear. Other areas were cultivated by a new group of French scholars.

American Judaism's impressive development in the decades after the Second World War was achieved thanks largely to social trends within the Jewish community and in America generally.[24] The old tension between the German and east European stock faded away as the native-born majority of American Jews constantly grew. As the prospering third generation of east European immigrant descendants reached maturity, in the course of nature they acquired decisive influence in the Jewish community. After relative immobility during the Great Depression and war years American Jews joined the white middle-class migration out of the cities into often newly built suburbs. The cities with their congestion and social and racial problems were left behind for fresh, uncrowded surroundings. Hardly any Jews remained within such cities as Newark, Detroit, Washington, and Cleveland after 1965, and city synagogues followed their Jews to the suburbs. Together with newly founded suburban congregations they attracted Jews who had not been affiliated in the city but felt the necessity of affiliation when they moved to towns which stood where a few years earlier there had been potato fields. Besides, for Jewish education, which was now desired, the children of suburban families had only the synagogue's afternoon school to go to. Suburban Jewish community centres, whose main activity was recreation, supplemented and sometimes rivalled the synagogues. Orthodox synagogues and their people for the most part stayed in the city, and so did some élite Reform synagogues. The Conservatives gained the most

---

[24] Articles by Jack Wertheimer in the *American Jewish Year Book* admirably synthesize the communal picture: 'Recent Trends in American Judaism' (vol. 89, 1989, pp. 63–162), 'Jewish Organizational Life in the United States since 1945' (vol. 95, 1995, pp. 3–98), and 'Current Trends in American Jewish Philanthropy' (vol. 97, 1997, pp. 3–92). All contain valuable historical perspective. The *Year Book* is an indispensable source on American Jewry.

from suburbanization and became the largest but not the best defined Jewish denomination.

Orthodox Judaism overcame the weakness in its image as a religion for poor foreign immigrants. Its overlap with the Conservatives, exemplified in numerous congregations and in the careers of many rabbis, was also discarded. American Orthodoxy, whose leader was the eminent philosopher and Talmudist Joseph B. Soloveichik, defined itself more precisely. Thus, an Orthodox synagogue could now be identified by its *mehitza* separating men and women during worship. Separation of the sexes became more widespread in other spheres as well. The modern orthodox, as they described themselves, claimed to be fully American and also, unlike Conservative and Reform counterparts, to represent genuine Judaism. Orthodoxy became more rigorous than it had ever been in America. Even so, by the 1960s sectarian or Hasidic Orthodoxy was questioning the orthodoxy of modern Orthodoxy. These sectarian Orthodox were largely post-war European immigrants at first. Even with an increasing number of native Americans in their midst they dwelled close together and avoided accommodation with American life. They gladly employed American technology while minimizing secular education and viewing negatively Zionism and the state of Israel. In a unique position was the *Habad* Hasidic sect,[25] which carried on missionary work for Orthodoxy among Jews and skilfully employed publicity and the mass media under its highly charismatic leader, the Lubavicher rebbe Menahem M. Schneerson. The characteristic institution of Orthodoxy was less synagogues than yeshivot, which not only educated children with sexes separated but fostered long-term, intensive Talmud study by young men. Its foremost institution was Yeshiva University, which combined secular with yeshiva studies. A large number of Orthodox young men attended a yeshiva for some period in America or Israel. Modern Orthodoxy also took up long neglected women's education, already practised by the other denominations.

Reform Judaism expanded from its solid, established base. Against strong opposition by a 'classical Reform' minority most congregations

[25] This is an acronym for *H*okhmah (wisdom), *B*inah (understanding), *D*aat (knowledge), the principles of its first rebbe Shneur Zalman of Lyady (d. 1812). The American rebbe was seventh in the dynastic succession.

resumed some long discarded traditional ceremonies. Zionism was no longer the divisive issue it had been, and the extreme anti-Zionist American Council for Judaism, of Reform orientation, shrivelled. Reform sought to establish itself in Israel against bitter Orthodox opposition. As the denomination most affected by intermarriage, it altered the definition of a Jew by accepting paternal and not only maternal descent. The issues agitating Reform hardly touched traditionalist Conservative Judaism. That movement's swelling membership in its approximately 800 affiliated synagogues included only a small minority who observed such fundamentals of tradition as Sabbath and *kashrut* despite its professed principles. Synagogue attendance was quite small except on major holidays. Conservative Judaism's scholarly product, however, was impressive and it enjoyed some educational success particularly in summer camps and youth programmes. The denomination also committed itself to day school education. Its rabbinic leaders were themselves quite traditional and the atmosphere at its central institution, the Jewish Theological Seminary, was still more so. The Conservative rabbinate attempted to apply its principle of adapting *halakhah* to modern needs by such measures as promulgating a slightly revised prayer book[26] and solving the classic problem of the *agunah*[27] by a supplementary clause in the marriage document (*ketubah*). By 1980 the new movement for women's equal religious rights became forceful and the ordination of women as rabbis was a rising issue.

Conservatives and Reform alike, and unaffiliated Jews particularly, were affected by the rising intermarriage rate. Among the Orthodox the rate was very low. It was an ironic sign of Jewish acceptance into American society that objections from the non-Jewish side, which was sometimes wealthy or distinguished, to marrying a Jew were few and muted if any. Only a minority of intermarriages resulted in the conversion of the non-Jewish partner to Judaism and the raising of offspring as Jews. Most intermarriages brought dissociation from the Jewish community, although intermarried Jews seldom converted to Christianity. By 1980 every third marriage of a Jew had a non-Jewish partner.

---

[26] The English translation was considerably more revised than the Hebrew text.

[27] A 'chained' wife whose husband disappeared or refused to give her a document of divorce (*get pitturin*), which prevented her from remarrying.

The American Jewish community became financially vast even when Jewish hospitals are not included. Several thousand rabbis, teachers, social workers, executives, clerks, secretaries and maintenance workers were in its employ, generating a yearly payroll of perhaps 3 billion dollars. Private businesses deriving livelihoods from Jews such as manufacturing and selling kosher food products, catering, managing Jewish resort hotels, funeral establishments, and cemeteries, did more than 3 billion dollars of business yearly. The value of synagogues and other community buildings had to be tens of billions. All this had no central organization. Most local communities had a community council whose principal power was to express Jewish public opinion. Among the major organizations informal functional arrangements prevailed but with rivalry and duplication. Thus, the American Jewish Committee, American Jewish Congress, Anti-Defamation League, and (in a minor way) the Jewish War Veterans were preoccupied with combating anti-Semitism and improving relations between Jews and other ethnic and religious groups. They were in the forefront of the struggle for equal rights for Blacks in the United States. All jockeyed for prominence and funds, and developed individual philosophies and methods. Thus, the pro-Zionist American Jewish Congress abandoned its aspiration to be a Jewish congress of sorts, but fostered liberal legislation, initiated court cases, and followed a rigorous interpretation of Church–State separation. Its rival, the older and better supported non-Zionist American Jewish Committee, was professedly élitist, moderate in its liberalism, separationist but not doctrinaire on Church–State issues, and preferred skilful work behind the scenes for objectives similar to those of the Congress. It had excellent information and library services. The Committee's prominent monthly *Commentary* had a counterpart in the Congress quarterly *Judaism*.

Local Jewish institutions were supported locally, but a few which catered to a broader clientele such as hospitals in Denver and Los Angeles conducted nation-wide fund raising. The central institutions of the religious denominations for the most part raised money 'within the family'. However, Brandeis University, a newcomer, raised independently tens of millions. Cultural and educational purposes had to get by with skimpy funds.

American Jewry possessed a large fund-raising
local needs and especially for the United Jewish A[
prodigious amounts for Israel and overseas needs. Lo
had long maintained federations for unified fund rai
which gradually expanded their work into commun   ....ng. The
United Jewish Appeal likewise began in 1939 as the fund-raising federation for overseas needs of the Joint Distribution Committee and the
United Palestine Appeal, and the smaller National Refugee Service for
refugees arriving from overseas. The United Israel (successor to Palestine) Appeal combined the appeals of the Jewish National Fund and
Keren Hayesod. These organizations carried on rivalry and politicking
for larger shares of the funds raised, and intricate arrangements were
devised for dividing them. The contentious issues derived from the Jewish situation: overseas versus domestic needs; the dividing of overseas
funds between European relief (Joint Distribution Committee) and
building Israel (United Israel Appeal). During the Second World War the
money available to the Joint for its rescue work was tragically limited,
but after the war sums unprecedented in Jewish or American philanthropy poured in. The United Jewish Appeal raised $35 million in 1945,
but its income skyrocketed to $200 million in 1948. This amount and
that raised in following years owed much to devoted volunteer workers
and famously effective high-pressure techniques, and to American prosperity. But the fundamental reason was the deep feeling over Holocaust
survivors in Europe and their resettlement in Israel, and the needs and
perils confronting the new state. The years Israel was at war—1948,
1956, 1967, and 1973—became the peak years of American Jewish fund-
raising. Thus, annual giving in the 1950s and early 1960s was $110
million to $130 million, but the Six Days War raised it to $318 million
and the Yom Kippur War of 1973 brought $686 million into the 1974
campaign which began soon after.[28] Yet even in the best years hardly
50 per cent of adult American Jews donated. In addition to the United
Jewish Appeal various Israeli institutions carried on American appeals.
Yet this too does not complete the assistance to Israel, since the purchase of Israel Bonds was also regarded as a philanthropy. Actually Israel

[28] If one reckons the declining value of the dollar the $200 million of 1948 was not
less than the $686 million of 1974.

Bonds was an investment which unfailingly paid interest and redeemed principal at maturity. An important development once Israel ceased being a controversial subject and became a common American Jewish interest was the unification of previously separate local campaigns for federations and the United Jewish Appeal. In one city after another the two often rival causes were harnessed together in a single campaign. This process began in the 1950s and did not end until campaigns in the largest community, New York City, combined in 1973.

Most of these sums, and those for the maintenance of the American Jewish community, came from a small number of rich men (but seldom women). Not surprisingly they had the decisive voice in their local community's allocation of the money it had raised. They received flattering attention when they visited Israel. American Jewry as a voluntary body not supported by taxes depended on such donations to maintain its communal life; in its deepest concerns the community was not and probably could not be a democratic body. However, there was articulate Jewish public opinion expressed through the pulpit, the Jewish press, and public meetings and lectures.

Israel was American Jewry's greatest cause. It was no longer the preserve of the American Zionist movement, which dwindled once American Jewry as a whole took over support for Israel. American Zionists' failure to undertake *aliyah* practically disqualified them in Israeli eyes as true Zionists. American Jews not only gave money but bought Israel Bonds on a massive scale as an investment and also conducted exhaustive lobbying. American presidents, secretaries of state, and every congressman and senator were made fully aware of Israel's needs and the aid the United States was urged to provide. Lobbying, however, did not create the deep American sympathy with Israel but built upon it. Israel was regarded as a democratic state—the only one in the Middle East—which took in refugees from the Holocaust about whom the democratic world felt guilt, and was a David under attack by bullying Goliath neighbours.

The Jewish State

The first decree of the new state, an appendix to its declaration of independence, was the abolition of the British White Paper of 1939. Mass immigration began immediately. The 650,000 Jews of 14 May 1948 numbered 716,000 six months later, 1,672,000 in 1957, and 1,932,000 in 1961, constituting at the time approximately 80 per cent of the country's population. Of the population increase of 1,910,000 from 1948 to 1970 62 per cent was due to immigration, including the Israel-born children of immigrants. Statistical experts calculated that without immigration after 1948 Israel's Jewish population would have been no more than 700,000 in 1952, 756,300 in 1957, and 800,000 in 1962. One far-reaching result of Jewish immigration, in Zionist terminology the 'ingathering of the exiles' (*kibbutz galuyot*), was a great increase in the country's prosperity after initial difficulties. The addition of capital from loans and donations enabled Israel's vast increase in manpower to be productive, to satisfy increased domestic demand and to reach foreign markets.

Considering its tremendous costs and difficulties there had to be deep faith in the principle of unlimited Jewish immigration. The first immigrants after independence were the 25,000 'illegal' immigrants detained by the British in Cyprus. By the end of 1948 another 103,000 arrived, mostly Holocaust survivors from displaced persons' (DP) camps and elsewhere in Europe. These survivors whether coming alone or as new families carrying babies born in DP camps were worn and penniless but hopeful. They were mostly Jews originally from Poland and the Baltic states, and there were also Romanian Jews who were permitted to leave that country. In that first year alone 203,000 Jews arrived, and from 14 May 1948 to the end of 1951, 684,000 Jews flooded the country, doubling its Jewish population. They were almost evenly divided between immigrants from Europe and America (few) on one hand and Asia and Africa on the other. The European survivors of the Holocaust followed the method of mutual aid, especially by those who came from the same home town. Earlier arrivals helped the later ones with temporary housing and referral to jobs, and the entire group assimilated quite rapidly into the new society. Many hastened their absorption by military service alongside native Israelis during the War of Independence. By the end of 1957, a little less than a decade since the state was founded, 898,000 Jews had come to Israel. The Jewish population of Israel was then 1,672,000, besides 213,000 non-Jews. Between 1957 and 1969 398,000 more Jews came, and the state's Jewish population at the end of 1970 was 2,559,000, of whom 422,000 were not Jews.

Israel was not satisfied with the merely negative step of abolishing the White Paper. In 1950, as immigrants were pouring in, it enacted the Law of Return which proclaimed that 'every Jew has the right to come to this country as a settler'. This was a cardinal principle of the Jewish state which was constantly reiterated in public and private. Ben-Gurion, who expressed Israel's Zionist ideology in this as in many other matters, declared that the ingathering of the exiles alone justified the Jewish state. Besides, Israel needed Jewish population. Great efforts were made to teach at least basic Hebrew to all newcomers by using many innovative methods which attracted international attention from linguistic experts. Foreign as were these arrivals in culture and language, Israel was sure their children would grow up as Israelis. Younger adults to age 40 could be retrained vocationally and become self-supporting while they made a productive contribution to Israeli society. The sick, aged, and handicapped had to be taken in as part of their families or as a humanitarian matter. If they had undergone the Holocaust the Joint Distribution Committee's Malben programme in Israel looked after them.

Especially dramatic were the exoduses from Yemen and Iraq, who came as cohesive groups. About 47,000 people, almost the entire Jewish community of Yemen, was allowed to leave and proceeded to Aden, from which they came by air to Israel in 1949 in an operation called Magic Carpet. Yemeni Jewry was a poor, deeply traditional community living since ancient times in a remote, little known country. They were craftsmen, especially weavers, silversmiths, and leather workers, and had lived in a fully Jewish culture with appreciable Jewish learning of a distinctive Yemeni style. Yemeni Jews had been brought to Palestine as labourers before 1914 and some lived in America. In 1950 the mass arrival of Iraqi Jewry began. They had been a prosperous, largely modern community of 125,000 people whose pedigree extended back to the

Babylonian exile of biblical times. The main city, Baghdad, was the home of 90,000 to 100,000 Iraqi Jews, where they had a distinct dialect of their own. Iraqi Jews enjoyed full rights, but the undertone of antagonism in the newly independent land rose to a peak during and after the Second World War. The establishment of Israel, considered an enemy country, undermined the Iraqi Jews' position further, and the killing of several rich and prominent Jews was a warning light. Emigration emissaries from the Jewish state operated in Iraq, at first secretly, and when its Jews at last received government permission to leave they were ready to go. They had to sign away their citizenship and leave behind nearly all their possessions. In 1950 and 1951 120,000 of Iraq's 125,000 Jews left their extensive property, took the negligible sums of money allowed them, and came to Israel by an indirect air route via Cyprus. During the peak from March to June 1951 70,000 made the trip. The Iraqi and Yemeni communities arrived *en masse* with many of their leaders, bearing rich historic traditions and a store of distinctive customs. Among the Iraqi arrivals were about 3,000 Jews from Kurdistan in northern Iraq, possessing a distinct culture and a language descended from ancient Aramaic.[29] In 1961 Israel also had about 60,000 Jews of Iranian origin, of whom some 37,000 were born there. Iranian and Indian Jewry were probably offshoots of Iraqi, one could say Babylonian, Jewry. The large majority of the Jews of Bulgaria and Libya also left their countries.

Immigration had ups and downs after the great burst of 1948–51. Thus, 1952–4, 1958–60, and 1965–8 were down years but the up years came nowhere near 1948–51 records. (Only the recent mass arrival from the tottering Soviet Union equalled it, but Israel by then had a Jewish population about 4 million and an economic level resembling western countries.) Late in the 1950s came immigration from north Africa, primarily Morocco, and from Hungary after the suppression of the 1956 uprising. Besides Jews from oriental lands, Europeans continued to arrive. After the uprisings against Communist rule in Poland and Hungary in 1956 the exit gates were opened and a mass of Jews left from those countries, 50,000 for Israel.

Merely to house and feed the immigrants and in the longer term to find or create jobs for them was an almost superhuman task. Prime

[29] Moshe Gat, *The Jewish Exodus from Iraq 1948–1951* (London, 1997).

Minister Ben-Gurion, who dominated the political scene, rejected suggestions to slow down immigration, pointing to physical dangers faced by oriental Jewry and the possibility that permission to leave their respective countries might be revoked. During the 1960s Moroccan Jewry also broke up, with its middle class mostly emigrating to France and the poor majority coming to Israel. All the time a trickle of arrivals came from western Europe and English-speaking countries. With prosperous countries to go back to not many remained, unable to take the hardships that other immigrants had to accept.

Lacking sufficient housing for the immigrant masses, the government was compelled to resort at first to tents with facilities for collective eating. It soon replaced them with temporary, slightly better 'transition camps' (*ma'abarot*), composed of rudimentary but private prefabs. Newcomers had to live there in miserable conditions of health and environment for periods up to three years until permanent, modest housing was built. Immigrant families, mainly oriental, who occupied these temporary quarters were subjected to aggressive 'Israelization' by representatives of the Jewish Agency, now responsible for bringing and absorbing (the term used) immigrants, which aimed at correcting their 'primitive' way of life. The majority of these teachers and social workers were adherents of labourite secularism. Their message was divorce from ethnic traditions and language, and detachment from religion. This was the period when the labour parties possessed triumphal self-confidence and political power, and with these convictions their functionaries dealt with immigrants. Religious parties in Israel and abroad repeatedly protested but did not have much success. Few could resist coercive Israelization then, but resentment was long-lasting until it came to open expression a full generation later. Energetic efforts were made to end the *ma'abarot*, yet some towns had their origin in these ugly settlements. By 1955 *ma'aborot* disappeared from the landscape.

The government was committed to agricultural settlement as a Zionist concept and a practical measure for growing more food. Few newcomers were willing to go to *kibbutzim*, whose collectivism and secularism (except for the few religious *kibbutzim*) repelled them, and the *kibbutzim* made little effort to broaden their social base. They drew most of their new members from their own progeny and graduates of Zionist youth movements in Israel and abroad trained for *kibbutz* life, as well as individual youngsters who came through Youth Aliyah and other programmes. To be sure the *kibbutzim* underwent a great expansion, from 149 in 1948 to 231 with 93,000 inhabitants in 1969, affiliated with four ideological movements. Newcomers, however, favoured *moshavim* where private family life and farming were combined with finances on a collective basis. The 77 existing *moshavim* of 1948 and the 269 founded thereafter until 1970 were frequently traditional in religion and way of life. They were home to 122,000 people. There was also a small *moshav shitufi* movement, more collectivist in farming than the *moshav*. During and after the *ma'abarot* period groups of new arrivals were often transported directly to the site of new *moshavim* which, with assistance, they were expected to build.

The *moshavim* had a larger population than the *kibbutzim* but lagged behind them in agricultural productivity and innovation, not to mention intellectual fertility and political influence. The *kibbutz* federations were a guarantor of government loans for their development, and affiliated *kibbutzim* received generous education budgets. Men from *kibbutzim* were prominent as officers in the Israel armed forces and in politics; one or more *kibbutznikim* (the term universally used for members) were usually found in cabinets and as many as twenty sat in the Knesset. Ideology was dominant, and *kibbutzim* split and *kibbutz* federations were founded on account of seemingly small differences in way of life and socialist principles. Gradually new, unexpected problems arose. The percentage of *kibbutz* children who remained on home turf became lower and hired labour, an almost scandalous violation of principles, became common although efforts were made in many *kibbutzim* to end it. One interesting source of labour was youths from many parts of the world, many of them not Jewish, who came as volunteers to experience collective life. A problem of a different kind arose when agriculture became secondary to industry after most *kibbutzim* set up factories and workshops whose products reached the world market. *Kibbutz* production amounted to some 12 per cent of Israel's gross national product, but the moral and political influence of *kibbutzim* slowly declined.

The summit of Israel's social and labour institutions was the Histadrut, the short name for the General Federation of Jewish Labour in

Palestine. After 1966 the 'Jewish' was omitted to indicate the equality of Arab members. With 1,038,000 members in 1969 including 319,000 housewives and youth, it was the largest organization of any description in the country. Histadrut elections were conducted under party labels and Mapai was dominant. The Histadrut was not a union in the customary sense. The functions of negotiating wages and working conditions came under a Trade Union Department, and agreements tended to cover wages in the entire economy with intricate linkages between the scales in different occupations. Most organized workers were government or government corporation employees, and the Histadrut was weak in organizing labour in the fast-growing private enterprises. The Histadrut's most important activities were in welfare and entrepreneurship. The array included its Kupat Holim health insurance which provided socialized hospital and medical treatment, and Solel Boneh, the giant builder of housing and public works which also operated abroad, besides a publishing house, sports teams and the daily newspaper *Davar*. Even before the founding of the state the Histadrut was becoming heavily bureaucratized and losing touch with its members, and this condition worsened with the years. Most members were solely interested in medical insurance, and the sight of the Histadrut's massive headquarters buildings in Tel Aviv and other cities helped to alienate them.

No country matched in tempo or proportions what the state of Israel accomplished in its first twenty years, and it did so while under constant external challenge to its very existence. World-wide public opinion was strongly pro-Israel on account of Israel's enlightened social pioneering and out of respect for previous Jewish suffering. Democratic Israel standing up to Arab dictatorships was a widespread, inspiring image. Zionist ideology, central to the state, laid great emphasis on return to the land and the indispensability of self-reliant defence. Israelis did return to the land and the soil of Israel, wasted for centuries, flowered. The new states of Africa, beset by the problems of food supply, called on experts from Israel to guide their agriculture. Israel grew much of the food it needed while also exporting the products of its agriculture.

Israel's extraordinary social and economic development and its fantastic immigration figures took place under the rule of Ben-Gurion's Mapai and behind the shield of the Israel Defence Force (*Zahal* = *Z'va*

Haganah le-Yisrael). Although Mapai never had a Knesset majority, it brought other parties into a stable coalition which the 'Old Man' headed until 1963 with a two-year break from 1953 to 1955 when the courtly, cultured Foreign Minister Moshe Sharett occupied the office. The main coalition constituents were Mapam, the United Workers Party largely controlled by the *kibbutzim* of Ha-Shomer Ha-Tsa'ir, and the religious Mizrachi and Hapoel Hamizrachi parties, soon combined as Mafdal, the National Religious Party. Mapam was pro-Russian for years despite their own Mordecai Oren's imprisonment, but continued revelations of Soviet tyranny culminating in Khrushchev's 'de-Stalinizing' speech of 1956 (revealed to the world through Israeli intelligence) brought a final break. Other parties were in and out of Mapai-led coalitions, such as the General Zionists, mainly a liberal party favouring free enterprise. The Communists, subservient to the Soviet Union, were kept out on principle. So was the 'Freedom (Herut) movement' headed by the former *Etzel* commander Menachem Begin, which was considered too extreme in its nationalism and lacking allegiance to parliamentary democracy.

All the parties especially of the left formed and reformed, allied and broke alliances. Mapai was produced by a merger of 1930, but a 'Faction B' broke off in 1944 and found its way to Ha-Shomer Ha-Ts'air and together they founded Mapam, the United (!) Workers Party. In its cabinets Mapai always held the key portfolios of defence, finance, and foreign affairs and others besides. Its leaders also headed the Histadrut and the Jewish Agency, the conduit for the immense sums donated to Israel. Moreover, Mapai appointees headed powerful government corporations in transport, housing, shipping, banking, and other fields. The 1940s and 1950s were the heyday of Mapai power, usually in coalition with Mapam and Mifdal as junior partners who received patronage crumbs. Mapam in a sense stood for the fading socialism of the leftist government. Mifdal stood for Orthodox Judaism and generally followed Mapai's leads on other issues. It succeeded in founding a religious state school system and establishing kosher food rules in government eating places, Sabbath observance in the public realm, Jewish law to govern domestic relations, exemption from military service for the comparatively few yeshiva students some of whom served anyhow, and an 'arrangement' (*hesder*) which combined army service with yeshiva study. These long-lasting religious provisions were known as the status quo. The religious establishment, headed by chief rabbis, was under Mafdal's strong influence. The *haredim*, ultra-Orthodox, avoided recognizing the state after a few years' early flirtation, and Mafdal functioned as their broker until ultra-Orthodox power grew in the late 1970s and they became independent. In contrast, most of the labourite left was secularist and considered that the new state's repudiation of the burden of *galut* tradition included religion. Yet political exigencies and nostalgic personal memories of eastern Europe where most labourite leaders originated led them, if reluctantly, to their agreements with religious parties. Their affiliated *kibbutzim*, ideological spearheads, were, however, militantly secularist. Many composed secular texts and rituals to replace religious ones for events such as Jewish holidays, boys' Bar Mitzvah, and burials. Religious persons were considered not quite Israeli. Most of the arrivals from oriental countries, however, were not strictly Orthodox, but secularism was foreign to them.

Israel's political parties competed not only over power and its rewards but over opposing visions of the state of Israel being built. Political life was intensely partisan, and parties disputed bitterly with their rivals. Each party was ruled by an almost self-perpetuating oligarchic executive, and party discipline among Knesset members and other political bodies was strict and not forgiving of dissenters. The functioning of the parties gave Israel's political life a tone resembling the states of central and eastern Europe. There was a furtiveness about some parties, especially on the left, reminiscent almost of the Russian underground under the tsars. On the other hand parliamentary government, the rule of law, and the rights of citizens, given imperfections, resembled those of a western democracy, which were also not perfect. However, in matters pertaining to state security laws were strict and secret trials could be conducted. It took a Supreme Court ruling to end newspaper censorship, a practice remaining from the British.

The powerful parties could have easily crushed Israeli democracy had they desired. The state's leaders had only superficial knowledge of western democracy, and their experience of political life was not with British or American government but with Polish dictatorship or Russian despotism. The practices of Israeli democracy derived not from the thought of Jefferson, Locke, Mill, or Lincoln but rather from the traditions of the *kehillah*. It had not been democratic in operation, but members of the community possessed an emphatic sense of equity and individual rights, and a practice of protesting energetically when these seemed to be violated. *Kehillah* oligarchs who failed to show proper regard for people's rights were inviting trouble. Like the *kehillah* Israeli democracy was procedurally weak and parties were powerful and internally secretive, but rights were respected, public opinion was articulate, and an independent, impartial judiciary functioned effectively.

Israel's political and economic life was highly politicized, but its cultural, academic and military affairs were relatively free of political interference. The Hebrew University reluctantly lost its monopoly of higher education after the religious Bar-Ilan University was established and particularly when its own Tel Aviv branches combined to found the independent Tel-Aviv University in 1964, which grew rapidly and competed with its parent. These universities along with those at Haifa and Beer-Sheba and the Weizmann Institute of Science won international reputations as scientific and scholarly centres. They gradually dropped their élite character except for the Weizmann Institute and undertook to educate masses of students for the anticipated technological society which, it was hoped, would also be cultured and Jewish. Although internal politics which occasionally burst into the open complicated university affairs, academic appointments and scientific research were generally of high quality.

Absence of politics also reigned at the Palestine Symphony Orchestra, renamed the Israel Philharmonic Orchestra, the country's foremost orchestra. Founded by the violinist Bronislaw Huberman with refugee musicians and its first concerts in 1936 conducted by the sympathetic Arturo Toscanini, the orchestra was acclaimed during its regular foreign tours. There were several lesser ensembles alongside; opera was yet to be. Habimah, the theatrical company whose origins reached back to Russian revolutionary years, continued its career in Tel Aviv with the sprightly newcomer Cameri Theatre and other troupes as well. The creative imagination of established painters and sculptors as well as newcomers celebrated the land and its people in different ways. Many institutional and entrepreneurial publishers were active, and in the 1966–9 period an annual average of 2,700 publications appeared. Lectures and performances, exhibitions and publications, numerous daily newspapers and sporting events provided Israel, despite limited funds and a small population, with a cultural diet rich enough to rival that of capital cities in the west. This cultural distinction was widely recognized and aided Israel to be recognized as a modern nation resembling the west. A cultural orientation towards the Middle East was spoken of but little realized in practice.

All this had to be backed up by tangible military force. The foundations of the Israel Defence Force (IDF) were laid in the years following the War of Independence. All fit young men except the then few yeshiva students who claimed exemption were required to serve usually for three years with shorter terms for older men who arrived as immigrants. Many of the physically handicapped argued their way into the ranks for special tasks, while many conscripts vied for places in the paratroops, the General Staff's reconnaissance, and other élite combat units. Not to serve at all was considered disgraceful and handicapped career prospects. Like the arrangement for students to combine yeshiva study with military service, there were small 'reserves' (*'atudot*) of talented young scientists, musicians, and athletes. After conscript years discharged soldiers performed reserve duty of about a month yearly. During full mobilization in the wars of 1967 and 1973 the IDF could deploy 250,000 to 300,000 reserve and conscript soldiers. A law to conscript young women for shorter terms of non-combat service met with impassioned religious opposition on grounds of morality, and a conscience clause allowed them to substitute 'national service' for military duty. The IDF's ethos of aggressive response to border provocations and raids, and seizing the offensive in combat, was incorporated into the training of soldiers. The army repeatedly proved itself in Israel's wars, often to world-wide applause and the respect of military staffs in many countries.

Israel set itself the goals of entry into the society of nations and close links with the Jewish world. It was admitted to the United Nations in 1949, and by then had received recognition from more than fifty countries. The Arab states demonstratively boycotted Israel at the world forum, but the gifted eloquence of Israel's ambassador Abba Eban, later foreign minister, filled the house anyhow when he spoke, especially at times of crisis. Israel also sought to join other international bodies, whether scholarly and scientific or athletic.

At the same time Israel was the acknowledged centre of the Jewish world. At first its centrality was ideological and philanthropic, but by approximately 1970 its Jewish population was approaching that of the United States and Israeli centrality was obvious. Declarations by Ben-Gurion and other leaders that the Diaspora had no future were in accord with a tenet of Zionist ideology which not all Zionists accepted but Israeli leaders believed. Such declarations and accompanying calls for *aliyah* from the west including the United States irritated Americans and others, especially wealthy non-Zionist Jews whose political and financial support was wanted. The immediate issue was settled by a written agreement between Ben-Gurion and Jacob Blaustein in 1950 by which the United States was admitted the land of American Jews and calls from Israel for *aliyah* stopped. Strongly motivated American Jews might settle in Israel if they wished. However, the fundamental issue of relations between the Jewish state and world Jewry had to be a matter of long-range concern. Were their respective Jewish identities similar? Did Israel's centrality in the Jewish world mean Israel's dominance? Would they lose interest in one another and drift apart? What collaboration if any could there be beyond financial and political support, which anyhow was becoming less essential? Could the supposed historical model of Babylonia–Jerusalem creative partnership be reproduced? Such questions were not answered by the deliberations of numerous conferences. The writings of philosophers and scholars carried influence but it would be the course of events in the political, social, and cultural spheres that would eventually decide. Thus, concern for Israel came to a peak during crises when its very existence lay under threat, especially in the wars of 1967 and 1973. Another meaningful sphere was *aliyah* from western countries, which although small was especially significant because no danger was compelling immigrants to come from there. The western newcomers were members of the professional and technical élite including physicians, scientists, university lecturers, and businessmen, many of whom arrived with independent means. Others came to Israel to retire. Graduates of Zionist youth movements were conspicuous.

The history of the state shows its inner development controlled by the imperatives of defence. After the armistices which ended the War of Independence in 1949 the army sagged for several years. In spite of United Nations patrols Arab terrorists infiltrated Israel and committed murders. The army retaliated, sometimes severely, and the military or diplomatic measures to be taken were often an issue within the government. By 1956, with the army reconstructed and substantial arms shipments received mainly from France, a more militant mood took over when Ben-Gurion returned to the prime ministership after breaking with his successor Sharett and pushing him out. Constant terrorist raids out of Egypt led to Israel's strange alliance with Britain and France, who wanted to secure Nasser's downfall. In a slashing four-day military campaign Israel gained its objective of ending the terrorist menace from the south. However, the British and French who landed simultaneously at Port Suez pulled out in the face of furious opposition at home and American anger. Israel withdrew from the Gaza strip, and with a United Nations Emergency Force patrolling the area it gained border peace in the south until 1967.

The years from 1967 to 1979 form a period of radical shift in Israel's foreign and domestic affairs. Israel's supreme crisis of 1967 was brought on by Egypt's Nasser, who dismissed the United Nations peacekeeping force without even an expression of opposition by them. He blockaded the Straits of Tiran, an act of war, and with Russian encouragement massed troops at his border with Israel. Confident of his army's ability, Nasser was apparently dizzied by his pan-Arab ambitions and his own bombastic, nearly genocidal rhetoric. Israel mobilized fully and waited tensely for weeks during negotiations for tangible support by friendly powers. When they left Israel standing alone supported only by words of sympathy the frightful spectre of the Holocaust crossed many minds. Israel struck back on 5 June 1967 and the outcome in six days was catastrophic for the army and air force of Egypt and for those of Syria and Jordan who joined Egypt. Thanks to its speedy, overwhelming victory Israel almost doubled its territory, with the Golan Heights captured from Syria, the Sinai peninsula from Egypt, and the west bank of the

Jordan river, including east Jerusalem, from Jordan. The world's acclaim was hearty but short-lived. Israel, like the Jewish people, received sympathy as a victim but not as a victor. The New Left, at the peak of its clamorous influence, railed at Israel for defeating righteous 'Third World' countries.

The Six Days War concluded with Israel in a position of confident strength. The lands it occupied generated the central political and military issue in its history after 1967. There was deep satisfaction that the entire old city of Jerusalem including the Wailing Wall, renamed the Western Wall after its Hebrew name, came under Jewish control. By all but universal Jewish agreement unified Jerusalem was to be the capital. The hitherto sedate city entered a period of dynamic growth in its population and economy. It was likewise agreed that the little-inhabited Golan Heights, out of which Syrians for years shelled Israeli settlements below, would also be held, and Jewish settlement there began. The gravest question concerned the west bank of the Jordan, which many significantly called by the ancient names Judaea and Samaria. The extraordinary victory of 1967 aroused messianic expectations among many religious Jews. In the view of messianic and right-wing Zionists the west bank, heavily inhabited by Arabs, had to be settled for nationalist and religious reasons; none of the land could be returned in any peace deal. Alleged security requirements were also invoked. Thus commenced the hotly contested process of establishing settlements in the west bank, including areas close to Arab towns like Hebron and Nablus (biblical Shechem). Labour governments, in office until 1977, discouraged but did not completely prevent settlement.

Within weeks of the Six Days War an Arab conference at Khartoum announced that they would not recognize Israel, negotiate for peace, or make the slightest concession. There were tentative negotiations for peace anyhow and plans for new borders involving almost complete Israeli withdrawal, in which the United States and European countries were participants, but they got nowhere. Israel was confident of its strength in a period of prosperity, and felt it could wait indefinitely since 'time is on our side', as the saying then went. Meanwhile Egypt was rebuilding with Russian aid under its new ruler Sadat, who succeeded after Nasser's death in 1970. Intent on restoring the military balance,

Egypt in alliance with Syria struck again on 6 October, the Day of Atonement, 1973. Israel's lack of preparedness on that day became the subject of bitter controversy for years, especially as it became known that intelligence reports of Egyptian war preparations had been misinterpreted because fixed doctrine held that they 'would not dare' to try again. After initial setbacks in the north and south the IDF, mobilized with frantic speed, went on the offensive. The IDF with resourceful bravery crossed the Suez Canal and surrounded an Egyptian army. Meanwhile the Syrian offensive was driven back and Damascus lay open. American arms flowed in and the American Secretary of State Henry A. Kissinger intervened and arranged a cease-fire three weeks after the war began. He also negotiated cease-fire lines between Israel and Syria in 1975 by flying continuously between Damascus and Jerusalem, so-called shuttle diplomacy. Almost 3,000 Israeli soldiers died and a far larger number of Arabs lost their lives in the Yom Kippur War; the Israelis lost in 1967 numbered fewer than a thousand.

Many consequences flowed from the Yom Kippur War, beginning with a 'war of the generals' over the conduct of the war itself, which stirred public disdain. The six years' euphoria between the 1967 and 1973 wars ended in a downcast public mood and a vehement protest movement. Mapai's long record as the party of achievement and military success was shaken. A new political phenomenon was external political pressure groups and the parties' attention to them. Out of post-war protest came Peace Now (*Shalom 'Akhshav*), while the renewed Fidelity Bloc (*Gush Emunim*) for west bank settlement gathered momentum. It was the protest movement which forced Golda Meir from the prime ministership and Moshe Dayan, its main target, out of the ministry of defence. Yizhak Rabin, Golda Meir's successor, was not politically successful and the decline of the Labour Party continued, beset by financial scandals. The extraordinary feat of freeing Israeli hostages by the airborne raid at Entebbe airport in Kenya in 1976 provided only temporary political relief.

In May 1977 came the 'overturn' (*mahpakh*), as it was called, the loss of power by the Labour Party. In its place came the Herut Party in alliance with the National Religious Party (Mifdal). The new prime minister was Menahem Begin, the one-time *Etzel* commander, and the speaker of the Knesset and future prime minister was Yizhak Shamir, once commander of the Sternists. This was far more than a change of regime, for Mapai had held power not merely since the state's existence but still earlier, from 1933. It was deeply significant for Israeli democracy that the defeated party yielded power at once despite anger and chagrin at an election result which some of them thought beyond belief. This was the ascent to power of right-wing Zionism, committed to the unpartitioned or 'greater' Israel. Socially it was the rise of Israel's oriental population, who had long been antagonized by the patronizing dominance of Mapai and Ashkenazim. There was much irony here, because Begin was a thoroughly east European Ashkenazi, but an outsider to power like his voters. Mifdal was also mainly Ashkenazi although its religious Orthodoxy was in constant confrontation with the secularism of its one-time political partners on the left.

This was an unlikely coalition to make the peace with Egypt which Mapai had long sought without success. After a secret meeting in Morocco between Foreign Secretary Moshe Dayan, who had gone over to the new regime, and Egyptian representatives, Anwar Sadat offered to come to Israel to talk peace. Begin officially invited him, and in November 1977 the highly improbable happened when the Egyptian ruler's plane landed in Israel and was received graciously by President Navon, Begin, and an Israeli entourage. Sadat met Israel's past and present leaders and presented his terms in a speech to the Knesset—he wanted his captured lands back and Palestinian Arab rights recognized. Only then could there be a treaty of peace. Negotiations were prolonged and arduous and the process was brought to termination in marathon sessions at Camp David, the American presidents' retreat in the Maryland mountains, with President Carter participating. Sadat got Sinai back, evacuated by the few Israeli settlers with the coastal town of Yamit intentionally destroyed. Cultural, travel, and diplomatic arrangements were also made. A peace treaty was signed in April 1979, and it took Mapai votes to secure its ratification in the Knesset. Most of Begin's coalition voted against the treaty, quite possibly to retain ideological 'purity' with its approval already assured. It was a 'cold' peace, but it was peace.

Nothing substantive came for years from the Palestinian provisions of the peace treaty. But by 1980 Israel was nearer peace and its once 'outsider' Jewish population was very much in power politically if not economically. Further developments would come with time as the Jewish state continued its stormy progress.

In Conclusion

Through more than three centuries of the modern age of Jewish history we are able to view the heroic, timid, courageous, and bestial qualities of humanity in full display. One notes persistence of Jewish dignity and cultural life in the early modern ghetto, without which the Jews would have sunk to a rabble. The turn to emancipation rewarded personal ambition as never before and brought forth adaptability, but also timidity in asserting rights and Jewish identity in the large society to which the Jews were admitted. Mass migration required the courage and resourcefulness of the common man and woman. The bestial malice of the Holocaust shows that sadistic, ideologically driven mass murder can also inflict an atomic holocaust on the human race. The courage of self-renewal is seen in Zionism, which restored youth and freshness to weary Jewish spirits and worn Jewish bodies.

The philosopher of history Nachman Krochmal, ruminating during the 1830s in Galicia, saw vast cycles in Jewish history. Unlike other nations whose histories ended in one cycle, the spirit of Judaism enabled the Jews to begin again after a cycle ended. Krochmal did not carry his scheme past the period of late medieval persecutions and expulsions, which continued to 1640 in his reckoning. Historians may venture to continue Krochmal's cycles at their risk. Modern Jewish history could be interpreted as a period of growth and flourishing as Krochmal would have it, but how would one conceive of the Holocaust catastrophe and the triumphant founding of the Jewish state in the same decade? Schemes, even as learned as Krochmal's was for its time, may not hold up against simple observation, not to mention detailed historical investigation.

The Jewish people re-entered history in the twentieth century. Their corporate structure in the Middle Ages before the age of emancipation had resembled that of other social and religious groups and they functioned in history with some skill in that framework. Jewish emancipation in the era of revolutions deprived them of historical standing as a group although certain individuals rose high, but religious life was readily recognized. It was new movements in the Jewish world and a freer atmosphere in the post-Second World War democracies which enabled the Jews to act politically as a community. As a state Israel acted in spheres unknown to the Jewish group for centuries, mainly military and economic, while functioning as the centre of the Jewish people. Future histories of the Jews in modern times will place the Jewish people linked to the state of Israel in the course of historical development.

Index of Names and Places

Abdullah, King of Jordan 393
Abramsky, R. Yehezkel 290
Acheson, Dean 393
Adenauer, Konrad 402
Adler, R. Nathan 126, 143, 147
Adler, Victor 229
Adrianople, Jewish community 193
Ahiyah of Shiloh 79
Alexander I, Tsar 124
Alexander II, Tsar 170, 185–90, 239
Alexander III, Tsar 239, 241, 247
Altmann, A. 90
Amiel, R. 335
Amschel, Solomon 114
Antonescu, Ion 367
Antwerp 16
Ashkenazi, Haham Zvi 63
Ashkenazi, R. Gerson 41
Ashkenazi, R. Jacob 40
Ashkenazi, R. Zvi 40, 45, 53, 56, 57
Askenazy, Szymon 300
Asquith, H.H. 273, 275
Athias, Joseph 45
Auerbach, Berthold 226
Auschwitz-Birkenau (camp) 355, 360, 369–70, 373, 376
Axelrod, Pavel 335
Ayllon, Solomon 53

Baal Shem Tov, R. Israel 54, 63, 74, 77–80
Babel, Isaac 291
Bachrach, R. Yair Hayyim 52
Balaban, Mayer 301
Balfour, Arthur 276

Balkan states 195
Ballin, Albert 259, 260
Baltic states 20
Baltimore 277
Baron, Salo W. 28, 82, 328, 382, 414
Bauer, Otto 229
Bavaria 40
  Communist revolution 305;
  family life 150;
  pogroms (1819) 135
Bea, Cardinal 397–8
Beer, Jacob Herz 140
Begin, Menachem 403, 427, 434, 435
Beiliss, Mendel 248
Bellow, Saul 414
Belzec (camp) 355
Ben-Gurion, David 345, 384, 385, 388, 391, 392, 401, 422, 424, 426–7, 431, 432
Berakh, R. Berekhiah 71
Bergelson, David 291
Bergen-Belsen (camp) 376–7
Berlin, anti-Semitism 219, 222;
  Jewish community 41, 95–104;
  and Jewish Enlightenment 83–4, 89;
  and modern Jewish history 25
Berlin, Naftali Zvi Yehudah 183, 250;
  Ha'amek Davar R. 181
Bernadotte, Count Folke 394
Bernays, R. Isaac 142
Bernstein, Eduard 225, 306, 335
Bernstein, Leonard 413
Berntein, R. Philip 380
Bessarabia, Jewish community 367
Bevin, Ernest 387, 388, 389

Bialik, Hayyim Nahman, '*In the City of Slaughter*' 246
Bialystok, ghetto 356, 361
Bing, Berr-Isaac 109
Birobidzhan (Jewish Autonomous Territory) 405
Bismarck, Prince Otto von 218, 219, 222, 226
Blaustein, Jacob 403, 431
Bloch, Joseph Samuel 231
Blum, Leon 321, 335
Blumenfeld, Kurt 310
Bodin, Jean 60
Boeckel, Otto 222
Boegner, Marc 364
Bohemia 40, 73;
    population growth 67–8;
    religious tolerance 99;
    role of *kehillah* (community) 8
de Bonald, Viscount, '*On the Jews*' 116
Bonaparte, Louis 113
Bonaparte, Napoleon see Napoleon I
Bonn 114
Bontoux (bank employee) 233–4
Bordeaux, Jewish emancipation 108
Boris, King of Bulgaria 361–2
Borochov, Ber 257–8, 341
Boston, Jewish community 277
Brand, Joel 373
Brandeis, Louis 327, 331, 340–1
Brandeis University 418
Brandes, Georg 253
Bremen 120
Breslau, rabbinical school 160
Bresslau, Harry 221
Buber, Martin 308–9
Buchenwald (camp) 377
Buenos Aires, Jewish community 217
Bukovina, Jewish community 367
Bunim, R. Simha 185
Bursa, Jewish community 193

Calahora, Dr Matthew 34
Calvin, John 118n.
Cardoso, F., *Las excelencias de los Hebreos* 46
Cardoso, Isaac 22
Carter, Jimmy 435
Casimir, Jan, King of Poland 30
Castro, Americo 13
Catherine the Great, Tsarina 124
Cerf-Berr, Herz 97
Chamberlain, Houston Stewart 307; *The Foundations of the Nineteenth Century* 222
Chamberlain, Joseph 255
Charles II, King of England 44
Chicago, Jewish community 217, 277
Chmielnicki, Bohdan, and Cossack invasion 28–31
Churchill, Winston 338, 347, 373
Class, Heinrich, '*If I Were the Kaiser*' 222
Clay, General 380
Clermont-Tonnerre, Count Stanislas de 107–8
Cleveland, Jewish community 217, 277
Cohen, Nehemiah, and Sabbatianism 51–2
Colbert, Jean-Baptiste 60
Collins, Anthony 84
Cologne 114, 159
Constantinople 45;
    Jewish community 11, 192–3;
    slave market 30
Copeland, Aaron 413
Corfu, Jewish community 11, 193
Coughlin, Charles 329–30
Cracow, anti-Jewish feeling 32, 34, 68;
    Jewish community 295;
    Swedish conquest (1655) 32
Cranborne, Lord 383–4

Cranz, A.F., 'The Search for Light and
    Truth' 96
Cremieux, Isaac-Adolphe 148, 156,
    194
Crete, Jewish community 11
Crimea, Jewish resettlement 288–9
Croatia 362
Cromer, Lord 255
Cromwell, Oliver 42, 43–4
Cunningham, Sir Alan 392
Czarniecki 32
Czerniakow, Adam 352, 357, 359

Da Costa, Uriel 46
Dachau (camp) 377
Daudet, Alphonse 232
Davidson, Israel 328
Davis, R. 15
Dawidowicz, Lucy 377
Dayan, Moshe 434, 435
Delmedigo, Yosef Shlomo 27
Derzhavin, G.R. 165–6
Detroit, Jewish community 217, 277
Diderot, D. 86
Dinur, B. 24
Disraeli, Benjamin 136–7, 198, 237
Dmowski, Roman 299
Dobruschka, Moses ('Junius Frey') 110
Dodd, W.E. (US Ambassador) 315
Dohm, Christoph 105;
    'Memorandum on the Condition of the
        Jews in Alsace' 97–8;
    On the Civil Improvement of the Jews
        98–9
Dov Ber of Mezerich ('the Great
    Preacher') 80–1, 92
Dresden, Jewish community 59
Dreyfus, Alfred 234–5, 238
Dreyfus, Mathieu 234
Drumont, Edouard, La France juive
    233

Dubno, Solomon 93
Dubnow, Simon 23n., 272
Duhring, Eugen 222
Dutch Surinam 127, 202

Eban, Aubrey (Abba) 389–90, 393,
    431
Eger, R. Akiva 144
Eichmann, Adolf 316, 365, 368, 370,
    373–4;
    trial (1961) 401–2
Einhorn, R. David 205, 206
Einstein, Albert 308, 340
Eisenhower, D. 377, 380
Eisenstadt, Jewish settlement in 18
Eisner, K. 305, 307
Ellis Island, New York 260
Emden, R. Jacob 63, 64, 65
Encyclopaedia Judaica 309
Endelman, T. 94
Engels, Friedrich 224
Erter, Isaac 173
Estonia, Jewish community 287, 303
Ettinger, S. 20, 82n.
Evian Conference (1938) 317–18
Exodus 1947 (immigrant ship) 388
Eybeschuetz, R. Jonathan 63

Feinstein, Moses 328
Felix Libertate society (Amsterdam)
    113, 118
Felsenthal, R. Bernard 254
Filderman, Wilhelm 367
Fischhof, Adolf 156, 158–9
Fleg, Edmond 235–6
Ford, Henry 215, 322;
    'The Cause of World Distress' 322
Fourier 232
Franconia 40
Frank, Anne 362–3
Frank, Dr Ilya 166

Frank, Eva 76
Frank, Jacob 74, 75
Frankel, R. David 90
Frankel, Zacharias 138, 144, 145, 160, 280
Frankfurt 118, 120;
    ghetto 132;
    Jewish community 159
Frankfurter, Felix 331
Frankl, Ludwig August 192, 194
Franz Josef, Emperor of Austria 158;
    opposition to anti-Semitism 231
Frederick II, King of Prussia 61, 91, 103;
    'General Jewish Regulations' 62
Frederick William, Elector of Brandenburg 41
Frederick William II, King of Prussia 103
Freehof, R. Solomon 397–8
Freeman, E.A. 237
Freud, Sigmund 232, 341
Friedjung, Heinrich 229
Friedlander, David 103
Frizel, I.G. 165–6
Furtado, Abraham 109, 117

Gans, E. 138
Gaon of Vilna 72–3, 125, 181;
    and Hasidism 82
de Gaulle, Charles 348, 411
Gebhardt, C. 22
Gedera (Palestinian colony) 251
Geiger, R. Abraham 138, 143, 156
Ginzberg, Asher 254, 274
Ginzberg, Louis 327, 328, 414
Ginzburg, Baron 242
Gladstone, William 237
Gobineau, Count de, *Essai sur l'inegalite des races humaines* 233
Godard, Jacques 108

Goering, Hermann 318
Goethe, Johann von 88, 104
Goitein, Shlomo 414
Golan Heights 432, 433
Goldmann, Nahum 390, 402, 403
Goldmark, Josef 156
Gomel, martyrdom 30;
    pogrom (1903) 246
Gordon, Judah Leib (Leon) 189
Gottlober, A.B. 189
Graetz, Heinrich 24, 138, 156;
    Geschichte der Juden 221
Grant, Ulysses 208–9
Greenberg, Clement 414
Grégoire, Abbe Henri 105, 106
Gromyko, Andrei 391
Grosz, Andor 373
Grotius, Hugo 60
Gruenebaum, Yizhak 296, 297, 383
Gruner, Dov 388
Guedemann, R. Moritz 231

Haase, Hugo 307
Hagiz, R. Moses 53
Haifa 200, 275
Halberstam, R. Hayyim 185
Halévy, Jacques 139
Hamburg 120;
    as emigration port 259–60;
    Jewish community 159;
    Jewish settlement in 16;
    New Christians in 16;
    Reform Judaism 141–2
Handelsman, Marcel 300
Hanokh ben Shmaryah, R. Manoah 27
Hardenberg (Prussian chancellor) 121
Harrison, Earl G. 379–80
Hayun, Nehemiah 53
Hayyim of Volozhin, R., *Nefesh ha-Hayyim* 73

Hebrew University 345, 346, 429
Hebron 196, 198;
    massacre (1929) 344
Heine, Heinrich 136, 138
Heinemann, Isaak 223
Henry, Lt. Col. 234
Herder, Johann von 102–3, 104;
    The Spirit of Hebrew Poetry 102–3
Herut (Freedom) Party 427, 434–5
Herz, Henriette 89
Herzl, Theodor 214, 232, 251–5;
    Der Judenstaat 252–3;
    The New Ghetto 252
Herzog, R. Isaac 346
Heschel, R. Abraham 397–8
Hess, Moses 148;
    Rome and Jerusalem 256
Hesse, H. 40
Heydrich, Reinhard 311, 318, 354, 365
Hilberg, R. 377
Higham, John 260
Hildesheimer, R. Esriel 145
Himmler 311, 318, 365, 376
Hindenburg, President 312
Hirsch, Baron de 262
Hirsch, R. Samson Raphael 145
Hirsch, R. Samuel 205, 208, 252
Hirschell, Chief Rabbi 143
Hirschenson, R. 335
Hitler, Adolf, and Arab leaders 384;
    attempted assassination (1944)
        371;
    genocide policy 311;
    ideology 307–8, 354;
    influences on 230;
    rise to power 308, 309;
    and Scandinavia 361; *see also*
        Holocaust;
    Nazism
Holbach 86
Holborn, Hajo 87–8

Holdheim, R. Samuel 142
Horner, Henry 331
Horthy, Admiral 368, 369
Howe, Irving 414
Huberman, Bronislaw 429
Hugenberg, Alfred 306
von Humboldt, Wilhelm 89, 120–1
Hundert, G.D. 34
Hyman, Paula 236

Ignatiev (Russian minister) 240, 241,
    242
Ignatius Loyola, St. 13
Isaac, R. Jacob 185
Israel, J.I. 24
Israel of Zamosc 89–90
Izmir (formerly Smyrna) 35–6, 50,
    193

Jabotinsky, Vladimir 337, 343
Jacob, Dinah 112
Jacob Joseph of Polnoyye, R. 80;
    Toldot Yaakov Yosef 81–2
Jacob, Rabbi, on Polish invasion 33
Jacobson, Israel 120
Jaffa 200, 275, 338
Janowsky, Oscar, *A People at Bay* 298
Jellinek, Hermann 156
Jellinek, R. Adolf 231
Jerusalem 390, 391, 393, 399n., 433;
    influence of Constantinople Jewry
        193;
    Jewish community 195, 196–8;
    Jewish-Arab conflict 343–4
Jewish Theological Seminary (US)
    326, 327, 414, 417
John XXIII, Pope 397, 398
Joseph II, Emperor of Austria 73;
    reforms 99–101, 104
Josephthal, Giora 403
Judah the Hasid 54

Kaganovitch, P. ('Der Nister') 291
Kahn, R. Zadok (French Chief Rabbi)
    235, 253
Kant, Immanuel 134
Karo, R. Joseph 2
Kassel, Jewish community 59
Kasztner, Reszoe 373–4
Katz, J. 25
Kautsky, Karl 225
Kazin, Alfred 414
Kellenbenz, H. 45
Kenez, P. 285
Kennedy, D.M. 349
Khazar kingdom 19
Khruschev, Nikita 406, 408, 427
Kiev, Babi Yar massacre 358
Kiselev, Count 172
Kishinev, pogrom (1903) 245–6
Kissinger, Henry 434
Kluger, R. Solomon 185
Knodel, John E. 151
Kook, R. Abraham Isaac 335, 339
Koppel, Jacob 63
Kosciusko 122
Krochmal, Nachman 24, 173, 436
Kun, Bela 306;
    Communist junta 302
Kuranda, Ignaz 155
Kurdistan, exodus of Jews to Israel
    423;
    Jewish community 195
Kuyper, Abraham 219–20

Ladislas IV, King of Poland 28, 29
Lafayette, General 109
Lainez, Diego 13
Lamdan, Isaac, '*Masada*' 286
Landau, R. Ezekiel 63, 72, 73–4, 95,
    100–1, 145;
    Noda biYhudah 74
Landau, S.H. 335

Landauer, Georg 305
Latvia 295;
    Jewish community 287, 304
Lavater, Johann 91, 92
Lazare, Bernard 234
Leavitt, Moses 403
Leeser, R. Isaac 206, 210, 211
Leghorn (Livorno), Jewish
    settlement in 15
Lehman, Herbert 331
Leipzig, Jewish community 59
Lenin, V.I. 244, 245, 272, 281
Leopold I, Emperor of Austria 40–1,
    58
Leroux 232
Lessing, Gotthold 88, 90, 134
Levi, Avigdor 90
Levi, David 85n.
Levi Isaac of Berdichev, R. 81
Levin, Judah 169
Levinsohn, Isaac Ber 175–6;
    Hefker Velt 176
Levinson, Adam ha-Kohen 189
Levinson, Micah Joseph 189
Lewandowski, Louis 139
Lieberman, Saul 414
Liebknecht, Karl 306
Lifschitz, Hayyim 63
Lilienblum, Moshe Leib 189, 249,
    252
Lilienthal, R. Max 178–80;
    Maggid Yeshuah 179
Lincoln, Abraham 208–9
Lipsky, Louis 341
Lloyd George, David 275
Locke, John 60, 90
Lodz, ghetto 351–2, 356, 357, 359,
    361;
    Jewish community 216, 295
London, immigrants' arrival in 260,
    261;

London, immigrants' arrival in (*cont.*)
  Jewish community 146, 159, 216,
    410;
  United Synagogue 320;
  in World War Two 347–8
Long, Huey 329
Lopez, Dr Rodrigo 16
Losener 313
Louis XIV, King of France 60
Louis XVIII, King of France 119
Lübeck 120
Lublin, expulsion of Jews (1761) 34;
  ghetto 354, 360;
  Jewish community 216;
  liberation (1944) 376;
  Russian attack 31
Lueger, Karl 228–9, 230
Luria, R. Isaac 48
Luxemburg, Rosa 306
Luzzato, Rabbi Simone 60;
  Discourse on the Jews of Venice 17
Luzzatto, Ephraim, love poems 93
Luzzatto, Moses Hayyim 63–4;
  'The Path of the Just' 64
Luzzatto, Samuel David 138, 156
Lwow, anti-Jewish riots 34;
  and Cossack invasions 29, 31;
  ghetto 360, 361;
  Jewish community 216, 295;
  pogrom 282;
  in World War Two 351, 353
Lysenko (Soviet scientist) 405

MacDonald, Ramsay 344
McMahon, Sir Henry 273–4
MacMichael (Palestinian High
  Commissioner) 389
McNarney, General 380
Madagascar, proposed ghetto 354
Magnes, Judah 346
Mahler, Gustav 232

Mahler, R. 66
Maimonides, R. Moses (philosopher)
  2, 49;
  Guide for the Perplexed 90
Mainz 114
Malakh, Hayyim 54
Malamud, Bernard 414
Malbim, R. Meir Leibush, *Ha-Torah
  veha-Mizvah* 181
Malesherbes, Count 98, 105
Mannheimer, Isaac Noah 156
Maria Theresa, Empress of Austria 73,
  89
Marr, Wilhelm 222;
  'The Victory of Judaism over
    Teutonism' 218
Marshall, George C. 393
Marshall, Louis 333
Martov, Iulii 245, 281
Marx, Alexander 328
Marx, Karl 137
Maurras, Charles 236
Maury, Cardinal 108
Medem, Vladimir 244
Mehemet Ali, conquest of Palestine
  197
Meir, Golda 405, 434
Meir, R. Isaac 185
Meir, Rabbi 40
Menasseh ben Israel, R. 42–4, 60
Mendel, R. 185
Mendelssohn, Felix 137, 139
Mendelssohn, Moses 25, 57–8, 87, 88,
  90–3, 97–9, 137, 189;
  Bible translation 93, 95–7, 145;
  conversion of daughters 102, 136;
  *Jerusalem: or, On Religious Power and
    Judaism* 96–7
Mengele, Josef 360
Metternich, Austrian Chancellor 132
Metz 105

Meyer, Jonas 133
Meyerbeer 139
Mickiewicz, Adam 76
Mikhoels, Solomon 405
Minsk, ghetto 356;
   Jewish community 216
Mohilever, R. Samuel 250
Momigliano, A. 136n.
Mommsen, Theodor, *Auch ein Wort
   uber unser Judentum* 221;
   The Provinces of the Roman Empire
   221
Montagu, Edwin 275, 276
Montefiore, Claude 275
Montefiore, Leonard 380
Montefiore, Sir Moses 148–9, 170,
   201, 211
Montesquieu, Baron de 85
Montgelas 121
Montreal 212, 217, 261
Morais, Sabato 206
Moravia, Orthodox Judaism 145;
   religious tolerance 99
Morgenthau, Henry, Jr. 331, 375
Mosley, Oswald 320–1
Munk, Salomon 138
Murphy, Robert 365
Muscovy, invasion of Poland 32;
   Jewish settlement forbidden 31
Mussolini, Benito 362

Nadav, M. 34
Napoleon I (Bonaparte) 110;
   and Eastern Europe 122–6;
   invasion of Palestine (1799) 197;
   Jewish policies in France 115–19,
      130, 146;
   and West European Jews 115,
      120–1, 146
Napoleonic Wars 110
Nasser, President 432, 433

Nathan of Gaza (Nathan ben Elisha
   Hayyim) 49–50, 53
Nathanson, R. Joseph Saul 181
Nemerov, Ukraine 28–30, 33
New York, immigrants' arrival in 260,
   261;
   Jewish community 202, 217, 277
Nice, refugees from Nazism 363
Nicholas I, Tsar 100, 162;
   Jewish policies 167–72, 177–80,
      181
Nicholas II, Tsar 241, 248, 271
Nieto, David 56–7
Nordau, Max 253, 335
Notkin, Nota 166

Odessa, Jewish community 216;
   Jewish self-defence 284
Ofen (Budapest), Jewish settlement in
   18
Offenbach, Jacques 139
Oistrakh, David 406
Oppenheimer, Joseph Suss 58
Oppenheimer, Samuel 41
Oren, Mordecai 405, 406, 427

Padua, University of 21, 56, 112
Palmerston 148, 199
Papal States 133
Paris, Jewish community 111, 146,
      159, 216
Passfield, Lord (Sidney Webb) 344
Patto, Samuel 111
Patton, George 379
Paul VI, Pope 398
Peel, Lord 345
Pelley, William Dudley, Silver Shirts
   movement 329
Perl, Joseph 173
Pernerstorfer 229
Persia, Jewish community 149

Petah Tikvah (Palestinian colony)
251, 338
Pétain, Marshal 363
Peter the Great, Tsar 123
Petlura, Semion 285–6
Philadelphia, Jewish community 216,
217, 277
Picquart, Colonel 235
Piedmont 133
Pilsudski, Josef 297
Pinsk, anti-Jewish feeling 34
Pinsker, Leon 249, 252;
Autoemancipation 249
Pinto, Isaac, Apologie pour la nation
juive 87
Pius X, Pope 274
Pius XII, Pope 362, 375, 391
Plehve (Russian minister) 246
Podolia, as Sabbatian centre 64
Poliakov (railway contractor) 187, 242
Posen, anti-Jewish feeling 34
Poujol, Some Observations about the
Jews 116
Prado, Juan 46
Prague 73;
Jewish settlement in 18
Pressburg, anti-Jewish riots 157;
Jewish settlement in 18
Preuss, Hugo 304
Priestley, Joseph 85n.
Prokofiev, Serge 405
Proskurov (Ukraine), pogrom (1919)
284–5
Proudhon 232
Proust, Marcel, Remembrance of Things
Past 233
Pulzer, P. 230

Rabin, Yitzhak 434
Randall, J. 96
Rapoport, R. Solomon J.L. 138, 173

Rathenau, Walter 307
Ratti-Menton (French Consul) 148
Reich, Leon 297
Reines, R. 255, 256
Renner, Karl 229
Reubell 108
Revah, I. 14, 22
Revel, Bernard 326
Rhineland 40;
French conquest (1795) 113–14
Rhodes, Jewish community 11
Riegner, Gerhart 371
Riesser, Gabriel 156
Rifkind, Simon 380
Ringelblum, Emmanuel 353, 360
Rishon le-Zion (Palestinian colony)
251
Rivkes, Rabbi Moses 39;
on Russian invasion (1655) 31–2
Robles, Antonio 43
Rohling, August 231
Rome 133;
ghetto 112
Ronsard 12
Roosevelt, F.D. 317, 325, 330–1,
365–6, 375
Rosenzweig, Franz 308–9
Rosh Pinah (Palestinian colony) 251
Rosman, M.J. 69, 80
Roth, Cecil 94
Roth, Philip 414
Rothschild, Edmond de 251, 252
Rothschild family 153, 154, 233–4,
275, 320
Rothschild, Lionel de 160
Rothschild, Nathaniel 240
Rousseau, Jean-Jacques 86–7
Rubinow, Isaac M. 329
Ruderman, D. 56, 94
Rumkowski (ghetto dictator) 351,
356, 357

Sabbetai Zvi, acclaimed as Messiah
  27, 47–52;
  becomes Muslim 52–3;
  conversion to Islam 34
Sadat, Anwar 433, 435
Safed 196, 198;
  killing of Jews (1929) 344
Safran, R. 367
St Louis, Jewish community 277
Saint-Simon 232
Salanter, R. Israel 183
Saliege, Archbishop of Toulouse 364
Salonika, Jewish community 11,
  35–6, 193, 367;
  slave market 30
Samuel, Herbert 337, 338
Satanov, Isaac, *Zemirot Assaf* 93
Schechter, Solomon 280
Schiff, Jacob H. 244, 262, 271
Schiller, Friedrich 134
Schipper, Ignaz 301
Schlegel, Friedrich 104
Schleiermacher 104
Schleunes, Karl 313
Schneerson, R. Joseph 290
Schnirer, Sarah 301
Schnitzler 232
Scholem, Gershom, *Sabbetai Zvi: The
  Mystical Messiah* 47, 48–9, 52–3,
  54–5
Schonerer, Georg von 228, 230
Schonfeld, R. Solomon 380
Schorr, R. Moses 301
Schorsch, Ismar 226–7
Schulte, Eduard 371
Schwartzbard, Sholom 286n.
Seligman, Joseph 209
Shaftesbury, Lord 84
Shamir, Yitzhak 435
Shanghai, German Jews in 318
Sharett, Moshe 391, 402, 427, 432

Sharif Hussein 274
Shinar, Felix 403
Shneur Zalman of Lyuzny, R. 81, 125
Shostakovich, Dimitri 405
Siberia 242, 373, 406;
  exile to 244;
  Jewish colonists 171
Siena 112
Silver, R. Abba Hillel 329, 384
Singer, I.B. 414
Singer, R. Simeon 254
Sinzheim, R. David 117–18
Slansky, Rudolf 405
Slonimski, Antoni 300
Slonimsky, Hayyim Zelig 176
Slovakia 373;
  rebellion (1944) 366–7
Smith, Gerald L.K. 329
Smolenskin, Peretz 189
Smyrna (Izmir), Jewish community
  35–6, 50, 193
Sobibor (camp) 355
Sofer-Schreiber, R. Moses 144–5, 303
Sokolow, Nahum 274
Soloveichik, R. Hayyim 183
Soloveichik, R. Joseph 328, 397–8,
  416
Soloveichik, R. Joseph Baer 183
Spektor, R. Isaac Elhanan 181, 240,
  250, 326
Spinoza, Baruch 22, 46, 55–6, 60, 83
Spire, Andre 235–6
Stahl, Friedrich 136
Stalin, Josef 405–6, 408
Stanislawski, Michael 168–9, 180
vom Stein, Baron 121
Steinschneider, Moritz 138, 156
Stoecker, Adolf 218–20
Stolypin (Russian reformer) 248
Stresemann, Gustav 306
Stuyvesant, Peter 202

Sulzer, Salomon 139
Sweden 32, 373, 375
Switzerland 373
Syria 336–7, 432, 434;
  and Israel 393–4
Syrkin, Nachman 256, 257–8;
  The Jewish Question 256
Szold, Henrietta 327

Tchernikhovsky, Saul, '*On the Blood*'
  286
Teller, Pastor 103
Teresa de Jesus of Avila, St. 12
Thiers, Louis 148
Thiery (lawyer) 105
Tiberias 196, 198
Ticklin, R. 143
Tindall, Matthew 84
Tishbi, I. 64
Tiso, Fr., President of Slovakia 366
Toland, John 84
Tolchin, martyrdom 29, 30
Tolstoy, Count (Russian minister) 240
Toscanini, Arturo 429
Touro, Judah 201
Toussenel, Alphonse, *Les Juifs rois de*
  l'epoque 155, 233
Treblinka (camp) 355, 359
von Treitschke, Heinrich 220;
  Ein Wort über unser Judentum 220–1
Trilling, Lionel 414
Trotsky, Leon 281
Truman, Harry S. 379, 380, 384, 391,
  393, 412
Tunisia 363, 365–6, 411
Turkey 373;
  and settlement of Palestine 253; *see*
  also Ottoman Empire
Tuscany 133
Tuwim, Julian 300
Twain, Mark 198

Uganda, offer of Zionist settlement
  255
Uvarov (Russian education minister)
  178, 179

Venice 45, 112, 133;
  Jewish settlement in 15
Verona 112
de Vigny, Alfred 232
Vilna 72–3;
  banning of Hasidism 81, 82;
  congregation 177;
  ghetto 352–3, 356;
  Hasidism in 125, 126;
  Jewish community 216, 295;
  refugees from 40;
  Russian attack 31–2
Vital, D. 273
Vital, R. Hayyim 48
Vives, Juan Luis 12–13, 15
Volozhin, yeshiva 182–3
Voltaire (Francois Marie Arouet), anti-
  Semitism 85–6, 87

Wallenberg, Raoul 375–6
Walsin-Esterhazy, Major 235
Warburg, Paul 329
Weizmann, Chaim 256, 274, 337,
  338, 339, 340–1, 343, 344, 345,
  384, 402
Weizmann Institute 429
Wessely, Naftali Herz, '*Poems of Glory*'
  93;
  '*Words of Peace and Truth*' 101–2
West Bank, settlement of 433
West Indies 202;
  abolition of slavery 129;
  Jewish community 127, 212
Westphalia 120
White Russia 172
Wilamowitz-Moellendorff 223

Wilhelm I, Kaiser 218, 219
Wilhelm II, Kaiser 267
Wilson, Harold 389n.
Wilson, Woodrow 271, 276, 340
Wise, R. Isaac Mayer 205–6, 209, 210,
    211;
    Minhag America 206
Wise, R. Stephen 332
Wisliceny (Nazi) 366, 367
Wolf, Lucien 275
Wolf, R. Abraham 141
Wolffsohn, David 255
Wolfson, Harry 328, 414
Worms 111, 114

Yemen, exodus of Jews to Israel 422,
    423;
    Jewish community 195
Yerushalmi, Y.H., *From Spanish Court
    to Italian Ghetto* 46

Yeshiva University (US) 326, 416
Yiddish Scientific Institute (YIVO)
    301, 382
Yizhak, Rabbi 179

Zadok of Grodno 54
Zalkind-Hourwitz (anti-rabbinic Jew)
    105
Zangwill, Israel 255
Zerahiah ben Mas'ud 93
Zhitlovsky, Chaim 272
Zikhron Yaakov (Palestinian colony)
    251
Zinberg, Sergei 291
Zola, Emile 232;
    'J'accuse' 234–5
Zoref, Heshel 54, 78
Zunz, Leopold 156;
    'The Sermons of the Jews in their
    Historic Evolution' 138

Subject Index

absolutism, dynastic 58;
    enlightened 105, 165, 166;
    Russia 218, 241
academies *see* yeshivot 71
Action Française 236
administration, communal 3, 7–10,
    37–9, 429
Agrarian League (Germany) 223
agriculture 406;
    education in 201;
    Russian colonies 171–2;
    United States 262;
    Zionist 314, 341
Agudas Yisroel 300, 301, 304, 385
Ahad Ha-Am 274
Algeria 363, 365–6, 411
aliyah 386, 431
Allgemeine Zeitung des Judenthums
    (newspaper) 147
Alliance Israelite Universelle 149,
    235;
    schools 194, 195
Alsace 40;
    expulsion of Jews (1940) 363;
    family life 150;
    and French Revolution 106–7;
    Jewish community 97, 146;
    Jewish emancipation 108–9, 111;
    Jewish population growth 67;
    Napoleonic decrees 119;
    returned to France (1919) 321
American Indians, as Jews of Ten Lost
    Tribes 42
American Jewish Committee 330,
    403, 418
American Jewish Congress 332, 418

Amsterdam, education system 46;
    Felix Libertate society 113, 118;
    French conquest (1796) 112–13;
    Jewish community 21, 44–6, 83,
    146, 216;
    New Christians 15, 16;
    role of *kehillah* (community) 7;
    Sabbatianism 53
Ancona 112
Anglo-Jewish Association 275, 320
Anti-Defamation League 418
anti-Semitism 98–9, 396, 397;
    among students 160;
    Austro-Hungarian Empire 217,
    228–32;
    Britain 236–7;
    and emancipation 131;
    France 148, 217, 232–6;
    Germany 135, 217–28, 233;
    Jewish reactions to 221, 226–8,
    230–2, 238, 242, 246–7, 330–1;
    nationalist 228–9, 237–8;
    political activity 222–3, 228–9,
    238;
    racist 214–15, 222, 228, 233, 299,
    307;
    rise of 213–15, 217;
    Russia 218;
    and social exclusion 208–9, 223–4;
    and socialism 224–5;
    in state institutions 223–4;
    United States 208–9, 325, 329–31,
    412–13;
    Voltaire 85–6, 87;
    in World War One 268, 269, 304–5;
    see also Holocaust; pogroms; riots

antinomianism, and Sabbatianism
47–8, 50, 51, 53, 54–5
Arabs, and Axis powers 384, 386;
British obligations to 344;
French sympathies for 411;
in Palestine 336–8, 343–4, 345–6;
and partition 390–2;
refugees from Israel 394
Archives Israelites (newspaper) 147
Argentina 261, 262, 401
Ashkenazi Jews, Amsterdam 44;
Britain 44, 146;
cultural interests 26–7;
France 411;
Israel 435;
Jerusalem 198;
Palestine 339;
population growth 191;
United States 191
Assembly of Jewish Notables (France)
116–17
assimilation, and emancipation
130–1
Atlantic trade, expansion 15, 35
Australia 191;
Jewish community 212
Austria, anti-Semitism 217, 228–32;
emancipation in 156;
empire 158–9, 181;
German annexation (1938) 316;
Jewish community 287
Austrian Israelite Union 231

Balfour Declaration (1917) 199–200,
225, 273–6, 288, 337, 340, 343–4,
346
Balkan crisis (1875–8), and anti-
Semitism 236–7
banditry 62, 111–12
banking 153–5, 233–4;
and Great Depression 328;

political involvement 154–5;
and railway construction 154
Bar Mitzvah 327
Bat Mitzvah 327
Belgium, Holocaust 363
Bible 2;
translations 93, 95, 309
Biltmore Programme on Palestine 384
Bilu (settlement movement) 250–1
birth control 5, 150
birth rate, after World War Two
400–1;
declining 287–8;
displaced persons 378–9 *see also*
population growth
Black Death, and anti-Jewish feeling
35
blood libel 75, 148, 166, 245
B'nai B'rith 262;
Anti-Defamation League 330
Boards of Guardians 320
Boer War (1900–2), and anti-Semitism
236–7
Bolsheviks 245, 271, 281, 293
Brazil 262;
Jewish community 201–2
Brichah (flight) 381, 386
Britain, American colonies 201, 202;
anti-Semitism 236–7, 320–1, 348,
410;
Ashkenazi Jews 146;
Balfour Declaration (1917)
199–200, 225, 273–6, 288, 343–4;
central and eastern European Jews
44;
Deism 84;
'dual obligation' to Jews and Arabs
344;
east European immigrants 260;
economic role of Jews 59;
emancipation in 130, 133, 160;

Britain, American colonies (*cont.*)
  emigration from 410;
  expansion of overseas trade 15;
  expulsion of Jews (1290) 11–12, 42,
    43;
  German Jews in 315, 317, 319–20;
  and Holocaust 321, 374, 375,
    386;
  Jewish Board of Deputies 275;
  Jewish charter requested 42–4;
  Jewish community 146, 161, 237,
    287, 319, 410;
  Jewish Enlightenment 94;
  Jewish organizations 320–1;
  Jewish population growth 67;
  Jewish rights 129;
  Jewish settlement in 41–4;
  New Christians in 16;
  Orthodox Judaism 320;
  and Palestine 321, 336–7, 343,
    345–6, 348, 380, 383–4, 385–91;
  population growth 150, 152;
  post-war conditions 410;
  protection of Jews in Ottoman
    Empire 199;
  Reform Judaism 142–3;
  resettlement of child survivors 380;
  Sefardim 44, 143, 146;
  support for Arab state 273–4;
  synagogues 143, 280;
  in World War Two 347–8, 386–7;
  Zionism 255, 320, 340
Brody (Polish Jewish community) 67,
  81
Bulgaria, exodus of Jews to Israel
  423;
  Holocaust 361–2;
  Jewish community 362
Bund (revolutionary organization)
  243–5, 272, 281, 289, 298, 300
burial, as Christians 42;

permission for Jewish cemeteries
    43, 98;
  societies (Russia) 163

Camp David agreement (1979) 435
Canada, Jewish settlement 127,
    211–12, 262
capitalism 61, 74;
  and anti-semitism 224–5, 257;
  Jews associated with 228, 229,
    232–3, 236
censorship 170, 428
Central British Fund for German
    Jewry 314, 320
Central Committee of Liberated Jews
    379, 380
children, brought to Palestine 327;
  in Holocaust 354–5, 377;
  rescue and escape 319–20, 381,
    383;
  resettlement in Britain 380 *see also*
    education
Christian Social movement
    (Germany) 219
Christian-German Eating Club
    (Berlin) 104
Christianity, attitudes to Jews 3–4;
  concord with 160;
  conversion *see* conversion;
  debate with Judaism 3, 20–1, 42;
  official recognition 209, 210
civil improvement, calls for 98–9
clothing industry 187, 264, 324;
  labour movement 279
Cold War 404, 405
colonization, in Russia 171–2;
  Zionist 196
Communism 286;
  and anti-Semitism 293, 302;
  Germany 306;
  Hungary 302;

Israel as bulwark against 391;
Jewish involvement 290, 292–4,
305–6, 334;
United States 331;
view of art 291;
and Zionism 334
community, and 1848 revolutions
156–7;
conflicts within 70–4;
membership 3;
obligations to 3;
in Russia 180–1;
under Napoleon 119
'community of Israel' 147
concentration camps 311, 312, 316,
355, 358–60, 361
concessions, leasing 10
Conference on Jewish Material Claims
403–4
conscription, of children 168–70;
Russia 167–70, 176, 181, 186, 199;
see also military service
Conservative Judaism, United States
144, 206, 280, 302, 326–7,
415–16, 417
consistory system 119, 133, 146, 321;
France 133, 142, 146, 235, 280,
321
conversion, Germany 136–7;
Russia 165, 168, 178, 186;
United States 209–10
Council of the Four Lands 44, 53,
71–2, 122
Council for German Jewry 320
councils, regional 9–10
court Jews 58, 83
court, Jewish (*beth din*) 74, 100, 194;
secular 74
credit institutions, Muslim 36 *see also*
moneylending
Crémieux decree (1870) 365–6

Crimean War 167–8, 197
cultural life 21, 135, 436;
achievements 396;
Britain 320;
France 321;
Germany 308–9, 312, 336;
in ghettos 352–3;
Israel 429–30;
north-south divided 26–7;
Palestine 345;
Poland 300–1;
reconstruction projects 382;
Soviet Union 405, 406, 407–8;
United States 278, 324, 333,
413–15;
and Zionism 335–6
Czechoslovakia 295;
anti-Zionism 405;
German Jews in 315;
German rule 317;
Jewish community 287, 302–3;
minority rights 287

Damascus affair (1840) 148, 194
debt-collection, by court Jews 58–9
Decembrist group, Russia 166–7
deism 46, 84–7
Democratic Fraction (Zionist) 256
Den' (newspaper) 176–7
Denmark, Jewish community 141,
362, 409
despotism, enlightened 105
devekut (communion with God)
79–80, 83
diet, Hasidic laws 125;
of immigrants 265;
kosher rules 74n., 110, 427
displaced persons (DPs) 378–82, 409,
412, 421
divorce 6, 117–18, 417
Dreyfus affair 232, 234–5

education 57;
  Amsterdam 46;
  Britain 410;
  and choice of occupation 160;
  elementary 6;
  Germany 312;
  in ghettos 353;
  girls 201, 301, 327;
  Iran 195;
  Israel 427;
  and Jewish Enlightenment 177;
  Ottoman Empire 194;
  Poland 174, 301;
  prohibition of religious education
    289;
  rabbinical schools 328;
  and religious tolerance 100, 101;
  religous basis 6–7;
  Russia 177–80, 182, 187;
  and social advancement 404, 407;
  Soviet Union 405, 407;
  United States 210, 326;
  Yiddish 301
Egypt, expulsion from 411;
  and Israel 393–4, 432–4
emancipation 397, 436, 437;
  and anti-Semitism 131;
  and assimilation 130–1, 159;
  attitudes to 104–5;
  Austria 156;
  and autonomy 129, 131, 146;
  definition 128–32;
  disadvantages 131–2;
  Eastern Europe 122–6;
  France 108–10, 129, 156;
  Germany 113–14, 156, 159–60;
  and ghettos 132;
  Habsburg lands 164;
  Italy 112, 133;
  Netherlands 133;
  opposition to 121, 128–9, 156;

Ottoman Empire 194;
  Poland 122–3, 296;
  reaction against 116, 132–3, 134–7;
  and Reform Judaism 146–7;
  and regeneration 133, 147;
  Russia 271;
  of serfs (1861) 186;
  under Napoleon 115–21, 132–3;
  United States 127, 204–5;
  and Zionism 252; *see also* slavery
Enlightenment 55, 61, 72, 83, 84–8,
    128;
  reaction against 134–5
Enlightenment, Jewish 24–5, 64, 72,
    73–4, 83–4, 88–94, 124, 125;
  and education 177;
  literature 93;
  opposition to 145, 177, 189–90;
  Russia 166, 172–7, 188–90;
  and secularism 189;
  and settlement in Holy Land 248–9
Eretz Israel see Palestine
estate management, Poland 68–70
Etzel (military group) 387, 388–9

family life 5–6;
  household size 10n.
Fascism, Britain 320–1; *see also*
    Nazism
Finland 373;
  Holocaust 361;
  Jewish community 361
France, anti-alien law (1938) 321;
  anti-Semitism 217, 232–6, 321,
    363–4, 398n.;
  consistory system 133, 142, 146,
    280, 321;
  Deism 84–7;
  emancipation 156, 411;
  expulsion of Jews (1306–94) 12;
  German Jews in 315;

Holocaust 363–6, 410–11;
and Israel 411;
Jewish community 59, 146, 260,
287, 321–2, 409;
New Christians 15, 16;
North African immigration 411;
population growth 150, 151;
post-war community 410–11;
Reform Judaism 142;
refugees from Nazism 321;
Revolution *see* French Revolution;
and Syria 336–7;
Vichy regime 363–6, 398n.;
in World War Two 348
Franco-Prussian War (1870) 149
Frankism 65, 73, 74–6, 110;
and Hasidism 74–5;
and Roman Catholic Church 75;
see also Sabbatianism
Freedom (Herut) movement 427,
434–5
Freemasonry 233
French Revolution 24–5;
complaints about Jews 105–6;
effects outside France 111–12,
120–1;
Jewish emancipation 106–10, 129;
Reign of Terror 109–10

Galicia (Austrian Poland), Jewish
community 100, 163–4, 173,
215
Galveston movement 262
General Zionist party 342
German culture in United States
204–6
German Democratic Party (DDP) 306
German National People's Party
(DNVP) 306
German People's Party (DVP) 306
Germany, acculturation of Jews 159;

anti-Semitism 217–28, 233, 305–8,
309–18;
conversions to Christianity 136;
court Jews 58–9;
Democratic Republic 402n.;
east European immigrants 260;
emancipation 120–1, 131, 134–7,
156, 159–60;
emigration from 151, 202–4;
expulsion of Jews (1350–1500) 12;
expulsion of Polish Jews 316;
Federal Republic 402–4, 409;
Hasidism 126;
invasion of Russia (1941) 348, 354,
358;
Jewish community 17, 18, 287,
314;
Jewish Enlightenment 88–94,
134–5;
migration to Palestine 314–15;
nationalism 129, 135;
Nazi definition of Jew 313;
Nuremberg laws 312–13;
Orthodox Judaism 144–5, 160;
population growth 67–8, 149–52,
409;
Reform Judaism 140–2, 143–4,
146–7, 160;
regional councils 9–10;
religious toleration 62;
reparations for Holocaust 402–4;
restrictions on Jews 312–14;
romanticism 135;
Weimar Republic 304–9;
in World War Two 318;
and Zionism 273
Gestapo 312, 316, 317, 318
ghettos 26, 436;
and emancipation 132;
Italy 17;
Poland 351–2

Grand Sanhedrin (France, 1807)
  118–19, 120
Great Depression, and anti-Semitism
  213–15;
  and immigration 315–16;
  and Palestine 344;
  Poland 297, 298;
  United States 322, 328–9, 332–3
Greece 192, 193, 362
guilds, craft 8, 11, 20, 100, 121, 134

ha'avara agreement 345
Habsburg empire see Austria
Hadassah (women's Zionist
  organization) 327
Haganah (defence) 385, 387, 388, 392
halakhah (divinely ordained law) 2, 6,
  56, 61;
  and Conservative Judaism 326–7;
  modern adaptations 417;
  and Reform Judaism 142, 143;
  restrictions on commerce 74;
  and Zionism 250
Hapoel Hamizrachi (political party)
  334, 342, 385, 427
Hashomer Hatazair (kibbutz
  federation) 346, 385
Hasidism 23, 63, 72, 73, 77–83,
  124–6;
  controversy over 81–3;
  and Frankism 74–5;
  Galicia 164;
  and modernity 126;
  persecution of 124–5;
  Poland 184–5;
  and political reform 185;
  principles and leaders 77–81, 83;
  and rural Jews 82;
  Subcarpathian Ruthenia 303;
  in United States 416
Haskalah see Enlightenment, Jewish

hazakah (tenure rights) 10, 39, 70
Hebrew language and literature 3, 20,
  414;
  enriched by Enlightenment 93–4;
  forbidden in Soviet Union 407;
  historical study 137–9;
  in Israel 414, 422;
  names 342;
  in Palestine 336
Hebrew Sheltering and Immigrant Aid
  Society (HIAS) 261
Histadrut (General Federation of
  Jewish Labour) 342, 345, 425–6,
  427
historical principle, applied to
  Judaism 137–9
Hitler-Stalin pact (1939) 294
Holland see Netherlands
Holocaust 349–50, 436;
  Belgium 363;
  Bulgaria 361–2;
  denial of 354n.;
  euthanasia 354–5;
  evidence 350, 353;
  Finland 361, 373;
  France 321, 363–6, 372, 410–11;
  Hungary 368–70, 372, 373–4,
  375–6;
  intentionalist-functionalist debate
  311, 349n., 354;
  Italy 362;
  Judenrat (council) 355–7, 370;
  killing methods 358–60, 369;
  Lithuania 372;
  Netherlands 362–3;
  North Africa 365–6;
  Norway 361;
  numbers 357–8, 360, 361, 377;
  organization 318;
  Poland 350–7, 358–61, 365;
  preparations 354–5;

reactions to 271, 347, 374–6, 386;
rebellion 356, 360–1, 366–7;
reparations 402–4;
rescue and escape 361, 362, 367,
    368, 372–6, 383;
resistance 356, 370–2;
Roman Catholic Church 372, 375;
Romania 367;
Slovakia 366–7, 373;
Soviet Union 357–8, 372, 404–5;
survivors 376–8, 401
Holy Roman Empire, status of Jews
    18
Holy Society (*hevra kadisha*) 8
humanism 21
Hungary 294, 373–4, 375–6;
anti-Jewish riots 157;
emancipation 157;
exodus of Jews to Israel 423;
ghettos 369;
Jewish community 59, 215, 287,
    294, 302;
Orthodox Judaism 145;
uprising (1956) 412

India, Jewish community 423
infanticide 5
informers, economic 70–1
Inquisition 12–13, 14, 43, 62;
in Latin America 201–2;
Portugal 62
Iran, education 195;
exodus of Jews to Israel 423;
Jewish community 194–5
Iraq, exodus of Jews to Israel 422–3
Islam, and Sabbatianism 50–2, 53
Israel, Arab refugees 394;
army 430, 432;
British policy 393;
centrality to Jewish world 431, 437;
culture 429–30;

and Egypt 432–4;
founding 391–3, 396;
and German reparations 402–4;
immigrant absorption 421–2,
    423–4;
immigration to 393, 397, 400, 410,
    421–2, 431–2;
and Jewish people 400;
kibbutzim and *moshavim* 424–5;
peace with Egypt 435;
political life 425–9, 434–5;
Reform Judaism 417;
and Russian Jewry 405, 408, 409,
    423;
secularism 404, 428, 435;
Six Days War (1967) 394, 411, 419,
    430, 431, 432–3;
and United Nations 390–1, 394,
    430–1, 432;
US policy 393, 431;
War of Independence (1949)
    393–4, 422, 432;
Yom Kippur War (1973) 419, 430,
    431, 434; *see also* Palestine (Eretz
    Israel)
Israel Bonds 419–20
Israel Philharmonic Orchestra 429
Italy 4;
emancipation 133;
establishment of ghettos 17;
and French Revolution 112;
Holocaust 362;
Jewish community 17–18, 146,
    362, 409;
in World War Two 362

Jesuits, and New Christians 13
Jewish Agency for Palestine 333, 343,
    383, 387, 390, 391, 402–3, 424,
    427
Jewish Anti-Fascist Committee 405

Jewish Association for the Protection
    of Girls and Women 261
Jewish Brigade 386
Jewish Colonial Trust 254
Jewish Colonization Association (ICA)
    259, 262, 277
Jewish Cultural Reconstruction
    382
Jewish organizations, after World War
    Two 379–80, 381–2;
    Alliance Israelite Universelle 149;
    and
    anti-Semitism 226–8, 231;
    Austrian Israelite Union 231;
    B'nai B'rith 211;
    Board of Delegates of American
    Israelites 211;
    Board of Deputies of British Jews
    211;
    Bund 243–5;
    Centralverein deutscher
    Staatsbuerger jüdischen Glaubens
    227–8, 231;
    Deutsch-Israelitischer
    Gemeindebund 226;
    development 148–9;
    France 321–2;
    fund-raising 419–20;
    for German Jews 320;
    Hovevei Zion 249–51, 254;
    Israelitische Kultusgemeinde 231;
    Jewish Board of Guardians
    (London) 263n.;
    Jewish Territorial Organization
    (ITO) 255;
    and migration 261–3;
    military groups 387;
    Palestine 385;
    philanthropic 270;
    and reparations for Holocaust
    402–4;

Soviet Union 408–9;
    under Nazism 314;
    Union of American Hebrew
    Congregations 211;
    United States 412–13;
    Verein zur Abwehr des
    Antisemitismus 227;
    women 327;
    Zionist 254, 335
Jewish Territorial Organization (ITO)
    255
Jewish War Veterans 418
Johnson Act (US, 1925) 322–3, 332
Joint Distribution Committee 270,
    300, 314, 341, 366, 374–5, 379,
    403, 405, 409, 419;
    Malben programme 422
Jordan 432–3
journalism 134, 278, 413–14

kabbalah (mysticism) 23, 27;
    and messianism 48–52
kahal (community executive) 9;
    and conscription 168;
    powers of 69–70
kehillah (community) 3;
    finances 37–9;
    and Israeli democracy 429;
    regional councils 9–10;
    right of settlement 8–9, 39;
    social functions 7–10
Keren Hayesod (Palestine Foundation
    Fund) 340–1, 419
kibbutzim 341–2, 380, 385, 424–5
Kiddush ha-Shem (conscious
    martyrdom) 29–30
kosher foods 74n., 110, 427
Kristallnacht (1938) 316–17
Ku Klux Klan 322
labour movement 244, 279–80,
    324–5, 331

Labour Party (Britain) 267
Labour Party, Israel (Mapai) 342–3,
    345, 385, 391–2, 425, 426–7,
    434–5
League of German Nationalist Jews
    310
League of Nations 343
Liberal Judaism 227, 410
liberalism 218;
    Austria 228;
    flourishing (1850–70) 158–61;
    and nationalism 155
Libya, exodus of Jews to Israel 423
literature 21;
    American 414;
    anti-Semitic 232–3;
    Jewish Enlightenment 93;
    midrashic 138–9;
    rabbinic 181;
    responsa 74;
    Yiddish 176, 180, 291, 335–6; *see
    also* cultural life;
    Hebrew language and literature
Lithuania 294;
    Council of Lands 39;
    expulsion of Jews (1915) 270;
    Jewish community 287, 294–5,
    303–4;
    minority rights 287;
    population growth 66;
    refugees from 44; *see also* Poland
Lumen gentium (Papal decree) 398
Lutheran Church, and anti-Semitism
    226

Maccabi (Zionist athletic
    organization) 335
Mafdal (National Religious Party)
    427–8, 434, 435
Mapai (Labour Party) 342–3, 345,
    385, 391–2, 425, 426–7, 434–5

Mapam (United Workers' Party) 427
Marranos (New Christians) 12–16, 36,
    62;
    returning to Judaism 15–16, 45–6
marriage 5;
    arranged 151;
    civil 111, 117;
    intermarriage 407, 410, 417;
    taxation of 39;
    women's rights 417
martyrdom 29–30;
    group 29
Marxism, and Zionism 257–8
Mensheviks 245, 281
merchant banking 153–4
messianism 46, 47–52;
    Christian belief in second coming
        200, 209;
    influence 52–5;
    and mysticism 73;
    pilgrimage to Holy Land (1700) 54;
    Sabbatian 22;
    Sefardic 22–3
midrashic literature 138–9
migration 436;
    and anti-Jewish riots 157;
    and anti-Semitism 258–9;
    Australia 191;
    from eastern Europe 324;
    from Germany 135, 151, 159;
    homogenizing effect 334–5;
    illegal 344n.;
    and population growth 1, 214,
        215–16;
    process 259;
    quotas 314–16, 322–3;
    restrictions 263, 287, 314–16, 318,
        322–3, 332, 346, 375, 380, 408–9,
        412;
    and smuggling 259;
    sources and causes 202–3;

migration (*cont.*)
South Africa 191;
statistics 203–4, 215–16, 277;
to Western Europe 214, 216, 238,
260;
warnings against 258;
welfare organizations 261–3; *see
also* Israel;
Palestine;
United States
military service 119;
Israel 430;
obligations 117;
and religious tolerance 100;
restrictions on Jews 223–4, 242;
under Napoleon 110;
World War One 268;
World War Two 347, 348, 350, 364,
373, 386
Mizrachi (political party) 334, 342,
385, 427
modern history, definitions 23–5
modernization, Germany 88–9
moneylending 10, 19–20, 36, 66;
Alsace 152;
and anti-Semitism 222;
complaints about 105–6;
criticism of 329;
Jewish law 118;
under Napoleon 116, 117, 119
Morocco 363, 365–6, 411;
exodus of Jews to Israel 423, 424;
Jewish community 149
mortality rate, in ghettos 351,
352
mortality rates 150;
Palestine 196
music, religious 139
mussar ethical movement 183,
301
mysticism see *kabbalah*

national minority rights 271–2,
282–3, 295, 296–7;
Poland 295, 296–7;
Ukraine 283
nationalism 102, 128–9;
after World War One 294;
Germany 129;
Jewish 189;
and liberalism 155; *see also* Zionism
nativism, United States 322
Nazism 13;
admiration for 297, 308, 310;
ideology 307–8;
international protests against 332;
Jewish organizations and 310, 314;
on Judaism and Communist 293;
refugees from 317–18, 332–3, 344;
rise to power 308, 309;
and Zionism 310, 314–15; *see also*
Holocaust
Neolog Judaism, Hungary 302
nepotism 70, 71
Netherlands, consistory system 133,
146;
emancipation 133;
expansion of overseas trade 15;
German Jews in 315;
Holocaust 362–3;
Jewish community 16, 42, 146,
287, 409;
Jewish population growth 67;
Reform Judaism 142–3;
religious toleration 42;
in World War Two 362–3
New Christians 12–17, 35, 45–6, 62;
anti-Judaism 22;
sceptics and rationalists 22
New Deal (US) 279, 325, 329, 331
nihilism, Frankism 74–6
North Africa, expulsion from 411;
in World War Two 385–6

Norway, Holocaust 361;
  Jewish community 361
Nostra aetate (Papal decree) 398–9
Nuremberg laws 312–13
Nuremberg trials 377

occupational groups 152–5, 159,
  160–1;
  immigrants 264;
  Ottoman Empire 192–3;
  Palestine 200;
  Russia 166, 170–1, 187–8;
  Soviet Union 407;
  United States 325, 412–13
Old Regime 129
oligarchy 331–2
Olympic Games (1936) 313–14
Oriental Jews, France 411
Orthodox Judaism, acculturated 145;
  birth rate 400;
  Britain 320, 410;
  Germany 144–5, 160;
  Hasidic sects 416;
  Israel 428;
  Palestine 339;
  Poland 174;
  and sectarianism 145;
  Slovakia 303;
  Soviet Union 408;
  United States 205, 211, 326–7, 412,
    415, 416;
  and Zionism 256
orthodoxy, in New Christians 21–2
Ottoman Empire 10–11;
  break-up 194;
  economic decline 35, 66–7;
  education 194;
  emancipation 194;
  Jewish community 35–6, 192–4;
  Jewish merchants 35–6;
  lack of Enlightenment 192;

  and Sabbatianism 50–2;
  Tanzimat (reform movement) 194
Pale of Settlement (Russia) 162, 170,
  186, 241–2, 292
Palestine (Eretz Israel) 288, 298;
  aid to settlers 250, 251, 253;
  Anglo-American Commission of
    Inquiry 387–8;
  Arab state 346;
  Arab-Jewish conflict 327, 336–8,
    343–4, 345–6;
  British policy 273–6, 310, 321,
    336–7, 343, 383–91;
  conditions for settlement 248–9,
    314–15;
  development of harbours 200;
  displaced persons and 379, 380–2;
  German Jews in 318;
  ha'avara (transfer) agreements 315,
    332, 345;
  Haganah actions 385, 387, 388,
    392;
  and Holocaust 374, 375, 383–4;
  illegal immigration 378, 379,
    383–4, 388;
  Jewish community 149, 193,
    195–201, 249, 338–9, 341–3,
    385;
  as Jewish national home 333;
  Nazism and 310;
  partition 345–6, 390–2;
  Peel Commission report (1937)
    310, 390;
  plans for practical development
    200–1;
  politics 342–3;
  population growth 195–6, 198–9,
    338–9, 344–5;
  spiritual status 200; *also* Israel
Palestine Jewish Colonization
  Association (PICA) 251

Pan-German League 222, 228
Panama scandal (1899) 234
pantheism 46, 55
Passfield White Paper on Palestine
   344
patriotism 121; *see also* nationalism;
   Zionism
patriotism, American 204–5;
   and Reform Judaism 147
patronage 192, 199
peddling and street selling 207–8,
   264, 324
Peel Commission report on Palestine
   (1937) 310, 345–6
philanthropy 8, 419–20;
   and development in Palestine
   200–1;
   for German Jews 314, 320;
   and migration 261–3;
   for Russian Jews 270;
   to overseas Jews 211;
   United States 211, 418–20;
   women's groups 327
philosophy, study of 56–7
pietism 92
Poale Zion 256–7, 258, 272, 289,
   340
pogroms 243;
   archives 283n.;
   Bavaria (1819) 135;
   Berlin (1923) 305;
   Bolshevik opposition 281–2;
   Gomel (1903) 246;
   government involvement 247, 286;
   Kishinev (1903) 245–6;
   Kristallnacht (1938) 316–17;
   and Manchurian war (1904) 247;
   Poland 282–3, 297, 381;
   Romania (1941) 367;
   Russia 234, 239–41, 247; *see also*
   riots

Poland, anti-Semitism 296, 297–9,
   381;
   as Ashkenazic Jewish centre 18–19;
   Austrian *see* Galicia;
   Congress 162–3;
   Council of the Four Lands 44, 53,
   71–2, 122;
   cultural life 300–1;
   Deluge (1648–60) 27–30;
   economic decline 33, 36–7;
   education 301;
   estate management 68–70;
   Four Years' Sejm (1788–92) 122;
   General Gouvernement 350–1;
   Hasidism 184–5;
   Holocaust 350–7, 358–61, 365;
   invasions of (1648–67) 27–33;
   Jewish charters 19–20;
   Jewish community 11, 20, 36–7,
   287, 295–6, 350–7;
   Jewish emancipation 122–3;
   Jews forcibly returned (1938)
   316;
   migration from 202, 344–5, 423;
   national minority rights 295,
   296–7;
   New Christians in 17;
   Orthodox Judaism 174;
   population growth 65–6, 67, 163,
   164–5;
   rebellion (1863) 190;
   regional councils 9–10;
   Renaissance 20–1;
   republic proclaimed (1918) 282;
   revolt (1794) 122;
   role of *kehillah* (community) 7–8;
   Sabbatianism in 51, 53–5;
   socialism 229;
   Ukrainian uprising (1648) 28;
   under Napoleon 122–3;
   uprising (1830–1) 162–3;

in World War One 268–9; *see also* Ukraine
polygamy 117, 339
population growth 1, 65–8;
  after World War Two 400–1;
  Ashkenazim 191;
  Britain 150, 152;
  central and western Europe 287;
  displaced persons 378–9;
  eastern Europe 287;
  France 150, 151;
  Germany 67–8, 149–50, 151–2;
  Israel 421, 431;
  laws to inhibit 134;
  and migration 214, 215–16;
  Palestine 195–6, 198–9, 338–9, 344–5;
  Poland 65–6, 67, 163, 164–5;
  reversal 410;
  Russia 163, 164–5, 292;
  significance 1;
  stagnation 66–7, 151–2;
  statistics 215–16;
  United States 203–4, 323–4, 412;
  and urbanization 216–17
Portugal, American colonies 201, 202;
  expulsion of Jews (1497) 11, 12;
  Inquisition 62;
  Marranos (New Christians) 12–15
'Portuguese merchants' see Marranos (New Christians)
poverty 170–1
Press, Jewish 45, 95–6, 176, 189, 211, 219, 278, 301, 321
printing and publishing 134;
  Amsterdam 45–6;
  Hebrew press 176;
  Israel 430;
  restrictions on 290;
  Russian 176–7

prisoners of war 370
prostitution 261
Protestant Churches, and anti-Semitism 364;
  rapprochement with Judaism 400;
  sects 20–1
Protocols of the Elders of Zion 293, 305, 320
Prussia, Jewish emancipation 120–1;
  Jewish settlement 18, 41, 67
Prussian Act (1812) 134
'purity of blood' 13

rabbinic Judaism 21–2; *see also* orthodox Judaism
rabbinic scholarship 2–3, 56–7, 59, 328, 411, 414–15
rabbis, rabbinate, admission of women 327, 417;
  career 6, 9;
  'Crown rabbis' 182;
  fears of office debasement 71–2;
  literature 181;
  Reform 142;
  training 178–80, 182–3;
  United States 326
racial purity doctrines 233
racism, United States 322; *see also* anti-Semitism
railways, financing of 154, 187
Raszvet (newspaper) 176
Red Cross, International Committee 374
Reform Judaism 104, 120, 140–4, 146, 280, 334;
  Britain 410;
  and emancipation 146–7;
  Germany 160;
  and *halakhah* 142, 143;
  in Israel 417;
  radical 142;

Reform Judaism (*cont.*)
United States 147, 205–6, 208, 211,
326, 327, 415, 416–17
refugees, from Nazism 317–18,
319–20, 332–3, 350;
internment 348;
Palestinian 394
regeneration 105, 133
religious tolerance 61, 91–2;
advocacy of 84, 85;
benefits 60;
and coercion 105;
and education 100, 101;
on Joseph II of Austria 99–100;
Papal attitudes 61–2;
and regeneration 105
reparations 402–4
responsa 74
Revisionists 343, 345
revolutions, (1848–9) 155–8;
belief in 243–8;
Russia 271; *see also* French
Revolution
riots, anti-Jewish (1848–9) 157;
and Dreyfus affair 234–5; *see also*
pogroms
Roman Catholic Church, and anti-
Semitism 224, 226, 228, 230,
233, 299, 306–7, 329–30, 364,
398n., 399–400;
Council of Trent 397;
Counter-Reformation 17;
disestablishment 236;
and Frankism 75;
and Holocaust 362, 366, 399, 400;
and Marranos (New Christians)
12–15;
Papacy 15–16, 17;
Poland 37;
rapprochement with Judaism
397–400;

and religious toleration 61–2;
Vatican Council (1962) 397–9;
and Zionism 391
Romania 295, 304;
Jewish community 215, 287
romanticism 102
royal protection 37
rural Jews, and Hasidism 82
Russia, abolition of Jewish autonomy
180;
absolutism 218;
anti-Semitism 218, 238–41;
conscription 176, 181, 186, 199;
Constitution 247–8;
conversions 186;
Decembrist group 166–7;
education 177–80, 182, 187;
Jewish Autonomous Region
(Crimea) 288–9;
Jewish Commissions 281;
Jewish community 123–5, 163,
215, 287;
Jewish Enlightenment 173–7,
188–90;
Jewish Statute (1804) 124;
migration from 204, 259;
occupational groups 187–8;
Pale of Settlement 162, 170, 186,
241–2, 292;
policies on Jews 149, 162, 165–7,
239–42;
population growth 163, 164–5;
Revolution (1905) 244, 258;
Revolution (1917) 271;
revolutionary movement 243–8;
rule in Poland 122–3;
taxation 180–1;
war with Japan (1904) 247;
in World War One 270–1
Russian Orthodox Church 123,
286

Sabbatianism 22, 23, 46, 47–52, 62–5,
200;
and antinomianism 47–8, 50, 51,
53, 54–5;
code language 63;
influence 78;
and Islam 50–2, 63;
Muslim converts 53;
in Poland 51, 53–5; *see also*
Frankism
salons 104
sanitation and public health,
Jerusalem 198
Science of Judaism 104, 137–9, 144,
173, 309
Sefardic Jewry 16, 22–3;
Amsterdam 44;
Britain 143, 146;
economic decline 191–2;
England 44;
France 108, 411;
Palestine 339;
United States 191
serfdom 37, 67, 69;
emancipation 186;
Poland 36
Shaw Commission on Palestine 344
shipping, river traffic 68–9
Shulhan Arukh ('Set Table') 2
Simpson Report on Palestine 344
slavery 11;
abolition of 105, 129, 186
smuggling 170;
in ghettos 352;
and migration 259
Social Democrats (Austria) 229
Social Democrats (Germany) 219,
223, 267;
and anti-Semitism 224–5, 229, 238,
306
Social Democrats (Russia) 245

socialism 155, 214;
and anti-semitism 224–5, 229;
establishment of Bund 243–5;
in Palestine 339;
Poland 229;
United States 331;
and World War One 267;
and Zionism 256–7, 272; *see also*
Communism
socialist Zionism 272, 334
South Africa 191, 212, 261
South America, anti-Semitism 397;
German Jews in 318;
Jewish settlement 127, 201–2, 212
Soviet Union, anti-Semitism 397,
405;
cultural life 406, 407–8;
decline 409;
exodus of Jews to Israel 423;
German invasion (1941) 318, 348,
354, 358;
Holocaust 357–8, 404–5;
Jewish communities 400, 405,
406–7;
Jewish national movement 408–9;
New Economic Policy (1921–8)
288;
refugees in 373;
treatment of Jews 281–2, 288–9,
290, 292;
suppression of Judaism 405–6;
and Zionism 391; *see also* Russia
Spain, American colonies 201, 202;
expulsion of Jews (1492) 11, 12, 22,
24;
Marranos (New Christians) 12–15;
'purity of blood' 13;
refugees in 372
'Spanish merchants' 42, 43
Spartacus League 306
Stern gang 387, 394

sweatshops 153
Sykes-Picot agreement (1916) 273–4, 336
synagogues, alterations to services 140–1;
  Britain 143, 280;
  building of 139;
synagogues, alterations to services (*cont.*)
  France 411;
  Orthodox 416;
  post-war rebuilding 409;
  Reform 417;
  Soviet Union 405, 408;
  suburban 415;
  United States 327

Talmud 2;
  scholarship 72–3;
  'trial' of (1756) 75
Talmud Yerushalmi 73, 181
Tanzimat (Turkish reform movement) 194
tax farming 10
taxation 9;
  by court Jews 59;
  by Jewish community 37–9;
  community role 7, 8–9;
  for 'improvement' 163–4;
  Russia 180–1
Thirty Years' War 27
Torah, Mishneh Torah ('Supplemental') 2;
  oral tradition 2, 3;
  role in Hasidism 79–80
trade and commerce 58, 68–70;
  employment in 20, 152–3
trade unionism 214, 279–80;
  Palestine 342;
  and revolutionary organization 243–5;

United States 324–5
transport, advances in 191

Ukraine, Hasidism 184–5;
  Jewish agricultural colonization 171–2;
  Jewish community 20, 27–8, 287;
  national minority rights 283;
  pogroms 239–41, 247, 283–6 *see also* Poland
Union generale des Israelites de France 364–5
United Jewish Appeal 419–20
United Nations 389–90;
  Relief and Rehabilitation Administration (UNRRA) 381;
  Special Committee on Palestine (UNSCOP) 388, 390–1
United States, anti-Semitism 208–9, 325, 329–31, 412–13;
  Ashkenazim 191;
  Civil War 186, 204–5;
  community leadership 331–2;
  Conservative Judaism 144, 206, 280, 302, 326–7, 415–16, 417;
  conversion to Christianity 209–10;
  cultural life 278, 324, 333, 413–15;
  education 210;
  emancipation 127, 129–30, 204–5;
  German culture 204–6, 315–16;
  Great Depression 322, 328–9, 332–3;
  and Holocaust 374–5;
  immigration see migration;
  Industrial Removal Office 262;
  international influence 277;
  and Israel 404, 418–20, 431;
  Jewish community 126–7, 201–11, 215–16, 404, 411–20;
  Jewish labour movement 244, 279–80, 324–5, 331;

nativism and racism 329;
Orthodox Judaism 211, 326–7, 415,
   416;
population growth 1, 323–4, 396;
racism and nativism 322–3, 325–6;
Reform Judaism 142, 147, 205–6,
   208, 211, 326, 327, 415, 416–17;
Sefardim 191;
in World War One 271;
in World War Two 348–9;
and Zionism 327, 340, 384–5, 388,
   391, 393, 420
universities 293, 413;
anti-Semitism 223, 231, 299;
Israel 429;
Jewish studies 328, 411, 414–15
urbanization 159, 187–8, 405,
   406–7;
and population growth 216–17

vagrancy 153
Vichy regime see under France
Vienna 89;
expulsion of Jews (1421) 40;
expulsion of Jews (1670) 41;
Jewish community 18, 159, 216,
   230–1, 316;
Jewish settlement in 18;
religious tolerance 40, 99, 100;
third Jewish community 41
Vienna, Congress of 132

war crimes trials 356n., 401–2
War Refugee Board (US) 375
Warsaw, ghetto 351, 352–3, 359,
   360–1;
Jewish community 216, 295;
non-toleration 68;
pogrom (1881) 240
Warsaw, Duchy of 122–3; *see also*
   Poland

wealth 120–1;
confiscation in World War Two
   382, 402
women, business role 5;
education 201, 301, 327, 416;
military service 430;
religious role 5–6, 151, 417;
status 150–1, 327
World Jewish Congress 371, 374, 402
World War One, and anti-Semitism
   304–5;
effects 268, 304–5;
and national unity 267–8;
opposition to 267
World War Two 318, 347–86;
Jewish soldiers in 347, 348, 350,
   364, 373, 386; *see also* Holocaust
World Zionist Congress 254–5, 390
World Zionist Organization (WZO)
   214, 254, 255–6, 338, 343, 344

Yad Vashem (scholarly institution))
   404
yeshivot (religious academies) 6, 71,
   182–3, 301, 344, 416, 427–8;
modern 73;
Orthodox 145;
United States 326
Yiddish 40, 334–5;
decline 404, 407–8, 414;
education through 290–1, 301;
in France 111;
and Jewish Enlightenment 175;
literature 176, 180, 291, 335–6;
newspapers 278;
opposition to 189, 336;
and Russian revolutionary
   movement 244, 245;
secular 278, 279–80;
suppression 405;
theatre 301

youth movements, *kibbutzim*
424–5;
Poland 350, 360–1;
Zionist 372

Zeirei Zion 340
Zionism 148, 225, 232, 235, 303,
436;
aid to migrants 314;
colonization 196;
Zionism (*cont.*)
Democratic Fraction 256;
and emancipation 252;

ideologies 200, 214, 227, 248–9,
252, 255–8, 300, 301, 308,
339–43, 342–3, 346, 385, 422,
426, 431, 433, 435;
and Nazism 310, 314–15;
opposition to 245, 253, 254, 275–6,
289–90, 333–4, 337–8, 405, 406;
organization 214, 249–51, 252–5,
254–5, 272–3, 289, 327, 334,
339–41, 384–5;
projects 309, 333, 335–6, 337;
and socialism 272, 334; *see also*
under individual countries;

Made in the USA
Coppell, TX
18 January 2021

48366585R00266